Men
Astutely
Trained

For my itinerant family

Contents

Preface

In Europe no valid claim can be made for a definite Jesuit style, its canons precisely laid down in Rome, and in the Americas there is even less justification for such a statement. The various regions adapted certain stylistic features, according to the exigencies of the time and place and the abilities of the builders, and out of them they created something original.[1]

I

A pair of full-length portraits by Peter Paul Rubens hangs in the National Museum in Vienna. One is of Saint Francis Xavier, missionary to the Indies. The painting shows him baptizing exotic figures, converting strange lands in the name of Christ. The other is of Saint Ignatius Loyola, healing souls and casting out demons. The portraits are larger than life, or so they seem. The presentation is monumental, the raiments richly colored, the gestures grandiose.

The portraits evoke the activist and the contemplative sides, the exterior and the interior, of the Society of Jesus. This antiphony pervades the lives and the work of Jesuits, but its expression varies across time and place. The Jesuit experience in the United States is of a different order from the rhetoric and iconography of Europe, and regional variations within the United States have to be respected in summarizing this experience.[2]

The crucial challenge, however, comes in framing the question at the outset. This book is not so much about the contrast between European and American Catholicism as it is about the interaction between Catholicism and the American way, as seen through the eyes of Jesuits in the United

States. What Thomas Fleming wrote about the missing agenda of Irish American literature can be taken, with some adjustment for historical setting, as the program for this study of the Society of Jesus:

> Most Irish-American novels tend to be hermetic. They explore the joys and sorrows, the pathologies and corruptions of the tribe and leave the non-Irish reader on the edge of sadness, not really giving much of a damn. The Irish-Americans themselves often boycott the best books for telling the truth and persuade the gullible that vaudeville turns like Edwin O'Connor's "Last Hurrah" are the real thing. Only a few writers have perceived that the important story—in the last 30 years, at least—has been the Irish encounter with the other side of the hyphen, with America.[3]

My concern is with the curious encounter between two cultures that have much in common, made up as they are of layers of the pragmatic and the transcendental, but that also represent rival ways of life. My theme is the ambiguous meeting between a "nation with the soul of a church" and a religious organization with a commitment to the mundane.[4]

II

Late on a Sunday morning in New Orleans, in his office at a radio station owned at the time by Loyola University, Fr. Thomas Clancy reminisced about his years during the seventies as provincial superior—chief executive officer—of the Society of Jesus in the southern states. A Southerner himself, Clancy is a raconteur. The novelist Walker Percy was a longtime friend. His reputation as a man with a tale for every occasion has made him something of a legend from the Deep South to its northern borders. Clancy has a doctorate from Oxford, and he has written about the history of the early Jesuits. But now he was holding forth about recent times. He talked about coming to grips with problems inside the society that hampered Jesuits in their work with those outside the order.

> After I was in for two years, we figured maybe we had 60 alcoholics, out of about 400 people. I said, if we could rehabilitate 40 of these 60 alcoholics, this would make up for every priest that's left in the last twelve years. So let's rehabilitate.
>
> It was not a general thing. It was one-on-one. I would fly into Tampa. I would show up for a dinner [at a Jesuit residence]. And everybody would say, "What the hell is *he* here for?" And then, after dinner, I would grab this guy. You couldn't tell them two days beforehand because they'd *kill* themselves drinking. So you say "Let me see

you for a minute." And the guy would go, "Uh-huh." And you'd say, "I'm really concerned about your drinking problem. I personally think you're an alcoholic, or pretty close to it." "Well, who told you that?" he'd say. "Well, you know," I said, "you drink an awful lot. I mean, accidents and so forth."

He had an explanation for everything. So, after an hour, I say, "Well, listen, this is a plane ticket. Tomorrow morning, at 9:10, you're going to Guest House [a detoxification center for clergy] up in Michigan." He says, "I'm not going up there!" I said, "So-and-so will take you out. I've already arranged it." He says, "Well, look, the reason I don't want to go is that no one knows I'm an alcoholic!" I said, "You jerk! *Everybody* knows you're an alcoholic! People in *El Paso* know you're an alcoholic!" And so, he would go up there.[5]

Clancy, who was in his early sixties at the time of the interview, entered the Society of Jesus in the 1940s. His career spans the decades of growth before the 1960s and afterward the years of declining numbers, ideological furor, sagging morale, and efforts to regroup. He talked, always concretely, without interpretive adornment, with a palpable suspicion of generalizations, of the changes and the responses to them.

Early Sunday mornings, Clancy visits a penitentiary to say Mass for the inmates. "This morning I had eighteen male prisoners, and I asked one of them to read part of the service, and only two of them volunteered, and neither one of them could read." He continued:

I have to talk to them. And they don't want to hear me talk about social justice. Of course, they like to hear about capital punishment. They want problems solved that they have right now. They're hurting right now. They want some kind of affirmation of themselves.[6]

The plain talk sounded elliptical. My acquaintance with Jesuits went back to the late fifties and early sixties: high school at Brooklyn Prep, now Medgar Evers Community College; higher education in St. Louis and Washington—nine years altogether of Jesuit schooling. But I had been away for a while, and now familiarity was mixed with strangeness, in part because I wasn't sure what I was looking for, and in part because Jesuits themselves had changed. The years since the sixties, after the Second Vatican Council, were a puzzle; the waning years of immigrant Catholicism when I had grown up, with "Jebbies" at the helm of the ethnic subcultures, had drifted into nostalgia; and the centuries before, when Jesuits set out from Spain and Portugal and Italy as "hammers of the Protestants" and as missionaries to the Indies and Brazil and the wilds of North America, seemed antiquarian curiosities.

There was a cryptic abundance to these impressions. The sense of mystery and possibility that comes when one's own experience links up with glimpses of the unknown was powerful. So was the ambivalent perception of damaged goods, of things faded and submerged. "I've reached the point," Flannery O'Connor wrote, "where I can't do again what I know I can do well, and the larger things that I need to do now, I doubt my capacity for doing."[7]

III

Catholicism is closer to a ponderous anarchy than to a monolith. G. K. Chesterton and James Joyce, among others, have said as much, and the mingling of bric-a-brac and sublimity in the Vatican collection expresses a certain unkempt grandeur that has been a feature of the church even during its severest periods of centralization. The mélange of diversity and cohesiveness makes it difficult to grasp what has changed and what has stayed the same in Catholicism. Survival has not meant stability. After acquiescing to the claim of his inquisitors that the sun was still fixed in cosmic space, Galileo muttered *"Eppure se muove!"* ("Yet it moves!") He might as well have been speaking about the church itself.[8]

The Society of Jesus is a mutation within Catholicism. One of the more rational pillars of the church, the order also retains some of its polymorphous sprawl. The origins of the Jesuits lie at the crossroads of sixteenth-century Europe. Social transformations that had been gestating for a millennium converged and picked up speed.[9] Jesuits bear the marks of the epoch of their founding. They incorporate more acutely than other groups in Catholicism the tensions between modernity and tradition.

Over the past few decades three things have happened to the Jesuits: They have lost about a third of their manpower. The society has changed from a rule-governed hierarchy to an organization that looks more like a role-driven network in which Jesuits search for, rather than being assigned to, jobs and tasks. And the normative world of the Jesuits—their sense of meaning, purpose, and community—has altered as well.[10]

In order to understand these changes, it is necessary to backtrack a bit. My primary focus is neither on the early days of the Society of Jesus, when it expanded rapidly across the globe, nor on the most recent period—the years since the sixties during which it has undergone a decline in membership and a rethinking of its mission. I concentrate on the decades from around the turn of the century to the verge of the Second Vatican Council. This period was the fulcrum time between past and present. Analysis of these deceptively quiet years reveals, as if in slow motion, the accumulation of tensions inherited not only from the Counter-Reformation but also conflicts that had been building up since the French Revolution and the onset of industrialization in the nineteenth century.[11]

IV

The Society of Jesus has been extraordinarily influential. As late as the 1980s, a leader of the Italian Communist party could declare, somewhat enigmatically but without sounding ridiculous, *"Il modello della nostra cultura politica sono i gesuiti"*—"the model of our political culture is [formed by] the Jesuits."[12] The order is by no means representative, in a statistical sense, of the pressures of modernization, nor has it customarily been at the vanguard of this process. Still, the saga of the Jesuits encapsulates not only the multiple strains in Catholicism but also aspects of the metamorphosis of the West.

In some quarters it is customary to think of religion as a matter of abstractions and absolutes—of universal, Platonic certainties. It is a short step from this view to a vision of the religious temper as a manifestation of fanaticism and closed-mindedness. For all their reputation for militarism, Jesuits—"the swift, light cavalry of Christ"—lean the opposite way. This characteristic style is as much a cultural property of the organization as it is a psychological manner of individual Jesuits.[13] As a multinational institution that has been in existence for nearly half a millennium, the Society of Jesus has cultivated a tolerance of diversity and cultural eclecticism that for some observers borders on incoherence and casuistry.[14]

Although a depiction of the "typical" Jesuit as Hamlet with holy orders would be misleading, it is true that many Jesuits incline toward self-scrutiny and subtle distinctions. They tend to deal not in generalities and certainties but in the refractory and the ambiguous. It is this awareness of—indeed, this taste for—complexity that the Italian Communist recognized in the order. It is the knotted humanity of the Jesuits, he suggested, that has encouraged a sympathy for compromise and that has elicited fascination in return.[15]

The clash between tradition and modernity is reflected in the Jesuit experience as a distinctive, never quite resolved but nonetheless recognizable pattern, embedded in particulars. Nuance is crucial. The concreteness of this counterpoint makes the experience accessible. The profusion of specifics and the crisscrossing of purposes also make for elusiveness. One man's moral complexity may be another's equivocation.[16] In the eyes of their critics, Jesuits have often been seen as little more than nimble reactionaries.[17]

What is this experience and how is it related to the dialectic between tradition and modernity? Imagine modernization as a mix of three elements.[18] The emergence of Western Europe involved the consolidation of the political power of nation-states, a process that took place over the protests of forces pulling in the opposite direction, toward a decentralized order.[19] The rise of Europe also involved the deployment of investment capital for economic growth. This change was resisted by sectors that favored a more distributive, egalitarian order. Both developments engendered characteristic lines of division: one between political elites and contenders for power—regional interests, minorities, and so on—and the other between social classes. Both entailed tangible, more or less computable outcomes.[20]

A third ingredient of modernization was less palpable but equally critical. The cultivation of human capital meant systematic education. In this field Jesuits were innovators and came to excel. The Jesuits' dedication to pedagogy assumed still greater proportions in the United States, where they trained large numbers of immigrant and postimmigrant Catholics and some non-Catholics as well. By the end of the 1980s there were more than one million graduates of the twenty-eight Jesuit colleges and universities in the United States.[21]

The tension intrinsic to this component of modernization may appear less substantial than the conflicts engendered by state building and the accumulation of physical capital. Jesuits were not alone in believing that learning and virtue were reconcilable. It was Samuel Johnson who stated that "the end of learning is piety."[22] Nor were they alone in assuming which took precedence if conflict did arise. It was Ralph Waldo Emerson who argued that "character is higher than intellect."[23]

Despite these earnest resolutions, however, discrepancies between knowledge and ethical mettle did not disappear. Secularization came to be defined as the attenuation of the bond between knowledge and morality. Not only did the ties between cultural development and political and socioeconomic progress come to seem vague and naive; in the eyes of many traditionalists and not a few neutral observers, the connection between learning and values came undone.[24]

The change can be understood by imagining another grand process—democratization—set alongside each of the three components of modernization. With regard to the political dimension of development, it makes intuitive sense to associate democratization with forms of decentralization. By the same token, an emphasis on economic distribution connotes social democracy. Though not uncontroversial, such correspondences are at least defensible.

Democratization becomes more enigmatic when applied to culture. Yet, obvious or not, it is the extension of democratization from the political and economic to the cultural sphere that has thrown the Society of Jesus into the most serious crisis in its history. It is the pervasiveness of this process that makes the predicament of the Jesuits part of a larger drama.

The conceptual difficulty comes from the slipperiness of "progress," "development," and similar notions when applied to moral change. Without such trend-like constructions, democratization loses meaning. Consideration of two points may help at least to clarify the problem.

First, Jesuits sometimes understood the dialectic between knowledge and virtue as a union or harmonious balance and at other times as a creative tension; the resolution was unsteady. Intellectual and ethical change of some sort, to some degree, was acceptable.

Second, for Jesuits, cultural advancement has involved something besides stern didacticism or a psychological game of contrarities between knowledge and virtue. Rectitude has also meant mastery of the passions and corporate loyalty. The cultural realm is therefore multidimensional rather than bipolar and divorced from organizational realities. Furthermore, self-control and institutional allegiance are themselves ambiguous. While discipline matters, so does liberation. The bedrock intuition of Jesuit spirituality stresses the supremacy of affection, shaped and refined but not, ideally, suppressed. It is this rhythm of the emotions that formed the ground base of the Society of Jesus beneath democratization and that was interrupted by it.

V

The political and economic quarrels involved in modernization clearly represent conflicts in the public realm. Cultural democratization, whatever it means, is not so readily categorized. It spans the shifting interstices between the public and private spheres.

As far as Catholicism and the Jesuits are concerned, two features of cultural democratization are especially problematic. One involves the difficulty of upholding an ethical heritage in schools that have become inexorably secular.[25] The dilemma is perpetuated by rival loyalties: to the teaching *magisterium* of the church on the one hand and to the marketplace of ideas on the other.[26] A related dilemma has to do with the family and the areas of sexuality and the status of women.

Both school and the family are pivotal to Jesuits because they perform socializing functions, transmitting norms from one generation to the next. They are considered to be the building blocks of social order. The family in particular is seen as the redoubt of hierarchy, inculcating preconscious understandings and shaping firm identities, no matter what inroads democratization might make in the public sphere. It is the primal school of the affections.[27]

From this perspective, ideals that are supposed to govern conduct—far from being spectral entities—are inextricably bound up with idiomatic structures of authority and intimate hierarchies like the family, and with the role of women. The decay of traditional values is not an abstruse turn in the history of ideas. The apparently vaporous process of cultural democratization means the democratization of everyday life.[28] It is the down-to-earthness, the immediacy and sensuousness, of this development that gives it such resonance among Jesuits. The boundaries between public and private spheres, that once seemed secure, that preserved a zone of authority for religious organizations and a haven for their members and for those to whom they ministered, and that permitted them to exert a modicum of influence on the secular world, have been reshaped.[29]

VI

In Europe and parts of Latin America, less often in the United States, Jesuits have at times engaged in the politics of symbolic and moral causes and have assertively defended their material interests. The Society of Jesus has also been subject to spasms of inner turmoil that, in addition to affecting its work *ad extra*, have an importance of their own. The variable connection between the inner and outer worlds of the order is a major thrust of this book.

Beneath the legend of political intrigue and derring-do, of black popes and back-door machinations and exquisite duplicity, the power exerted by Jesuits has been largely indirect.[30] The Society of Jesus is the carrier of a moral culture whose logic is driven by contradictions straining toward integration, toward transcendence of a kind. The tension between virtue and knowledge, I have argued, has fueled the dynamism of the order.[31]

A plausible though incomplete account of the crisis of the Society of Jesus would point toward the erosion of its dominant position on the knowledge side of the equation. Jesuits worked themselves out of a leadership role in education by training generations of laypeople who eventually surpassed them and whose offspring, with wider options available, no longer sought the expertise of Jesuits in such numbers. Jesuits empowered their pupils. The Society of Jesus has left behind a variety of cultural institutions and objects, and the order has become, in effect, its admirers. But Jesuits themselves have been left behind.[32]

The trouble with this line of reasoning is that it fails to consider changes in the ethical component of human capital formation and, more broadly, in the hold the Society of Jesuits has exercised over the moral and social imagination of Catholics.

The rationale of character formation associated with the Jesuits is one of recurrent conflict between aggression and compassion—between courage and affection; between the church militant and the church maternal. A correlative struggle can be discerned between the need to preserve a durable identity, something like a psychic anchor, and the need to navigate within the implacable diversity, the catholicity, of the church. Traces of this dualism can also be detected in episodes of an almost sepulchral asceticism set alongside the joyous effulgence of the baroque.[33]

The psychic economy of Jesuits, then, encompasses tradeoffs between divergent and seemingly contradictory goals. This imparts a nervous energy to individual Jesuits, as well as some instability to the society.[34] These tensions are patterned, structuring principles. The contradictions underlying Jesuit life are overarching polarities and animating countercurrents. It is when such antinomies become less compelling, when the inherited categories of behavior and meaning give way, as happened with the age-old division between male dominance and female subservience around the time of Vatican II, that the dynamism of the hierarchy faltered and Jesuits became disoriented.[35]

The challenges faced by Jesuits have institutional as well as psychological ramifications. Jesuits are engaged in corporate activity as well as intrapsychic management. The Society of Jesus is both a service agency and a socialization mechanism. In addition to the difficulties encountered in trying to train their members, Jesuits have confronted obstacles in their efforts to translate individual "character" into collective action.

Part of the problem of institutional design is historical. The organizational hierarchies that suited an earlier age, presumably reflecting the self-discipline and sense of order of Jesuits themselves, no longer provide credible models for professional networks and formidable bureaucracies such as those of modern universities.

Another aspect of the problem is more circuitous. In contrast to many institutions with expressly political or economic goals, the bottom line of the Society of Jesus is relatively soft. "How does one measure," one Jesuit asked me, "the progress of sanctifying grace?" Jesuits come up against the paradoxical question of how altruism is to be rewarded and the slightly more amenable problem of how generosity and benevolent impulse can be channeled into reliable behavior. The order's goals are multiple and some are incommensurable; feedback is uncertain. There is no unequivocal chain, no causal bridge, from micro-intentions to macro-outcomes, no algorithm for assembling collective outputs out of the depths of individual character. Yet the link between motivation and behavior, and procedures for corporate action, count supremely in organized religious life. Otherwise, Jesuits might as well return, like troglodytes, to solitary contemplation.[36]

Within Catholicism, and among the Jesuits, the indeterminacy inherent in the problem of aggregating the dispositions of individuals into a cohesive organization, when the goals of the enterprise are diffuse, has generated three responses. Although they may be compatible with it, none of these alternatives corresponds to democracy. One has been an insistence on hierarchy, as if top-down control were needed to focus and shape the profusion of subjective wills. A second reaction has been the flip side of this: piecemeal, expedient empiricism, a casual pragmatism, a seemingly haphazard adaptability.

A third response has been symbolic. It has meant reliance on collective aesthetics—that is, on allegory, parable, and metaphor as emblems of communal suffering and purpose and as signs of identity. From this viewpoint, the religious institution itself is something of a shell. The work of storytelling, the implicit framing of the community and the myth-making go on without respect for organizational charts or dogmatic correctness.[37]

It would be a mistake to reduce Catholicism to opera and the Society of Jesus to *spectaculo*.[38] Still, it is helpful to take an interpretive as well as an analytical view of the cultural devices—the instructive rhetoric and riveting fables—that made sense of the mission of the Society of Jesus and fostered the allegiance of individuals to the collective enterprise. Instead of searching for ladders between the micro- and macrolevels of the institution—levels that are nebulous to begin with—one can envision the order as an ensemble of delicately aligned dimensions, a configuration vulnerable to change, encompassing cultural as well as organizational and psychological realities.[39] What might these cultural filaments be?

Through the years leading up to Vatican II, Jesuits operated within a symbolic framework that gave tacit meaning to the hardships of immigrant and postimmigrant Catholics. This cultural membrane encompassed two not altogether compatible visions. The family was at once the primary human unit, joining intimacy and order, and an allegory—sometimes simplistic, in other versions more sophisticated—of the larger collectivity. The family has been to Catholic social order what class has been to social conflict in Marxism, and what the individual has been to the capitalist market, and the voluntary association to democratic theory.[40]

The other image cast the Society of Jesus itself as a peripatetic band of virtuous achievers who stood apart from the entanglements of the familial environment and from ecclesiastical routine. The figure of the *homo viator* as an emblem of the pilgrim soul predates the Society of Jesus. But among religious orders it is one that the enterprising, cosmopolitan Jesuits, known for their versatility and mobility, developed to an exceptional degree. It was a vision with powerful associations in the polyglot yet parochial world of immigrant Catholicism.[41]

Jesuits gave themselves to the task of providing meaning and hope, not certainty or happiness. They did this through their mystique as a kind of itinerant family, enfolded within the provisional settlement of the larger community, as well as through the training they provided in skills and critical thinking. When the set of myths began to lose meaning, and when their expertise became less precious, Jesuits entered into turmoil. How this metamorphosis came about is the story that unfolds in the following pages.

VII

One doesn't plow straight through a book of this length; one deals with it. Here are some tips.

• Among the myths that have come to enshroud the Society of Jesus is one to the effect that Jesuits are extraordinarily articulate. Many Jesuits can give polished and moving renditions of their lives and work. Jesuits can also be as oblique and reticent, as normal and boring as the rest of us when it comes to matters that concern them most.

The world of the Jesuits is not all words, not is it simply the sum of inner states. It composes a material culture, too. I hope there is enough descriptive accuracy and implicit conceptual architecture, as well as oral history, in my reconstruction of preconciliar, mostly East Coast and Midwestern Catholicism—the boiled food and lumpy sofas, the sidewalks inlaid with chewing gum, the tasseled offwhite window shades and the polychrome statuary—that a good deal of analytical commentary can be foregone. This means that it is probably only a venial sin to skim the Introduction.

• It is natural for Catholics of a certain age to view this time, from the receding of the immigrant era to the beginning of the sixties, as encapsulating a childhood and an innocence irretrievably lost, the years of crayon-colored saints, batty nuns, and the thin white smoke of incense. "Bittersweet" is the buzzword for that wistfulness.[42] Opposed to this is the notion of the modernity, the growing-up into assimilation, by which that tradition was transformed out of recognition. In fact, however, it may have been the other way around. Catholic childhood, a time of marvels, cannot be equated with innocence, any more than can fairy tales be understood without knowing about magicians, witches, and the folly of adults. It is the belief in the innocuous progress of the postwar years, of "the American century," when both prosperity and traditional Catholicism were at high tide, that in retrospect seems quaint in its materialism and tidy idealism.[43]

• This story is about a way of life unfolding over the course of about half a century, at multiple levels. Demographic, organizational, cultural, and psychological changes are intertwined. Yet changes in one dimension—say, the institutional—do not always mesh instantaneously with changes at another—for example, the psychological—and patterns of causation are complex. The impression can be like that of watching fast and colorful action through a lens that keeps scenery and figures at various distances all more or less in focus. It is tempting to view everything from a single angle. Thus, one might reduce the narrative to a kind of manic psychodrama, with interludes of lyric quietism, or to an analysis of organizational stagnation, or to an interpretation of the dynamics of the symbolic capital of the Society of Jesus. None of these perspectives is wrong, but each is incomplete.

VIII

The bulk of the financial support for this study came from the National Endowment for the Humanities. Generous financial assistance was also furnished by the German Marshall Fund, the Social Science Research Council, the Fulbright Commission, the Horace H. Rackham School of Graduate Studies and the Institute for Social Research at the University of Michigan, and Arizona State University. My former colleagues at Vanderbilt University stimulated me to think about the parallels between the unsettled traditions of big-city Catholicism and the unmaking of the Old South.[44]

Peter Dougherty, my editor, guided a complicated project to completion, and convinced me that the Finnegans Wake of footnotes belonged at the back of the book. Eileen DeWald, Robert Harrington, and Sue Llewellyn gave superb long-distance support during the finishing stages. Robert Mester and Patti Webb provided indispensable research assistance; Joyce Meyer and Deborah Eddy transcribed dozens of interviews. Saint Genesius, patron saint of secretaries, works in mysterious ways.[45]

This book has been about eight years in the making. The fondest memories from this time are of half-a-year's stay in Dublin. I wish to express my gratitude for the hospitality extended to my family and myself by Colette Delaney and Paddy Hannigan, by Helen and Kevin Burke, and by Tom Garvin and the late John Whyte.

Whenever I got to feeling sorry for myself about the occasional rebuff suffered in trying to find out "how this outfit really works," I considered how other institutions might have reacted to similar snooping. In the land of the Jesuits, I came across very little of the unction of the horrified, almost no "Here, let me give you some literature" ploys. On the whole, Jesuits reacted generously and thoughtfully to my importunings. In reporting on his research about the adventures of an eighteenth-century Jesuit and the Chinese covert he brought back with him to France, Jonathan Spence captured an experience not unlike my own:

> Unlike some modern guardians of our fate, [Fr. Jean-François] Fouc-
> quet did not attempt to prove his own innocence by erasing the past

from the record. Instead, he carefully kept and filed away every memo and letter that came his way, even if the material did not show him in a pleasant light. He copied and recopied many such items, convinced that the record in its totality would vindicate his views of his own rightness. I don't happen to think that Foucquet was right in the way he treated Hu, but I am only able to make that judgment because he lets me. Thus even if I believe I have confronted him successfully Foucquet remains, in a way, the victor.[46]

My greatest debt is to the individuals, most of them Jesuits and former Jesuits, who have taken part in the study, through interviews, arranging access to archives, and commenting on preliminary drafts. They are too numerous—more than two hundred—to mention here by name. None of them bears responsibility for my errors of fact and interpretation.

This book is dedicated to my wife Josefina and our daughters Graça and Julia. They put up with "all those church books around the house." Josefina saw all along what the project meant to me. I am more grateful than I can say for her willingness to see it through good times and bad.

PMcD
Aldeia de São Pedro,
Portugal
Summer, 1991

Introduction

Of the many changes associated with the Second Vatican Council—the conclave of cardinals, bishops, heads of religious orders, their advisers, and assorted observers that took place from 1962 to 1965 and that divided an archaic from a partially updated church—two stand out. One was the globalization of Catholicism. The shift from a Eurocentric to a multicultural vision corresponded to a tipping of the demographic scales within the church from the Northern to the Southern Hemisphere. A second change was the accent on social justice.

Several aftershocks of these changes—notably, the falloff in religious vocations—were unanticipated. Yet the changes themselves were cumulative rather than wholly unprecedented. They were prefigured in earlier transformations. For more than a century prior to Vatican II the migration of European Catholics to North America had been propelling a massive demographic realignment. By the 1950s English-speaking Catholics had become economically dominant, with considerable organizational clout, in the midst of a legacy that was still Latinate. A parallel change involved the participation of immigrant Catholics in the industrialization of the New World. An uprooted peasantry and an emerging working class were thrust into a culture of prodigious abundance.

The American offshoot of Catholicism grew in numbers and wealth. The dispersion of Catholics from the European matrix posed challenges to a church that, institutionally and doctrinally, was straining for control in the wake of the French Revolution. Urbanization and the growth of the working class drew the attention of ecclesiastics to the social question. At the heart of these geographic and social movements was a pair of preoccupations: the striving for material improvement and concern with safeguarding the family. These were the supreme imperatives of American Catholicism as they were for most newcomers to the United States.[1]

The connection between the pair of goals was uneasy. Change on one side—an increase in family income, for instance—might alter the division of labor and power between husbands and wives and between parents and children. The nexus of mobility and tradition was dynamic, and such equilibrium as might be attained was unstable. Historical transformations of momentous proportions were acted out from day to day in the intimacy of the household.[2]

Three things were at stake. One was the split in gender roles over the allocation of domestic labor, of child rearing and in general of work in and outside the home. The family and the status of women in the family resonated with abiding values against the mutability of the wider world. They took on a near-mythical fixity that became all the more appealing with the vagaries of migration. How were these hierarchies to withstand and adapt to the American enterprise?

Another locus of contention was the division between generations. The aspirations of second- and third-generation ethnics differed from the expectations of those who had come before. The spread of education and accelerating social mobility stretched the bonds between successive cohorts of the Catholic subculture.

Still another source of tension lay in the fact of migration itself—in the uprooting and mixing together of people from largely parochial backgrounds in a great cosmopolitan venture. Their traditions differed, their intercourse was complex, and the transition they underwent was multidimensional. The diversity of origins and the proliferation of opportunities were vertiginous. For a while the binding element was Catholicism.

II

It seemed that there was so much in us that only storms, terror and the fury of life could purify; so much in us of the achiever, the macho, the frantic and the appetitive, the willful failure. Indeed we were a complicated lot.[3]

This book is a study of the prelude to revolution. It encompasses the period from around the turn of the century, when the Catholic church began to take the social question seriously while at the same time clamping down on intellectual dissent through the antimodernist crusade, to the mid-sixties, when the Second Vatican Council inaugurated its attempt at *aggiornamento* ("updating"). It concentrates on the largest male religious order within Catholicism, the Society of Jesus.

Revolutions in the accepted sense involve the overthrow of institutional power and the dispossession of material property. Nothing like this transfer and redistribution of physical capital happened with Vatican II. Nevertheless, something approaching a revolution took place among the Jesuits. Change came about not in the face of pressure from the outside but largely as a result of discontent in the leadership and among the ranks with what came to be seen as an overly embroidered and increasingly counterproductive tradition.

Equally as significant as the genealogy of the revolution was its substance. Catholicism is perhaps the largest Western institution in which authority has been bound up with questions of sexuality and the segregation of roles by gender. In the sixties, rebellion against authority was fused with attacks against the regulation of sexuality. The church that, in the United States, had ridden out—and prospered from—political and economic reforms was hard hit by the crisis in the protocols of everyday interaction and by the challenge to privileges that had been thought to be private "since time immemorial."

The multiple collisions of the sixties were the outcome of emotional as well as intellectual and moral transformations. While many of its manifestations were at the time scandalously physical, involving the rejection of restrictive codes of dress and speech, change also involved an upheaval in mental constructs and moral values—in meanings, goals, and the framing of human endeavor. The revolution that struck the Jesuits was both corporeal and resonant of a transformation in intellectual and ethical positions that had been solidifying since the Counter-Reformation and the reaction of the Catholic Powers to the Enlightenment and the French Revolution. Underlying a growing but still somewhat clerk-ish split between intellectual and ethical standards of conduct and social order were profound fissures between moral composure, emotional expression, sexuality, and male identity.[4]

Almost inevitably, the excitement surrounding the Second Vatican Council obscures the years leading up to it. While in retrospect it is virtually impossible not to view these decades as a prelude to a revolution of sorts, the period is also of interest in its own right. It constitutes an interlude—a bubble of stability—between the trauma of migration and the belated encounter with modernity. It is this deceptively becalmed period in American Catholicism, from around the turn to a bit after the middle of the century, that stands as anomalous in balance with the tumult that followed and the wrenching transformations that preceded it. This problematic, tension-ridden slice of tradition forms my main subject. The revolution itself is something of an anticlimax, and the very recent years of an attempted Catholic restoration are scarcely treated at all.[5]

III

Founded in 1540, in early modern Europe, the Society of Jesus quickly gained a reputation as a shaper of human capital. Jesuits set themselves up primarily as a network of educators rather than as an organization with an unequivocal product. However bent on bringing a measure of rationality and renewed acceptance to a corrupt church, Jesuits never made a clean break with the past. Instead, they fixed on the papacy as the embodiment of tradition. Nevertheless, their commitment to the development of human resources set the Jesuits apart from wholly obscurantist elements in traditional Catholicism.[6]

The Society of Jesus has had chronically to reconcile loyalty to an ancient hierarchy with outreach to the secular world. Through most of the nineteenth and the first half of the twentieth century, the European branch of the Society of Jesus remained the product not only of the Counter-Reformation but of a virulently conservative reaction to the French Revolution. In the United States, however, while these quarrels were not completely forgotten, distinctive tasks and conflicts were layered over them, and the responsibilities that the Society of Jesus took on in North America differed from those facing its continental counterpart. The selective conservatism of the American branch of the order mirrored the dispositions of its immigrant constituents at least as much as it did the ideological battles of continental Europe.

Diversity, contradiction, and even discontinuity—the order was abolished a few years prior to the French Revolution, only to be resurrected in the early years of the nineteenth century—have made for a picaresque history. Tradition for the Jesuits has been a series of fleeting equilibria, and the geographical heterogeneity of the order has fostered variation in its operations and its ideology even during periods of composure. Although some of the mystique of the Society of Jesus may stem, as Jesuits themselves used to observe, from the fact that every fifth Jesuit seemed to be writing about the exploits of the other four, it is true that much of the history of the order reads like a *tremendista* novel, replete with heroics, disasters, dizzying ups and downs. An enduring paradox of the Society of Jesus is the coexistence of its volatility and longevity.[7]

Recent Jesuit history is summarized in the next section by way of background to the central themes of the book. Before entering into this chronicle, however, it is worth highlighting the key changes undergone by the Society of Jesus. One of these is quantitative; the others are harder to put numbers on.

Figure 1 shows the ascent and decline of membership in the Society of

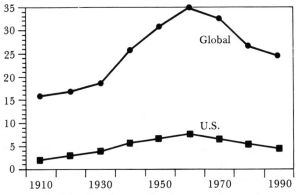

FIGURE 1. Membership in the Society of Jesus (in thousands), 1910–90

Jesus from the second decade of the century, just after the American "assistancy" (region) gained separate administrative status from the English branch, to the beginning of the last decade of the century. Membership in the international order peaked at over 36,000 men in 1965. By 1990 it had fallen below 25,000. In the United States during the same period membership fell from more than 8,000 to fewer than 5,000.[8]

The numbers for the society worldwide and for the society in the United States appear to rise and fall in tandem. On closer inspection, however, a significant twist emerges. Figure 2 traces the growth and drop-off in American Jesuits as a percentage of the world total. The Americans increased steadily as a proportion of the global society from the turn of the century until the sixties. Then, approximately one out of four Jesuits was an American. Their relative magnitude has since slipped, to less than one out of five. Jesuit numbers have fallen overall, and the decline of the

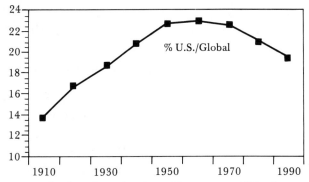

FIGURE 2. American Jesuits as Percentage of Total Membership in Society of Jesus, 1910–90

Americans has been especially pronounced in the wake of the rising numbers and the expectations that accompanied them prior to the Second Vatican Council.

A fuller account of the factors contributing to the downturn will be given later in these pages. For now it is the swelling in Jesuit numbers, not the decline, that merits attention. The first lesson suggested by the statistics is the brevity of the American moment in Catholicism. The ascendancy of the Americans spanned no more than a decade or so from the early fifties to the mid-sixties. After that, the momentum in recruitment, not only among the Jesuits but for other religious orders as well, passed to the Third World.

The growth side of the curve matches the period covered in this study. The demographics behind the trend are so important for understanding the ideological and institutional evolution of the Society of Jesus in the United States that a word of explanation is needed. Briefly stated: The approximately one hundred years from the middle of the nineteenth to the middle of the twentieth century—the "golden century" of growth in the immigrant church—corresponded to the high tide of the cult of male celibacy in American Catholicism. The expansion of clericalism had its roots in the German, and particularly the Irish, segments of the immigrant and postimmigrant communities.

The idealization of female virginity was nothing new in the church, especially in its Mediterranean and Latin American branches.[9] In the United States during the nineteenth century the cult of domesticity and delicacy became normative for married women, particularly although not only for Catholic women.[10] But none of this translated in like measure into the sanctioning of celibacy for men, certainly not for Latin males, among whom vocations to the priesthood were notoriously few and whose adherence to the vows of ordination was in any case an object of skepticism on the part of the laity.

By contrast, famine, land hunger, and rules of inheritance that favored one son to the exclusion of other male offspring combined with a legacy of sexual asceticism to generate large numbers of applicants to the priesthood among Irish men and boys.[11] In a cultural afterlife for a code whose demographic rationale was disappearing, the pattern thrived in the Irish American enclaves of the United States. Religious vocations were also numerous among German Americans. Aside from whatever contribution an authoritarian family structure might have made to this growth, the sheer volume of immigration from Germany overtook the flow from other nations during the final decades of the nineteenth century, and vocations to religious life among German Americans increased in absolute terms. While Irish immigrants dominated the influx between 1830 and 1870, Germans became the largest group from 1870 to 1890.[12]

Male celibacy was a form of popular heroism in the subculture of immigrant and postimmigrant Catholicism.[13] It inspired prodigies of hard work and organizational inventiveness, and it waved the banner of tradition. But much of what was taken for clerical tradition and providential expansion was the byproduct of a demographic fluke. The numbers could not be sustained.[14]

American Jesuits were profoundly affected by this confluence of demographic incentives and cultural forces. The ideological climate that shaped Jesuits in the United States was predominantly Latin. But the institutional landscape—with the crucial exception of the parallel system of Catholic schools—was overwhelmingly American. Neither the confessional nor the militant leftist parties of continental Europe were present in the United States.[15] The American political environment channeled the partisanship of Catholics into outlets that, to the Roman mind, seemed perilously nonsectarian. The energies that European Catholics invested in Christian Democratic parties and Catholic trade unions went into the ethnic but officially secular Democratic machines of the cities of the United States. As if in compensation, American Catholics supported an infrastructure of private education that surpassed the system of Catholic education in Europe, and it was to the secondary and higher reaches of this network that Jesuits in the United States devoted most of their labors.

Finally, the emotional and psychosexual disposition of the Jesuits in America was characteristically Irish, with a strong admixture of German severity.[16]

The ideological template and the institutional realities of immigrant Catholicism went separate ways. Although a Latin ambience suffused the life of the community as a resplendent liturgy, in its intellectual guise religious culture was confined mostly to theology, which had little to do with daily concerns or social policy. Organizations and associational rituals on the other hand—the offices of political clubs, union halls, communion breakfasts, and the like—had clear significance for personal contacts and bread-and-butter issues. A pragmatism persistent in its disregard for ideas typified the politics of the Catholic enclave.[17]

Religious professionals, including many Jesuits, nurtured an affective orientation of obsessive restraint, and strict sexual decorum was taken as a model for the laity. Ritual and personalism—a busy mixture of formality and face-to-face interaction—characterized the world of immigrant Catholicism. A folk minuet of propriety and tribal populism governed everyday life. These habits defined the quotidian relations of authority and the modes of collective expression. They stood at a second remove from—in effect, taking the place of—ideas and overt sexuality.

The ideological, organizational, and sexual components of the immigrant way of life did not so much clash as hang together in unsteady suspension. Their compartmentalization smoothed the interaction of the subculture with the American scene. A de facto privatization prevailed over ideological rigidity and outright political reaction. It shielded tradition, preserving it in the form of an underlying inertia of popular customs that were only loosely connected to religious dogma in the theological sense or to political platforms. The effect was to foster adaptability without the loss of cultural identity.[18]

These demographic, organizational, and cultural trends were also associated with a pair of collateral and less conspicuous changes. One of these touched on the Society of Jesus as an organization, the other on the inner life of Jesuits.

On the organizational side, it is instructive to consider the Society of Jesus as an arrangement for satisfying three types of needs for its members, in addition to providing services to others. When an organization like the Society of Jesus fails to meet these needs, its survival is threatened.

The most tangible of these is mastery, the sense of exerting control over an area of performance such as, in the case of Jesuits, education. While not all Jesuits are involved in education, the bulk of them have been and continue to be teachers. To the degree that the order has a bottom line, it is reflected in enrollments, graduations, grades, academic budgets, and the like. By the 1960s the Society of Jesus in the United States was becoming a victim of its own success. The growing sophistication of Catholics, many of them educated by Jesuits, together with the increasing size and complexity of the schools, undermined the capacity of Jesuits to determine the course of their pedagogical and other institutional activities. They no longer had a corporate sense of dominating their environment.

Meaning is a less tangible condition of the survival of organizations such as the Jesuits. Specific tasks make sense within a larger set of goals. Otherwise, individuals tend to pursue objectives that may or may not coincide with those of the organization. In service organizations in which profit does not constitute the payoff and in which the ethos encourages sacrifice, overarching goals help sustain motivation.[19] Virtue is not the sole reward of altruism. Sustained idealism works by fulfilling evidently needed functions and generating gratitude and even a modicum of power by association with a cause and corporate success, and it may depend as much on belief in the effectiveness of prescribed behavior as on zeal or charitable impulse.[20] It was the wider rationale of services, and with it the role of the priesthood, that was shaken with the demise of the immigrant subculture in postwar America and the revision of the conceptual framework of Catholicism during Vatican II. The sense of clerical mission waned together with the Jesuits' air of competence and control.

Last, organizations such as the Society of Jesus must provide emotional support for their members. Although this function is hardly confined to religious groups—one thinks of the bonding that occurs among men in combat—solidarity is critical to an organization that, besides doing its job, stands as a family for its members. The society is more formalized than a social movement and many small groups, yet it is also an organization that has to furnish affective sustenance to its members. Though from a narrowly bureaucratic perspective this function might seem less tangible than the imperatives of mastery and meaning, it can scarcely be thought of as abstract. An important element of this support was the prestige and élan that accrued to Jesuits as leaders of Tridentine Catholicism, the Counter-Reformation movement-fortress that took shape at the Council of Trent (1545–63). The diminution of the communal ambience of Catholicism with the suburbanization and social mobility of the postwar years, coming as these changes did alongside the decline in managerial capacity and the questioning of a venerable world view, cut into the tacit bases of emotional support and threw the Society of Jesus into crisis.

The gradient from mastery through meaning to emotional gratification goes roughly from hard to soft organizational properties. Mastery would seem to be the sine qua non of organizational viability. Even if its bottom line eludes precise estimation, the Society of Jesus resembles any organization that is in the business of converting part of its surroundings into a predictable output. But just as clearly Jesuits participate in a special class of organizations not only because of the relative immateriality of the order's goals but also because of the commitment it requires and the sense of belonging it engenders in return.[21]

Religious orders like the Society of Jesus strive to mesh the dimensions of action, understanding, and emotion that intersect much more casually in the ramshackle comprehensiveness of Catholicism. The Society of Jesus is altogether too complex for this integration to be attained in practice, yet the ideal is more serious than mere rhetoric. It resembles a motivational metaphor.[22] As the metaphor approximates not only a preference but a perception of organizational reality, an institution becomes virtually indistinguishable from an enveloping way of life, grounded in behavioral, cognitive, and affective reinforcements. Besides being a mechanism for action, it constitutes a context of understanding and a habit of feeling. The perceived integration of the three dimensions makes change along any one of them hard to disentangle from the rest. Around the time of Vatican II, all these supports came undone for the Jesuits.[23]

The predominantly psychological traits that comprise the matrix out of which the Jesuit outlook has developed can also be thought of in three dimensions. Like the institutional and cultural properties of mastery, meaning, and emotional support, these more individualistically psychological features underwent change with Vatican II. And, like their organizational counterparts, they have rarely been in equilibrium.

A major rationale of the lengthy training of Jesuits—it may take up to fifteen years—has been to inculcate a set of values and goals that are supposed to stay with the members of the order and guide their actions in distant places and institutional contexts outside the reach of centralized surveillance. This is character as consistency: dependability, endurance, willpower, internalized obedience. Character is also understood as conscience, as the discernment of choices and the adherence to convictions that might fly in the face of institutional demands.[24]

The distinction between consistency and conscience is not axiomatically invidious, with the latter ranking above the former. Character as consistency may require loyalty to a set of norms, of which organizational rules are a special case, that engenders a sense of reliability even in the view of those who reject these norms. It entails the construction of a sense of personal continuity, a creation of the self that tends to be deeply problematic in times marked by rapid cultural change, such as the formative years of early modern Europe, and not unlike the more recent decades of the postmodern era.[25] Similarly, character as conscience may facilitate adaptability to unforeseen circumstances—a kind of common sense and trust in individual judgment—rather than signifying a principled rejection of conformity. Still, there remains an unresolved tension between consistency, often bound to obedience and corporate loyalty, and conscience, whose connotations are more plainly individualistic.[26]

The clash between these understandings of character has furnished the Society of Jesus with a restless energy, and it has occasionally burst forth in the shape of severe conflicts between hierarchical authority and an anarchistic streak in Catholicism. Officially there is not much legitimate middle ground between obedience and rebellion; flexibility is not organizational pluralism or personal autonomy. Crosspressure of this kind parallels the agonistic pulls at the heart of Ignatian spirituality. It also helps account for the swings between turbulence and orderliness in Jesuit history.[27] Its various manifestations will be a leitmotiv of the following pages.

The Jesuit frame of mind is thus both tenacious and precarious. What might trigger a shift from creative tension to turmoil? Whether as consistency or conscience, character stands midway along a continuum that runs from the superficial to the abiding—between mere opinions and preferences, which are changeable, and identity, which is close to immutable.

Character is arduously constructed. Identity, to simplify, is virtually given, inherited.[28] It serves as a ballast in the recurrent struggles between character as consistency and character as conscience. Identity is both psychosexual and, in the case of religious groups such as the Jesuits, corporate.

Changes such as the erosion of the ethnic ghettos, transformations in family structures, and the hugeness of organizations may fracture the social underpinnings of identity and set in motion crises of character, not to mention brusque changes in opinion. To some extent, the balance between character as consistency and character as conscience depends on collective buttressing and a prerational sense of identity. Constancy without conscience tends to be associated with dronelike obedience. Conscience without consistency, a flitting from one cause to another, impedes commitment and vitiates collective life.[29]

The triad of identity, character as consistency and character as conscience has in one way or another always been in conflict among Jesuits. Their inconclusive dialectic has provided the order with much of its dynamism. Vatican II precipitated a sharp alteration in the intrapsychic balance of Jesuits—specifically with regard to the anchoring of corporate and psychosexual identity.

Categories such as these are heuristic devices for making sense of the highly charged transformations that burst on the Jesuits in the 1960s. The historical foundations of identity shifted out from under the Jesuits. Some of these antinomies—the inherited polarity in gender roles, for example—persist institutionally but, like rhymed poetry after the advent of modernism, they came to lack not only acceptance but also, even among practitioners, the conviction of times past.

This process can be unraveled in concrete terms. In some instances in the course of its history the Society of Jesus seems to have been in control of its fate. The order produced cultural artifacts of great value; Jesuit pedagogy is perhaps the most enduring monument to its creativity. But on numerous other occasions, heroics and system alike proved futile, and on still others Jesuits simply didn't know what they were doing. These misadventures were not fatal, however. Such setbacks did not differ wildly from the commonplace inefficiencies of organizational life, and even if Jesuits failed to learn with maximum efficiency from their mistakes, these defeats entered the collective wisdom of the order, building its reputation for tenacity. They proceed by trial and error. It took them several decades to develop an organizational formula for evangelizing the natives of Latin America—"the reductions" that gathered tribal peoples into regulated enclaves—only to see the settlements abolished several decades later.[30] Historians used to write that in the glory days of the order scarcely a column of soldiers, explorers, and trappers sallied forth from the French settlements in North America without a Jesuit or two at its head. As Jesuits themselves like to point out, such accounts neglected to mention that they were lost.[31]

Yet even when they were lost or experimenting with eclectic abandon, Jesuits usually had a firm sense of mission. The series of changes in which the Society of Jesus was caught up during Vatican II can be visualized as a peeling-away from the outer to the inner layers of Jesuit reality, from action and purpose to the self. For a time, not only did Jesuits not know what they were doing—they didn't know who they were.[32]

IV

So we took ship, somewhere in the late fifties, with a sublime wide-eyed confidence. The world looked stable; not at all like molten water; the church was a sound vessel; the Jesuits a skilled crew.[33]

The experience of the Jesuits in the years leading up to the council can be divided into two phases. The first opened in the early decades of the century and closed around the mid-forties. This period witnessed the collapse of the *ancien régime* in Europe, economic depression, the rise of fascism and communism, and the absorption of immigrant communities in the United States.

In Europe the Jesuits set up "centers of social research and action." The first, and the one that became a model for the rest, was the Action Populaire in Reims.[34] During the 1930s the superior general of the society enjoined the American Jesuits to "marshal forces against communistic atheism and work for the establishment of a Christian social order."[35] The chief experiment along these lines in the United States was the Institute of Social Order, headquartered for most of its existence in St. Louis. (Soon after World War II, similar operations were launched in Latin America and the Philippines.)[36] This period also saw the inauguration of schools of social work affiliated with Jesuit universities at Fordham in New York, Loyola in Chicago, and elsewhere; the simultaneous opening of faculties "of commerce and finance"—the early business schools—in the same locations; and the training of selected Jesuits in the social sciences.

The waning years of the nineteenth century and the early decades of the twentieth encompassed countertrends that mirrored persistent tensions within Catholicism and between Catholicism and secularism. Besides efforts to preempt radical labor movements, the founding in 1909 of *America*, the Jesuits' "journal of opinion" in the United States, signaled an attempt to reach out to a modernizing environment. These were also the years of the backward-looking pontificate of Pius X, who followed his predecessor's condemnation of "Americanism" in 1899 with a repudiation of the generic heresy of "modernism" in 1907. Ventures in dialogue with a world in intellectual ferment, undergoing colossal structural transformation, were conducted under ecclesiastical surveillance and, in the United States, largely from within the confines of immigrant ghettos. [37]

Although the size and the diversity of the subculture defeated impeccable control, the drift of enclave Catholicism was toward mildly progressive authoritarianism. Priests cared for the flock and received deference in return. Jesuits attuned to the ultramontane pretensions that were widespread among the brethren in Europe propagated a conservatism with an ideological edge, but most settled for apolitical discretion.

The mores of the enclaves, particularly as they were crystallized in traditional family structures, seemed sufficiently hierarchical, and the Catholic minority itself was still insufficiently secure, that efforts somehow to overcome the larger culture remained hypothetical and indeed unintelligible. The effective campaign of the church militant was not offensive but rather one of self-congratulation. Entente was preferable to warfare. Catholics kept to themselves; intermarriage was rare. Most of the time, the world was within walking distance, and propinquity governed what doctrine could not.

Organizational developments were driven at least as much by demographics and market demand as by dogma. Intellectual dissent was rare, yet organizational expansion and innovation went on apace. Women were able to enroll in the numerous professional schools Jesuits had attached to their universities long before female students were admitted into their undergraduate colleges. Expedient reforms like these responded to the demand for applied education on the part of the immigrant community, at the same time that they helped finance the classical parts of the curriculum. [38]

Ideological niceties were lost in the press of business, as was much intellectual curiosity. The fact that institution building in the United States was self-funded also gave American Catholics a measure of autonomy. [39] As for the Jesuits, the confidence that the Society enjoyed from the Vatican gave its members a good deal of operational discretion. Unlike ordinary priests, Jesuits were not under the rule of local bishops. The result was a certain freedom in the field that got the job done and was largely devoid of ideas. On the one hand, doctrinal conformity was vigorously pursued. On the other hand, theological debate tended to be so stratospheric that its effect on day-to-day activities went largely unnoticed. Ordinary faith was reinforced through a seemingly unintelligible but emotionally comprehensible liturgy in which individual expression and participation were submerged in a collective cadence. Ideas were academic and European; institutions were home-grown. [40]

Efforts originating in Europe to develop a social doctrine that advocated a "vocational order" as an alternative to capitalism and communism were pursued up through the thirties and early forties. Skepticism about economic liberalism and political democracy, both identified with Protestantism, and dread of a socialism that was equated with a stridently anticlerical communism characterized the undertaking.[41]

Cast this way, the problems themselves sounded un-American, and the vocabulary of the proposals for solving them never took hold in the United States. "Corporatism" as propounded by Catholic political theorists had a medieval flavor. Their ideas about social peace seemed to have more to do with maintaining the preindustrial harmony of guilds, in an organic and static hierarchy, under a halo of religious community, than with managing the boisterous mobility and booming productivity of "America, Inc."[42] What Americans understood as business organizations—as capitalism—continental Catholics took to be "estates," status groups, and occupational categories that were low on mobility and had a strong antimarket slant. There were no Christian Democratic parties in the United States that might serve as interlocutors between the two interpretations of corporatism.

The corporatist model, elaborated by German Jesuits attached to the Gregorian University in Rome, became compromised with the policies of the authoritarian regimes in Italy, Portugal, and Spain, and its formal trappings fell into disrepute with the victory of the democracies. Yet corporatism of a de facto variety, involving capital-labor bargaining, comanagement schemes, and a directive Keynesian role for government gained acceptance in Western Europe—in Germany and France, for example—and to a lesser extent in the United States as reconstruction proceeded during the Cold War. Despite the differences in legal contexts, there was common ground between Catholic and secular versions of corporatism in their focus on bureaucracies and organized interests as the fundamental units of civil society, in place of diffuse classes and atomistic individuals. Shorn of their antiquarian rhetoric, social engineering and managerial *dirigisme* emerged in the guise of a depoliticized pragmatism that paid off for consumers.[43]

The prosperity ushered in by the postwar boom further undermined the appeal of a social doctrine that presupposed conditions of scarcity and prized stability over growth and mobility. All the same the number of Jesuits increased through the remainder of the forties and most of the fifties and early sixties. In part because of the need to process large numbers, and in part as a reaction against what was perceived as a swelling and insidious materialism, the training of Jesuits continued to be regimented. Secondary and higher education pretty much monopolized the activities of the society in the United States. The social *magisterium* was peripheral to the growing attraction of religious life; the number of Jesuits engaged in "the social apostolate" remained small. Despite occasional exhortations by the leadership of the order, the social analysis and action undertaken by Jesuits during this time were marginal to their other commitments.[44]

This second period, then, which got under way as soon as the end of the war was in view and which lasted through the early sixties and the beginning of the council, was characterized by a conservatism or indifference with respect to economic and social issues and by a sustained asceticism regarding questions of personal morality.[45] But it was also during this time that some American Jesuits, led by John Courtney Murray, began to cultivate relatively enlightened political ideas. Murray provided legitimation for religious tolerance and political pluralism and helped rid Catholic political theorizing of much of its antimodernist verbiage, making possible a rapprochement with the liberal tradition. A conservative in matters of economic policy and personal morality, Murray nonetheless managed to reconcile institutional Catholicism with "the American proposition"—that is, to demonstrate the compatibility between parts of the Catholic tradition and Anglo-American pluralism.[46]

In one respect the innovation was anticlimactic. Catholics had been living under the American dispensation as fervent patriots and were striving for further assimilation without troubling themselves about the theoretical propriety of one political system or another in the light of church doctrine; on the whole they seemed oblivious to the need for justifying what they had already welcomed in practice.[47] It was the way Murray reached his conclusion about the soundness of pluralism, through an affirmation of historical change, as much as the live-and-let-live conclusion itself (that pluralism was, after all, acceptable) that proved to be pathbreaking for Tridentine Catholicism. A methodology that stressed the need to come to terms with historical processes departed from the ideal of eternal verities and unchanging principles as the standard against which institutional arrangements, and by implication moral laws, were to be judged. Murray's stress on the dynamics of intellectual discovery contrasted with the ideal of a static revelation and reinforced his approval of an anti-triumphalistic, minority role for political Catholicism.

This appreciation of historical contingency and process was to become the hallmark of Vatican II. Acceptance of the pluralism advocated by Murray cut the legitimacy out from under roughly half a century of antimodernist defensiveness and organizational encapsulation that had fortified the Counter-Reformation, anti-Enlightenment tenor of Catholicism. It is the tightening-up and the crisis of this intellectual and institutional environment that forms the context of my study.[48]

The years following the council, like those before, can be divided in two. After an initial euphoria that exceeded the tempered optimism of men like

Murray, the coincidence of the council and the turmoil of the sixties traumatized the Society of Jesus. Like many other religious groups, the Jesuits
moved toward the left on public controversies; a few became active in the
antiwar and civil rights movements. In Latin America some embraced liberation theology. The political liberalism espoused by Murray began to look
tame and antiquated balanced against calls for a drastic overhaul of social
structures.[49] Departures mounted, the number of recruits fell. The reduction in numbers facilitated the customization of training. This process had
been underway in any case as the norms of the old template system of
formation were rejected and as men entered the society, on the average, at
a later age and with higher levels of education.[50]

This third period of downsizing and comparative radicalization lasted
through the tenure of Pedro Arrupe, a Basque who acted as the order's
superior general from 1965 to the early eighties. When a stroke incapaci-
tated Arrupe in 1981, the papacy took the unprecedented step of appointing
caretakers to run the society until a new general was elected in 1983.

A fourth period dates from the beginning of the eighties. The leadership
of the order has tried to improve relations with the Vatican and the ecclesiastical establishment, without jettisoning the reforms of the Arrupe years.
Membership has continued to decline in industrial societies, but growth is
vigorous in parts of the Third World, particularly in South Asia.[51]

V

We brought a weighty cargo aboard. You must understand, to grasp
the depth of our foolishness, that we were enterprising, disciplined,
respected abroad, even subjects of a glittering folklore. We were also
men of the world: travelled, mature to a degree. Quite a crew. And yet
foolish, far from the wisdom required for a steady crossing and a safe
outcome.[52]

A major contention of this study is that reforms internal to the Society of
Jesus—in governance, in the training of younger Jesuits, and in particular
with regard to the expression of emotion—are more significant, even if more
tortuous and less visible, than the revamping of the order's preferences on
political and social issues. These internal reforms and the psychic and
organizational struggles they have provoked distinguish post- from preconciliar Catholicism more fundamentally than do calls for social justice and
political activism. The stoic spirituality that undergirded the sacrifices of an
earlier time was to some extent undone by the achievements it helped to
produce.

What changed with Vatican II was not so much the social ideology of the

Society of Jesus—this goes back, in outline, to nineteenth-century critiques of capitalism[53]—as the cultural ground and the social code, the assumptions about the hierarchies of daily life and mastery of the emotions on which Jesuit identity had come to be built. The old ethic of long-suffering and natural organic order lost plausibility. No equivalent blueprint took its place.

Thus, the transformations undergone by Jesuits—stirring quietly from the turn of the century until the depression, then becoming more visible in the postwar period and picking up speed with Vatican II—can be thought of as layered over and loosely connected to one another, with those toward the inside being more threatening and painful than accommodations taking place nearer the surface.

One bundle of changes was political. These encompassed the acceptance of religious toleration and political pluralism vis-à-vis denominations and systems of government at variance with institutional Catholicism.

For the Society of Jesus, whose mission had come to be shaped by a Counter-Reformation militancy and an anti-Enlightenment conservatism, the political turnabout was major.[54] John Courtney Murray had to endure some years of silence, ordered by the Vatican and enforced by Jesuit superiors, before his ideas were vindicated. But vindicated they were. Openness toward other religions and governments was not applied, as Murray foresaw from his own experience, in equal measure to the intramural structures of the church. Almost certainly, this is one reason why the change with respect to political and religious liberty, controversial as it was, went through.[55]

Another set of changes took place in social and economic philosophy. The encyclicals issued during the Vatican II era nudged the ideological center of gravity of Catholicism to the left. There was an admixture of precapitalist traditionalism in this posture, going back to the teachings of nineteenth- and early-twentieth-century popes, with a strong whiff of nostalgia for a rustic steady state. Some of the pastoralism and medievalizing fustian had been dropped by the 1930s. The audience envisioned for *Quadragesimo Anno* in 1931, or rather the ultimate target of the encyclical, was the Catholic working class of industrial cities. However, the imagery of left versus right misses the increasingly dominant orientation, which was geopolitical, from a Eurocentric to a more global, North-versus-South perspective. The movement was encouraged by the demographic momentum of Catholicism in the Third World in conjunction with preexisting strictures against mass consumerism and materialism.[56]

Whatever its ideal preference for one type of regime over another, the church has had long experience dealing with a variety of political arrangements. Similarly, the social doctrine of the church could be sufficiently commodious to accommodate a diversity of understandings without generating firm commitment among the poor or serious discomfort among the powerful, or vice versa. Alarm and support depended on the attention given to social issues, relative to traditional moral peculations. A hallmark of Catholic social thought, as compared to moral theology, was ambiguity. Conciliation was the dominant theme. After Vatican II the dominant rhetoric took on a progressive cast.[57]

A third set of issues touched both the institutional and ideological core of Catholicism. These have involved questions of sexuality and authority that are intimately linked in the patriarchal church. Alterations in the church's position regarding political regimes and religious denominations and in its policies on social and economic issues could be treated as matters of opinion. They did not cut to the doctrinal quick. But questions regarding sexuality and affectivity went deeper, and in no other area of the church were personal and organizational dilemmas so closely linked.[58]

Choices in this domain are nowhere near so malleable as are preferences on political and social questions. Although a number of changes, in emphasis and to a degree in substance, have taken place in the social and political thought of the Society of Jesus, Catholicism has budged scarcely at all in the areas of sexuality and authority. In a patriarchy the institutional consequences of reforms in what might seem to be merely symbolic quandaries about the role of women are very great. The connections between gender inequality, psychosexual identity, and organizational authority are, or used to be, extraordinarily tight in Catholicism. Change here poses a crisis of individual and corporate identity and purpose, centered on the working out and sustenance of a male role and personality in opposition to women. Identity has turned out to be vastly less mutable than opinion. The issue is doubly explosive: psychically visceral and bound up with institutional stratification. The dual menace is licentiousness and the usurpation of authority.[59]

The notion that recent changes in the Society of Jesus have unfolded with increasing difficulty, with each successive layer being more treacherous than the previous one, makes sense once it is recognized that the dynamic parallels the turn, sanctioned by the Second Vatican Council, away from the Ptolemaic cosmology inherited from traditional scholasticism. Just as the earth was supposed to be the core of a series of concentric spheres that made up the heavens, so the family and gender relations stood at the epicenter of social creation.[60]

The concept provided a tangible, experiential analogue for the larger world and the position of individuals in it. The family was seen as transcendent in its particularity, at once local and universal, the elemental social organism. This made it intuitively graspable, in local terms, as a phenomenon that incarnated a global communion and cause. The imagery was especially vivid for immigrant Catholics living out the twofold drama of primary group preservation and economic mobility. The family was the last bastion of religious authority and social order. The household economy was perceived as the kernel of a global community.

It might also be noted that since the church is not a typical producer organization with an unequivocally economic bottom line, it has been able to finesse and give ground on political and social matters insofar as they do not affect the organization so directly as questions of internal authority and sexuality. In the Society of Jesus, the symbolic and psychic resonance of familial imagery has had a clear institutional equivalent. Hence, issues of power and sexuality and the links between them are extremely sensitive. The abandonment of positions on these issues would come closer than alterations in social and political theory to a paradigm shift capable of transforming the being of Catholicism.[61]

While the link between gender hierarchy and power is exceptionally strong in Catholicism, it is not unique. Conflict about change in this area, acute in the church, can be visualized as an instance of a broader struggle over the expansion of democratization that took place earlier in political and economic realms, toward the domestic and otherwise private sphere. The process, unfolding with the evolution of mass society, has involved a movement toward and a battle over the democratization of everyday life that is not exclusive to Catholicism or the Society of Jesus.[62]

VI

The symbolic charge with which Catholicism invests the family, the role of women, and allied matters exhibits elements of both continuity and change. The family has been constant or at least steadier in importance than other areas of concern.[63] The adamancy of the church regarding this bundle of issues might be laid to the appeal of holding fast in the midst of flux. However, "the family" is not only a sign of a hoped-for stability of the intimate but also a metaphor for broader collectivities—for social, political, and global community. Variations on this metaphor reflect different understandings, loosely characteristic of different historical circumstances, of the linkages between personal morality and public order. The metaphors vary in the closeness or distance imputed between private and public spheres. They have acted as guides to framing the myriad problems that Jesuits have faced in serving the immigrant and post-immigrant subcultures of Catholicism. Four such variations emerge in Catholic lore and Jesuit usage, in rough chronological sequence from the past to the present.[64]

The earliest depicts the family as a microcosm of good government, a blueprint for patrimonialism. Distinctions between public and private are

incidental, matters of scale rather than qualitative differences. The fit between the two spheres is tight. The best rule is personal, the best regime is
monarchical. The model is literal and integralist. Its most grandiose application is the joining of church and state. Failing this, it surfaces as a
yearning for a prelapsarian or heavily agrarian utopia. The family is not only
a metaphor for community; it is a model of social hierarchy, elite rule, and
moral behavior.[65] Society is homologous with the family, only bigger. The
family encapsulates a cosmology, a way of life. Historically, the model
crystallizes the self-contained world of the immigrant enclave.

A second, Aristotelian variation is considerably more widespread across
denominational and cultural lines. The family is seen as a linchpin of social
order. The connection between family and governance, while attenuated
and far from the one-to-one bond of the integralist vision, remains critical.[66]
The model tolerates diversity but not discontinuity. The family acculturates
successive generations in virtues and skills—respect for authority, work discipline, and so on—without which the larger society could not function and
which the state itself could not instill except at the cost of intolerable control. The foundational model is better geared to an industrializing ethos
than the nostalgic ruralism of the integralist vision. It smacks less of parochialism and superstition, it allows for a realistic pluralism in forms of
government, and it is compatible with a pivotal mixture of traditional and
modernizing values: the inculcation of the work ethic and respect for authority.[67]

The foundational model shares with its primitive counterpart a conviction
that the family has a direct if long-term impact on politics and society. It is
a stable or very slowly moving center around which the realms of the secular
world orbit at faster speeds. It supplies the outer spheres with preconscious
norms. If these steadying customs and pieces of wisdom had to be purpo-
sively invented, the larger world would wobble and begin to oscillate wildly
and eventually collapse. The family is a moral gyroscope. Without it, gov-
ernability would vanish. The model is Burkean in its reverence for tradition
and the remedial powers of the local. It is organic, too, in the belief that
individuals and small primary groups are not only part of but contribute to
the functioning of the larger whole.

It bears stressing that the foundational model does not require a simplistic
congruence between family structure and political organization. The family
acts like a pivot rather than a scaled-down state. Around this hinge, variation
in political form is possible. Without it, however, any political form is likely
to be unstable. The family is no longer viewed as a realistic metaphor, a kind
of diorama, of social order but as an indirect cause of it. This vision of the
family, which presupposes resilience, gives the core unit adaptability.[68]

A third construction of the family is a weakened version of the second; its intellectual lineage can be traced to the Augustinian vision of the two cities. It reverses the belief in the impact of micro-level roles and values on the macro-order. Here the family is besieged, an embattled bastion of virtue on the brink of disintegration under the pressures of mass society. It is a countercultural sign that no longer influences a society gone out of control, rather than the cornerstone of a subculture engendering a broad stability, much less a miniature state. Now the family has lost its capacity to project norms outward. Successive generations—the more recent, the more susceptible—are in jeopardy of becoming entranced by the technology of the second industrial revolution, by the ruinous values propagated by the mass media. Although the temporal correlation is imperfect, the defensive image of the family and of social decay does in fact appear to be associated with the later stages of industrialization.[69]

Privatization is one reaction emerging from this vision of the family as an island about to be swamped by permissiveness. Politics is severed from the personal realm. Another reaction is defensive but activist: political mobilization against forces like the state and the media that seem bent on reducing traditionally autonomous zones. Recognition that the family may no longer be the *primum mobile* of the social order, to be replaced by class or perhaps by some inchoate technological repertory and a proliferation of social movements, is another response.[70]

A fourth model is more expansive and archetypal. The family becomes the family of man, the human community. The world is an ecumenical global village, its biota intricate with harmonies, sharing a common fate. Stewardship and conservation take priority; long-standing antagonisms between tradition and progress are obsolescent in a new age of solidarity. It is the population of this world to which many of the postconciliar encyclicals are addressed.[71]

This image of communal diversity, catholic with a small *c*, has both traditional and modern connotations. It resonates of meditations from the perspective of geological time and from the Mediterranean basin at the origins of the church. It corresponds as well to a growing internationalization of the economic order. It also comes close to blending with another understanding of the human condition, and particularly of the role of the Society of Jesus, in Catholicism: that of the pilgrim whose dwelling is the world instead of a particular locale.[72]

A twofold pattern of contrast and holism underlies the perception of communities as variously triumphant, as pockets of security against chaos, under siege, or at mystical peace. The second and the third—the Aristotelian and the Augustinian—are agonistic, stressing tension and conflict between inner and outer, private and public worlds. They display masculine tendencies. The fourth, family-of-humankind model is irenic, and the first—though potentially explosive—espouses an integration of private and public realms. They have a feminine cast.

To recapitulate: the familial metaphors are first of all emblematic of variably strong and weak linkages between private and public spheres, between "morality and politics." In addition, their temporal evolution is an allegory of the church's perception of its fluctuating fortunes over the course of secularization—roughly, a declension from the Constantinian ideal of the union between church and state and an edenic pastoralism. Finally, the pulsation between agonistic and irenic orientations, between conflict and conciliation, is symptomatic of dualities within the Society of Jesus itself.

VII

Variations in understandings of the family as a metaphor of social order and solidarity track the changing fortunes of ethnic Catholicism in the United States fairly well. Through all these variations, the family has signified the repository of traditional values. Jesuits as defenders of this order were closely tied to this collection of sexual and social norms.[73]

Alongside this domestic imagery is a cluster of symbols that has set the Society of Jesus apart from the secular clergy and members of other, more monastic congregations in Catholicism. "Mobility" stands in contrast, and in partial complementarity, to "family." From the outset, the leadership of the Society of Jesus conceived of the order as a group of men who combined strict obedience with the capacity to move from locale to locale and from one type of work to another. Unlike parish clergy, Jesuits were supposed to be on the move, or at least available to change places and jobs. Mobility was functional as well as geographical. "Mission" was understood to mean both a task on which Jesuits could be sent and a foreign destination.

The imagery associated with the commitment of the Society of Jesus to availability and movement was cosmopolitan. "There are missions," wrote Jerónimo Nadal, one of the first Jesuits, "which are for the whole world, which is our house. Wherever there is need or greater utility for our ministries, there is our house." "The principal and most characteristic dwelling for Jesuits," he continued,

> is . . . in journeyings. . . . Since this is the case, they consider that they are in their most peaceful and pleasant house when they are constantly on the move, when they travel through the earth, when they have no place to call their own. . . .[74]

On the other hand, as the references to "house," "dwelling," and the like indicate, mobility presupposed the preservation of community and of familial ties. This sense of belonging was often bolstered, in a mild paradox, by militaristic rhetoric. In mundane terms, the network was held together by an insistence on regular correspondence.[75]

The two metaphors of family and of pilgrimage, while complementary, are also in tension. Through all its variations, the family connotes the primacy given in Catholicism to communitarianism and to the survival of the species. The *homo viator* suggests individualism and a certain solitary salvation.[76]

While the Society of Jesus never lost its cosmopolitanism, in practice Jesuits often became accustomed to living out their lives in one place, carrying out the same chores year after year. During the period of immigrant Catholicism, this meant for the most part attachment to the high schools, colleges, and universities of the order. The legend of mobility often came down to an apotheosis of self-abnegation and bravery in harsh, forbidding places made endurable by companionship. It meant the celebration of male spirituality that simulated a quest and trials that were only bearable in common. One Jesuit, writing of a Good Friday devotion restricted to males as it was conducted in Chicago during the 1930s, captured this ambience and the bonding that resulted from it:

> The massive doors of "our" church closed and were barred. Inside the church was packed with men, only men, in dark suits, hat in hand or a cap tucked into a pocket, and somewhere a rosary they were never without. A tremendous black cloth that hung from the ceiling of the sanctuary hid the altar. On the altar steps were chairs for the overflow crowd in the pews and standing in the aisles. I was fortunate to have had a place on the top altar step facing the sea of reverent faces. . . . The music of the famous organ thundered and rolled through the cavernous church, leading a thousand male voices in well known Latin hymns as tribute to the power and majesty of God. . . . It was an age of Faith without questions, doubts, arguments or irrational options about life and death. At three o'clock the men emerged, newly energized by this spiritual experience they took home to wives and children, that made life more Catholic for all.[77]

VIII

Collective representations are not institutions or social structures. Taken alone, they risk becoming vacuous dramatizations or being limited to literal accounts of power relations in small groups.[78] Questions of family structure, of sexuality, of the role of women—together with the continuities and conflicts expressed in age and generational differences—stand at the center of the tensions and obsessions within the Society of Jesus. But they are not the whole story. The interplay between parochial attachments and cosmopolitan influences is also crucial in situating the work of the Jesuits in the American Catholic subculture of the immigrant and postimmigrant years. These factors are not without cultural resonance. But they take us beyond a focus on psychosexual symbolism and interpersonal microworlds toward the contrast and partial compatibility between the European cultural matrix from which the Society of Jesus came and the institutional landscape in which Jesuits settled. The question bears on the adaptation of multiple European legacies to the American context.

At the time that the social *magisterium* received its initial formulation with the encyclical *Rerum Novarum* in 1891, North America was still mission territory in the eyes of the Roman Curia. The Catholic population of the United States, while growing, was smaller than that of Europe, and the attainment of economic hegemony by the United States was some decades in the future. The cultural dominion of the Roman authorities remained firm. Theological currents flowed from Europe to the United States.[79]

After two world wars the demographic and economic bases of Catholicism had altered drastically. The American Catholic subculture had expanded and was on the verge of assimilation. Corporatist prescriptions had lost their luster because of their association with the discredited regimes of Latin Europe, much as Marxist ideals were tainted by Stalinism, and the southern and eastern European provenance of both schools of thought offended the palate of Anglo-American liberalism.[80] In theology and philosophy American Catholic intellectuals continued to be shaped in the European, particularly the French and German, mold. But on economic and social questions American and European Catholicism followed separate paths. Confessional parties and labor unions of Christian Democratic inspiration were as foreign to the American political landscape as were socialist ideologies and organizations.[81] Conversely, the near-transcendent bountifulness of the United States and the relentless optimism of its citizens baffled the leaders of European Catholicism, including those responsible for managing the Society of Jesus.

American exceptionalism failed to arouse grave alarm so long as the acceptance of democratic and capitalist values by the faithful did not jeopardize their allegiance to Catholicism. If proof of fidelity were needed, it could be found in the growth of religious vocations coming from the American branch of the church.[82] If it seemed intellectually laggard, the American context was nonetheless innocent of the ideological polarization and anticlericalism that plagued the church in continental, especially Latin, Europe. The failure of Catholic institutions of higher learning in America to rank with their secular peers was compensated for by the geographical coverage of the system and the doctrinal fidelity it ensured.[83]

On the whole, then, intellectual exchange between Jesuits in the United States and Western Europe during the decades preceding Vatican II was confined to theology and philosophy, and it was decidedly asymmetrical. The European influence on the life of the mind was as overwhelming as it was virtually nonexistent in social and political practice; influence ran almost entirely one way in the former domain and was practically absent in the latter.[84]

The distinctiveness of the American condition that shaped the operations of the Society of Jesus in the United States was founded on a relatively flexible structure of economic opportunity, a comparatively open system of political participation, and a certain though far from complete separation of religious from economic and political power. In contrast to North America and, indeed, most of Northern Europe, the countries of southern, Latin Europe were characterized by rigid class hierarchies, closed political systems, and a proximity between Catholic ecclesiastics and political and economic elites. The identification of the church with the defense of economic hierarchy and political exclusion in Latin Europe reinforced intransigent reaction on one side and anticlericalism on the other. The intertwining of economic, political, and religious power left almost no middle ground between ins and outs. Revolution was pressed as an alternative to an inflexible social order.[85]

Economic, political, and religious-versus-secular divisions were less strictly superimposed in other parts of Europe. Especially toward the north—in the Netherlands, Germany, and Belgium, for example—where Catholicism did not exercise a near monopoly over religious affiliation, the church kept its distance from national, usually Protestant, elites and encouraged the formation of Catholic labor organizations and political groups. The preservation of moral order was not identified with the defense of the economic status quo, and moderate social reform was promoted.[86]

Three structural traits, then, differentiated northern European from Latin Catholicism. There was no religious monopoly, a condition that encouraged economic and political elites on Catholic and Protestant sides to compete for rather than coerce the allegiance of the middle, working, and peasant classes. Religious animosities were not equated with diametrically opposed social and political philosophies.

Second, although economic stratification was fairly steep, in northern Europe the franchise was extended, permitting a struggle for economic advancement through, rather than outside, the political system. By contrast, access to political participation was nonexistent or came later in the countries of Latin Europe.

Third, while social hierarchies perpetuated a sense of class differences, the Catholic business and middle classes in northern Europe were sizable enough to make organized bargaining a feasible operation, not just a paper, "corporatist" ideal as it was in Spain, Portugal, and Italy, where polarization between classes prevailed. To the north the tonic was social welfare and moral sobriety, high on class consciousness but wary of revolution and disorder.[87]

These differences with Latin Europe made the northern European current in social Catholicism seem less bizarre in the North American setting. The Catholic subcultures of Austria and Germany bore some resemblance to the religious enclaves of their counterparts in the United States. Religious coexistence that allowed for a certain neighborly fraternization was the norm; tolerance rather than total segregation was acceptable.[88] German immigrants settling predominantly in the Midwest brought over elements of moral traditionalism and working-class mutualism. The intellectual features of the reform tradition were secondary to the pragmatic legacy of Catholic unionism and associationalism in the old country.[89] In contrast, while the Italian immigrants cherished ritual and popular liturgy, they brought nothing in the way of Catholic social thought—a construct that, if it caught their attention at all, they almost certainly associated with the defense of the upper classes. The aesthetics of the liturgy, along with the institutional infrastructure—the schools and the parishes—of the Catholic subculture, outweighed the intellectual content of Catholicism for most of the laity and, probably, for clergy and religious as well.[90]

The Irish stream in European Catholicism became so powerful in North America by virtue of numbers, language, and early arrival that at first glance it may seem to have washed over the northern and southern continental currents. But the dominance of the Irish did not go unchallenged, and it did not last. Far from being singular, the success of Irish Americans was broadly similar to that of other groups, particularly the Germans.[91]

Some of the historical memories borne by the Irish—for example, the struggle against landlordism—had parallels in the background of other Catholic immigrants. The Irish were closer to earlier American settlers by reason of their experience with colonialism. Their precocious expertise in mass political organization, before the onset of industrialization, was reminiscent of the sequence of political mobilization undergone by Americans since the Jacksonian era.[92] But German Catholics underwent a comparable experience during the *Kulturkampf* of the last decades of the nineteenth century, and this persecution honed their organizational skills.[93]

The adherence of the Irish to democracy was neither anticlerical nor class-consciously revolutionary. In this, too, they resembled the northern

Europeans. They did not reject capitalism in principle. Their social resentment had been directed against foreigners who controlled property and opportunity more than against a set of economic principles. They were outsiders pressing to get in more than revolutionaries bent on overturning the system.[94]

While devotionalism among men as well as women was a hallmark of the Irish, their piety stood out more in contrast to the laxity of Latin males than it did when compared to the Germans.[95] The Catholic church had a confessional monopoly in Ireland, and Irish immigrants carried this piety with them to the United States. Piety took active form in church attendance that regularly surpassed not only comparable behavior among many Protestant denominations but also the rates of electoral turnout in the general population—a demonstration of the church's capacity for social organization that was not lost on political managers. Religious zeal among Irish and Irish American families was also reflected in the very high incidence of religious vocations. Popular idealism was channeled into clerical life.[96]

Irish American religiosity and sentiments of nationalism were well publicized. The annual Saint Patrick's Day parades were a stroke of public relations genius. For the most part, however, this visibility was an East Coast phenomenon, and dissemination of the myth to the rest of the country was speeded by the adoption of stage Irishness on the part of the motion picture industry.[97] Concentrated in the Midwest, German Americans were in fact more assertive than the Irish in promulgating social Catholicism.[98] Overall, it is their resemblance to Catholics of Irish descent in adapting to American conditions, and their numbers in the Society of Jesus, as in the American clergy generally, that marks the historical record.[99]

The Irish and the Germans preserved their religious identity in the United States while adapting to its political mores. In Ireland the affinity between politics and religion at the psychological and quotidian social levels was sufficiently close so that a confessional party was not needed,[100] and the parochial bond between ward and parish carried over to the United States, where the obstacles against forming such partisan organizations on a national scale were overwhelming in any case. The influence of the church over the popular hierarchies of everyday Catholicism—the family and the parochial-school system—reduced the need for the creation of a European-style confessional party.

Religious doctrine and political opinion were compartmentalized within the subculture. On the whole, Irish American politics was ideologically shapeless. In contrast to the Spanish case and the Latin syndrome generally, religious fealty among the Irish was not identified with economic and political beliefs. The Irish had been more united against their economic and political oppressors than they had been stratified socially among themselves. Fervor organized around the primacy of class struggle was difficult to sustain in an atmosphere of piety and backslapping.[101]

The Latin ethos, on the other hand, bred rigid views on social hierarchy, political exclusion, and economic dominance, but as a matter of course it allowed for considerable latitude in personal and sexual morality.[102] Vocations to religious life were uncommon; class politics flourished. Conversely, Irish religion bore an almost preternatural resemblance to the privatized ethos that had evolved from American puritanism: strict in matters of personal morality but comparatively tolerant and opportunistic about economic and social policies. Irish American as well as German American Catholicism tended to be authoritarian *en famille*, while maintaining a penchant for bargaining and compromise in the public arena.[103]

The mainstream of American Catholicism during the decades of immigrant absorption was Irish, with a rising influx from Germany. Nativist animosity was strong; discrimination reinforced a measure of working-class solidarity in the Irish American ghettos. Nevertheless there was a genuine commonality between the host and the transplant cultures, manifested in the appeal of nationalist sentiment and patriotism over class identification and in the Irish facility for mass politics.[104] Even the nature of their religiosity, whose ritual and organizational trappings set them apart, turned out to be compatible with the American political and economic scene. Sociability was layered over a strict sexuality. For the most part, politics and personal morality were kept separate. More of the heroic and sacrificial strain in the Irish legacy went into the priesthood than into politics, and this was made up of moral fervor and practical service.[105]

On balance, then, the energies of immigrant Catholics went into institution building. A mania for problem-solving that bordered on the intellectually oblivious was both a blessing and a curse. The Americans were immunized against the schematic abstractions of continental social and political theory, and they looked out efficiently for their own.[106] But the pragmatism and parochialism of immigrant and second-generation Catholics did not equip them for critical insight into the American dream. Suspicion of alien ideologies was prone to translate into anti-intellectualism. The clergy, including the Jesuits, were numerous and respected, and their moral injunctions were obeyed or at least considered to be legitimate.[107]

On the other hand, the church's political and social admonitions were selectively received. The parish church transmitted a distinctive moral and sexual ethos, and the network of educational facilities, with Jesuits at the helm, equipped Catholics to cope with industrial society.[108] But there were no Catholic vehicles such as separate political parties for translating the social *magisterium* into policy. The Irish- and German-dominated immigrant communities could realize many of their objectives at less cost by accommodating, and in places taking over, the existing political machinery at the same time that their religious associations stayed intact. The settlement worked for a while. Very few members of the subculture were spurred toward intellectual or artistic achievement out of anguish over a gap between institutional accomplishment, social mobility, and religious or ethical principles, over which a tribal sentimentality, robust and maudlin, fell.[109]

IX

Two other factors separated American from European Catholicism and affected the conditions under which Jesuits in the United States operated. One was the question of race. The issue was age-old in Europe and a version of it began to take on vicious proportions during the thirties, as anti-Semitism revived in the form of Aryan eugenics. But the American problem of "interracial relations" between blacks and whites was barely visible in Europe, and only slightly more so to the faithful in the United States, since blacks made up an exiguous proportion of Catholics. No doctrine had been formalized. The issue seemed peculiarly American rather than Catholic. Eventually, the vagueness of Catholic teaching in this area worked to the advantage of church progressives. The lack of guidelines and prohibitions emboldened a few American Jesuits to take courageous stands in favor of racial integration in the thirties and forties, ahead of some liberals in the Protestant denominations.[110]

What might be called the arcadian syndrome also had a European analogue but, like the question of race relations, it was suffused in the United States with indigenous connotations. For Catholics and other minorities, the "land of opportunity" meant social mobility and assimilation into the American way. For Catholic immigrants in particular, success came through the growth of manufacturing and the proliferation of blue- and white-collar jobs in cities. In time the process called forth the expansion of governmental action to contain the hardships wrought by industrialization.[111]

The response of Jesuits to this economic and political transformation ranged from rejection to ambivalence. Purists attacked capitalism for abuses they thought would lead inexorably to communism and moral laxity, and they railed against a swelling public bureaucracy. They advocated a return to rustic simplicities and dreamed of the restoration of a manorial way of life, self-sufficient like a feudal demesne that stymied the state-building ambitions of monarchs and fended off modernity and the market economy.

Pastoralism enjoyed a vogue from the beginning of the century through the thirties. Beyond an appreciation of Gregorian chant and neo-Gothic stained glass, however, it did not resonate among the majority of American Catholics who were city dwellers. It had some aesthetic but few directly social or political consequences. [112]

Ambivalence was more common than revulsion among Jesuits. Industrialization was assumed to be irreversible. Though not without its attendant problems, it was taken for granted, as was the development of democracy in the American case. The practical task was not merely to come to terms with economic and political innovations but to take advantage of what was desirable in them. Again, the dominant posture was one of outsiders looking in, gazing through the shop window, rather than of prophets turning their backs on modernization.

Nevertheless, escapist as much of it was, the rejection of industrialism proposed by the neomedievalist minority cannot be dismissed as an inconsequential aberration or as peculiarly Catholic. With the Latinate jargon removed, and with the glorification of a Eurocentric feudalism excised, the writings of this handful of Jesuits reverberated with anxiety over the loss of a yeoman America that struck a chord among Protestants as well as some Catholics. Images of village assemblies, of the "city on the hill," and the spirit of small towns—the frame houses, the smithy and the spreading oaks, the paths edged with wildflowers—were not far distant in spirit from the communitarianism of the papist urban ghettos. Generations of recently citified males who knew nothing of European history could share in the drama of innocent competition, under unchanging rules in which individuals might excel and shine like heroes, on the green fields of baseball parks. [113] Intellectuals and cultural leaders from the postbellum years of the nineteenth century through the 1930s and indeed beyond also experienced pangs at the loss of an earlier America, sentiments that to them expressed communitarian yearnings buried in anonymous cities. Some were Southerners, others were metropolitan political commentators with genteel leanings, still others were immigrants from eastern Europe who confected an America of gentle lawns and leafy towns that expressed popular longings for safety at the end of a history of wandering. [114]

Mirages of agrarian harmony, of self-reliant homesteads, invocations of the principle of subsidiarity—in effect, a gospel of local control—against the depredations of an intrusive state, and paeans to the family differed in detail. But each in its way was a cry in defense of collective identity. The agrarian vision that enjoyed some popularity in the twenties and thirties was more of an aesthetic than a social ideal for American Catholics, and it was peripheral to the programs that Jesuits developed to deal with the consequences of industrialization. Yet there is one thread that binds together preindustrial,

industrial, and indeed postindustrial thinking in Jesuit commentary. The pastoral ruminations of Jesuits in the early decades of the century might better be understood as images of a purified domesticity than as designs for a frictionless polity, and as talismans of the countercultural potential in a subculture headed toward assimilation.[115]

PART
ONE

Ordina quest'amore, O tu che m'ami.

—Jacopone da Todi

The towns of French Lick and West Baden nestle together in the Cumberland foothills on the Indiana side of the border with Kentucky, sixty miles northwest of Louisville. Toward the end of the eighteenth century, while chasing Indians in the area, the explorer George Rogers Clark came across bison trails that led to salt traces and mineral springs. By the middle of the nineteenth century a local entrepreneur was bottling "Pluto Water" in homage to the god of the underworld. Nowadays the street that runs south from the grounds of the French Lick Springs Golf and Tennis Resort bears the name Larry Bird Boulevard, in honor of the town's favorite son. There is an ice cream and soda shop across the way.

About a mile up Broadway Boulevard, just off Highway 150, stands a colossal round building that was once the West Baden Springs Hotel. From the turn of the century until the Great Depression, the structure was touted as the eighth wonder of the world. It was "the Mecca for fun and pleasure in the Midwest." Al Capone and his entourage frequented the casino. The Monon Railway had summer runs from Chicago, Indianapolis, St. Louis, Cincinnati, and other towns and cities in the region to cater to the vacation crowds. The Cubs and the White Sox used the resort area for spring training.

"The principal feature of the hotel," reads a local history, "is the Grand Rotunda, with the largest and finest promenade in the world. This immense Rotunda is covered by a glass and steel dome 200 feet in diameter, having an inner circumference of 600 feet, the center of the dome being 130 feet from the ground. This dome has the distinction of being positively the largest ever constructed in the world."[1] The rotunda, fitted with statuary, fountains, and tropical plants, was flooded during the day with a northern glow, and at twilight the building took on the aspect of Xanadu, set in the heartland of America.

Over Labor Day weekend in 1943 more that two hundred Jesuits from across the United States convened under the dome at West Baden. By that time the old hotel had been the property of the Society of Jesus, in use as a seminary, for nine years. Although a good many resolutions were passed, the Indiana meeting itself did not produce great changes in the Society of Jesus. The significance of the West Baden gathering was that it lay at the watershed of seminal events and social changes that ultimately transformed the order. The social and intellectual aftermath of World War II pushed the Jesuits into unexplored territory—in the direction, as it happened, of the Second Vatican Council.[2]

For more than a decade a scattering of Jesuits had been engaged in "the social apostolate." Their efforts had been improvisational, the results uneven. The objective now was to pull ideas and resources together. The times were pivotal, yet the leadership of the society was unsettled. Wlodimir Ledochowski, the Polish aristocrat who had governed the society since World War I, had died in 1942, and the war prevented the calling of a congregation of Jesuits to select a new leader. During the interim, until 1946, the American Jesuits were managed by the "American assistant," the Very Reverend Zacheus Maher, a dour Californian who had directed the growth of the University of Santa Clara.[3]

As recently as 1941 nearly nine million Americans had been out of work. By 1943 full employment was attained. The desolation depicted in *The Grapes of Wrath*, published in 1941, was replaced by the expansive optimism of the musical *Oklahoma!*[4] Economic depression was vanishing with the war effort, yet the boom in consumption and mobility was still some years away. A few Jesuit colleges and universities, their cash-flow problems aggravated by the draft, feared that with so many men in uniform they would not be able to survive the drop in enrollments if hostilities lasted much longer. This led them to reconsider their prohibition against admitting women.

For the most part, however, the massive institutional and demographic changes that came to be identified with the postwar boom remained pent up. Anticipation ran high. Immigration to the United States had crested just prior to World War I. By World War II many immigrants and their children had weathered the depression and were approaching prosperity. Almost imperceptibly the social bases of enclave Catholicism and with it the subculture of the ethnic ghettos were beginning to slip away.[5]

Nineteen forty-three was also the year of *Divino afflante Spiritu*. An encyclical drafted by the German Jesuit Augustin Bea, this document opened the way to Catholics for critical and historical study of biblical texts, an enterprise in which Protestants had been engaged for nearly a century.[6] It prepared the intellectual ground for the *aggiornamento* that was to take place twenty years later. The next year, in Pius XII's Christmas address, a pope for the first time extolled the virtues of democracy.[7]

Except for the likelihood of a surge in enrollments once the war was over, it was scarcely possible to foresee what was to come. Memories of economic hardship were vivid, and Jesuits lived in a conceptual universe bounded by the categories of scholastic philosophy. Like every "house of formation," the seminary at West Baden was set in the countryside, a refuge from the lures of the city. Frugality reigned. Only rarely were the men allowed to listen to the radio. Debating tournaments, athletic competitions, and the occasional screening of films brought in from the outside after being vetted by the *patres graviores*, the senior fathers, served for recreation. The regimen was largely monastic.

Austerity was associated with success. By the standards of the time the

Jesuits had done well by their immigrant and postimmigrant clientele. A few of their schools had been hurt by the depression, but almost all of them stayed open. Enrollments held steady or showed modest increases. Except for a downturn attributable to the draft, the number of Jesuits had grown, not spectacularly but with comforting regularity. At the time of the West Baden meeting there were approximately 4,500 Jesuits in the United States, slightly more than half the number which the American branch of the order would reach at its peak in 1965. The scale of operations was small. The pace of change was slow, or so it would come to seem.

A system of high schools, colleges, and universities, spread through the United States, overshadowed the lesser activities of the American Jesuits. Social ministry made up a miniscule portion of their work. The marginality of this line of activity was not without advantages. Precedent came in isolated fragments rather than as a seamless tradition. One strand of experimentation was made up of a miscellany of initiatives—the Jesuit schools of social work in Manhattan and on the North Shore of Chicago, and later in Boston and St. Louis, parish work among immigrants in East Coast and Midwest cities, chaplaincies in prisons and hospitals—some dating back to the turn and the early decades of the century, and a few to the century before.

Professional schools like those at Fordham were quickly integrated into the Jesuit educational establishment. In exchange for the training they provided, these faculties became cash-cows for the universities in which they were located. The market in social services and the need for personnel trained in these areas burgeoned during the depression. Within the order, however, the professional schools did not have the prestige of the liberal arts colleges. Though few Jesuits worked in them except for the obligatory deans, they enjoyed more respect than chaplaincies and parish chores, which were plainly incidental to the thrust of the society. The schools "belonged" and their activities added up; revenues were generated and graduates were produced.[8]

Another influence on the Jesuits' ventures in social ministry was formal and more centralized. It came from Europe, filtered through Rome, in papal encyclicals about the social question, in response to the rise of fascism and communism on the continent and toward the East. The schools of social work in the United States arose out of local conditions and were created by enterprising Jesuits who recognized the demand for training in the new white-collar occupations. They taught practical skills, and they were eclectic triumphs of institution building. The legacy of Catholic social thought, codified in Rome, was ambitious in a different way. Its agenda was ideological as well as practical. The social encyclicals envisioned an intellectual and educational project that rose above training and implementation and aimed at shaping policy. In Europe this meant working through church-sponsored organizations—Catholic trade unions, Christian Democratic parties, Catholic action groups—that had virtually no equivalent in the United States. It was revulsion at the idea of communism, which rivaled Catholicism in its claim to totality, and a distaste for the vulgarities of capitalism that drove this counterattack.

The dream of a political economy that was distinctively Catholic and that offered an alternative to capitalism and communism entered the United States from continental Europe during the mid-thirties in the guise of an attempt by the Jesuits to introduce a blueprint for a "Christian social order." The effort, taken seriously by few American Jesuits and understood by hardly any, all but died in the planning stage. It was resuscitated in the early forties with the establishment of the Institute of Social Order, an operation the Jesuits hoped would combine social philosophy, propaganda, and action. This was the grand design the assembly at West Baden was called to inaugurate.

Then there were the labor schools. These stood apart from the faculties of social service and, to a degree, from the Institute of Social Order. They emerged in the latter half of the thirties, in the New York area, in Philadelphia, and in a scattering of other places such as Kansas City, Missouri, near Jesuit colleges or high schools, offering night courses to workers who were about to organize industrial unions under the facilitating legislation of the New Deal.

The labor schools were organizational curiosities. Some proved to be useful and fairly durable. Unlike the schools of social work, they were not spontaneous developments. Unlike the Institute of Social Order, they went their own decentralized way. They came into being at the urging of a papacy worried about the communist menace and anxious not to repeat in America the often-antagonistic relationship with working-class militants that had characterized church-labor dealings in nineteenth-century Europe. Jesuits saw themselves as competing with communist organizers for the loyalty of at least the Catholic share of the urban working class. But they could not bring themselves to mount a coordinated crusade. The labor schools were pretty much one-man shows, run by generally flinty Jesuits impatient with theory, usually imbued with anticommunism, and irritated by their low standing vis-à-vis the society's accredited educational institutions. They were mostly ignored as well by their European brethren, who shared their anticommunism but who were baffled by the political terrain on which the church stood in the United States.

The decades preceding World War II revealed two partly disparate trends to Jesuits with an eye on social problems in the United States. The Catholic population increased enormously on the wave of immigration and the undercurrent of high birthrates. But especially during the thirties, Catholics, most of whom belonged to the working class, suffered economically.

The social work faculties, the Institute of Social Order, the labor schools—not to mention the schools "of commerce and finance" that were precursors of business administration departments—and the law schools were all geared toward accommodation, of a kind, with industrial society. There were practically no social incendiaries among the Jesuits then. Yet many Jesuits resisted a wholehearted embrace of industrial capitalism. Some kept their distance on progressive grounds. They were Roosevelt Democrats for whom the principles of laissez-faire economics were tied to Protestant individualism. Some were leery of a government that provided a modicum of welfare but that threatened to intrude on the prerogatives of the church. Others went in a different direction, toward the past. For them the object of criticism became industrial society itself. They dreamed of a return to self-sufficient farm communities.

The prose poems in which some of these idylls were described made them out to look more like European fiefdoms than frontier patches and home-steads cleared and settled by an American yeomanry. But the arcadian imagery was not wholly fanciful. Through the thirties, the Rose Hill neigh-borhood in which Fordham had been established in the Bronx was still semirural, before the boulevards and other monuments to urban planning had been set in place; and as late as the twenties, before the subway lines made development profitable, much of Brooklyn was exurban scrub and potato and onion fields.[9] The pastoral evocations also touched off reminis-cences, sentimentalized but not so distant, of "happy times among our own" in the misty vales of Ireland.[10]

Nonetheless the shrinking of the rural sector as a way of life was unde-niable. The few Jesuits who persisted in this vision found themselves in the company of aesthetes and reactionary diehards without political influence.[11] What was infinitely less clear by the early forties was the future trajectory of the new industrial society. Full employment was a welcome surprise but presumably transient. The Jesuits at West Baden met in anticipation of renewed class conflict once the wartime boom was over. The divisions between rural and urban sectors had subsided; the United States had become an urban nation. But antagonisms between capital and labor were expected to resurface.

If there was a common assumption among Jesuits who thought about such matters, it was that the working class, like the Catholic community itself, would continue to grow. The subculture would expand without be-coming diluted. Postwar prosperity and the assimilation it fashioned undid this expectation. For the time being, however, the overlap between working-class status and Catholicism allowed socially concerned Jesuits to get a hearing that the busy and politically not-very-conscious majority of their peers might not otherwise have given them.

Three other developments—mostly nontrends before the forties, since the movements looked infinitesimal then—turned out to affect the American Jesuits powerfully after the war.[12] One was the increase in white-collar occupations, especially the service sector. Another was the related acceleration in the growth of higher education. The enactment of the GI Bill spurred an upsurge in college matriculation. The rapidly increasing proportion of Catholics attending colleges and universities, from a pool that was also growing in absolute size, placed enormous strains on the Jesuits.

A third trend was the growth of female participation in the work force. Immediately after the cessation of hostilities, many women returned to full-time housekeeping in an apparent restoration of the antebellum balance. But the long-term trend was upward, and it picked up speed two decades after the war.[13]

These changes transformed the socioeconomic composition of the Catholic community and the bases of family structure. They shifted the focus of social concern from the transition to industrialism, and from the struggle between management and labor, toward a panoply of other controversies. Issues that had been taken as private became matters of public dispute. Democratization cut into the household and into the church. Political currents coursing through the society at large worked their way into the interior of the Society of Jesus.

But this is to get ahead of the story. In 1943 such changes lay in an unimaginable future.

1

Parishes, Prisons, and Schools of Social Work

Hell's Kitchen on the West Side of midtown Manhattan was among the rowdiest of the Irish neighborhoods—Red Hook by the Gowanus Canal in Brooklyn was another—clustered in the cities on the Eastern Seaboard during the nineteenth and through much of the twentieth century. A few Jesuits, apparently no more than three, led by William Stanton, set up temporary residence near the district in the 1890s. The expedition took place soon after Leo XIII had issued the first of the major encyclicals on the social question. Among Protestant ministers, stirrings of the social gospel were already evident, and journalists had for some time been publicizing the horrors of the slums crammed with immigrants.[1]

The Jesuits' foray was a reconnaissance detail; their task was to preach missions—the Catholic equivalent of revivals—during the weekends to assist a pastor who, though not a Jesuit, was "a graduate of Ours." The contrast between their academic surroundings, where they taught a classical curriculum to high school boys, and the Hell's Kitchen setting struck the Jesuits forcefully.

> Across a narrow court in the rear of the priest's house loomed up a dingy building whose upper story windows were boarded up, as no one would live on the third floor where a woman had been murdered. Around us the tenants sang, fought, and swore whenever they sounded too deeply the depths of the foaming cup; and more than once was the silence of night broken with cries of "Help," "Murder," or the brawling of a notorious "gang" that infested the parish, and gave the neighborhood the dubious reputation it enjoyed in police court circles.[2]

Amid this violence priests and patrolmen tried to establish themselves as symbols and enforcers of order. Irish or of Irish descent, the police were tough but not alien, and the priests were lettered and therefore paragons of gentility, due respect. "Usually when the hubbub became intolerable," Father Stanton observed,

> the pastor rebuked the roisterers from his window, or, when mild means failed to bring about peace and quiet, he went down into the streets or alleyways and there by threats, expostulations and the menace of his imposing presence secured a truce from disorder and riot. A better reign of law, order, and sobriety soon began to be apparent to all, especially to the policemen, who admitted that the pastor was doing the work of a squad of officers.[3]

As a rule the respite was only momentary. The piety of the parishioners of Saint Ambrose did not extend to abstention from drink. After the preaching of a weekend mission, so it was claimed, 250 men enrolled in the Holy Name Society, and most of them presumably took the pledge. But temptation was ubiquitous; every block was studded with bars. In an effort to reinforce the newfound sobriety of the devout, four police officers were stationed "in disguise [as layabouts] standing at the corners of 54th Street and 10th Avenue, from 11 p.m. until an hour after midnight."

The parishioners were soon back to carousing. Although repelled by the noxious ambience of the place, Stanton and his colleagues do not seem to have fallen into condemnation of the laxity of the poor. The Jesuits recognized that alcohol provided one of the few means of relief from exhausting work. The "social glass" enabled the men to express themselves in conviviality or to vent their frustrations in occasional brawls after long hours of having to behave themselves:

> Turbulent in their cups, blasphemous in their rage over check or reproof at home, neglectful of their children, and a source of misery and scandal to all, these unhappy souls kept their respect for the priest, and doubtless would have died to defend him, or the faith that yet possessed their hearts. . . . Saturday night came on apace, and with it came pay-night drinking. In this, and other parts of New York, there is usually a saloon on each of the four corners made by the streets that at right angles cross the long avenues. In and out of these well-lit bar rooms move too many of the poor, the weary, the homeless, or the vicious of the big city. For five or ten cents they can procure the Horatian "ex lex et bene potus" state [lawless and deep in their cups], which they fancy brings recreation to their tired bodies, or releases their spirits from the remembrance of the week's toil, or perhaps frees them for a time from their sense of hunger and misery. But much of the dissipa-

tion comes from the social glass, from the drink *pour rire*. Pails and half kegs of frothy decoctions are brought home, or into stables, or, as we found to our sorrow, into the junk shops and wharf houses not far from us.[4]

By the Jesuits' account the neighborhood was a raucous shambles. The men were almost all unskilled laborers. Many were stevedores, casual workers called out intermittently from lines that formed in the morning on the docks.[5] The single women, if they could, found employment as chambermaids. Families lived at close quarters, the tenements stank, the sidewalks were loud and, although not filthy, irregularly clean.[6] The Irish custom of marrying late or not at all guaranteed that a fair number of males would be roaming the streets on weeknights and Sunday afternoons, in varying degrees of intoxication and sexual frustration. The women, unwelcome at the pubs, drank at home.[7]

In Stanton's view the neighborhood seemed to lurch from one catastrophe to another, always on the brink of disintegration. Once, when a policeman tried to haul a drunk to the station house, a riot nearly ensued.

One of the mob seized an empty iron ash barrel, and hurling it at the doughty policeman, knocked him insensible before us. The prisoner was freed, and in the twinkling of an eye, everybody rushed away and disappeared on the avenues or behind their own doors. It looked like a murder, and none of them cared to be accused of having a hand in it. Silence, a strange silence, just as a sudden death casts over a place, filled the entire street. The gang had been sobered at the sight of the officer falling in his blood to the ground. He was, however, not fatally injured. The numbers on his helmet and its leather band had saved him from the full force of the blow inflicted. We did our best for him and returned to consider the ways and means of reforming such ungodly characters as we had just beheld in full Saturday night revel.[8]

Most of the problems that preoccupied Jesuits in social ministry during the following decades were previewed in Stanton's description. Family life was precarious. The environment not only provided innumerable occasions of sin; it also deprived the inhabitants of opportunities to obtain the skills that might ensure their survival and perhaps gain them a measure of comfort and decency. There was little virtue and less material consolation in being poor.

Whatever dramatic heightening he may have resorted to in detailing the ways of the habitués and denizens of Hell's Kitchen, Stanton did manage to suggest the Jesuits' own confusion as they struggled to find ways to help the immigrants. He diagnosed the problems but could not find solutions. The missions were doubtful mechanisms for saving the souls of the immigrants and of no use for their betterment in the here and now. The place alternated between pandemonium and prostration. Camping in the slums, rather than providing treatment—a concept that barely existed at the time—was a salvage operation on the part of the Jesuits.

Stanton refrained from righteousness. While his analysis was conventional, he conveyed a sense of dismay and frustration instead of blaming the victims. The care he lavished on local color had the purpose of reminding his fellow Jesuits, most of whom worked at some remove in the schools, about the continuing poverty of many urban Catholics. What is most remarkable is the impression Stanton transmits from up-close inspection that the real menace of the disorder in places like Hell's Kitchen was not revolution of the poor against the rich but self-destruction. The immigrants were feckless, wallowing in drink, unable to help themselves or to correct the conditions that kept them in poverty. Almost none of the dread of class warfare that permeated the social encyclicals drafted by European Jesuits appeared in Stanton's documentary.[9]

The adventures and picaresque calamities that befell the Jesuits in Hell's Kitchen, though extreme, were not completely unrepresentative of their work in urban communities in the United States during the high tide of immigration. The clientele was composed almost exclusively of Catholics—in this case Irish, in others Italian or German—who settled in urban areas. The stevedores and their families lived in misery, and they were susceptible to the coercion and bribery of the thugs and criminals who ran the docks. But other immigrant Catholics—some of the transport and construction workers—were slightly better off, and as the nineteenth passed into the twentieth century modest signs of progress and mobility appeared in the neighborhoods.[10]

In the 1920s the Jesuits had a struggling parish downtown on the East Side in the Bowery, centered around Nativity Church, that catered to Italian immigrants. Fr. Dominic Cirigliano, a young curate, noted that while the area was still poor it was no longer a rank slum. "Twenty-five years ago it was a 'City of Iniquity' and the dives and cabaret halls and the tempter's gentle voice induced the careless passerby to sin." By the end of World War I the neighborhood had improved. McGurke's Suicide Hall, named after the customers who drank themselves into the grave, had closed. So had the Granite Club for prizefighters, the Owl Hall for "midnight wanderers, and Little Jumbo for reckless desperadoes."[11] While Cirigliano neglected to mention that some of this improvement must have been due to the passage of Prohibition by the Protestant majority, the immigrants he dealt with were no longer the dregs of society. Some upward movement had taken place.

Even so, poverty was extensive, and the area retained a few unsavory customs. Especially at night, Cirigliano observed, "one must keep close to the buildings for fear of getting hit on the head with bundles or other things thrown from the windows above." Worse than these physical hazards and deprivations were the perils of religious pluralism in a strange land. For Cirigliano and his fellow Jesuits the chief menace was the *cauda serpentina*, the snake's tail, of Protestant proselytizers, inspired by the social gospel, who "began by gaining the body first" in order to wean the soul from what they viewed as "centuries of ignorant and superstitious environment." Father Cirigliano resented their resourcefulness and professionalism. He complained that "the Protestants have wealth, we have poverty; they have countless social workers hunting up children and parents, we have none; they have all kinds of natural attractions for mother and child, we scarcely have any; we have to cope with worldliness and with the power of gifts and money."[12]

The sense of an embattled church with growing needs and never enough resources stayed with American Catholicism well into the middle of the century. But the social foundation of this defensiveness was changing. The ignorant "mariners," as immigration officers classified them, of the docks of Manhattan were close to the bottom of a motley horde. While many Catholics continued on their rough-and-tumble course, an emerging sector—a proto middle class—was both docile and buoyant, expecting better times. They sacrificed for the education of their children, and they supported the projects of priests and nuns without question. This stratum of the subculture promoted a life of hard work in the hope of happy endings. Migration liberated them from economic fatalism, and they strained for a heroic reversal of their experience in the old world. Some connection appeared between effort and reward. Their hardy optimism brimmed over into pageantry and a pragmatic devotion to education. Parishioners found the wherewithal to erect stupendous neo-Gothic churches, laced with stained glass, embellished with alabaster and marble finishings, stuffed with pastel-colored plaster statuary, and redolent with flowers in smoked glass vases set around raised altars. To almost every one of these churches was attached a kindergarten and an elementary school staffed by nuns, supported by the collection plate, raffles, and bingo nights. Ambition was joined to religious celebration.[13]

The Jesuits' accounts of their experiences in the slums of New York City can be treated as an only slightly folklorized anthropology of this ethnic skein. The same material was transmuted for commercial purposes into the slapstick and romance and moralistic denouements of the vaudeville shows, nickelodeons, and silent film shorts that began to enthrall immigrant audiences soon after the turn of the century. The immigrants were on their way to assimilation, yet they showed few signs of secularization or anticlericalism. They clung to the traditional rituals, to the warm candles, the curling incense, and the rolling Latin of the liturgy, and the hushed dark interiors of the churches with their solid oaken pews. The immediate past of poverty and hooliganism was mythologized into bittersweet sentiment.[14]

Jesuits like William Stanton, who seems to have been reasonably typical, spent most of their time outside the desperate slums of the East Coast. In contrast to the Jesuits, the diocesan clergy and "the good sisters" were considerably more numerous and spread throughout the parishes of the big cities. The Jesuits had virtually no leverage with the "notorious junkshop gangs" and "ungodly characters" of Hell's Kitchen. They had no schools in such areas. And aside from the few sorties into administration like the operation at Nativity church, parish work was something that the Jesuits customarily left to the diocesan clergy.[15]

Nevertheless, in those days the cultural and physical distance between the truly wretched and the immigrants clinging to the fringes of respectability was not overwhelming, and the Jesuits were in no real danger. They shared much the same dense parochial world. Stanton proposed no remedies for the misery he encountered. On the other hand he was reluctant to castigate the slum dwellers. The dominant drive, he suggested, was to escape the slums. Some tried to do so through drink. Others managed to keep their families intact and set their children toward success within the enfolding family of the parish church and school. The Jesuits concentrated on what they saw as the future of the Catholic community and on what they felt they did best; after a fashion, the order was cost-effective. It was in high school and college education that Jesuits performed their characteristic service.[16]

II

Teaching did not take up all of the Jesuits' time, however. A few French and German, and later Irish American, Jesuits established a base for early versions of social work in the prisons and hospitals that the municipal authorities began to erect to deal with the immigrants who began entering New York in large numbers about a decade before the Civil War, with the onset of famine in Ireland. Through the nineteenth century and on into the twentieth, most of these facilities were located on islands in the harbor and in the East River where the sick, the insane, the destitute, the criminal, the luckless, and the otherwise undesirable could be quarantined. Across the river in Brooklyn the Jesuits built a high school on the foundations of what used to be a jail and, before that, an insane asylum. Before the Statue of Liberty was erected on it, Bedloe's Island (today Liberty Island) was a site for hangings. The French Jesuit, Henri DuRanquet, remembered accompanying twenty-five convicts to the gallows.[17]

The largest of the hospitals was on Blackwell's—later Roosevelt—Island, along with an almshouse and, for a time, a mental hospital. On nearby Randall's Island there was a foundling hospital, a prison to take in the overflow of inmates from Blackwell's, and a reform school, called the House of Refuge, for orphans and young vagrants. The incidence of mortality on Blackwell's Island was high. The common diseases were cholera, typhoid, smallpox, and tuberculosis, with a smattering of leprosy. Six funerals were the daily average. "Our work," DuRanquet wrote, "is something like a permanent mission, enabling a good many poor people to square their accounts with Almighty God." Some of his fellow priests died of diseases contracted from the inmates. [18]

The Jesuits comforted their captive audience, engaging in the corporal works of mercy, visiting the sick and the imprisoned and administering the sacraments. "I spend about three hours every evening," DuRanquet reported, "in visiting them from cell to cell. . . . I speak to them through the bars. When you can thus speak to these people, one by one, you can do a great deal with them. A number of Protestants become Catholic, on the average, one every month. I try to get them books. While speaking to them through the bars I hear their confession. I say Mass for them only once a month, and often give forty or fifty Communions, eight or ten being First Communions."[19]

Warding off the incursions of the Protestants and preparing the poor for death were the main accomplishments of the Jesuits. They proselytized and consoled. Even then, however, there were glimmerings that prison and hospital work along traditional lines might not be the most productive use of their skills. Another priest who worked on Blackwell's Island, Ernest Ryan, was ahead of his time in the advocacy he brought to his work. He operated like a ward boss on a small scale, exploiting loopholes in the law for his clients. He cultivated his cronies in the legal profession, negotiated sentence reductions, and arranged bail.[20]

On weekends Fr. John Hart, who taught at Xavier High School in downtown Manhattan, used to take a rowboat across to the House of Refuge to teach catechism there. He came to a mixed judgment about the correctional system. Like Xavier, the House of Refuge was run as a military school, complete with uniforms. Hart extolled the discipline, similar to the ethos inculcated in Jesuit schools, that the system instilled in the youthful inmates. Nevertheless, Hart observed, "nature is strong." The place was isolated, and Hart recognized the difficulty that some of the boys had in adapting to the schedule of a bustling metropolis when they were released. The reformatory encouraged punctuality and respect for procedures but also a certain dependence, prolonging childhood.

The activities of the Jesuits around Hell's Kitchen, at Nativity Parish, and in the prisons and hospitals of New York City were all devoted to Catholics. Despite the reputation that Jesuits brought with them of cultivating the European upper classes, they were concerned with poor, some of them destitute, Catholics. During this period there were very few well-off Catholics in the United States for Jesuits to bother with.

Usually these charitable operations were not run by the Jesuits and so they were marginal to the society's operations. Accounts of the Jesuits among the human wreckage of New York, like those of William Stanton, were published as "edifying letters," following in the line of the *cartas edificantes* that Jesuits had sent centuries before from outposts in North and South America and Asia. But few Jesuits actually pursued these activities. Rank-and-file members of the order were not expected to take up such work in great numbers.[21]

Nevertheless the precedent was kept alive, as was the sense of adventure and sacrifice in the service of hard cases, and a sensitivity to class distinctions never seems to have been as acute within the American as it was in some European branches of the order, where the *Jesuite de salon* was a legendary figure. The main difficulty appears to have been less an insufficiency of motivation—many Jesuits were accustomed to hardship—than bewilderment about how such efforts might be structured for efficient results. The question came down to organizational strategy and practical imagination.

III

The schools of social work that began to emerge in the early days of the century under Jesuit auspices were more representative of what was to become the dominant thrust of the order in the United States. Not only were they linked to the existing network of colleges and universities and hence more structured on the Jesuits' own terms; they were also geared to training a clientele of the upwardly mobile rather than to comforting society's losers. Their educational and organizational talents gave the Jesuits a chance to reach a receptive audience on a regular basis.

The beginnings of these institutions can often be traced to the enthusiasms of one or another enterprising Jesuit, responding after a fashion to the doctrinal mind of the church. Although the authorities of the order had to be consulted and give the go-ahead, planning took second place to daring in filling the needs opening up in the market for urban services. The schools that succeeded responded to a demand for training in the new white-collar occupations. The fact that some of the ventures were incubated at the periphery of the order's main operations probably gave them freedom to experiment. None of them fit the liberal arts program laid down in the *Ratio*

Studiorum, the traditional guidebook of Jesuit education. In such cases, the legacy of Jesuit adaptability might be invoked. The beginnings of some of the professional schools were only a little less haphazard than those of the prison and hospital chaplaincies. In most cases they seem to have searched out and quickly found a viable balance between innovation at the margins of the order and incorporation into its academic establishment.[22]

A striking feature of the early undertakings in social ministry, particularly social work education, was how many of them spun off as specializations from a broadly labeled "lay apostolate," a set of activities that involved giving retreats and organizing devotional associations—confraternities, sodalities, and the like—for the growing Catholic middle class. Some of this entailed individual spiritual direction. Like psychoanalysis, it was directed at a comparatively articulate clientele. Manual laborers rarely participated in this development, even though they were thought of as its eventual beneficiaries. The social work schools were born out of an exuberant amateurism that evolved from pastoral care into professional training.[23]

The career of Terence Shealy exemplifies the pattern. He had been brought up "amid scenes of wild grandeur and beauty" in County Cork, had written a poem entitled "To My Mother in Ireland for my First Mass" that made the rounds of the Catholic press, and by the first decade of the twentieth century had established himself in New York as an exceptionally eloquent speaker.[24] He helped set up the law school at Fordham. In 1909 he was directing retreats for "Catholic gentlemen" from the New York area. Many of them were alumni of Jesuit schools, and they contributed to a fund that by 1911 enabled Father Shealy to open a retreat house, Mount Manresa, on Staten Island.

Under Shealy's leadership, the initiative that started out as the Laymen's Retreat Movement became the Laymen's League for Retreats and Social Studies.[25] He had taken to heart the directives of Leo XIII, originating in the final decades of the nineteenth century, about the perils of capitalism and the appeals of communism. He railed against both, though there was little doubt about which was thought to be the greater danger.[26] "The objects of this work," outlined in a statement presented to John Farley, then archbishop and later cardinal of New York, "are to prevent the spread of false doctrines and to combat Socialism, especially among the laboring classes." Archbishop Farley welcomed the undertaking. "The new feature, i.e., Social Studies," he responded, "is highly to be commended for reasons too obvious to the man of the world to call for special mention. Social questions are uppermost in the minds of thinking men today, and calling for solution such as only careful study by the members, and clear exposition by the leaders of your League, can deal with successfully."[27]

In 1911 Shealy inaugurated the league's educational activities with a series of twelve lectures defending the idea that "Socialism, in its Principles, is Irreligious and Immoral." A columnist for the *Wall Street Journal*, Thomas Woodlock, presented a course of six lectures in defense of the proposition that "Socialism in its proposals is impracticable and impossible."[28] The goal of the School of Social Studies was "to promote the study by Catholic men and women of the great social questions which are of vital interest in our time, and thus to train a corps of competent writers and lecturers who will spread among Catholics a sound knowledge of social facts and of the Christian principles in the light of which these facts must be interpreted."[29] The model of enthusiastic laymen operating under the guidance of the clergy was in line with the strategy, officially called Catholic Action, then favored by the papacy.[30]

The school—more accurately, a speakers' forum composed of dedicated volunteers—lasted nearly eleven years, ceasing operation with Shealy's death in 1922. It succumbed to the drawing power of the School of Sociology and Social Studies, which Shealy had also founded at Fordham University in 1916. Loyola University in Chicago inaugurated its school of social work at almost exactly the same time.

By this time an institutional formula had come into view. The tide of immigration was at its crest. Some of the newcomers were in desperate straits, and many of them needed help. Others were college material, and almost all the men and some of the women were in search of jobs. The antimodernist mentality inhibited the Jesuits from pursuing what urges they might have felt toward academic excellence of the sort prized at some Ivy League and state universities. The idea at both Fordham and Chicago was to prepare tuition-paying students for jobs as city or state social workers. They granted professional degrees, certifying graduates for white-collar positions. This was the most institutionally durable outcome of the early Jesuit explorations in social ministry.[31]

IV

Terence Shealy was an orator and an organizer, not a scholar. He published little on social issues himself.[32] Other Jesuits who taught in the embryonic schools of social work and sociology departments did, however, produce books that convey the tenor of thinking about social issues which they tried to communicate to their students through the early decades of the century.

The books were of two kinds. One was an assemblage of practical remedies, how-to manuals for community action and self-help, often with documentation on the social ills of the day. The other type might also take the form of edited volumes interspersed with commentary. But whether compilations or original works, those in the second category were more conceptual. They were geared primarily to the interpretation of papal social doctrine for an audience of American Catholics.

Fr. Joseph Husslein favored the theoretical approach. Born in the German-American community of Milwaukee in 1873, Husslein belonged to the same generation of Catholic social thinkers as Monsignor John Ryan, the "Right Reverend New Dealer" who wrote the landmark letter for the American bishops on the state of the economy in 1919.[33] He had been associated with Terence Shealy at the founding of the school of social work at Fordham, and he returned there to teach during the late twenties. Most of Husslein's long career—he died in 1952, at the age of 79—was spent in St. Louis. There he founded the school of social work at the local Jesuit university. Beginning in the 1930s he edited a line of texts on social problems directed at students in Catholic colleges; among the best known were two stout volumes on papal social teaching, entitled *Social Wellsprings*.[34]

It was just before coming to Fordham that Husslein began his work as a social commentator. Between 1909 and 1911 he published more than a dozen articles in the national Jesuit magazine *America*; many of the pieces were concerned with the dangers of socialism. He joined the staff of the magazine in 1911 and kept his affiliation with its editorial board until the end of the twenties. In 1912 he published the first of his ten books of social commentary and analysis, a series that terminated thirty years later with the second volume of *Social Wellsprings* in 1942.[35]

Husslein's output spans the period of social Catholicism defined by *Rerum Novarum* (1891), the first of the social encyclicals, punctuated by *Quadragesimo Anno* (1931), and brought near to a close with the approach of prosperity during the postwar era. Papal pronouncements were the source of his framework, and the immediate inspiration for his early writing was the experience of accelerating social change—industrial concentration, mass mobilization, and the collapse of the old regime in Europe and Russia—culminating in the upheaval of World War I. The Great Depression prompted Husslein to compile his commentaries on the encyclicals themselves.

Husslein aimed much of his fire against "the selfish spirit of rationalistic capitalism that sprang into being after the Reformation and continued its development until the great world war." The besetting sin of modern economies was liberal individualism:

> The gospel rule of charity, the laws of justice and the sanctions of religion were all obliged to yield to the overmastering considerations of profit, rent and interest: in a word, to the absorbing ideas of personal gain. This became the sole motor power of the entire system as the

idea of religion was eliminated from . . . business transactions. . . . It is the economic expression of liberalism and rationalism, and therefore of modern paganism pure and simple.[36]

What had been lost with the rise of individualism and the "merciless exploitation of capitalism" were not merely religious values such as respect for authority but communal association and fraternal sentiments as well. In Husslein's view the precapitalist world of Europe was both more ascetic and more egalitarian—spiritually and materially more democratic, or authentically populist—than the systems that followed. Its key institutions were the guild, which Husslein took to be the precursor of labor unions, and the family.

These social units complemented one another. The corporate bodies were an extension of the household; the public sphere complemented the private realm:

> Each guild constituted, according to the mind of the Church, one great family. Spiritual as well as temporal benefits were sought by the members during life, and masses were offered for their souls after death. Apprentices, journeymen and masters were still united by identical interests. Poverty, as it exists in our day, was practically unknown.[37]

The egalitarianism that Husslein attributed to the medieval system derived not only from the supports the guilds and ecclesiastical institutions, such as the monasteries, gave to their members and dependents in time of need—a kind of floor below which individuals were not supposed to fall—but also from prohibitions against the accumulation of wealth—a ceiling above which individuals were not supposed to rise. These were norms of social control and distribution, the analogues of political checks and balances.

> The object was to prevent any single man or group of men from controlling the labor market or monopolizing a local trade. Every man was enabled to gain an honest livelihood, and no man was permitted to grow enormously rich through the labor of others.[38]

The paradox of the argument consisted in the combination of economic egalitarianism, promoted by the guild system, and the hierarchy that characterized the other key institution of that lost era, the family. If Husslein's reconstruction of the medieval order is taken literally, the factor of utmost importance in the scale of everyday social stratification—the elemental building block—seems not to have been class, or even the distinction between the temporal and spiritual spheres, but rather gender and the dominance of male over female necessary for "right order." The family, stable and hierarchical, was the linchpin of society.

In a ringing paragraph Husslein stressed the contrast between the ideal of the patriarchal family and the breakdown of this ideal brought on by rampant individualism:

> There are in fine many phases of the great woman problem. Some of these are intimately connected . . . to a false idea of equality and independence. If woman sets aside her modesty, as many people openly advocate; if woman loses her domestic affection, her religious instinct and devotion, her womanliness; if she no longer recognizes her true ideal in the Mother of God, whose soul was wrapped in her Child and Savior, and whose heart was obedient to Joseph her husband, then paganism has returned and the deluge is upon us.[39]

The subversion of domestic stability was encouraged not only by abstract notions of individualism but also by economic circumstances that impelled women to work outside the home. The oversupply of labor precipitated by the entrance of women into the market threatened to drive down their husbands' wages. For both economic and moral reasons the place of women was in the home:

> "Women," as Pope Leo XIII warns us, "are not suited for certain occupations; for a woman is by nature fitted for home work, and it is that which is best adapted at once to preserve her modesty, and to promote the good bringing up of children and the well-being of the family." Conditions which drive the mother from the home into the factory, likewise expose the children to every form of vice and irreligion. It is the duty of the State, furthermore, to prevent the employment of women in occupations detrimental either to their physical or their moral well-being or the well-being of their children. . . . While the adult woman workers should receive at least a living wage, the adult male laborer should receive no less than a full family wage. This will either enable him to marry or to support, in Christian decency, the wife and children whom God has already given him.[40]

In summary, the communalism Husslein wanted to revive was a mixture of corporate egalitarianism and familial hierarchy that was to foster economic security, moral virtue, and social order. Personal rectitude, inculcated in the home, was the foundation of social stability. The organization of daily life at the level of the family was a microcosm of the larger society.

As for economics, Husslein avowed that his program was anticapitalist in its attack on the free, impersonal, frighteningly abstract, and curiously righteous market of nineteenth-century theory. His idealized medievalism gave the critique a more properly preindustrial slant. From either perspective capitalism was "an economic monstrosity of pagan selfishness."[41] Its riches were seductive, as the inequality it fostered was cruel. His criticism of socialism was slightly less scathing. As a political platform it was atheistic, and it preached class hatred. But in spirit socialist doctrine amounted to a later-day Catholicism in its detestation of individualism, its horror at the atomizing effects of the market, and in its advocacy of communal solidarity and welfare. Socialism at least seemed to retain an ethical drive. The danger of capitalism was that its evils made socialism of the atheistic variety attractive. Catholicism was closer to a socialism defined as fraternity than to a capitalism that was ruthless in its pursuit of progress:

> Suppressed Catholicism is at the center of the great social unrest. Suppressed Catholicism is the spirit struggling for liberation beneath the crackling, breaking, bursting shell of an unnatural and un-Christian social order. It is the pre-Reformation spirit of social freedom, which the Church alone can prevent from degenerating into lawlessness or injustice once it has achieved its liberation. . . . Catholic state action in favor of the people is even today confused with Socialism, to the great gain of the latter, whose borrowed plumage hides its real nature. . . . Whatever popularity Socialism may possess is entirely attributable to its camouflage Catholicism.[42]

This line of reasoning was bound to appear strained to many Americans. Even Catholics, who might be more sympathetic to the medieval imagery, were apt to dissociate the social and political from the cultural and aesthetic streams flowing from any reconstruction of the Middle Ages. One stream was pious and pleasant and as evanescent as incense; the other was serious, realistic, and practical. The failure of Husslein to separate these currents made him appear to be more of a crank than in fact he was. The high-toned homiletic pitch of his writing, appropriate in sermons on personal morals, seemed poetic and therefore impractical when he touched on social and economic matters.

Husslein's panegyric to medieval society was not matched by close analysis of current social realities. At times Husslein tended toward the rhapsodic, and he lapsed into a florid anti-intellectualism:

> More can be accomplished by the pure preaching of the Gospel than by all the wisdom of our social experts. . . . A Saint Francis of Assisi is of more avail for the true regeneration of mankind than a host of sociologists, and a Saint Teresa of Carmel than a hundred social institutes.[43]

Embedded in the rhetoric, however, was a point of view that enabled him, like other more-or-less eccentric advocates of social nostrums, to press causes and alternatives that were not inherently bound up with the resurrection of a reactionary dreamworld. He argued not only for a reduction in the work week but also for "democratic industry"—that is, for co-ownership by workers and entrepreneurs of the means of production and for similarly progressive policies that the Catholic bishops, at the prodding of Husslein's colleague John Ryan, advanced in their 1919 "program of national reconstruction."[44] Husslein drew on a common stock of utopianism shared by some radicals of the left and the right during a period when the cause of rural society had not quite been lost before the onrush of industrialism. One side saw themselves as the vanguard of the future, the other as restorers of a golden past, and the epithets of sentimentalism and superstition and secularism and false science flew between the opposing camps. But the inspiration and some of the ideas behind the mutual rejection of unbridled capitalism were not altogether at odds.[45]

Husslein's writing exhibited the classic flaw of visionary literature: a lack of follow-up and specificity about the application of old truths or revolutionary predictions to current conditions. The problem was aggravated by the inclination of Husslein to let imagery soar past graphic communication and take the place of ideas themselves. His metaphors were the conservative equivalent of revolutionary slogans. They mimicked the paradoxes of Chesterton and the witticisms of Belloc. Thought was truncated for the sake of Ciceronian effect.

Few leftists of the time would pay attention to a social program that was steeped in religion. Perhaps more grievously, such a discourse could not get a hearing from the secular center and the progressives, the influentials of American politics. Husslein was in a bind that several Jesuit social commentators who came after him would also encounter. He packaged conservative proposals in semipopular form on the supposition that his main antagonists were revolutionaries on the left. He did not, nor did the revolutionaries, advance democratic propositions in analytical form for a specialized audience. The aura of sectarianism was thick on both sides. Both were effectively shut out of policy debate. This was the route taken up by academic social scientists and rare journalistic philosophers such as Walter Lippman.[46]

Because the links between imagery, analysis, and policy formulation were patchy, it is unclear whether Husslein seriously intended a restructuring of the institutions of industrial society along the lines of artisanal guilds and corporate bodies. Enough of this ornamentation is present in his writings to make the "dotty curmudgeon" label stick. In fairness, however, there is a finger-exercise quality to his organizational speculations that suggests self-doubt or perhaps lack of genuine interest in the realism of such a scheme. Husslein wanted to recapture what for him was the sober communal ambience, the still feel, of medievalism. He saw the preservation of the patriarchal family, rather than the reform of public institutions, as essential to achieving something between the evocation and the restoration of this lost world. If a causal chain existed, perfection of the former, familiar sphere was a prior step to the consolidation of the latter, public realm. Maintaining the microstructures of traditional authority seems to have been considered a necessary and possibly a sufficient condition for the rehabilitation of the social order in the aggregate.

Yet the connection between stability at lower levels and preservation of the overall system was never specified. Large-scale organizations—for example, business firms—seemed relatively intractable, and so the fantasy of restoration turned into a view of the family as the core of social order or, failing that, as a shelter from the harsh world of economic oppression and competition. The sacredness of the family radiated like scattered haloes, strewn in a dark landscape, that could not be gathered up.

This indeterminacy aside, Husslein's discussion became so interlarded with special pleading for Catholic causes—against secular education, for example, and the evils imputed to the Reformation generally—that its message could not have reached far beyond selected corners of the Catholic ghetto.[47] The potential audience was still sizable, however. It was drawn from a large, mostly immigrant constituency of Catholics who were shepherded behind the walls of the parochial-school system. But while the Protestant-bashing and the cries from the heart may have had some appeal, it is doubtful whether Husslein's flights into social philosophy could have held such an audience, their eyes fixed on practical realities and social assimilation, for long. Toward the end of his life Husslein may have recognized the indifference with which American Catholics treated the social *magisterium*, and his writings concentrated on matters of pastoral psychology.

When laid out retrospectively in analytic form the social message dispensed by Husslein seems a composite of incompatible or at least divergent priorities: relative egalitarianism in the workplace, patriarchy at home, and a dour morality suffusing public and private spheres alike. His philosophizing makes greater sense once the context within which he wrote is recognized. A style that drew on analogy and metaphoric resonance and an occasional historical anecdote was not alien to immigrant Catholics. Husslein's disinclination for strictly analytical sociology paralleled his disdain for the heartless calculus of the market. Within the Catholic subculture of the time, he managed to sound avuncular: learned and analogical without being inordinately ponderous. His was an energetic, not a melancholy, conservatism. Husslein's writings might not have been read thoroughly or taken seriously. He did not pretend to be an original thinker; he spent more time in academic administration and in editing and publishing the manuscripts of others. But his own books were decorous and full of strange lore. His writings were integral to the atmosphere of American Catholicism in the early twentieth century, as venerable as the dust on volumes lining library shelves. It was not so much their content that mattered as a cast of mind that withheld enthusiasm for modernity out of moral repugnance.

The likelihood that few American Catholics actually read his books and articles does not controvert the fact that Husslein sided with the poor during a period when such views were often considered imprudent and possibly subversive. He began writing at a time when the transition to consumer capitalism had yet to be consummated in the United States and when social philosophies of industrialization were hotly contested. His policy recommendations, though shaped by the Catholic subculture, were no more bizarre than many of the other political panaceas then competing in the marketplace of ideas.[48]

Husslein was an advocate for the welfare of the immigrant communities. If his position was not altogether coherent, neither was the situation of the immigrants themselves. Many of them were miserably poor, but others were climbing upward. Living conditions, neighborhood alignments, and urban coalitional possibilities varied from region to region. While assimilation might eventually reduce the divisiveness of ethnic loyalties, the same process could also work to augment class differences. The Irish contingent may have looked upon Husslein's praise of corporatism with baffled tolerance. Such notions, however, were not so strange to German American Catholics. The precocity of Husslein's interest in social issues and the distributive slant he gave his analysis of these issues derived not only from the immigrant experience but also from the scholarship, originating in the nineteenth century, of German and Austrian Jesuits with strongly positive positions on state intervention on behalf of communal welfare.[49]

Insofar as public and business institutions were concerned, the orientation espoused by Husslein was distributive rather than egalitarian. In ideal terms these institutions were to act benignly, like the church, through a code of patrimonial honor and service. The severe morality instilled by a disciplined family life, cultivating endurance, would counteract tendencies toward dependence. The minihierarchy of the family and the larger body of the church would be firm but kind.

As for the modern industrial world, Husslein did not hold out much hope for the regeneration of impersonal institutions. The customs and associations of an idealized preindustrial Europe would not be reborn in the United States. Yet this stratified pastoralism remained as an absolute, in part perhaps because of its very unattainability. Traces of virginal utopianism, impregnable in its timelessness, against which actual politics was to be judged, when such matters were considered at all, persisted among Jesuits up to the eve of Vatican II. This was a spillover from the prevailing integralism. While the connections between private morality and public order might not be very rigorous and were ultimately mysterious, the goal of a moral infusion from the first to the second stayed in place.

Forsaking the dream of an American corporatism as impractical did not lead Husslein to embrace a democratic liberalism, much less to accept a liberated private morality. The foreignness of his ideas was not simply an ethnic oddity. Their German roots, tangled together with the antiliberalism of Latin Catholicism, were alien to most American Protestants and practically unknown to or about to be forgotten by many American, especially Irish American, Catholics.[50] The implications of his reasoning put him at odds with a dominant value of American democracy that process and political procedure mattered, at least as much as their outcome. The tone of Husslein's program was drawn largely from Europe, and from a lost Europe at that, and his writings suffered from an exoticism similar to that which placed socialist ideas imported from eastern Europe and Russia at a disadvantage in American eyes.[51]

Husslein reasoned by analogy. Latent contradictions and loose ends did not bother him much. The dominant Anglo-liberalism of American social thought was not immaculately consistent itself, and the audience that he addressed was unlikely to be upset by supposed incompatibilities between patriarchy at home and democracy in public. In fact, there was little if anything that might contradict Husslein's insistence on family values and self-discipline in the respect accorded the same norms by Protestant denominations at the time. His views on the micropolitics of ordinary social institutions—notably, the family—were strictly authoritarian but not wildly out of line with the Puritanism of early-twentieth-century America; the franchise had yet to be extended to women. Husslein's ideas lost much of their strangeness when set inside the walls of the immigrant subculture. There were few Catholic intellectuals, or Catholic businessmen, to challenge his romanticized medievalism.[52]

Furthermore, while the social policies advocated by Husslein were progressive, he draped his skepticism about democratic government in the effulgent patriotism common to American Catholics at the time. The common enemy was a corrosive bohemianism. The socialism that in principle inspired a sympathetic hearing because of its supposed coincidence with the Catholic sense of economic justice drew criticism from Husslein not only because it was a latter-day rival of what he claimed to be genuine Catholicism but also because it pressed for "perfect sex equality" and was the creation of "free thinkers and free-love agitators." The place for women was "on their knees at home," in prayer.[53]

Husslein had a vision of the future that in some ways suited the ordinary wisdom about material progress in America. He favored, although he did not give overwhelming priority to, economic growth. He advocated a more equitable distribution of wealth. He was conventionally, even enthusiastically, patriotic. But his understanding of historical development did not admit of change in the microstructures of everyday life, particularly the family. Social order, the functioning of impersonal institutions, whether capitalist or egalitarian, depended on intimate hierarchies and a communally supported "character." In this he did not deviate greatly from the assumptions of many earnest social reformers and indeed of some radicals who were more interested in class struggle than personal liberation.

Husslein then made a quantum leap in claiming—fuzzily and through images but nonetheless positing as an ideal—that the family was a mini-model of the perfect state. His theory of social change implied not merely stasis but a return to a prelapsarian state of familial simplicity and maternal austerity. At this point he parted company not only with political theory as understood by intellectual elites in industrial democracies but also with the vanguard of artistic modernism that formed the Lost Generation and even with some aestheticians on the right who envisioned a sleek new order molded over the regeneration of an impassioned primitivism.[54]

V

The books produced by Fr. Henry Spalding, who organized the sociology department at Loyola University in Chicago, were not exercises in theory. As the title suggests, *Social Problems and Agencies*, a compendium edited by Spalding, was problem oriented.[55] This guidebook to policy and practice opened not with a reference to papal teaching but with a chapter on immigration—a phenomenon of personal interest to most Catholics at the time—and "Americanization," the ideal toward which immigrants struggled. The book was illustrated with graphs and line drawings depicting fluctuations in employment, the advantages of the eight-hour as compared to the twelve-hour day, and trends in food prices. Much of this information, Spalding acknowledged, was supplied by the United Brotherhood of Maintenance of Way Employees and Railway Shop Laborers, the United Mine Workers, and other groups in the labor movement. The audience for Spalding's "textbook for students in the social sciences" was composed of Catholics, most of them lay people, training to become social work professionals, rather than philosophically inclined clerics.

Although Husslein's and Spalding's books were keyed to different levels, their appeal was confined mostly to Catholics. At the end of each chapter of *Social Problems and Agencies* were "topics for discussion," and the questions assumed that students shared a frame of reference made up of the neighborhoods and parishes of urban Catholic communities. "The St. Vincent de Paul Society looks for personal sanctification as the principal motive of its members. How is this achieved?"[56] "If all nations were of the Catholic Faith, would arbitration be more easily applied to labor problems?"[57] Spalding did not bother to evoke a world of jongleurs and guilds. He assumed that his readers were drawn from Catholic neighborhoods and that they would want to know the rules of social life as they knew their prayers.[58]

Both Jesuits backed labor unions and supported the struggles of the working class, many of whom were Catholics. Both rejected the idea that the economic hardships faced by ordinary Americans might be exaggerated, or that the free market would by itself engender an equitable social balance. Where Husslein's approach was theoretical, Spalding's was catechetical. Both were moralizing, and the effect was much the same. The following passage, written by a journalist for the United Mine Workers Union newsletter in response to an antilabor tract, was lifted verbatim from the original to form part of chapter three of *Social Problems and Agencies*:

> They do not tell you about the armed gunmen and thugs in the private employ of non-union coal companies in West Virginia, Kentucky, and elsewhere, who roam over the hills with a roving commission to assault, shoot, and abuse men and their families who dare to join the union or speak in favor of organization! They do not tell you how these gunmen bully helpless people; how they evict them from their homes and throw them and their little belongings out on the mountainside or roadside when the family has no other place to go! . . . Resistance in or out of court is useless, because the power of the coal company is supreme. They own the land, the highway, the court, the sheriff and everything else, and the miner has not a chance.[59]

A fundamental contribution of the texts prepared by Husslein and Spalding was to reinforce the legitimacy of working class culture and labor agitation—of the right to organize, if not of the full slate of radical demands—that were taking shape in the immigrant communities of the urban centers of the East Coast and Midwest. Their work represented a Catholic variation on the tenets of the Progressive movement. They were consistently critical of big business, which was viewed not only as monopolistic but as the monstrous product of Protestant individualism. Perhaps because the reforms espoused by the Progressives showed a Republican bias against the machine politics of the big cities, which were largely Catholic-run under the Democratic party, neither Husslein nor Spalding dwelt on urban corruption.[60] And in their defense of family hierarchies and the sexual division of labor, Husslein and Spalding shared some of the ethical traditionalism of the populists. They preached a composite of social policies that might benefit or at least protect American Catholics without undermining the traditional way of life of this constituency.[61]

On paper this was a parareligious curiosity, not a secular ideology. What saved the program from quick extinction, aside from its appeal to a sizable electoral bloc, was that overarching logic was not a paramount criterion of American political thought. Although it could not be expected to dominate or even to flow smoothly into the mainstream, the kind of thinking represented by Husslein was consonant with several elements of a freewheeling pluralism, and the emphasis given to family morality redeemed its latent social radicalism. Within the family most Americans were not democrats, and many were troubled by the boundless avarice of public life.

Rather like the tips and advice put together by Henry Spalding, the books assembled by Husslein indicated that he was an idealist and a man of action, an institution builder. Rigorous concepts mattered less than diffuse ideals, combined with a belief in mobility that was as deeply held as social dogma. Most of the time Husslein managed to stay on the safe side of eccentricity. An edifying imprecision added a Catholic stamp to common sense and practicality. In the end the constituency of Husslein, Spalding, and their colleagues was made up of immigrants and second-generation ethnics who had vivid memories of the differences between social authority and family hierarchy. They made shrewd distinctions between order in the household and claims to piety on the outside.

VI

The direct results of the writings of Husslein and his colleagues on the national scene seem to have been negligible. They do not appear to have influenced labor legislation. Their contribution was cultural rather than strictly intellectual. They helped sustain a left-of-center legacy during a period, from the turn of the century onward, when the bulk of Catholics in the United States were being drawn into the toils and charms of American capitalism.[62] They nurtured their critical perspective by means of traditional appeals, mixing calls for social reform with invocations of a moral sobriety based on what they supposed were traditional family structures. The corporatist nostalgia in which Husslein's thought came packaged festooned a vision of a reformed capitalism held together, not by a remote democratic state but from the bottom, by the industriousness of virtuous families.

This posture had limitations that went deeper than occasional reliance on an arcane vocabulary and antiquarian allusions. It was founded on a set of concepts that were not just static but backward looking. The scholastic categories that rescued Husslein, Spalding, and their colleagues from uncritical acceptance of the boosterism of the times also diverted them from creative engagement with the dynamics of American society, even though this mode of thought put them on the fringes of contact with cultural conservatives. Perfection was in the past, a lost Eden. Material progress might be acknowledged and even encouraged, but it stood ultimately in defiance of the norm that sought restoration of a way of life that was both more heroic and more humane than "the present catastrophe" but that, since it neither existed in the past nor had a chance of coming into being in the future, invited ridicule or a tacit compartmentalization of private religion from collective action and public policy. What was protected was an intellectual innocence that was captive to an elevated play of words.[63]

However, once the antiquarian drapery is sheared away, a crucial set of questions emerges from the importance that Husslein and his associates attributed to primary units—chiefly, the family—in shaping social order and protecting traditional values. The question concerns how values formed in intimate groups might be aggregated into larger collectivities or, alternatively, how intermediate institutions might shield individuals from an encroaching government. Husslein never answered this pair of questions; indeed, his phrasing of them was uncertain. Nevertheless, he succeeded in inching toward problems of analytical interest and practical importance even though he posed them strangely and his answers were sketchy.

It is symptomatic of the conceptual difficulty he faced, and not just an indication of his taste for metaphor and analogy, that a miasma of imagery clouded the extrapolations that Husslein tried to make between the microexperience and macro institutions. He seems to have favored taking the family as a nearly literal microcosm of an ideal social and political structure. But the state-in-miniature construction of the family could not withstand the smallest movement toward modernity. This meant a fall from grace. Depicting the family as a ministate smacked of institutional triumphalism and absolutist thought. Even the defense of its less grandiose variant, positing the family as a building block of stability on a larger scale, required working through a very complex and problematic causal chain. It was an ethical standard, not a scientific law.

Although he favored an assertive role for the church, Husslein seems to have settled for the defense of the family and familylike institutions in their role as subcultural guardians against a secular array of business organizations and state agencies. Whether families, church groups, and the like might make up a countercultural challenge to the prevailing order was another matter, to be considered as assimilation gathered momentum. For a time, given the size of the Catholic ghetto, the squads of priests and nuns supporting it, and the insecurity of an immigrant populace, the encapsulating model seemed to be a realistic strategy.

In Husslein's time the Catholic church was still very much on the defensive in the United States. Broadcasting a militant ideology could bring down the wrath of a hostile majority, but on the inside a certain triumphalism kept up the solidarity of the tribe. This ambivalence probably accounts for Husslein's shifting back and forth between prudence and in-house chauvinism, between weaker and stronger readings of the social functions of the family. A younger generation of Jesuits whose writings began to appear after World War II, with fewer illusions about the future of Catholicism as a majority denomination, would more readily dispense with historical fantasy and promote the male-headed family and the parochial-school system as guarantors of a minority way of life.[64]

From the beginning, even as Husslein spun fables of a premodern utopia, the schools of social work went their pragmatic, adaptive way. They grew in competence and professionalism, performing a genuine service. But as far as ideas were concerned they turned inward. In part because it was not their purpose, they did not attain intellectual excellence. One price paid by the early Jesuit social analysts and advocates for encasing their appeals within the boundaries of the Catholic ghetto was that they and many of their readers often could not distinguish between countercultural criticism of some validity and the preaching of cranks. Eccentrics and fools, like prostitutes and others who were banished from the schemes of puritanism and productivity, finally had their place in a social order that was hierarchical and formally intolerant but routinely forgiving and even indulgent. The ethic was familial, not juridical.

The potential for controversy raised by the oddity of Husslein's writing was handled by compartmentalizing private virtue from public policy. Few Catholics quarreled with his depictions of the lyrical hierarchies of family life. Everyone who reached the age of reason was supposed to know that Husslein was using figures of speech and that literal application of Catholic social thought was to be curbed by prudence, not left to innocence or enthusiasm. Thus understood, the social *magisterium*, far from dictating policy, provided an unobtrusive tonality and diffuse idealism within which the work of institutional service was performed. For American Catholics this division of labor separated religion from politics. It also kept ideas separate from organizational life.

So, along with religious zealotry, intellectual creativity drained from the subculture. The absolutes that characterized Catholic moral teaching were supposed to be superior to the circumstantiality of social thought. For the latter, perfection was unattainable; for the former, it had already been reached. An operational divide existed between social and ethical theory. Political thought, as opposed to practice, was relegated to the realm of aesthetics, living on in dreams of an old-fashioned domesticity.

2

Social Principles and Political Tactics

In 1866 in a town outside Vienna, at the onset of the last great age of the Austro-Hungarian empire, the wife of Count Anton Ledochowski bore a son named Wlodimir. Of Polish origin, the Ledochowskis were known as a "pious and capable family." The count was a royal chamberlain at the Hapsburg court. A brother went on to become a cardinal and prefect of the Sacred Congregation for the Propagation of the Faith, head of what was once called the Inquisition. Another son of the count became a general in the Austrian army during World War I. There were also two daughters, both of whom became nuns, one establishing the Ursulines in Poland and the other directing missionary work in Africa. Wlodimir himself entered the Society of Jesus. He became general of the Jesuits in 1915. He died in Rome in 1942.[1]

Ledochowski's tenure as general spanned a period that opened with the crumbling of the *ancien régime*, covered the rise of communism and then fascism, and witnessed the onset of World War II.[2] It was a period, his obituary noted, of "rapid and confusing changes brought about by gigantic national expansions and the resultant jealousies, by new conceptions, most of them anarchical, in science, in general culture, in social theory, in religious and philosophical speculation, while concomitantly the very existence of Western civilization was threatened by internecine wars in Europe and the rapid rise of outside powers hostile to the Christian tradition."[3]

Ledochowski fitted the mold of antimodernist Catholicism. A reactionary, he was optimistic that secularism was on the verge of exhausting itself. The times were ripe for a revival of tradition. "Towards the end of the past century," he wrote early in his term, "we were able to note a great change in men's way of judging and thinking. Freethinkers, after more than a century of contempt of God and religion, tolerated by them only for the benefit of the ignorant masses, promised that science would solve all the problems of life. . . . The souls of men are feeling ever more and more the terrible void created by the conspiracy of governments to tear away modern generations from Christ and His Church."[4] The origins of "the evil days on which we have fallen" could be traced back beyond the turmoil of the nineteenth century, to the "tremendous catastrophe" of the French Revolution, and further still, to the "so-called Reformation." Ledochowski was ready to deploy his men on a new crusade that he felt would outshine the Counter-Reformation.

As early as 1916, writing from Switzerland, where the Jesuit curia had been transferred for the duration of the war, Ledochowski noted that "on the solution of the so-called social question, the fate of modern society seems to depend. The Sovereign Pontiffs, who from their lofty watchtower behold the condition of the human race, have again and again exhorted Catholics to take part in social works." The general wanted his troops to refrain from direct political activity. While he applauded the recent opening of the School of Sociology at Fordham and a similar venture at Loyola University in Chicago, the role of the Jesuits was to "explain the principles of the natural law, the laws of the Church, the teaching and admonitions of the Sovereign Pontiffs regarding social and Catholic action, and at the same time show how these principles should be used to solve various practical questions, in order that every enterprise may be correctly undertaken." He left it to "capable laymen, with united efforts," to work out the destiny of these undertakings. Jesuits were to be teachers and moral guides, not social activists.[5]

The strategy was two-tiered. Catholic social principles were enduring but their application was circumstantial, The task was one of deductive application, not of revision of dogma. In addition, while Jesuits were not to participate in day-to-day politics, they could serve as advisers, cajoling the powerful. Both parts of the strategy posed difficulties. Not much time passed before the suspicion emerged that a key problem was how to derive practical applications without changing doctrine. Aside from this puzzle, there arose varied interpretations of what the educational role of Jesuits meant in social and political matters. These readings ranged from informal chats or abstract disquisitions to a ventriloquist model in which "capable laymen" mouthed fixed principles.

Ledochowski had almost nothing to say in public about the social question. Behind the scenes, though, he remained active. In 1930 Pius XI entrusted him with the preparation of what was to be issued the next year as

Quadragesimo Anno, the encyclical marking the fortieth anniversary of the first major papal statement on the relations between capital and labor. The work of drafting the commemorative encyclical fell to "the German fathers," principally, Oswald von Nell-Breuning. The project was carried out in secrecy. With an occasional assist from "a few brother priests" and the Latin translators, Nell-Breuning wrote the encyclical, passing on typescripts to Ledochowski, who passed them on to the pope.

The restricted circle within which the encyclical took form, in conjunction with the peculiarities of the situation of the papacy in Italy, left its marks. The document confirmed the place of social concern alongside spiritual consolation on the ecclesiastical agenda during the depression. On the one hand, like most such statements, the encyclical aimed for generality. But in effect it was addressed only to Catholics and could indeed best be appreciated by those with a feel for the vortex of church-state relations in Italy.

The encyclical was compromised by prudential references to the feats of Italian fascism, and it suffered from a detailed and soon-to-be-dated exposition of the virtues of corporatism and class harmony through consultation among occupational groups.[6] An unacknowledged agreement between Mussolini and the pope might be detected regarding the merits of corporatism as compared to alternative political systems, at the same time that there existed a rivalry over whose version of corporatism would meet with acceptance. They shared a hatred of maximalist socialism and a disdain for Anglo-American liberalism. The collaboration between Pius XI and the Jesuits reflected a combination of imperial strategy, personal whim, revulsion for communism and capitalism both in principle and in practice, and scholastic systematization that set the tone for official pronouncements and commentary on the subject for another three decades. Forty years later, in 1971, Nell-Breuning poured out his regrets:

> The final say as to what was to be incorporated in the encyclical could . . . be made only by Fr. Ledochowski, the man appointed by the Pope. He accepted my material and as a rule agreed to my proposals. When, as an exception, he denied his approval, it was not because he was of another opinion on the subject and thought he understood it better, but as a matter of expediency. He did not want to awake sleeping bears (whether Vatican or fascist) needlessly. . . . Formally, the whole responsibility lay with Fr. Ledochowski, though in fact he depended on me in technical questions. When I think back on it today, it seems to me that such a procedure, that allowed the whole bearing of an official document to be determined by a consultant . . . without

establishing any countercheck worth mentioning, seems frighteningly irresponsible.[7]

The publication of *Quadragesimo Anno* gave a stamp of approval to social concern among some clerics and other attentive Catholics accustomed to giving priority to higher things. But the specifics of the encyclical, with its talk of corporatist assemblies for improving the state of industrial relations, were not suited to the American scene. The organizational logistics sounded exotic and, if taken literally, damaged the credibility of the doctrine from which they were supposed to have been deduced.[8]

Nothing much happened in the United States. Encyclicals were better suited to delineating what was forbidden or recognizing changes that were taking place than to advancing positive programs for shaping social realities, and policies could not be mandated from above in democracies. The Roman authorities quietly scolded the Americans for their indifference to the social *magisterium* and their isolationism regarding the threats of fascism and communism that were consuming Europe, while seeking to mobilize their resources and energies behind a political and social counteroffensive. Ledochowski grew chagrined at the lack of response to papal social teaching among the American Jesuits, who were the most rapidly growing segment of the society. As the end of the 1930s neared, membership in the American assistancy surpassed that of Spain, making the Americans the largest single group in the order. Their near-total silence was influential and therefore irritating.[9]

II

In the mid-1930s, in a letter "on combatting Communism," Father Ledochowski commissioned the Jesuits of North America to lead "the way in our Society's project of a worldwide systematic warfare against the common enemy of Christianity and civilization."[10] The general's delegate for launching the project was Fr. Edmund Walsh, founder of the School of Foreign Service at Georgetown University, and later, during the Cold War, a confidant of Senator Joseph McCarthy.[11]

The appointment of Walsh, whose celebrity as an expert on international affairs and on the Soviet Union in particular had been launched by his relief work in Russia in the aftermath of World War I, signaled that Ledochowski was intent on redirecting the resources of the American Jesuits against communism.[12] Although Walsh did not stay with the new project for long, his brief efforts at translating the urgings of the general for the American context gave a preview of the dilemmas that Jesuits would encounter later in trying to adapt theory to practice.

Toward the end of 1936 Walsh wrote a letter to the American provincials in which he attempted to set out the norms under which Jesuits in the United States were to operate as they engaged in social action in greater numbers. Walsh assured his colleagues that a store of Catholic social doctrine existed from which practical solutions, and not merely philosophical attacks on communism, could be drawn. Reasonable answers were in hand. What was needed was the proper mix of prudence and zeal, the traditional dose of courage and diplomacy that Jesuits had shown in the past. Ideas, propelled by conviction and channeled through common sense, could move toward implementation. Walsh's memorandum combined the features of a pep talk with cautionary admonitions.

> We have a new mandate obliging us to give wider circulation to the Encyclicals in which the outlines of the true Christian State and a rational economy are drawn in firm and enlightened language. In those classical expositions of Catholic sociology will be found concrete measures of a very practical character: just wages, the rights both of Labor and Capital, the right use of property and money, the rights of workers to associate in unions for their own protection and advancement, a just and equitable distribution of profits, the necessity for a reform of banking and credit, correction of the abuses of financial power, the social obligation attaching to wealth and the corresponding duty of governments to assure that justice and equilibrium be maintained in economic relationships. Here are specific and constructive measures in abundance which we should and must advocate.[13]

Yet, even if Jesuits could assume that they were in possession of principles that only needed to be applied to remedy the ills of American capitalism, Walsh was aware that important questions remained. The correctness of the doctrine did not relieve Jesuits of the obligation to respect the rules of American politics as they moved from the realm of ideas toward political reform and regulation. Persuasion not just of princes but of numerous other influential figures was needed.

Furthermore, a distinction had to be drawn between the prevailing economic and social system, afflicted by numerous injustices, and American political democracy, in which Jesuit undertakings were prospering. The distance between the ethics and economics of capitalism on the one hand and liberalism as a political process on the other might be obscure to the Roman mind, but for Walsh it was an essential piece of practical wisdom. A significant implication of this line of reasoning—one that Walsh declined to spell out, probably in deference to integralist sensibilities—was that the virtual fusion of religion and politics favored by European conservatives was a dangerous fiction, even as an ideal, and had no place under an otherwise eclectic Americanism. Separation of church and state was an absolute tenet of the civil religion of the land. The notion of joining the two was incomprehensible in the American setting. To Walsh's way of thinking, an equally serious difficulty was the failure of the continental mind to distinguish politics and economics—in particular, to understand the differences and reciprocity between capitalism as an economic system and democracy as a system of conflict management under which minorities, including Catholics, might protect their interests.

In the end, Walsh proposed, there did not seem to be an inherent conflict between American public philosophy and Catholic principles, certainly none that was worth forcing a quarrel about. While some tension might arise between Catholic teaching and social-reform movements of secular origin, he held to the idea that there was no ultimate incompatibility between the message of the encyclicals and the American way. Walsh spoke a language of open-mindedness and avoided the temptation to escalate specific conflicts into symbols of larger contradictions. Changes could be made incrementally, and policy disputes could be dealt with and probably settled piecemeal. Political reason operated empirically and, as far as possible, dispassionately. Ideological maximalism was to be avoided.

> Since the strengthening of our own economic structure is a powerful means of combatting Communism, it is clear that His Paternity would not wish us to omit sound constructive commentary.
>
> I find no reason, then, for the slightest relaxation in the effort to discover and profit from the various experiments now being conducted in that field. Where they are in accordance with the very ample recommendations of the Encyclicals, they should be commenced; where they are conflict with Catholic morals and ethics they should be rejected. Such a factual and objective study of the most important problem facing the present generation is the very root purpose of . . . "An Integrated Program of Social Order" on which we are now working. We intend the word "order" to mean *"apta dispositio plurium ad unum,"* the *"unum"* being the social reign of Christ to be achieved through the enlightened proposals of the Sovereign Pontiffs in their Encyclicals.[14]

The social *magisterium* according to Walsh was a series of "very ample recommendations," not categorical injunctions. He focused on generalities about process and style, on matters of good judgment and civility that Jesuits could recognize and agree on, and he skirted generalizations about substantive issues that might trigger questions of principle. He wrote as an emissary between the Latin and Anglo-American worlds, and the result was a pocket manual of church-state diplomacy.

Walsh stressed that while Jesuits could get involved in the development of ideas and practical solutions to social problems, they were not to identify these recommendations with partisan alternatives or with a blatant preference for one type of political system over another. The objective was political "presence." The imperative for Walsh was not overt power but diplomacy, combined with a reputation for political judgment that, instead of requiring him actively to seek influence, drew others to him. Political instinct, not theory, was his strong suit. His position left unclear where policy formulation ended and the exercise of political influence might begin. But commitment of a type that condemned the governmental apparatus as such, going from disagreement on particular issues to sweeping condemnation, was not to be countenanced:

> We do not intend by the word "order" any favored political regime, as if Jesuits—who are members of an international body that functions in every land—stood for some one form of social control or governmental organization above all others. To be sure, as Americans we believe that the constitutional democracy under which we live in the United States is for us the best guarantee of religious and civil liberty. But wherever other forms are chosen by the sovereign will of the nations in question, we leave to them the natural right of free and unquestioned choice in determining their domestic policy. [15]

In the American case, then, the promotion of papal economic and social teaching need not and should not entail the installation of alien, corporatist political mechanisms. The triumphalist strategy would almost certainly provoke a disastrous reaction against Catholics. If influence was to be extended, principles were to be expressed in line with a tact adapted to political realities. Although other political arrangements—for example, communist regimes—might be censured, prudence as well as a natural patriotism dictated that the American constitutional formula should not be criticized.

Sensitivity to the difficulties of translating Catholic social principles into practice in an overwhelmingly non-Catholic environment was the closest that Walsh came to the substance of public policy, and his recommendation seems to have been that implementation could be handled on a case-by-case basis. He kept returning, without vehemence but somewhat less blandly, to the procedural question of clerical participation in politics. If, as Walsh claimed, the passage from general principles to detailed applications could be comparatively brief, it might appear that Jesuits need not stick with theory but could thrust themselves into political action.

Here again, however, prudential factors were paramount. While Walsh left the door open to partisan involvement in selected situations—chiefly, moral issues that the church took to be its domain—he insisted that an indirect, pedagogical role should be the norm for Jesuits, in conformity with the position of the general and with the regulations of the society itself:

> I interpret the emphasis in the General's letter as a warning against entering too deeply in our publications into the particular manner, the specific legislation or the machinery which could be adopted to bring about these socially desirable improvements. It is not a prohibition against suggesting definite ways and means in harmony with the guiding principles of the Encyclicals. But the final execution and local application of such programs should be left to laymen and those charged with the temporal administration of civil society. . . . [T]he Jesuit's vocation lies in the spiritual domain, as a teacher, an expounder of principles and a moralist. But obviously he may be a teacher of economics, of sociology, of international law as well as of ethics, philosophy, and theology. We all know that the history of the Society is replete with eminent examples of distinguished service in all these fields. Since, however, in modern times economics, sociology and law are so intimately connected with politics and involve legislation by party governments, the delicate problem arises of determining where intellectual and moral guidance ends and where political leadership begins. The former is clearly within our vocation. The latter is definitely forbidden.[16]

In a democracy full of contending interests, approaches to power and methods of influence that relied on the confessor-to-the-king model were no longer appropriate. With the rise of mass politics and the media, governmental decision making had become an object of greater public scrutiny. Even if Jesuits felt that they possessed a stock of extraordinarily useful policy guidelines, they were not in a position to impose them as absolutes. Persuading or converting a handful of eminent personalities might be a reasonable option, and indeed it was one that a few talented Jesuits had used with success in the courts of Europe. But the rules surrounding intraelite consultation and the offering of advice differed in aristocratic and democratic polities. In the United States, this was permitted and it flourished, but it was not the only game in town. Influence, Walsh implied, was liable to be diluted, and results correspondingly partial. When it came to political practice, Walsh was less concerned with the abstract dialectic of absolute and relative truths than with securing a niche from which to exercise a bit of influence among numerous competitors. He operated more like an entrepreneur in the marketplace than a general out to conquer an empire.

In addition to appreciating the political mechanics behind the advancement of group interests under democratic conditions, Walsh recognized the diversity of opinion that was bound to arise among Jesuits themselves, whatever the supposed unity of Catholic social doctrine. The assumption of a stock of certainties was as misguided as the expectation of sovereign influence.

> Just when, where and how we may in exceptional cases adopt publicly a strong crusading attitude on a national issue outside the domain of faith and morals is a question to be decided in the instance. . . . This at times may be necessary when a moral or religious element appears to be involved. Any such program adopted by a group of Jesuits acting collectively will ordinarily be interpreted by the public as a Jesuit doctrine. That involves such a grave responsibility that extreme caution and mature deliberation is required, since sharp differences of opinion will be encountered in the Society as among any similar group of educated men when debatable problems in economics are discussed. And if the endorsement happens to be in favor of a measure of controversial character that later meets repudiation by the people, serious consequences could follow for the Society in the United States. The recent repudiation of Father Coughlin by the millions who were supposedly loyal followers is a case in point.[17]

Here Walsh reiterated a strategy that had been gaining some currency, though imperfect legitimacy, in ecclesiastical circles since the French Revolution. A partial and perhaps even complete separation of church and state might be as beneficial to the interests of Catholicism as a religious monopoly. But a pluralism from which religious contention had been largely expunged, normal as it might appear in the American context, remained controversial among Jesuits in Europe, where confessional parties and Catholic trade unions competed against an ideological left.

Walsh did not pretend to anything but pragmatic accommodation to American exceptionalism. Caution and adaptability were his watchwords. The one clear and consistent thread in his argument was belief in a broad compatibility between Catholic social doctrine and American political philosophy and, especially, the institutional mores of American politics. Walsh did not raise the hackles of principle except to suggest in passing that on certain matters of faith and morals—not "debatable problems in economics"—the Society might have to take a strong stand.

His letter was long and sinuous. The circumlocutions reflected a need for maintaining flexibility amid the multiple actors and contingencies of American politics without abandoning Catholic dogma. The solution—which Walsh characteristically never quite put in so many words—was to downplay doctrinal specifics on both sides and to take advantage of the genius of the American system, which institutionalized maneuverability and compromise. The assurances that Catholic social principles could readily be put into practice were a bit ritualistic. Passion in the defense of the faith did not override Walsh's sense of the institutional limitations that surrounded the options available to American Jesuits in advancing papal teaching.[18]

The social *magisterium*, then, was not like a prescription that needed only to be swallowed for an illness to be cured. Walsh's tenure in Washington as director of the Georgetown School of Foreign Service honed his astuteness about the constraints on the exercise of power. He had the intuition of a successful organizational operator. He also had a strategic agenda that gave priority to geopolitical power struggles over domestic issues of social equity. In this regard, although the substance of his views was conservative, his style of thinking resembled the perspective that a generation later would place global imbalances ahead of class tensions in the social teaching of the church. For the time being, this perspective confirmed him in his inclination to stay above the tangle of difficulties involved in sorting through the application of corporatist social theory, with its strange talk of *Stände* and *ordines* ("social estates" and "occupational groupings"), to the American scene.

Walsh did not conceive of a social science in purely academic terms, any more than he derived the ideas he cared about by way of deductive abstraction from scholastic manuals. This practical slant, together with his personal experience of the ways of Washington politics, relieved him of the schematic innocence displayed by some of his colleagues. But it also shunted him away from intellectual advances in politics. The *magisterium* was simply given, a marvelously stable and vague platform—a label and an identity—from which to launch campaigns to influence policy. As a body of ideas, it was insufficiently defined to merit either elaborate defense or to provoke serious attack or even rethinking.

Walsh lent visibility among American Jesuits to a social campaign that Ledochowski wanted to mount on a world scale. But he knew little economics or sociology himself, and he was so busy traveling and managing the Georgetown operation that his contribution was confined to arranging for the publication of *Informationes et Notitiae*, a periodic compendium of anticommunist news items and essays for circulation within the Society of Jesus. He took little interest in the organizational details of getting his fellow Jesuits involved in social analysis and action. With the School of Foreign Service, Walsh had created a niche ingeniously suited to the world of Washington politics. He had become an insider, practically an institution by himself, and he saw that nothing was to be gained by the advocacy of strange ideas. He sensed that coordinating the activities of Jesuits on a national scale was as unwieldy a logistical task as the conceptual chore of explicating the links between theory and practice was insoluble.

Walsh quickly lost interest in the operation. Much of the collective response to the general's directive was concentrated instead in the Midwest and on the East Coast, and it involved many of the same Jesuits who were to meet at West Baden in 1943.

III

During the last years of the depression leading up to the outbreak of World War II, Jesuits in the United States responded in two ways to the directives from Rome regarding social ministry. First, they tried to develop a grand design, a social blueprint, that would meet the economic and political challenges of the 1930s. They labored away at a theoretical task of precisely the kind that bored Edmund Walsh.

The conceptual venture itself took two forms. Some projects, such as the flirtation with small-scale farming and agrarian cooperatives, reflected the mixing of the rural interests and life experiences of individual Jesuits with a taste for medieval corporatism and preindustrial peace that was more common among the general run of Jesuits, all of whom had been exposed to the philosophical legacy of the Middle Ages. Their quarrel was with modernity itself. Their utopianism sought a refuge from the modern city. The fact that most American Catholics were city dwellers ignorant of the scholastic theorizing from which the schemes for social reform drew thickened the air of fantasy that clouded this part of the enterprise. But there was also a nativist American strain in the advocacy of a return to the soil, and this prevented the small movement from becoming another weird ethereality of imported Catholicism.[19]

The second response, the creation of the labor schools, adhered less closely to a contrived nostalgia. Jesuits in this camp accepted industrialization, rejected socialism, but questioned capitalism, if not very articulately then at least by their actions. The movement was aimed at an urban working class which could not be sealed off from the modern world within a religious ghetto even if many of its members were more than just nominally Catholic.

In contrast to the intellectually top-heavy programs developed in the name of a Latinate Catholicism, the labor schools were largely pastoral improvisations without much prestige among the weightier Jesuits. They sprang up with the permission and indeed at the prompting of authorities in the society, on the expectation that somehow they would develop into a coordinated force. Centralization did not take place. Some of the schools evolved into dumping grounds or petty satrapies for crusty Jesuits without pull among their more intellectual peers. Others—rather like parishes whose variety resisted a coherent overview—defied synoptic planning because, inserted in local conditions, they "went native."

The outline for the "Establishment of a Christian Social Order" emerged in 1935 and 1936 from meetings among Jesuits in the Midwest and New York. For the most part, XO, as the plan was called for short, stayed on paper, forgotten in the files. A few elements, however, fared better than others. The suggestion that schools for workingmen, and not merely symposia on social topics for the middle class, should be promoted was taken up. This entailed closer contact with the working class than was implied by the model of the school of social service two decades earlier at Fordham.

Even if the labor schools did not function under an established plan, as envisioned for the society's educational institutions in the *Ratio Studiorum*, they responded to the Jesuits' tradition of activism. The labor schools required little intellectual or logistical overhead. The investment in manpower and money was small, and most of the Jesuits who took part in the schools were volunteers possessed of a missionary zeal.

The grand design itself reflected the conceptual boundaries within which the Jesuits operated. In line with the primacy that the general had accorded to the educational role of his men, the starting point was to be a manifesto summarizing a "Catholic Program of Social Justice." The goal was to develop a set of "brief, challenging assertions [covering] the essential Catholic positions with regard to God, Man, Religion, Church, State, Society, and Human Rights, meeting *directly* the Communist position on each of these topics."[20] What evolved was a series of sprawling agendas, listing areas of concern across the spectrum of American social and religious life in the 1930s. Attention was to be given to social security, to atheism, to labor unions, to race relations, to youth, to the family, and so on.

Principles and proposals for action were categorized under headings and subheadings, and the lists ran parallel without much indication of how one followed from the other. The problem areas were susceptible to infinite subdivision and refinement, yet the application of Catholic principles to social realities by way of deductive reasoning proved to be more difficult than the supporters of XO had anticipated. The expectation that an overall vision was available or that the Jesuits were capable of reaching it increased their frustration.

What emerged was ad hoc brainstorming. Under the label "Information and Propaganda" came the suggestion that "each University, College and High School should have study clubs or a *Social Justice Academy*, to which the more intelligent students could be invited for a further investigation and discussion of the problems, and other extra-curricular activities." Jesuits were also urged to be active "among workers and the poor, in transient camps, patriotic organizations, employers and heads of industry, among the police (to ensure a more Christian method of dealing with Communists when necessary), and in the army and navy." Efforts on the part of Jesuits were to be international as well as domestic. "To meet Communist activities along these lines, co-operation should be promoted among Catholics of Latin America and the United States dependencies in opposition to an un-Christian policy of imperialism, such opposition to be based upon Christian principles of international ethics." Finally, under the category of "Spiritual Orientation," it was proposed that "fervent prayers, particularly those of the Contemplative Religious, should be enlisted for XO; and public prayers, e.g., novenas directed toward the work."[21]

As the lists of suggestions and possible projects proliferated, the difficulty of reaching agreement on priorities grew. The need for consensus on a positive model of society and politics that went beyond criticism of secular solutions considered to be dubious or evil was a standard refrain. "The attack upon the enemies is far less important than the presentation of the Catholic answer." However, no such consensus—no "unified, coordinated, practical plan"—emerged.[22] The vast scope of the program nullified attempts to orchestrate its components in a manner that the Jesuits hoped would be both logical and visionary.[23]

Although the desirability of such an ideal lingered, Jesuits began to sense and tacitly to admit that the dream of synthesis in social ministry was indigestible. It was easier to agree on the identity of the evils to be combatted. The outstanding ones were atheism and communism. These were the twin demons that Father Ledochowski and recent popes had singled out for counterattack in the midst of a crisis thought to be "the most important since the reformation."

A third target generated less unanimous militancy across the Society of Jesus as an international body. This was represented by "the dangers of Dictatorship, probably the more immediately perilous, as pagan in philosophy as Communism, as destructive of personal liberty, religious freedom, Christian democratic principles."[24]

Not many American Jesuits were as concerned about or sympathetic to the modern versions of rightwing European politics as was Ledochowski himself. They had little awareness of fascism in the abstract, a condition that isolationism reinforced. This created a delicate situation. Antifascism of a kind was sanctioned by the tribulations of Pius XI with the regime that had been consolidated in Italy under Mussolini, whose attempts to curb the independence of church-sponsored youth groups and newspapers were a persistent source of friction.[25] Furthermore, the thoroughly Italianate papacy became increasingly exasperated with the Teutonic pretensions of national socialism, and sensitivity to being patronized as a tired culture eventually led to anger at the racial doctrines of the Nazis.

On the other hand, some varieties of fascism worked to the advantage of Catholic interests in Europe. The corporatist government of a former seminarian, Antonio de Oliveira Salazar, had saved Portuguese Catholicism from radicalism.[26] Its constitution claimed the medieval guild system as fundamental to its lineage. The wall paintings and mosaics commissioned by the corporatist state were as rapturous about the dignity of labor and social hierarchy as the murals of Diego Rivera were indignant at class oppression and religious obscurantism in Mexico. The Portuguese path was praised by some Jesuits, for example, by Walsh and his protégés at Georgetown, as an exemplary counter to communism.[27] And, despite the harassment suffered by Catholic Action at the hands of Mussolini, the concordat between the Vatican and the government stayed in effect, providing financial and material support to the church and giving it a monopoly over religious life in Italy.

Finally, civil war was brewing in Spain during the 1930s, and the defense of ecclesiastical interests by the Nationalist forces, marshaled by Franco against atheistic communism, made strenuous antifascism difficult.[28] The issues raised by this conflict began to cut deep and close to home, even for some American Jesuits whose politics bordered on isolationism or whose tastes ran more to theology than to public affairs. Matters of principle were joined with corporate interest; international solidarity with suffering Catholics was invoked.

In 1932 the society had been expelled yet again from Spain, this time by the Republican government, and most of its schools had been closed. Later that year a news item in *Woodstock Letters*, the quarterly published at the society's theologate in Maryland, reported with the impassioned precision of an atrocity story that

> with the closing of the twenty-six schools, 14,599 students were deprived of the instruction of their 709 Jesuit teachers. Left to the Jesuits are two observatories, the scientific review, *Revista Ibérica*, and the leper colony at Gandia. In the aggregate, the pupils of the Jesuit free schools in Spain numbered not less than 400,000.[29]

Solidarity with the Spanish brethren was encouraged by frequent allusions to the work that Jesuits had doggedly carried out in Spain and by comparisons of their efforts with the sacrifices made by American Jesuits. In 1935, on the twenty-fifth anniversary of the opening of the Jesuits' prep school in Brooklyn, *Woodstock Letters* noted that a parish priest had managed to work in praise

> in behalf of the Spanish Jesuits who have suffered so much in the recent cruel persecution in Spain. . . . [W]hile he does not know any of them personally he knows that they receive the same training as the American Jesuits, and he will leave it to the American people, and

especially to Catholics, to judge how well they serve God and their country.[30]

So, Jesuits might work up emotions about a far-off conflict in light of the society's long history of adventure in foreign lands. Questions of political theory, which few Jesuits had thought about, got tangled up with the imperative of defending Catholicism and the demands of corporate loyalty.[31]

Jesuits tried to thread their way through the confrontation in Europe and the less polarized situation in the United States. Their hope of finding a consistent political formula proved chimerical. The ambivalence involved in condemning fascism in some places and coming to terms with it in others manifested itself in the difficulty that Jesuits had in devising a third way that would avoid the perils of communism and the threat of atheism in its various guises—for example, as anticlerical liberalism or, in the United States, as materialistic capitalism.[32] Condemnations of communism alone could lead the society into uncomfortable alliances. The Jesuits resolved that "with those who combat Communism on Christian principles we will ally ourselves; with those who oppose Communism for patriotic or business reasons merely we will use their machinery but we will not ally ourselves openly with them."[33]

A strategy that tried to balance attacks on communism with criticism of fascism was also tenuous. Fr. John LaFarge, then beginning a distinguished career at *America* magazine and already a national figure in ecumenicism and race relations, warned flatly that "Father General will not approve a direct stand against Fascism." A proposal to work around this obstacle led LaFarge into a bit of casuistry and an acerbic exchange with the more reactionary Walsh. "We can indirectly meet the threat," LaFarge argued, "by advocating a Christian program, positive and negative, that of itself will exclude Fascism. We will include in our stand the repudiation of a totalitarian state. Therefore it is not a nominal attack, but positive in our own program, and negative by the repudiation of the totalitarian state."

"What if we're questioned about Fascism?" Walsh asked.

"*You* might lecture against it," LaFarge snapped.[34]

So the XO plan was torn by equivocation regarding the softer and stronger forms of fascism. Nostalgia for preindustrial incarnations of corporatism, fashionable in then-current understandings of the Catholic political tradition, according to which the thirteenth was "the greatest of centuries," mitigated criticisms of modern authoritarian regimes.[35] By and large Jesuits were repelled by the "pagan" or "profane" brand of fascism and its fascination with futuristic technology and the mobilization of mass society.[36] They were less put off by forms of authoritarianism identified with the preservation of traditional values and with the imagery of family and farm. While such embellishments were irrelevant to Jesuits in the labor schools, who ignored theory almost completely, they were reminiscent of the medieval atmospherics common in the theologates. Social order and ethical rectitude of a rustic sort, a moral and political economy based on austerity, competed with social justice in industrial settings for thematic dominance of the program that the Jesuits were striving to develop.

Not all the influences shaping the thinking of the American Jesuits on politics during the thirties were of Latin origin, even though these sources were the most articulate and prestigious. Recollections of Ireland transmitted by parents and grandparents were of famine and the miseries of migration, but there were also imaginings of a pristine, prefamine Ireland that lent an appealing glow to ideas about the virtues of a return to agrarian simplicity. If a literal ruralism was impossible, if a back-to-the-farm program would not work, then a neighborly sturdiness unsullied by material excess would suffice. The parishioners of the big cities, sheltered behind church, school, and adjacent convent, could not be as protected from modernity as were rural dwellers. All the same, memories of farm life were still alive, and urban parishioners were never far from clergy who reminded them of the old ways.[37]

The associations conjured up by images of a postcard Ireland were not unlike Currier and Ives depictions of a rural America of soft grass, majestic skies, and homes with friendly porches. Formal arguments in favor of changing the American political system, democratic as was the Irish, were impossibly speculative. In contrast with fantasies of this sort, the idea of leaving traditional mores undisturbed had the appeal of common sense. The objective was the restoration and preservation of a social order that was in its foundations hierarchical and familial. Catholic order was embedded in vernacular hierarchies, in the day-to-day authority patterns of the common people. There was a reassuring affinity between this sentimental but sober image of social reality and the abstractions of Latin social theory.[38]

Orientations toward fascism were further complicated by philosophical misgivings about capitalism and democracy. Jesuits traced the individualistic roots of both systems to the Reformation, and they were not intellectually prepared to look on liberalism as a corrective to either fascism or communism. The argument that Joseph Husslein had made two decades earlier for the protection of community in the face of uninhibited competition and individualism was echoed in the praise heaped on the organic stasis espoused by the corporatist states of Europe. In 1935, Fr. W. X. Bryan, visiting West Baden from Loyola College in Montreal, argued that "Civil Society, as willed by the Creator, is the natural extension of the family." He continued:

But modern states are the result of man-devised institutions divergent in aim from the primary end of civil society. Therefore a return should be made towards the God-willed, organic, natural, functional organization of civil society. But as God allows man to work out his own temporal welfare by the use of his faculties of intelligence and free-will, this return must be brought about by the establishment and strengthening of functional, occupational organizations freely entered into, and sanctioned by state authority, so that, ultimately, ideally, the state should be governed by chosen representatives of the functional groups composing it.[39]

This was about as close to an unadulterated brief in favor of continental corporatism as American Jesuits were apt to hear. Father Bryan stopped short of calling for the introduction of corporatist political institutions in North America. They might be the next best thing to a social arrangement that was "the natural extension of the family." But implantation of the model depended on a uniformity of religion and a bareness of industrial development that did not obtain in the United States. Even under predominantly agrarian conditions—Ireland came close—the system stayed mostly on paper.[40] Corporatism was shelved as hopelessly idealistic, like a bright glimmer destroyed in the transition from image to system, and Bryan went on instead to extol the virtues of local cooperatives.

After some discussion of cooperatives, and some questioning of the feasibility of producers' cooperatives, and an explanation of the words "changing basis of legislative representation from the present arbitrary geographical to the natural functional system," Father Bryan's paper was accepted.[41]

Such ideas might have had repercussions of sedition. But the talk was mostly a verbal game, and the words did not have real consequences. Few among Father Bryan's listeners either distinguished sharply or made a close connection between corporatism as a formal, national system and as a loose network of cooperatives. The words sounded alike although one, *corporatism*, was expressly political and the other was not. While producer and consumer cooperatives were not completely off the map of American Catholic consciousness, they were often located in small towns and rural areas, far from the workaday experience of most American Jesuits and their Catholic countrymen. Edmund Walsh was right: Toying with ideas about altering an entire political system was very heady business. Taming ruthless competition did not mean the abolition of capitalism and the ascent of socialism in the abstract. Similarly, the promulgation of cooperatives did not entail the triumph of fascism or corporatism or any other ism. They were scattered, not ideologically charged, social experiments; they were reasonably safe pilot projects. In practice, on the ground, the social logic of Catholicism was local.[42]

Thus the task of deriving a social blueprint from the deposit of papal teaching and scholastic principles turned out to be daunting not only on account of conceptual insufficiency but also for reasons of prudence and practicality. The political enmities and class alignments that made Catholics receptive to authoritarian corporatism in parts of Europe did not exist in the United States. Spain was the most dramatic but not the sole instance of a political tangle in which the Jesuits found themselves tied to the *ancien régime*. Southern and eastern European Catholicism of the sort with which Ledochowski was familiar had a stake in the contribution that the likes of Salazar and Franco could make to the defense of the old order.[43] This expedient was missing from the largely aesthetic dalliance with medieval corporatism that could be found among some of the American Jesuits. Still, defense of the faith was a long-standing priority of the Society of Jesus worldwide, and policy set by the general could not be ignored.[44]

The Jesuits' rejection of two objectionable—in the view of some of them, extreme—political options did not enable them to settle on a third course. The "pagan, totalitarian state"—nazism or communism—was wholly unacceptable. But rampant capitalism joined to a licentious individualism was only a bit less repugnant. The republican ethos was considered an offshoot of Lutheranism and of the Enlightenment. To the Catholic mind of southern Europe both alternatives had been befouled by anticlericalism and laicization. With some versions of corporatism, however, it was possible to strike a deal. The authoritarianism of Salazar and Franco—and even that of Mussolini—served to protect the church from presumably greater evils.[45]

A pair of calculations born of circumstance helped the American Jesuits to avoid declaring themselves in favor of even the soft version of authoritarianism. The first was the understanding that social structure and cultural ethos, as enshrined in family habits, mattered more than did external political form. The Irish example and the ties of sentiment suffusing it, together with the sternness of the German family, spoke volumes compared to the flamboyant loquacity and frank sensuality of the Latins.[46] The attempt to deduce political institutions from ideas was dangerously gratuitous if the desired results could be obtained "organically" by caring about the underlying anatomy of authority, the family, and the Burkean order that went with it. For practical purposes the American offshoots of the Irish, and in a somewhat different fashion the Germans, furnished the right combination of political adaptability and moral abstemiousness. This stood in contrast to perceptions of the Latins, or at least the Spanish, who reversed the mixture:

political inflexibility but emotional and, in particular, sexual demonstrativeness.[47]

Second, the American Jesuits worried that authoritarian measures adopted in the name of anticommunism violated the rules of the pluralist entente and could backfire on the Catholic minority in the United States. They had much more to gain than to lose by working within the system and keeping their distance from extremists; an all-out crusade on behalf of a lost cause, however noble, could not be a "just war." On one occasion Jesuits in the Chicago province resolved to "oppose the activities of the American Legion in outlawing radical meetings as threatening liberty of speech and as possibly becoming a boomerang some day, if for instance they judge the doctrine of the Church or the work of ECSO [XO] as UnAmerican."[48] A few days later, however, "the question of co-operating with other anti-communistic movements—American Legion, Elks, Paul Reveres, Chambers of Commerce, the Hearst papers, Father Coughlin, etc.—was discussed, but without decision."[49]

On balance the XO experiment advocated a measure of political tolerance, not forthright liberalism. It emphasized social progressivism, and paternal control, as against what Jesuits tended to consider the run-amuck individualism of post-Enlightenment politics. It was compatible with the try-this-on-try-that-on experimentation and working-class slant of the New Deal.[50]

On the surface the intellectual ambience of the Jesuits in the United States was heavily European. Systematization was still the *beau idéal* of seminary learning. But the content of the social *magisterium* had not attained the centrality of dogma in more traditional fields such as moral theology. What had developed instead was a verbal small world in which hierarchical imagery and polysyllabic abstraction, giving the appearance of ideology, thrived. The continental discourse was not compelling or concrete enough to determine policy either in the fledgling social apostolate or in the routine works of the society, such as the schools. But it sustained a malaise— hardly a full-blown attack, but some hesitation—with the realities of Anglo-American pluralism.

The operative culture of the Jesuits in the United States was more profoundly Irish and German than Latin. The machinery of politics and family morality counted for more than ideas. The Jesuits were in the business of the production of services for large numbers of Catholics, primarily education and training rather than the advancement of knowledge. Political ideology was usually as distant from the daily operation of their institutions as were original ideas.

Nevertheless, once in a while, questions of social principle, intuitions of social wrongs, or a combination of the two shone through the ordinary pragmatism of the operations of the American Jesuits. The suspicion of untrammeled political liberalism that the Latins disliked occasionally surfaced among the Americans, but more as a philosophical than a live practical issue, for Catholics had done well politically in the United States. There was probably a greater tendency to direct criticism toward the economic sphere, in which memories of Malthusian policy disturbed the Irish, and in which there were as yet few Catholic capitalists.

The Jesuits detected a twofold problem with the American business classes. They were critical of the inclination of some capitalists to do business regardless of ideological labels; specifically, to support diplomatic recognition of the Soviet regime and to trade with it. Such men were not to be trusted on questions of principle. Beneath their cosmopolitanism, they were mere profit-maximizers.

Conceivably more serious was the difficulty that forthright criticism of American capitalism on the part of Jesuits might cause some benefactors to cut back on their donations to the schools, retreat houses, and other works of the order. Here costly conflict might arise. Jesuit administrators were urged to "make a survey of the past ten years to discover:

> a. The number of BIG GIFTS actually given by wealthy benefactors to the Society, compared with
> b. The amount of support we have received through the tuition, contributions, Sunday collections, stipends, and small gifts coming from the middle class groups and the poor, now so terribly tried by the depression.
> It will be important to see that OURS are made aware of the fact that the friends of the Society have not been the rich and influential but the middle class upper and lower, and the poor.[51]

The difficulty turned out not to be threatening. During the thirties and the following decade the Jesuits knew hardly any of the truly high and mighty in the United States, and they ran almost no risk of alienating or being taken seriously by them. The diagnosis of the last paragraph was accurate: Support came from the donations, multiplied many times, of little people. Nevertheless, as Catholics moved upward socially, middle-class sensitivities had to be taken into account. Their allegiance was never in doubt, nor was their willingness to sacrifice. But the shoestring nature of private educational budgeting counseled prudence.[52]

IV

So the development of theoretical positions on social and political issues was not a Platonic exercise for American Jesuits. The conceptual apparatus and modes of expression available to them forced the discussion into a scholastic framework. Yet while the tone of the debate might be academic, their organizational situation made them vulnerable and placed a premium on practicality. They had to take into consideration pressures from within the ecclesiastical hierarchy, particularly the European branch, the institutional commitments and ideological posture of the society vis-à-vis the authoritarian regimes of southern Europe and the potential backlash from financial patrons.

To a greater or lesser degree all these constraints were matters of internal church politics. But social ministry was a mission directed toward the outside, taken up not only to care for Catholics but also to face and possibly win over secular competition. Unlike the schools, however, it was a field without walls. The intellectual maps were skimpy, compared to the store of preexisting doctrine in moral theology, and the organizational architecture was undeveloped. This indeterminacy allowed for experimentation with new fashions in communication.

The Jesuits were concerned about ways to disseminate their message to a large audience. They were conscious of their elitist image and of the liability this could pose in their efforts to reach the common man. The United States was huge, and the logistics of spreading the social *magisterium* were daunting. In the new age of the media the task was not only or even mainly one of influencing elites but of propaganda to reach the immense diversity of the United States.

A few Jesuits experimented with ways to overcome the tradition of relying on the cultivation of leaders, notables, and other influentials. Fr. Daniel Lord, the editor of *Queen's Work*, a magazine for sodalists, and former adviser to Hollywood on decency in motion pictures,[53] who was to convene the meeting at West Baden in 1943, noted "the difference between communist propaganda and ours. They don't hesitate to be popular:

a) They have common-mindedness; we lack it.

b) They are not ashamed of cartoons and songs; instances [of] communist young people singing red songs in N.Y. L's and subway trains. . . .

Their approach is primarily emotional, ours primarily intellectual.[54]

The Jesuits did not settle on a single method for communicating their program, any more than they were able to come to a consensus on the substance of the program. Two aspects of the new media were of interest: the tools themselves—the equipment that amplified the voice and multiplied messages by previously unimaginable factors—and the ebullient popularizing manner, the salesmanship, that could be put to the service of a cause as well as a product. In the thirties, the few Jesuits who took the mass media seriously embraced the popularizing manner and not, since the start-up costs were formidable, the machinery itself.

The irrepressible Father Lord adopted a more populistic and quasi-evangelical approach than the journalism espoused by John LaFarge, editor of the weekly *America*. He wrote dozens of peppy declamatory pamphlets with such titles as "Death Isn't Terrible," "Prayers Are Always Answered," and the like. Starting in 1931, he organized the Summer Schools of Catholic Action (SSCAs). These were weeklong sessions, mainly for high school students and women religious, that offered liturgy, religious counseling, and social uplift. Even though there were few black Catholics to take advantage of the opportunity, the program had caused a stir by its policy of nondiscriminatory participation. By the late 1930s the SSCAs were touring on a schedule that covered a good deal of the East and Midwest, with a stopover in New York as well.[55]

Lord's style in combating racial segregation gave a preview of changes to come in the next decade. No Catholic teaching on the matter had been enshrined. Just as he improvised with methods for spreading the *magisterium*, Lord patched and filled where doctrinal substance needed definition. He worked the purlieus of institutional respectability.

It was through the writing and production of his trademark pageants, song-and-dance spectacles often staged in his home base of St. Louis but also taken on the road, that Father Lord tried most energetically to spread the moral and social gospel of Catholicism. The spectacles—Lord pounding away at the piano, spotlights turning from one end of the proscenium to the other, much flapping of drapery and theatrical gowns—were the multimedia events of the era.[56] The pageants were animated images, histrionic extensions of the colorful perorations of Joseph Husslein. "The Social Order Follies," which enjoyed a week's run at the St. Louis University Auditorium, opened with the chorus singing "Good Evening, Mr. Ritz," and included a ballet number, entitled "The Women of the Spanish Revolution," that "tells dramatically the relationship of Women to the Civil War in Spain."[57]

During the mid-thirties Lord also mounted a lecture series entitled "Social Order Mondays." These talks, delivered by Lord and his Jesuit colleagues in St. Louis, covered such topics as "Can Civilization Be Saved From Ruin?" "The High Cost of Business Selfishness," and "Is Democracy Doomed?" In addressing the last question, Fr. Edward Dowling elaborated on the notion that the Protestant Reformation from which Anglo-American democracy developed was "the only revolution in history that went backward, the rise of the rich against the poor." The rebellion of Luther had brought in its train not only political upheaval but also capitalist individualism and social injustice. The politically hierarchical yet socially egalitarian medieval vision depicted by Husslein gave way, so the story went, to inequality and the disintegration of community.

After this obligatory swipe at the Protestants, however, and after pointing out the forgotten Catholic roots of limited government, Dowling emphasized the least-of-all-evils status of democracy. At the end of the day he was a patriot. "As a Christian and as an unworthy heir of nineteen hundred years of Christian ethics, I believe in democracy. Those who prefer the opposite can point to Italy and Russia and Mexico and Germany."[58] Despite its faults, democracy somehow functioned. The politics that shielded Catholics from persecution, even if it prevented the community from gaining the power it deserved, differed from an economic system that fostered both exploitation and mobility. For American Catholics, history was confused and its lessons were ambiguous. The medieval past had become a Gothic cemetery, a memory to be mourned and celebrated but not a set of guidelines for the future. The message was much like that of Edmund Walsh: The Catholic tradition and the American venture were compatible.[59]

The talks were florid but far less rabid than the broadcasts of Charles Coughlin, the radio priest from whom the Jesuits distanced themselves.[60] The rhetoric employed by Lord and his colleagues was an attempt to popularize Catholic social philosophy. This was a necessary step, Lord assumed, to putting it into practice in the American setting. The difficulty was that the philosophy had a static, agrarian, and European cast in a country that was dynamic, industrial, and unreceptive to ideas with a foreign gloss. The disjuncture between packaging and content was glaring. The archaism of the message—especially the medievalism and the fulminations against individualism—lent the perspective a critical angle of vision, not to say a peculiar aesthetic glint. However, it also gave the impression that twentieth-century ideas, and much of the thought of the preceding two or three centuries for that matter, could be dismissed. As the expressive creativity of the American South during the same period demonstrated, this was not necessarily an impediment to artistic innovation. But as a political program preached to a mainly urban audience it was gravely flawed.[61]

Father Lord's fascination with the possibilities of the mass media placed him among the progressives of the Society of Jesus. Yet his habit of pitching what he said in the chipper tone of an enthusiastic high school teacher, as if he were striving to keep the attention of bright-but-distracted adolescents, belied this modernity. There was an ironic convergence between Lord's bubbly manner and the fantasy of a European past whose reality Americans wanted to forget; both were somewhat childlike. In fact, Lord did not resort very often to the archaic themes in vogue with his colleagues. His gift was for topicality charged with a zeal that conveyed conviction rather than doctrine. He was a splendid classroom performer made larger than life by the stage. He conveyed a positive mood, above all the sense that Catholics could be at home and happy in America while holding on to their moral traditions. Self-affirmation mattered more than doctrinal specifics.

The organizational consequences of Lord's dramatizations and exhortations appear to have been sparse. The SSCAs were inspirational, but the actions that participants were supposed to follow up on during the rest of the year were ill defined. The world, even the relatively sheltered one of the Catholic subculture, was not a classroom. Like a latter-day circuit rider, Lord tried to disseminate a Catholic mentality, duplicating the subculture by traveling across its constituent enclaves. It was unclear whether the communal psychology of Catholicism could survive apart from the ethnic and parochial supports of its separate components, and Lord's road show was ahead of its time in attempting to stitch together the network of an America-wide Catholicism. Furthermore, although he wrote hundreds of pious expostulations limited to a Catholic audience, he played down the sectarianism favored by some other Jesuits and in this way prefigured a less tribal, more ecumenical Catholicism.

It was the effort at popularization itself, rather than its content or even its impact on the audience, that constituted a breakthrough. The freewheeling manner, generous with respect to denominational and racial boundaries, sent a significant message. Lord's style implied an attempt to win legitimacy for a media-conscious approach to social evangelization. The strategy meant reaching directly out to the mass of the citizenry, or at least to Catholics among them, rather than relying almost exclusively on the inherited policy of influence through contact with leaders. It drew sustenance from the long-standing priority that the Society of Jesus gave to pragmatism and adaptability and, to a degree, from the Jesuit tradition of cultivating theater as a means of edification. On the other hand it offended the Jesuits' equally venerable sense of hierarchy and respect for decorum, and Lord never escaped being criticized as a vulgarian.[62]

Lord himself felt ambivalent about his work. Although the constraints were formidable, they were not insuperable, yet he shied away from making use of radio and motion pictures as if threatened by the impersonality of the media and by the lack of control that collaborative production implied. A quasi-charismatic figure, he tried instead to magnify his enthusiasm through constant travel and pamphleteering until these exertions finally proved too much for him.

Although his energy and style of work were exceptional, the rush of activity Lord generated was symptomatic of challenges facing the Society of Jesus as a whole. There was a democratic cosmopolitanism to the new technology that evaded received ideological and institutional categories. The media and the popular culture spreading with them were beginning to penetrate subcultures and cover over regional differences. At the same time Jesuits were struggling to promulgate a social doctrine that rang false or seemed irrelevant for the nation as a whole and even in its Catholic corners. Considerable tension existed between the hierarchical and strongly preindustrial components of the social *magisterium* and the emerging, postindustrial ramifications of the new means of communication. The media were a new mixture of showmanship and salesmanship, intriguing because they suggested the possibility of diffusing messages that were really images, without having to define them rigorously, and they also suggested ways to mobilize the loyalties ensconced in the neighborhoods and parishes without having to erect alternative popular organizations. Images that did not depend for their coherence on logic could be diffused widely and rapidly. All this hinted of an alternative realm to the classic pedagogy and the solid institutions of the brick-and-mortar era.

V

Lord's brand of outreach through entertainment was an attention getter even if the social message got lost in the spectacle itself. In the 1930s most Catholics were urban workers and members of the lower middle class, financially strapped and eager for more stimulation than they got from Sunday sermons.[63] In a few years, together with other Americans, they would form a huge market for boldly packaged appeals that might have some political content in addition to their glamor. Lord looked ahead to the future of religious propaganda and political marketing through the mass media.[64]

Another Jesuit, John Rawe, turned to agrarian simplicity as the Catholic response to the strains of industrialization. His book *Rural Roads to Security*, coauthored with Luigi Ligutti, bore the subtitle *America's Third Struggle for Freedom*.[65] The first two struggles were for political independence and the abolition of slavery. The third was to be for social justice.

Like Husslein, Rawe traced the roots of modern social distress to the rise of liberalism. Rawe, however, came across as less of a medievalizer. A native of Omaha, raised on a farm, he had a feel for the soil and small towns. More easily than Husslein, he evoked images of eighteenth- and early-nineteenth-century America without the trappings of gothic Catholicism. His views paralleled those of the Southern Agrarians, with whom he had contact. While the grieving of the Agrarians over a vanished antebellum society was analogous to the nostalgia for the Middle Ages fashionable among Catholics at the time, there was little taint of continentalism in Rawe. He glorified the American yeomanry, and the times he yearned to restore were Jeffersonian.[66]

Still, Rawe's diagnosis of the causes of contemporary social evils was virtually indistinguishable from Husslein's:

At the very time when wars were being waged for political independence, there was injected in the veins of American industry a deadly virus which would tend more and more to paralyze the mind and spirit of American manhood. . . . America fell heir to the liberalistic system which Europe had fostered. When the renaissance individualism cast off moral restraint through the influence of the Reformation, the road was paved for a materialistic philosophy. . . . The discoveries of science in the eighteenth and nineteenth centuries coincided with the liberalistic stream of philosophy, ever deepening and expanding the glittering sea of modern Capitalism. Heavy machinery, power, crowded factories, congested cities, large-scale production, greater and still greater profits and investments complemented each other, and accelerated the evolution of liberalistic industrialism. And so, with every new stage of the swirling cycle, liberty retreated farther from the wage earner, as economic necessity left him ever more helplessly at the mercy of the capital which he serviced.[67]

The key to combating the "spicy entertainments and gaudy baubles" of modern industrial society lay in a return to the soil and in the restoration of "some natural economic functions to the family."[68] An organic order was to be founded on the moral economy of this "natural unit." The spread of family farms was to be encouraged. Smallholdings that were practically self-sufficient would be bulwarks against the ethical and the material depredations of the market:

Families . . . are the units which compose the State. The State is an outgrowth of the single family, a natural expansion because an increase in the number of single families necessitates order and guidance. . . . Destroy the individual family and ultimately you destroy the State. Likewise the religious, moral, economic, and social health of the State is conditioned by a like prior health in the family.[69]

The family was the building block of sound government. Cities ruined the family. The strengthening of family life and the rejuvenation of honest politics therefore required a return to the soil. Rawe vehemently denounced city life, especially the assault on economic security, moral propriety, and demographic robustness that prevailed in large metropolitan areas. In cities and "fashionable suburbs" birthrates declined alongside the state of morals. Rawe brought an occasional touch of black humor to his string of jeremiads against big-city decadence and effeminacy:

A steady decline in birth means, first of all, that we become a nation of old people. . . . The business of producing baby shoes is on the downward trend. The buying group in our nation dwindles. The demand for our industrial and agricultural products shrinks. There comes a smaller demand for housing, clothing, and even for what is called the luxuries of life. The attendance at football games will drop. Old folks do not go to these pageants of youth. Perhaps the best business to enter will be the production of false teeth.[70]

The American metropolis could virtually be given up for lost. This prospect was all the more alarming, Rawe concluded, in view of the fact that 80 percent of Catholics in the United States were city dwellers. For this reason, he argued with disconcerting optimism, "no policy of the church could be more sound and forward-looking than that of building up vigorous country parishes." Rawe feared that the American countryside would fall victim to the same blight that had afflicted the cities. The depression had jeopardized homeownership. The rate of tenancy, he noted, "has moved up from 25.6 per cent in 1880 to 42.1 per cent in 1935." Citing Oliver Goldsmith's paean to the deserted village, he warned that the separation of residence from the place of work inexorably created rootless families:

The American commercialized family may travel as a unit, sleep as a unit, consume goods as a unit, but it no longer produces wealth as a unit from its own productive property . . . the life of the American family as a basic natural productive unit is well-nigh destroyed. Food, clothing, and shelter, the basic essentials for living and the sources from whence they come, are gathered up into the huge interlocking hands of commercial owners and distributors. With this continued centralization and industrialization of food, clothing, and shelter, the last vestiges of American freedom and security are lost.[71]

"The homestead way," a compound of private ownership and autonomy from the outside world and, on the inside, a bastion of paternalism and natural, organic order, was Rawe's proposal to prevent the spread of the peregrine family. He saw it as an alternative to the twin products of heedless industrialization, capitalism and communism. It was this version of Americanism, rather than derivatives of a class-ridden Europe, that would protect the family, nourish society, and make for stable government. He envisioned a purified localism beyond the reach of a corrupting cosmopolitanism:

Strange as it may seem to the self-satisfied, capitalistic mind, blinded by profit and power, and the communistic mind, blinded by hatred and power, it is only in the hands of such small family-based owners of productive property that democracy, culture, freedom, religion, and life itself are safe and secure. The man and his family, living on a few acres of their own land with a culture that is agrarian and a religion that is Christian, is the last bulwark against an extreme enslaving centralization and its final collapse into the hands of the Red Commissars. The homestead and its family is the last bulwark in an urban civilization which is losing its property and freedom and failing to reproduce itself.[72]

Rural Roads to Security was composed of variations on the themes of the family as the bedrock of a moral social order and the family farm as an economic unit that avoided the wage slavery of capitalism and the state slavery of communism. Since Rawe had little use for urban modernity, especially on a large scale, he made no mention of the "vocational orders" of an industrial corporatism that European proponents of middle-way solutions favored. Instead, he praised the virtues of the cooperative movement and of small-scale production generally, and he made a point of describing experiments in Nova Scotia and New Jersey along these lines.

These cases were isolated—*decentralized* is Rawe's word—and it is difficult to see how they fit into the comprehensive agrarian system that Rawe advocated as national policy. Nevertheless, the model islands of virtue and modest prosperity were described in bright detail. Photographs showed the shopwork at Assumption High School in Granger, Iowa, where the boys learned practical activities like furniture repair, mechanical drawing, and metalworking and the girls were instructed in needlepoint and rug hooking.

Again and again Rawe waxed lyrical about the invidious contrast between countryside and city. In such passages his book became a Sears catalog in reverse, preaching the benefits and the virtues of self-sufficiency:

> For physical well-being, there is no work like the work on a farm. The sunshine and the air, the bronzed countenance of the boy, the rosy cheeks of the country maiden! Compare that physical existence with the stuffy, sunless apartment dwelling, with the chemical smells of a shop. Compare the song of the birds soaring overhead with the shrill noise of trolleys and trucks, with rumble of subways, with jangling of bells. . . . How can a girl prepare herself for motherhood, her highest ideal, midst the nerve-wracking artificial life of a city, standing on her feet all day, and then snatching a restless sleep from a bed pulled out of the wall?[73]

The imagery stressed reproduction and wholesome simplicity, even austerity, within the enfolding security of nature, in contrast to mass production and frivolous consumerism.

Are you a boy, and do you like a machine? Do you want the city where man-made machines make a machine out of a man? . . . Cannot men rise above machinery and understand the powers of nature—the strength of a kernel of corn and the tiny flower seed? The farmer plants it and plans its proper place on his farm and around his home. Gentle mother earth nurses it in her bosom, the sun warms it, the rain moistens it and it bursts forth.[74]

In the midst of numerous illustrations and mythopoeic descriptions, the link between these pockets of frugal productivity and rural virtue at the local level and the development of the larger social system was obscure. When theory faltered, Rawe resorted to anecdote rather than analysis. One of his most breathtakingly embroidered yarns was the parable of the communist and the cow:

Recently an American Communist became the owner of a two-acre homestead and a cow. Soon it was the cow and her productivity, her contribution to economic security, that turned him and his family once more into the pursuit of democracy, once more into the pursuit of its own good and the good of the community. The ownership of the cow changed the man's philosophy. Sound thinking was restored. Where hard and straitened circumstances had before raised a difficulty about a just and loving God, land and cow—principally the cow—brought back a firm belief in God. God was after all just and loving, working for man's benefit through creatures. Here, through the cow, came a new security, a new promise, setting right a false philosophy more quickly and more conclusively than any raise in wages, or a new gadget or uncertain stock would have done. . . . The privately owned, food-producing cow reformed the father and the family that had been all but ruined by inadequate wages, uncertain employment, and relief allotments.[75]

The expostulations about farm and family came crashing down in bathos. Just as these two entities were the elementary particles of a society that somehow held together in sympathetic vibration with the smaller units, the building blocks of Rawe's method were images of utopia not ideas for planning. Like Husslein he dealt in dreams and evocative detail.

The style was odd but not completely eccentric in a time of multiple conflicts and swirling transitions between capital and labor, from rural to urban, and between producer and consumer cultures. Rawe's agrarianism built on nostalgia for an American past of Jeffersonian yeomanry and for the robust calm of classical, Virgilian tillers and shepherds. The thirties were vintage years for utopias—some of them backward looking, others indistinguishable from science fiction. It was the last decade before such schemes became pathological or ludicrously innocent with the devastation of World War II, and until New Jerusalems sprouted again in the sixties in the aftermath of sustained abundance. The preindustrial dream propounded by Rawe was only mildly bizarre in comparison with some rival visions of the time—for example, with the Townsend plan, and the tendency to invest programs for rural reconstruction with claims about the salvation of civilization, or at least of democracy, was not unknown in connection with the success story of the era, the Tennessee Valley Authority.[76]

Besides, Rawe was not a Luddite. He favored manufacturing, and even cities, on what he viewed as a human scale. His ideas anticipated the small-is-beautiful platform that Schumacher and his followers were to push in the 1960s. In addition, Rawe wanted to restore a true Americanism, not replace it with a foreign model exhumed from an era before the discovery of the New World. His denunciations of "liberalistic industrialism" and his praise of a stolid civic republicanism were consonant with the critiques of hedonism and utilitarian nihilism and the breakdown of communitarian spirit that gathered force generations later.[77]

Yet the agrarian myth propounded by Rawe was by the 1930s an ideal whose time had passed. Nearly 30 percent of the work force was still in agriculture, but this figure was shrinking fast. Demographic and economic momentum favored the cities. The rural communities praised by Rawe were not simply decentralized, scattered about the countryside. They were also to be insulated from urban life. In their self-containment, they formed a simulacrum of the cultural and social shelter that the Catholic urban ghettos on the Eastern Seaboard attempted to provide. As his favorable references to Scandinavia suggest, the program prescribed by Rawe may have been politically viable in countries, unlike the United States, with a still-modest industrial base and, unlike some peasant societies, with a low demographic concentration.[78]

Several related limitations of Rawe's work exemplify in extreme form the difficulties that characterized the reflections of his Jesuit contemporaries on social issues. The sealed-off nature of the economic system proposed by Rawe reflected a penchant for holistic, synoptic thinking that he shared with Husslein. The subculture of Catholicism was enclosed in urban enclaves and a school system that circumscribed the experience of its inhabitants. Physical separation was complemented by a frame of reference that formed an intellectual universe unto itself. Even though Rawe stood outside the urban environment, he was well within the conceptual bastion.

For all the detail he lavished on his hymns to the family and the small farm, Rawe's forte was the making of homely poetry out of a way of life. The task of proposing specific policies for the creation of intentional communities was beyond him. He was a kind of Edgar Guest of regional planning. There was a zany sweetness to his choice of illustrations. Joseph Husslein had a taste for the exotic; he was fond of contrasting the intrinsic democracy of the medieval guilds with the awful despotism of pharaonic rule: the bad pyramids versus the good cathedrals. But Husslein never broached, as Rawe did, the subject of communism or capitalism in the same breath as the cow of noble domesticity.[79]

Rawe's vision was as charmingly apolitical as it was dubious on intellectual grounds. It was impractical not only in its remoteness from the concerns of an increasingly urban Catholic constituency but also in its neglect of the politics of implementation. The gap between theory and practice was bridged neither by a program of political organization nor by a method of systematic reasoning and testing. Rawe called up cravings for a small, secure world and relied on exhortations to a return to natural law and eternal, cyclical verities.[80]

The failure to consider political mechanisms of coordination was not altogether surprising, given the separation of religion, or religious actors, from politics that was supposed to hold in the American scene and in light of the reluctance on the part of most Catholics at the time to press for political alternatives outside the American way. The veto on political specifics exacerbated a tendency toward abstractions and absolutes that ran counter to the style of American politics. A halo of aesthetic moralism emanated from the assortment of policies and programs that composed the neomedieval and agrarian approaches to social ministry.

VI

An ambiguous idealism stymied efforts on the part of Jesuits during the 1930s to come to grips with social problems under American conditions. The material circumstances in which immigrant Catholics lived and the class origins of many Jesuits encouraged support for welfare programs and distributive policies at the same time that their ethnic and religious identification curbed the appeal of radical options.

Jesuits found themselves hard pressed to furnish what they were accustomed to giving the Catholic community—intellectual leadership—in the social field. For many of them it was unfamiliar ground. Negotiating this territory was made all the more awkward by an expectation that an overview, at once comprehensive and practical, could be developed for the American terrain. In practice, when carrying out their accustomed chores in the schools, Jesuits performed credibly and sometimes with distinction, and they were sought after as spiritual guides. But the articulation of social theory eluded them. The commentaries that Jesuits provided on social problems during these years may have been even more frequently marred by non sequiturs and juxtapositions of the sublime and the ridiculous than the visionary average for the period. "Poor Johnnie Rawe," some of his peers observed. "He thought he found the answer in a pile of manure."[81]

Unreality was compounded by the remoteness of the utopian style from the immigrant Catholic constituency. The return-to-the-soil alternative evaporated not only because it flew against the tempo of American industrial growth. It also lacked demographic backing among American Catholics, most of whom lived in cities, outside the South. The dream had a nostalgic appeal, like Currier and Ives prints, for city-dwelling immigrants. The familial imagery symbolized moral purity, and the parables of discipline and sacrifice called them to hard work. But there was little ambition to return to the past.

In part the problem was the Eurocentric doctrine that Jesuits were charged with adapting to the American scene. Associations of the European past with a distinctly unromantic poverty and powerlessness were still vivid among immigrant Catholics. There was some poignancy and even genuine poetry to the writing of men like John Rawe, but much of its poignancy came from the impression it gave of expressing private longings without public consequence. A way of thinking that prized changelessness and a kind of imperial universality tended to perpetuate political naiveté, when it did not favor outright authoritarianism. It discouraged and silently discredited the application of ideas to political realities. This did not prevent displays of moral concern and adherence to a steady idealism. But social principles remained on a pedestal, removed from policy.

The danger of an ideological, principled authoritarianism was slim even among American Jesuits who thought about politics. Nevertheless, some possibility of going this route can be seen in the logical implications of the thinking set forth in *Rural Roads to Security*. Rawe came up against, but never quite confronted, a problem similar to the one Husslein had skirted: how to assemble benign microcosms into a workable whole. For Husslein the foundation was the family, set inside the Catholic ghetto. For Rawe it was the family set inside the farm. In his efforts to knit together the dispersed communities of American Catholics Daniel Lord also broached the problem.

One solution to the task of shaping a collective identity was to foster homogeneity within separate parts of the subculture. The farm families of Rawe's philosophy were decentralized but not very diverse. However, exclusionary sameness were much less of a possibility in the ethnically mixed urban ghettos. The comparative cosmopolitanism of the Jesuits probably kept them from playing to the biases and bigotry of localism and from encouraging an enforced uniformity of the kind latent in Rawe's musings. The equation of moral with racial purity was avoided. But the filaments binding the heterogeneous Catholic community remained invisible. No Catholic political party of the sort that came into being in Europe was in the offing, and despite the efforts of pioneers like Daniel Lord the new media of mass communication did not furnish a bulwark of Catholic identity.

Because theory produced so little in the way of results, some Jesuits simply ignored logical formalisms without losing their moral fervor. Others retained parts of the ideological dressing—particularly anticommunism—and pressed on with action programs such as the labor schools. A small number released their impatience with abstraction in furious activism. These activities provided a service to working-class Catholics, who composed a major political force, without calling into question the social order.

3

The Labor Schools

I

The School of Social Studies that Terence Shealy inaugurated in 1911 held its first classes at Xavier High School, facing uptown on West Sixteenth Street in Manhattan. A few blocks downtown, in lofts at the top of narrow seven- and ten-story buildings, garment workers trimmed and sewed twelve hours a day, six days a week. In July and August they took breathers by stepping out onto newly installed fire escapes at the back of the buildings, away from the heat that gathered beneath the ceilings and that the fans moved around but failed to dissipate. Some of their output was sold at Ohrbach's, the cut-rate department store some blocks to the southeast on Union Square, where soapbox orators, political organizers, and assorted ideologues harangued passers-by.

Classes on the social question were held in the basement of the high school. Adjacent to the school on the west was Saint Francis Xavier Church, the seat of a parish run by the Society of Jesus. Its Victorian baroque spires were as tall as the surrounding buildings. The Jesuit residence adjoined the church on the east. In the previous century it had been the home of William Cullen Bryant, poet, essayist, and enthusiast of Garibaldi. The street was lined on both sides with sycamores, and except on Sundays it was noisy with traffic.

In Shealy's time the lecturers and the audience at the school were almost exclusively middle- and upper-middle-class Catholics. This was the forum that was transferred in the nineteen-twenties to the Fordham School of Social Service, moving to slightly grander quarters in the Woolworth Building. When the Xavier Labor School opened on Sixteenth Street in the middle of the depression, the clientele was made up of workers, predominantly unskilled laborers, most of them Catholic.[1]

By 1935, as the depression deepened, John Lewis, Philip Murray, and other labor leaders split from the American Federation of Labor. The CIO—

the Congress of Industrial Organizations—was formed for the purpose of gathering unskilled and semiskilled laborers into unions that crossed the old craft lines, an undertaking that was facilitated by the Wagner Act and the generally supportive New Deal administration. Competition between radical and moderate currents, and between clean and corrupt factions, for the domination of this mass of manpower was intense.[2]

The Jesuits who set up shop in the basement of the high school plunged into a political maelstrom. Socialists and communists had been agitating among the proletariat in cities on the East Coast and the Midwest since before the turn of the century, and Protestant adherents of the social gospel had been active before World War I and the Russian Revolution.[3] Several conflicts buffeted the labor movement at once. Although New Deal legislation removed technical impediments against the right to organize, some bosses continued to resist the formation of industrial unions with goon squads and payoffs to the police. Strong-arm tactics carried over into faction fights over the control of particular unions, once they existed as legal entities. Fair play was not the norm. These were eminently political battles. Jesuits in Europe, where Catholic trade unions and Christian Democratic parties enjoyed some success, watched the battles over ideological dominance of the labor movement with interest and intermittent comprehension.

Two other sets of controversies stimulated less confrontation and violence. The "how much" issues over wages and benefits became matters for periodic negotiation. In certain cases, however, apparently institutionalized procedures turned out to be very precarious. The right to strike was a bargaining chip that workers in semipublic utilities—the transport workers were the chief example—could resort to only at the risk of legal entanglements and at the cost of alienating public opinion, expressed through man-in-the-street tirades published in tabloids like the *Daily News*.

A final bundle of issues was related to questions of workplace democracy, the participation of labor in company planning and profits, and the like. Such questions were high on the agenda of Catholic social theory, and they were live issues in the countries of northern Europe, where Catholic trade unions were forming. But they were rarely at the front of American labor politics, and they became dead letters with the advent of postwar prosperity.

II

Philip Carey arrived at Xavier as a young Jesuit in 1940 and stayed for half a century, until his death. His recollections of the Catholic immigrant subculture square with the more polished reports of William Stanton about the roughhouse crowds in Hell's Kitchen:

> The problem then was socialism, and the socialists had a school over here on 15th Street, 7 East 15th Street. It was founded by a poor minister that ran away with somebody else's wife. We'd have no trouble with that kind of socialism nowadays, because we've come a long, long way.
>
> But it was a time when we were trying to work amongst the Irish. When the Irish came here after the Great Famine of '47, they weren't stupid, really, but they were totally unlettered because England would allow no schools. And they were so diseased that when they reached land, up at the Canadian border, they were kept out with rifle power. When they got settled down here, it was around Chatham Square. It was called the Five Points. There was a murder every night. Then it was the Civil War that saved the Irish. That was a terrible blood bath. Only the rich man and the dandies could buy themselves out by paying the bounty, and the Irish were dying at Antietam and Gettysburg. After that, there was a long struggle up.[4]

One of the earliest church-related labor schools in New York was begun by the Catholic Workers under the inspiration of Dorothy Day. During the mid-thirties a few rooms on the eighth floor of the Woolworth Building became the headquarters of the Fordham School for Workers. The Jesuits tolerated this group of Christian anarchists and apparently gave them the run of the offices for a nominal fee. But their own operation, the offshoot of Terence Shealy, was eventually moved uptown out of range of the radicals. Almost simultaneously, the Jesuits inaugurated the Xavier Labor School and, across the river in Brooklyn, the Crown Heights School of Catholic Workmen.[5]

The Jesuits themselves stayed clear of organizing work. *Rerum Novarum* and later *Quadragesimo Anno* legitimized attempts to encourage working-class movements. But the doctrine was arcane in American eyes, and the Jesuits who engaged in the social apostolate were not known for scholarship. For their part, neither the leadership nor the rank and file of urban Catholic labor showed enthusiasm for direct involvement of the clergy in union affairs. This left education, for which they were best known, as the Jesuits' entrée into the working-class movement.

Links between the labor schools and the mainstream of Jesuit education were not close, however. The schools represented a partial break with tradition. They improvised on earlier experiments that failed or that, like Shealy's work, evolved along other paths. They were ventures in adult education. The decision of the Jesuits to focus in a systematic way on a lower-class audience, though not unprecedented, was something of a novelty. The students were neither adolescents nor doctors, lawyers, and other respectable Catholics but adult working-class males who came once a week, usually from eight to ten or ten-thirty in the evening, for courses in parliamentary procedure, methods of public speaking, and the like. These practical classes were the drawing cards to which offerings in Catholic social doctrine were appended.

In some areas Jesuits had considerable expertise. Courses in public speaking were an updated version of rhetoric out of the classical curriculum. The strategy of responding to the market for applied education duplicated the one that Terence Shealy had hit on decades earlier in attracting lower middle-class students to the Fordham School of Social Work, and indeed it did not differ much in timing and method from the way in which the Jesuits' "schools of commerce and finance," which began with night courses in subjects like accounting, got started. The classes in practical skills were time-honored Jesuit ventures in adaptability.

The Jesuits also handled such topics as labor ethics, emphasizing the reciprocal rights and obligations of labor and capital. But they did not dominate the curricula of the workers' academies as completely as they did in their high schools and colleges. Most instruction was conducted by "reliable, experienced Catholic laymen. Jesuits tend to be too academic and theoretical in treating these men, and there is the additional difficulty that in such classes the men in trying to show the proper respect for priests feel constrained and not free to air their difficulties."[6]

The lay speakers came from varied backgrounds. A few were Fordham graduates, lawyers, and businessmen who had gained debating experience in organizations such as the Catholic Evidence Guild. In the early days some were college professors who "did not know the problems of workers nor the language to be used (never more than two syllables and always in concrete terms if possible)." As the thirties gave way to the forties, however, an increasing number were leaders of union locals and working men themselves.[7]

The distinguishing feature of the schools was not humanistic education, then, but training in techniques that might prove useful in labor-management negotiations. The schools offered specific services designed to develop particular skills and they did this, much of the time, for a working-class clientele that had no hope of escaping its class origins but that wanted job security. Carey taught rudimentary sessions for sandhogs, men who dug and cleared subway tunnels. For unskilled laborers, survival during the depression meant avoiding falling into the ranks of the unemployed. Even after the right to organize had gained legal sanction, such men were on the brink of joblessness and drifting. Stories went around of men tying the laces of their shoes together and carrying them around their necks, to save leather, as they trudged from place to place looking for work. Insecurity such as this gave their dealings with management an urgency that bargaining over wages and benefits generally did not have.[8]

Dogma usually stayed in the background. In Philadelphia, what began as a labor school cast in the same mold as the ones in Manhattan and Brooklyn became an institute of industrial relations that stressed cooperation between employers and workers. Employers and city officials as well as working men were admitted to the classes.[9] But in the early days the schools gave priority to training workingmen in bargaining and organizing techniques. Disagreements over the makeup of the student body revolved around whether a union card was required to establish credentials for enrollment or whether yet-to-be-unionized workers could also be admitted. Corporatist doctrine prepared the ground for the evolution of some of the schools into labor-relations institutes, an option that was taken up with increasing frequency after the war when the unions had developed their own educational programs.[10]

Thus, overt propaganda in the name of corporatist principles was downplayed, and concepts such as workplace democracy did not penetrate the trenches. The schools had an ideology by default, however, and it was anticommunism. The Jesuits saw themselves as rivals of communist agents in the labor movement. In New York they were particularly worried about the hold of the left over the Transport Workers' Union, most of whose members—trolley car operators, bus drivers, track repairmen—were Irish.[11] The men were led by Mike Quill, a former militant in the Irish Republican Army and doubly a nemesis to the Jesuits because of his marriage to a Jewish labor organizer whom they suspected of being a Communist operative.[12] The ethnic and ideological anomalies were compounded by an anticlericalism that some Jesuits thought approached the hatred of radical factions of the Spanish working class for the ecclesiastical establishment.

> Many of the men bitterly resent the action taken by the Irish Bishops and the Irish Clergy during the trouble with England. This spirit of anti-clericalism is nourished at the Union meetings by the Union leaders who constantly repeat such questions as: "When you had no union, and when the Company used to kick you around like dogs, where was the Catholic church and the Xavier Labor School then? When you tried to throw off the yoke of England, didn't the priests tell you to keep your chains and remain slaves? Now they want you to be slaves of the Company again."[13]

Some of the militants among the transit workers had been recruits of the IRA who had emigrated to New York in the 1920s after the partition of their homeland. A few were dedicated socialists. Many were young men schooled in violence, similar to the inhabitants of Hell's Kitchen, without interest in political ideology or religious doctrine, so ignorant that they were liable to confuse communism with the eucharistic-sounding "communionism." They were apt to look on the classes in parliamentary procedure and debating protocol that the Jesuits offered as so much lace-curtain sermonizing. "On the simplest level," one historian has written,

> the IRA men were a particularly tough group, men who had "gone through hell" together in Ireland. Having faced British and Irish guns, lived in flight, and in some cases gone to jail, they found company supervisors and their plainclothes agents, the much-hated "beakies," less intimidating than others might. Generally at an age when they hoped to begin families but still had few responsibilities, they were more willing than most to take their chances in trying to improve their lot.[14]

The communists had some success among the leadership of the TWU. But most of the rank and file remained indifferent to grand strategy and ideological niceties, and the brawling gave way gradually to the burdens of domestic life and flipping through the pages of the *Police Gazette* at the barbershop. Many of them kept up a Catholicism of sorts through fraternal associations that gave the men a chance to eat and drink together. Sentiments of ethnic bonding, family ties, and a growing patriotism overcame class militancy, political radicalism, and international solidarity.[15]

Fr. James McGinley, who would later direct a reorganized version of the Institute of Social Order, captured the riot of cross-purposes and the burlesque of idealism and material interests that typified union politics in New York City during the thirties and forties. At one level were the labor leaders, ablaze with slogans after the fashion of autodidacts, and their rather more educated advisers, engrossed in a shifting maze of ideological alliances and personal allegiance. "They changed tactics," the saying went, "more often than they changed their shirts." At another level were rank-and-file members who enlisted in competing factions and caught pieces of the changes in partisan lines. McGinley wrote an acid description of the tactics behind "much T.W.U. propaganda, so tragically all embracing at times." According to him:

> Only sheer opportunism could roll into one column "burst our chains," Daniel O'Connell, the Corporal Works of Mercy, and the American Labor Party. This was the amalgam of an unabashed sales talk which wanted the people of Spain to succeed in "bursting their chains" too, while urging an agreement between the Vatican State and the Moscow government.

Such convenient juxtapositions became unpleasantly arrogant on occasion. When T.W.U. picketed the home of a civil servant who ceased paying dues . . . one zealot for the cause jumped to the vantage point of a cart, pulled a large Crucifix from within his coat, held it high, and pointed to its Burden as the image of "the one I follow." He then defied anyone to state that the speaker was a Communist.[16]

McGinley and to a lesser extent Carey sensed that the Jesuits were unable to have as great an impact on the course of labor-management relations as they wished. The church had come on the labor scene late. Caution as much as outright reaction was its rationale. Many comfortable churchmen and a number of immigrants who had struck it rich disapproved of union activity; in the forties and fifties Cardinal Spellman became the symbol of this clique. At the same time, however, *Rerum Novarum* sanctioned labor's right to organize. Convincing business interests and civil authorities to recognize this right often brought on bloody confrontation. Reconciliation and mediation, not agitation and mobilization, were the roles preferred by almost all clerics. Catholicism was a church after all, not a sect. Involvement in organizing the unrepresented risked violating the circumspect spirit of the social encyclicals and alienating powerful economic groups. In counterpoint, Jesuits like McGinley and Carey felt that the church could not afford to lose a numerically vast working-class following.

Another factor keeping the Jesuits in an advisory and pedagogical role was the disinclination of workingmen themselves, Catholics and non-Catholics, to express their demands in either ideological or religious terms. The Jesuits had something to offer the men—training in public speaking, a place to congregate once a week or so for useful and occasionally edifying instruction, where their wives could not pester them about drinking away their money, and a sympathetic ear for the family troubles that defeated the urban poor as often, it seemed, as did problems on the job. But these pastoral remedies could not be organizationally or politically decisive compared to what the unions managed to accomplish on their own. The unions were aggressively pragmatic, not inveterately anticlerical. The Irish American workingmen did not care about the intricacies of a social doctrine that had been elaborated with Latin and northern Europe in mind, nor did they show much taste for secular ideologies. The same mentality that endeared the ornate ritual rather than the abstract theology of Catholicism to them also helped inure them to radical socialism.[17]

The workers expected Jesuits to be decent men and to counsel them with their personal difficulties. They were looked on as chaplains, not commanding officers. The division of labor between political and priestly functions was clear though respectfully unspoken. Even had the men been more disposed to ideological appeals, whether from the left or from the church, their leaders were jealous of their autonomy and distrusted meddling from clerics much as they resented the maneuvers of managers. The workers kept their economic interests uppermost. McGinley assessed the situation with sympathy:

> This record of achievements must be at the heart of any attempt to explain the zeal, cohesiveness, and impersonal loyalty which characterized the union's rank and file. Most rapid transit workers thought in terms of their organization as such—its proved effectiveness and not its personal leadership. As long as that leadership continued to "deliver" in the form of increased economic security, they were content to go along.
>
> The charge of Communism was often leveled . . . without any evidence and only as a screen to hide the denial of workers' rights. . . . [T]here were men and women workers who did not know they had any worker rights, so effective was the intimidation practiced on that railroad for years. T.W.U. changed this. . . . What is the conclusion? Merely this, that where others were less industrious, T.W.U. sowed and reaped after Communism helped break the ground. . . . Rapid transit workers were "organization conscious" in a deep sort of way, especially where there were memories of earlier days. . . . They were loyal to a union which succeeded in their behalf without exorbitant fees. To them, the philosophy of its current leaders was merely a sign that others were in default. . . . About the organization being "red," they were easily and rightly insulted, for T.W.U. membership was not "red." About the leaders being overexercised as to the things that were "Communism," the members departmentalized their minds and had no desire whatsoever to wield any influence in the matter. . . .
>
> New York City, private and public, had only itself to blame, not its Communism, and certainly not its rapid transit workers. The latter lived and worked in an atmosphere charged with traditions, if not actual memories, of acute industrial injustices. . . . On these injustices radical leadership fed and became strong, and though an unwelcome guest, it filled a chair left vacant by others.[18]

A discouraging implication of this diagnosis for the Jesuits was that the workers treated Catholic social doctrine as casually as they reacted to political ideology, and that they viewed the peccadillos of the leaders of their unions as pagans must have followed stories of the goings-on of the gods.[19]

Not all of McGinley's colleagues shared his equanimity. The Jesuits felt embattled by Communist incursions in other fields—among public school teachers, for example. Many labor organizers in New York were Jewish; the membership of one large union—the garment workers—was overwhelmingly Jewish.[20] Ethnic and religious rivalry heightened ideological competition. The temptation to define the labor schools in terms of what they were against, around common enemies, to shape them around an exclusionary Catholicism, was practically irresistible. As a rule the Jesuits who worked in the labor schools were not the intellectual cream of the order, and they were sensitive about being patronized by their peers. This lack of prestige made them all the more touchy, and they had reason to feel threatened by secular activists and professionals who were often better educated and much less inhibited about organizing for political ends. Unappreciated by many of their fellow Jesuits and frequently outmaneuvered by their competitors, the labor school priests were anxious to find acceptance among the workers themselves.[21]

The ideological tone of the schools was conservative, but shades of anti-communism existed among the Jesuits. Fr. Philip Dobson, who headed the program at Xavier for a few years before the arrival of Carey, and who later opened a labor school across the Hudson in Jersey City, was more strident about his political stand than was Carey. Under his direction courses for teachers in "Americanism and Education, from the Catholic viewpoint" were offered at the Xavier Labor School:

> Every Tuesday evening for twenty-four weeks an average of one hundred and fifty teachers came to the Xavier Theater to hear lectures on various phases of Education, Americanism, Democracy, Racism, etc., by prominent Catholics, who were also fearless and uncompromising. Only Catholics were invited to lecture to this group, and with one or two exceptions, only Catholics who were educated in Catholic schools, because it was our experience that almost all Catholics educated at secular schools are unsound on the fundamental questions of the origin of authority and of rights, free speech, tolerance, democracy, the will of the majority. Their views are usually so liberal that they are more naturalistic than Catholic.[22]

Although the labor schools spread to nearly a dozen cities, they rarely moved in the same league as the major players. No Jesuit labor school was set up in Pittsburgh. None was established in Detroit, where the United Auto Workers held sway and where union membership was split among blacks, white Southern Protestants, and Catholic immigrants of predominantly Eastern European origin.[23] For a brief period the demographic and political environment favored the Jesuits' expeditions in the labor area. The majority of the workers with whom the Jesuits came in contact were Catholics, and this tie paid off after the war in helping to rout communists from the unions in the New York area. But the demand for their services in labor politics never reached the support attained for their work in secondary and higher education.

III

Few of the Jesuits connected with the labor schools were equipped to compete with union organizers on the left.[24] This failure to engage the opposition on intellectual grounds bothered European Jesuits, particularly the leadership in Rome. Appraisals of the labor movement of the kind made by McGinley, who stressed the reformism of American workers and documented their communal attachment to Catholicism, together with their indifference to Catholic doctrine and Communist ideology alike, did not overcome the frustration involved in trying to extend the influence of the church into labor politics.

Once the right to organize in the first instance had been consolidated, Jesuits understood their task as that of wresting control of key unions from Communists and mobsters. The outcome of these struggles depended largely on the emergence of a broad conservative and social democratic settlement that took shape during the Cold War. Carey and his colleagues played appreciable if secondary roles in this denouement, but their performance did not live up to the grander ambitions of European Catholicism.[25]

Another area of policy, involving questions of workplace democracy, was one where Jesuits might have been expected to make a significant contribution. In addition to favoring concepts of the social wage, corporatist theory was more open to comanagement and profit-sharing proposals than the ideologies of private property and wages for consumption prevalent in the United States. But organizational mechanisms like the Christian Democratic parties of Western Europe, which pressured central governments to enact industrial and labor measures into legislation, were not in place in the American scene. In contrast to the supportive moves of the New Deal administration on the question of industrywide labor organization, enabling legislation was not forthcoming in the area of workplace democracy. Comanagement and similar ideas caught the interest of a few labor leaders—notably, Philip Murray, who was a Catholic. But in the United States such programs stayed off the agenda of labor politics.[26]

For the American Jesuits, an alternative to ideological combat, as well as a backup to the provision of educational services, was pastoral care. The social encyclicals had recommended retreats for working men and spiritual counseling of various sorts as measures that might serve as ideological inoculation.[27] The inspiration for such programs was not merely anticommunism, however. The priests were also driven by personal identification with the trials of working-class life that almost all of them had grown up with. Spiritual retreats were an extension of the counseling and emotional problem solving that Philip Carey and his colleagues were called upon to do almost daily. They afforded the kind of one-on-one contact that Jesuits who did not consider themselves intellectuals or teachers were good at and felt comfortable performing. "The motivation," Carey recalled, "was that horrible, terrible thing that came from the Depression. The absolute collapse of a whole society. The fact was that men were walking around like something out of . . . like zombies. Men like my brother, he was a Fordham grad. For three solid years he walked the streets every day looking for work, couldn't get any. And he'd come home and throw himself on the couch in absolute desperation, just completely wiped out. And so our work was an answer to this. As one of the men said, 'Oh, what the hell, the social encyclicals— they're dusty books on a priest's shelf.' It was not the way it reads in books at all."[28]

Carey's anticommunism was more a matter of ethnic rivalry and the territorial possessiveness of a gang tough than a reflection of class entrenchment. His father had been a streetcar conductor, and his political sympathies did not extend to big business. The flair for human contact and the personal touch that may have impeded his view of the big picture served him well in small groups. A good deal of his daily work involved lending a sympathetic ear and helping resolve family disputes. He was a master of kindly discretion, adept at knowing what not to say. Long sermons on the dangers of communism, he perceived, would tire most of the men. In the pretherapeutic ethnic neighborhoods, there were bartenders and priests. When he was not giving classes in labor ethics or attending to cases of personal hardship among his working-class contacts, Carey kept busy organizing activities for Catholics of various classes and ages. There was no coherence to the stream of things to do except the ups and downs of working-class and small-business families, the jagged rhythm of minicrises, as seen from street level. The programs were nearly indistinguishable from the gamut of parish fare.[29]

Carey directed spiritual retreats as an avocation and no doubt as a change of pace from his work as social advocate and confidant of workers, civil servants, and small businessmen. One of his main audiences consisted of Catholic boys enrolled in the public high schools of New York City. These institutions, Carey was convinced, had fallen into the hands of the followers of John Dewey and other secular humanists, and little good could come of them. Some of the boys had not managed to pass the entrance exams to the Catholic secondary schools. Some were of families too poor to send them to the college preparatory schools run by the Jesuits. They were not leaders in the making.

Except for the difference in age, the clientele was the same as the one Carey was trying to reach in the labor school at Xavier. The notes that he drew on in preparing talks for these retreats capture the ambience of innocence, muted sexuality, symbolism, and romantic militarism designed to galvanize the idealism of the young.

> Story of Father Sherman, S.J. and his father General [William Tecumseh] Sherman—"Father, I am going to make a retreat." The General was up in arms immediately—"Son, no man ever dare mention that word in my presence." The son explains what he means by retreat. The father answers—"That's all right. It's a great thing. But you've got the name wrong, that's not a retreat, that's a council of war." Who is sitting at the council table? You and Jesus Christ. What are you going to discuss? Your plans for winning the battle of life. [30]

The talks were cast at and slightly above the level of the boys' everyday language. The imagery and the stories elicited and reinforced yearnings for achievement and dedication. Carey went back and forth between curious allegories and commonplace examples, making striking connections, opening panoramas:

> Story of the young knights with their stainless swords unsheathed for the veteran to touch them with his battle-scarred sword that they might imbibe some of his courage. . . .
> The first thing we wish to do is to stand on a hill with Christ with a pair of powerful field glasses while He points out to us the whole battle-field of life. We can get a good look at that battle-field if we answer these questions. Where did you come from? What are you here for? Where are you going?
> You didn't choose the time, place or circumstances of coming into this world. God did. God made the world and everything in it and God made you. Maybe some of you fellows like to build model airplanes. Well, if you get the material together and take a lot of time and trouble in assembling your plane when you get it all done, to whom does it belong? To you. Why? Because you made it. It's the same way with God. [31]

In the midst of the homely and the melodramatic examples Carey inserted a political message, drawn from the events of the day. Like many other Jesuits, he was worried by the zeal displayed by rivals on the left:

> What He asks of you—nothing easy—the Cross—strength—loyalty—trust—sacrifice. What other causes ask of the youth of today. Frightful sacrifices. Youth must die at the barricades. Youth must work on star-

vation rations. Youth must throw its labor with this five-year plan or that five-year plan. You must obey a leader blindly. . . .

Vincent Sheehan in his "Personal History" tells us with enthusiasm of the young woman communist he met in his journeying; he saw her in Spain, in Russia, in China, on a half-dozen battlefronts. He likens her to a flame for she simply burned with enthusiasm for the cause. She darted here and there like a flame, glowed like a flame, shone with the light of a flame, and in the end died like a flame. [32]

The response appropriate to such a challenge was not passion or effusion, which were fleeting and unmanly. Instead it was to be both "the answer of reason" and "the answer of love." The crucial idea making this synthesis possible was that "love isn't sentiment, or words or emotion. Love is measured only by sacrifice."[33] Affection alone tied one down, and made men sappy. Prolonged tenderness was weak and effeminate. Dedication, commitment, self-denial—these liberated human energies for greater causes.

The lesson was not one of self-realization but of devotion and generosity, albeit of a somewhat restricted and communal variety. Collective identity anchored and provided the context for character in a sense recognizable by immigrants laboring to realize themselves through their children, undeterred by the lures of immediate gratification. Toughness, true grit, and fortitude were nurtured in the enfolding community within which sacrifice was honored and chivalry was idealized. The real heroes were those who sacrificed themselves for the sake of others.

The message fell on a transitional generation. To American-born high school students, dedication to a public cause outside the immigrant subculture was not a tradition nor did it promise mobility. Before the rise of the Kennedys it was not an option. Yet the subcultural enclosure was about to crumble. While it held, a vocation to religious life instead of abnegation and service in public life remained the primary expression of idealism.

Irish asceticism added a cultural twist to the religious lesson contained in the retreat notes. The call to sacrifice and discipline was bound up with sexual control. The highest virtue was not public service but self-denial through celibacy. The fact that sex rather than social concern fascinated the adolescents to whom Carey ministered was hardly surprising. It was the degree to which the retreats directed this energy toward chastity and discipline rather than toward more expressive or more outwardly altruistic channels that caught the tenor of the subculture.

A way of interpreting the world that in theory might have been shaped around ideological polarities, between the political left and right, or structured along the division between private satisfaction and public service was based instead on a struggle between asceticism and the pleasures of the senses. The moral fiber that was thought to be the foundation of social order came down to sexual continence. The odor of a constricted Irish Catholicism was strong:

> Some fellows never commit a sin against holy purity. Others have real serious problems. . . . Sex is holy. God made it. If you know the sublimity of it, most of the difficulty disappears. . . . In a very few years, you will all make some promise, whether to a girl in marriage or offer the use of sex to God in the priesthood or the vows of religion.
> Learn to use the proper terminology for sex, so that you don't get vulgar. . . .
> Description of the world as two camps. The battle of life. Now we ask the Commander-in-chief to show us how to fight. . . . What are the points to guard against? *Money*—taking it easy—this world no place for a sissy—anything for pleasure—Christ had the Cross—taking a chance on purity—Christ wants strong men.[34]

Money was not identical to sex—the notion of "filthy lucre" sounded too Protestant—but the analogy was plain. The pursuit of wealth, like the pursuit of pleasure, made one soft. Virtue required mortification. Austerity was preferable to material comfort, just as chastity was greater than sexual gratification. Aside from the lures of money, the two other worldly temptations to guard against were "honor" and "pride":

> *Honor*—popularity—anything to be one of the crowd—ashamed of your faith—not in Spain—being dominated by others—being a big shot . . .
> *Pride*—rebelling against authority—obedience is the virtue of the strong—obedience closes up the ranks—example of Protestant churches—respect for the clergy, loyalty to the Church—those who cast off authority pay in the end.[35]

The notes that Carey drafted for the juvenile retreats were a popularization of the spiritual exercises that Ignatius had written down centuries before. The stress given to self-denial as a precondition for sustained service made sense in light of the physician-heal-thyself principle. It also rang true in a subculture in which physical deprivation and the memory of starvation were still familiar.[36] The idealization of chastity and the voluntary embrace of poverty associated with supreme religious devotion had significance in themselves, within the tradition, but they also had the function of symbolizing the conquest over the material constraints that weighed down most members of the Catholic community. In a few years the attainment of material abundance by large numbers of American Catholics, and the alternatives thus opened up to them, would render this mode of spirituality less meaningful.

IV

The Jesuit who brought the pastoral approach most successfully to workers was Fr. John Delaney, who worked at Xavier from 1940 to 1943. In the late 1930s Delaney took a doctorate at the Gregorian University in Rome, where he wrote a thesis on the ethics of workers' rights, and he worked for a while at Vatican Radio, which was in the society's charge. It was his performance at Vatican Radio that brought Delaney to the attention of Wlodimir Ledochowski. The general sent him back to New York in 1940 to establish the Institute of Social Order as an American replica of Action Populaire, the think tank run by the Society of Jesus in Paris.[37]

The assignment was made without consulting the other American Jesuits who had been working toward patching together the Institute of Social Order out of the remains of the XO. Delaney's energy and verbal facility obscured from Ledochowski his lack of interest in ideological disputation. His gift was for personal contact. He built on his familiarity with the mores of American Catholicism by channeling the prestige of the priest's role into the mediation of family troubles. He extended the counseling of individual workers, which his labor school colleagues had begun in conjunction with their classroom activities, into workshops and retreats—the Christian Family Movement and the Cana Conferences—in which wives participated with husbands.[38]

Delaney saw family, not class, relations as the building blocks of social order. He worked well within the tradition of social concern and practice as understood by Catholics in the United States. He fitted the widely shared definition of the good priest. He was a case worker rather than a community organizer, and his operation was more like a crisis clinic than a labor school. His overriding concern was for the stability of the family in the midst of rapid social change:

> The ISO hopes to lay particular emphasis on the Family. If it is true that even the Catholic Family is not entirely what it should be—the sacred unit of Catholic life—the fault is undoubtedly a lack of a sense of responsibility, a lack of education, spiritual and economic, for family building. Young men and young women must be carefully educated to the unselfish responsibility necessary for making marriage a success. They must be brought to realize the amount of preparation and hard work and study necessary to make the family a *center—a unit*

of prayer, in education, in recreation, in productive activity through Home Economics.[39]

Delaney portrayed the home as a warm hearth. Nurturance and affection, qualities that were not prominent in the chillier depictions of conjugal austerity among the Irish, were intrinsic to the nature of the good family. These qualities were in turn indispensable to the cultivation of traits that the family had to strive to attain: character as "unselfish responsibility" and habits of hard work. Affection and discipline gave the family resilience and made it productive.

The family retreats were enormously popular. If Delaney had an overall plan, it was somehow to coordinate these diverse activities as they spread across the United States. But before the age of mass travel and communications, this goal did not have much practical significance, and even at the time Delaney was not known for his fund-raising capacities or institution-building prowess. His was a one-man operation, confined to New York City.

What was new about Delaney's work was his capacity to project a loving rather than an astringent model of the family and to preach this message convincingly in a way that moved Jesuits a step outside the classroom, further into the streets and the homes of Catholic urban communities, without binding them to the parish routine they disliked.[40] Delaney brought organizational creativity and a recognition of the companionate as well as the traditionally sanctioned, reproductive aspects of marriage to "Catholic family life," the theoretical cornerstone of social order. While his views on social and sexual matters in the abstract conformed to Catholic conventions of the period, his actual treatment of the family placed husband and wife as a couple before patriarchal ideals of moral order. As far as Delaney was concerned, the practical foundation of social order was the stable and sexually faithful married couple.[41]

By Delaney's own account the headquarters of the Institute of Social Order at Xavier High, still in the basement alongside the church, was a combination drop-in center and base of experimentation for making contacts with a world defined not primarily by class but by denomination:

Come in next Sunday and you'll see fifteen couples—husbands and wives—here for our first "Family Day of Retreat.". . . They'll be here from eight in the morning until six in the evening. They'll offer Mass together in a nearby chapel, breakfast in our retreat dining room.
They'll have conferences and roundtable discussions in our library; in their free time they'll be browsing through books and pamphlets on the family.
If you had come in last weekend you would have seen sixteen work-

ing men sitting in the same library in perfect silence. They too were in
retreat, a workers' retreat. On other occasions you might see a group of
college girls discussing the Mass. Or if you go downstairs, you might
find our psychiatrist handling a very practical case of child delinquency
with a much worried parent. . . .

We are not always around. Shadow us for a month or so, and you'll
find us slipping into union meetings, addressing union members, and
sometimes even men and women on strike. You'll find us talking at
labor schools, lecturing before groups of employers, social workers,
teachers, students, interracial forums, industrial conferences, Communion breakfasts, educational conferences, open forum discussions. . . .

Does it all fit into a pattern? At first sight it seems a hodgepodge of
all different sorts of work. Actually, it does follow a pattern, a social
pattern, a complete pattern, a completely Catholic pattern. . . . Carry
the principles of Christ into the family, into the neighborhoods, into
business and labor and the professions, into politics, and you Chris-
tianize these social units.[42]

The model that Delaney developed for the Institute of Social Order was
improvisational and pastoral. Within this setting all were welcome. Priority
went to personal contact. Delaney was eclectic in his intuitions and in the
programs he fostered. His role was that of the priest as lay therapist. The
workingmen he talked with and celebrated Mass for brought their wives
along, and as word of the family sessions spread other workers got interested
in the offerings at the Xavier center, not so much as a base of union activity
but rather as a kind of parish hall. Delaney provided a setting for participation and interaction, for cultivating the consolations of a reciprocal awareness of common pain, during a period when the stress of coping with
industrial jobs and numerous children, the hardship of the market and the
grind of domesticity, weighed on both husbands and wives.

Under Delaney the Xavier Labor School did not spend much time propagating a social philosophy of militating for social change. The guiding idea
was to build not on dogma but on the generic goodwill expressed toward
workers by recent popes. This was conveyed through the personality of the
priest. The sureness of Delaney's touch was exhibited in the delicacy with
which he modulated pastoral and political matters. He understood instinc-
tively, from the taboo against discussing religion or politics in saloons, that
bringing up social and political issues could precipitate more feuding than
solidarity among workingmen.

Delaney organized weekend retreats for workingmen. What Terence
Shealy had attempted to do through retreats directed toward professionals

and rising members of the Catholic middle class Delaney tried to implement through workers themselves.

> Our Labor Schools simply cannot succeed in their purpose unless side by side with their educational program there is also a spiritual program based on retreats. Only retreats will give to our workingmen that enthusiasm for Christ and that unselfish zeal that will make them real leaders in a campaign to put Christ and Christ's principles into Labor.[43]

The workingmen's retreats faced material difficulties that programs for better-off Catholics did not encounter. Most of the men could not afford to stay away from home the two nights required by the closed weekend retreats, and some could not easily pay for the breakfasts and lunches on Saturday and Sunday. Delaney solved these problems by adapting a schedule and system of voluntary donations begun by another New York Jesuit, Fr. John Gallagher, in the late thirties. The "order of time," as Delaney announced it, let the men get home at night. The schedule of the typical day included some discussion of social issues with traditional religious devotions:

8:00	Mass—Short Introductory Talk
9:00	Breakfast
10:00	Talk—Meditation
11:00	Free Time
11:30	Talk—Meditation
12:30	Lunch
1:30	Round Table Discussion on the Family
2:45	Rosary in Chapel
3:15	Talk—Meditation
4:15	Coffee
4:30	Round Table discussion on the Ideal Catholic Workingman
6:00	Talk followed by Benediction[44]

The retreats gave Delaney occasion to exercise his talent for putting the men at ease. The notes that he printed in the ISO bulletin, then three or four mimeographed sheets, were aimed at the diocesan clergy, whom he urged to offer weekend retreats for their parishioners. The essential step, Delaney emphasized, was to get away from the punitive overtones that most of the men had associated with religion from their primary school days: "Not God, a policeman with a big stick, not God majestic, immense, Creator of heaven and earth, far-off, untouchable, but the God that Christ revealed, Our Father."[45] The sympathetic deity of Delaney's homilies matched his vision of the married couple as the warm core of the family.

Delaney emphasized themes common in the social Catholicism of the time, such as the dignity of labor. He gave the theme a traditional emphasis, reminiscent of the medieval motif of death as the great leveler, by suggesting that the powerful might not be truly respectable and that the humble might in their fashion be saints. "Among the saints . . . there is St. Joseph, the Carpenter, all the hard-working fishermen among the Apostles . . . Stephen, the first Martyr, a waiter . . . and some day soon, we may hope, Matt Talbot, the Dublin longshoreman."[46] The status of individuals within the social hierarchy did not determine their worth. The message touched personalist and populist chords; it did not stir partisan sentiment directly.

Like Carey, Delaney worried that most Catholics did not compete well with Communist militants in their dedication to labor causes:

> A point our workingmen grasp easily is the comparison between the enthusiasm and zeal of Communists for a false cause and the indifference of Catholics in the cause of Christ. Communists and Catholics in Labor Schools; Communists and Catholics in selling their wares in daily contact; Communists and Catholics in Union interest and Union activity. The obedience, the unity, the generosity, the self-sacrifice of Communists. And Catholic workingmen for Christ?[47]

Similarly, like Carey, Delaney could not fathom the difference in social and political consciousness between American Communists and Catholics. He perceived that the communists had a cause, and he admired them for their adherence to it. It did not occur to him that attention to the ceaseless round of family problems and reminders about the dignity of the poor in the eyes of God might support a certain passivity regarding the larger society.

In the end analysis did not matter to Delaney. He was able to convey a sense of concern for social fairness in his demeanor, amiable and egalitarian as it was, and through his dedication. He exuded human warmth. If there was a phenomenon, besides individuals themselves, that Delaney vibrated to, it was not political debate but liturgy as collective expression. His calls for active lay participation in the Mass placed him among the clerical progressives of the time. Ordinary Catholics, he believed, wanted more in the way of religious involvement than what the old devotionalism provided them:

> Wearing medals, making this, that and the other Novena, eight, ten and fifty-three day devotions, special devotions to any number of Saints are all good, provided they are not replacing the essential devotions. So many of our Catholics seem to know the Saints better than they know Christ.[48]

Whatever their effect on workers, the activities developed by Delaney failed to rally much support inside the Society of Jesus. In the eyes of the international—that is, the European—leadership of the Society of Jesus, retreats for workingmen were not enough to meet the Communist challenge and the potential disaffection of the proletariat. Delaney's approach, while commendable, was hard to replicate without an exorbitant commitment of manpower. He was an evidently holy and engaging man. It was not his opinions on social issues that bothered Jesuit decision makers, for these were correct enough, but the fact that his style of work could not be readily duplicated, at least in the service of the combative objectives that had been set for the society by Father Ledochowski.

The disappointment expressed with the limitations of Delaney's experiment itself revealed three problems with the ambitions of the Society of Jesus in social ministry. Most obvious were the misapprehensions and frustrations built into the idea that the American Jesuits should duplicate the political and institutional model of their European colleagues, just as they followed them in moral theology and metaphysics. The Christian Democratic model could not be exported to the United States.

Second, criticism of Delaney reflected uneasiness with simplistic notions of a direct link between family propriety and social order. The best that might be said about the social repercussions behind his focus on the family was that, while the correlation existed in theory, the multiplier effect was tenuous and slow. It needed reinforcement from political parties and elites.

Finally, the role that Delaney created for himself seemed too close to that of the parish priest burdened with the pedestrian obligations that Jesuits traditionally avoided. While he was popular and very busy, Delaney was neither so entrepreneurial nor quite so charismatic as Daniel Lord. In addition, he did not fulfill the other option of the Jesuit role model, which was to develop professional competence—for example, as an educator—beyond his priestly functions. He was a dedicated amateur, the decent man whom his admirers treated as they might the discovery of a restaurant that would be spoiled by undue publicity.

Late in 1942, after Wlodimir Ledochowski died, Fr. Zacheus Maher, the head of the American branch of the Society of Jesus, removed John Delaney from the directorship of the Institute of Social Order.[49] After the war he took up the same type of work in the Philippines, and thousands attended his funeral.

V

The labor schools and the Institute of Social Order, with which the schools were affiliated, were unable to reconcile two divergent tendencies in the Society of Jesus. One was the call to action. Such enthusiasm as accompanied the founding of the labor schools reflected a desire to stop talking about, and start acting on, social questions. The order's tradition of pragmatism provided Jesuits with some backing for getting on with the work.[50] The inspiration and guidelines for social action were thought to be timeless. Ideas themselves were not supposed to be problematic. The challenge was to get something done.[51]

The push toward action ran into a pair of difficulties. Jesuits had to be watchful about crossing the boundary between advice and political action. In the United States the opportunity to engage overtly in politics was smaller, because the cultural prohibitions were greater, than in Europe and Latin America. In addition, while almost all socially conscious Jesuits stayed out of conventional politics most of the time, the abrasiveness of some of the labor school priests in dealing with colleagues and clients was a serious problem. The urge to dominate in the politics of interpersonal relations was more of an issue that was ideological zealotry.

Conversely, however great the need might be, the constituencies that might favor priestly involvement in social reform were unclear. Labor chieftains were protective of their turf, and the rank and file preferred to have the Jesuits as counselors, educators, and interlocutors than to see them at the head of the column. Clerical participation was situation specific, decided by rules of thumb. The reputation that Jesuit social activists such as the labor priests gained for being loners was not merely a reflection of their crusty personalities but also of the circumstantiality of their roles.[52]

The other tendency in the society viewed itself as intellectual. Especially at the level of higher education, the prestige of teaching in the "real" schools far outweighed the sacrifices and the dreariness that were thought to come with toiling in the labor institutes. For some Jesuits the order provided a mechanism of mobility and security up from the working class. They kept a sentimental yet physically distant attachment to their origins, through expressions of admiration for popular mores, often of times gone by. The labor schools were not folklore. They were a live reminder of social conditions that might better be forgotten, and at any rate their achievements seemed small in comparison with the evident success of the Jesuits' educational operation. The high schools, colleges, and universities were institutionalized. They combined the predictability of academic routine, relative clarity of purpose, control over substance and procedure, and the capacity to give both teachers and students a sense of accomplishment. Forays into social ministry were organizationally risky, and they were perceived as intellectually unsatisfying.

4

"Une Longue Patience"

Social Order, Social Reform, and John LaFarge

I

If social ministry among the Jesuits had a gray eminence, it was a man who was identified solely with neither the activist nor the educational wing of the society. John LaFarge, scion of a family of artists and architects, joined the Jesuits at a comparatively late age, having already been ordained to the priesthood.[1] LaFarge's childhood had been filled, like that of the offspring of the James family, whose members he knew, with travel to Europe. He spoke fluent German and French, and he had attended Harvard. The fashions and controversies that engaged the European intelligentsia were not alien to him.[2]

With this background, LaFarge would normally have been sent to teach at a Jesuit institution of higher learning. Instead, because of fragile health, his superiors sent him to a parish in Maryland, to work of a kind customarily reserved for retired or less cerebral Jesuits. There he spent fifteen years.

LaFarge performed his pastoral rounds in an area that had been the first in which Jesuits settled when they arrived in the English colonies of North America. Thus he worked as a parish priest in a region that for the Jesuits was charged with high adventure and romantic tradition. The band of Jesuits who set to work in the area during the eighteenth century, before the suppression of the society and some decades prior to the onset of revolution on the continent and in the colonies, had incorporated themselves as "The Gentlemen of Maryland" to shield themselves from the anticlericalism and anti-Catholicism of the times.[3] His experience in the Tidewater put LaFarge in touch with an odd corner of American Catholicism. Some of his parishioners were black Catholics, and some of their ancestors had been slaves of the Maryland Jesuits during the previous two centuries.[4] LaFarge also numbered black Protestants among his acquaintances. Regular contact with the poor and concern for ecumenical relations were exceptional among American Jesuits at the time, and the combination of such interests was all the more unusual.[5]

Two other factors added to LaFarge's distinctiveness. Saint Mary's parish was set in rural Maryland, and his stay there spurred his interest in the problems of farm communities—a curiosity that had first been aroused, almost certainly by way of the artistic ambience of his family household, through exposure to the late-nineteenth-century aesthetic and social organicism propagated by John Ruskin and William Morris.[6] LaFarge had the taste of an intelligent American aristocrat for sensibilities and schemes that were uplifting yet offbeat. He called John Rawe "an agricultural genius," and he heaped praise on the Creighton University Rural Life Institute that Rawe had founded outside Omaha. Rawe died when he was barely forty, of a disease contracted on an Indian reservation. LaFarge's eulogy captured the blend of concreteness, pedagogical enthusiasm, and noble dottiness transmitted by Rawe's own writings:

> Through the cooperation of Omaha businessmen [Father Rawe] had obtained the use of the Omar Farm, a magnificent tract of several hundred acres with a fine residence. There he was able to work out his plans with eight carefully selected students. . . . The farm was a combined poultry and dairy farm. The former owners had run a tremendous, elaborate sort of poultry scheme with thousands of chickens bred in wire cages. From a biological standpoint the breeding process was perfectly successful. The hens grew large and fat and toothsome. The only disadvantage was they developed neuroses and at the slightest noise would pump their heads against the cages. Father Rawe liberated the neurotic hens and had equal success without the disastrous consequences. The most striking feature of the Omar Farm was an earthworm ranch, a big wooden barrel filled with countless squirming earthworms. These were Father Rawe's pets, for he was an enthusiastic believer in organic agriculture. . . . He had taken everything into account, the whole scope of public relations with Catholics and non-Catholics alike, the farmer as a citizen, as a consumer and distributor, the farmer as part of the whole social, religious, and political organism.[7]

LaFarge had also ministered to the urban poor. His description of a stay among the social rejects on Blackwell's Island is done with a lighter touch than the accounts left by Henri DuRanquet and John Hart, but it is equally jarring. LaFarge brushed his account of the aftermath of a near drowning with a wry humor that placed ethics by committee, not personal idiosyncrasies, in an ironic light. "My first feelings," he wrote, "were pretty much of terror." He details the event:

> Shortly after I arrived on the Island, Father Ryan, a frail elderly man, had rescued a fellow from drowning in the river by jumping overboard and bringing him to shore. He was cited for a hero's medal before the board of a famous foundation. . . . [T]hey asked Father Ryan what he was thinking about when he jumped overboard. "I saw a man in the water," he said, "and I thought I had better pull him out." They then decided that he should have been conscious of the fact that he was performing an heroic act. Unfortunately, the idea of heroism had never occurred to Father Ryan, so the medal was not bestowed.

Unlike his predecessors at the penal institutions on the East River, and in contrast to Rawe, LaFarge revealed by droll indirection and knowing understatement a sense of the politics of social control that ran through the arbitrariness of life and death among the downtrodden:

> Gloomy and depressing as the institutions were, another side to the life began to dawn. A hospital, after all, is not just a building housing patients; it is also a family with a life of its own and a spirit of fellowship. With Tammany in supreme control of Blackwells Island, the administration was not ideal. Yet a friendly spirit prevailed among the officials, the nurses, doctors, wardens of the Work House, matrons, and everybody else. . . . Chief Warden of the prison was James Fox, a great friend of Father Casey, a warm-hearted, enlightened man who introduced a simple form of shop work for the prisoners and did as much to rehabilitate them as possible. Even the women prisoners with their bedraggled careers revealed to me much that was hopefully human beneath a forlorn exterior.
>
> During my eight months on the Island I administered the Sacrament of Extreme Unction three thousand times.[8]

LaFarge had been around. The fact that he never held a full-time position in a Jesuit school—the tour of duty common in the curricula vitae of his confreres—completed his exceptionalism. His range of interests and experience in rural and urban areas, with Catholics and non-Catholics, with blacks and whites, and with the affluent and the poor, was unprecedented. His versatility was certified by a career that ran in reverse. He gained prominence after a modest beginning in parish work, even if the parish was not an ordinary one. Jesuits who lived long enough normally followed the opposite tack, retiring or winding down to parish work after a career in the schools.

Jesuits without formal ties to the schools run by the society, but with energies and talents that qualified them for bigger things than pastoral work, often seemed to gravitate toward the media. In LaFarge's time this meant semipopular writing. LaFarge began writing when he was in Maryland, and he spent most of the second part of his life as a journalist and essayist. In 1926 he was appointed associate editor of *America* magazine. In 1942, a year before the West Baden conference, he was made executive editor of *America*, the Jesuits' "journal of opinion."

II

Articulate, socially concerned, and diplomatically astute, LaFarge took part in the initial planning for the Institute of Social Order. In 1935 he was appointed secretary of the interprovince committee charged with coordinating the social action initiatives undertaken by Jesuits in various parts of the United States. The job proved to be frustrating. The obstacles to planning posed by the administrative autonomy of the provinces, each reporting directly to Rome, were heightened by the power of LaFarge's ideological and bureaucratic bête noire, Edmund Walsh. Father Walsh stood to the right of LaFarge, and he was used to running his own show. Though, LaFarge complained, "I had at that time assurance from practically everybody that they were willing to cooperate with me in working out a constructive and permanent program," it seemed that:

> This assurance . . . was not given by the Rev. Chairman [Walsh] of the committee itself. He was absent from the two first meetings and later took a position that the views of the various delegates could not be harmonized and so the proposal had best be allowed to lapse. His major emphasis was laid upon the approval given to reports about the committee which were sent to Rome and the retention of his scheme for the publication of *Informationes et Notitiae*, without the slightest change in form or scope.[9]

Walsh was so engrossed in charming his Washington contacts that he abandoned whatever empire-building ambitions he might have had for the ISO. Although Walsh was exceptional by virtue of his near-celebrity status, his relationship with the social institute project typified a problem—indifference in practice on the part of the local leadership and the rank and file of the order rather than personal or principled hostility—that plagued enthusiasts like LaFarge throughout the course of the experiment. The press of ongoing business kept Jesuits who were ensconced in the institutions of the society from paying close attention to the pioneering enterprise. They had little to gain from it in comparison to their fulfilling and time-consuming work in the schools.

From the start Father Ledochowski, as general of the society, viewed the plans for a Christian Social Order project—the Institute of Social Order, as the undertaking soon came to be called—as a national and indeed continental operation, to cover the United States and Canada. The only existing Jesuit operation of comparable scope in North America was *America* magazine. The staff had written often on social and political issues—for example, about the persecution of the church by the revolutionary regime in Mexico and, rather more favorably but rarely enthusiastically, on the economic policies of the New Deal. Together with Francis X. Talbot, the editor in chief of *America*, and Wilfrid Parsons, a former editor, LaFarge made up a triumvirate that sponsored and provided an institutional haven for the chancy, extra-academic endeavor when it set up shop in New York in 1940. Though the operation at *America* was not tied to teaching, neither was it a shop of activists. The hope was that it might develop into a think tank, a research-and-dissemination center, to guide the society's work in social ministry.

Two years before, in the summer of 1938, LaFarge had toured Europe, and it was then that he established firsthand contact with the Jesuits' premier organization in social analysis and action. Action Populaire had been set in motion in 1903, about a decade after the issuance of *Rerum Novarum*. The institute had a full-time staff that ranged between fifteen and twenty Jesuits, "the very aces of the four French Jesuit Provinces," as LaFarge described them, "a galaxy of the cleverest and most useful men with particular qualifications."[10] Together with a few lay assistants, this team worked under the direction of Père Maurice Desbuquois, an energetic leader who had been with the organization since its inception, disseminating pamphlets on social and political questions, organizing discussion groups, and building a network of contacts with national elites and regional notables.

LaFarge was so taken by the bustle of activity around Desbuquois that he resolved to make the New York Social Action Institute, as he called it, "an American *Action Populaire*." Equipped with competence in the major European languages and with a curiosity honed by his cosmopolitan background, LaFarge seemed to have the skills and interests required for absorbing the conceptual tools of contemporary European Catholicism and not merely the ornaments of its past.

With LaFarge's sophistication came a dose of caution, however. In contrast to the more sweeping visions afloat at the time, the plan he laid out in 1939 on the "scope and method" of the proposed institute was remarkable not for its substance or system building but for its care about tactics and administration. Partly for reasons of in-house diplomacy, and perhaps exasperated with the poor results generated by the synoptic mania of the early XO sessions, LaFarge gave the magnitude of the plan cursory treatment. Exhortation and histrionics were absent. He looked instead at the means for achieving goals.

During his European tour LaFarge had stopped in Rome to discuss the meandering course of the social action programs in the United States with Ledochowski. The "wiry, vivacious" general

> was deeply concerned, as was obvious, over the Communist issue, and grasped it with great clarity as a world revolution. He had already written to the entire Society alerting its members to the danger and urging their prayers as well as deep analytic study of the situation. As a Pole, he was particularly aware of what was happening in Russia. At the same time, he felt that nothing could be accomplished by a purely negative approach. His view was in accord with the broad position taken by Pope Pius XI. . . . The Pope insists on the revival of social studies and an active, effective correction of grave social evils.[11]

Aside from curiosity about the ominous developments in national socialist Germany, however, and an assurance after listening to a radio transmission of one of Hitler's speeches that "there will be no war," Ledochowski was silent about the authoritarian movements that had come, or were about to come to power in Portugal, Austria, Spain, and parts of eastern Europe.[12] LaFarge himself had grave misgivings about American progressives who discounted criticism of the Soviet Union and its allies. Neither he nor other Jesuits had patience with the ideological principles supposedly at stake in the power struggles between Trotskyites and Stalinists, and they lined up as a bloc against the anticlerical Loyalists in Spain. LaFarge did not demur from the general's priorities. The purpose of the social action institute, he stated in the preamble to his memo, was "to combat Communism and other subversive movements"—that is, totalitarian fascism—"and to promote a Christian social order."[13]

These goals repeated the ambitions set down originally in the mid-thirties. They were vast and vague. Aside from the advantage of enjoying the approval of the general, the halo of indefinition surrounding the objectives had the potential for encouraging flexibility in implementation. LaFarge spotted the opening. Instead of proposing a smorgasbord of tactics for reaching goals that bordered on the intangible, he eliminated schemes that he sensed would not work because they stood too far outside the society's own areas of competence or because the payoffs were small in proportion to the manpower required.

Thus, LaFarge rejected "direct personal contact with the masses of the people" as strategically inefficient. This tactic was a poor investment that yielded little influence in return for the time it consumed. "A large amount of our care would be given to the instruction and direction of women, who flock to such affairs, and would be involved with local parish and diocesan organizations."[14] Besides discarding the counseling of women as a chore that Jesuits had treated very gingerly in the past, LaFarge's dismissal of this option was an admission that his own pastoral experience, during which he managed to write and to mix with an assortment of constituents, was unrepresentative of parish routine. In rejecting standard pastoral work, he was following traditional Jesuit judgment on the small value of such activity in the larger scheme of things.

He also drew on Jesuit custom in pressing for two alternatives: the use of "various forms of written and spoken propaganda . . . and the training of leaders for direct personal contacts." As an editor of *America* and the author of several books and pamphlets LaFarge was already proficient as a journalist. Though he recoiled from showmanship of the kind that came spontaneously to Daniel Lord in the Midwest, he knew that the message of Catholic social doctrine had a distributive and for some a latent populist cast. The challenge was to shake off its hierarchical trappings and reach a mass audience. The paternalistic substance had to be packaged in a popular style.

> After a careful survey of the ground the S. A. I [Social Action Institute] might undertake a popular type of periodical, similar to the *Peuple de France*, an *America* for the masses. We may also see our way to organized radio or platform talks, etc. There should be issued a weekly mimeographed sheet giving the latest "inside information" to key people. Also leaflets, throwaways, etc., for distribution to the masses.[15]

The priority that LaFarge gave to the media in the mission of the new institute meant that many of its activities would come under the aegis of *America*. The magazine had a national presence—visibility across the Catholic community—together with a list of subscribers. The idea was to reduce the financial and psychological start-up costs of institution building and to guarantee that the enterprise maintained intellectual vitality and did not slip into repetitive sermonizing. Research undertaken at the social institute would help inform the journalistic activities of *America* with a longer view. As editor of *America*, LaFarge would be situated at the command post as Jesuit social ministry radiated outward.

While LaFarge saw *America* as a vehicle for bringing Catholic social philosophy to national attention, he understood the limitations of the personnel who would be responsible for carrying out this task. His fascination with the Action Populaire was not an uncritical case of Francophilia. In his judgment the low level of editorializing by *America* on social issues, not to mention the incoherence of the labor schools, made the French model, whatever its faults, attractive by comparison:

> There is [an] absence of any powerful editorial concentration upon a positive and systematic social program, of a type that will appeal to the working man with the ease, the spiritual and emotional dynamism of Communism and Socialism. The attitude toward labor is predominantly critical. Though the criticisms are often thoroughly justified, they are not conveyed through a medium which appeals to the working man; they are not conveyed in the tone of a man who is in daily contact with labor movements and personalities. The impression conveyed is of a group of men who are in much closer personal contact with the employers and employing classes and are emotionally more sympathetic to the same.[16]

LaFarge also had doubts about the substance of the teaching itself insofar as it was supposed to apply to the American context. The papal encyclicals seemed obsessed with class even as they tried to diminish its force in relation to higher things; the letters failed to mention other lines of social antagonism. On the other hand, LaFarge was bound to be put off by what he took to be the hyperbolic importance the Communists assigned class conflict in the United States.[17]

With regard to Catholic doctrine, it was not as if there were a product of irrefutable depth to be taken off the doctrinal shelf, waiting to be marketed properly. The onus of static hierarchy behind the patriarchal benevolence of *Rerum Novarum* and *Quadragesimo Anno* might not be corrected by popularized presentation. In the hands of many of its interpreters the *magisterium* was handled as a statesmanlike defense of privilege; social order meant the manipulation of tradition. Obeisance to antimodernism required LaFarge to walk a tightrope.

Like most of his fellow Jesuits, LaFarge was distressed about the drive Marxism engendered among its militants. He worried also about the complacency of Catholics, Jesuits included, who had been sheltered from debate in the secular world. The *magisterium* was fuzzy, the stress on equilibrium encouraged reactionaries to cultivate a tactical blandness and genteel concern, and antimodernism protected those who might develop the social teaching of the church from sharpening their focus in give and take with critics. Infatuation with the conciliatory produced little intellectual crackle:

> The other handicap, closely related to the preceding, is an habitual conservatism; what I frankly think is an extreme conservatism. There may be arguments for such a conservatism; some of them are eloquent

and weighty, but the working men are not looking for conservatism, but for social change and for thoroughgoing and concrete remedies for their acute economic plight. The attitude of *America*'s editorials has not grown less conservative but more and more so; has grown rigid, where social matters are concerned. . . .

I am not saying that it may not be *America*'s best policy to continue in its present line of being predominantly critical, concentrating on certain movements and personalities which offend Catholic convictions and are in the public eye. But I do not think such a policy will allow us the cooperation we need with the ISO. I believe, also, that the good our work is doing the Catholic public, and it is very great, is somewhat disadvantaged by the loss of influence we might otherwise have, as a periodical, over the non-Catholic public.[18]

LaFarge did not expect creativity on the printed page from the handful of Jesuits, like Philip Carey and John Delaney, who were in touch with workingmen. His disappointment was reserved for the narrowness of the opinion makers whose parochialism filled the pages of *America*. The personnel problem was not just a matter of crusty personalities. "I do not deny," he noted after praising the brilliance of the Jesuits clustered around Action Populaire, "that it is much easier to fulfill this requirement in France than the U.S. where we are struggling with our immense educational burden."[19] The obligations of the American Jesuits to their high schools and colleges had become as much of a drag on their intellectual flexibility as doctrinal inhibitions.

III

LaFarge was cosmopolitan not only in the range of his knowledge and interests but also in the smoothness he brought to the internal workings of the church and the order itself. In trying to extend the audience for Catholic social doctrine beyond the American Catholic enclave, LaFarge felt that the Society of Jesus had no choice but to take into account the demands and constraints at the interior of the ecclesiastical hierarchy, together with the ways of the broader culture. This sensitivity to the clientelism and personal stakes that could speed or block new ventures within the clerical bureaucracy was an important factor keeping LaFarge in favor even when his projects did not work out according to plan. Individual clerics might gain and lose power, but the culture of personal connections persisted. Faces changed but personalism remained.

The institutional overhead was so labyrinthine that reform, if it came, came slowly in small increments, at heavy costs in time and almost superhuman persistence. The internationalism of the Society of Jesus, like that of the larger church, was dazzling but deceptive. The polyphony of languages that in the aggregate suggested a panoramic intelligence up close revealed a cosmopolitan veneer that expressed intensely local concerns in infinitely different ways. The geopolitical fancies of the multilingual Wlodimir Ledochowski derived from the specific concerns of Italian and eastern European politics.

LaFarge understood the game but never quite mastered it. Institutional overhead also meant organizational depreciation, the wearing down of the capacity to maneuver toward change without exhausting heroics. LaFarge was the equal of most European Jesuits in external cosmopolitanism, in linguistic versatility, in his acquaintance with the ways of the world of *Realpolitik*. His savoir-faire also extended to the inside of the church. His peripheral vision was extraordinarily wide in both spheres. This dual feature of LaFarge's intelligence was quickly recognized, and it made him a welcome participant in a variety of ecumenical ventures. In addition, his tenacity suggested a dependability and character, even a certain guilelessness—perhaps an American innocence—in the face of stupendous obstacles, not covered by suaveness alone. In some corridors of ecclesiastical power an ultimate cynicism and weariness reigned, traits that found a place for men like LaFarge who pushed and pushed again but whose exquisite feel for limits did not quite upset the ways of authority "from time immemorial." He was a politician of some probity, and this opened some doors for "Uncle John." But an irenic temperament was insufficient to make the intellectual breakthrough in social thought that he seemed to aim for, and it inhibited LaFarge from going down certain indelicate trails. In the Catholicism of the time there could be no such thing as a loyal opposition.[20]

The feeling for the tradeoff between internal resources and external results that appeared in his consideration of propaganda techniques emerged in LaFarge's insights into the other means of influence he favored: the "selection and training of leaders." The Catholic bishops and their staffs were an important part of *America*'s readership. They looked to the Jesuits for intellectual guidance. They also protected their turf. The society's decision to push ahead with the Institute of Social Order created a potential rival to the bishops' own National Catholic Welfare Conference, which had been established after World War I.[21] One of the motives behind LaFarge's desire to house the Institute of Social Order within *America* was to avoid calling episcopal attention to the Jesuits' possibly competing operation.[22] Similarly, in considering which sectors of the Catholic and non-Catholic worlds might furnish the most influential, and teachable, contacts, LaFarge sorted through a number of options before settling on the secular clergy:

It is necessary to make some selection at the start: certain groups

(a) to whom our efforts *ab initio* should be mainly directed;

(b) who will be most accessible and most ready to second our efforts; and

(c) whose influence will reach furthest.

Two groups appear to fall most readily under these categories: labor leaders and the clergy. To these might be added, if the opportunity therefore can be created, some of the leading Catholic employers, and religiously-minded non-Catholic employers.[23]

The importance given to conciliation among classes in Catholic social doctrine permitted LaFarge to entertain the possibility of drawing employers as well as workers into the activities of the institute. But the indeterminacy of the social *magisterium* was just as important as the principle of conciliation. Room for interpretation was great, but goads to action were few. While practically no one opposed the social *magisterium*, incentives to divert resources from schools and parishes to social ministry were almost nonexistent. LaFarge spent more time trying to coax coalitions from suspicious or offended camps within the church than in bringing labor and management together. He treated doctrine not as a blueprint but as a vessel, capacious and set on a steady course, in which to carry forward the causes he believed in. (Race and international relations—two areas on which the church had not pronounced—happened to be closest to his heart.) Experience entered his calculations more powerfully than did dogma. The following appreciation of the educational competence of his Jesuit colleagues and their role compared to that of the diocesan clergy is indicative of his pragmatism:

So far, efforts made by our various Schools of Social Science here in the East to arouse a sympathetic and receptive attitude among the labor leaders have not been very successful. Their point of view remains strongly utilitarian, and they are difficult to convince of the need of any solid social teaching. This is natural, in view of their own lack of educational and spiritual background, and the very type of action and atmosphere in which they have shaped their own successful careers. Obviously, the problem is that of forming a new type of labor leader, which means the training of younger men who can win their way to such positions. To succeed, however, in this difficult task we need all the help and cooperation possible; hence the need of very definite aid from the clergy.[24]

The implication was that the diocesan clergy was less elitist—perhaps less intellectually talented—but also more educable and enthusiastic about the social apostolate than most Jesuits. They would be available in large numbers, too. Recent graduates of diocesan seminaries were not yet bogged down in parish administration, nor were they tied to the operation of schools as the Jesuits were. Because he understood that it would never have the resources in manpower of the Action Populaire, LaFarge strained to come up with an organizational formula that would extend the impact of the Institute beyond the efforts of the few Jesuits who would be available to serve as full-time members, while at the same time keeping the operation in clerical hands.

LaFarge showed flexibility regarding the mix of Jesuit control and clerical influence generally. But even within the hothouse ecclesiology of the period this was a rather fine distinction. The fundamental strategy of long-term guidance was one that LaFarge had enunciated in the 1930s and that he gave no evidence of changing in later years. In reporting on his liaison with the Southern Agrarians and the mostly German American clerics involved in the National Catholic Rural Life Conference, he took for his model a variation on the Action Populaire that had been established by Jesuits in Quebec. "There," LaFarge wrote,

> the clergy worked out the principles, and their lay associates worked out the immediate and technical applications, the laymen taking the sole responsibility for the latter. This keeps us clergy and Jesuits out of controversial special issues, while it enables us to get across what is really essential.[25]

As for Jesuits themselves, LaFarge recognized that not all of them were clever or endowed with the capacity for leadership. In a letter to a Jesuit scholastic who had sought his advice about sparking ideas and action in social ministry, LaFarge summarized his philosophy in a way that combined the wisdom of learning to work with available resources and a dose of organizational ruthlessness. He laid down his vision of the links between personal serviceability and corporate effectiveness. It was an eloquent recipe more than a precise formula:

> Any priest who has real patience and intercourse with a friendly group can accomplish much even if he is not particularly gifted. The men who do most for the Society in the long run are as a rule not those with brilliant talents but those who use what talents God gives them with great perseverance and total singleness of purpose.[26]

LaFarge's recommendations did not win out on the scale he desired. Few of the suggestions he made took root. Neither *America* nor the Institute of Social Order became a center for the training of secular priests in social doctrine.

However, the staff residence of the magazine in Manhattan was open to socially conscious clerics who stopped in New York for a touch of intellectual stimulation and urbanity, perhaps on their way to Washington or Rome and back again as they traveled the routes of Catholic charitable agencies. *America* was not far out in front of educated Catholic opinion on political and social issues. But the atmosphere at the combined office and residence on the Upper West Side was congenial and heady compared to the near suffocation of some of the isolated parishes that the visiting clerics worked in, and conversation over preprandial drinks carried a glimpse of new horizons and an awareness of the tides of ecclesiastical power.[27]

LaFarge's dream of creating an American version of Action Populaire was not realized. At the same time that he was reporting to the general on the tribulations of getting the social apostolate organized in the United States, and receiving encouragement about the significance of such work in combating communism and restoring social harmony, Ledochowski was selecting John Delaney to head the Institute of Social Order. The general's grand designs were those of an autocrat, and he commissioned Delaney for the position in the same personalistic way he set Oswald von Nell-Breuning to the task of drafting *Quadragesimo Anno*. From 1940 to 1943, the command post of the ISO was lodged in downtown Manhattan alongside the Jesuit high school and parish church on Sixteenth Street, not at the offices of *America* uptown, and the split between the activist and the intellectual ambitions of the project was reinforced.

LaFarge had an appreciation of the structural pressures exercised by social forces. But he also saw that much depended on accidents of personality, even if he would have drawn back from the hypothesis that the system of clerical decision making was a codification of personal caprice. He put his finger on a crucial factor in the success of Action Populaire and, by extension, on one of the major obstacles to planning its replication:

> I was forcibly impressed by the fact that the success of this undertaking was not due so much to any scheme of organization as to the person of its Director. . . . Indeed it is difficult to describe its organization; it is rather a group of active workers gathered around one man who possesses an extraordinarily constructive mind and has gradually won recognition for his ideas against the dead weight of skepticism and the pressure of opposition and misunderstanding.[28]

A highly personalistic manner of policy formulation went hand in hand with a penchant for big-picture divagations on geopolitics. The clubby pattern was the Jesuit version of a cigars-and-brandy style of decision making. But outside the overcommitted educational establishment there was virtually no equivalent of a skilled bureaucracy or network of competent professionals to back up the structure of command. The Society of Jesus was stretched thin. Two Jesuits, not the fifteen or twenty who worked regularly at Action Populaire, were assigned to assist John Delaney, whose modus operandi was in any case individualistic.

IV

LaFarge was a man of insights rather than systematic ideas, who had chronic difficulty finding institutional lodging for his proposals. He was at once mired in and marginal to the organizational apparatus of the Society of Jesus. He tried to turn his interstitial position to creative use. He looked on tradition instrumentally, as a set of accumulated skills and lessons of experience. The Jesuit legacy was more circumstantial and fortuitous than it seemed in hagiography or patterned retrospect. Because this history had not followed a preordained plan, LaFarge believed that it could be nudged in new directions. Jesuits were activists. Moreover, many of the consequences of their actions were inadvertent.[29] From this perspective LaFarge derived much of his wry humor about the vagaries of the exchange between order and reform, and from the habit of dispassionate assessment also flowed his conviction that Jesuits should go for the long term, building on their strengths as educators and cultivators of leaders rather than getting involved directly in either union organizing or the care of souls. He was fond of citing a favorite apothegm of his father's: "Le génie est une longue patience."[30]

Another asset was his cosmopolitanism. The urbane LaFarge cast his writing in a nonsectarian though still religious idiom. At times his forbearance with what he saw as the shallowness of American culture wore thin, and he lamented the "plain, somewhat materialistic American thought that anything producing results and making the wheels turn around must be pretty good."[31] On balance, however, he moved smoothly in varied environments. His effective parish was made up of a broad, interdenominational spectrum of progressive interests and shapers of opinion.

Yet LaFarge did not have leverage where it counted, inside the educational apparatus of the American branch of the Society of Jesus. Recognizing the problem did not solve it. He had practically no say over the allocation of Jesuit manpower, most of which was in the schools. This institutional problem bordered on the intractable.

The other serious obstacle in the way of the social institute project was posed by the limitations of the intellectual system within which LaFarge and his colleagues functioned. He possessed a remarkable practical sense, and he scanned the range of social problems more widely than did most Catholics. His eclecticism did not, however, develop into a social philosophy or set of analytical perspectives, beyond the somewhat remote categories of the encyclicals, that could come to grips with the dynamic nature of the American experience. The "total singleness of purpose" that might energize "great perseverance" was missing.

LaFarge's fascination with Action Populaire reflected a love of ideas and of intellectual system more than it did a liking for a particular organizational format. For the same reason, he was bored and repelled by the fragmentary tactics of the labor schools. Most American Jesuits seemed to consider papal social teaching uplifting but irrelevant to their work: a museum piece, beautiful and untouchable. LaFarge was not so casual about the *magisterium*, but he too found that it could not be imported whole into the United States. To some extent apart from its totalizing vision, Communist theory was looked on as especially threatening because it placed enormous stress on action, *praxis*, as Jesuits themselves did. The search for system was not merely a neurosis of cerebral types in the society. It also reflected a need to give order and meaning to the miscellany of nonroutine work engaged in by the likes of the labor school Jesuits.

LaFarge could identify social problems that did not fit the categories of scholastic thought. His political antennae were sensitive. But his formidable intelligence, moral commitment, and common sense had no method to draw on for getting back and forth from recognition of issues to the means of analyzing them. He was aware of the difficulty, just as he hinted at the inadequacy of literal translations of papal doctrine to the American scene. In comparison with most of his peers, LaFarge went a long way toward overcoming the scarcity of resources and stimulation:

> I had spent many years in practical pastoral work when theoretically I should have been working for degrees in sociology, social ethics, or political science. When stationed at Leonardtown I did borrow a case of books on some of these topics from the Congressional Library in Washington, through the kindness of its librarian . . . and did a little exploring in spare moments. But without guidance one could not get very far. However, I had the advantage of having already probed into a number of problems of our time.
>
> All this made me desire to keep the line entirely clear on two cardinal points: First, the complete integrity of personal responsibility before God; for we cannot fob off on society or circumstances what in the last analysis is an affair of our own personal conscience. Second, the scope of that claim on our integrity; for the burden of our conscience is not confined to purely personal matters.[32]

When he did manage to take up social issues at length, LaFarge showed insight that departed from the blame-the-victim penchant of much Americanism and indeed of American Catholic individualism. Like other commentators arguing from a Catholic perspective, LaFarge viewed the family as the fundamental unit of society. But he did not isolate lax family structure and faulty parental discipline as the sole or even principal causes of the breakdown of morality, the explosion of sexuality, and the general shiftlessness and poverty of ambition that some analysts attributed to the poor and, especially, to African Americans. On the contrary, LaFarge argued:

> It would seem to be the logical course for the good of society as well as the charitable course from the standpoint of Christian neighborliness to surround such a group with every circumstance that could possibly aid them in conforming to the accepted moral standards, instead of conniving at the perpetuation of conditions that lead to its infraction. Elementary social psychology has no difficulty in indicating these favorable circumstances. Whatever tends to the moral and spiritual integration of the individual and of the social community tends to safeguard these moral practices which are necessary for the very preservation of human existence.
>
> The young man or woman who can look forward to an honorable and useful career opened to them by opportunity is much less exposed to the demoralizing temptations of sex indulgence than those who can see in life but a gamble, in which the highest gains are doubtful and the losses well-nigh inevitable. [33]

LaFarge had an instinct for the structural and circumstantial preconditions of "sin" rather like the peripheral vision that helped him navigate the back channels of ecclesiastical and civil organizations. It was this awareness that kept him from trafficking in hortatory commonplaces and righteous denunciations of individuals. [34] This was not a social *Weltanschauung*, but it went beyond psychologizing.

V

In the late thirties LaFarge came very close to contributing to a major advance in Catholic social doctrine. In the spring of 1938, while staying at the Jesuit curia in Rome during his European tour, he was told that "the Holy Father wants to see you." The next day Pius XI received him in private audience. On the desk before him was a copy of LaFarge's early book on interracial justice. [35] "I read your book," the pope said, speaking in French. "I like it. I want you to write an encyclical on racism for me. Write it as if you were the Pope. And don't tell Father Ledochowski about this." [36]

Although the summons was unexpected, the urgency of Pius XI about racial issues was not surprising. The racist propaganda of the Nazi regime was becoming insupportable to the pontiff, already impatient with what he viewed as Teutonic arrogance. The pope was probably not well informed about segregationist practices in the United States, but he was resentful of German pretensions to cultural and biological superiority in Europe. La-Farge's writings against the pseudoscientific bigotry of the period caught his attention.

"I felt," LaFarge said later, "as if the rock of St. Peter had fallen on me." Despite the prohibition against doing so, LaFarge told Ledochowski of the papal command. The general reacted with an exasperated, "The Pope is mad!" and then assigned Fr. Gustav Gundlach, a German Jesuit who had written ponderous tomes of economic theory and was unwelcome in his homeland, to collaborate with LaFarge in drafting the encyclical. The pair spent the summer of 1938 in Paris at the headquarters of *Études*, the Jesuit intellectual journal, writing the document. Its working title was *Humanae Generis Unitas*—"On the Unity of the Human Race."

In the fall LaFarge returned to Rome "exhausted." The draft was given to Ledochowski; soon LaFarge was back in the United States. Some months later, hearing nothing about the fate of the draft, Gundlach passed on a copy to one Father Rosa, a Jesuit colleague who edited *Civiltà Cattolica*, in the hope of speeding up its review in the papal chambers.[37] Within a month, however, Rosa was dead of a heart attack. A draft of *Humanae Generis Unitas* had reached the pope anyway. But Pius XI himself died in February 1939, and his successor did not take up the project.[38]

Although he made no breakthrough in social theory, LaFarge was ahead of his colleagues in calling attention to issues that captured the attention of Catholic radicals a generation later. The system builders among his fellow Jesuits remained enthralled by a romanticized corporatism; in turn many Jesuit activists were resentfully anti-intellectual. It may have been LaFarge's subdued interest in the schematics of the *magisterium*, together with his evident social concern and the extraecclesiastical cosmopolitanism of his mind, that gave him the resources to map out new areas without forcing them into a whole. He was a moralist and a diplomat, not a visionary. The Institute of Social Order drifted further out from under his control, and he went on to pursue in his writing the interests that genuinely moved him: race relations and peace.

In 1940 France fell to the Germans. The Jesuit who had once been LaFarge's role model, Père Desbuquois, together with many of the French bishops, supported the Vichy regime.[39]

5

"Men Astutely Trained in Letters and Fortitude"[1]

One of the rhythms of Jesuit seminaries during the time before the Second Vatican Council was cyclical. The academic year followed the round of the calendar of the saints. It began with the feast of the birth of the Blessed Virgin on September 8. The training of incoming candidates to the Society of Jesus, admitted late in August, began at that time, and the formation of men in their second and successive years began again. Fall, winter, spring, and summer were filled with major holy days—Christmas, Easter, and so forth—and with commemorations of Jesuit saints: the founder, Ignatius, on July 31; the missionary, Francis Xavier, on December 3; the Counter-Reformation polemicist Robert Bellarmine, doctor of the church, on May 13, and so on through the year. Enfolded within this seasonal cadence was the daily order of prayer, study, exercise, recreation, and meals, with wake-up at five, or in a few places five-thirty, and lights-out at nine-thirty at night. Diurnal regularity flowed into annual predictability, imparting an arcadian calm. One year was much like the last, and the next would be nearly the same. The ringing of the bells signaled the divisions of the day as the seasons divided the stations of the year, turning in time. The seasons came and went and came again.[2]

Another pattern was cumulative and hierarchical. The training of Jesuit priests took fifteen years. It began with the novitiate, which lasted two years. This period was devoted to prayer and spiritual testing. When the third autumn rolled around, candidates took their first vows and were permitted to use "S.J." after their names. They were issued birettas, the stiff, square black hats with three ridges on top, to be worn at meals, Mass, and other communal occasions. The scholastics then began the juniorate, a two-year period dedicated to the humanities, mainly to the reading of Greek and Latin classics.[3]

The novitiate and the juniorate were typically housed in the same large building, with the novices on one floor and the juniors above. After this, the young Jesuits moved on to the study of philosophy, which took three years. The philosophates were separate establishments, still away from the cities but at some distance from the novitiates. The classes were held in Latin.

At the end of the seventh year, after completing philosophy, Jesuits left the countryside and began three years of regency. This usually meant high school teaching. At the start of regency the average age of Jesuit scholastics was twenty-five.[4]

After regency Jesuits returned to the countryside. They began four years of study in theology, "the queen of the sciences." There were five Jesuit theologates in the United States. The one at West Baden in the low hills of Indiana was a combined philosophate and theologate, and at its peak the community numbered more than 250. Ordination came at the end of the third year of theology, after thirteen years in the society. The Jesuit said his first Mass the next day, with his family and relatives in attendance.[5]

There was still another year of theology and then a year of tertianship, at a location in yet another rural setting. The tertianship was designed as a recapitulation, more mature in tone but nonetheless a renewal, of the novitiate experience in which the Jesuit priest was supposed to do little studying and a good deal of praying.[6] Here again, as in the novitiate, Jesuits made a long retreat, that is, the full Spiritual Exercises over a period of thirty days. Finally, after fifteen years, they took up their life's work. Most Jesuits went to teach in the high schools and colleges run by the society.

II

The system of formation was self-contained, repetitive, and evolutionary. Especially in the beginning, in the novitiate, periods of prayer, work, reflection, and recreation were parceled out at precise intervals, the briefest being fifteen minutes. The division of the day became less punctilious as Jesuits moved through the course. By the time they began regency, supervision loosened up a bit. But there were still common times for rising and for meals;[7] Jesuits still moved in groups. This was the third steady pattern, the unison of the collectivity, the reinforcement of belonging. Litanies were still recited by the whole community assembled before dinner in the evening.[8]

What change occurred was expected to occur. As the quotidian order, the monastic ground base, changed from day to day, the course of study from one year to the next went its accustomed route. The spiritual observances that took place on October 17, 1937, would also take place on that date in 1938, and in 1939, and on into the future; and the times of rising, eating, and going to bed would be the same. The daily rhythm was constant. Change emerged slowly, from year to year, in small increments. Novices became juniors, juniors became philosophers, philosophers regents, regents theologians, and theologians priests. The schools, retreat houses, parishes, and chaplaincies awaited the Jesuits when they completed their training. Jesuits almost never left a system that enclosed their lives from adolescence until the grave.

Patterns of stratification were woven into the turning of the days and years. The line of command went from superiors—the rector, the novice master, and so on—to the student Jesuits. Among the students the sharpest division was between those training for the priesthood and those undergoing formation as "temporal coadjutors"—the Jesuit brothers. The course for the brothers was shorter and less taxing academically. Their work was chiefly manual. Many were cooks, barbers, carpenters, gardeners, tailors, stonemasons, and, as the century wore on, electricians and automobile mechanics. Their chores supported the larger operations of the seminary system and, in the cities, the administration of Jesuit schools.[9]

The priests-in-training were divided into those destined to become fully professed Jesuits, permitted to take the fourth vow of obedience to the pope and qualified thereby to be appointed to certain positions of authority within the order—to become major superiors—and those who were not.[10] The latter would become "spiritual coadjutors," ordained with the powers of the priesthood but subordinate to the former, who would become the fathers of the fourth vow. The initial sorting into the short course and the long, as the tracks were called, took place toward the end of the philosophical studies, before the Jesuits left for regency. Scholastics who received a grade of less than six out of ten in a comprehensive oral exam, conducted in Latin, would be assigned in the theologate to separate and less strenuous classes. This was the short course, even though it took the same number of years to complete. The academic load was lighter and the intellectual give-and-take not so intensive.[11]

Numbers made for ritual, division of labor, and hierarchy. In the thirties and on through the late forties and fifties, the cohorts entering each of the five novitiates in the United States often totaled between thirty and forty, sometimes more than fifty. Processing these quantities of candidates encouraged the proliferation of rules. The numbers also encouraged camaraderie and a sense of continuity. Instead of having the rules laid out at length by the novice master, their practical operation was explained to novices when they arrived by those a year ahead of them. Adherence to externals fostered the evolution of esprit de corps and, it was hoped, steady growth in the spiritual life. One Jesuit who went on to become a provincial superior after Vatican II recalled the incantatory, systolic beat of the training and the feeling it created.

> Birettas and litanies, gone; reading at table, gone; first and last visit, gone; monthly permissions (remember them?), gone; Long Order and Short Order, gone; exhortations and *casus conscientiae*, gone; Excitators and Visitators, gone; culpas and refectory penances, gone; and other things in the Custom Book, including presented menus for First and Second Class feasts, gone.
> The "long black lines" in corridors from chapel to refectory to recreation room, etc., gone; "Benedicamus Domino" to start the day and "Deo Gratias" at table, gone; and *bells*—bells for rising, bells for meditation, bells for Mass, bells for breakfast, bells for classes, bells for examen, the Angelus, bells for lunch, bells for spiritual reading, bells for litanies, bells for dinner, bells for the end of rec, bells for points and examen, the De Profundis . . . all gone.[12]

The system was one of cycles and levels, over a fairly stable flux of numbers. The cycle of the day nested within the turning of the seasons, and the phalanxes of Jesuits wound on in procession through the phases of their training toward their assignments in Jesuit institutions where they lived in communities that kept the old protocols. As the course of formation proceeded, for those who proved apt, the life of the mind was emphasized. But always subtending the intellectual concentration and the steady progression was the basal metabolism of the order itself. The formalisms became second nature. They were organic and timeless, enclosing the minihistories of individual Jesuits. Activities that were tuned to the schedule of the bells and that moved with the ritual of the seasons, back and forth and around, like paths in a formal garden, were the behavioral correspondences of the images that the Jesuits used in prayer.

III

The externals, molded over the years, were elaborate, dense, and rich, and the orderliness they were designed to inculcate and maintain displayed considerable variety.[13] The regimen was monastic, with militaristic overtones, but not always ascetic. Abstinence alternated with ample meals and an occasional near banquet in celebration of the saints. These were the "first-class feasts." Nevertheless, through the thirties and forties, numbers were greater than money, and the routine was essentially frugal. The Great

Depression affected the Jesuits as well as those on the outside. It was thought fitting to observe the vow of religious poverty with some rigor. Indeed, several houses of formation could exercise no choice in the matter, having little or no funds to buy food. They lived off donations or by borrowing from better-off Jesuit residences.

In the typical seminary a *haustus* might be held late in the afternoon, around four or four-thirty. A snack, typically coffee and rolls, swallowed in silence and standing up, was made available in the refectory. This was a daily affair. The setting could be fancier for a special community event, when a rare "grand *haustus*" might be held. In 1933 the baseball team formed by Jesuits who were studying philosophy at St. Louis University in the city visited suburban Florissant to play against a team formed by the juniors. If a full supper was not served, the *haustus* prepared for meetings like this would consist of "candy, cakes, fruit and a drink: chocolate, malt milk, etc."[14]

Comradeship developed in the midst of hierarchy. Classmates often tried to work out the personal difficulties that one or another of them might have before bringing such problems to the attention of superiors who were so busy with the droves of men in formation that they might disregard or simply not notice the growing pains of individuals. The standardized training created a store of experience and a language for Jesuits to share. Cozy shelters, tacit exceptions, and ways to maneuver around the regulations evolved:

> What happened was, as numbers grew, and so on, there came to be a greater and greater reliance on the system. It was kind of like a Henry Ford assembly line, or a sausage factory, you know. You put the guys in this end, you put them through this meat grinder, and what comes out the other end is a fully formed Jesuit. . . .
>
> It was more system-oriented, more group-oriented. You stayed with your class. I think the sharing mattered, though it's not the same kind of sharing, for instance, that younger Jesuits today would talk about when they talk about faith-sharing. But there was a group sharing of ideals, and the healing of hurts and so on went on more at a peer level. I mean, if you had a problem, you'd go in and sit down with two or three close friends and you'd talk about it and you'd grouse about it, and guys would try to encourage you. And then if they felt that you were *really* having a problem, then they might go and see the superior and say, "You ought to talk to Monahan, 'cause he's really having trouble." The superior wouldn't know that, you see.[15]

Large numbers made it possible for individuals to hide problems. The numbers and the ritual reinforced one another. They also allowed for and produced a degree of eccentricity. Tiny deviations, "mannerisms," may have been symbols of defiance; they were also expressions of humanity. They were tolerated and even valued, becoming part of the ritual itself.

Frankie Smith's one of the common legends of the Chicago province. There are guys to this day who can still, and do, imitate Frankie and some of his mannerisms. He was an elderly Jesuit when we were at West Baden, who wasn't teaching. He seemed to be doing some writing. He was kind of the resident . . . what? Well, "clown" 's a bad word. But everybody went to Frankie to confession and stuff like that.

The nice thing about Frankie was that he routinely damned superiors. Whether superiors did good or ill, it made no difference to Frankie. Because one of his favorite sayings, although he was actually quoting somebody else, I guess, was, "The scum rises to the top!"

You would meet him, Frankie would stand outside the refectory and grab the first guy who came by and begin to tell him a story. And if you were still eating breakfast you could hear his voice echoing out in the corridor. Frankie was out there performing, you see. Anyway, everybody knew Frankie, and Frankie's attitudes toward superiors, which were a joke. Nobody took them seriously. I'm not even sure he took them seriously.[16]

The toleration of personal quirks and characters gave a natural ornamentation to the rigor of the training, which was so stark and set that minor departures from routine could become the stuff of in-house legend. The cult of local color was the Jesuits' way of making the system their own, without changing it.

The rigid processing was not dictated entirely by numbers. Hierarchy was a principle as well as a function of size. A cat-and-mouse game tended to develop between superiors and scholastics that would take the form of generational conflict after the war. In the thirties and the forties, however, methods of control that were personal and capable of instilling resentment and fear were part of the communal norms that individuals generally accepted.

There was a great gulf between the scholastics and the superiors. Sort of like people who say, "I'd only go to a doctor if I were really sick." A conference with the novice director was a formal affair. You sat in a straight-backed chair. If he wanted to see you, a note went on the board for all to see: *P. Magister vult videre: C. Flanagan* [Father Master wishes to see the novice Flanagan]. To get a "vult videre" was not a desideratum. The superior was generally thought to be in the business of telling you what you'd done *wrong*.

This explains the "charm" of Frankie Smith. . . . Superiors liked to "allow" subjects to imitate them, et cetera. It reinforced [the impression] that they were on top.

Novices were supposed to "manifest" other novices who had "done wrong" so one might be called in to be told one had been "manifested."[17]

In compensation there were the reassuring numbers, the steady procession of the seasons and the sedimentation of tradition that instilled a sense of purpose and even grace. "Christmas at Milford," the same Jesuit remembered,

was quite beautiful, especially your first. You did your Advent fast and I think Christmas Eve was a fast day, too. You went to bed and were awakened by caroling at about 11:30. It really was as though you were in heaven. You got ready and went to midnight solemn Mass— followed of course by two others. You had no one else but fellow Jesuits. Not even phone calls were allowed.[18]

IV

Beneath the rules and the collective rhythm was the primordial encounter with the divine. This was the experience of rapture that lay beneath the formalism and that the pattern of recurrence and ascent to full membership in the society was designed to nurture and preserve and put to use. These are memories of that exhilaration from a Jesuit who entered the novitiate at St. Andrew's-on-the-Hudson, near Poughkeepsie, New York, in the late 1930s:

I think that [feeling] can be put rather simply. I don't say that everybody would agree with the way I formulate it, but I think what I'm saying is a thing that's basically true for everybody. The noviceship was valuable because it introduced us to what Christianity is really about. I remember that before I went there I was talking to a priest I knew at Fordham who helped me make the application to the Society, and he said to me, "You can't live the life of a Jesuit without a personal love of our Lord." That was the classic phrase that was used. As a phrase it might not stand up to linguistic analysis. What would be an impersonal love? But I think it's fair to say that really what Christianity is about is about encountering God in Jesus, that's the whole essence of it. That this is eternal life, to know "the eternal Father in Him Whom You have sent." And when this priest said to me you can't lead the life of a Jesuit without personal love of our Lord, I recall feeling a kind of a chill, or a certain apprehension. I cannot recapture exactly what I thought about our Lord at that time. I certainly believed in our Lord. But I don't think our Lord was for me much more than any other historical figure. I would not have put him in the same class as Washington, or Plato, or Mozart. But he was, really, a kind of historical figure although I had, I suppose, a simple, scarcely formulated devotion when I went to communion. I had never read the scriptures. I had been in Catholic schools all this time and I'd never read the scriptures. So what the noviceship experience was basically about was encountering Jesus. The whole framework—the routine, the schedule—you were with other young men your own age, you had these daily conferences with the master of novices. For the first time in your life you had prolonged, regular periods of prayer.[19]

The novice had time and was in a setting to press toward intimacy with the divine. The bucolic surroundings, the ritual, the sense of community with others desirous of the same communion, and the counsel of the novice master moved him toward this sense of intimacy and personal encounter and back toward daily life again:

I was fortunate in having a master of novices who had a special gift, I think, for introducing young men into the life of prayer. And then developing a set of aspirations for service in the church that would grow out of this kind of intimacy with our Lord. And that, I think, is the great thing. It's hard to express in a way that doesn't sound conventional or pietistic. But that is actually what it's about. . . .

I don't ordinarily say this sort of thing because it's too personal. But I would say that the happiest years of my life were the noviceship years, because of this sense of the discovery of our Lord, which is the discovery that every Christian is supposed to make. Catholicism is not about the church, not about the Pope or about dogma. It is first of all about the Word made flesh. That's what you discovered in the noviceship. And that's why it was a kind of springtime of the spirit. That's why it has, in recollection for me, always a springtime freshness. A great watershed. I tend to think of my life as, in many ways, beginning then.[20]

The novice was born again. He had experienced love, or had come close to an emotional fulfillment that he wanted to hold on to and grasp again, though he might not be able to understand the feeling or to express his reactions to it. At the core of the tradition and the ordering of memory and the conventions of interpretation there were passion and a streak of anarchism, a perception of liberation, and simplicity. There was an intuition that something transcendent might be real, and the sensation was at once crazy and deepening. The Jesuit recognized that the combination harked back to the ancient days of Christian spirituality, to:

> the tradition that people of the fourth century, mostly laymen, in the Egyptian desert invented, the fathers of the desert, the early ascetics who went out and lived in hermitages, because you could do that in a dry climate. They're the ones who created the Christian ascetical tradition. It passes down through the Middle Ages. Rodriguez, the seventeenth-century Spanish Jesuit, Alphonsus Rodriguez, codified it, passing it on, in *The Practice of Perfection and Christian Virtue*. . . . The fathers of the desert, right at the dawn of this tradition, discovered and gave Western civilization the idea of eternity, which it had not had before. Some of these fathers were very steely. They are these little sayings of the fathers, little short things that some compiler preserved just by traveling around talking to people. One old man said to someone who was laughing, "We are to be judged in sight of heaven and earth! And you laugh?!!!"[21]

The motive force released by this mix of sensations was great. It combined youthful exuberance and trust in the future with pride in tradition. The convergence of personal commitment with codified imagery was so powerful that it could not be soon forgotten. The intensity of individual experience entered into the ubiquitous rhythms of clock, calendar, and personal community.

The strictness of Jesuit formation in the days before Vatican II was prompted by the need to put the energy from this subjective and still untamed drive to joint use. The organizational corollary of the personal zeal of the novices was a sense of participating in a great adventure, a communal enterprise that made the discipline of the long training bearable and even an exciting challenge.

In the summer of 1925 a novitiate opened in Milford, Ohio, about twenty-five miles northeast of Cincinnati, to house the growing numbers of candidates entering the society in Missouri, the largest of the provinces west of New York, New England, and Maryland. The novices came by train from the motherhouse seminary, Saint Stanislaus, located in Florissant, outside of St. Louis. One of the novices, Frank Wilson, was appointed *manuductor* ("beadle," or "diarist"). His assignment was to record the happenings of the day. Earnest and ornate after the style of the time, his diary nevertheless captures the zeal and devotion of the thirty novices—most of them of Irish and German descent: Hallahan, McQuade, McEvoy, Malone, Wesselkamper, Schwakenberg, and so on—who made the journey under the direction of Fathers Mitchell and O'Hern:

A drizzling rain could, in no wise, hinder the Fathers and Brothers, Juniors and Novices at St. Stanislaus from giving us a most warm and hearty send-off as we left the Novitiate for Milford. It was, exactly, 7:20 A.M. (St. Louis time). The trip up to the Union Station in St. Louis took one hour and ten minutes. All left the bus which had conveyed us thither and gathered in the station—bag and baggage. . . . As the train was about ready to pull out, Bishop Murphy of Belize [British Honduras] arrived. He, together with Fr. Provincial, came into the car, gave us their blessing and departed amid lusty applause. Precisely at 9:00 [the] Baltimore & Ohio Limited left the station.

All day long we travelled. On the way we passed through Vincennes, Indiana—old Vincennes—a place famous in American History. At 7:40 P.M. (Cincinnati time) we arrived, and were met at the station by Rev. Fr. Brockman and a number of generous Catholic gentlemen . . . who conveyed us to the novitiate. We arrived at our new home at 9:00 . . . a drizzling rain heralded our arrival. . . . A visit to the chapel was our first thought. . . . After supper, curtains were put up in the dormitories and we retired after an adventurous day—adventurous, at least, for a novice of the Soc. of Jesus. . . .

Nothing else but the Fatherly Hand of Providence could have guided our venerable superiors to this lovely spot at Milford. Tucked away in the midst of high hills—itself on a hill—it presented a wild, rugged appearance with its rocky glens and wooded lands. The encroachments of civilization have done much to mar this natural rugged beauty but only enough to render it admirably suitable for the purposes of a Novitiate and still preserve a [good] deal of its pristine beauty.

The following day saw the beginning of much needed work. The generous spirit shown from the start made possible the most phenomenal progress, and on this day of our writing, not even a week after our arrival, our Novitiate presents a settled, homelike appearance.

Thus began under such happy auspices the new Novitiate at Milford, Ohio. May God bless it and prosper it and may He send forth from it men firmly grounded in the spirit of St. Ignatius—men of generous heart and powerful physical constitution equipped, themselves, to vanquish Satan and to snatch from the jaws of Hell souls who were made for Heaven and Happiness. Such is our one desire. Benedictio Dei descendat super nos et maneat semper.[22]

Devotions were modulated as always by the ringing of the bell. The day was subdivided, the novices had periods assigned for all of their duties, everyone was kept busy. The regularity of the life was the steadying counterpoint—a rhythm of activity upon activity, then prayer and meditation, then meals, then activity again—of the exultation of the encounter with the divine that the young Jesuits experienced during the early days of their training, often in the course of the thirty-day retreat that took place in the first autumn of the novitiate. Thought was supposed to be secondary to physical work and prayer. The repetitious tempo of a shared life girded religious commitment through habituation and collective movement. The novices absorbed the regimen through doing and from one another, and the ritual of it absorbed them:

> It was shared, like a bootcamp. It was part of your fiber. Everybody did it. And people who were thirty years your senior had done it. Whether they did it at Milford or Florissant, it was the same thing. And you could talk about it. You could make parenthetical references to snippets of rules that everybody recognized. You might be doing it in jest. But it was all part of the fabric, of the fiber.[23]

The energy that was left over went into activities, such as athletics and glorification of the militaristic traditions of the society, that encouraged the competitiveness, cohesiveness, and responsiveness to command distinctive of the order. The imagery was of adventure, sacrifice, and masculine toughness. Its purpose was to shape the mystical abandon and the expansive, directionless emotion that the scholastics hoped to experience in the novitiate. In the 1920s, to celebrate the centenary of its founding, the seminary at Florissant published a booklet addressed to "the fine Catholic fathers and mothers who bravely dedicated their sons to the service of God." The recourse to martial references seemed a natural conceit:

> Two years of hard spiritual training wait for the young Jesuit on his entrance into the Novitiate. He learns in this drill school the discipline of Christ's skirmishers. He prays with new depth and fervor, and for thirty days he lives through the Spiritual Exercises which changed Ignatius the Soldier of Spain into Ignatius the Soldier of Christ. He studies with exacting care the spirit of the Society, its soldierly obedience to the commands of God's representatives, its zeal for souls, its fervent devotion to the King. But most of all, in every action of his day he strives to copy in his soul the image of Christ, his Commander-in-Chief.[24]

The novitiate was not a school. The development of a disciplined spirituality was the objective at this stage. Some reading, almost entirely of religious classics, went on. But the power of the novitiate was not conveyed primarily through written materials. It came instead through repetitive behavior in groups and a tuning in to aural signals—the indefatigable bells—and a modicum of oral communication, between silence at meals and periods of prayer and collective worship, in rudimentary Latin. Silence and the sound of rustling cassocks came before articulation. The regularity of the schedule, bolstered by the shielding of the men from the outside, stood for a kind of certainty. In this way the novitiate transmitted a sense of primeval order, purpose, and solidarity. The sense of security was strong. Certainty, security, solidarity—it was first of all a way of life and only secondarily a matter of conscious belief:

> The work-a-day life of the novice begins. It is, for the most part, the same routine day after day. He arises at five-thirty in the morning, a trying hour in winter time, but ameliorated by turning out in the company of some hundred others who assemble with him in the Community Chapel for the first morning visit to our Divine Lord in the Tabernacle. Then he meditates for an hour. . . . Meditation is followed by Mass and Holy Communion, and afterwards a hearty breakfast. . . . From breakfast to dinner and again from dinner to supper, he is carried through a bewildering variety of duties for each of which a little bell is rung, and at that sound he is expected instantly to leave off what he is doing and turn to the next duty. The sound of the everlasting bell soon begins to be an annoyance. Later it becomes a trial, and then a real cross to be borne, until at last, like anything else, custom makes it first tolerable, then a mere matter-of-course. Certainly the bell is an effective means of teaching the foremost lesson that every Jesuit must learn, prompt obedience.[25]

The sounding of the bell was clear and steady; so was its purpose.

> Some of the duties to which the bell invites him are: To read the Imitation of Christ, or some other spiritual book, to hear a conference or sacred lecture from the Master of Novices, to attend class for a brief period, to examine his conscience, to sweep the house, to wash dishes, help in the kitchen, on the farm, or at a dozen other manual tasks, to recreate with two companions allotted to him, to read the life of some Saint, to visit the Blessed Sacrament, to say the beads in bands of three walking in the open air, to prepare the points for the meditation of the following morning, and, at last, to retire to his bed in the dormitory for an untroubled sleep of seven or eight hours, uninterrupted by the fatal bell. . . . By these duties he is formed to the chief habits required of a Jesuit; by the bell to obedience, by the household work to humility, by recreation with prescribed companions to charity, by his constant spiritual occupations to familiarity with God and the saints. It is all devised by long experience with an eye to the desired result.[26]

V

Two years of regimentation and cadenced training in obedience in the novitiate gave way to the study of the humanities and philosophy. This five-year sequence—the juniorate and the philosophate—amounted to a college course for the Jesuits. The dropout rate in the days before Vatican II was low, so numbers remained large and the schedule structured.[27] The military allusions continued, but the program shifted from an almost exclusive emphasis on supervision and religious drill to greater stress on the combative and competitive ethos of the society. The idea now was to learn, and formation became more academic. Articulateness was prized:

> He realizes now that it is a part of his professional life-equipment to be familiar with language and literature; and, furthermore, the training of the last two years has fortified his soul with strong supernatural motives for applying himself to study. He means to promote God's glory, to widen the influence of the Church, and to slay heresy outright by the two-edged sword of tongue and pen.[28]

The philosophy course was designed not only to transmit the traditional content of scholastic thought but also as an exercise in assertiveness training. The mock debate was an important mechanism in the cultivation of this style.

> Not only are the lectures in Latin, but the scholastic disputations also. Fencing has been called the philosophy of dueling; with better reason the disputation may be called the duelling of philosophy. The weapon is the two-edged rapier of the syllogism. This is what happens. Three times a year a bulletin published from each class announces a list of theses or philosophical propositions, and at the end of these the names of three capable students are appended; the first is to champion, the others are to impugn the scholastic doctrine. When the appointed hour arrives, the defender takes a chair facing the assembled community. . . . The professor, silent now but watchful, sits among the other professors, while the duel proceeds. Swords are crossed at once. The objector singles out one of the theses to be defended, and makes the preparatory lunge by peremptorily denying it. The champion has a few minutes to define, explain and demonstrate his position, and then begins the battle royal of wits; syllogism after syllogism flashing forth from the objector, each met and parried by the defender with swift riposte of distinction or denial, until the signal is given for a similar performance from the second objector. It may also happen that the defender fails to parry, and is actually "cornered" by his astute antago-

nist; then, lest error should seem to prevail over truth, the watching professor comes to the rescue and indicates a means by which the defender may extricate himself and his doctrine. Such is the quarterly disputation. Similar exercises are held semiweekly in the comparative privacy of the classroom.[29]

The transition from the novitiate to the academic phases of Jesuit formation built on virtue—the practice of piety and familiarization with the liturgical routine and hierarchy of religious life—and moved toward the acquisition of skills, specifically, the development of an assertive masculinity. Combativeness, controlled by obedience, was emphasized. Verbal competitiveness was fostered; aggression was ritualized. It was not a movement from spiritual to real-world concerns, for both stages were stylized. The movement was rather from the feminine to the masculine pulls of Jesuit life.

Through both phases solidarity continued to develop, abetted by the common timing of activities for each cohort. In the small world of the seminary, regularities were everywhere, and the smallest of changes detectable. Little deviations were woven into the pattern. Rumblings and inflections that elsewhere would have gone unnoticed became the stuff of high nuance. The experience was pervasive, so much so that it seemed scarcely necessary to state, except by indirection, the feelings generated by it. For some Jesuits insistence on the use of Latin inhibited expression. "You couldn't say," one Jesuit recalled, "what you really felt." But others were not bothered by such constraints. For them the common signs of the routine virtually dispensed with the need for personal communication except in an improvised patois of Latin laced with Latinized English. It was as if the predictability of the rules and the richness of the ritual left interpersonal turbulence to settle to the bottom and freed the Jesuits for the exchange of gossip that depended on and could not disturb the larger bonding. Neither personal identity, collective purpose, nor overall meaning was at stake.

Spiritual fervor, obedience to the organizational hierarchy, competitiveness, a measure of combativeness—what was lacking still was service. The experience of apostolic work came after the philosophate, in the three years of regency. In August of their seventh year in the society, the scholastics were notified of their new assignments. Their names were posted on a bulletin board alongside the names of the places where they would be the next autumn. Almost all of them went to teach in the high schools.

Now abnegation took outward form. Discipline merged with sacrifice for the sake of the students, and both of these were joined to the pedagogical methods of the society. Release from the monastic isolation of the seminary also provided motivational sustenance.

The approach, consolidated at the end of the sixteenth century, had by the twentieth century gained in its conservative as well as character-forming purposes. It had become an illustrious tradition. This passage inflates the rigors of the pedagogical method but it states clearly the two general goals behind the classroom specifics: devotion to systematic application—learning through endurance—and the development of moral sensibility, the cultivation of conscience. These were the twin foundations of character and possibly of success:

> In his teaching [the scholastic] is guided by the same system of education which was responsible for his own training. This system, known as the *Ratio Studiorum*, is guaranteed by long experience and sound psychological principles. With it as his guide [he] is freed from the necessity of making his classroom an experimental laboratory where, as in so many of our modern educational institutions, students are subjected to trial and error methods. He is more interested, too, in training than in mere book learning. The bulk of Latin, Greek, or mathematics learned may not outlive graduation day, but habits of application, accurate thinking, and honest solution will carry over into life's activity in any sphere. Nor does he stop at professional or vocational training. Life is much more than just making a living. [His] ambition is to train for life. He tries to inculcate a sense of responsibility, the courage to face and attack life's problems, right attitudes on social and moral questions.[30]

Training in hard work ("habits of application") was the primary skill transmitted. Content and facts might be memorized but it was the feat, the act of accomplishing, that mattered more than the substance. The discipline meant not only obedience; it was also geared to bolster the self-confidence that came from mastering what seemed impossibly difficult. An ethical tenor ("right attitudes on social and moral questions") was added to the cognitive toughening. Here, too, the emphasis was on ardor and courage rather than specific content, even though correct positions ("right attitudes") were assumed to be discernible. For the students, character grew out of dedication and a diffuse ethical consciousness that came from the self-denial built into carrying out the obligation to steady work. The acquisition of certain skills, in particular, compositional facility, took precedence over the sciences, which formed part of the curriculum but which most Jesuits themselves were not prepared to teach. At its best the system was supposed to produce a modern variant of the versatile Renaissance ideal: the cultivated Christian gentleman.[31]

For the Jesuits themselves, the teaching experience, outside the seminary as it was, still took place under more-or-less controlled conditions. The predictability of academic chores helped the scholastics make the transition from seven years in the hills. The combination of traditional system and youthful enthusiasm consolidated religious commitment in a relatively un-reflective way, without a search for explicit causes. This account from an official pamphlet, though a bit idealized, conveys the climate of energetic dedication that the scholastics brought to the schools:

> His first appreciable break in the day's work comes only after the evening meal when he spends an hour of restful but most enjoyable recreation with his fellow scholastics. These nightly sessions are not the dull, sober meetings one might suspect. "I want you to laugh, my son, and be merry in the Lord," was the advice St. Ignatius gave. . . .
>
> Recreation over, the young Jesuit is back to his work either correct-ing papers or preparing the next day's classes. So ends his scholastic day. It is a day of genuine self-sacrifice in which he puts himself com-pletely at the disposal of his boys. He has no office hours. There are no ties of home or family to distract him. He has no salary to measure his work by. His own convenience, his own comfort, his own needs are sacrificed to the duties of his vocation.[32]

In the seminary, routine had sharpened a sensitivity to fine distinctions and magnified small deviations from the expected. Now, during regency, num-bers continued to encourage solidarity along generational lines. The fol-lowing recollection captures the quality of the differences—many of them unspoken, emanating from procedures and the physical distances of the institutional environment—between the younger and older men.

> Just structurally, you had the fathers' rec room, and you had the scho-lastics' rec room. And periodically some of the fathers used to come down and be in the scholastics' rec room, because that was *alive*. There wasn't one guy in my class who would go to the fathers' rec room if he was offered a chance to do it, unless they were serving French [cuisine] or something. The impression we had of it was, these guys would all come in there, and they sat around the room, and they read newspapers, and maybe commented to one another on the ball score or something in the headlines. But there was very little conversa-tion and certainly not much sharing. Whereas the scholastics' rec room was hilarious. There were eighteen scholastics in there, they were all talking about things that were vital to the life of the school: this kid, that activity, what are we gonna do about this, what happened there? Whereas at least our impression, since we didn't go to the fa-thers' rec room all that much anyway, but our impression was that the fathers sat in this kind of smoke-filled room, smoking stogies, reading newspapers, and saying nothing. To anybody. It was that *structure*.

The fathers sat at certain tables in the refectory, the scholastics sat at other tables. The only thing we did together was go to chapel and say prayers. And, you know, this was consecrated. The term that was used was "division." And so when we were novices, novices didn't mix with juniors, except on set days called "fusion days." Philosophers didn't mix with theologians, even though they were in the same building. It wasn't allowed. If you were caught, you were "breaking division."[33]

The four-year study of theology that followed regency was the penultimate stage of formation. Jesuits returned to the countryside and to instruction and disputation in Latin. Classes remained large. In the United States, scholastics were assigned to five theologates from twice as many provinces. A rigidity of regulations, geared to processing large numbers, was layered over a question-and-answer style of classroom presentation. The system prospered; attrition was still fairly low.

The culture of the theologates held fast through the thirties and forties, as did their rural ambience. The Jesuits lived close to nature, and aloof from the world, chattering as best they could in Latin, most of the time in English. The growth in numbers gave little encouragement to self-doubt. The current of the days flowed steadily. Small events and tiny departures from routine came to the surface like bubbles. On Thursday, September 19, 1946, the scholastic who was responsible for keeping up the theologians' diary at West Baden noted telegraphically: "Drinks on [election of] new General [Fr. John Baptist Janssens] after dinner." A curious vigilance was maintained regarding links to the world outside. Thus, it was recorded that the "Monon sleeper service between Chicago and West Baden [was] resumed" on Sunday, September 29. On Wednesday, October 30, there were two showings, at two-thirty and six forty-five, of *The Bells of St. Mary's*. Things slowed down as the fall term progressed. Punctiliousness edged up. On Friday, All Saints' Day, it was noted in red pencil that the Office of the Dead had been read "five minutes too late," at five-fifteen. The smallest of fluctuations gained notice. On Sunday, November 10, "three new napkin boxes replaced the single box to speed up traffic [at meals]."[34]

Estrangement from changing times surfaced in oblique ways. Aggression was redirected as sacrifice and apologetics for the church militant. The student theologians, it was thought, were "spoiling for a fight":

[F]rank and open discussion is given not only to opposing Protestant doctrines but also to the so-called higher criticism of the past century and the Modernism of our own that would reduce Christianity to a collection of ancient myths or a passing answer to purely subjective needs. Their claims are put forth boldly and met squarely with convincing arguments . . . conviction is strengthened by a study of the history of the Church. The young theologian sees the Church rise and spread miraculously over the globe; he sees it survive such violent attacks from without and strife from within as would have crushed any merely human organization.[35]

. . . For a little while, perhaps, it may seem like heavy plodding, for the work requires long hours of study with deep thinking, rigid logic, abstract penetration into the mysteries of God's dealing with men. But gradually something else dawns on him. Something of these truths of religion he has known from catechism days, and still more as his religious life enlightened him from year to year. But till now he had no adequate realization how impregnable is the rock upon which they were built, nor how marvelously organic is the whole structure of revelation, like some great oak-tree, no branch superfluous, no leaf pasted on adventitiously.[36]

Formation came full circle in the final year. During tertianship, Jesuits renewed their experience of "days of communion with God."[37] For many it was a time of rest, a sabbatical, before taking up their commitment to the long, hard work of the society.

VI

Woodstock College was the flagship theologate of the Society of Jesus in the United States. Located in the Patapsco Valley twenty-five miles west of Baltimore, it had opened its doors in 1869, less than three months before the start of the First Vatican Council, when papal infallibility was pronounced.

Woodstock served as a model for the final stages of the training of Jesuit priests in the United States. The setting in the rolling hills of Maryland was bucolic; the air was damp and fresh, still touched even that far inland with the tang of Chesapeake Bay. It was not until after World War I that electric power lit the halls and rooms of the main building and its annexes.[38] By then the theologate also had its own printing press. "Its own vehicle of expression," a Jesuit historian noted proudly, "quickly won for the seminary a respected place among Catholic scholars in the United States and Europe and even occasionally notice from secular scholars and the sensational press."[39]

The seminary had the charm and rustic vigor of an extended retreat, a utopian isle apart from the seductions and perils of industrialism. Physical exercise was regularly scheduled, and there was plenty of time to observe and catalog the flora and the animal life of the area.[40] Scholastics formed the Woodstock Walking Club and strolled the grounds of the seminary singing to the tune of "Tarara Boom de Ay:"

> Some odd miles from Baltimore
> Is the college I adore,
> Where I work till I am sore,
> Heaping up a lot of lore.
> When I feel the agony
> Brings a weight of woe on me,
> Then I take a walk with thee,
> Glorious W.W.C.![41]

The detachment of Woodstock typified, on a slightly grander scale, the self-sufficiency of Jesuits in other houses of formation. The seminary and its grounds composed a physical image that magnified the customs and ideals of a protected subculture.

Food and lodging were taken care of, the regimen was predictable, and, after a while, once the scholastics got used to the routine that accompanied the provision of the basics, the steadiness of formation had the effect of releasing psychic time for intellectual speculation as well as spiritual contemplation. But Woodstock was a somber garden planted in the ideological climate of the period of its founding. Belligerent antimodernism marking the ideological tenor of the place, just as the rhetoric of recruitment pamphlets and the regimentation of behavior gave it a tincture of militarism. An immobile scholasticism shaped the curriculum.[42] Intellectual stasis was entwined with the tactile sacramentalism that invested the changing of the seasons and the migrations of the birds, and the stony abstractions of theology, with an aura of naturalness and inevitability. The rock was impregnable, the structure of revelation "marvelously organic." The liturgical cycles and the formal truths of Catholicism were both timeless. Feminine nature and masculine system were one:

> One of the most notable of the ten original faculty members was Camillo Mazzella (1833–1900), a native of Vitulano, Italy. He was the school's first dean and its strongest driving force. Less than two years after arriving at Woodstock he had prepared for printing on the Woodstock Press a 612-page textbook, *Proelectiones de Virtutibus* (1871), a work strongly marked by neoscholasticism. In the preface to the book, Mazzella boasted that his goal was "nova non docere" [to teach nothing new].
>
> Another Italian faculty member was Aenilio de Augustinis (1829–98). He laid no claim to the dangerous gift of originality in theology, for originality bordered too closely on the precipice of heresy to suit his mind.[43]

By the 1930s and 1940s, some of the strange edges of the system had been rounded off. But the process amounted to an indigenization of a conservative worldview rather than a cultural renovation. There were flights of fancy but little creativity. The vaulting aspirations and agonistic imagery were encased in a constricted intellectual system.

Energy abounded. "There was a great sense," a Jesuit recalled, "that you *ought* to be doing something to *better* yourself—if not learning to type, then to write; if not to write, then to speak; if not to speak, then to speak a foreign language."[44] One such project that the theologians at Woodstock devised in the early thirties was a mimeographed florilegium called *Spare Time Essays*. The contents comprised musings of a mostly philosophical and poetic nature, with a rarer piece on social questions. Mr. Francis G. Reed wrote on "The Law of Entropy and Order in the Universe"; Mr. F. Marshall Smith on "Our Economic Difficulties"; Mr. James Conway gave an appreciation of Hilaire Belloc; and Mr. A. G. Shirman contributed a Latin poem dedicated to the French Jesuits martyred by Native Americans, set to the beat of *Tantum Ergo Sacramentum*.[45] Thomas Henneberry, who later became superior of the New York province, delivered himself of a piece of juvenilia under the title "The Ideal Poet." The point of the essay was that poetic achievement was the product not only of a religious sensibility but of a mind in possession of religious truth:

> Why are the lights so dim? Why is criticism so superficial? Why has the bulk of English poetry fallen so far short of the ideal? . . . [T]he Reformation is the cause of this blindness to possibility, this meek acceptance of what is offered. The Reformation overtook England at a very unfortunate moment. . . . With the passing of Catholicism went also the certitude of an invisible world; men were left with opinions and passed to negations; they had problems but no answers; riddles but no solutions. English poetry from that day to this is poetry sung in the dark; it is a growth living in an unnatural soil; it tries to ignore Christianity.[46]

The prevalence of such views among the clerical elite of Catholicism through the first half of the twentieth century was evidence of the damage done by antimodernist injunctions. The mentality was bound up with the preconceptual symbols and the soundings and recurrent flows of the methods of training. This virtual fusion of the artificial and static and the apparently natural and continuous helped sustain the system and also made it difficult and painful to distinguish the two when change came.

There was a bellicose poetry to the writing in *Spare Time Essays*. The pieces had a youthful boisterousness that strived for the serious and the assertive. They were polemical exercises. Some of them reached beyond simile and Ciceronian rhythms, but they did not escape a schoolboy earnestness in which imagery and verbal cleverness overcame analysis. Metaphorical imagination was cultivated at the expense of ideas.

Somewhat as rhyme and meter set up rules to enhance literary skills and effects, the method of training provided numerous tests and constraints that were useful for the toughening of character and whose repetition had a ritualistic beauty. But toward the later stages of training, especially when it turned toward academic achievement, the method showed its limits, so that, by the time they earned their degrees in the sacred sciences, usually in their early thirties, Jesuits tended to be agile and pertinacious but intellectually innocent. Even within the context of the times, the scholastic framework creaked. It required propping up in the form of rationalization and compulsory memorization.

VII

The twin pillars of the formation system were the sense of overflowing love—of transcendent devotion that Jesuits encountered or felt they encountered in the novitiate—and the discipline that surrounded them, persistently though not quite relentlessly, through the course. Discipline, regular devotions, and the academic sequence made up the channel into which emotion flowed. They were the mechanisms by which heroic yearnings and generous impulses took on value, indeed became values—of reliable conduct, sacrifice, competence—that gave form to an enclave Catholicism in the modern United States.

Energies were shaped in academic competition and released in allegories of military combat. Commitment to service during regency provided further training and gave a measure of personal satisfaction. The experience entailed intense interaction with relatively tractable outsiders, followed by withdrawal back into the cloistered world of the seminary. Liturgical ritual and the flow of the seasons reinforced the rhythms of obedience and the hierarchical patterns of the community. There seemed to be a natural order to things, a way of life so cohesive that the abstractions of the classroom blurred into the long pulsations of the course of training. The ceremonies were sensual and tellurian in their regularity, like the rocking of a cradle. They conveyed an unspoken security beneath the disputations over points of doctrine and the tension of the stylized academics.

Afterward, with the process of information behind them, Jesuits felt they knew what to expect. They would most likely be assigned to another Jesuit school in the same province in which they entered the order. As long as this sequence and these institutions stayed in place, Jesuits could work and live out their lives in familiar surroundings. The environment was known and reasonably controllable. The stages of the cycle of life were linked, the ties between inner and outer worlds were unbroken:

> Every Jesuit of my era went through *exactly* the same training, and exceptions were rarely made. Somebody might have an extra year of regency, or go on to a year of study and fall behind his class. But, by and large, everybody went through four years of novitiate and juniorate and three years of philosophy and three years of regency and four years of theology and that was it, followed by one year of tertianship with practically no intermission.
>
> That was all set in place. It was like the Church. There hadn't been any changes, you didn't anticipate any changes. It was the way it always had been. Which wasn't true. But I mean at least in our memory it was the way it always had been and it was always going to be.[47]

It was still possible in the thirties and forties for Jesuits to reach a kind of maturity in the system. "Meaning" was not a widespread issue; the sense of purpose, of mission, was still in place. There was still a great deal to be done in the Catholic subculture. The schools continued to grow and needed tending. Furthermore, the hope of some lively and ambitious Jesuits was not directed at retrenchment and the defense of tradition, at mere defiance of modernism, so much as it was at demonstrating how modern accomplishments could be welded onto traditional values.

Yet, during the same period, signs of imbalances and pathologies in the system began to appear. For a process that had been fine-tuned over centuries, an extraordinary amount of care continued to go into making the program function according to plan. The written record—the rules posted by rectors, the correspondence of superiors, and similar materials—leave the impression that as times changed (for the worse, so it was perceived), vigilance increased. New rules were added, almost none were abandoned. Prohibitions outweighed incentives. Refutational minutiae swamped exhortations to keep up with new developments. For every danger that caught the eye of a superior like an incoming round from the enemy camp, a defense shot up. Many of the regulations were not enforced meticulously, but their proliferation reveals concern about fortifying the Jesuit ethos and Jesuit achievements in a hostile environment.

The intellectual covering around the mystical core—scholastic philosophy and theology—had grown increasingly stale. Because this shell was thought to be practically immutable, most Jesuits spent less time attempting to adapt the ideas to contemporary realities than mastering their formal intricacies and tinkering with their paralogical properties. The underlying idea was to train the mind, but telesis stopped short of engagement with the world beyond the pale of the miniature system of the seminary.

Discipline and industriousness, designed to turn the exuberance and generosity of the novitiate days into long-term commitment, began to sag under the weight of regulations. Character as endurance was built up through repetitive behavior. The system prevented the seminarians from getting soft, from holding on to a smiling, adolescent spirituality. They were to grow into a tough, even aloof, maturity.

At least three escapes were available to Jesuits whose endurance was pressed to the limit. Intellectual games provided one outlet. These were a kind of doodling, finger exercises that were not entirely unproductive, for habits of thought were cultivated that formed a free-floating resource for the educational institutions. Although creativity was not a major goal, versatility was prized.

A second and probably more common alternative was to accept the arbitrary elements of the grind and the occasional penalties and reprobations as tokens of suffering that were opportunities to grow in the spiritual life. Tribulation was inevitable in any case, and given the correct perspective it could be sanctifying. It constituted fodder for the eventual harvest.

Rueful humor also spiced acceptance of the chain of vicissitude and virtue. In practice, control could not be complete:

When I entered, I had some unfinished dental work to be done. My hometown dentist recommended a Cincinnati dentist he knew. In terror I presented this idea to the novice master, since we never went into the city. For some reason, it was okayed.

Okay. But because I was a "religious," I had to be assigned a "companion," since religious couldn't travel alone. I was at the time a healthy 18-year-old American who had negotiated trains and planes on my own by that time. This involved a 45-minute city bus ride. We didn't wear our cassocks. We wore dark suits and ties and had some prayers to say, as I recall, on the bus.

The purpose of the rule of "companion"—to keep nuns from being attacked—hardly applied in our case. Since we were both lively youths, we found our way to the roof of Cincinnati's tallest hotel, to have a look around: something we didn't report back home. But the *feeling* was that we'd been allowed to visit Mars.

Am I clear? I think we did a lot of these silly things because some Europeans somewhere thought that's what makes people holy. . . . Asking permission for *each* shower was another. A priest stood in the hall. We all filed by on a hot summer day after lunch, sometimes saying "shower?" and he'd keep nodding. He couldn't say this was idiotic. Someone above would tell him to do it, and ultimately Rome sanctioned this nonsense.

Wearing a T-shirt while swimming was abandoned just before I came—chinks in the armor, you see.

It was the stressing of the minutiae as the main point that was the error. Silence was treated as a great virtue. You "broke" silence, and the silence after 9 P.M. was called "Sacred Silence."[48]

For some the system missed, or did not cope very effectively, with the depths and terrors of spiritual and emotional life. The attention to personal development and the exercise of self-discipline that depended on the supervision and assistance of older mentors turned into a system of surveillance that for some Jesuits lost its utility and possibly its meaning. There was clearly a childish side to the long discipline and close inspection. Although the awareness was rarely articulated at the time, some Jesuits later had inklings of themselves as stunted adults.[49]

One side effect was a kind of melancholy enclosed by the Spartan rigors of a training set in the increasingly artificial, lovely, and isolated gardens of the seminaries. Keeping busy did not suffice to ward off monotony and doubt: "As I went through philosophy-in-Latin, I and many others sensed 'I'm not getting this but somehow I'm getting through.' It did no good to tell authorities this. Methods weren't going to change."[50]

It is hard to talk of an empirically typical, real-life Jesuit of the times, since the pool of candidates was large, the composition of recruits was varied and the templating force of the training never so powerful as it might have appeared. The idealized outcome seems to have been a Jesuit who was strong and capable of withstanding material hardship. The tales of torture and martyrdom of Jesuit predecessors legitimized this toughening, as did the practices of physical penitence. The model was one of a muscular Christianity and imperturbable masculinity. Collective identity was not in doubt. The long training emphasized individual character in the sense of endurance; it was difficult to conceive how conscience might come in conflict with the demands of service, for the cause was good. The Jesuit was also kind, but in a rather detached way. He might in addition exhibit a certain wit and sense of the absurd that grew out of familiarity with the oddities of a religious training with military overlays.

The anxiety for toughening and for maintaining control turned inward. As the surrounding environment became increasingly lax in the eyes of superiors, the prescriptions of formation grew increasingly harsh. Attention was redoubled on the rules and the disciplinary side of religious life. The intellectual foundations of the system were not questioned, and geographically the formation process was insulated from the outside world. Conceptual and physical isolation encouraged a regulatory pattern making, and this in turn expanded the area of the prohibited and the forbidden. With the intellectual and institutional parameters of the society out of reach, the mind of superiors turned to improvement through the tightening of discipline and order. Zeal meant scrupulousness in adherence to the rules. The spiral of competitive piety tightened.

The *Constitutions* and other documents of the society standardized most of the norms for the behavior of Jesuits. They remained in Latin, of uncertain salience to English-speaking Jesuits, until after Vatican II.[51] While taking none of these away, each community added regulations of its own. The seminary at Florissant was the oldest and largest in the Midwest, and over the years Jesuits there had accumulated lists of "permissions" that had to be sought from three different superiors—the dean in charge of academic matters, the rector in charge of spiritual things, and the minister in charge of material items and behavior in general.[52]

The dean's permission was to be obtained, inter alia, to practice music, to have more than three library books at a time, and to procure books from any but the juniorate library. The rector's permission had to be sought to go to St. Louis and to write letters. Thirty-one items came under the purview of the minister. These included permission to use the telephone, take long walks, play the Victrola, and to be dispensed from speaking Latin after supper.

In Jesuit houses of formation there had also evolved a tradition of confession of *culpas* (faults) in chapters, that is, before meals. At Florissant, from a list of twenty-five possible transgressions and defects, scholastics were expected to write down "at least five." Only three of these were read aloud, however, "so that the reading of Chapters may be finished in good time." Common faults involved "violation of silence," "violation of modesty," and "violation of the rule which forbids touching another." Others were made up of a miscellany of great and little deficiencies: "obeying with reluctance" as well as "carelessness in the observance of obedience," "want of punctuality" as well as "not doing things at the proper time," "criticizing new undertakings and refusing to support them," "bearing oneself with coldness, arrogance, condescension, reserve, or peevishness in dealing with equals," "speaking to others harshly, peremptorily, or sarcastically," and "violation of the rules of the library."[53]

The ranking of the faults according to seriousness was left unspecified. The list formed a collection built up from general laws ("violation of modesty") and observations of particular offenses ("selfishness at table, in games, at work") that could become very grating among people living together at close quarters around the clock. Some distinctions are so fine that to the outside observer they border on the redundant. "Frequent displays of pride" are difficult to distinguish from "speaking boastfully of oneself" or from "doing or saying things that reflect credit upon oneself." Other *culpas* reveal the tacit hierarchies of community life. "Bearing oneself with coldness . . . in dealing with equals" is blameworthy but evidently not so serious if "subordinates"—for example, coadjutor brothers—replace "equals."

This was an empirical listing, not a classification with subheadings and a deductive scheme behind it. The lack of an explicit rationale resembles the initially arbitrary but eventually predictable ringing of the bell that regulated seminary activities from waking to sleeping. A similar effect was generated by the patterning of prayers by days within seasons, according to agricultural cycles, in the breviary that contained the office read by priests for an hour every day. A natural mystery still seemed to cling to it.

As early as the 1940s, however, a sense of absurdity showed through the air of mystery. The custom was to submit *culpas* in writing to the local superior. At the Jesuit residence at St. Louis University, a bit of an uproar was created when one of the older scholastics slipped a list to a superior so dulled by the drone of the ceremony that he read out the charges before grasping their content. The scholastic had accused himself of "returning overdue library books, of arguing too long that the truth might appear, and of making a fool of myself by imitating the actions of superiors."[54]

VIII

After the death of Wlodimir Ledochowski in 1943, at the beginning of the three-year interregnum before a new general could be elected, the American assistant, Zacheus Maher, made a visitation—an inspection tour—of the various Jesuit houses in the United States. The outcome of this trip was a document, eighteen single-spaced pages in length, of admonitions and recommendations. Maher was an obsessive disciplinarian. Although it was sent to every rector of the society in the United States, the report was never officially promulgated. Left to stand, parts of it might be carried out at the discretion of local superiors.

The report is significant in two respects. It illustrates one extreme of the range between the oppressive and the permissible in the society at the time, a possible norm, rather than a depiction of real behavior.[55] Second, while the regulations were probably not consensual even as a set of norms among superiors who were supposed to enforce them—some of the provincials were commonsensical and humane—the existence of the report is indicative of a personalism taken to the level of systematic management. The paradox of rigorous personalism inadvertently brought out the sediment of caprice and vagary in the tradition and served eventually to drain meaning from it.

Maher arranged the exhaustive list of misdemeanors and petty evils for efficiency. The ordering was "alphabetical for convenience of reference," starting with problems related to "athletics in our colleges and high schools" and ending with "women employees." Since the moral system itself was taken for granted, he avoided situating the serial presentation in a larger rationale. Few justifications were offered for specific items.

The themes running through the catalog of distractions were austerity and authority. "[W]ho if not we should offer our whole person to labor, to go against our own sensuality, our carnal and worldly love, and to make the offering of greater worth?"[56] Maher's prefatory remarks were taken up with praise of the heroic abstemiousness of the recently deceased Father Ledochowski. His observations also reflected a queasiness about the simultaneous promise and allure of the United States, and he brooded over the recesses of evil and weakness in the midst of outward success and the sinful impulses that needed always to be tamed:

> During his long generalate there was no respite for him, no surcease, no "breaks," to use a current term. His days were full and his nights were crowded. Day after day, year after year, the problems of the Society were presented to him and received careful attention. Every moment of the day and many hours of the night were consumed in their study and this in spite of pain and sickness, in spite too of the unbelievably many demands on his time, some reasonable, some unreasonable; yet if he could contribute to keep this battalion of the Church always fit, always ready for action and in action, he would make the contribution no matter at what cost to himself. . . .
>
> I assure you that he held [the American assistancy] in high esteem, that he was humbly yet sincerely proud of its achievements, grateful for the many splendid things done, appreciative of the loyalty and generosity of the men, convinced that America offered as fine material as any other country for preeminence whether in learning or in sanctity. But he knew too that precisely because of the American outlook we were exposed to influences which, unless carefully guarded against, would work harm to that genuine spirit of the Society, the maintenance of which was his supreme objective. . . . He wanted us to be more prayerful, more observant of those externals of discipline which contribute so much to the preservation of the inner spirit. He prayed that we might be less "*effusi ad exteriora* [enthusiastic about externals]," less caught up with sports and "*nugacitates* [trifles]," more generous in self-denial, more all-embracing in mortification, more strict in our estimate of what is befitting poverty, more outstanding in all perfection proper to the Society.[57]

Some of the prohibitions were inspired by temptations peculiar to the double demons of modernity and the American way. Under "Baseball,

Professional," Maher noted, "Ours are not allowed to attend professional ball games whether baseball or football nor to listen to such on radio."[58] The menace here was not only the frivolity of attending sporting exhibitions, as Maher was inclined to call them, but the insidiousness of the new media—a subject that would become a major preoccupation after the war.

The next admonition came under the title of "Brothers, Coadjutor." Here Maher dwelt on matters that were of general concern within the hierarchical traditions of the order:

> There is need of emphasizing to them from the outset that they are not scholastics and that they must not expect the same kind or frequency of recreation as that granted to the scholastics. For them there are no regularly recurring *gaudiosas* [feasts], villa days, outing, etc. to which have a "right." It stands to reason, however, that the Superior may grant these occasionally as may seem good.
>
> Industry and obedience are two virtues to be insisted upon with them. Care must be exercised in the reading matter allowed the Brothers.[59]

The longer the list went on, the more evident became a problem that Maher seems to have sensed but failed to act upon. The multiplication of rules made enforcing them all the more difficult. On the one hand fresh temptations sprouted like weeds; on the other, it was impossible to control the spread of imperfection by external surveillance. In Maher's eyes, the culprits remained those who flouted rather than those who made the rules. But he also recognized that attempts at total monitoring were self-defeating. The downward dynamic of control and evasion might be self-perpetuating. Under the category of "general observance" Maher lamented that

> The general tone of some houses, the conduct and common procedure, often give one the impression of a club rather than a religious house. Men come and go as they will, and behave pretty much as they feel inclined. This manifests itself primarily in what is the outstanding fault of the Assistancy, the failure of Ours in the colleges particularly to rise on time in the morning, to make their visit and meditation, to say Mass fittingly, with due preparation and thanksgiving. No new rules are needed, and there is Fr. General's beautiful letter on the subject; but we do need Superiors who will put their hand to the work, at no matter what cost to themselves, of seeing to it that what has been established is observed.[60]

But the perception of accelerating moral deterioration in the world outside made the regulatory escalation difficult to stop. Maher urged redoubled vigilance on the part of superiors as a way to enforce rules already in place as he added injunctions of his own devising.

He warned at length about the dangers of slacking off during the course of training. His fear was twofold. There might be a connection between intellectual curiosity and a questioning of moral restrictions and, even if there were not, generational bonding might provoke resistance against authority. At points like these, regardless of his evaluations, Maher's report can be read as a perceptive document not only of perennial difficulties in the traditional format of tradition but of a gathering historical storm:

> Philosophy is a very dangerous period in the formation of our young men. For the first time they sense larger liberties. Fervor readily declines. Those who try to be more exact are laughed at by some, and they themselves are apt to become more lax, noting the divergence between theory and practice in the matter of observance. The nervousness we note in some arises from the endeavor to adjust their knowledge of what should be done and their experience of what is done, often with the connivance of Superiors. Hence the great need of guidance; of a good spiritual Father wholly dedicated to his work. . . . Watch carefully and observe all prescriptions regarding newspapers, magazines, radio, songs, games, plays, movies, concerning all of which wise regulations have been laid down.
>
> In the novitiate all of our young men are given the conviction that they must possess mortification of some sense pleasure if they are to advance in the spiritual life and become the supernatural force for Christ that the Society expects them to be. After the novitiate a large number lose this conviction as an active principle in their lives. There is a rather common cause of this loss. It lies in a certain *crowd-spirit* or *group-spirit* that begins to show itself in Philosophy (sometimes in the Juniorate) and grows in its evil influence until the end of Theology.[61]

Thus Maher traced the erosion of spiritual fervor to the growth of a defensive solidarity in the ranks of the scholastics and to a dalliance with intellectual fashion. The former suggested group autonomy, the latter individual freedom. Within a more flexible framework these developments might have indicated movement toward maturity. To Maher they were indications of a loss of control. He recognized that the fault might not lie entirely with weak individuals. Yet he returned to the conventional belief that the nub of the problem was not in regimentation but was instead a matter of insufficient motivation. It was the person who was to be transformed, not the organization. "Methods weren't going to change":

> This spirit has its origin regularly with a few men of inferior ideals but who are rather forceful in expressing their ideals and have an indirect

way of showing disapproval of the practice of high ideals on the part of others. Thus in a silent imperceptible way they rob their fellows of the convictions they possessed in the novitiate and impose upon them their own convictions. And this not only in the case of weak men who never possessed convictions, but even in the case of many young religious of fine spiritual gifts who give promise of becoming men of real holiness.[62]

Time operated in two ways to reduce the zeal of the novitiate. Some scholastics became more difficult to handle as they grew older. Intensive training in the spiritual value of obedience did not overcome a drive toward independence and self-assertion. Indeed, for some Jesuits, this resistance was a direct byproduct of the routine of seminary life, and it was prized by certain superiors who detected in it the capacity for future leadership.

Second, even success in instilling clockwork regularity bred trouble. Control was fugitive. As the novelty of the seminary regimen wore off and as routine set in, it became harder to fill up psychic time from day to day. The motivation to excel was no longer satisfied with living up to what seemed to be increasingly picayune injunctions. Idealism joined with human frailty in reacting against the boredom of following the rules.

> The group-spirit generally operates [through] a vague feeling that the ideals and convictions of the novitiate are for the novitiate. After the novitiate, or at least after the juniorate, a man has to be practical and not visionary; a man would be singular if he did not do as the crowd does . . . one must be sociable and acquire adaptability; severity of one's life will drive people away . . . after all, a man must have some breaks in his life. . . . Gratification of the senses grows in its demands—a cult of the comfortable—almost complete neglect of our few positive practices of penance—disregard of our fine modesty in managing the body—little guard of the senses—then the cigarette habit. . . .
> Then the pleasures of the table take on a bigger interest in their lives with little thought of mortification—movies, public games—all forms of amusement—have an undue interest and place and are indulged in at the expense of obedience and poverty.[63]

There was also the issue of sex. Maher brought it up under the rubric of "Chastity," noting that "the struggle for the Holy Virtue is continuous." The question aroused a number of detailed animadversions about occasions of sin. The fundamental rationale for celibacy was treated obliquely, the assumption being that it was understood and accepted. Maher was writing a practical manual of contingencies, not theology. The effect was to surround a core element of religious life with peripheral repression and the prospect of petty and never-ending peculation.

> So much militates against Angelic Chastity in this our day that Superiors must be ever on the alert to correct those defects and to remove those occasions which may endanger Holy Chastity: neglect of spiritual exercises; novel reading; improper magazines and newspapers; worldly songs and music; improper home movies; attendance at public movies; too much visiting of externs, both by day and by night; neglect of the rule of companion; too free association of Ours, whether priests or scholastics, with girls; lack of vigilance on the part of Superiors, some of whom judge these matters too lightly. If there is solid evidence for suspecting the existence of a fault in this regard, the matter must be investigated and strong action taken. Men accused of these faults are not to be readily believed if they deny them, the more so in the light of the blameworthy contention of some that one is free to deny his guilt to his Superior "until proven guilty."
>
> Anonymous letters, though per se they do not admit credence, may nevertheless afford the occasion of prudent investigation.[64]

By the standards of the social and cultural transition—the American era of prosperity and mobility—that was to arrive soon in the postwar period, the norms assembled by Maher into a directory of rules would quickly seem constricted and pointless. Even at the time he wrote the compilation was understood to be a mistake. It was received in silence, with embarrassment. Maher had crossed the border that tried to balance sanctions and incentives. The legalistic tracery gave the appearance of righteous futility. The system was coming under such pressure that plugging one leak served only to open up another somewhere else, and so on without cease. The emphasis on the attainment of individual holiness and the protection of organizational unity was so pervasive as to border on being divorced from the goals of service, and whatever intellectual coherence the system had was obscured beneath the serial listing of temptations and prohibitions. The regulatory refinements, the increments of control, the fussing with the inevitable failure to reach perfection threatened to displace inducements to sacrifice on behalf of others. Memories of the distortion of *cura personalis,* "personal care," into the surveillance and manipulation of a regimented religious life would provoke bitter criticism in the years after the war, as the system became increasingly unwieldy.

> The individual was suspect in his own organization. His immediate superiors . . . were to be suspect of him, and they in turn were to be suspected by higher ones. Thus, you had great achievers operating in a

system that had no place for recognizing achievement—only finding fault or, if they were lucky, sin. There was no corresponding set of rewards, or awards, for having done well. Each fault was to be examined and rooted out but we came away with hands empty of reward. You finished three hard years in a high school and received nothing— not a dinner out, not a pen set, nothing. Perfection was expected.[65]

The intellectual framework of Jesuit formation made less and less sense outside the confines of the seminary and the subculture surrounding it. The system turned in on itself. The standardized mechanisms of individual progress in the spiritual life were becoming disengaged from personal, expressive needs and from the corporate need to develop ways of acting in a world that was overtaking the Jesuits.

The methods of training used by the Jesuits in the nineteen thirties, the forties and through most of the fifties were almost exactly the same as the procedures that had been set in place in the previous century. Concessions to modernity—electric lighting, the occasional phonograph—were limited. Correspondence was monitored. Radio listening was scrupulously rationed. The seminaries were marginally more comfortable and efficient. Large numbers of candidates were successfully processed. Materially and logistically, the system functioned.

Intellectually, however, the process of formation had gone backward. As the twentieth century approached its midpoint, seminary instruction slipped farther behind the changes that had taken place in the world outside. Still the system appeared successful. The number of recruits held up. New schools were established. Almost all the feedback was positive. There was little stimulus to change.[66]

The Catholic subculture was still in place, and the order still had a clear purpose, with visible goals to reach. The sacrifices and stupidities could be justified in the name of a worthy cause. Decades later, when the underpinnings of that external mission had eroded, the intellectual and especially the affective undernourishment within the order quickly lost its rationale. For the time, though, it was still possible for the best and the brightest of the Jesuits to believe that the order could keep up with and in fact influence the direction of the modern world without jettisoning the accoutrements of tradition. Zeal and willpower remained plentiful.

Praxis

The conference held at West Baden over the Labor Day weekend in 1943 was as much an effort to loosen the bonds of the past, without declaring the objective loudly, as it was to build on tradition. The success of the Jesuits in education meant that the schools tied down most of their manpower and inhibited experiments in areas such as social ministry. As the Catholic population became more mobile, the Society of Jesus became less so.

Wlodimir Ledochowski had noted the problem. He was as favorably impressed with the work of Action Populaire as he was chagrined by the slow progress being made toward duplicating its accomplishments in the United States, and he reminded the American provincials of his dismay. Zacheus Maher reiterated this concern, quoting the late general, in a letter to Daniel Lord that served as his welcoming remarks to the men assembled at West Baden:

> I regard your ministry of the education of youth highly, and have done all I could to further it. There is a danger, however, lest it become your only ministry, the others being regarded as secondary. It was the mind of the last Congregation that the Social Apostolate should be promoted now more than ever before, an apostolate, however, in which your Assistancy has not done enough as yet. I am certain that you will undertake this work with your accustomed alacrity and that through it you will render a great service, greater perhaps than you now realize, not only to the Church and to the Society, but to your own beloved country as well. [1]

The intent of the West Baden meeting was to get a critical mass of Jesuits directly into the business of influencing social change. But the ideas behind this objective and how they were to be carried out were obscure. Nor was it clear whether Jesuits would actually be taken out of the schools and reassigned to social programs. Despite these uncertainties, the appointment of innovative leadership to guide the undertaking signaled that the project was taken seriously by some powerful Jesuits. Neither John LaFarge nor John Delaney, already active in the movement behind the development of a social action center, came out of the schools. And Daniel Lord, another formidable Jesuit who had been in on the initial planning and whom Maher had designated to head the Institute of Social Order early in 1943, replacing Delaney, was not identified with the educational operations of the Jesuits.

The achievements for which Lord had become best known were the growth of the sodalities that spread through the high schools and his promotion of the Summer Schools of Catholic Action. He furthered these activities through the pamphlets that poured from *The Queen's Work*, headquartered in St. Louis. Lord was an entrepreneur and a showman. He generated numerous projects out of his own efforts, with few resources. The loaves-and-fishes effect intrigued Jesuits who saw social ministry as a hodgepodge of solitary activities in which costs were clearer than benefits. Lord's organizational talents might help gather up the pieces of the social apostolate and put them on a viable footing. Revenues from the sale of devotional pamphlets, together with honoraria that he earned from lecturing, were fed back into *The Queen's Work* to keep its diverse operations solvent. Success at self-financing was not common at the other main national activity of the Jesuits, *America*, which required a regular subsidy from the provincials. Lord's ability to sustain a paying operation recommended him to Jesuit authorities who were more familiar with the brick-and-mortar side of institutional education and its financing than with noble but possibly misguided ventures in social action and analysis.

Faint gusts of uncertainty and change stirred the atmosphere surrounding the West Baden assembly. By 1943 several previously quiet anxieties regarding social ministry were gaining notice. Catholic social doctrine now appeared to be an incomplete blueprint at best. Jesuits retained a hope that the *magisterium* could provide a full, coherent, and universal guide to social reality. But in the meantime the doctrine seemed a muddle alongside the clarity and fixity of Catholic moral dogma.

Two recent learning experiences contributed to skepticism about the workability of the social *magisterium*. The first was uneasiness with the meager results of a decade of probing through the labor schools and the XO project. There was a tiresome inconclusiveness to these experiments. Second, by the end of 1943, it was becoming apparent that the Allies were winning the war. The authoritarian wave of the twenties and thirties was receding. This did not eliminate the possibility of conflict between the forces of democracy and communism, and on the domestic front between capital

and labor. But it reduced the wisdom of an authoritarian or heavily corporatist response to class struggle. The vapors of Latin hierarchy that hovered
over the *magisterium* as formulated in the thirties now appeared not only
exotic but damaging. Southern European fascisms could not be held up as
models of social order by Jesuits in the United States. For these reasons,
Jesuits began tentatively to take a more realistic view of the social *magisterium*. They did not altogether relinquish the idea that a total system could
somehow take shape, like bits of metal suddenly magnetized around the
lodestone of tradition. The unchanging precepts of systematic and moral
theology remained the standards by which other branches of knowledge
were judged. But the dream world, deductive vision of social order no longer
carried great conviction.

Another shift that partly inspired and was partly hidden by the West
Baden meeting lay in the awareness that social ministry could not be considered simply a matter of common sense and good will on the part of Jesuits
who might be available to do the work. Just as doubts about Catholic social
doctrine did not take the form of outspoken criticism, Jesuits were loath to
admit that they were unprepared for and possibly incompetent to take on the
social question. The West Baden meeting served as a pep rally to overcome
defeatist premonitions. Yet Jesuits were aware of their shortcomings as social
analysts and activists. Even though a can-do orientation prevailed, recognition of these deficiencies managed to surface at the Indiana meeting. It
was not until after the ambitious plans laid down by the meeting fell through
that Jesuits agreed on the desirability of professional training in social work
and the social sciences.

The incipient loss of innocence regarding the solutions to be drawn from
Catholic social theory and the glimmering awareness of the complexities of
social reality and of the inadequacies of Jesuits to deal with these problems
reinforced one another. They pointed toward a middle ground in which
professional competence, secular learning, and political know-how came
into play. This was the arena of policy formulation in the United States,
where dogma and amateurism could not guarantee success. One task of the
West Baden meeting, then, was to bring coherence to social ministry as an
intellectual project. Another was empirical and practical: to help Jesuits gain
skills in the implementation of social projects. The assembled Jesuits were
caught between a time when the old certainties were no longer so convincing and before they had gained much expertise in practice.

Still another challenge was institutional. Social ministry remained not
only an intellectual but also an organizational orphan in the Society of
Jesus. The social work schools had caught on, and so had the schools of
commerce and finance. But operations of this type did not reach the working class as students and participants. Besides, they were ignored by the

American intelligentsia. Many of the squabbles that erupted in efforts to find suitable housing for ventures in social ministry were routinely blamed on the personal cantankerousness of administrators and reformers. Their infighting and foibles kept up the supply of anecdotes about the "characters" and "screwballs" who were looked upon by ordinary classroom Jesuits as maintaining in their colorful way the baroque tradition of the domestic politics of the order. Yet the logic of the movement for establishing social action and analysis as a ministry of the society also raised important strategic and philosophical questions about the demographic and financial constituents of the academic establishment, about the place of secular learning, and about the tradeoffs between thought and action. Jesuit social activists complained about being patronized by their colleagues in education. The schools in turn felt defensive about the pretensions of social ministry.

Since the social activities of the society remained at the margins of the order's established organizations, individual initiative played a crucial role. To some extent, this bore out the commonplace that strong personalities, whether charismatic or abrasive or both, shaped an inchoate enterprise. The assignment of men like Lord and LaFarge to leadership positions in the movement seemed to confirm this pattern.

There was more to this side of the undertaking than the antics of colorful figures, however. Because it was institutionally marginal, work in social ministry tended in fact to be improvisational. It got less support but was also less subject to supervision. Pockets grew up around the periphery of regularized activities—not a vacuum exactly but rather zones of potential innovation and deviance—where character as predictability might give ground to courage and conscience. Forays in social ministry that might have passed as gestures in ordinary charity, or that required some daring and solidarity in the face of resistance from outside forces, came also to be laden with a symbolic charge about the authority structure internal to the Society of Jesus. Efforts to explore the relatively unknown territory of social action raised questions about the supposed fixity and completeness of doctrine and about the internal stratification of the Jesuit order.

II

Although they had reason to be insecure about the application of precepts to practice, the Jesuits who gathered at West Baden still operated under the dominion of custom. "Social principles" as they were called—not hypotheses or policies—might need some adapting to the American context. But the possibility of major change in the doctrine itself was off the agenda.

Whatever revisions and amplifications were to take place would occur from the top down.

Acceptance of the untouchability of the main lines of Catholic doctrine meant that the Jesuits learned less than they might have from secular sources in their attempts to elaborate a social program. Scholarship in the social sciences tended to be ignored or to be looked on with suspicion. The expectation was not only that change would come from the top but that the renovation would be in the nature of a *magisterium* modified in phrasing and emphasis but immutable in its essentials. New material had to be either reconciled with Catholic dogma or rejected. Doctrine itself could not be revised.[2]

In part because it could not be handled frontally, this dilemma manifested itself indirectly. Intellectual quandaries were displaced onto bureaucratic politics. The administrative obstacles were real enough in any case. There was considerable worry about how the ambitious venture in social analysis and action was to be set on course inside the Society of Jesus. The inspiration for the project was international, and its scope was to be national. Yet the managers of the order were the provincial superiors who controlled manpower in their bailiwicks. How was enthusiasm among Jesuits at the grassroots to be mustered for an undertaking that had the blessing of a recently deceased general but that enjoyed doubtful support from the provincials, who made day-to-day policy and guided implementation in the United States? The unassailability of doctrine had its bureaucratic analogue in a hierarchical management style that did not favor novelty from below and that could stall directives from the top by allowing existing organizational commitments, most notably to the schools, to tie down resources.

Even if some reassignment of manpower were feasible, the competence of Jesuits outside their accustomed fields was questionable. The training that American Jesuits received failed to acquaint them with economic and political matters, and it did not prepare them for active roles in social reform. Academic prestige within the order went to the eloquent and to those with a flair for classificatory thinking. The logic chopping honed by the course of formation seems also to have been unsuitable for, and may have discouraged, those Jesuits with a penchant for direct social action.

Nevertheless, the publicity surrounding the West Baden meeting kept public affairs on the agenda of some Jesuits who would otherwise have confined their attention to the routine activities of the society. Issues emerged on which Catholic social thought had not formulated positions. These issues went beyond the standard fare of church-specific questions such as the question of governmental aid to parochial schools. Race relations formed one such catholic-with-a-small-*c* issue; the maintenance of peace in the coming postwar period was another. The first issue was distinctively American, and the second concerned the role of the United States during the postwar years; neither had been of much concern to the Roman authorities. The distance between constantly changing current events and the supposition of a distinctive Catholic viewpoint on public policy occasionally prompted the Jesuits to hit on fresh ideas. Partly out of ignorance, they did not have a stake in some of the conventional wisdom about the American way of life. The line between heterodoxy and eccentricity was fine.

The areas in which official Catholic teaching was mostly silent were often those that had been made visible by secular groups on the left. Jesuits responded to an agenda set from the outside at least as much as they were trying to establish social priorities of their own. There was also some inclination to outbid the competition. Jesuits might embrace with some vehemence a progressive position on the right of labor to organize rather than fall into an unreflective conservatism.

There was a good deal about the social line of the Society of Jesus that was simply undecided; indeed, there was not much of a recognizable social program at all. Doctrinal incoherence and lack of expertise left open the possibility of productive ferment. The absence of system did not compensate for the amateurism in social matters induced by the course of training, and it did not spur many Jesuits to undertake firsthand research on social conditions. But it did constitute a protoecumenicism and a certain openness regarding knowledge of the things of the world that was to build in the years after the war and on into the sixties and Vatican II. In some cases, as in the fight against racial discrimination, gaps in doctrine and tradition created an opening that permitted some Jesuits to overcome the dictates of venerable prudence and act courageously ahead of their time.

The downside of amateurism was righteousness. If the *magisterium* could not be changed, then social reality itself might be, without regard to theory and similarly artificial constructs. Doctrinal rigidity and organizational arbitrariness bred an anti-intellectualism among some though not all of the Jesuits who turned to social activism in the forties, going their own often bitter ways, at the margins of the philosophical and institutional establishment of the order. The stifling aspects of the formation process produced some obstreperous Jesuits who rankled at what they considered the abuse of authority and the weakness of their peers for intellectual vapidity. They were shaped by and reacted against this environment. Their views tended to be progressive and their manner high-handed. The battles they fought were not only against social injustice but also against the protocols of obedience within the Society of Jesus.

III

The scholarly, patrician John LaFarge and the ebullient Daniel Lord were temperamentally worlds apart. But, like LaFarge, Lord appreciated the need for finding historical precedents for the programs that were to be proposed at West Baden. This was the rationale behind Lord's invocations of the encyclicals and his depiction of Christ as "the true revolutionary."[3] If the social *magisterium* was to be understood as timeless or nearly so, it was necessary to recover buried principles.

Just as urgent as this cultural adjustment was the practical necessity of situating new initiatives within the chain of command of the order. Here, too, Lord showed an understanding of the intramural politics of the society, even if he was eventually even less successful than LaFarge, whose victories were themselves limited, in turning the structure of governance to new goals. Without a go-ahead from the provincial superiors, who decided what Jesuits could and could not do, just as the general had the first say over what Jesuits should do, the Institute of Social Order would be stillborn.

The task of launching ISO as a national operation was complicated by the circumstances of wartime and by the death of Wlodimir Ledochowski. Communication with Rome, though possible, was time-consuming and unreliable. As the American assistant, Zacheus Maher was next in command of Jesuits in the United States. But he had little juridical power over the provincials, and in an organization with a bent for legalisms Maher's mandate was ambiguous. He settled for the role of strong-willed caretaker. He referred matters like ISO, that involved reorganizing the institutional pillars of the society, to committee. His responses to the frequent requests that came from Lord for putting organizational power behind the ISO were guarded:

> My sojourn in the States is accidental: we are building up a permanent organization which will have to continue in operation when the Assistant is back in Rome. Hence, while I am prepared to act as temporary Organization Chairman, to bring such authoritative action into play as may be necessary, I do not think that the Assistant should figure as a member of the permanent setup. Rather, the top governing body should be the *Coetus Provincialium* as it is for all our Assistancy activities. In the JEA [Jesuit Educational Association] the term "Board of Governors" is used. This might well be employed here too.[4]

Lord's answer to Maher's demurral revealed his apprehension about the intellectual and administrative magnitude of the job he was taking on. The move from New York to St. Louis was not merely geographical; it reflected a deliberate strategy that the Institute of Social Order was to be national in scope. But the lines of authority remained decentralized, under the direction of the provincials. "May I ask if you are sure that my job is interprovincial?" Lord inquired:

> Of that I am not certain. I asked for it a number of times, but, perhaps through a slip of memory, I cannot recall that the appointment or the office in St. Louis was ever made inter-provincial. That would make some difference in my relationship to the other provincials outside of St. Louis. Fr. Brooks [Peter Brooks, provincial superior of Missouri] was not sure either. . . .
>
> I am convinced that my job in the Social Order program should be that of an executive secretary who coordinates and keeps in touch with the Committee Chairmen. I am not sufficiently the expert to direct these men or to be the "Big Man" standing before the country. Rather, I'm the person who does the detail work of coordinating, etc., along secretarial lines. . . .
>
> My job should be announced as Executive Secretary or Organizing Secretary, or what you wish to call it. But everyone concerned should be given a command over the joint signatures of yourself and the Provincials to get behind this and go to work.[5]

Maher was supportive in his prudent way on specifics that did not touch patterns of authority within the order. He did not discourage Lord from taking up the issue of racism in Catholic schools, for example. On the question of admission of blacks to the society he counseled extensive consultation. Insofar as the issue of race relations touched on questions of authority and procedure inside the order, Maher temporized. As it happened, the recruitment of blacks into the society, and the allied issue of the integration of Jesuit schools, emerged as full-blown controversies within the year, as students flocked back to the schools after the war.[6]

In the meantime Maher urged Lord, who preferred discussion to peremptory decision making but who valued action above all, to exercise his own judgment and authority and get on with the work of the West Baden meeting. To some extent it was possible to separate the task of rallying the provincials behind the Institute of Social Order as an undertaking that they should collectively support—even if it stood apart from the direct control of any one of them—from the risks that the American assistancy might run were ISO to become embroiled in matters of public policy where church doctrine was ill defined or over which American Catholics could become divided. The former problem was internal to the society. The latter raised issues concerning the relations between Jesuits and the greater world. Both involved questions of power, but each might be less explosive if managed on its own.

John LaFarge sympathized with Lord's plight. As the other major national operation of the society, *America* also depended on the favor of the provincials, and the workaday incentives of the provincials led them to tend their separate gardens. LaFarge wrote to Lord immediately after the West Baden meeting:

> There will have to be a follow-up or two on the question of authority, on the authorization of this work, for there is always the inevitable inertia to be met back home, particularly in the case of Superiors who did not attend the meeting and who only hear of it in a remote sort of way. We must remember it was all very clearly visualized for us at West Baden, but that visualization may not penetrate very far into the back lands, as it were, and will need to be reinforced by a considerable amount of pressure from above. At some time, not too soon, but at an opportune moment there will have to be another authoritative push from the Rev. Father Assistant [Maher]. That should be carefully prepared for, not wait [sic] until there is some kind of a crisis and some acute cry of distress but a good deal of thought given as to the proper timing and psychological moment for such a move to be made.
>
> There will have to be clarification between just a smaller group of us as to just what the authority is and where it all is derived.[7]

The managerial limbo in which ISO floated was indicative of a blind spot in the hierarchical structure of the society. Operations parallel to the chain of command were anomalous. The Jesuits' educational network, vast as it was, fitted within the order's traditional canons of management. Demands on manpower had not yet quite outrun supply—that was to happen after the war—and the provincials retained control over appointments to administrative slots in the high schools, colleges, and universities within their territories, and over the assignment of Jesuits to and from teaching positions.

The Institute of Social Order conformed partially to this pattern. Daniel Lord served as its director at the pleasure of the provincials as a body. But in another way the operation departed from normal procedure. The financial success of Lord's activities gave him a bit of independence from the provincials. Giving the go-ahead to ISO cost the provincials nothing. It did not require a huge investment to start up. On the other hand, its activities were difficult to monitor. From Lord's perspective the financial promise of ISO did not compensate for his inability to add Jesuits to the enterprise as might be needed to get beyond the Midwest and mount a truly national operation. The imagination behind the Institute of Social Order was still European, a centralized idea disembodied in the American decentralized institutional landscape. There was no counterpart to the Christian Democratic organizational framework to give it shape from coast to coast.[8]

The ebullience Lord displayed when he had a target in sight got diluted in the amorphousness of ISO, and he modestly admitted the limitations of his intellectual resources. He also understood that the materials he had set to work with presented difficulties of their own. Yet another sprawling agenda emerged from the West Baden meeting. It was reminiscent of the lists that came out of the first meetings in the mid-thirties.

The usual excuse—that the generality of the social *magisterium*, together with its supposed unchangeability, rendered much of it ambiguous and difficult to translate into policy—had started to wear thin. Lord took another tack. Now that he had become the most visible Jesuit in the area of social ministry, he was obliged to take social doctrine seriously. Beneath the apparently innocuous circumlocutions of the encyclicals, Lord reasoned, readers could find a critique of unbridled capitalism. Regardless of the assurances made by Jesuits like Edmund Walsh, it was conceivable that Catholic teaching could come into conflict with cherished American beliefs. The energetic proliferation of social goals and programs coming out of the West Baden encounter might belie disagreement among Jesuits themselves about the hard truths of the gospel and the encyclicals.

Lord raised the issue with the provincials and solicited their reactions. At the time Catholic social doctrine meant almost exclusively papal teaching with regard to class conflict and the rights of labor. It was in the context of possible conflicts between this focus of the *magisterium*, the interests of the large blue-collar constituency of American Catholics, and the economics of supporting private educational and other service institutions in a capitalist America that the issue arose. The dilemma was not merely procedural or hypothetical. Money might be at stake. In his letter to the provincials Lord broached the problem forthrightly:

> At a meeting with Father Assistant, Father Talbot, Father LaFarge and myself, we were discussing the ISO and its future and an important practical question was raised. Naturally the ISO is not a purely educational project. It will in the course of time find itself progressing from theory to practice with the necessity of taking stands on social questions. We thought of such things as individual strikes, our attitude toward income taxes, and things of that nature.
>
> Inevitably it will be impossible for the ISO to present Christian social justice or to actuate for its own institutions the Papal social programs without taking sides on heated questions. We may even find ourselves affronting possible benefactors. *America* in the past has had

this frequent experience, so have many of Ours who have been interested in Labor Schools or in work for the labor unions.

We can assure you, of course, that the ISO will never be "red" or dangerously advanced, but the Papal pronouncements themselves have an unpleasant sound in many a Catholic ear, so we frankly wondered whether the Provincials were aware of this entirely practical problem. When possible benefactors are affronted by the plain statement of Catholic principles will they seem disloyal to the Society? Will the ISO be regarded with suspicion by superiors if in the interest of justice it offends at times those who may regard themselves as friends of the Society?[9]

Lord succeeded in piquing the interest of at least three of the provincials. The responses that survive are a mixture of confidence in the social doctrine itself, tact about forestalling avoidable conflict, and a general air of assurance that the society in the United States had been and continued to be capable of weathering incidental turmoil without undue risk. Leo Sullivan, provincial of Chicago, was the most succinct:

With regard to your previous letter about the possibility of offending benefactors and other prominent Catholics by taking sides on controversial issues, my only comment would be that we shall have to be careful always to be very sure of our facts before we take sides. Then if the benefactor happens to be on the wrong side, there isn't much we can do about it. We certainly should not compromise principles for the sake of possible financial gain.[10]

According to Sullivan, not only were ethical guidelines clear-cut—Catholic doctrine was secure in this regard—but the objective conditions that related to morally charged issues could be unequivocally ascertained. Theory was unequivocal, and evidence could be mustered. Thomas Shields, the provincial of New Orleans, took a similar position, with a shade more emphasis on the need for circumspection:

In reference to the I.S.O. and questions of justice which offend some, it seems to me you have to present the truth and "let the chips fall where they may." Naturally it is expected that the I.S.O. will use prudence, but at the same time will not compromise on principles or truth. I mention prudence, for there might be some who present the facts in a manner which might do more harm than good. If there are such men, they would have to be careful to moderate their presentation.[11]

Shields understood that personal style might be as important as substance in coming to terms with controversial issues, and he favored the diplomatic

route. He assumed that such problems were symptoms of personality difficulties and lack of balance, not signs of unquiet conscience. And like
Sullivan he assumed that both principles and the facts themselves ("truth")
could be determined incontestably.

James Sweeney, provincial of the then combined Maryland–New York
province, stuck to practical considerations. His supposition seems to have
been that there was no real danger of conflict between Catholic social
doctrine, as it might be applied in particular cases, and American business
practice:

> You have brought up an interesting point about putting into practice
> the principles underlying the I.S.O. It is here that the experience of
> the *America* editors will aid you. During the present conflict, we have
> had little trouble about the stand of *America* and the various questions
> that are hotly debated elsewhere. The same could not be said during
> the last war. It would be well for you to confer with some of the lead-
> ing industrialists, such as Mr. Grace or Mr. Raskob, when an issue
> does appear. As far as I know, these men have been very sane in their
> dealings with labor problems. I should mention in passing that we
> have few benefactors in this part of America.[12]

The provincials were not gravely worried that a countercultural movement might be mounted by the Society of Jesus, in the name of Catholic
social doctrine, against the canons of American capitalism. Friction there
might be, but confrontation was unlikely. They assured Lord of support.

The responses of the provincials appear to have been prompted in good
part by the willingness to stand up to criticism in the defense of principle.
Jesuit leadership took pride in withstanding criticism, which after all was
often made up of mere opinion and emotion, unsupported by evidence
much less by revelation or the dictates of natural law. The provincials were
also sensitive to the criticism that the order was given to equivocation and
hairsplitting rather than to taking costly stands. In addition, the fact that the
provincials themselves were not responsible for the actual running of the
high schools, colleges, and universities may have lent their assessment of
possible difficulties an insouciance that Jesuits in charge of "the works"
might not exhibit.

Moreover, the leaders of the Society of Jesus in the United States had not
come under serious threat at the hands of the economically powerful. Father Sweeney noted the paucity of big-time benefactors. The context within
which Jesuit operations—the schools being by far the most significant of
these—were conducted through the thirties and much of the forties insulated them from the pressures of high finance. While the total number of
Jesuit schools in the United States was considerable, each of them still

tended to be intensely local, relatively small, and virtually self-contained. Budgets were met mostly out of tuition fees paid by the innumerable Catholic families accustomed to supporting a parochial-school system they considered their own. Finances were also underwritten by various sorts of donated and noncontractual labor—for example, the unsalaried contributions of Jesuit instructors and administrators. Lay teachers were not paid as well as their peers in secular institutions.

The infrastructure of the Society of Jesus was set in a comparatively poor but populous subculture. The depression of the previous decade had placed some of the schools in jeopardy. Saint Peter's College in Jersey City closed for a while, and the University of Detroit went into receivership. None of the schools were well-off, not even those, like Boston College and Georgetown, that would become prosperous decades later. But their troubles could not be attributed to the withdrawal of support by large benefactors; there was almost no support of this magnitude to begin with. Few such figures had emerged among American Catholics. The schools had yet to produce a critical mass of wealthy alumni, and the professional fund-raising and allied techniques that came later, at the tail end of the postwar period, were unknown during this period.

Catholic social doctrine, when it was not a mild irritant, seems to have been almost wholly irrelevant to the workings of American capitalism of the time. To the dismay of some of their more class-conscious European counterparts, it was all but invisible to Catholics aspiring to a piece of the American pie. By the same token, the pressures of American capital—grand capital, anyway—seemed to have been only faintly bothersome to the operations of the Society of Jesus in the United States. Jesuit operations in the American assistancy constituted a collective abstraction for what was really a composite of local interests and pressures; the whole was less than the sum of its parts. The Jesuits had to remain alert to the habits and prejudices of small businessmen and advertisers. But by and large the Society of Jesus in the United States seems to have had some of the virtues as well as the innocence of a venture whose modest size and ambitions did not enter into competition with the larger social and cultural context. For the time being the Jesuit schools had gained a small niche outside the main arena of the American educational economy. As if in compensation for their inability to influence national social policy through centralized organizations like ISO, the small scale and decentralization of the ongoing activities of the American Jesuits gave them a kind of indestructibility in the face of the hazards of economic fortune.

Finally, the responses of the provincial superiors to the query sent by Lord may be more remarkable for what they did not say. There was no mention of a division between the activities of the order and the interests of ordinary, lower-middle- and working-class Catholics. No doubt this is largely attributable to the fact that Lord phrased his question in terms of possible friction between the Jesuits and economic elites. Even so, alienation on the part of the masses of Catholics was practically inconceivable, since they made up the vast majority of the clientele of the Jesuit educational system.

In the end it is significant that Lord framed his question the way he did, suggesting that whatever economic danger the society faced in the United States came from upper-class elements. In Latin Europe the supposition was the other way around; the menace to the church came from the bottom of the social hierarchy. By either count, however, the question verged on the hypothetical. As much as it occupied the attention of Catholic social thinkers in Europe, class conflict was a tractable issue in the United States, and it was undergoing a further transition away from the core of social contention.

IV

There is no indication that Daniel Lord had race relations in mind when he laid the question of disgruntled benefactors before the provincials. He was worried instead that the economic message of the encyclicals might sound " 'red' or dangerously advanced" to American businessmen, a small but growing number of whom were Catholic. Catholics among the working class were much more numerous. Hence, the potential for dividing American Catholics on economic policy was a demographic reality. By contrast, blacks made up an exiguous portion of the Catholic population. Aside from LaFarge and less than a handful of others, Jesuits had been silent and inactive in the field of race relations. [13]

In the spring before the West Baden assembly, Daniel Lord sent postcard questionnaires to the 5,664 Jesuits in the American assistancy. "In the social world," he asked, "where do your instinctive interests lie?" He offered twenty-two different categories to choose from, including "recreation," "radio propaganda," "liturgy," and "political sciences, etc." Half of the Jesuits responded. Among these men the most popular field turned out to be "education," checked by 24 percent, followed by "retreats, etc." (23 percent). "History" came in third with 7 percent. [14]

Even though Lord had tried in phrasing the question to confine responses to socially relevant areas, the profile of "instinctive interests" was not encouraging with regard to social activism. The responses reflected the absorption of manpower by the schools and a dedication to spiritual counseling. "Race relations" was not offered as a category. The issue scarcely existed.

By the same time the following year, however, the issue had come to a boil, and was decided, in St. Louis, where the reorganized Institute of Social Order was setting up its headquarters. The issue involved the admission of blacks to St. Louis University. During the academic year 1942–43, Peter Brooks, the provincial superior of Missouri, urged the university administration to consider the possibility of racial integration. In the fall of 1943, at around the same time of the ISO conference in West Baden, Fr. Patrick Holloran, the president of the university, launched a fund drive for the construction of housing for veterans who would soon return as students. Describing his plans in a letter sent to friends and benefactors of the university, Holloran, in deference to Brooks's prompting, mentioned the difficulties faced by black Catholics in gaining access to higher education.

There was little reaction until the late winter of 1944. Fr. Claude Heithaus, an assistant professor of archaeology, spoke out ardently in favor of racial integration at a student Mass. Defending Catholicism and segregation in the same breath was a hideous contradiction, he declared, tantamount to justifying "Christian cannibalism." "Of course," Heithaus continued with mounting sarcasm, "you may think of tolerating it for a 'greater good.' "[15]

The university newspaper, of which Heithaus was the moderator, printed his sermon the same day. Tempers flared once the issue went public. Holloran reproved Heithaus for his indiscretion. Heithaus received letters of support from LaFarge, Lord, and several leaders of progressive civic groups. The Jesuits in St. Louis could not reach a consensus. In April Holloran turned down the application of a graduate of the black Catholic high school in the city for admission to the university. Heithaus and a Jesuit ally, John Markoe, pastor of a black parish, protested to Joseph Zuercher, the new provincial, who notified Zacheus Maher, the American assistant. Before the month was out Holloran reversed his decision. Blacks were to be admitted to the university, starting that summer.

Heithaus continued to write "interminable and highly emotional letters" to the provincial and to publish articles, criticizing the slow pace of integration at the university and in the archdiocese. He was supported by another Jesuit, George Dunne, who had arrived from California (with a doctorate from the University of Chicago) to work at the Institute of Social Order. Heithaus was reprimanded by the rector of St. Louis University, who expelled him from the Jesuit community; he took a position as a chaplain among the Native Americans at Fort Riley in Kansas.[16] Dunne was sent back to California. Markoe continued to work at Saint Malachy's parish in the city. Maher chastised Holloran for failing to deal with the ethical issues raised by the reformers, and the expulsions were left to stand.[17]

The integration of St. Louis University was a breakthrough. It occurred in the absence of support from peer institutions in the area, and it took place a decade before the Supreme Court's decision prohibiting segregation in public schools and about fifteen years before the integration of Southern universities got underway. The episode reveals the mix of idealism, caution, and strong personalities at work inside the Society of Jesus, within the distinctive parameters of St. Louis Catholicism.

The impetus for racial integration came from within the order, not as a result of prompting from the outside.[18] Once cast in moral terms the issue was difficult to keep down. However, although the movement welled up from inside the order, the outcome depended to a large extent on facilitating conditions in the social environment over which Jesuits had no control. Prudential considerations came into play. The costs in community relations and financial support of a decision one way or the other had to be weighed. These assessments were more uncertain than the deductions from principle or the hard facts that the provincials envisioned when speculating about the relations between the society and its benefactors *in vacuo*.

The balance of external forces did not exert great pressure against the decision to integrate St. Louis University. On the contrary, demographic circumstances appear to have created a favorable climate for desegregation on a small scale. St. Louis was a border town, and the prospect of integration was therefore sensitive. But the Catholic community was buffered from segregationist pressures of the magnitude that prevailed farther south. No racist demagogue emerged among Catholics in St. Louis, as happened a decade later in Louisiana with the appearance of Leander Perez, devout segregationist of the bayou country.[19]

Whites in St. Louis were themselves heterogeneous. Catholic and Protestant ethnics in St. Louis were probably not as walled off from one another as were the Irish from Protestants in Boston. Interdenominational chats were not uncommon in the bars, on the porches, and across the backyard fences of the neighborhoods of south St. Louis. Catholics and Protestants of German extraction were numerous, and they shared a nonsectarian dedication to soccer. The city conformed more closely to the melting-pot model, with less of an obsession about fraternizing with one's own kind, than was usual in some other urban settings. Habits of religious coexistence flourished. Though there was no groundswell in favor of racial integration on the part of the white community, there was little organized opposition either.[20]

In addition, black Catholics in St. Louis were few, although their relative numbers were larger than in some northern cities, and not many non-Catholics, black or white, attended Catholic colleges and universities. The specter of sudden, large scale integration was therefore not as menacing as it was in the Deep South. Gradual amelioration rather than massive transformation was the scenario. Barbershops, movie houses, and eateries in St. Louis, including those around St. Louis University, remained segregated into the late fifties and the beginning of the sixties. The issue at the university in the mid-forties was limited to the classrooms.

Furthermore, while racial integration was not a traditionally Catholic ideal, segregation was not a cultural tenet of Catholicism either, and discrimination had identifiably negative connotations. It also would not do to support a practice identified with some Protestant denominations and sects known for their anti-Catholicism. The indeterminacy of Catholic doctrine did not rule out (and for some individuals even encouraged) moral concern. For Jesuits like Heithaus and Dunne, the moral ethos of Catholicism, not doctrinal specifics, rendered segregation indefensible. The absence of these specifics gave the advocates of integration an opportunity to demand change, just as the demographic configuration of St. Louis served to neutralize segregationist constituencies.[21]

A final consideration was institutional. A Catholic high school for blacks existed in St. Louis. The financial costs of segregation at the secondary-education level were bearable. The economic burden of establishing a separate college or university for blacks was not. As more black Catholics readied themselves for higher education, the pressure to admit black students into Jesuit colleges and universities was bound to increase. The Catholic subculture was committed to providing its members with the full gamut of formal education. The integration of St. Louis University was a reasonable response to these developments. Segregation was morally objectionable, and its economic tenability was on the decline.

Desegregating St. Louis University involved risks. The decision to integrate the school placed it ahead of Catholic parishes as well as public and other private educational institutions in the area. Yet the episode reveals more conflict within the Society of Jesus than between the order and opponents outside.

The conflict posed a moral quandary. There was the "sin of segregation," and there was the question of corporate solidarity.[22] The outside ramifications of the conflict were partially separable from the intraorganizational struggle between authority and conscience. The society's chain of command could require obedience, but it could not claim indisputable competence over moral principle. The case set up a sharp conflict between adherence to individual beliefs and the dictates of organizational unity.

At the same time, the issue was as much about communal solidarity as it was about hierarchy or the principle of obedience. The prodding in favor of desegregation, to begin with, came from the authority structure of the order, which gave legitimacy to the insurgents' demands. The decision of a few Jesuits to break ranks with their superiors by publicizing the issue was not just an act of rebellion. It was also an intimation of a nascent self-confidence that no longer identified American Catholicism with tribal loyalty and local prejudice, and that pressed its criticism of the internal workings of the church. In this respect "the scandal" in St. Louis was a harbinger of the self-scrutiny and explosive changes of coming decades.

V

In August 1944 Zacheus Maher solicited the advice of John LaFarge on a battle brewing in the pages of the ISO bulletin about the tactics of dealing with communism. At the same time that St. Louis University was moving toward racial integration, an exchange of bad-tempered letters between Jesuits was developing into another threat to decorum and authority. LaFarge seized the opportunity to open a discussion of how American Jesuits might clarify their position regarding the recruitment of blacks into the society. The expulsion of obstreperous Jesuits from St. Louis for the sake of preserving internal discipline, even as their views won out in the external setting, had not settled the question of how the Jesuits might set their own house in order with respect to racism.

LaFarge opened his reply to Maher with a commonplace about the need to fight communism with a positive program:

> The strength of our position against Communism, I believe, is much impaired if any impression is created that the Christian social reconstruction program is primarily motivated by combat as such against Communism. The attack on Communism, as I see it, will be only effective when it is simply the natural corollary of a Christian program of integral social justice and social charity which is independent of such extraneous considerations and would be wholly operative even if there were no Communism or any other error to contend with. I see the error as a stimulus and a warning but not as a motivation.[23]

The stress on virtuous motivation in this otherwise unexceptional statement is notable but not out of the ordinary. There were some stands, stemming from simple justice and charity, that Jesuits had to take and adhere to even if they were not pressed by their rivals. LaFarge emphasized purity of intent rather than dogmatic injunction; he was not a formal theologian. The stance was easily recognizable by his religious colleagues as one that tapped "supernatural" inspiration.

Thus, although he was about to break new ground, there was little in his opening words to set off alarms. LaFarge wrote with high-toned civility. He did not make a sharp distinction between the facts of the case, as he saw them, and the ethical imperative to set things right. While he separated the attack against communism from the promotion of social reform, he did not distinguish between the detached analysis of social wrongs and the urge to rectify them. Nor—at least for the moment—did he go into what might be the costs of advancing social change in the face of opposition.

All of this accorded with the broad and generally bland norm of integrating values and action central to "a Christian program of integral social justice and social charity" and with a disdain for scientific analysis as opposed to spiritual motivation and sympathy for the oppressed. Another implication of LaFarge's reasoning, however, was less comforting. The preservation of internal unity that depended on an outside enemy might muffle critical thinking and productive dissidence. Counter-Reformation Catholicism was prone to a garrison state mentality. The Jesuits liked to think that they could generate a social program from the inner resources of Catholicism, and that they could do so without fomenting fratricidal quarrels. This was too much even for the boundlessly courteous LaFarge, dedicated to *la longue patience.* He sensed the difficulty of reconciling the two goals. He recognized, as had Daniel Lord, that appeals to conscience might not be innocuous calls to virtue after all. As the episode at St. Louis demonstrated, disruption had its uses.

So the stage was set for placing ethical imperatives on a par with ordinary conciliation and internal peace. LaFarge was about to recommend a policy that would require more courage than might be forthcoming from a prudential calculus. An adept of the ecclesiastical logic that verged on but did not quite pass into non sequitur, LaFarge turned from the immediate difficulties surrounding the renewed Institute of Social Order to make a suggestion that was masterful in its use of conservative Catholic imagery for the promotion of his favorite cause:

> As I join the rest of the ISO in prayer to Our Lady of Fatima for its success, I cannot help but asking would not Our Lady's blessing be more assured, her intercession be more material and fervent if we were to exemplify in a more striking and tangible way the reality of our social conviction?
>
> Might not such an act of holy boldness open sources of grace which now lie closed? It seems to me that by audacity, not by timidity, our Lady's potent favor can be won. Such an instance might be were we to lay too many human considerations aside and receive a qualified Negro alumnus at one of our Jesuit schools as a Scholastic Novice in either the New York or the Maryland Province.[24]

So LaFarge, with his usual aplomb and his feel for the unspoken rules for nudging Jesuit superiors, clothed a proposal for major change in traditional language. Maher readily understood that such a move might put the leadership of the Society of Jesus a step ahead of the reformers who decried racism in Jesuit schools. He responded by asking whether LaFarge "was speaking merely in the abstract or of an actual case." LaFarge replied that he was thinking of

> a young Negro, who has made an excellent record both in studies and in conduct at St. Peter's College, Jersey City, son of a fine Catholic colored physician of that city and a good mother, [who] applied to our province for admission. He was received in kindly fashion by Fr. Provincial, but informed that we could not take him, since there would be no place to use him in the New York Province.[25]

LaFarge was a pragmatist—he was not prone to extended abstraction—but he was also a moralist. His manner was that of a dogged idealist. The particular instance raised a general issue, and he pressed his case, still with courtierlike delicacy, on Maher. He draped his advocacy of "an act of holy boldness" not in confrontation but with studied consultation and a touch of temerity.[26]

> I am mentioning this matter to you, not with the idea of pursuing the matter from above, but with the idea of learning what might be your own mind on the matter before I take it up with Father Sweeney [the provincial superior of New York]. I do not mean your mind on this particular instance, but on the general principle of refusing admission to an *otherwise qualified*, fully qualified candidate, solely upon racial grounds. I should like, in other words, to feel some assurance that I was upon relatively safe ground before approaching the Provincial. But I would not quote you or throw anything back upon you, although after taking it up with him I would report results.[27]

For LaFarge integration was more a question of political will, of implementing through institutional means a general ethical imperative, than of establishing or disputing doctrinal positions. On the other hand, though LaFarge would shortly lay out a map of the social terrain indicating the conditions under which Jesuits could combat segregation without incurring intolerable losses, the program was not to be simply a matter of opportunism or preemption. Rational deduction from timeless principles would no more impel Jesuits to act courageously than would mere pragmatism show them the right course. For reasons that had more to do with historical accident and reasons of state than with amaranthine truths, the papal encyclical on racism that LaFarge helped to draft had never been issued. Available doctrine was bereft of explicit guidelines. LaFarge took the tenor of church teaching to favor—at a minimum, not to stand in the way of his position. The fundamental idea was simple; it was expressed with customary sinuosity:

Even if by meticulous, human calculations, we may be able to allege
reasons against admitting a Negro into the Province, is there not a special blessing to be obtained from our Lord, through the intercession of
Our Lady, in a clear, *domestic* exemplification of the entire Catholicity
of the Church?

I see this from many angles: as an exemplification of our mission
ideals at home, and *inter nos*. As an exemplification of the social program, making a tangible and even, for some, a slightly sacrificial example of the same. And also as test of our own personal humility,
upon which all else is built. This is a frankly supernatural viewpoint:
but it is such a viewpoint which is the basis of such a devotion as that
of Our Lady of Fatima.[28]

LaFarge knew that Catholics did not perceive racism as a Catholic issue.
The advantage of this peripherality was to render it manageable. By the
same token, the low salience of the issue was an impediment to rallying
Jesuits around the cause. LaFarge insisted that action against segregation
should be driven not only by moral considerations—after all, secular liberals
had their standards, too—much less out of competition with communism,
but by a superethical, "supernatural viewpoint." This, he argued, would
give a distinctively Catholic air to the movement. But LaFarge was leery of
an escalation of dogmatic fervor that might set Jesuits quarreling among
themselves again and threaten authority. This was a tender point with Maher. On balance, LaFarge argued, the movement required only a "slightly
sacrificial example" and not an exorbitance of zeal. He concluded his recommendation for desegregating the society on the chord of optimism and
diffidence that was his trademark.

Personally (this is merely my own opinion) I do not think there would
be any such insuperable difficulty in placing a Negro Jesuit in our
Province, right in our own home works. People would take him for
granted much more readily than one suspects, and he would have the
cooperation of many more men among Ours than one may now anticipate.[29]

For more than a year LaFarge and Maher kept up a correspondence about
the ethics and tactics of racial integration. In May 1945, "having been asked
several times to declare what should be regarded as the position of the
Society in America towards the admission of otherwise properly qualified
negro applicants," Maher circulated among the provincials "some useful
remarks made by a Father whose judgment I know you respect" but who had
requested anonymity for the moment.[30] The cautious statement, rendered
in the axiomatic style of scholastic Thomism, was sent to LaFarge, and he

seized the opportunity to prod Maher toward a less accommodating position.

The response of LaFarge is remarkable for its careful unfolding of the strategic, tactical, and ethical parameters of what he thought should be the policy of the Society of Jesus on race relations. His ethical appeal was set within a framework of politically astute and sociologically sophisticated judgments about the ideological and regional grounds across which Jesuits had to maneuver. He began with a panorama of strategic practicalities:

> There is the viewpoint evidently considered in what is here given: viz., admission of the Negro as a blow to the serious heresy of Racism and, by the same token, a strong affirmation of our belief in the universality of the Church, in a practical not merely theoretical way.
>
> There is also the expedient angle of the question of Communism. We cannot afford to let ourselves be exposed in any weak manner to Communist attacks, when this can be avoided. The presence of an occasional Negro in our ranks is an answer to a very frequent and harmful type of Communist propaganda. This applies not merely to the local scene, as e.g. if we had a Negro Jesuit in the N.Y. Province, but to the world scene: e.g. the effect produced on foreigners, our missions, as in China or India, if we can point to a Negro Jesuit in the U.S. . . .[31]

In stressing the mundane aspects of a decision to press forward with integrating the order, LaFarge characteristically noted the potential benefits to the society—enhanced credibility, better public relations—and the costs: action had to be taken, verbal gymnastics did not suffice. The Society of Jesus had effective control over integrating its own ranks. Even though some negative consequences might be anticipated, the costs of doing nothing were higher than whatever pain might be entailed in pressing ahead. Desegregation was an investment, with acceptable risks, and an obligation, driven by a decision about right and wrong. It was a wise move.

With this strategic vision as a background, LaFarge turned to the question of how Jesuits might handle the integration of their educational facilities. Universal solutions could not apply. The Society of Jesus did not exercise the same control over its schools as it did over its members. Uniformity could not be imposed. Tactical precision was needed:

> With regard to the schools, I would only add that some form of educational care for the Negroes in the secondary stage (whether by separate high schools, in some regions, or by admission to our high schools, in other sections), will greatly help in assimilating them at the college level.

In the *strictly Northern cities* (Chicago, Detroit, Philadelphia, etc.) there can be no question even of separate high schools: regarded as Jim Crow, etc.

In the *border towns*, like St. Louis, Cincinnati, Baltimore, etc., the general sentiment of intelligent Negroes appears to be that they are not concerned about sharing them with whites in the secondary stages: it is on the college level that they resent the discrimination. . . . But this cannot be said of a real Northern town. A "Negro high school" in New York is an impossibility. [32]

LaFarge saw the experience at St. Louis University as a pivotal case. Change there had been set in motion by a coalition of strident idealists and reform-minded managers but it had been made feasible by distinctive demographic and institutional equilibria and shifts in the area. Outside of brief references to pockets of Jesuit presence in New Orleans and Southern Alabama, he said little about the Deep South, a Protestant preserve.

Having distinguished among the contingencies besetting and abetting reform, LaFarge then circled back to the ethics of the question. The twist now came in his desire to fortify conscience with an unequivocal norm, to give a potentially disruptive condemnation of racism a backup in official teaching. This was the impetus that the aborted *Humanae Generis Unitas* was supposed to have supplied:

Even in the border cities, the existence of a separate high school can only be regarded as a temporary expedient: it cannot be accepted as a permanent arrangement.

It is for this reason, and for the whole matter of meeting squarely the issues both of Communism and Racism, that I hold we should clearly register in every part of the Assistancy our unqualified rejection of the principle of compulsory segregation as a permanent, untouchable means for adjusting the relations between the races: such rejections being understood as quite abstracting from the question as to how far segregatory practices may be tolerated for the time being according to certain circumstances and places, but only as exceptional, temporary measures, which our students and our people—and Ours themselves—should be sedulously educated and cleansed away from.

If the correct *principle* were once stated, and a break made in *principle* from the traditional racialist absolute that segregation is scared for fear of intermarriage, etc., all other problems could be worked out in [a] normal, prudent and rational manner. [33]

Maher welcomed LaFarge's comments. A follow-up came from LaFarge at the end of June. He responded with tact and sober imaginativeness:

I am glad to know that you found anything of practical value in my remarks on the interracial situation. . . . You will observe the way in which I phrase the matter with regard to the Negro high schools in the border cities. I do not want to concede too much in this respect. With sufficient courage and determination something can be done interracially even on a high school level in certain places and instances. But, as I said, it is not just the capital issue in those locations. [34]

LaFarge's exposition of the case for integration demonstrated his capacity for holding several factors in mind at once—social and political as well as moral—without losing the central thread of the argument. For LaFarge this was the ethical imperative of acting against racism. But LaFarge was an exceptional man. His field of vision was very broad, and his ability to move from one level to another without resorting to platitudes about balance and due proportion was rare. It was unclear what lessons might be drawn from his example about the institutional workings of social ministry. The incidents at St. Louis University represented a specific case of indeterminacy of doctrine and creativity of action. The events raised questions about the gaps between principle and practice, about the tradeoffs between zeal and prudence, and about the connections between social order and reform on the outside and the maintenance of control inside the Society of Jesus. By the standards of an official doctrine that claimed to be comprehensive, they showed how chancy and confused the links between ethics and politics could be. [35]

VI

The margin of doctrinal uncertainty regarding racism not only created high drama and institutional anxiety. It also triggered a traditional Jesuit bias toward action. Doctrinal ambiguity did not mean decisional paralysis. The absence of explicit moral guidelines highlighted the need for behavior informed by diffuse ethical concern. Strength of character was crucial in the absence of clear principles. But prudence and corporate unity were also powerful values in the society. In St. Louis individual conscience was pitted against organizational authority. These opposing forces caused the Jesuits in St. Louis to split things down the middle. Racial integration was achieved, but dissidents who advocated reform at the cost of hierarchical solidarity were punished. Idealism was not suppressed, but individual courage was not rewarded. Conscience had personal costs.

Among Jesuits conflicts between adherence to conscience and obedience to the organization could ultimately be settled in favor of the latter. But educated opinion was not to be routinely flouted. Persuasion was preferable to coercion. The paradox of esteem for and distrust of individual conscience was symptomatic of a profound ambivalence in the Society of Jesus. Recourse to the definition of truth by hierarchical authority was a sore point for an organization that had come to specialize in education and that needed intellectual credibility.

In the relatively new and dogmatically ancillary area covered by the social question, active concern for the underprivileged had counted for more than doctrinal correctness or sociological sophistication. Anticommunism was taken for granted, and this was often as far as an interest in ideas went. A spirit of pragmatic charity directed the schools of social work; theoretical puzzles were finessed. In addition to encouraging the provision of needed services, the priority given to good works had the advantage of avoiding ideological confrontation with reactionaries in the church. The priority was to get on with helping the needy. There were few stimuli for an intellectual approach to social ministry.

In the aftermath of the events in St. Louis, however, the limitations of this low-profile, no-waves approach began to emerge. Charitable pragmatism lacking in intellectual stature depended on an ethical concern and for some a sacrificial zeal that could crystallize into mindless righteousness. Circumspection kept the peace at the cost of intellectual mediocrity, but anti-intellectualism could also turn dissent into fanaticism. A manly pragmatism that eschewed ideas was not as practical as it seemed. Courage that came down on the side of virtue in some situations could prove an embarrassment in others. Coping with social complexity and change required intellectual and professional competence as well as moral commitment and diplomatic skills.

Social ministry might be especially vulnerable to seizures of zealotry. In place of the firm, austere, and readily understandable "principles" of moral theology that imparted virtue through the application of "right reason," it dealt in hypotheses and experiments. One option besides the Pyrrhic one of imposing theological purity in social ministry suggested itself. If the social *magisterium* provided few guideposts for individual conscience, education in the secular sciences might at least provide competence.

In 1934 Father Ledochowski had issued an *instructio* to stimulate "special studies."[36] Selected Jesuits were to be encouraged to undertake graduate work at non-Catholic universities in nonreligious subjects, including the social sciences. Upon completing their doctorates they were to return to Jesuit schools to teach and conduct research. The early results were modest. The normal course of training was already so lengthy that Jesuit students started late in secular universities, and wartime exigencies reduced the number available for academic specialization. The low point was reached in 1943–44, when seventy-six Jesuits—less than 2 percent of the total manpower in the American assistancy—were enrolled as graduate students. Of these most were in traditional fields—philosophy, literature, history—in Catholic universities.[37]

Thus, just as Jesuits were trying to restart their efforts in social ministry, the society found itself shorthanded. Zacheus Maher gave a sympathetic hearing and some backing to LaFarge's progressive views. But his fixation was control, and he was disquieted by the slackening that might ensue from exposing younger Jesuits to secular learning outside the confines of the seminary. For Maher, shaping their ethical earnestness through professional education came second to correcting what he saw as the casualness of younger cohorts of Jesuits in manners and possibly morals.

Early in 1943 Maher detected an incipient generational rebellion. He wrote to Daniel Lord in connection with an article that Lord was drafting about methods for preparing retreats for Jesuits. At the time that he offered these observations to Lord, whose own manner occasionally skirted the irreverent, Maher was compiling the list of admonitions designed to regulate the lives of Jesuits throughout the American assistancy:

> Your long experience and your authority will go far to impress this [the need to stay within the framework of the Spiritual Exercises] on our young men. There is a growing tendency among some of our young priests that one must be a smart-aleck in story and conduct, or must speak after the manner of Walter Winchell to make a hit, never realizing that just by acting thus they lower themselves in the eyes of the very audience they seek to win. Many talk too much about sex, and too plainly.[38]

Soon after the West Baden assembly, committee chairmen of the reconstituted ISO met in Chicago to sort through ways of implementing the Indiana program. Complaints vented at the Chicago sessions by older Jesuits, the men charged with leading the movement in social ministry, hinted not just at generational differences, which might be handled as part of the normal cycle of maturation, but at a possible historical transformation, an intimation that the society might be approaching a watershed. As happened in St. Louis, but with a less spectacular denouement, discussion of social policy turned to attacks against the ways of the society itself. "I must confess," Maher wrote to Lord:

> that I was greatly disturbed and saddened at the meeting to hear the strictures passed on the Society and her method of training by men of mature judgment and so prominent in their respective positions; almost, forsooth, as if whatever good there may be in any of us is there

in spite of rather than because of our formation, spiritual and intellectual, in the Society.[39]

In the absence of clear directives about the course of ISO, Lord had designed the West Baden assembly as a brainstorming marathon, with an unfettered exchange of opinions on the spectrum of social issues. He covered insecurity about substance with ebullience and the production of vibrant newsletters. Many Jesuits appreciated the participatory exercise. But some expected to receive clear marching orders, and dismay crept in with the realization that whatever certainty and practical utility the *magisterium* was supposed to provide tended to evaporate under the give-and-take of discussion. None of this impelled consensus about the future of the ISO. Strong leadership was the solution that Maher proposed for both procedural democracy and whatever objective ambiguity might afflict the *magisterium* itself:

> They (the chairmen of the various ISO committees) must be under the unified direction and stimulation of your good self. I appreciate your attitude toward authority; yet the exercise of authority is essential to the existence, let alone the well-being, of any organization. Some dread the very concept of authority as if it necessarily implied dictatorship, which it does not. You will find the men looking to you for guidance and inspiration.[40]

Perhaps because Lord was on edge about the shapelessness of ISO, Maher's admonition struck a nerve. Lord had a facility for galvanizing large numbers of people in short bursts, and he had a pastoral touch. But he knew he could not lead the ISO forcefully without ideas. Ideas in social ministry were in short supply, and so was competence.

Stung into defense of his troops, Lord responded with a concreteness that contrasted with Maher's *obiter dicta*. He understood that his colleagues' grumblings could not be blamed on immaturity and rebelliousness. Maher had treated authority and obedience as abstract principles. But what absolutes were there to follow in social ministry? The fault was with the insufficiency of training and experience in the field:

> I personally felt during a large part of that discussion that we of the older group are quite out of touch with what is being done for the Scholastics at the present time. . . . The older men remember back to the days when we got the splendid fundamental training of the Society and were then expected to do almost anything. They still think of their own experiences. The men around that table had had very happy experiences in the sense that they were quite able to meet the Society's demands upon them out of their fundamental training. Yet many of

them had regretted that they lack the specialized training which would have fitted them for what they regard as higher efficiency.[41]

There had been no special studies for these Jesuits. The gap between what was expected of them and the resources at their disposal heightened their anxiety. They were amateurs being asked to ready themselves as professionals, and bravery and improvisation were no match for complexity. Their predicament was the same as Lord's, and he sympathized:

> It has been my policy in dealing with Jesuits to encourage as much as humanly possible every frankness on their part. The type of man who comes to a meeting of that sort is a Jesuit deeply in love with the Society and his own life, but he is also a man who is well aware of his own limitations and who tries to differentiate between his own culpable lacks and the things he feels he might have gotten with better direction. . . .
>
> I am having a great deal of difficulty in getting the men to write, even to contribute small squibs or book reports. The universal answer is that the secretarial work involved, the mere task of typing, is so heavy and time-consuming that the average professor never gets around to it. . . . They cannot turn out the type of work that the Society expects. Father [Wilfrid] Parsons at the meeting lamented the fact that he had no secretary at all and someone laughingly recalled the fact that [Francisco] Suarez [Spanish Jesuit theologian, 1548–1617] had seven. . . .
>
> You are kind to re-express your desire for unified direction. I shall do everything possible to see that the direction is given, but I want the men to know always that their wishes and their initiatives are most important to me in whatever plans we make.[42]

The Jesuits who would normally lead the way, those in their forties and fifties, were almost all teachers, now willing to stretch their range toward social issues. But they could not deduce practical solutions to American social problems from a Eurocentric *magisterium*. They were expected to generate useful policy recommendations without calling into question the received wisdom of Catholic social thought. The men sensed that they were out of their depth. Some began to suspect that the terms of the undertaking itself might be flawed.

Although it was scarcely visible at the time, the stage was being set for tension and challenge to authority among Jesuits. The zeal of many of the younger men would be tempered with age. What was novel was the self-doubt of the older cohorts, which could not be dismissed as a crisis of the life cycle. It betokened instead a historical lapse. The course of training showed signs of having failed the generation of Jesuits whose role it was to mediate between the oldest and youngest of them. Toward the end of the war, some of them were beginning to feel out-of-date. They had been given firm answers to old questions.

The integration of St. Louis University represented a spectacular change. It was also part of a larger, less conspicuous movement. A few Jesuits had begun tentatively to move beyond the kinds of issues that were of concern to the ethnic ghettos in which they flourished. Reformers found themselves not only out in front of their constituents but also ahead of their own institution and its ideology as codified in doctrine. The intellectual synthesis and organizational unity enforced by antimodernism were starting to fail.

John LaFarge assessed the situation for Zacheus Maher, who had sought his advice after a copy of yet another fiery message addressed by Heithaus to Joseph Zuercher, the Missouri provincial, had been received. LaFarge commented in the approved manner on the need to respect authority. Even so, his emphasis was on tact rather than strict obedience:

> The tone of Fr. Heithaus' letter is indefensible. He says at great length
> things that could have been briefly put, he indulges in taunts and
> irony that are entirely out of place in writing to anyone, least of all to
> Fr. Zuercher, to whom at least he might have extended the courtesy of
> assuming that Fr. Zuercher was just as unwilling to condone injustice
> as he (Fr. Hh.) was.[43]

LaFarge broached two difficulties that gave the challenge to authority, significant as it was for the domestic traditions of the Society of Jesus, greater importance than a simple case of in-house politics. One was the implacability of ethical concern, with or without dogmatic backing. The other was the need for competence, for complementing prudence with expertise. Each of these was a two-edged sword. The enthusiasm of the novitiate helped drive Jesuits through the long formalities of training; it could also burst forth in impatience with institutional prevarication. Education lent polish and imparted skill; it also expanded the critical facilities.

> While badly and improperly put, however, many things Fr. Hh. says
> are true. . . . Even though Fr. Hh. be silenced, others will say what
> he is saying, and continue to say it, despite all attempts at repres-
> sion. . . .
>   Incidentally, with regard to men like Hh. and others, of one idea or
> another, it seems to me so many of our clergy, in general, lack a clear
> idea of methods of social reform. There is a recognized way of going
> about these matters: a series of steps to be taken, of means to be used.

They, and obviously others, would be spared many a headache if these methods were followed.[44]

There was a joint nebulousness and intractability about trying to reconcile incompatible objectives that drove even the imaginative LaFarge to banalities about the need for "balance and proportion." Right after the West Baden meeting, he reflected on the role of younger Jesuits and, by implication, on the coming turmoil in the society:

> A considerable amount of rather [careful] thought will have to be given by higher and local Superiors to the whole question of the Scholastics' participation in this work. This participation is invaluable as a preparation for the future and as a dynamic means of realizing the whole matter. On the other hand, there is the question of balance and proportion. Discouragement and hasty regulations would do very great harm and, on the other hand, [a] certain prudence has to be observed. I think whatever policy is adopted in that matter by Superiors should be something that has been carefully thought out and rather maturely deliberated.[45]

Efforts to push forward in social ministry raised unforeseen difficulties. On the one hand, social issues proved amenable to experimentation and even courageous action. This made for progress. The breakthrough against segregation was the prime example. On the other hand, such actions raised questions, still barely audible, about what was changeable and what was not in Catholicism. The ideal of a comprehensive social *magisterium* was coming perilously close to the status of a myth.

Discussions of political and social controversies spilled over into challenges to authority. The hierarchical style of the society did not preclude discussion altogether. But the exchange of opinions and information—embodied in the system of consultors, for example, and in the periodic correspondence required of administrators—had the function of binding the community of Jesuits together at least as much as it did of winnowing the false from the true. Flexibility, adaptability, pragmatism were all permissible in social ministry. But pluralism as a method and a principle was as yet a murky and uncertain tendency. It lacked the legitimacy of tradition.

VII

The organizational design for the Institute of Social Order that emerged from West Baden was cumbersome. On paper it encompassed nearly two dozen working groups. There were "content" committees concerned with substantive issues such as labor, international relations, and the like, and there were the "channeling" committees charged with facilitating implementation and with disseminating precepts that were supposed to flow from the content committees. The organizational chart of the ISO was taking on the gravity of a Teutonic guidebook to the Vatican, cataloguing the real and the not-so-real with impartial thoroughness.

The fatuity of the arrangement was not immediately evident. The elaborate categories might eventually shake down into a more efficient plan. The West Baden meeting itself was judged a positive step. Many of those who were skeptical about the project and the abilities of the organizer of the assembly were caught up in the initial enthusiasm. LaFarge himself reverberated to the energy generated by Lord:

> In every respect the meeting seemed to be a most marvelous success.
> The enthusiasm and the extraordinary work of organization shown by
> Father Lord was universally acclaimed and vastly surpassed all expectations. It was a splendid affair and was both congenial and deeply spiritual.[46]

LaFarge was not just engaging in the habitual gentilities. In patrimonial systems, principles were enacted through personal stratagems. He was capable of treating institutional formulas with aristocratic nonchalance. He was convinced that neither formal authority nor fixed doctrine would move Jesuits to effective social action. This pastoral intuition led LaFarge to stress ideas and moral indignation, shaped through experience, over received principles and orders from above.

The division of power between the multifarious commissions of ISO and the commanding role that LaFarge, still holding up Action Populaire as a model, wanted for his team at *America* had not been specified. Whatever its format, LaFarge was pleased to observe, ISO served to rally the troops. The complex structure may have had a theoretical completeness, yet there were nowhere near enough Jesuits to make it more than a letterhead venture. This was a bothersome inefficiency. But it was not a serious threat to what LaFarge hoped would be the manageable and intellectually decisive role of *America*.

LaFarge returned to the theme that ran through his thinking on race relations and Action Populaire alike: the priority of combining ideas with moral urgency. Organizational contrivances were merely means to ends, to be devised to suit conditions:

> A tremendous motive force is needed. Very soon all the enthusiasm
> will be dissipated, and what I am particularly afraid of is that uncertain
> reaction which comes from the feeling that something which was
> started with great enthusiasm has been allowed to lapse. One never can

get it again. It is always a warmed-over dish if we attempt to recapture it. . . . It cannot be kept up unless there is somebody taking up and pushing the thing all the time.

I cannot see this done just by any mere organization. A certain amount of personality must go into it. Father Lord has shown this personality. It brought him out in a somewhat new light, a more serious light, if one might say so.[47]

LaFarge knew that the reservoir of the social *magisterium* was low. In order to maintain an ethical drive behind the venerable personalism, guidelines were needed. The corporatist principles that had developed over the early decades of the century were too vague or foreign to be binding. LaFarge was willing to forsake the XO platform that Jesuits had cobbled together in the thirties and to adopt the social program set out more recently by the National Catholic Welfare Conference. The freedom of action of the society remained intact either way. "You may say," LaFarge wrote to Maher,

> [we] Jesuits should have "something distinctive," not just be tagging after the U.S. Bishops. Granted, but that "something distinctive" can be in our *interpretation* and *application* of the program. It is couched in fairly general terms. I can readily give, offhand, a dozen instances in which wide variations of interpretation are possible. So there is plenty of room for what is a Jesuit policy, as compared to theirs, if such be desired.[48]

LaFarge did not specify what these interpretations might be. Instead he attempted to sketch in a framework that would bind together the multiple sources and motives of social action. He envisioned a synthesis between theory, understood as concepts derived from natural law, and commitment, understood as a transcendental passion to fight injustice. So ideas and idealism were joined. Added to these would be an empiricism—a professional, scientific respect for social facts:

> The particularly Jesuit contribution to social-order thought consists in the *balance* that the Society traditionally has taught and practiced between three fundamental elements in the whole picture.
>
> a) our precision as to the *natural order*, e.g., of justice, as opposed to a false supernaturalism, and a cowardly opportunism;
>
> b) the vigor, on the other hand, of our *supernatural motivation*, drawn from the Kingdom of Christ; and
>
> c) our attention to *concrete reality*, to genuine knowledge, as seen in Jesuit insistence upon "exact study" and thorough formation, in other than social fields.[49]

This statement was a grand rationale rather than a concrete platform for the social involvement of the Society of Jesus in the United States. It represented an advance over the belief that a comprehensive social vision was already in place, waiting to be put into practice. The world according to LaFarge could be approached at three presumably ascending levels —facts, ideas, and ideals. This was a slightly more analytical rendition of his habit of dealing with social activism by way of tactics, strategy, and ethics.

The scheme was content-free, a property that reflected LaFarge's desire to provide a general method without becoming entangled in substantive issues. It also left out practical politics. The model was another stately ship, motionless in the water as if in a bottle on a shelf. It was organizationally disembodied, and it was silent about questions of authority. Institutionally, for the moment, LaFarge played deaf and dumb.

Flexibility with regard to dogma may have facilitated progress of sorts, but it was also too vaporous to constitute a point of view that might be developed through cumulative debate, and in any case the institutional formulas for sorting out and consolidating new ideas continued to be elusive. Although LaFarge could not say as much, the difficulty was not just that Catholic social principles were so arcane or broad that conscience was frustrated in seeking guidance. The *magisterium* did not favor the institutional autonomy of units within the church that might be necessary to thrash out practical ideas. Both pluralism and intellectual "progress" were of dubious value in balance with the reaffirmation of unity and the wisdom of the ages. The emphasis on corporate solidarity blocked original thought. This was why the Jesuits sometimes had to stake out a position in defiance of organizational authority.

LaFarge circled the dual problem without explicating it. It was literally and symbolically unthinkable. The lack of ideas was not only a function of a fogginess inherent to lofty thoughts. The absence of intellectual creativity could also be caused by the institutional hierarchy itself. There was an unacknowledged no-man's land between the ideal of synthesis and the fear of doctrinal chaos.

LaFarge refrained from raising the organizational cul-de-sac to a question of principle itself. He confined his reflections to the existing array of individual and institutional actors. He had no faith in the capacity of ISO to forge a social vision. Daniel Lord generated enthusiasm, but in the Society of Jesus social programs were not hammered out, like political platforms, in conventions. On the other hand, the Jesuit schools did not offer a hospitable intellectual or institutional base for the new undertaking. LaFarge fell back on the notion that the staff of *America* could provide the ideas that ISO would put into practice:

It seems to me that an error will be committed if the ISO will set up a high policy-forming board which will determine attitudes of Jesuit social policy on the various issues as they appear day by day, such as the legislative projects, bills in Congress, the complex international peace and reconstruction issues, etc. This work, it seems to me, should be the work of the staff of *America*, who should be chosen for their ability to work on just that sort of thing. . . .

The general staff of the ISO would seem to me to determine things of a practical character, within the specified scope of coordinating Jesuit activities, providing service of [sic] those engaged in them, devising methods of popularizing and applying our social policies, etc. But the wider and more complex issues should be the care of the *America* staff.[50]

This was a streamlined staff model. *America* assumes the work of the content committees, which suffered from a surfeit of participation. LaFarge counted on expertise to give shape to the goodwill of Jesuits in the field.

Even with this slimming down of intellectual responsibilities, however, the organizational strategy depended on human resources that were difficult to muster either in St. Louis or New York. Institutional entanglements and intellectual confusion formed a vicious circle. Tradition could not simply be fine-tuned or reformatted. LaFarge continued to be listened to respectfully. But he was growing old, and his plans were filed away and forgotten.

Lord kept the movement, as he called it, busy through the end of the war. Annual conventions were held. He hoped that the project would catch on as the Jesuits had built colleges and universities in the United States, through grit and good fortune:

We realized that this was a period when we could start universities on a nationwide scale, but it was a moment that might pass and never come again. So, though we had neither money nor resources, though we were inexperienced in the university forms, we built and annexed and ventured into new fields. We have a long way to go, and you young priests will have to push forward your work. But we had to act fast, courageously, and sometimes apparently against sound judgment and prudence.[51]

VIII

Efforts to reignite the Institute of Social Order in the early forties were full of promise, frustration, and surprises. The promise came from the hope that ideas and ethical impulses could be mobilized effectively behind social ministry. The frustration arose from the unwieldiness inherent to the ambition of the enterprise and from the preexisting organizational commitments of the Society of Jesus itself. The materials at hand, in manpower and ideas, might be inadequate to the task.

The surprises—notably, the breakaway from racial segregation in advance of what was not happening in other, presumably more modern institutions— were both exhilarating and alarming. It was hard to draw lessons for the future from such experiences. The Society of Jesus had turned the corner toward integration, but the episode's implications for strategy in social ministry were unclear. The conflict that resulted simultaneously in desegregation and the exiling of Claude Heithaus and George Dunne suggested the dangers as well as the promise of coming out from under the habits of tribal unity. Jesuits had opened up new territory, but they weren't sure where they stood or where they were going. [52]

Some Jesuits like John LaFarge and Daniel Lord worked at the tortuous reconciliation of divergent goals. Others ignored the problem as insoluble and plugged along. At one level the difficulty was the practical one of gaining competence and a degree of mastery over the new areas of social action. At another, the task was to provide a rationale for what remained to be accomplished in light of what had already been achieved. This required situating social ministry within the intellectual legacy and the institutional infrastructure of the society.

By the end of the war Jesuits had started to recognize that the search for overarching political and social formulas, common to both the European and the North American contexts, was chimerical. The dream of universalism was itself a piece of parochialism, a fantasy of cultural imperialism. It was a leftover of the ultramontane mentality. Nevertheless, if social ministry was to gain the prestige that education enjoyed among Jesuits, such activities had to confront organizational and intellectual challenges. Four related questions gained in urgency. What was the corporate feasibility, the organizational effectiveness, of social ministry relative to other activities— mainly educational—of the society? What was the relevance of the social programs of the Society of Jesus as American Catholics stood on the verge of economic and cultural assimilation? What might be the repercussions of promoting a social agenda *ad extra*, on the outside, for the structure of authority of the Society of Jesus itself? Finally, how were all these dimensions of social ministry—the intellectual, the activist, the organizational—to be joined within an ethical framework that the society could call its own and defend as integral to Catholic tradition?

PART
TWO

Amor non tenet ordinem.

—Saint Columbanus

As World War II drew to a close Jesuits began to consider the course their work would take in peacetime. How was the Society of Jesus to adapt to a United States that had changed on a colossal scale, while retaining its leadership in the Catholic subculture? In 1939 the gross national product had been $90 billion; by 1945 it was twice that size. Between 1940 and 1944 the nation's output of manufactured goods trebled. The divorce rate that in 1940 stood at sixteen out of every one hundred couples climbed to twenty-seven per hundred by 1944.[1] The country had overcome economic depression and was about to emerge victorious over its foreign adversaries. Wartime mobilization brought in its train a democratization of expectations and lifestyles, an expansion of numbers pressing after opportunities, that the Jesuits knew they had to prepare for. Speculation focused on the future of their schools.

In 1943, while still an unknown instructor of philosophy, more than a decade before he became editor of *America*, Thurston Davis published a brief article entitled "Blueprint for a College." The plan that Davis set forth in the pages of the *Jesuit Educational Quarterly* was drawn up along the lines of a seminary. In spite of the anticipated flood of veterans, enrollment at the model school would not exceed one hundred. The student body would be exclusively male. The faculty would be all Jesuit, "seven priests and two scholastics." It was to be an elite liberal arts college in which "intensity would be the keynote." The aim of the college was

> to prepare young men, by thorough grounding in the classics, philosophy, history, science, and religion, for careers in the following fields: journalism and creative writing, the theater, the radio, social work and labor-union leadership, politics, school and university teaching . . . the "cultural" professions. . . . The ideal of "lay vocations" will be instilled into the students. . . . The fathers of the faculty will maintain contact with graduates through a carefully organized alumni society. After ten years there will thus have been created a small group of active Catholic laymen, placed strategically in the more vital centers of American life within a given area, who by reason of their training and by more or less constant contacts with their Alma Mater will form a very potent instrument of intelligent Catholic action.[2]

Davis's college was very nearly a *collège* in the European sense, what Jesuits in the United States called a preparatory school, extended through the years of undergraduate education. The broader ambitions of the plan rested on European premises about the role of religion in public affairs. The intellectual rationale of the school was continental and classical; over the long haul the institution was also supposed to be eminently practical in the American context.[3]

205

Davis's view of "the cultural professions" took the American Catholic experience selectively into account. The category was not limited to the intelligentsia, still a minuscule part of the community. Yet it was not broad enough to encompass business "statesmen," also a small portion of the subculture. Both the academic and entrepreneurial sectors would grow in the postwar years, and in different ways their interests would diverge from the mixture of traditional learning and service that Davis posited as the basis of Jesuit schooling. His conception of educational excellence and clerical influence was better suited to poor, overwhelmingly Catholic countries—Ireland, Spain, or parts of Latin America—and to the countries of Western Europe where Catholic trade unions and political parties were functioning, than to the postwar United States.

Davis stressed education in the liberal arts, the staple of Jesuit schooling, as a preparation "for life and making a living." He also stressed the long-term practicality of his ideal campus for Jesuits who, instead of catering to the crude pragmatism of "vocationalism," as they were called on to do under wartime conditions, could return to teaching what they knew best: literature, classics, philosophy, and religion. Over the years, he believed, this wide coverage would have a greater payoff than would narrow specialization.

Davis invoked another Jesuit heritage, emphasizing the need to train leaders and gain influence in a world seen as increasingly threatening. Scholarship for its own sake or the cultivation of knowledge and taste as mere refinement—either one was in vain. Davis issued a call to arms.

> The coming generation of Catholics faces a showdown, and we Jesuits should attempt to fit them for the battle of the next half-century. It will be a half-century dominated by a monster secular press, class struggle, godless universities, and tremendous technical achievements in many of the means used to form public opinion. These are but a few of the fronts on which battle will be joined, and it will be a battle for the culture and the soul of America. It will be won or lost in the newspaper, the theater, on the radio, in the labor union, the city hall, and the classroom. The Church needs leaders in these storm-centers of American life, leaders in the cultural professions. We are assuming here that intensive liberal training in a small Jesuit college, where the full impact of a zealous Jesuit faculty can be brought to bear on the intellectual and religious formation of each student, will still produce such leaders.[4]

The goal was to multiply among lay cadres the mixture of conviction and versatility, the air of adventure for a cause, that lent grandeur to the Jesuit legend. Davis wanted to form articulate, humanistic conservatives who would set forth to shape public opinion. Education increased the chances of mobility for the capable and the talented, but immediate gain was not the primary objective. Jesuit schools were to specialize in the values of the rounded life instead of in training for myopic and materialistic pursuits. In Davis's perspective the cultural professions dealt in ideas, ethics, service, and, ultimately, power. The goal of the Society of Jesus should be to shape the shapers of opinion.

Although the rhetoric and vestiges of the spirit of his vision turned up in parts of the society's educational system during the following decades, Davis's "blueprint for a college" did not become a reality.[5] The idea of establishing a traditional alternative to what he later called the "educational Jacobinism" of mass society, of carving out a niche specializing in the classical humanities, was not implausible.[6] The school he envisioned was of manageable size. But whether such an institution could be a vehicle of cultural and political influence was doubtful. The problem was one of extrapolation from the confined setting of a semimonastic world to the wider environment. The aim of shaping the direction and the policies of the larger society in the United States, never far from illusory, grew further out of reach in the wake of World War II. The flow of influence went the other way around, conditioning the options of the Society of Jesus.

The strategy Davis laid out presupposed historical conditions that were fleeting in Europe and that never existed in the United States. The outcome of World War II eliminated or called into question old political combinations. The defeat of fascism meant the obsolescence of outright authoritarianism in industrial countries. The alliances that the church had struck with the dictatorships in Portugal and Spain lingered and for a time, with the Cold War, these links would grow even stronger. However, the monopolistically Catholic, hierarchial state had begun to lose its luster as the standard against which political arrangements were to be judged. In Italy the church settled into an electorally successful coalition with the Christian Democrats. In the Netherlands, Belgium, and West Germany political institutions of Catholic origin flourished.[7] In the United States, which lacked a tradition of confessional parties, no such mode of influence was possible.

The scheme—essentially a clone of European political Catholicism—advanced by Davis remained the norm for American Jesuits who thought about such matters as late as the 1940s, and into the early fifties. To be sure, Jesuit educators modified the classical prescription to suit curricular needs, and while they gave lip service to the goal of training leaders it was hard to take seriously the objective of expanding Catholic influence if by that was meant the conversion of large segments of the American system to Catholic values. This was so much oratorical embellishment. The European ideal was legitimate but inoperative; the American methods worked but they lacked respectability. The European norm offered reasonable educational standards. It was as a political model that it proved infeasible. The resemblance of the idealized *collège* to a seminary isolated in the countryside evoked not only fantasies of the mastery and influence associated with the glory days of ecclesiastical power in predominantly Catholic settings but also images of an arcadian innocence untouched by the industrial world it sought to control. As a protective mechanism against the evils of modernism, it had a certain consistency. But as a device for spreading Catholic influence beyond the quarters of the subculture, it was naive.[8]

Whatever his failings as an architect of political power, Davis sensed the need for a conceptual framework that might give coherence to the sprawl of liberal arts and professional schools run by Jesuits in the United States. The faculties gathered under the Jesuit system performed a variety of functions that in reality did not have much internal consistency. The professional schools were eminently useful. They provided instructional services to a Catholic clientele in search of upward mobility. But they lacked the cachet of liberal education. Such undertakings as the labor schools and the schools of social work did not have the intellectual stature of the curriculum, requiring classical Latin and Greek, leading to the bachelor of arts degree. Besides, they were not for elites and "leaders of men" who might be taken as seriously for their culture as for their financial success or practical abilities. The difficulty was not only a matter of snobbery or style; the professional schools were not seedbeds of ideas.

The GI Bill promoted an upsurge in enrollment that threatened to overwhelm the traditional pedagogy of the Jesuits, making the liberal arts colleges and their professional school appendages more like one another. The infusion of funding proved irresistible. As one Jesuit recalled:

> Many schools, I think, had scraped along through the Depression and it was touch-and-go if they could make it. But with the war, the schools found the government would *pay* to bring men in to be trained; the Navy V-12 program was one [such program]. In at least one case, the SJs moved out of their residence to fit in yet more students. Small schools became big ones. Then as the men came back from the war, the G.I. Bill let them get educated at government cost.[9]

The educational theory of the Jesuits had not caught up with the expansion in numbers. *Faute de mieux*, the model proposed by Davis survived as a norm according to which Jesuit schools were granted status or relegated to the less than ideal. Jesuit institutions were at a tipping point as the United States entered the postwar years. On the one hand, there was a realistic expectation that Catholics were approaching a postimmigrant stage. Soon they could make their political presence felt with increasing force. On the other, it was doubtful that Catholics would bring a distinctive cultural and intellectual message, one that could speak to the larger society without capitulating to it, on their way to assimilation.

Besides the institutional obstacles against transplanting Catholicism with a European cultural and social tenor in the United States, economic factors undercut the assumptions on which Davis projected his hopes for a renaissance of Jesuit education and influence. The boom of the postwar years in Western Europe and the United States undermined a social doctrine that had been elaborated in a context of scarcity. In the United States the assimilation of the Catholic subculture accelerated with prosperity. The austere message of the social encyclicals, already hidden under a ponderous and alien vocabulary, was all but forgotten.[10]

As the postwar era dawned, then, Jesuits in the United States faced two new challenges. The adaptation of European Catholicism was at an institutional impasse. Literal importation depended either on a monopoly of political power, as in Spain, or on a Catholic duplication of business, labor, and party organizations of the sort that existed in the Netherlands. Neither of these circumstances obtained or was going to develop in the United States. The absence of an organizational alternative to the ideal of religious monopoly still on the books in Rome fixed American Catholicism in a second-tier footing in the eyes of European conservatives, despite its economic and demographic power. In the United States it confirmed the air of fantasy surrounding Catholic social and political teaching. Antimodernism was more of an irrelevance in the American context than an anomaly that might spur change. It was this institutional mold that John Courtney Murray broke. After Murray, Jesuits ceased to be prisoners of the self-induced fiction that political pluralism inhibited the realization of Catholic values.

The second challenge was moral rather than explicitly political. Jesuits in social ministry had striven to help the Catholic working class cope with the hardships of American capitalism. Fuzzy as it was, the *magisterium* was at least minimally compatible with industrialization. Its agrarian variant aside, Catholic social teaching sought to mediate, not evade, the conflicts and rigors of the process. But prosperity seemed only to marginalize the social *magisterium*. Moreover, the consumerism of successful industrialization threatened to erode the temperateness and everyday asceticism on which Catholicism thrived. The good life, the American dream, was coming true. It was particularly insidious in respect of the sexual and familial mores of the Irish Catholicism that dominated the church in the United States. Even if the institutional vehicles of Catholic influence were miraculously to take root in American soil, the social bases of the values of traditional Catholicism were receding. Just as Catholics were coming to political maturity and as Jesuits were about to abandon illusions about the inferiority of pluralism, the structural underpinnings of virtuous toughness were slipping out from under them, like the shifting of tectonic plates.[11]

The vastness of these developments made them difficult to comprehend. Their workings were obscure even when the tensions they embodied burst forth in the sixties.[12] It was natural to assume that Jesuits would be equal to the task of reconciling the contending forces and crosscurrents of the postwar years as they had been reasonably successful in shepherding Catholics toward the far side of the immigrant enclaves. They were expected to remain steadfast but also were expected to stay in touch with intellectual and cultural advances.

In 1940 Pius XII sent the first of several messages urging an energetic yet controlled adaptation of the Society of Jesus to novel challenges. Technology could be absorbed, it was supposed, without transforming the institutional or doctrinal core of Catholicism. Jesuits would continue to be at the cutting edge of tradition:

> The new times in which we live demand, it is true, even in spiritual
> lines new undertakings, works and safeguards, by which suitable provi-
> sion may be made for the changed and increasing needs of this our
> age. In keeping with your ardent zeal do not neglect these means and
> strive to bring it about that whatever this adult age may introduce may
> contribute in fuller and fitter measure to strengthening at home and
> extending abroad the Reign of Jesus Christ. Yet let your Institute, so
> dear alike to Us and to you, be ever the same; the spirit whence it de-
> rives its nutriment, the same; the same, finally, that enthusiastic obedi-
> ence and devotion by which you hold fast, unfalteringly to this
> Apostolic See.[13]

It was not just that Catholicism would remain unaltered in its essentials. The church would exert a net influence on the world, rather than being changed by it. The Jesuits were to be vigorously, at once boldly and persuasively conservative. The holistic mentality turned syncretic, generating a hodgepodge of contradictory tendencies that eventually burst at the seams.

The papal injunction meant abjuring ideas that gained currency among members of the clerical avant-garde in France and northern Europe in the forties and fifties. It also meant a preoccupation with social order and sexuality "in a world full of nervous excitement and devoid of any discipline."[14] While there might be selective concessions to modernity in some of the externals of Catholicism, the inmost restrictions regarding authority and sexuality were to hold. The Society of Jesus was out of touch intellectually. To this was added an affective costiveness. For some Jesuits these combined deficiencies burst forth in the sixties as mindless activism and rage.

In the meantime the piling up of obligations, the constant spurring to mastery on top of renewed strictures, did not make for coherence. The strain of reconciling disparate objectives increased psychic pressures. Jesuits were kept at a distance from developments in high culture, as they had been from the beginning of the antimodernist campaign, yet they were expected somehow to respond to and influence these changes. They were also unprepared for the emergence of a popular culture that seemed increasingly permissive and expressive of a rootlessness and absence of habits of deference, on a mass scale.[15]

One turn of events, however, enabled the American Jesuits to postpone their encounter with the problems of postindustrial society. The mandate to expand the Jesuit presence, in conjunction with the tightening of internal controls and the growth of resources in manpower, coincided with a shift in population from the center to the periphery of Catholicism. Some energies that might be directed at internal scrutiny could be transferred outward. The end of the war cast the Jesuits on the international scene. The financial support that the American branch of the society gave to its brothers in Germany and other devastated parts of Europe constituted the beginning of this movement. By 1945 the American Jesuits made up not only the wealthiest but also the largest group in the order, surpassing the Spanish contingent in size.

An even broader demographic shift was underway. Toward the end of the 1950s the population of Latin America overtook the population of North America. Latin America, while predominantly Catholic, was notoriously short of priests. The internationalization of the Society of Jesus attained its zenith during the years preceding Vatican II. Missionaries spread through the Third World, with a concentration in Latin America.

In the midst of these changes the American Jesuits were busy and apparently successful. Their dynamism overflowed into expansion overseas. The surplus energy reflected some boredom and incipient frustration with their

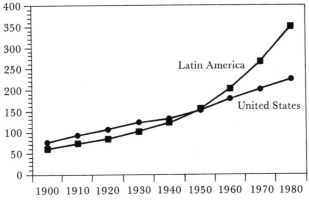

FIGURE 3. Population Growth (millions) in Latin America and the United States, 1900—80

work in the United States. The pioneering days of American Catholic education were giving way to demands for the absorption of numbers and the competition for public funding at the college and university levels. This stage of institution building presented dangers of its own. It was unclear whether Jesuit colleges and universities could compete with their secular peers. As the size of their institutions grew, the work of academic professionalization also became increasingly bureaucratic and impersonal, and there was some reluctance to persist in the management of what might be constrained to be a merely adequate enterprise. Steady application did not pay off in a corresponding control of the environment of higher education. Either the Jesuits kept on performing the same educational services, or they took the gamble of competing with their academic rivals.[16]

The foreign missions opened an alternative. They presented a new challenge in fresh surroundings. They promised not only sacrifice but a change from an environment that for some appeared to be too comfortable and secure and for others too complex and unwieldy. The institutional infrastructure of American Catholicism no longer provided quite so engrossing an outlet for Jesuit energies. Some Jesuits concluded that they could make a greater difference overseas, in less-worked-over areas.

Not all of the energies of the American branch of the Society of Jesus focused on the exterior of the church, whether domestic or in foreign countries. The impulse to evangelize and convert large numbers implied unshaken belief and a certain satisfaction with conditions on the inside. But some Jesuits began to feel that while many of the brick-and-mortar chores of American Catholicism had been nearly completed, quantitative accomplishment could not be taken as a substitute for dealing with subtler challenges. One of these was the quality of the schools themselves, particularly the colleges and universities. This was the main institutional referent of the debate over American Catholic intellectual life that culminated in the late fifties. Another sign of restlessness with the status quo was the interest that some enterprising Jesuits took in the mass media.

The debate over educational quality has significant implications. Especially since the last decades of the nineteenth century the intellectual heritage of Catholicism had been set forth as a rich treasure of fixed truths. The monotonous mediocrity and downright inferiority of some of the products of this tradition, however, gave rise to suspicions about its claims to certainty and creativity. But the issue was not wholly academic. The intellectual and moral perfectionism, the encroaching impeccability, that underlay the triumphalistic mindset left almost no room for appropriation of the tradition on the part of younger generations.

The institutional creativity of the American Jesuits reached a plateau after the war. At about the same time the intellectual legacy of Catholicism showed signs of exhaustion, even to its devotees. It was laden with the fullness and the stasis of age. Regardless of its intellectual merits and defects, the completeness imputed to the scholastic synthesis prevented those who inherited it from making it their own. The immobility of the conceptual edifice generated undercurrents of resentment against authority. The synoptic pretensions were preposterous on intellectual grounds, and they were emotionally unwise. The psychodynamics of knowledge stimulated rebellion rather than transmission across generations. At about the same time that opportunities for service and self-realization opened up outside the United States—notably, in the vast areas of Latin America with numerous Catholics and very few priests—doubts about the rationale and interior structure of the church and of the Society of Jesus began to shake the motivational ground on which Jesuits had traditionally stood.

In isolation each of these transformations and latent shifts was massive. Together, they threatened to overwhelm the Jesuits. The challenge Thurston Davis perceived was nebulous and less tractable than the adversaries that had come before.

7

Political Change

The defeat of the Axis powers was welcomed by the Society of Jesus in the United States. "The last good war" was the culminating demonstration of the patriotism of American Catholics. Jesuits served as chaplains in the armed forces. Some were decorated; one received the Medal of Honor. Their reports stirred memories of the glory days of the society, when missionaries underwent hardships with preternatural endurance.[1]

From "somewhere in China, en route to the U.S.A.," Fr. John E. Duffy, a secular priest, wrote to Fr. John Hurley, wartime superior of the Jesuit mission in the Philippines, informing him of the death of a Jesuit.

> Father Hausmann, S.J., died about January 20, 1945 on Jap P.O.W. transport of starvation, malnutrition and exposure. I have his stole and rosary and I will turn them over to Father Provincial in New York. Fathers Stuber, Zerfos, Vanderlauden, McDonald, McManus, Carberry, Hausmann and Cummings died on this trip. I alone survived among the priests and I have been a hospital patient since my arrival at Maji, January 30th. Fathers O'Brien and Scecina are believed to have survived but I am not certain. We had 17 chaplains on the transport which left December 13th. Taylor and myself alone survived and about 200 of the 1619 who started the journey still live. Two ships bombed from under us; one ship's propeller torpedoed and the fourth a funeral ship. If you have the list of those I buried in Guagua fishponds, and the names of the two Marines who carried me on the Bataan march, may I ask you to send them to me. . . . I hope you and the Jesuits have all come through safely. Understand Manila is in ruins.[2]

The letters of L. R. Hugh, a Jesuit who attained the rank of lieutenant commander with the Pacific Fleet, reflect a lighter side of the war. His description of dockside festivities in Hong Kong captures the innocent comedy of American abundance, generosity, consumerism, and flirtation that softened the grueling all-male world of combat.

> The ship turned itself inside out for the nuns and the nuns played ball like professionals—and I don't mean wartime ball-players. The Captain turned over the Admiral's suite to them. On the way to lunch I took them through the ready room. They wanted to know what a "Mae West" was. While I was explaining, one of the pilots came over and pulled the string, puncturing the CO_2 bottle and inflating the life preserver. . . .
>
> The first thing the Captain asked was: "What do the nuns need, Padre?" He phoned the doctor and got medicine. He phoned the supply officer and, among other things, gave them twelve cartons of chewing gum. That was funny. You should have seen their reaction when he asked them if they chewed gum. They just giggled; they didn't want to admit it, and they wanted gum too badly to say no. . . .
>
> I had to take a large parachute bag for them to carry home their spoils. Just before they left the Captain called Mother Superior in alone and gave her two bottles of whiskey; and like a Mother Superior, she said naught of it.[3]

The account of Father Hausmann's death was absorbed into the society's heroic past. The anecdotes of Father McHugh were touched with the coyness and bravado of an American musical, and they pointed to a future of sunny abundance.[4]

II

The position of the Catholic church in Spain appeared fairly secure despite the victory of the Allies in Europe. Franco had kept the country neutral, and Catholicism continued to be the official religion of the Spanish state.

The problem posed by the situation of Catholicism in Spain for the Society of Jesus was no longer one of religious persecution. The difficulty was symbolic and conceptual, with implications for ecclesiastical policy outside of Spain. It stemmed from the partnership between the church and a dictatorship that granted a religious monopoly to institutional Catholicism and wide influence over the educational system and the cultural media. The confessional state fulfilled the political wishes of nineteenth- and twentieth-century popes. Ceding management of the schools to the church guaranteed that Catholicism would exercise control over crucial sectors of the intellectual as well as the religious life of the country. Ecclesiastical dominance was identified with the suppression of democracy.

The question was not whether Franco and his followers had the right to impose such an arrangement on Spain; this might be dismissed as a local matter. But—so authorities and scholars in church circles contended—a matter of principle was also involved: Was the formula generalizable, and desirable, elsewhere? The triumph of the democracies put this equation in doubt. The alliance between church and state might be sustained for a while in the name of anticommunism, but this differed from justifying it as a political solution in its own right, expressing timeless ideals. The realization dawned among some Jesuits that the church might be on the wrong side of a turning point in political evolution.[5]

In the late thirties, during the Spanish Civil War, John LaFarge and his colleagues at *America* placed the American Jesuits squarely in the Nationalist camp. By the mid-forties LaFarge had begun to change his mind. This switch came about partly because the Nationalists no longer required the same degree of support, now that Franco was in power and they were fully able to protect the church, as they had during the time of open warfare with atheists, socialists, communists, and the left in general. LaFarge also cast an eye toward the future. The Spanish political system was not, he suspected, as stable as its admirers wished. In 1945 LaFarge outlined his misgivings in a letter to Zacheus Maher:

> For a very long time I have kept a most careful file of everything that I could lay hold of that could give any information about conditions in Spain and invariably, in recent times, these things point to the conclusion that the position of the Falange is anything but steady. Indeed one often wonders if Spain has ever had or ever will have a government that can be really stable. The tragedy of the Franco situation which appears to me is that hope of a stable government was actually roused in the minds of so many Spaniards only in turn to be disappointed.[6]

For many clerics at the time, government stability was the political analogue of eternal truth. It was therefore alarming to raise doubts about the life expectancy of the Spanish regime. If the government was not as enduring as it seemed to be, then its value as a paradigm of church-state relations diminished. LaFarge understood that a quandary was in the making. The idea of a settlement that involved a permanent union of Catholicism with any political regime had long been recognized by diplomatic practitioners like LaFarge as dangerous. Recognition of the danger might have taken a bit longer in coming in the case of Spain because of the triumphalist aura surrounding the conclusion of the Civil War and the longstanding association of *hispanidad* with the defense of Christendom.[7] For all this, as a long-term commitment the coalition of church and state—especially an authoritarian state in democratic Europe—was unwise. "I personally think it is a dangerous mistake," LaFarge wrote,

> to tie up . . . the Catholic cause throughout the world to the existence of the Franco regime, indeed to any given political regime. It always has a fatal reaction on the Church in the long run and I consider it a highly imprudent position for us to try to maintain that the only alternative to a one hundred per-cent endorsement of Franco is out and out Communism. That sort of simplification of the issue, in my mind, plays simply into the Communists' hands.[8]

LaFarge's objective was the age-old one of leaving the church room for maneuver. While he did not advocate militant opposition to the regime, he counseled against unconditional commitment to a possibly losing alliance. He wanted to make sure that the church could extricate itself from a short-sighted coalition. In particular, LaFarge wanted to avoid an irrational attachment, displayed by maximalists on the Spanish right, that took the Franco regime to be the living quintessence of Catholic ideology, victorious over communism and superior to democracy. Such intransigence left no opening for reform or escape. It jeopardized the credibility of the church not only among opponents of the regime but also among its more cynical supporters. The issue was taken up in the pages of *America*, and LaFarge explained his position in a follow-up letter to Maher:

> My article on Spain in this last issue was partly inspired by a careful study of the material sent to us by our own Fathers connected with the *Fomento Social*. The fundamental idea of what I have written is that the way out of the labyrinth seems to be the encouragement of the soundly, truly Catholic, progressive element in Spain.[9]

This tilting away from Francoism was matched by the cautiously favorable response that *America* gave to the worker priests in France. In light of the subsequent squashing of the worker priest movement by Pius XII, this mild thaw in the Cold War mentality proved futile. Yet an important principle was at stake behind the play of political convenience. LaFarge took what amounted to be a methodically novel approach, in Catholic circles, to a significant theoretical problem. His tack was neither purely topical nor wholly moralistic. The "careful study" of the evidence he had gathered differed from the hortatory, emotional pragmatism cultivated by many Jesuits. Nor did LaFarge deduce his way from abstract principles to the conclusion that Spanish fascism might be a poor coalition partner and a dubious and possibly repellent model for the church to emulate in other parts of the world. He detected the possibility that the system established by Franco might be a poor bet on historical grounds, unable to deliver on the promise of stability and the monopoly of power that formed the real basis of much of its appeal. While such dominion might not be a bad thing, it was risky to raise it to the level of a permanent ideal of "the Catholic cause throughout the world."

Politics was indeed the art of the possible; political formulas were relative. Timing mattered. LaFarge had an instinct, unimpeded by dogma and stimulated by strategic interest, for how contingency might confound timeless abstractions. This was an insight that he shared with his colleague John Courtney Murray, who joined the staff of *America* for a short time in 1945. It was Murray who was to use it to develop an alternative to reigning notions of what constituted political perfection in Catholicism.[10]

III

In 1953 the Vatican renegotiated a concordat that extended its influence in Spain while granting the government veto power over appointments to the Spanish episcopate.[11] This quid pro quo was typical of a decade of politically and theologically reactionary Catholicism. In 1950, the same year in which he issued *Humani Generis* warning against "errors, false opinions, and dangerous tendencies of our day," Pius XII proclaimed as binding truth the dogma of the assumption of the Virgin into heaven. In 1953 he ordered the suppression of the worker priests' movement on the grounds that it was "contaminated with the Soviet virus." In 1954 he canonized Pius X, who had set about persecuting the modernist heresy earlier in the century.[12]

Toward the end of the decade, frustrated by the persistent strength of the political left in Italy and appalled by the spread of consumer values in the country—television came to Italy in 1954—Pius XII's mood became increasingly apocalyptic. He consulted medical charlatans, and his wide-ranging allocutions rambled and were tinged with the bizarre.[13] The pope had reason to be pleased with the success of Catholic political parties and labor unions in parts of Europe. Political Catholicism reached its apex in Western Europe during the late 1950s. But even these victories were not absolute. They fell short of an ideal that preyed on the mind of the Vatican since the loss of the papal states in the nineteenth century, the onslaught of modernism, and the Communist ascendancy in Russia and Eastern Europe. This was the dream of a truth, integrating the realms of morals and politics, that defied change and transcended space. When the Society of Jesus held its thirtieth General Congregation in 1957, Pius greeted a delegation of

Jesuits with an address that put a stop to any plans they might have had about coping with modernity by reforming the ways of the order. "The Society should do everything to ensure correctness of doctrine," a Jesuit historian wrote, summarizing the pope's address:

> Fidelity in obedience was to be central to its life. . . . Humility and abnegation were part of religious discipline. . . . Jesuits should willingly carry the cross. They were thus "instruments conjoined to God." In the practice of poverty, certain specific practices should be looked to with a view to correction, for instance, holidays outside a religious house, excessive travel, too many private instruments for work. Among the things that ought to be cut back was the use of tobacco. Jesuits in giving up tobacco, among other things, would be an example to others. By all means, modern methods and modern instruments were to be used and adapted to the work of the apostolate, but we should remember the Gospels and fallen human nature. Among the substantials [immutable principles] in the Society was the monarchic form of government. The Society should, above all, be faithful to what it is; otherwise, it would not be the Society.[14]

In 1954 an essay entitled "The Problem of Pluralism in America," written by John Courtney Murray, then a theologian on the faculty of Woodstock College, appeared in the Jesuit journal *Theological Studies*. For some ten years Murray had been publishing articles on such subjects as ecumenism and the ethical limits on warfare. This was the last piece of writing about religious tolerance and political freedom that he got into print before his superiors in Rome, conforming to the wishes of the Holy See, ordered him to drop the subject.[15]

Murray's contribution began with his treatment of the American variant of the liberal tradition on its own terms. The approach signaled an assault on the papal condemnation of Americanism that had inhibited intellectual advancement among Catholics in the United States since the last days of the nineteenth century.[16] His point of departure, that the political sphere had a certain autonomy, as did the religious, was traditional although not entirely uncontroversial, dating back to the Augustinian vision of "the two cities." His real target was twofold. One was the supposition that the Spanish solution, privileging Catholicism to the exclusion of other religions, embodied a timeless ideal. Instead, he argued, the situation in Spain was an accident of history that could not be raised to the level of universal principle.

In 1953, a few months after the Vatican had signed the concordat with Spain, and as it was becoming clear that Murray's line of argument was stirring consternation in Rome, he wrote to Vincent McCormick, who had replaced Zacheus Maher as the society's American assistant. He outlined his case against extracting eternal verities from the Spanish experience:

> I have said things about Spain, rather more dissection than criticism. Done with a view to showing that the Spanish legal system reposes on conditions of fact and is not some "ideal" transcription of pure Catholic doctrine. So, the fact is that Spain is not really Catholic but hopes to become so by the strong exercise of governmental authority. . . . I should be content to say that this is one way of doing things, seeking the triumph of the *res catholica*. But is it the only way, the "ideal" way? Instead of putting one's trust in the principles of governmental authority, might one not put one's trust in the principle of freedom? Or in some combination of both principles?[17]

This went beyond a simple espousal of common sense and pragmatism. Murray was raising up pluralism as a principle in itself. It was this shift, which assigned a positive value to nontranscendental diversity, not the negation of the Spanish example, that gave Murray's argument conceptual resonance:

> I should be prepared to defend the Spanish situation (or the medieval situation, or the situation in the post-Reformation German principalities) in its own terms, as an adaptation of Catholic principles to peculiar conditions of religio-social fact, to the specialities of a particular political tradition, etc. I would only balk at the bald assertion that "Spain represents the ideal."
>
> As I said, I want to defend the United States, but again in its own terms—and not as an "ideal," but again simply as a valid adaptation of principles to existent conditions.[18]

Murray's other target was the converse of doctrinal absolutism. It was the "wretched morass of expediency" into which Catholic practice about church-state relations tended to fall, regardless or perhaps because of the craving for providential truths in politics. The fallacy of the perfectionist mentality on display in the idealization of the Spanish case was that it led to sectarianism on the one hand and utter lack of principle on the other. Autocracy alternated ceaselessly with chaos. The modus operandi of this way of thinking was a de facto opportunism that substituted intrigue and betrayal for compromise.[19] The intolerantly secularizing "totalitarian democracies" of continental liberalism, foisting rationalistic models of statecraft on societies whose resilience lay in their historical peculiarities, were no better in this regard than traditional obscurantism. In the guise of reason they brought forth monsters of the inhumane.

Even though political outcomes under pluralism were uncertain, the system at least had rules, and these rules were workable. By contrast, absolutizing makeshift political arrangements created standards that existed only to be violated and evaded. The irony of dictatorships was that stability could not be enforced, and of the religious monopolies bound to them that belief could not be compelled. Both were prone to rebellion.

Elevating the Spanish solution to a principle of Catholic statecraft was a special case of the penchant for pulling sweeping generalizations from particular circumstances. It was a kind of sacramental thinking that invested a contingent reality with a symbolism that ignored historical specificity and change. The result was a spiral of ideological polarization and appeals to principle on the one hand, and irrational personalism and arbitrariness on the other.

> The Latin countries of Europe have displayed this spectacle of ideological politics, a struggle between a host of "isms," all of which pretend to a final view of man and society, with the twin results of governmental paralysis and seemingly irremediable social division. . . . [T]he experience of the Church . . . , especially in the Latin lands, has been alternately an experience of privilege or persecution. It was alternatively the determination of government to ally itself either with the purposes of the Church or with the purposes of some sect or other (sectarian Liberalism, for instance) which made a similar, however erroneous, claim to possess the full and final truth. The dominant conviction, whose origins are really in pagan antiquity, was that government should represent transcendent truth and by its legal power make this truth prevail. However, in the absence of social agreement as to what the truth really was, the result was to involve the Catholic truth in the vicissitudes of power. It would be difficult to say which experience, privilege or persecution, proved in the end to be the more damaging or gainful to the Church.[20]

In passages like these Murray revealed a revulsion at the operational code of Latin politics that seemed to belie his theoretical willingness to live and let live.[21] In defending pluralism, Murray was drawing, perhaps unwittingly, on an alternative tradition of Catholicism, embracing the plenitude of a variety that might include despots as well as democrats. Temperamentally, however, he was repulsed by the pretense to perfection in politics. He despised the squalor behind intellectual imperialism. In any event, his personal preferences did not vitiate the logic of his case in favor of pluralism, and later in his argument Murray would express reservations of his own about the workings of the American system.

The standard with which Murray proposed to replace the norm of political immutability and the cycle of despotism and anarchy that he felt accompanied it was a historical principle that recognized the significance of development in political systems—in particular, the breakthrough toward political freedom represented by the American experience. According to Murray, this evolution was in the direction not only of religious liberty but of civic tranquillity too. The trend represented a good in itself. Reconciliation was, after all, supposed to be at the top of the Christian agenda.

Murray drew on a number of arguments to avoid the criticism of relativism. He buttressed his point that "the American proposition" was indicative of a historical trend rather than simply exceptional, as he suggested the Spanish case was, by stressing the paradox of the comparative stability that this evolution had produced. The American experience had stood the test of time. Democracy in the United States was more durable than dictatorship or for that matter any government in Spain. And it was not just civil peace but pluralistic debate and the contention of rival opinions, that were good in themselves. Political comity depended on dialogue.

While the stress on peace and tranquillity fit with official Catholic opinion, the praise of pluralism had a heterodox touch. It was the positive appreciation of change, with the implication that political and social principles were historically contingent, that was the innovation overarching the set of specific arguments. Of practically equal significance was the idea that minority status, rather than majority much less absolute control, was an acceptable position for political groups identified with Catholicism. History had bypassed the old triumphalism.

Other American Jesuits besides Murray had defended the virtues of democracy. Chief among these had been the Fordham political scientist Moorhouse F. X. Millar, who claimed to trace the influence of medieval Catholic thought and especially of such Jesuit political philosophers as Bellarmine and Suarez on the framers of the American constitution.[22] Millar's argument was undermined, however, by a gratuitous anti-Protestantism, by the assertion that proponents of the Reformation, in addition to bringing an unwanted capitalism down on a poor but contented populace, had usurped the genuine liberalism of feudal Catholicism. What was fatal to this line of reasoning in the American context was that it looked to an irretrievable past as the solution to present difficulties. An ideal though quite impossible historical restoration, equivalent to the resurrection of the guild system, was supposed to return democracy to its pristine origins. Even if it were desirable in principle, the minority condition of the American Catholic community ruled out any thought of imposing such a system. Taking such ideas seriously, if only as an academic exercise, perpetuated idiosyncratic thinking that might pass muster as an aesthetic manifesto but invited ridicule if taken as a political program.[23]

Because the theory propounded by Murray acknowledged the evolving nature of political ideas and institutions, he departed from notions of what constituted "theory" and "principles" among many of his peers. The truths "we hold" develop and are corrected over time in civilized debate. This was one of the functions of pluralistic dialogue. The welcome accorded the historicity of collective norms, and the recognition of the indeterminacy of their outcomes, posed the major challenge to the classical certainties of Catholicism.[24]

Murray did not embrace the liberal tradition wholeheartedly. He returned repeatedly to the argument that pluralism depended on virtuous citizens. The deists who devised the American constitution were convinced of the capacity of the common man to govern himself because of their still-unshaken belief in the existence of natural law. Rights were feasible in view of shared assumptions about the regularities of objective reality and the moderating possibilities of a reason that was capable of grasping the laws of nature and society. In this the American ethos differed, Murray believed, from the offshoots of Roman legalism, which raised abstract formulations above common humanity and which, pitting reason against a slovenly empiricism, displaced practical incentives and sanctions with unreasonable regulations.

> Because it was conceived in the tradition of natural law the American Republic was rescued from the fate, still not overcome, that fell upon the European nations in which Continental Liberalism, a deformation of the liberal tradition, lodged itself, not least by the aid of the Lodges. There have never been "two Americas," in the sense in which there have been, and still are, "two Frances," "two Italys," "two Spains."[25]

Murray had a visceral distaste for Latinate schematics and a corresponding admiration for the rigors of natural law tamed by what he judged to be Anglo-American common sense. He also had something of a love-hate fascination with the irremediable antinomies of Latin politics ("two Italys," "two Spains"). Expunged from his political theory, this agonistic interplay emerged (as we shall see shortly) in his ideas about moral psychology.

By the late fifties, Murray was less sure that "the tradition of natural law, the foundation of viable politics, has the same hold upon the mind of America today that it had upon the 'preachers, merchants, planters, and lawyers who were the mind of Colonial America.' " As he put it:

> The tradition of natural law is not taught or learned in the American university. It has not been rejected, much less refuted. We do not refute our adversaries, said Santayana; we quietly bid them goodbye. . . . [T]he American university long since bade a quiet goodbye to the

whole notion of an American consensus, as implying that there are truths that we hold in common, and a natural law that makes known to all of us the structure of the moral universe in such wise that all of us are bound by it in common obedience.[26]

The subjectivity and personalism that Murray saw in the declension of the American ethos was inimical to the survival of natural law. Consensus was not only a function of the capacity to grasp objective reality—this was a scientific or a sociological concern—but of a shared moral heritage. For Murray the possibility of manageable change in the polity required ethical stability—reliability—among individuals. Political pluralism had to be founded on common decency. Character was the ballast that made collective transformations—in policy, in values, in organizations—feasible without violence. Citizens had to be able to trust one another.

As memories of the natural law vanished in most quarters, Murray held out hope of its persistence in the American Catholic community. He refrained from the Protestant-bashing that some of his predecessors, like Moorhouse Millar, had indulged in. But he took pride in a Catholic identity that stood apart from the American mainstream but that also, he felt, was a constitutive if unacknowledged element of the success of the American experiment:

> The men of learning in it acknowledge certain real contributions made by positive sociological analysis of the political community. But both they and their less learned fellows still adhere, with all the conviction of intelligence, to the tradition of natural law as the basis of free and ordered political life. Historically, this tradition has found, and still finds, its intellectual home within the Catholic Church. It is indeed one of the ironies of history that the tradition should have so largely languished in the so-called Catholic nations of Europe at the same time that its enduring vigor was launching a new Republic across the broad ocean. There is also some paradox in the fact that a nation which has (rightly or wrongly) thought of its own genius in Protestant terms should have owed its origins and the stability of its political structure to a tradition whose genius is alien to current intellectualized versions of the Protestant religion, and even to certain individualistic exigencies of Protestant religiosity.[27]

This subculture, unfortunately, was fast succumbing to assimilation. Murray was a realist, not a wishful thinker. On the whole he was not optimistic about the future of natural law as the underpinning of democratic civility. He feared the corrosive appeal of a secular humanism that rejected what, for its purposes, was an antiquated innocence. An insatiable skepticism devoured the legacy that nourished it; a vastation loomed at the end of modernism. Pessimism regarding the possibility of consensus in the absence of a natural law tradition led Murray to emphasize the need for hierarchial order to sustain pluralism:

> It is a Christian theological intuition, confirmed by all of historical experience, that man lives both his personal life and his social life always more or less close to the brink of barbarism, threatened not only by the disintegrations of physical illness and by the disorganizations of mental imbalance, but also by the decadence of moral corruption and the political chaos of formlessness or the moral chaos of tyranny. Society is rescued from chaos only by a few men, not by the many. *Paucis humanum vivit genus.* It is only the few who understand the disciplines of civility and thus hold in check the forces of barbarism that are always threatening to force the gates of the City.[28]

With the decay of natural law, the prospects for political stability depended on a keepers-of-the-flame rendition of democracy. At the center of the ongoing American experiment was a hierarchy of responsible elites. The internalized controls that fostered the civic virtues of the early republic had been diluted not only by the spread of secular humanism among the intelligentsia but also by the growth of mass society. The onslaught against democratic civility came from two quarters: from an elite that was overdosing on skepticism, and from a mass public devoured by consumerism.[29]

Murray was not an enthusiast of participatory democracy. Nor did he show much interest in the economic and social correlates of pluralism, even though in the later sixties, toward the end of his life, he started to turn his attention to the racial conflicts that he feared might undo whatever threads of consensus remained in the American social fabric. He thought more naturally in terms of character rather than class or ethnicity as a determinant of political behavior, perhaps because he was more concerned with public order than with policy. He also stood apart from the theorizing associated with the labor encyclicals, in which questions of social equity took precedence over those of political process, and over sociological speculation in a secular vein.[30]

For his time Murray was one of the most anomalous of figures, a Catholic Whig. Liberty was his foremost concern. In him were joined a commitment to democratic procedures, and a corresponding disdain for tyranny, especially of the Latin variety, with a belief in the need for an abiding system of personal morality. He favored limited political change that left individual ethics intact. On the one hand he was convinced of the wisdom of keeping the political and religious spheres separate; on the other he was not convinced that political liberty could endure without a foundation of extramaterial values. "The thing that we have not yet proved in the U.S. is that the social consensus, as at least moral, can be maintained in the absence of religious unity—in the presence of radical divisions. There are signs that the consensus is eroding."[31]

That Murray was able to develop a rationale for the separation of public and private life that commanded respect within a Catholic framework was a considerable achievement. The verbally still-prevalent—and tacitly ignored—view among Catholic ecclesiastics in the United States was that the perfect solution would be a very close and static match between the two, a variant on rudimentary familism, magnified to the nation-state and buttressed by guildlike vocational groupings. This was the model espoused by Husslein. It was a museum piece, a catechetical piety, that managed nonetheless to forestall an engagement with American realities while at the same time discrediting Catholic social thought. The conceptual apparatus and its terminological trappings were so severely European that the potentially germane preoccupations of the *magisterium* were lost on American Catholics. In Murray's eyes all this was hopelessly childish, a reduction of the complex to the simple and a chasing-after the universal that was blinded by an imperial myopia.

In the American case Murray justified treating the acceptance of political change as a desirable good by trying to show how support for this development rested, or had rested for a long time, on a substructure of shared values. Habitual discipline on the part of individuals was supposed to underlie, modulate, and make tolerable the vagaries of historical shifts in political institutions and social structures. Moral consensus about the indispensability of self-control supported collective diversity and political change; the self-discipline of citizens made possible the democratic control of rulers.

In defending the separation of church and state, then, Murray maintained a connection between quasi-religious mores and democratic stability. He discarded a simplistic transference of every day paternalism into political despotism, and he showed little patience with the idealization of stability as perpetual stasis. But there remained a link between personal virtue, the reachability of consensus, and nonauthoritarian governance. The health of the larger polity depended ultimately on individual restraint and communal norms operating lower down the scale of daily life.

Yet the prospects for the democratic civility favored by Murray had turned grim under what he saw as the deterioration of moral community. The transmission of democratic values depended on a historical continuity that was disintegrating. The logic of his analysis seemed to lead Murray to a political and ethical dead end.

In fact, however, although the strain of pessimism was strong, there was an existential element in Murray that went beneath conventional politics, lifting what might have been despair into a series of primordial contests that restored confidence and assertiveness. In his public writings hints of his deep passion surface in bold strokes that flash through the clouds of nuance and the suavity of tone. The preface to "The Problem of Pluralism in America," for example, concludes with a forthright, even arrogant, passage that is just as important as a statement of Murray's belief in the value of strong convictions to stave off an insipid relativism as it is a declaration of the superiority of religious belief over political truth:

> In pursuing the argument it is taken for granted that the principles of Catholic faith and morality are controlling. Religious faith and morals are not subject to judgment by the norms of any political and social system. The question sometimes raised, whether Catholicism is compatible with American democracy, is an invalid and impertinent question; for the manner of its position inverts the order of values. The question is whether American democracy—in our case as involving a theory of pluralism—is compatible with Catholicism. No other manner of putting the question would be acceptable to anyone who places the imperatives of consciences [sic], which mediate the law of God, above the imperatives whose origins are in human law and sentiment.[32]

Murray had a talent for combining stateliness with an air of primordial drama. "He entered a room," one Jesuit recalled, "like an ocean liner."[33] He could strike a chord between old-fashioned orotundity and the communication of a dread of the bottom falling out that smacked of lived experience. Here is Murray on the menace—presumably a variety of modernism—that subverts both reasoned discourse and traditional wisdom:

> This is perennially the work of the barbarian, to undermine rational standards of judgment, to corrupt the inherited intuitive wisdom by which the people have always lived, and to do this not by spreading new beliefs but by creating a climate of doubt and bewilderment in which clarity about the larger aims of life is dimmed and the self-confidence of the people is destroyed, so that finally what you have is the impotent nihilism . . . now presently appearing on our university campuses. (One is, I take it, on the brink of impotence and nihilism when one begins to be aware of one's own awareness of what one is doing, saying, thinking. This is the paralysis of all serious thought; it is likewise the destruction of all spontaneities of love.)[34]

Murray evoked a logic of the emotions that, for him, subtended creative analysis and prevented it from lapsing into shallow certainties. This logic reflected a struggle for self-definition that provided a psychic anchor in the midst of inexorable change. In setting out to explore the rationale of the American polity, Murray began with the ringing assertion that "What is at stake is America's understanding of itself." He continued:

> Self-understanding is the necessary condition of a sense of self-identity and self-confidence, whether in the case of an individual or in the case of a people. . . . The complete loss of one's identity is, with all propriety of theological definition, hell. In diminished forms it is insanity. And it would not be well for the American giant to go lumbering about the world today, lost and mad.[35]

The link between this rather feverish depiction of personal *angst* and national malaise, and between either of these conditions and the actual workings of democracy, is not altogether clear. The argument is dense and the phrasing histrionic. Working from the outside in, from Murray's observations about public life to his perceptions of its psychic grounding, helps recover the main lines of his reasoning.[36]

Political community, Murray contended, was forged through debate: "Civilization is formed by men locked together in argument." The civilizing feature of the dialogue that joined men in politics was its rationality. It was adherence to the rules of the game—the public ritual of partial victory and conditional surrender—that gave pluralism its capacity to accommodate dissension. Just beneath civil discourse, Murray insisted, lay the clash of brute interests and, worse, absolutes. For Murray discussion of issues could be as important as the actual decision if ultimate beliefs—ideologies—were not at stake. Politics worked when it did not slide into violence over irreconcilable values and identities. This was the main reason for keeping religion out of politics. Politics could not be catharsis. All of these precepts fell within the pluralistic dispensation.[37]

The question then arose as to how to prevent deadly quarrels without at the same time making politics a mere diversion in which strong loyalties and genuinely divergent interests failed to be channeled. A characteristic ambiguity of Murray's perspective derived from his cursory treatment of the socioeconomic bases of pluralism, of their relative manageability or explosiveness. He was given to switching between the autonomy of politics and the law, of institutions on high and the ethical consensus below, that purportedly kept political conflict this side of violence, sidestepping the social and economic interests at stake. It was difficult to visualize what specific social mechanisms, aside from the improbable bulwarks of natural law in a few educational institutions, might contribute in Murray's eyes to the transmission of the ethical consensus he felt was indispensable to democracy.

Although Murray was not much interested in the socioeconomic supports of democracy, he did not confine himself to the technicalities of constitutional law. He spoke of elemental, primal struggles that defined what mattered: masculine identity. His argument did not concern politics in the conventional sense. It was, however, of a piece with his thinking about the importance of collective identity and of "a natural law that makes known to all of us the structure of the moral universe in such wise that all of us are bound by it in common obedience" for sustaining political consensus. If there is a larger implication to Murray's observations about psychosexual identity, it seems to have been that when leading citizens—in effect, men—were secure in their identities, social vitality could flourish, a static conversatism could be avoided, while intractable questions and a debilitating irrationality were kept out of the civil arena. Men strong in their masculinity and steady in their convictions could distinguish between opposition and anarchy, avoiding the latter by tolerating the former.

For several years running—indeed, for nineteen out of twenty—Murray had been invited to give the preordination retreat for the theologians at Woodstock. From time to time he was also called upon to give "conferences"—that is, edifying lectures—to the community of priests and scholastics on topics of general interest. His notes for one of these talks were assembled in an essay, published shortly after his death, on "The Danger of the Vows: An Encounter with Earth, Woman, and Spirit."[38] The remarks were addressed to his fellow religious but the problem—"so many men of diminished manhood, of incomplete virility"—was not limited to priests; the afflicted males were "not necessarily more [numerous in religious communities] than in the world."[39]

The message was that "man becomes a man by the encounter with three elemental forces, and by the mastery of them—the encounter with the earth, with woman, and with his own spirit." The unifying theme is mastery. Thus, "man is not man until by his own hard work he has bent stubborn earth to his own purposes." Similarly:

in this wrestling with his own spirit, and with all the alternatives presented to it by circumstances and his own desires, a man becomes a man. He enters into possession of his powers, and of himself—becomes self-directed, self-controlled, able to think his own thoughts, feel his own feelings, meet his own friends with love, and his enemies without fear. . . . Through his life runs that thread of purpose, which is the mark of virility: I am come for this, I am not come for that.[40]

The encounter with woman was more complex but still "primal" and "elemental." In the first place, woman offered to man the "possibility of procreation, hence of manhood, of realizing himself as, under God, the creator, the active principle of generation." But woman had another and even more crucial role:

> More importantly, it is woman who offers man the possibility of head-ship, of entering into his native inheritance of rule—or realizing him-self as head, *Logos*, the principle of order, which by ordering life rules it. Woman is life, but not *Logos*, not the principle of order. . . . She is not her own ruler; man is to govern her.[41]

Domination of the female represented the triumph of reason—*Logos*, the word—over shapeless passion.

> Man does not know himself aright until he knows he is the head of woman, set above her, having her under his government. This is his part and person; and if he resigns it, he resigns his manhood. . . it is in his encounter with woman, with life, that man knows himself, achieves himself as *Logos*, who is to rule life and not be ruled by it. Through his encounter with woman there is offered him the possibility of achieving the triumph of reason over life (or the marriage of reason with life). Out of this encounter comes life that is human—untamed life in the bones of man is disciplined unto integrity, which is chastity, which is in turn the freeing of all the forces of life by their subordina-tion to reason. Again it is woman who puts within the reach of man the act of man—the act of self-rule, through rule of her. It is she who lets him become man.[42]

Murray was attempting to clarify the prerational coordinates of masculinity, which he associated with reason. The mastery of feminine unreason made the man and, by extension, subtended political peace. The struggle, if it was successful, reaffirmed a fundamental hierarchy: the stratification of the sexes. Historical development—not just cyclical change but evolutionary progress, touched though never fully dominated, by reason—presupposed stable male identity, and female subordination. The attempt, it would ap-pear, was to establish the foundations of political logic in passion—in pas-sion that was controlled, to be sure, but passion nonetheless, as if Murray sensed a need to recover the primitive emotion banished by his Hispano-phobia.

There was a necessity and permanence to this tension that at once ani-mated and moderated clashes over explicitly political issues. The exclusion from public discourse of the either-or conflicts symbolized by the male-female rivalry made civilized politics possible. Such conflicts were religious and therefore potentially calamitous in their intensity. But they were forever threatening to break through the veneer of pluralism. Religion and politics were immiscible, yet the tension between them was symbiotic: "the triumph of reason over life (or the marriage of reason with life)."[43] The higher morality was to keep moral issues out of politics, yet the compartmentalization was fragile, and some underlying code of private behavior was evidently needed to keep public life from becoming fragmented. This norm came down to masculine supremacy. Men firm in their identity could afford to be statesmanlike in public affairs. Otherwise, under the pressure of political dilemmas, politicians were liable to lack courage, to be irresolute and to fail to lead, or to compensate for their personal insecurities by escalating ideological combat.[44]

Murray knew that for some of his critics the advocacy of pluralism smacked of relativism, of a sort of polytheism of political idols. He sensed that the political and social assimilation of American Catholics would prove disillusioning if in the process they—that is, their leaders, in particular the clergy—lost their psychic core. His treatment of the attainment of masculinity through an agonistic dialectic of the sexes is intuitive and literally self-dramatizing. The pillars of rationality are sunk deep into a primeval softness. What is extraordinary about the piece is that it summons up the demons that seem to have driven Murray himself and the prerational antinomies that set the terms of identity and fixed the limits of change within the Society of Jesus.

The fire-and-ice tenor of the contrast made for high drama. Identity went deeper and had to be more abiding than ideology. It was a token of immortality, surviving history. At the same time, identity was bound up with an ideology of power. Murray connected the cerebral and the sexual in a way that makes it possible to understand the terrible seriousness with which ideas, especially ideas about sexuality, have been taken in Catholic officialdom and, in contrast, the relative ease with which the church abandoned its fondness for one type of political arrangement over another.

The pathos behind the advocacy of pluralism by Murray was that it was accepted in some measure for reasons of convenience. With or without Murray, the church found reasons to accept pluralism. Just as it was indelicate of Murray in the early fifties, when a concordat was under negotiation, to question the lessons of the Spanish solution for church-state relations, so in the late fifties it became seemly, when a Catholic with a serious chance of winning began his run for the American presidency, to acknowledge the beneficence of pluralism. It was a denouement by a complex of motives and organizational prerogatives that Murray in his wry, impassioned way understood.[45]

IV

The reactionary interests involved in the accord struck between the Vatican
and the Spanish government dramatized the major impediment to the acceptance of Murray's ideas, which was the papacy of Pius XII himself.
Eugenio Pacelli died in 1958. He was replaced by the aging-but-simpatico
Angelo Giuseppe Roncalli; Pope John XXIII.[46] Around this time Murray
began to publish again on church-state relations.

The factions inimical to the kind of thinking represented by Murray did
not vanish. The presuppositions about politics and patterns of internal authority that were brought to a culmination by Pius XII lingered after his
death. These forces were not an empty shell. The ideological rationale of
old-time Catholicism had been weakened, but the institutional context and
the habits of maneuver within which Murray's thought developed and
against which he reacted remained.[47]

A fundamental divergence persisted between Murray's cultural environment and the institutional atmosphere of the Roman hierarchy. Catholicism in America was a minority religion; in parts of continental Europe,
where ideological proclivities that Murray detested flourished, Catholics
were in the majority. Elsewhere in Europe, confessional parties were established elements of the political landscape. Catholicism was also a dominant presence in Latin America, where the liberalism prized by Murray had
a tenuous foothold in the face of recurrent crises of social distribution.
Thus, as it turned out, the influence of Murray's ideas was curtailed on the
left and on the right. Demographic and institutional configurations embedded in historical trajectories quite different from the North American setting
conditioned political tactics and expectations about doctrinal uniformity and
influence over governmental policy.[48]

Murray treated political ideas as cultural expressions that were close to
idiosyncratic in their contextual specificity. They were conditioned by historical circumstances but there was no particularly systematic variation, no
grand pattern, in similarities and differences from country to country. At
least, there was no such pattern that Murray bothered to explain with reference to social structures and economic interests. The family resemblance
prevailing in the politics of Latin countries was noted as a cultural syndrome. Murray was satisfied to leave the explanation of such phenomena to
others.

His focus on political ideas permitted Murray to concentrate on the
internal logic of their content and evolution, as a historian of theory rather
than a historical sociologist, and to make more refined discriminations
among the varieties of secular thought than the us-versus-them contrasts
drawn by some of his colleagues. If he discerned a larger pattern underlying

the development of political ideas, it was in the ways they reflected and magnified understandings of personal ethics and moral struggle. Even then, Murray preferred these connections to be oblique. A sophisticated realism ruled out fundamentalist notions of a direct line between solid citizens and good government. The connections, such as they were, between ethics and policy were circuitous. Yet a stable polity could not dispense with some carryover between individual probity and the formulation of public policy. Murray was careful to stress the conservative moral stratum underlying his advocacy of toleration and his appreciation of pluralism-in-principle. The hope of the political course followed by the American experiment rested on a tradition of natural law; if this tradition were neglected, the collective promise of this historical departure in democratic politics would be jeopardized. Murray emphasized that enthusiasm for American liberties in no wise indicated approval of continental liberalism or secular humanism, much less of socialist radicalism. Although it might be exportable in small doses, democracy American-style was not a universal panacea.

Such distinctions were lost on the papal mentality and the coterie of Vatican advisers. After all, Murray's work boiled down to a critique of the Latin legal tradition—of Roman law and the Napoleonic code—in both its conservative and radical republican forms. His criticisms cut both ways and they stung, all the more so because it was impossible to dismiss Murray as an American innocent of the lessons of history. His ethical depth showed that he was not a social engineer unacquainted with human frailty and the mark of Cain. It was this complexity and pessimism and the political lessons that were drawn from them that puzzled and disturbed European Catholics who were used to identifying the Americanist heresy with a superficial materialism and a kind of moral adventurism.[49]

Pius remained suspicious of the neoliberalism propagated during the Cold War by such American intellectuals as Reinhold Niebuhr and Arthur Schlesinger. It was a sober rendition of Americanism that placed compromise ahead of unconditional surrender on the part of adversaries and that seemed to counsel coexistence with evil. It dreaded ideological polarization. While it helped legitimize the postwar policy of anticommunist containment, and while it stressed the limits of politics for alleviating human suffering, the doctrine appeared too ready to downplay absolutes, including religious principle, for the sake of preserving an even-tempered incrementalism. The differences between such thinking and the ideas propounded by Murray were not conspicuous to the Holy See.[50]

To ward off this debilitating liberalism, Pius envisioned the expansion of a cultural apparatus that would furnish guidance across the range of social issues and would mobilize Catholic opinion to influence public policy. What he seems to have had in mind was the Christian Democratic party and its allied network of Catholic Action organizations as they operated in Italy, inflated to an international scale.[51] Since confessional parties along European lines were no more in the American political style than were militantly leftwing parties, the grounds for mutual incomprehension were great. A crucial discrepancy remained between a theory of pluralism that presupposed a minority position for Catholicism and a vision of political dominion, fortified by the Latin ambience, in which Catholics formed a majority.

The model favored by Pius was a singular combination of localism—a political formula inspired by the rivalry between the Vatican and Italian Communists—and appeals to universalism. The outcome was a contradictory mixture of increased centralization of papal authority and calls for mobilization on the part of the clergy and a zealous laity to spread Catholic values. In a radio message delivered in 1952 Pius proclaimed:

> Now is the time, beloved children . . . the time to take decisive steps and shake off this fatal lethargy. . . . An entire world must be rebuilt from its foundations, transformed from savage to human, from human to divine. . . . Just as on a day now long passed . . . We accepted the heavy cross of the pontificate, so also We do now bow to the arduous duty of being . . . the herald of a better world, willed by God.[52]

The strategy of *rinnovamento* was based on the premise that human resources could be galvanized in a modern-day millenarianism without changing the organizational rules or the ideological tenets of Catholicism. Control would be augmented; so would mobilization. Numbers would increase, and this could be taken as a sign of growth in ardor, without risking doctrinal change. The hope was not unfounded. At the end of the war, the Society of Jesus numbered about 28,000 men worldwide. By 1965 there were more than 36,000 Jesuits. Other religious orders, particularly ones committed to activism, also grew. The idea of fusing energy with strict obedience to command reflected the fascination that the military side of the Society of Jesus held for Pius XII. Theories of pluralism did not flourish in this ambience.[53]

One Jesuit showed extraordinary drive in responding to Pius's appeal. The Movement for a Better World founded by Fr. Riccardo Lombardi, who began his career on the staff of *Civiltà Cattolica*, combined revival meetings, spiritual exercises, and how-to workshops on parish work and social problems. The aims of the movement were as broad as the ambitions of Pius:

> The apostolic effort of the Catholic Church is so splintered into a multiplicity of disconnected initiatives that the proper organic functioning of the Mystical Body of Christ cannot perform its healing action on

the world around it. . . . There must be a unity of purpose, a unity of spirit and effort for all the world to see and feel. The progressive social apostasy of the last five centuries demonstrates the lack of such unity; it can be halted and turned back only by a Catholic Church functioning with maximum efficiency at its head and all its parts.[54]

During the 1950s Lombardi traveled through Italy and Latin America, preaching to large crowds. He became known as "God's microphone." Priests, nuns, and laity testified to the inspiration and renewed vigor gained from participating in the movement. Riccardo Lombardi was an Italian version of Daniel Lord. His capacity for mobilization and his dedication to the papacy suited the image that Pius XII had of the role of Jesuits. He drew on modern techniques, but his message was plainly traditional. Far from collapsing under their weight, Catholicism could turn new methods of communication to its own purposes. Changes could be piled on Catholicism without modifying its core; the whole structure could absorb them without bloat or contradiction.[55]

Lombardi stood to the right of Lord, however, and he seemed to have been less affable. In 1955 Lombardi had a run-in with Cardinal Roncalli, who was then patriarch of Venice and who three years later would succeed Pius XII. In a dinner speech of inordinate fervor Lombardi accused the Italian bishops of not living up to the Counter-Reformation precepts of the Council of Trent and reminded them of their obligation to carry out the vision of the Better World Movement, which offered hope of salvation to a Christendom in decline. Lombardi managed in one stroke to offend the future pope and the Italian episcopate as a whole.[56]

As preparations for the Second Vatican Council got underway Lombardi could not succeed in patching up the damage, despite assistance from the still powerful Cardinal Ottaviani, who had earlier been a prime mover in the silencing of John Courtney Murray.[57] The leadership of the Society of Jesus opened a prudent distance from the *Movimento*. The enthusiasm of its participants and the zeal of their leader were tinged with hysteria. Lombardi's rallies evoked memories of the fascist style. Frustrated in its attempts to gain an institutional niche within the church, the movement was becoming an emotional miasma. It threatened to burst the traditional organizational structures of Catholicism.

Lombardi called for a crusade against poverty in Latin America to offset the popularity of Fidel Castro. The reception of this and other projects of his by the Vatican was, Lombardi complained, "glacial."[58] In 1962, John XXIII arranged for the withdrawal from circulation of a book by Lombardi outlining reforms that the council should implement. In 1963 the Decree on Religious Liberty, written in large part by Murray, was promulgated by the council. Lombardi retired from the scene. He died in silence in 1979.

The withdrawal of Lombardi's official support signified a rejection of the overwrought militancy of the previous regime. The implication of the Lombardi affair was clear. The papacy of John XXIII was moving in a different direction without directly criticizing his predecessor.[59]

By the end of the 1950s, two features associated with the papacy of Pius XII had come to be judged as more harmful than the advocacy of pluralism and religious toleration associated with Murray and the Americans. One was the special relationship between the Vatican and authoritarian governments. This favoritism brought discredit on Catholic social theory by compromising corporatism with fascism. As LaFarge had feared, marriages of convenience that were looked upon as matters of principle made it difficult for the church to extricate itself from political alliances without drawing attention to its doctrinal inconsistencies.

Second, there were pathological elements to the pious transports of the likes of Lombardi. Such revivalism was doubly disturbing for its protestations of loyalty to the church. A holy delirium that led nowhere, it provided fodder for the movies of Fellini. Ironically, the moderation propounded by Murray, once scorned as "indifferentism," promised to restore a dignified balance to what had become a pharonic papacy. The ideas of the American offered a respite from the unseemly and the surreal.

V

Fortuna played a crucial role in the career of John Courtney Murray. The long-term intellectual change he wrought was bound up with dynastic politics and with sheer accident. This paradox was at the heart of his argument. Political formulas enshrined as absolutes were better understood as contingent. The attempt to derive all-encompassing principles from expedience and abiding traditions from circumstantial practice led to hypocrisy and intolerance. It also bred instability, and was therefore self-defeating. The search for political perfection violated the golden rule of moderation. It ended up perpetuating a cycle of tyranny and anarchy.

Murray caused a passing scandal. He pointed to the feet of clay on which the posturing after a singular ideal of statecraft stood. At one level he merely appropriated the hushed wisdom of court gossip—what everyone knew but no one would speak aloud—to the effect that when dogma is said to be fixed and hierarchy makes claims to unshakability, personalities matter all the more. Inflexibility hid the mortal flaw of dictatorships, which was caprice.

But Murray did more than demonstrate that the emperor was all clothes and hollow inside. While he did not invent a system to replace a discredited synthesis, he helped open up possibilities that had previously been forbidden. He made it legitimate for Catholic thinkers to acknowledge diversity and accept political change. A theory of how political or social transformation occurred was beyond him. He moved Catholic social thought away from its attachment to categorization and pointed it in the direction of the consideration of historical change, even though he never developed a dynamic system.[60]

Murray's achievement left room for ambiguity. Political systems that were largely circumstantial arrangements were easier to change than manifestations of universal and timeless principles. But Murray preferred an accommodating pluralism within political systems to brusque change from one type of regime to another. Incrementalism on the political surface was steadied by a community whose members shared ethical standards. This meant a polyarchy of civilized elites. On the one hand Murray forsook the thought-by-imagery depiction of the ideal state as a projection of the family. This was illusory in practice and damaging even as speculation. On the other hand he was not a Machiavellian. Personal, even religious, virtue that stood at some distance but not at a complete remove from the public sphere was necessary to stabilize the polity, not as a narcotic or prop to patriotism but as the courage to advance one's views forcefully and, if it came to that, to lose gracefully. Resolve and a certain courage were the gifts of character to civilized politics. Public life needed the reinforcement of stoic masculinity.

Two other sources of ambiguity were the spotty treatment Murray gave to the economic context of political pluralism and his sketchiness regarding the origins of norms. An Eisenhower Republican, Murray may have felt it superfluous or distasteful to go into detail about the capitalist underpinnings of American democracy. Without training in economics, he was not professionally equipped to do so, and he had no truck with the corporatist meditations of Catholic political economy. Just as his advocacy of pluralism made enemies among Catholic traditionalists, Murray's boredom with economics left him open to criticism from Catholic radicals.[61]

Socialization into habits of civility remained mysterious. The links between Murray's vision of political order and his views on the consolidation of identity through sexual combat are tenuous. The institutional connections between this moral ground and the world of public policy are at best fragmentary. The problem disappears if one assumes that Murray's political philosophy is simply an extension of his reading of natural law and that his real interest lay in the moral determinants of public order, broadly understood, instead of in the specifics of policy. The difficulty with this solution is that Murray felt that the social supports of natural law were collapsing even among the elites capable of grasping it.

Murray's reflections on gender relations are plainly incomplete as political theory, even generously defined. They are, however, diagnostic of a preoccupation with personal as well as collective stability. Murray might have been getting at what he thought was the linchpin of common morality in the development of masculine fortitude. Yet from another angle agonistic struggle had only the remotest connection with politics. Character does not put politics on autopilot; the problem of aggregating strong preferences remains. Murray's disquisition on male identity can just as well be taken as his thoughts on the sources of creativity and courage, in the face of psychic inhibitions and the resistance of the Catholic tradition.

For Murray, character meant first of all reliability—not certainty exactly, but a clear sense that opinions were not to be trimmed to every passing breeze. This is the steadfastness behind the declarative, here-I-stand tone of much of his argumentation. But character also meant conscience. It might lead not to obstinacy or rebellion—which Murray evidently disliked—but to a refusal to gainsay one's convictions. Rather than betray his cause, Murray suffered in silence.

Both understandings of character were seen as manly virtues, contrasted to a Latin, feminine excitability. Both constancy and the adherence to principle depended in turn on the strength of personal identity—on the *self*, one of Murray's favorite words. This identity was forged by men who wrestled with the irrational. It meant the attainment of control over impulse, yet it tapped into passion in order to redeem the self from a fixation with stability. Sublimation was precarious. "Man lives," as Murray said, "both his personal life and his social life always more or less close to the brink of barbarism." A ruthlessness of the emotions vied with the ambitions of reason.

Countercurrents that in later years would clash like a riptide crested in the person and the work of John Courtney Murray and came to fragile equipoise. Perhaps for the last time in a controversy surrounding a major figure in preconciliar Catholicism, before the apparatus collapsed, character as consistency and character as conscience stayed in balance. This precarious resolution—Murray was silenced but not exiled or expelled—may have been facilitated by the fact that, unlike the uprising mounted by Fathers Dunne and Heithaus in St. Louis, his dissent was based more on intellectual than moral grounds. Besides making a point of moral orthodoxy, Murray never accused his opponents of ethical laxity even as he came close to humiliating them for their stupidity and political obtuseness.

Murray's signal contribution was to map the middle ground that American Catholics felt they had already discovered but could not quite appropriate and settle into, the broad and abundant country that lay between an integralism that sought to unite politics and morals—in effect to join church and state—and a dystopia of boundless greed and competition. His pluralism meant not only a rebuttal of the Spanish model. By not bothering to comment on them, Murray also rejected third way, corporatist formulas that focused on the social organization of the economy; the implication was that such models might be fine for parts of Europe but were without interest in the United States.

In addition, Murray ignored the "holy family" ideal for governance that prevailed in the Irish Republic. There the sacredness of the family had been written into the constitution, and the operations of government, if viewed with discretion, were supposed to resemble the family of "the plain people," hazy and aglow with the nimbus of a folk democracy that was authoritarian in practice. It was all too literal and *simpliste* for the United States. The sophistication of Murray reflected a cosmopolitanism that not only sniffed at the localisms of the church but that also resisted the imperialism that sought to elevate these localisms into universal law.

Murray's recognition of the temporal contingency of political forms did not lead him to embrace a vision of a commonwealth held together by the crisscrossing of self-absorbed actors. Self-interest dominated, he suggested, but it could not rule alone. Yet the mechanisms for maintaining the overarching consensus he thought necessary for the survival of democratic civility were obscure. Mass society placed the moral culture of pluralism under siege. At the interior of Murray's thought was a binary, impassioned logic that tried to overcome the interminable vellcities of character while refusing the either-or solutions of ideologues in the public sphere. The linkage was unresolved.[62]

8

Corporatism, Journalism, and Internationalism

Through and for some years after the war American Catholicism continued to be rooted in the parish. The neighborhoods clung around the parish church. Alongside the church stood the rectory, and nearby was the convent that housed the nuns who staffed the elementary schools. Devotional pageantry and recreational clubs were interwoven with training in academic basics and the inculcation of doctrine. Feast days rolled around, each with its ritual and Latin readings in black missals with red tassels for place marks and gold leaf on the edges of filmy pages. Lines formed on Fridays in the pews beside the confessionals, below the plaques and recessed statuary illustrating the stations of the cross. All the secrecy and personalism of the community were enfolded there. These facilities, accessible and human scale, were based on and supported, and were designed to perpetuate, growing families. The parishes themselves functioned like extended families.[1]

Most Jesuits operated outside but not quite beyond the parochial setting. They ran the better high schools—institutions that recruited boys from various parishes and neighborhoods on a citywide basis—and the colleges and universities that drew on a still broader yet predominantly local clientele. The schools formed an outer ring with one side facing the wider world and the other turned inward toward the parishes and neighborhoods. As members of a religious order Jesuits stood apart from the diocesan system of governance according to which bishops supervised pastors, pastors directed curates, and so on down the line. Although the society was administered according to "provinces," and Jesuits "in the trenches" usually stayed in the region where they had entered the order, they could take pride in memories of mobility and a task-oriented rather than a territorially based mode of functioning. Compared to most other actors in the ecclesiastical context, Jesuits had a cosmopolitan flair.

The parishes were recognized as wellsprings of community. They were seen as preserves of innocence and manpower in the midst of secularizing cities. Whether they furnished adaptable bases for reaching out to the postwar world, however, was another question. The parishes were sources of religious vocations and a home to return to, but they were not agencies for a "rechristianization of the social order." Preserving the sheltered insularity of the parishes was a task left to others besides the Jesuits in the division of ecclesiastical labor. Jesuits were seen and tended to see themselves as poised on the border between traditional Catholicism and American modernity.

American Jesuits explored three avenues, in addition to their schools, to extend Catholic influence beyond the parishes. One involved a stop-and-go effort to adapt the principles of the social encyclicals to American conditions. The objective was to provide a Catholic perspective on the national economy, to make sense of and possibly redirect the larger forces that shaped the sprawling context within which Catholics worked and lived out their lives. Most of this task fell to the Institute of Social Order and the labor schools. But some of the work of intellectual translation was carried out by an occasional Jesuit, more or less on a free-lance basis, who came to realize that the European and medieval slant of the encyclicals was inappropriate to American Catholicism.

Cast this way, the goal was slightly less farfetched then the one that had been assigned to American Jesuits in the thirties. Then the presumption was that the realities of American Catholicism should be made to conform to a European model. Now the objective leaned toward adapting European ideas to the dynamics of postwar Catholicism in America. With the defeat of fascism, the re-emergence of the democracies of Europe and the upward movement of the American economy, the impetus toward assimilation gathered force. These trends all but overwhelmed attempts to incorporate Catholic social thought into the American setting. Cultural disparities aside, the great difficulty was the absence of the organizational scaffolding on which the Christian Democratic parties of Europe built their political power. While one or another prelate—a Spellman or a Cushing—might wield extraordinary influence, the organizational expression of American Catholicism was pretty much confined to the local level.[2] "The realities of American Catholicism" were dispersed across the parishes and dioceses, each with their own finances, and without ties to any national institution. Furthermore, after the war, this configuration of local churches began to change, as prosperity and mobility reshaped the parishes.[3] Between the parochial

and the international levels American Catholicism existed as a label for a
cultural presence. It was a collective but unevenly organized entity. Turns
in French theology and liturgical experimentation filtered through but the
organizational framework of the European church provided no model. Institutional decentralization and cultural diversity held together through a
doctrinal uniformity confined to moral and personal issues. Political and
social Catholicism along European lines scarcely existed in the United
States.

One vehicle that stood above the confines of the parishes was *America*,
the "national journal of opinion" in whose offices John LaFarge reigned
from the end of the thirties to the forties. The purpose of the magazine was
to interpret the world of politics and culture for a Catholic readership. It also
harbored the ambition of projecting the ways of the Catholic subculture to
a national, ecumenical audience.[4] Neither target quite came within range.
As the sophistication of the Catholic community increased, no single viewpoint or even a distinctive slant could be brought to bear on the issues of the
day, and the need to defend the community from attack could no longer be
invoked so readily as a bar against internal factionalism.

A third venture was international in scope. It entailed missionary expansion, especially to Latin America. From about the early fifties to the late
sixties, the involvement of American Jesuits as missionaries reversed the spin
of immigrant Catholicism in which ideas and manpower came to the United
States from abroad. Now the energies of American Catholicism found release overseas. At first the goal of the expansion was evangelical rather than
ecumenical or reformist, but the experience soon took on political dimensions with psychological undertones. American Jesuits were driven to come
to terms with their own limitations. Although features of Latin American
Catholicism were familiar and attractive, the Jesuits encountered social
complexities that could not be controlled or readily understood and that
called into question the functions of the church as a political actor and their
own role within the international organization.

II

Discussions of corporatism as an ideology of class reconciliation appeared in
various Jesuit publications during the Depression and the Second World
War, and developments in corporatist industrial and labor organization were
reported in these journals through the fifties.[5] It was not uncommon for
promising Jesuits to spend their year of tertianship in France, Belgium, or
England, perhaps with trips to Germany and Spain, where they pick up
information about corporatist social policy.[6] These writings demonstrated

that a corporatism of a sort was alive and perhaps undergoing a revival; but they were all reports from overseas, and their application to the United States remained unclear.

A last-ditch attempt to refurbish corporatist thinking for an American audience was made by Bernard W. Dempsey, a Jesuit from the Missouri province who had completed a doctorate in economics at Harvard under the tutelage of Joseph Schumpeter, the conservative economist and theorist of political pluralism. It was Dempsey who in 1936 had translated Oswald von Nell-Breuning's lengthy gloss on papal social teaching, issued as *Reorganization of Social Economy*. More than twenty years later Dempsey published his own summation, *The Functional Economy*.[7] His opus was an effort to update corporatist theory before it died of neglect, and its significance lies not so much in the outcome of this venture—it aroused little interest—as in its appreciation of the fluidity of the postwar American economy.

Dempsey retained the stress on moral sobriety and the condemnation of liberalism and communism that ran through the writings of Joseph Husslein and John Rawe. But he also tried to rid his book of nostalgia for an arcadia of sturdy yeomen and dutiful wives. Dempsey did not dwell on the institutional specifics of corporatist assemblies as the ideologues of Latin authoritarianism had done. These legalisms were treated as so much archaic ornamentation; they were irrelevant to postwar democratic economies.

The criticisms and prescriptions Dempsey set forth were geared to industrial society, to "the machine age." The theoretical principles and social requisites, not the bureaucratic shell, of a functional corporatism would safeguard the traditional hierarchies of small personal units. The conservative essentials—Thomistic philosophy, the patriarchal family, and patterns of ownership and production that were supposed to reflect vestiges of traditional cooperation—remained. The organizational manifestation of these principles and practices might take various forms. By the standards of neoclassical economics, the approach was odd; the focus on mutualistic arrangements seemed incongruous with Dempsey's acceptance of market competition. Still, while the theorems of Marshallian economics furnished a somewhat more accurate picture of the actual workings of the American economy than did the political economy of scholasticism, Dempsey's perspective was not antiquarian. He did not appeal for a return to the past. In general he praised the efficiencies of American capitalism and called for a more realistic interpretation of the way it actually functioned. To his mind, such a depiction would show that the operations of the modern economy corresponded closely to a de facto corporatism. Dempsey was less interested in political forms than in the social organization of industrial capitalism.

Like many of his predecessors, Dempsey traced the origins of what he judged to be the political and economic disarray of the moment to the breakup of Christian unity. The Protestant Reformation brought in its train a series of revolutions—the commercial, the industrial, the political—culminating in the present crisis. The opening pages of *The Functional Economy* could have been lifted from almost any Catholic tract of the twenties or the thirties assailing the depravities of modernism. Instability pervaded all levels of life:

> Disorder is the essential note of our society. . . . [I]n our generation, revolution and the dissatisfied attitude that makes possible the spread of revolutionary ideas are not limited to the forms of political organization. Every social institution is under fire and the whole question of the nature of man, the number, quality, and origin of his rights, if any, and the social institutions best suited to such a man, family, civil communities, industrial organization, are all called into question at the same time. . . . The consequence of the Protestant movement that concerns us now in the United States is that the ultimate effect of this principle of division in political life and the shattering of intellectual unity has been the complete disintegration of Christian society both internationally and domestically.[8]

Dempsey registered a sense of loss for a time when "there was in Europe a way of life accepted by all which made association natural, easy, and permanent" and he lamented, quoting Pius XI, the abolition of "that highly developed social life which once flourished in a variety of prosperous institutions organically linked with each other."[9] In some passages Dempsey preached with a vehemence that was indistinguishable from the certainties of turn-of-the-century Catholicism:

> The basic teachings of the Church on matters of this kind are not merely the subject of opinion or choice; they are simple truth and any economic program that is at variance with them will not work. . . . What the Church has to say on Christian living in industrial society is important because it is true.[10]

He railed against the depersonalization of market economies, the spread of "nameless multitudes," the separation of the world of work from the world of the home, and the deterioration of ancient patterns of authority and affection:

> We may ask, without denying other important causes, to what extent is juvenile delinquency due to the lack of parental authority, which in its own turn is caused by the insecurity of the father? Can a man spend forty hours a week in a situation that kills his self-respect and then be a wise and affectionate disciplinarian at home?[11]

Yet as much as he might mourn times gone by, Dempsey understood that restoring the past was impossible. Unlike Husslein, he was trained as an economist. His condemnation of Protestantism did not prevent him from applauding the progress ensuant on the demise of the guilds and the overthrow of monarchies. The medieval guilds, like present-day parishes, were disadvantaged by their smallness and their localism. They did not provide adequate mechanisms for coping with a mass society and international markets. In the hands of nostalgic historians they had become organizational mummies, romanticized talismans without relevance to present conditions in the United States.

> Chiefly [because of] their limited local activities, there is little for us to learn directly from the guilds, and it is unfortunate that some proponents of the program sponsored by Pius XI talk about reviving the "guild system." The guild system never functioned effectively beyond a local market and is known to most people through its faults and limitations rather than its very great virtues. The only thing that the guilds have to offer modern industry and commerce is a functional principle of organization both within an industry and in the relation of industry to the state and to other industries. [12]

Dempsey recognized that not only historical corporatism but also the vocabulary of corporatist ideas were alien to the United States; they tended to be associated with the fascism of recent times:

> The historic word for a guild cannot be used in America. Just as the world "undertaker" no longer applies to one who undertakes any sort of business enterprise . . . so the word "university," which was one of the common types of guilds, is now limited to a particular kind of association. . . . The same is true of the words "corporation" (a term widely used in the middle ages for guilds) and "order" (a word used in a slightly different sense); a particular guild might be referred to as a university or a corporation, but all the guilds taken together were the orders of the community. These words have in modern times been used by Hitler and Mussolini for organizations which had completely lost their autonomy and, in the most complete violation of the principle of subsidiarity, had become mere instruments for the achievement of political purposes. [13]

Dempsey was not a mathematical economist. He considered the vogue for abstraction in the academic discipline to be as useless as the fantasies of neomedievalism. He argued for bringing economic thought—inordinately deductive as it was, deluded by the spinning of marginalist theorems disembodied from historical reality—into line with practice, which he saw as approximating corporatism in all but name. Like his mentor Joseph Schumpeter, Dempsey favored an institutional economics that would impart a descriptive accuracy and some feel for historical setting. Similarly, he advocated an organization of production in which form would more closely follow function.

These forms were inchoate. They were novel relations of production, no longer closely tied to physical plants and fixed locations. New arrangements of human relations were emerging, in advance of academic theory, in the postwar period of rationalized manufacturing by huge corporations. These collectivities differed from manufacturing facilities and financial conglomerates; they were networks made possible by new modes of transportation and communication.[14] The task of economics was to revise intellectual frameworks in the light of this new reality rather than to shape working arrangements according to preconceived abstractions or after romanticized models of the past.

The operative economic groupings that were forming alongside giant firms were not broad classes but finer-grained occupations and professions. In the American case, Dempsey argued further, these entities worked for joint ends instead of being locked in zero-sum combat. In the United States, markets were so vast that neither classes nor large companies could conspire successfully against the public interest. The size and diversity of the American market meant that there could be something for everybody; competition need not be ruinous. Barriers to entry and factors of scale could not block initiatives from the bottom up. Because the corporate communities transcended geographical localities and small markets, they differed fundamentally from older small organizations defined, as parishes or mom-and-pop stores were, by their physical presence. They were less tangible but more powerful than conventional institutions. Their primary resource was know-how rather than physical capital.

> There exist, then, in the United States, genuine functional communities, large groups of people who have a common interest, a common task, and a common purpose. These persons, regardless of location, form a functional community quite as real and almost as important as the civil municipality. Among the metropolitan economic municipalities, Steel-town is just as real as Pittsburgh, and Motor-town is as real as Detroit. There are important small and middle-sized economic municipalities quite as real and as important as these economic metropolises.[15]

Thus, since the New Deal and the rise of labor unions, the United States had moved, uncertainly but nonetheless discernibly, in the direction of an operative corporatism. This period had also witnessed the progressive absorption of the Catholic working class into the economic mainsteam. The transformation of American capitalism meant not only the rise of huge corporations and industrywide unions but also the emergence of styles of work that depended on cognitive resources rather than physical effort. These communities of skill were not wholly compatible with either traditional or early industrial divisions of labor. They were networks in embryo. What amounted to a second industrial revolution was underway. The nature of work was changing, and the workforce was becoming more mobile.

Along with these changes came two difficulties. One was the growth of a central government whose size threatened the independence of lesser organizations, not only the unions but also business corporations. Dempsey believed that American manufacturing enterprises were less in need of government regulation than the dictates of centralist varieties of corporatism might require. Most big companies were geared to the production and distribution of consumer goods in a market controlled by popular demand. The American economy was market driven and thus democratically controlled. For this reason, government intervention could be kept to a minimum:

> To some people, the mere mention of giant corporations conjures up "malefactors of great wealth," by nature, the enemies of the people.
>
> Whatever may have been true in Europe, or even in America during the 19th century, with the corporations then regarded as big, many large American corporations dare not be enemies of the people. Of the twenty-one *industrial* corporations listed as having sales of over one billion dollars in 1954, eight of them have sales organizations that bring them in direct touch with consumers. . . . Seven more, the large oil companies, are also in contact with the consumer, through intermediate steps terminating in the filling station and the fuel oil truck. . . . If this is true of corporations that can properly be described as primarily industrial, how much more true is it of *distribution* businesses like A & P, Sears . . . whose product, through distribution channels, goes straight to the consumer?[16]

Dempsey, who was dean of the school of commerce and finance at St. Louis University during the 1940s, saw the major American corporations not as oligopolies, as some institutional economists did, but as harbingers of mass sovereignty. The American economy was a supermarket supplied by efficient factories and large farms. This was a far cry from the excoriations of mass society and from the austere, homey ruralism idealized by Husslein and Rawe. It represented a melding of the aspirations of postimmigrant

Catholics with the ethos of abundance of the Eisenhower era. Prosperity was revoking the anticapitalist suppositions of Catholic social thought:

> The peculiarity of the giant American corporation is that it is geared to mass production with a small profit per unit, rather than to wide loose margins on a small output produced at high costs. . . . This has two genuinely democratic connotations: first, that it is a good thing to produce even semi-luxuries for the great mass of the people (who must have incomes to buy them); and, second, that such companies simply dare not risk a serious impairment of their public acceptance. . . . This is the main reason why public relations has replaced public-be-damned policies.[17]

The claim that the U.S. economy was evolving in a direction compatible not only with popular tastes but also with Catholic social doctrine implied a historic revision of earlier Jesuit critiques of capitalism. Disorder might well be the hallmark of the times. Nevertheless, Dempsey expressed impatience with the inflexible categories of Catholic thinkers that prevented them from coming to grips with economic realities. The stable vantage point which they thought they enjoyed encouraged them to issue condemnations of the modern age, but it did not provide them with a means for analyzing change. The problem, moreover, was not just an academic question, of the capacity to discard old rubrics and apprehend hard facts. Social change was passing the traditional mold of Catholicism by. Dempsey pointed approvingly to the socioeconomic assimilation going on among Catholics in a way that paralleled Murray's acceptance of pluralism in politics:

> Large numbers of American workers are becoming investors, at least vicariously, and supplementing their wage earnings with payments which have their origin in interest, rent and profits. On such a large scale, and potentially a vastly larger scale, this is a new thing on the face of the earth, a genuinely American contribution to economic life, not perfect but amendable as it grows.[18]

American Catholics were moving into an era in which the impulse behind the growth of governmental programs was slowing down because the need for such policies was weaker. Dempsey did not argue for the liquidation of the welfare state. But he believed that market-driven prosperity and distribution by consumption would reduce its role.[19]

A second difficulty remained, however. Catholics might lose their moral compass in the midst of plenty, as Murray also suggested. Even as they rejoiced in their economic success and growing political importance, it was doubtful whether their religion had either contributed to this mobility or could protect them from being corrupted by it. Catholicism might be out-moded in America:

> Basic central notions have been largely ignored. Meanwhile, the en-cyclical [*Quadragesimo Anno*] has served admirably as a source of quo-tations in support of whatever anybody was in favor of, for whatever reason. . . . Talking about social justice as an objective condition can easily make us sound as though we thought it was a fine virtue for oth-ers to practice.[20]

Dempsey saw the importance of extending American Catholic horizons beyond a subculture nourished by the family and the parish. Sentimental attachment to a simpler past did not bind him to an uncritical defense of face-to-face associations. But he could not put much faith in rational or-ganizational mechanisms for sustaining personal integrity in the midst of the good life. Individual virtue in some of its forms, such as self-discipline, for example, might enhance collective prosperity, and indeed Jesuit pedagogy might be credited with fostering a Catholic variant of the work ethic. But abundance did not in turn encourage individual goodness; on the contrary, it might undo it. This was the irony of progress. Technological functionality and the increasing size and complexity of markets reduced the core of personal responsibility for the good life.[21] The subversion of traditional values proceeded with the decline of institutions that might protect the solidarity and moral order once supported by the small-scale mutualism of the precapitalist era. The attainment of abundance threatened to undo the virtues that had made success possible. The increased education and mo-bility that were making old-line institutions obsolescent also seemed to be undermining organizational loyalties and commitments of any kind.[22]

In the end Dempsey did not trust institutions. The rejection of a literal reading of corporatism that enabled him to envision its functional utility regardless of organizational surfaces also led him to ignore institutional devices of almost any kind as practical incentives either for stable collective behavior or personal morality. Like Murray, Dempsey had a sense of im-pulsive disorder, of a latent atavism that could wreak havoc on human institutions. "Anarchy in the civil order," he wrote, "and free love in the domestic order are the principle analogous to theoretical competition in the economic order."[23]

> The essential condition to the restoration of social order is the aboli-tion of class conflict. Improvement in the utilization, distribution, and administration of private property, and the resulting improvements in the production and distribution of real income are, to be sure, impor-tant aids in removing causes of class conflict, but the two goods—

knowledge and love—which can be truly and pre-eminently common (because they are increased and not diminished by sharing) are the factors which dissolve class conflict at its foundations.[24]

Dempsey was a moralist with pragmatic yearnings.[25] "Knowledge"—the cultivation of human capital—could foster "the flowering of functional communities." These would not be constructed through the social engineering he identified with central planning. But neither would technical expertise by itself make a solid human community. Science alone did not build character. "The better social order will be principally the work of a shared knowledge and of a social cooperation expressive of mutual love."[26] This was not so different from the imagined ambience of the guilds or the neighborliness of the Catholic parishes. But Dempsey had abandoned that model, mourning its passing—and he wrote about a decade before the metaphor of the global community as a family, the "mystical body," came into vogue. He groped in a limbo of concepts with extrarational properties, hoping to link individual ethics to collective outcomes.

The knowledge that Dempsey praised was a composite of old and new. It was a compound of secular know-how and craftsman's pride: skill with a sediment of tradition. In modern times it would take the form of specialization and the proliferation of invisible colleges of professionals that were somehow responsive to the collective good but protected to a degree from the market. Social reform was to be guided not only by knowledge but by a cooperative instead of a competitive ethic. Dempsey envisioned a network of sharers, rather than a market of competitors, that in outline and in spirit was to be much like the electronically linked clusters of computer users of later generations.

The functional "conferences" of modern corporatism, as Dempsey called professional associations, and their connections to industrial companies were depicted sketchily. The organizational side of Dempsey's model remained nebulous. In part this was because the economic system as perceived by Dempsey was itself inchoate, burgeoning between the free market of neoclassical theory and the oligopolistic concentrations depicted by institutional economists. The decentralized communities of spirit and skill that Dempsey envisaged as the lifelines of American capitalism were also analogous to the spatial segmentation of American Catholicism into spread-out parishes sharing a larger culture. In effect, it was this common culture, rather than the traditional organizations associated with the centralist heritage of Europe or the tangible mechanisms of secular society (such as business corporations) that formed the subject of *The Functional Economy*. Dempsey did not dwell on the implications of this centrifugalism for the Catholic hierarchy itself.

Much of Dempsey's work was derivative. His analysis of the large, consumer-oriented firms of American capitalism strongly echoes the early work of John Kenneth Galbraith.[27] The connections between these organizations and the professional and occupational networks were unspecified. For all his interest in institutional economics, the functional groupings of American corporatism remained spectral entities. Occupational networks and professional knowledge were capable of overriding the imperatives of a market of purely material things, but this was not quite the same as a community of meaning. Other Jesuits, as disinclined as Dempsey to examine formal institutions, would search for this bond in the mass media.[28]

The significance of Dempsey's writing stems from its transitional quality. By the time he produced *The Functional Economy* he had forsaken the formalized corporatism of his German mentors. The static categorizations of scholasticism were mostly gone. Times had also changed. The depression was over, and Western Europe and the United States were enjoying the fruits of Keynesian growth. Dempsey cast aside analytical classifications that were premised on chronic scarcity.

Yet Dempsey also sensed that abundance might be the undoing of traditional Catholicism and, more broadly, of tenuous community. His willingness to abandon received notions of social order, particularly as they depended on impersonal bureaucracies, did not provide him with a coherent view of emerging networks of production and exchange. Secondhand as many of his ideas were, their composite formed an intriguing oddity by its juxtaposition of traditional and futuristic themes. His intuitions skirted mystical possibilities. Two intangibles, knowledge and love, might overtake the material prosperity that precipitated religious decline—a preview of the antiinstitutional, personalist movements of the next decade. His advocacy of economic decentralization also had a less romantic side, prefiguring ideas about industrial organization and flexible manufacturing methods that would surface three decades later in the work of a new scholarly generation.[29]

III

The spatial equivalent of the conviction that Catholic doctrine was unchanging was belief in its universality. The *magisterium* held regardless of place and time. When it was not ignored altogether, the assumption of a nucleus of abiding generic verities could be treated more or less flexibly, more or less rigidly. Everything depended on how broadly or narrowly the nucleus was defined. In practice few Jesuits gave credence to the idea that personal ethics and public behavior could be all of a piece, and it was doubtful whether any such integration should seriously be pursued. Nevertheless, the idea of a holistic vision, somehow integrating private and public spheres, stood as background to the observations of Bernard Dempsey on economic, social, and political questions. This dream gave his writings and those of his predecessors, like John Rawe, the two-edged character of prophetic eccentricity.

On a day-to-day level, where ideas and organizations were supposed to meet, this way of looking at truth and falsehood created an insupportable dilemma for Jesuits in the United States. How could such fixity and uniformity be reconciled with a pluralist and predominantly secular environment? As long as Jesuits stayed within the Catholic enclave, this sort of difficulty was manageable. They tended to put it aside and get on with their work, with the result that speculative thought became an intellectual curiosity remote from reality. This strategy, workable within the confines of a parochial universe, became less feasible as Jesuits moved toward dialogue with their non-Catholic peers. John Courtney Murray proposed to solve the quandary by recognizing the historical contingency of political and social, if not moral, norms. He went beyond the acceptance of toleration as a functional convenience for Catholics in a minority position; he gave legitimacy to toleration as a good in itself. He lifted the burden of what amounted to a parody of "tradition," crystallized in Roman formalism, from the improvisations of American Catholic experience.

A second difficulty touched more directly on the internal unity of Catholicism than on the relations between Catholics and members of other denominations. It arose from the changing social profile of American Catholics. The supposition of a timeless, universally veracious Catholicism provided a common culture—an image of a way of life—that spanned the social and cultural heterogeneity of the immigrant faithful. When assimilation seemed far away and Catholics felt encircled, what outsiders thought, especially if those thoughts were critical, could be dismissed as erroneous and probably ill intentioned. Internal differences were secondary to communal solidarity.[30] But the crumbling of subcultural boundaries after the war, rising levels of education among Catholics, and their intermingling with other denominations cut into this line of defense.

Homogeneity of custom and even of belief no longer seemed secure. Uniformity in principle had been sustained in large measure by a parochialism of practice; intellectual unity depended on the replication of small worlds. The withering of these local supports made the mores seem petty and arcane, but the lingered for some time. The distance between habit and underlying social change made for awkward and occasionally surreal passages. Customs constituted a silent language, never fully articulated. Because the minutiae of tradition were felt to be part of a larger code, they formed a symbolic halo of their own, like cobwebs on an heirloom, which would disintegrate if they were touched. It was difficult to separate minor from important matters.

After the war, through the years leading up to the Second Vatican Council, the Society of Jesus in the United States found it increasingly difficult to maintain a sense of internal community while extending an effective liaison with the social and intellectual environment outside the Catholic subculture. These years can be read as a movement from a primitive, small-world holism to a more sophisticated perception of complexity, fragmentation, and incipient loss of control.

In May 1947, the provincial superiors of the American Jesuits gathered at Gonzaga University in Spokane, Washington, for their annual meeting. On their agenda were several items of great and small importance, treated serially. Among their other decisions, the provincials resolved to discourage the mounting number of requests for travel to attend national meetings on the part of Jesuits involved in professional associations:

> The question arose about the great number of national meetings of Jesuits at great distances from their place of work. The Provincials agreed that these meetings were too numerous, since instances were known of Rectors complaining about the inconvenience, expense, etc. sustained by the individual houses, members of whose community took trips to distant parts of the country for meetings of various national groups.
>
> In regard to the Jesuit Educational Association, it was thought that perhaps one meeting a year would be sufficient for the Executive Committee.
>
> It was determined to request of Father Lord at the next session what national meetings he considers really necessary for various groups of the ISO. He should also be asked to state objectives of the meetings.[31]

The policy of keeping Jesuits close to their home provinces worked reasonably well when the principal mission of the American assistancy was to build up a network of high schools and to develop a string of colleges and universities that provided instruction to local and regional clienteles. Each of these was a small market, and the ingenuity of the Jesuits lay in adjusting their pedagogy to local conditions. Greater cosmopolitanism was needed to cultivate a national audience, already educated, for whom a comparatively sophisticated interchange rather than instruction as tutorial would be the mode of address. For this job fewer restrictions—greater intellectual as well as physical mobility—were needed. The protective regulations of the subculture suddenly became petty and counterproductive.

A major vehicle for publicizing the Catholic point of view in the postwar period was *America*, the magazine edited by the Jesuits in New York. In 1944 John LaFarge had stepped up from managing editor to editor in chief. Even the celebrated LaFarge had to spend considerable time finessing the customs of the society that were hindering *America's* program of intellectual outreach. Difficulties with the regulations took numerous forms, but the underlying problem involved the balance between religious authority on the inside and editorial discretion vis-à-vis the public. The particular dilemma that happened to emerge toward the end of the war prefigured disputes over censorship versus journalistic freedom that cropped up in the following decades.

Every Jesuit residence, including the one on the Upper West Side of Manhattan out of which the staff of *America* worked, had a superior, the Jesuit in charge. In the educational establishments of the society, the superior had both spiritual and operational functions. The president of Fordham University or Boston College, for example, was responsible not only for running the institution but also for the well-being of the Jesuits who made up the community. The roles of inside and outside manager were undifferentiated.[32] However, at Campion House, as it was called, the editor was not the religious superior, and LaFarge bridled at the prospect of having to clear the contents of the magazine through another layer of Jesuit officialdom. In 1945 the provincials had decided in his favor, but the issue came up again the next year. In commenting on the minutes of the 1945 meeting, Zacheus Maher tried to settle the issue by affirming a hierarchy between competing principles, in favor of internal control:

> We must maintain that since all the members of the community, including the Editor-in-Chief, depend on the Superior not only in matters affecting religious discipline but in others as well (for in any house there is but one Superior) it cannot be maintained that he has no veto power over the Editor-in-Chief.[33]

LaFarge shot back that

> the very existence of AMERICA and its continued success depends on its Editor having a free hand in matters immediately pertaining to the periodical's editorial policy, stand on vital issues, etc. He is already subject to the veto power of the representative of the Board of Governors . . . the Provincial of the N.Y. Province.[34]

The provincials sympathized with LaFarge. It had never been the practice for a superior at the *America* residence to exercise control over what appeared in the magazine:

> The Fathers Provincial decided unanimously to permit the Editor and the Superior to carry on for the time being as here-to-fore, and that

meantime they would respectfully ask Fr. Vicar to reconsider his recent decision on the veto power of the Superior of Campion House.[35]

Such squabbles were aggravated by compulsive individuals like Maher, but the basic tension went beyond personalities. It concerned the tradeoff between two equally venerable features of the society's organizational culture, hierarchy and adaptability. In the case of the division of authority between rector and editor at *America*, the insistence on maintaining a standard rule, regardless of the setting, was so impractical that the provincials managed to defer the question in the name of common sense. To go by the book would also certainly have meant an inane sacrifice of efficiency, and even if the religious superior turned out to be a capable journalist, the rationale for maintaining an editor, even a titular one, became problematic. Evidently, some differentiation of functions was needed. Some compromise had to be worked out between the principles of authority on the one side and autonomy on the other.

The dilemma was postponed but not resolved. Similar disputes came to absorb more of the time of the leaders of the American assistancy. The shift from almost wholly local or in-house concerns to the consideration of national questions before a culturally mixed audience meant that not only the organizational but also the intellectual dimensions of institutional harmony had to be dealt with. When issues were of a religious nature, or when they were confined to the local arena, the appearance of Jesuit unity could be kept up. But as the society reached toward the national level, the complexity of issues and the heterogeneity of the audience made the propagation of the Catholic perspective less controllable. The certainty presumed to be characteristic of truths hived off under the rubric of religion did not carry over into political and economic controversies.

In 1948, for example, the provincials noted that there might be a danger of *America*'s taking a stand that, after research on the part of the Institute of Social Order, would have to be altered. From his headquarters in St. Louis the director of ISO maintained that "this will hardly be true of the main principles," insisting "on the need for controversy to stimulate thorough thinking" and discouraging "any effort to have a single official Jesuit opinion."[36] This issue, too, was shelved.

As the explosion in secular knowledge continued, both the Jesuits at *America* and those attached to ISO became increasingly perplexed by the gap between the deposit of faith and positions to be taken on political matters. Expertise had to be cultivated; credibility could not be maintained by decree. Even then, however, the fit between "faith and science" was not guaranteed. Traditional alternatives to competing for acceptance in secular terms through persuasion were problematic. Clinging to the old truths, or to

the belief that practical applications could be more or less commonsensi-
cally derived from them, or resorting to adherence by obedience, meant
perpetuating a simpler world in which Jesuits were never quite at home
either. Accommodating the new without contradicting the old required
stretching ingenuity to the breaking point. Spats between defenders of authority and proponents of intellectual novelty defied peremptory resolution.

At the same meeting in which they accepted the view of ISO that there
was no clash between the doctrinal core and circumstantial applications of
it in social and economic matters, the provincials found themselves unable
to fit courses in the social sciences into the classical curriculum of the
seminaries:

> A request that the Fathers Provincial devise means of making courses
> in social studies available to scholastics during the scholastic year was
> considered. This was judged impossible in view of the heavy schedule
> of class periods in our houses of study. It was recommended by the
> Fathers Provincial that this matter be further considered in the reports
> on the *Ratio* to be made by the scholasticate deans to Father Gen-
> eral.[37]

For the moment the issue was treated as a problem in logistics; the intellectual implications were set aside. But the inertia of innumerable minutiae
slowed adaptability. Traditions creaked under their own weight.

A corollary of the image of Catholic doctrine as timeless and universal
was that the *magisterium* tended to be all-embracing; the teaching was
supposed to be catholic in the sense of covering all persons. A premium was
placed on conciliation. On the one hand there was an intransigence to the
ideal of doctrinal impermeability. This carried a potential for movements of
"enthusiasm" and for clinging to certainty in sectarian terms. There was in
compensation an understanding that a kind of psychic diplomacy, a moral
economy of forgiveness and sub-rosa toleration, was needed to assuage conflicting claims. This melding made for pastoral kindness but intellectual
blandness and a cultural propensity for handling contradictions with verbal
finesse.

Catholics in the United States clustered in ethnic communities, and they
were still predominantly blue-collar and lower middle class. They made up
a large constituency and latent interest group on such issues as federal aid for
parochial schools. The mores of the subculture, the teachings of the church
and the economic interests of both might run against the American grain.
In addition, the Catholic community itself was expanding and becoming
differentiated. A bent toward conciliation and caution was politic, but a
circumspect manner could not suppress anxiety that arose from shifts in the

Catholic constituency and possible conflicts stemming from these changes.

After John LaFarge retired from the editorship, Fr. Robert Hartnett, a political scientist from the University of Detroit, took over the direction of *America*. Unlike some of the Jesuits who staffed the magazine in the thirties, Hartnett was an avid New Deal Democrat. Both he and Fr. Benjamin Masse, a Jesuit specializing in labor issues, had been brought on board by LaFarge for their progressive views.[38] But they lacked LaFarge's suaveness. On various occasions Masse was chastised for his prolabor stance. In 1946 the provincials heard the complaint that

> whereas Fr. Masse has many worthwhile things to say on industrial relations and the like, he at the same time betrays a bias in favor of Labor, giving no ear whatever to complaints against Labor. It was said that he would vastly improve his position were he to give Management a hearing; that he ought now and then to present the virtues of the other side and some of the defects of Labor; and that finally he ought to watch and weigh more carefully his sources of information.[39]

Six years later, in 1952, on the eve of the Eisenhower era, the same ideological slant came in for criticism.

> All the Fathers Provincial had heard in their own Provinces criticisms (whether few or many), mostly from Ours, of the editorial policy of AMERICA. They come to this: the magazine seldom seems to admit that the Federal Administration or Labor are in the wrong, so that it has a partisan tinge; topics that are "political" are treated when they seem to have no connection with matters of Catholic interest; offense is given to individuals.[40]

The left-of-center line taken by Hartnett and Masse represented the zenith of a strain in the social philosophy of the American Jesuits that expressed sympathy for the plight of working people. Parts of their perspective were also consonant with the conservatism of older Jesuits like Joseph Husslein. This current of thought was ambiguous in its attitude toward liberalism, consumerism, individualism, mass democracy, and the secular varieties of socialism, and it was interlarded with traditional scholastic suppositions about "right order." The hierarchical communitarianism of Hartnett and Masse sounded like a jeremiad against the rising class of Catholic businessmen and graduates of Jesuit professional schools who were more likely to read *America* than the union members whose cause the editors espoused. By the standards of the Eisenhower years there was a taint of un-Americanism about such thinking. It was sufficiently leftist to arouse suspicion or embarrassment among Catholics of the postimmigrant generation who were straining toward middle-class respectability, while the occasional references to interventionist models of managing economic conflict threatened to rekindle flashes of nativist resentment against a subculture still anxious to demonstrate its normalcy.

The prolabor stance adopted by *America* did not change drastically. Its importance, however, eventually receded in response to a jockeying for power inside the magazine. Editorial policy was moderated. Labor politics verged on becoming a nonissue. The pivotal factor was the absorption of the unions and Catholics in postwar prosperity. Somewhat as happened with John Courtney Murray's defense of pluralism, it was not so much that hearts and minds had actually been won over, and supposedly deep convictions changed, as that the issue ceased to be controversial because a change once perceived as menacing turned out to bring the comforts of realism and a feeling of insertion in the larger culture. During the 1950s American labor unions won concessions that diminished the radicalism of the thirties and forties, and American Catholics were becoming increasingly assimilated. The immigrant backdrop of the Catholic social ethics of the thirties was thinning out.

Through the middle of the fifties Hartnett and Masse gave a tinge of a social-democratic slant to the pages of *America* that was reminiscent of what had appeared in some secular journals on the left two decades earlier. But the magazine had neither a working-class base nor a secular intellectual readership. A good many of the subscriptions went to parish and episcopal residences, in addition to circulating among Jesuits themselves; working-class Catholics had never paid close attention to the magazine. In the eyes of some Jesuits, the defense of Catholic values seemed in danger of becoming entangled with too narrow a constituency. The editor of *America* had repeatedly to justify what other Jesuits, including the provincials, took to be the magazine's bias:

> Father Hartnett admitted some degree of justness in the criticism but denied that AMERICA was pro-Administration in a partisan way; rather, it sought to defend, as far as possible, the policies of the Government as distinct from the party in power, and considered those policies, in general, to be based on correct principles. He asserted that it is difficult to find any topic that is "purely" political; almost every question involves the prudential choice of means to morally important objectives. In the Editor's view, it should be the aim of the Review to discuss any and every topic that has news value. Offense has been given to some individuals, but in these instances the matter reported was accurately true, the phrasing might have been more tactfully chosen. There is a pro-Labor slant that is excessive, but this is due to the

impossibility of finding a writer who can present the opposite side competently.[41]

The justifications Hartnett set forth included tortured but not wholly fanciful theoretical distinctions—between the party in power and the government, for example—and an admission that the expertise of Jesuits in questions of labor-management relations was circumscribed by the largely working- and middle-class composition of the American Catholic constituency. As Bernard Dempsey had done in trying to visualize an American corporatism, Hartnett ran up against the problem that there were as yet few Catholic managers to provide coalition partners for a conciliatory capitalism, and in any case these men were unlikely to be receptive to either the depression-era progressivism or the war-enforced collaboration between capital and labor that they wanted to put behind them. Although this class of American Catholics did not come of age until the late fifties and early sixties, they were even then appearing over the horizon, and there was no need to offend them. Besides, labor itself seemed to want little part of class confrontation, and the social encyclicals prized harmony over conflict. By the beginning of the 1950s the institutional and demographic receptors among American Catholics for a strenuous Jesuit advocacy of the rights of labor had weakened.[42]

Had he been more agile in dealing with the severely conservative ambience of Irish American Catholicism in the New York archdiocese, Hartnett might have managed to sustain an assertively prolabor line a bit longer, even as the sporadic radicalism of working-class Catholics faded with prosperity. The international polarization of the Cold War helped distract attention from the domestic quarrels between management and labor that remained after the accommodation made possible by prosperity. It was a period in the subculture of Northeastern Catholicism when piety and patriotism were inextricably joined; chauvinism held sway over class divisions and even over the remnants of ethnic radicalism.[43] A vigorous advocacy of the rights of labor, at a time when working-class Catholics showed themselves to be increasingly content with the postwar settlement, struck many in ecclesiastical circles as imprudent. In 1952 the religious superior of the Jesuit community at *America* observed that

he [had] heard priests of the Archdiocese of New York and of other dioceses express dissatisfaction with the publication, and never hears any favorable comments from the clergy. He believes that Father Hartnett is competent in ability, incompetent in judgment; that his view is politico-scientific, not ecclesiastical; that he should be counterbalanced by an expert religious editor; that he should be subject to the advice of an "admonitor."[44]

So Hartnett got into trouble not only because of his prolabor position but also for his attacks on McCarthyism—a state of mind, espoused by Cardinal Spellman and other local notables—which pitted xenophobic Americanism against a cosmopolitan elitism.[45] On this issue he could not be accused of politicizing an area such as labor policy that might have a Catholic but not overly controversial tenor. Senator Joseph McCarthy, a graduate of Marquette, the Jesuit university in Wisconsin, who had gained notoriety in the early fifties, was ardently defended by conservative Catholic interests. Hartnett became embroiled in a polemic with various McCarthyites, including some fellow Jesuits, a few of them on his own staff.[46]

The pros and cons of McCarthyism were not the nub of the controversy. The larger uproar was about editorial freedom. Hartnett's desire to show that freedom of the press was taken seriously by American Jesuits was pitted against the institutional drive to maintain ecclesiastical unity and to avoid exacerbating divisions among the faithful. The tradeoff was between maintaining credibility through open discussion and the preservation of a community of opinion on Catholic and para-Catholic issues. In 1953 Hartnett was reminded that the *instructio,* the founding document of *America,* forbade the treatment of *res mere politicae aut saeculares* ("merely political or secular matters"). He responded that

> the staff has tried consistently to steer clear of topics that bear no obvious or important relation to the general welfare of the Church or of society. AMERICA [Hartnett], maintains, commands respect in many areas, and, as a weekly review of opinion, it must take definite and strong positions on specific current issues in the light of Catholic social and political principles. . . . If AMERICA is not known to express its own authentic opinion or to treat topics with authority, but is known to be inhibited, it will lose its value among thinking people. . . .
>
> Father Hartnett further stated that it would be practically impossible for AMERICA to carry on unless the Fathers Provincial support him in his editorial opinions and policies.[47]

The danger of scandal in the McCarthy affair was managed much as the controversy building up around Murray's speculations in political philosophy had been controlled, by an order of silence from the superior general in Rome. *America* stopped writing about McCarthy from mid-1954 until he died in 1957. Then the magazine noted the senator's passing in a small note, almost as an afterthought.[48] Hartnett went on leave in 1954. The next year he was replaced by the urbane Thurston Davis. Rather than a sharp turnaround in ideology, the new command brought in a change of editorial tone, wittier and less polemical, and greater harmony developed among the staff. A bit more attention was given to columns of spiritual contemplation and advice. The format of the magazine was modernized. Circulation increased.[49]

The battle over *America*'s editorial policy illuminated tensions internal to American Jesuits, during a period of growing social complexity. The working through of the controversy over McCarthyism at *America* was a clerical affair. Clarification of the rights and wrongs of the political issues was secondary to the maintenance of unity in face of outside observers.

Yet consensus presupposed a directness and clarity in the links between core beliefs and derivative applications that was less and less tenable and that could not endure by being handed down from a central authority. Such consensus as was reached risked being fabricated at the price of sacrificing creativity. This cost could be hidden as long as the self-referential standards of the Catholic enclave were kept in place. As that environment came apart, more time was spent in monitoring agreement. The dialect of internal control and dissent remained heavy-handed, suffocating intellectual honesty during a period when a previously captive constituency was moving away.

In 1954, at the height of the turmoil over McCarthy, the staff of *America* comprised fourteen Jesuits, a number approaching the size of the staff of Action Populaire during its heydey. But the growth in numbers did not promote unity of outlook, or even a critical mass of competent analysts. Hartnett pleaded that "the staff is unwieldy and should be reduced to eight or at most ten members":

> The staff is in the worst condition he has seen. He laments their lack
> of cooperation, with few exceptions; their limited capacity, both in
> work and ability; their immaturity; overspecialization; and failure to
> produce more copy and reviews.[50]

The presumptive doctrinal conformity of the waning days of the papacy of Pius XII, like the standardization of ritual, was ornamental. The complexity of public issues and the heterogeneity of American Catholics defeated attempts to propound a convincing synthesis on political and social matters. The split between the myth of an overarching community of belief, reinforced by the social homogeneity of the Catholic subculture, and the growing differentiation of knowledge grew wider:

> [Father Hartnett] explained how the policies of the AMERICA staff
> were established on the several major questions of domestic and for-
> eign interest. AMERICA, he said, as a review of opinion, sought to
> break down current questions to sound Catholic principles and to ex-

plain the relation of these principles to the development of the questions at issue. He pointed out that in obscure questions the policy of the periodical is often determined by the member of the staff with special competence on the subject. In this respect, there was noted the greater need of Associate Editors with wide interests and competence so that their contributions might be more beneficial to the establishment of editorial policy.[51]

It was an ethical imperative that *America* take authoritative and, if need be, courageous stands. But, the question of courage aside, and apart from the long-standing habit of favoring conciliation over polarization, it was not always (or even usually) clear what the authoritative or semiofficial posture of the church on the issues of the day was supposed to be. There were fewer absolutes than expected. Intellectual creativity was constricted; the uniformity imposed in the name of antimodernism was becoming dysfunctional. Still, in the absence of unambiguous principle, and with expertise divided, the tendency was to fall back on authority and to cleave to a careful medium.

The tiffs and scuffles at *America* formed part of a larger pattern, one that included the silencing of John Courtney Murray. In both instances, intellectual integrity was pitted against the power of authority. In the case of *America*, however, there was a larger component of home-grown political hedging. Jesuit superiors acted in the spirit of party managers unwilling to offend a significant portion of their constituents.

Hartnett stuck to his prolabor position, but he sensed that social militancy had not gained much support among Jesuits and was losing ground among Catholics generally. Ideology was thought to be coming to an end anyway, and prudence and delicacy of judgment were never out of favor. Hartnett became increasingly disappointed with the self-absorption and political indifference of American Catholics.

> The Editor understands the Fathers Provincial to want AMERICA to avoid what is seriously divisive of Catholics. But he feels that an uncatholic mood has overtaken a great deal of Catholic thinking about public questions; and, in particular, that anything like a vigorous presentation of what he and the staff believe to be the kind of application of Catholic social teaching incumbent upon us will prove offensive to many American Catholics.[52]

By the end of the fifties the incorporation of unionized labor ceased to be an issue for Catholics. Other issues would emerge, and the civil rights movement was gaining momentum. As the sixties opened, a former student of the Jesuits, Michael Harrington, published a book that drew attention to the persistence of poverty in an America of abundance.[53] But neither of these concerns was peculiarly Catholic; most American Catholics were white and increasingly well off, and their idealism was channeled toward international causes and movements such as the Peace Corps. *America* nurtured the traditional skills of eloquence and judicious commentary. In an interim of less than a decade, between the end of the fifties and the middle of the sixties, geniality and a smooth, almost canned circumspection reigned.[54]

IV

In the decades preceding World War II, most of the foreign contacts of American Jesuits were with their colleagues in Western Europe. There were some missionary expeditions, largely to colonial areas. In 1919 the Bombay mission was assigned to the mostly Irish American Jesuits of the Maryland–New York province. This arrangement did not last long, for the British administrators of the raj did not warm to the prospect of Irish American priests stirring up their Indian subjects, and the Bombay province was soon transferred to presumably more-imperial-minded Jesuits from Castille.[55] In 1921, however, responsibility for the Philippines was transferred from Spanish Jesuits to the same group of Americans from the East Coast of the United States. Still in the twenties, a few young American Jesuits were sent off on the papal relief mission to Russia, headed by Edmund Walsh, and others helped set up schools in Lithuania and Czechoslovakia. During the thirties and forties some California Jesuits, including the obstreperous George Dunne, went to China.[56]

These interwar excursions had started from a low base. Not until the first decade of the twentieth century did Rome officially acknowledge that American Catholicism was no longer a "mission church," and not until 1915, at their twenty-sixth general congregation, did the Society of Jesus separate the administration of its provinces in the United States from the English assistancy and recognize them as forming an assistancy on their own.[57]

In the twenties and thirties Latin American Catholicism had become visible to North American Jesuits through the campaign waged against the revolutionary regime in Mexico by Wilfrid Parsons, then editor of *America*.[58] Although the provincials urged Parsons to soften the tone of "certain censorious articles and editorials in *America* . . . in connection with the religious persecution in Mexico," they urged "no abatement in the agitation of the question and publication of facts authentically reported from Mexico, until American sympathy can be won for the suffering Catholics of that distressed land."[59] During this period, as North American Jesuits saw it, the main threats to Catholicism in Latin America, as elsewhere, were secular radicalism and a competitive Protestantism. Parsons felt that the appeal of the two movements depended on the attention they gave to social justice and human services, and he argued that the Jesuits should meet the challenge in like manner:

> The most effective way of counteracting the Protestant influence would be to begin in South America with social work and to follow this up with a pamphlet and doctrinal campaign. It was agreed that *America* should lend its assistance by exposing in the United States the Protestant activities in South America and their anti-Catholic propaganda.[60]

By the early forties, the American branch of the Society of Jesus had not only overcome its status as an outpost in mission territory, it was on its way to becoming a center of expansion itself. Europe remained the intellectual center of Catholicism. But the United States was now its quantitative core by reasons of manpower and money.[61]

Toward the end of the war, opinions regarding the role of North American Jesuits in Latin America were in transition. The defensiveness that had characterized attitudes toward the persecution of the Mexican church in earlier decades was giving way to optimism about the contributions that North American clergy might make to the Latin American scene. Jesuits began to express a can-do assertiveness that smacked of pride in the virtues of Yankee common sense and practical rationality. The spirit of adventure was mixed with caution, however. Jesuits retained a skepticism and some resentment toward the Protestant overtones of the ethos of efficiency. In addition, acculturation to the exotic was a feature of the expeditionary past of the society. This entailed, alongside the heroics, sobering lessons about the failures and the painstaking successes of the missions. Jesuits did not try to export an unabashed Americanism, and a willingness to endure martyrdom was not seen as an excuse for arousing hostility among benighted heathens. They showed foresight and sophistication as well as enthusiasm.[62]

The reflections of Fr. Peter Masten Dunne, head of the history department at the University of San Francisco, who toured Latin America in 1944, were marked by this ambivalence.[63] He did not dwell as Parsons had on the persecution suffered by the church in Mexico. Instead, as LaFarge had done in the case of Spain, he pointed to some of the historical compromises that, if left to stand, would hurt ecclesiastical interests in the future. He observed that "Brazilian Catholicism has not everywhere been of the finest type. It has often been easy-going and lethargic." He speculated that this lassitude might not be a character trait but reflect instead a history of religious monopoly on the part of the church. "Perhaps a little opposition [from Protestantism] will stir the Brazilian Church to still greater energy of action and still finer loyalty to high spiritual ideals."[64] Dunne stressed the need to match Protestant incursions with the drive that North American Jesuits, their competitive skills honed by experience in a pluralist setting, could furnish.

> Old, easy-going ways must be discarded. The Catholic Church has long been in possession. Let's recall the words of the Brazilian bishop stating that church-men had been easy-going there; had taken things for granted. "We knew that everybody was a Catholic". . . . Another Latin American bishop told me that more energy and organization was exactly what was needed. . . . If Protestants have a broadcasting system, let Catholics get a bigger and better one. Instead of spending $50,000 on a jeweled crown for a statue of the Virgin Mary, let them put the money into Christian social works. Let the parish priest at Christmas time instead of buying new candelabra for the altar of his church use the Christmas offerings to buy food and presents for the poor children of his parish.[65]

Dunne noted that the church in Latin America had so long been given over to a traditional emotionalism, gone soft in the absence of serious intellectual or organizational challenges, that it had "lost the men." The propensity for display over hard work that he detected in Latin America undercut a true, stoic virility even as it promoted shows of machismo:

> It gradually came to the point that the Church was considered to be for the women. That weakness which we call human respect got into the male psychology so that a man became ashamed to be seen at Mass, though he approved of his wife and daughter going, and even facilitated their religious practice. . . .
>
> The Latin with all his culture, courtesy, charm, and other amiable qualities, is not so strong a character as is often met with among the peoples of the northern races. He is easy going. A little negligence and disorder does not bother him much. He is sensitive and yields to what others might think. Human respect dissolves his courage. There is a certain sterner stuff in characters of the north which the Latin, by and large, does not possess.[66]

By this standard there could be no question of Latin American Catholicism influencing North America Jesuits. Influence would flow the other way around. "Emotion," Dunne stated flatly, "offers no solution."[67]

Nevertheless, Dunne could not remain insensitive to the attractions of the Latin mentality, which he perceived to be less singlemindedly calculating and hence more humane than its North American, Protestant counterpart. In a rhapsodic passage, Dunne suggested that the Latin psyche represented a harmonious mean—an androgynous resolution of the intolerantly rational and the volcanically expressive. Latins were not the problem solvers that North Americans made themselves out to be. This relieved them of the righteousness that came from identifying success as the product of hard work. But they were not happy-go-lucky primitives. On the contrary, their experience of defeat and tragedy, their closeness to suffering and capacity for emotional release, had given them a sophistication and an aesthetic sense that surpassed mere rationality:

> There is a certain emotional richness and refinement in the Latin psychology which is difficult for the colder North American justly to evaluate, because he often does not possess it. It is like the stolid Englishman unable to understand the emotions of the Irish. I have often thought that the refined and cultured Latin is the best rounded out of men, because he partakes of the qualities of both the sexes, the refined emotions of the woman and the intellectual strength of the man. . . .
>
> Take the Latin male: He will be sensitive to beauty, even if he be uncultured. With his powers developed by education and training, he will appreciate the good and the beautiful in all things. . . . Because of less emotion in the North, there is less of religious warmth, less of spiritual ardor. The saints of Christianity, you will note, have more often come from the South. This is one reason why Catholicism, with its warmth and supernatural devotion, is predominant in Latin countries, even if the male is estranged from the Church. The Latin has seldom made a good Protestant. The colder, if more practical spirit of Protestantism, has little appeal to the emotional ardor of the Latin.[68]

In attempting to dispel a single stereotype of culture "south of the Rio Grande," Dunne verged on perpetuating multiple caricatures of frigid Yankees and humid Latins.[69] Yet he managed to draw a wedge between the strengths and flaws of national character as cultural phenomena, on one side, and as causes of economic stagnation and political instability on the other. The latter could not be tied directly to the former. Dunne empathized with Latin Americans. He admired them, as it were against his better judgment, because they were not Protestants or, worse, English. It was collectively, in their institutions, in an organizational environment given to wasteful conflict, that they suffered by comparison with productive and politically stable North Americans. The pathology was organizational and educational, not one of character or temperament. For Dunne the ideal society seems to have combined the institutional sobriety and technological know-how of North America with Latin soul.[70]

The remedy for the "emotional richness" of Latin Catholicism was therefore not its replacement by the austere vigor of North Americanism—an

Fr. Wlodimir Ledochowski, born in Poland in 1861, governed the society as its Superior General from World War I until his death in 1942. The following year, a papal encyclical opened the way to Catholics for critical and historical studies of the biblical texts, an enterprise Protestants had been engaging in for nearly a century. Undaunted by incipient progressivism, Ledochowski was determined to direct the Jesuits in Europe and America in a moral crusade against the excesses of modernism. It was Ledochowski who supervised the writing of *Quadragesimo Anno* (1931), the landmark social encyclical. *(Courtesy of Special Collections Division, Georgetown University Library)*

In his letter, "Combatting Communism," Father Ledochowski commissioned the Jesuits of North America to lead "the way in our Society's project of a worldwide systematic warfare against the common enemy of Christianity and civilization." His choice for launching the project was Fr. Edmund Walsh, founder of the School of Foreign Service of Georgetown University, and an expert on international politics and the Soviet Union. *(Courtesy of Special Collections Division, Georgetown University Library)*

Although education was the traditional method of cultivating Catholic leadership among the Jesuits, the irrepressible Fr. Daniel Lord, seated here at center, adopted a more populistic, almost evangelical approach to spreading the social gospel and combating communism. By the late 1930s Lord had organized "Summer Schools for Catholic Action," primarily throughout the Midwest and the East. The SSCA offered liturgy and social uplift for high school students and men and women religious, and operated on the novel basis of nondiscriminatory racial participation. *(Courtesy of Chicago Province Archives, Society of Jesus)*

THE QUEEN'S WORK

presents

The Social Order Follies

Book and Songs
by the producer

Daniel A. Lord, S. J.

-------------------------!

NOVEMBER 20 to 27

St. Louis University Auditorium
3642 Lindell Boulevard
Tickets, $1.00—75c—50c

Note: All of the characters presented in this sketch are purely imaginary. Any resemblance to your friends or relations is entirely in your own mind, and you ought to be ashamed of yourself.

I
OPENING CHORUS

(The Whites):
Good evening, Mr. Ritz,
And Mrs. Vanderschnitz;
And Mrs. Forest Park and Mr. Cages.
Isn't it nice to know where you look
There are people from the Blue Book?
All our names are written in the Social Pages.

(The Reds):
Good evening, Mr. Trotski,
Mrs. Emma Not-so-hot-ski,
Mr. Blum and Mrs. Run-around-the-town-ski.
All the brave who do their stunt
For the bold, united front,
And whose names you simply can't pronounce-ski.

(The Whites):
We're surprised to see you patronize
This red, subversive enterprise;
We hear this is a Social Order Follies.
And all noble, true conservatives
Will use the best preservatives
To keep these chaps from slipping off their trolleys.

(The Reds):
These retrogressive dabblers here,
These retroversive babblers here
Who plan to do a Social Order Follies,
Are so blank-blank conservative
They really don't deserve to live,
Let's fling 'em to the dogs—we don't mean collies.

THE CHORUS:
The chorus now must hurry in,
And bid you not to worry in
The least about our Social Order Follies.
We'll tread upon no tender toes,
Bash no aristocratic nose;
We're only having fun about . . .
In just a little run about . . .
To tell a funny one about . . .

(PAUSE)

Well, him or he
Or them or they or she . . .
But never, never, never, never you!

(Waltz)
For you're perfection. No correction
Ever could add to you, friends.
Charming, gracious, strong, veracious,
Perfect in deed and view, friends.
Customs, races, people, places
Ought to be changed, it's true, friends;
But all our sketches
Are for the wretches,
None of them's meant for you, friends,
None of them's meant for you.

(The Whites):
Oh, this talk is quite persuasive,
Though the argument's evasive;
We'll admit that there's perfection in our party.
We advise you not to shock us, or
To castigate or mock us, or
You'll find our disapproval very hearty.

ACT ONE

Time: The present (or thereabouts).

Place: Thither and Yon.

Episode I

The Show Begins

The Conservatives Debate the Leftists

Until the Chorus Mercifully intervenes.

Opening Chorus: "Good Evening, Mr. Ritz."

"You're Perfection."

CONSERVATIVES

Captains of Chorus: Mr. and Mrs. Jack Schuler

Edmond Keane	Dolores Kenny
Margaret Menard	James Fabick
Wanda Atamanchek	Mary Loretto McCarthy
Elizabeth Jacobsmeyer	Charlotte Bussman
Eleanor Rohan	Marie Gebken
Loretto Barrett	Jane Dooling
Marie Burneson	Eleanor Henry
Mary Ann Whelan	Dorothy Wagner
Eleanor Kenny	Arthur Depenbrock

Mary Catherine Tammany

LEFTISTS

Florence Callahan	Dolores Weslick
Mary Helen Baudo	Harris Conway
John Dean Warner	Charles McNamara
Virginia Rohan	Frances Lenzen
Carmen Laferla	Louis Barth
Josephine Privitera	Bob Mahon
Anne Mosher	John Minton

Vincent Kelleher

The Lads of the Chorus

Michael Leis	Bill Walsh
Harry Corley	George Scanlon
Robert McNearney	Keith Morrison
Larry Mullen	Gene Buechler

The Maidens of the Chorus

Dorothy Henderson	Rosemary Boehm
Mary Frances Walsh	Pat Costello
Dianne Pauley	Virginia Fahroner
Jeanne Devaney	Beatrice Perez

Father Lord, based at the Jesuits' St. Louis University, was not beyond appealing to the faithful with a touch of show business. Above is the first page of *The Social Order Follies*, a musical written and produced by Lord in the mid-thirties and performed in the university auditorium. Note the ticket prices.

Fr. John LaFarge, the Harvard-educated scion of a family of architects and artists, toured Europe in the summer of 1938 and visited the European Jesuits' premier organization in social analysis and action, *Action Populaire.* LaFarge was so impressed with it that he resolved to make the Jesuits' New York Social Action Institute its American equivalent. Its purpose, he stated, was to combat communism and other subversive movements — totalitarian fascism, in particular — and to promote a Christian social order. In 1942 he was named executive editor of the Jesuit journal of opinion, *America. (Courtesy of Special Collections Division, Georgetown University Library)*

LaFarge, who had worked as a parish priest in rural Maryland, saw poverty up close. He was among the first Jesuits to campaign actively for civil rights and the breakdown of racial barriers in the Church. Here he is pictured among a group of school children from St. Mary's parish. *(Courtesy of Special Collections Division, Georgetown University Library)*

Woodstock College was the flagship theologate of the Jesuits in the United States. Located about twenty-five miles west of Baltimore, it opened its doors in 1869. Antimodernism marked the ideological tenor of Woodstock and scholasticism shaped the curriculum. Pictured are the Woodstock College refectory (1930s), the college band (1950s), and the printing press (1930s). The pressman is a Jesuit brother. *(Courtesy of Special Collections Division, Georgetown University Library)*

Pictured is the Grand Rotunda of the West Baden Springs Hotel in West Baden, Indiana. The hotel, purchased in the thirties by the Jesuits and converted into a seminary, was the site of the meeting, in 1943, of more than 200 U.S. Jesuits who convened to discuss the social changes in America which would affect their ministry and the order itself. Fr. Zacheus Maher, then the American Assistant — the leader of the American Society of Jesus — opened the meeting, where Fr. Daniel Lord tried to forge a plan for an active social ministry among the poor. *(Courtesy of Chicago Province Archives, Society of Jesus)*

Number 2   One Cent

CHALLENGE

"... Nearly all the evils of society prevail most where we live and not where Protestants live ... Eighty per cent of Protestantism is rural ... and it is in rural America where family life is most wholesome, and where the divorce rate is low ... On the other hand where the bulk of Catholics live, one-half of the marriages end in divorce ... We should long have been exerting leadership as campaigners for Christ."

These challenging words, reported by the *New York Times*, were hurled at all Catholics by Bishop Noll of the Fort Wayne Diocese at the National Catholic Conference on Family Life in Chicago.

———◆———

INFLATION

"It costs more to run a boy through a reformatory than through college." This is the testimony of Presiding Judge Michael Scott of St. Louis Juvenile Court.

```
UTOPIA
CITY OF THE FAR-SIGHTED
```

Skip It

When Joe and Mary go out to a movie, they agree to skip the food afterwards and instead, they buy a pound of candy and send it to a poor family in their community.

```
FOOD
for
THOUGHT
```

Pat on the Back

Pius XII says: "The American people have a genius for splendid and unselfish action and into the hands of the American people God has placed the destinies of afflicted humanity."

A Choice Bit

"It is the duty of the free Associations of workers, farmers, employers and professional people to assume their full responsibility for the ethical conduct of their own industry or profession and for the economic welfare of the community and all its parts." This is a choice bit from the "Declaration of Economic Justice," which was signed by 122 Jewish, Protestant and Catholic leaders.

True or False?

Get better politics in the United States or set up an altar every twenty-five years on which to offer the best blood of the country.

Hear Ye! Hear Ye!

Father Parsons, contributing editor of *America*, writes: "As for the Lilienthal affair, almost everything but the real issue came up in the hearings, and that was: who is going to own or control atomic energy, the state or private industry?"

THE RIGHT SPIRIT

The United States Chamber of Commerce is urging its members to help the labor unions fight Communism by working along with good union officials so that the rank-and-file will keep them in office and by refraining from tagging "Communist" on the name of a union official just because he drives a hard bargain.

———◆———

NO TWO WAYS ABOUT IT

The one and only way to fight AGAINST Communism is to fight FOR Catholic social and economic justice. Worth noting is the comment that the Hearst press' idea of social and economic justice is not the same as the Catholic idea.

———◆———

MONSTER

1945 produced 31 divorces for every 100 marriages. There were 25% more broken homes in 1945 than in 1944. The divorce rate for 1945 was highest in American history. 1945 gave birth to a monster.

```
MYOPIA
CITY OF THE NEAR-SIGHTED
```

A Small World

When Hector and Lulubelle go out on a date, they never do anything together for anybody else. Taxi or dad's car, movie, dance, food, good times are all for Hector and Lulubelle and nobody else.

DEDICATED TO INSPIRE AMERICANS TO WORK AND SACRIFICE FOR THE COMMON GOOD

In the late forties, the Institute of Social Order, then centered in St. Louis and headed by Fr. Daniel Lord, distributed its leaflet, *Spearhead for Social Action*, to Catholic laymen, many of them of the urban working class. It popularized the institute's position on the important social issues of the day.

AMERICANS

WISE

HARMONIZE

What OTHERS Are Doing

Ninety Plus

In order to do their bit for American relief in Italy eighth-graders and high-school freshmen in Washington, D. C., volunteered to sew and pack supplies at least one day a week all last summer—this in a city with a usual summer temperature of ninety plus and with the cool waters of Virginia beach only a stone's throw away.

Never Say "Die"

Arthur T. Vanderbilt, dean of the New York University School of Law, has spent much of his time and energy SINCE 1919, fighting for decent government in Essex County, New Jersey.

All Alone

Samuel Liberman, a merchant on the east side of Detroit, has done so much to better relations between Negroes and Jews in his neighborhood that he has been cited for his excellent work by the *Michigan Chronicle*, Negro weekly.

◆

Editor's note: The praise of certain actions of people mentioned in this paper does not imply praise of all their actions. Nor is there any attempt to judge motives.

IN FULL SUPPLY

Men and women whose full-time job is to take care of their own personal good.

IN SHORT SUPPLY

Men and women who work and sacrifice for their own personal good and for the common good, too.

WHAT CAN **YOU** DO?

On the Offense

You can bring SPEARHEAD home and tempt the rest of the family to read it.

You can spread the social attitudes of Christ far and wide in your community, your city, among your friends and acquaintances. You can make your own life square with these attitudes.

You can imitate the actions praised in this paper NOW or you can PREPARE to imitate them in the FUTURE.

You can make a hobby of some social problem in your community. (Your community is your city. Start there.)

You can lend not only a tongue but a hand. Better still, you can lend a brain.

STORY of the WEEK

"Accentuate the Positive"

Less talk and more action was the policy of Mr. Charles Vatterott, well-known contractor and builder in St. Louis, when he decided to attack divorce and birth-control by building Mary Ridge,—one hundred houses in a development for families with four children or more. Many of the families have seven or more children. He has hope of "accentuating the positive" again by erecting a similar project for Negroes. Hats off to Mr. Charles Vatterott.

◆

ASK ME ANOTHER

Many a member of the CIO, when asked how so few Communists can do so much, gives the same simple but direct answer: "They work like —." And, we might add, they work together.

◆

BLESSED ARE THE POOR . . .

Up from Dublin slums comes the only layman who has made a serious bid for beatification in Ireland. Matt Talbot is the man. He is a man of our times, too. 1925 was the year of his death.

Published weekly by the Institute of Social Order, 3115 South Grand Boulevard, Saint Louis 18, Missouri. Sold only in packages of 50 or more.
Copyright, 1947, The Queen's Work, Inc.

"He entered a room like an ocean liner," one Jesuit recalled of Fr. John Courtney Murray. Bold, brilliant, and innovative, Murray during the early fifties broke with the traditional European Catholic view of American democracy by espousing pluralism. For Murray, civilization emerged from "men locked together in argument," and the main feature of this political dialogue was rationality. Politics worked when it did not slide into violence over irreconcilable values. This, for him, was the main reason for keeping religion out of politics. He was temporarily silenced for his progressive views. *(Courtesy of Special Collections Division, Georgetown University Library)*

After Fr. John LaFarge retired in 1948, Fr. Robert Hartnett, a political scientist from the University of Detroit, assumed the editorship of *America*. Hartnett, an avid New Deal Democrat, gave the journal a strong prolabor editorial orientation. He might have succeeded at sustaining this line had he been more agile in dealing with the Spellmanesque ambience of Irish American Catholicism in the New York archdiocese. In addition, postwar working class Catholics found themselves increasingly satisfied with their conditions, rendering Hartnett's social democratic angle imprudent and old-fashioned in the eyes of some clerics. Hartnett later locked horns with the Jesuit-educated senator from Wisconsin, Joseph McCarthy. *(Courtesy of Chicago Province Archives, Society of Jesus)*

In 1949, John Baptist Janssens, the Belgian Jesuit who was chosen to succeed Father Ledochowski as Superior General, wrote a letter to all Jesuits urging them to greater efforts in the social apostolate. His moral conservatism and his anticommunism were balanced by the priority he gave to social justice. "To prevent our Society from justly being classified with the rich and the capitalists, we must direct with utmost zeal many of our ministries towards the poorer classes." *(Courtesy of Special Collections Division, Georgetown University Library)*

In 1949, Fr. Vincent McCormick (left) replaced Fr. Zacheus Maher (right) as American Assistant. Here they are seen with Superior General Fr. John Baptist Janssens. Aside from effectively silencing John Courtney Murray for proposing his theories of pluralism, McCormick worked to shape an overall educational policy for the Jesuits in America. McCormick understood education as a vehicle for ethical training and only secondarily as a scholarly enterprise. But secular values were soon to penetrate the seemingly peaceful Jesuit schools. *(Courtesy of Special Collections Division, Georgetown University Library)*

Fr. Robert Ignatius Gannon, president of Fordham University from the thirties to the fifties, was much in demand as an after-dinner speaker among New York-based groups like the Friendly Sons of St. Patrick, the Policeman's Benevolent Association, and the Holy Name Society. Gannon preached a tabloid conservatism. Of the Irish he would say with characteristic bravado that the ". . . true son of Erin is repelled by the hard core of Atheism, of dialectical communism, that unifies the theory and practice of the Kremlin . . . . Whatever can be said of Ireland, good or bad, this must be said: for centuries she has borne in her sacred flesh the mark of the five holy wounds . . . they will remain to the end the real source of her glory among nations." *(Courtesy of Fordham University Library)*

Pictured are a theology class and a "domestic exhortation," at West Baden College in the early 1950s (opposite page), and, just a few years later, an ordination of 38 Jesuits, at Georgetown University. By 1952 there were 7,000 Jesuits in the United States, well over double the number thirty years before. But by the end of the decade, the momentous changes in Catholic spirituality began to have their effect on Jesuit life. Said one Jesuit, "Back in novitiate I'd been slipped books by this Latin teacher . . . in structural linguistics. It was already in the late or mid-fifties, '57, '58, reading this kind of stuff and feeling that sort of vision of things was correct . . . ." *(Courtesy of Algimantas Kezys for the West Baden College photos, and Special Collections Division, Georgetown University Library, for the ordination photo)*

In the progressive tradition established by John LaFarge and John Courtney Murray, Fr. Gustave Weigel promoted ecumenism, inveighing against the Protestant and secularist bashing, ritualized in the *disputationes*, that kept Jesuits from fruitful exchange with the larger world. Weigel was a popular teacher at Woodstock and a close colleague of Murray. The liberalism of both Murray and Weigel struggled for acceptance in the fifties and early sixties as the American Society of Jesus faced the momentous spiritual and intellectual changes stirring in Catholicism on the eve of the Second Vatican Council, and the equally profound demographic and social changes caused by the assimilation of ethnic Catholics in the American mainstream. *(Courtesy of Special Collections Division, Georgetown University Library)*

impossible undertaking in any case and one of dubious value besides. The solution was managerial skill, teamwork, "the quality of cooperation, of organization, of cohesion." Sadly, "rancorous division had bedeviled the relationship of groups, passionate sectarianism has poisoned the cooperative spirit."[71] Dunne had the same distaste for secular-clerical hatreds and intractable antinomies as Murray revealed in his condemnation of the Spanish syndrome. Like Murray, he encouraged an ecumenical respect for the Protestant brethren and emulation of their genius for problem solving as a way of overcoming the no-win cycle of ideological confrontation:

> Many of the Latin-American clergy, secular and regular, Jesuits and Franciscans, would do better by the Good Neighbor, and be more constructive generally, did they understand rightly the Protestant of the North. . . . Such churchmen fail to appreciate the Protestant's good faith, his just spirit, his fine moral quality. They forget what Catholicism in the United States owes to Protestants. It is they who made the Constitution, model for all of Latin America; it is they who by demanding freedom of religious worship set the condition for the present flourishing condition of the Catholic Church. They are respectful toward the Church. They are not persecuting it. Latin-American Catholics cannot say the same for some of their own governments.[72]

Latin Americans veered between strident confrontation and outpourings of love, with long and possibly recuperative stretches of apathy and indolence. They lacked habits of competition and organizational know-how—two skills that Jesuits had nurtured to a fine degree. Jesuits were torn, too, between hard-driving practicality and discipline and a fascination with the exuberance of Latin America and the possibilities for accomplishment it offered. The hope articulated by Dunne was that Latin cultural identity and the warmth of personality he admired could be preserved as educational and institutional reforms directed energies toward material progress.

V

Around the end of the fifties and the early sixties, about fifteen years after the appearance of *A Padre Views South America*, requests for funds and personnel poured in not only from Latin America, where priests were traditionally scarce, but also from Japan, which was the single truly international mission of the society, staffed by Jesuits from all over the world, and where Pedro Arrupe, the Basque who would become general in 1965, was provincial superior. "A century earlier," the Jesuit historian James Hennesey noted, "it was not uncommon for Jesuits from the United States to beg funds in South America. Now their successors travelled south to assist the Latin American Church."[73] Jesuits from the New Orleans province began operations in Campinas, in the state of São Paulo; Jesuits from New England went to Bahia, in northeast Brazil; Jesuits from New York province began teaching at the pontifical university in Rio de Janeiro; the Wisconsin Jesuits, in addition to founding a university in South Korea, sent men to teach at the Catholic university in Salta, Argentina, and so on.

Some of the interchange went from South to North; a few Latin American Jesuits studied theology or the social sciences in the United States. But the dominant strategy of the society, set by the general in Rome, was to direct the flow of manpower and financial resources southward. The Cuban Revolution, led by a graduate of the Jesuits' law faculty in Havana, sounded the alarm. The demographic surge throughout Latin America was a longer-term consideration. In 1960, in tones similar to those used by his predecessor, Fr. John Baptist Janssens, superior general of the society, urged the American provincials to free more men from their high schools and colleges for work in Latin America. "Ideally, of course, it is desirable to have a very large number of Jesuits teaching in our high schools and parents are pleased with this," Janssens wrote:

> But conscious, as we must be, of the tragic lack of priests in so many parts of South America, can we in conscience maintain even so high a proportion of Jesuits in our high schools . . . ? Is it not our duty to enlist the help of more lay teachers so as to be able to offer greater assistance to the souls starving for want of spiritual sustenance? I would be happy to assign, e.g., the new Federal District of Brasilia to our American provinces.[74]

The North American provincials received Janssens's remarks hesitantly. "In view of the great and immediate need in Latin America," they asked rhetorically, "should we not consider suppressing some of the works which now occupy us here in North America?"[75] They had qualms about becoming overextended. Mere numbers, they reasoned, gave a misleading impression of the resources at the disposal of the American assistancy. The quality of the men who might be available for mission work had to be taken into account. Most of the best men were busy maintaining the Jesuit educational network in the face of postwar competition from other private and state-funded institutions:

> It certainly must seem strange to some of Ours in other regions that the American Assistancy, so rich in men, should seem to find it more difficult than some other Assistancies to release an abundance of men for work in the missions and in other Society projects. The explanation

may be that besides staffing six theologates for Ours and seculars, seven philosophates, one minor seminary (and soon a second), and forty-three secondary schools, it also operates twenty-eight universities, all within the continental United States. These works, especially the latter, are operating against the keenest academic and financial competition from secular schools and can continue to command respect from Americans only if they are staffed by talented and highly trained men.[76]

Even if more manpower had been available, the magnitude of the operation and their ignorance of Latin America were daunting. Enthusiasm and numbers could not overcome so many unknowns. "Great concern was felt by all the Fathers Provincial about the nature of the work to be entrusted to us, the location of it, and the details of jurisdiction." They quoted approvingly from a letter sent from the field by a North American Jesuit:

All possible effort should be made to determine well the type of work to be undertaken and the place. Experts should be consulted. The crisis in Latin America is very much a race against time, against a social evolution which is taking place at a terrific pace. We need priests as soon as possible.[77]

By the beginning of the sixties, however, the momentum in favor of expansion overcame fears about the complexity of the mission. The pope had himself requested that religious orders send 10 percent of their North American personnel to work in Latin America. The challenge assumed the air of a great opportunity.

Manuel Foyaca, a Jesuit in exile from Cuba, acted as the general's adviser on policy toward the Third World. Foyaca's social philosophy was taken straight from solidarism, the blend of anticommunism and antiliberalism formulated by German Jesuits like Gundlach and von Nell-Bruening.[78] This was mostly a rehash of *Quadragesimo Anno*, heavy with Latin abstraction and Germanic syntax. What caught the eye of the general and the papacy were the statistics Foyaca assembled showing the inexorability of population growth in Latin America. At the turn of the century, he pointed out, the continent had 70 million inhabitants. By the middle of the century the population had reached 163 million, and over the next decade, by 1960, it had surpassed 200 million. North America had been overtaken by the South as the growth area of Catholicism.[79]

The inauguration of a program to familiarize North American religious personnel with the ways of Latin America before they took up full-time work there helped reduce the anxieties of the Jesuit leadership about the magnitude of the challenge. This program was located at the Center of Intercultural Formation (CIF), at Cuernavaca in the state of Morelos, Mexico, with a branch in Brazil, and set up in conjunction with Fordham University. The guiding spirit of the experiment in Mexico was Ivan Illich, then a secular priest, who had worked in Puerto Rico. During the fifties his educational accomplishments in Puerto Rico caught the attention of Cardinal Spellman, who had grasped the significance of Latin America for Catholicism by observing the tide of Hispanic immigrants in New York City. He had also gotten to know Joseph Fitzpatrick, the Jesuit sociologist at Fordham who specialized in research on Hispanic subcultures.[80]

Born in Vienna, the polyglot Illich was an outspoken critic of American parochialism. Despite the harshness of his language, for a time the cosmopolitanism of his message had some appeal to American Jesuits who were insecure about their ability to transcend cultural barriers. Illich sensed that the rising interest in Latin America on the part of North American Jesuits reflected not only a response to a pivotal shift in the demographic balance between the two continents but also a search for new modes of activism, now that the majority of the Catholic immigrant working class had been assimilated and had lost what curiosity it had about political and social alternatives to the American way. "Latin America can no longer tolerate being a haven for U.S. liberals who cannot make their point at home," Illich noted with the acerbity that came to be associated with the CIF operation, "an outlet for apostles too 'apostolic' to find their vocation as competent professionals within their own community."[81]

The Cuernavaca school opened with several of the rising stars of international Catholicism on its faculty.[82] Language training and social science seminars were offered during the summer months to American and Canadian missionaries-to-be. The site became a meeting ground for the burgeoning network of Catholic social advocates, peace activists, and promoters of related causes. It was the springtime of the sixties. George Prendergast, a Missouri Jesuit visiting in 1963, left an account of the activities at Cuernavaca that captured the casual mixing of grand ambition and patchwork logistics:

> Cuernavaca was a beautiful place for the Lombardi retreat and the Illich seminar. We had fine quarters, excellent meals, and the Lord gave us excellent weather. . . .
>
> Father Lombardi made himself understood in English and got better as we went along. However, he could not follow the discussions. . . . Father Lombardi made several propositions to the group on the last day. He hopes the Conference will take up the Movement for a Better World. He thinks more good can come out of America for the Movement than out of Rome. . . .

One thing almost certain to come out of these Cuernavaca meetings will be a greater effort at coordinating the big contribution now being made by American (U.S., Canada) religious in favor of Latin America.[83]

Cuernavaca quickly became a crossroads through which ideas, personnel, and funds in international Catholicism were channeled. Improvisation and charisma prevailed over structure:

> Monsignor Illich did not appear until towards the end of the Lombardi retreat. He is a pleasant fellow, somewhat shy, very humble but quite lively, not too deep in either philosophy or theology (Rahner, Küng group), goes in strong for the liturgical-scripture spirituality now in vogue, and shows an inclination to find the church "wrong" in much of its approach to the problem of Latin America. However, he seemed to me to be quite candid, not hiding anything, very ready to discuss his views and even to modify them . . . (By the way I left him twenty dollars to help with future guests). As you probably know there are some good souls . . . who entertain deep fears all is not well in Cuernavaca. With religious coming and going all the time, with the Conference of Religious Superiors in such close contact with the place, with the blessing of Cardinal Spellman and the watchful eye of the Fordham people I don't see how the place can get very far out of line.[84]

Prendergast understood that the political alignments inherited from colonial times could no longer protect Catholicism in Latin America. Population growth added urgency to a social crisis bound up with the immobility of class structures. Unable to gain access to land and to sustain themselves in the countryside, increasing numbers of peasants flooded into cities. Prendergast summarized the hopes invested in the Cuernavaca experiment:

> Something like this has been needed for a long time. There is an intensive course in Spanish. The acculturation program strikes me as very important. I can never forget what a good father once told me in Progreso [Honduras] in 1953 (before the strike). "After all we are here as company chaplains." That is, real babes-in-the-woods entering upon an apostolate in a foreign country sick—at that time—of Yankee domination, and ready to curse everything coming out of Yankeeland.[85]

Prendergast sensed the dual nature of the challenge faced by Jesuits as they prepared for their work in Latin America. Ecclesiastical strategists hoped to pry the church away from its historical alliance with conservative elites before it was overthrown with them. There was a feeling that even the good works carried out under the old regime were no longer adequate for a more urban and crowded continent. Rejection of the political past did not automatically provide Jesuits with a vision and skills for the future. Hope in the new commitment to Latin America continued to be qualified by severe doubts about the capacity of Jesuits to live up to the task they had set themselves:

> There is also an effort at Cuernavaca to help the spiritual readaptation of the religious etc. coming for instruction. The change from one world to another can be spiritually difficult too. I was not surprised to hear them talk about the spiritual crises many go through. I can remember seeing some of Ours go through some pretty helpless weeks seeking a readaptation that didn't seem to be forthcoming.[86]

The institute at Cuernavaca expressed at a dramatic pitch the mixture of idealism and uneasiness, combining fear of failure with social guilt, common to American missionary planning at the time. Early in 1962, when the Conference of Major Superiors of Male Religious and the Mission Secretariat of the National Catholic Welfare Conference met in Washington to discuss Latin America, Illich attended, as did other leaders of the intercultural scene, including such Jesuits as Renato Poblete from Chile. The conference opened with a reminder of the origins of the concern for Catholicism in Latin America: the numbing demographics. By the end of the 1950s, it was noted, while there were more than forty million children in Latin America below the age of fifteen, only twenty-one million of them attended school. Catholic schools at all levels enrolled less than five million students, a minority within the bare majority that managed to matriculate at all. "Who is the minority that the Catholic schools serve?" the conference participants asked themselves. "The answer is that it is generally the very rich."[87]

The remedies proposed were on the whole reminiscent of the labor school and social think-tank philosophy of earlier times. However, it was not as if stale concepts were simply being applied to new problems. In the early sixties, at the beginning of Vatican II, the old intellectual system of Catholicism had not yet collapsed. It was showing signs of wear, to be sure, and anxiety about obsolescence and the loss of meaningful roles within the priesthood motivated Jesuits to sit through Illich's harangues. But the impulse to attack what was left of the conceptual edifice was not yet widespread among Jesuits. Even if preconciliar ideology was viewed as less and less satisfactory, it remained to be seen how this malaise would alter recommendations for action. Action was not yet conflated with anti-institutional movements. Commitment to the missions implied a certain relief from the constrictions of ecclesiastical authority at home. At the time, the experience represented something of an escape from, rather than an attack against, authority.

Thus, the approach of the Jesuits to Latin America in the early sixties was reformist and managerial. The number of missionaries grew, but operational change was moderate. The strategy presupposed a shift in clientele rather than a radical break in goals. The job was to administer scarce resources efficiently, to engender multiplier effects, by cultivating leaders from the lower, rather than the upper, levels of society.

> Father Poblete's thesis, then, is that to rectify the present errors, to make an impact upon the teeming problems, Catholic educators must work for social betterment. They must communicate Christian ideals— code, morality, liturgy—which make Catholics. Form and infiltrate. Begin this infiltration in strategic areas: in existing normal schools, in universities, in government. Influence students to go into teaching and to thus raise the status of teachers. Begin normal schools in underdeveloped or even developed areas.[88]

The meliorative optimism of the missionaries of the early and mid-sixties would jar in contrast with the radicalism and romantic intensity of the liberation theology that emerged toward the end of the decade and the beginning of the seventies. Exposure to the social disparities of Latin America, in light of the initial promise of the Alliance for Progress and the decade-of-development thrust, disillusioned some North American religious. But the hopeful pragmatism of the dawn of the sixties was not simply a mélange of inexperience and goodwill, and the later radicalism was not just a response to the stimulus of clearly worsening conditions in the objective world. A crucial intervening factor that separated moderate from revolutionary leanings among Jesuits was growing insecurity about the role of the priesthood itself. Jesuits had already expressed misgivings about the magnitude of the task facing them in Latin America and suddenly, just as they launched their expedition, some began to feel overwhelmed by events, by awareness of their dubious expertise, and by shock at the disjuncture between their idealism and the caste-like conservatism ascribed to the clergy in Latin America.[89]

The internationalization of American Catholicism continued through the sixties. In 1968, the peak year, there were just under 3,400 North American Catholic missionaries in Latin America. But 1968 was also the year of the conference of Latin America bishops in Medellín, Colombia, where resentment over the dependence of the South on the North crystallized, and it was the year as well as of *Humanae Vitae*, the encyclical that reiterated the ban on contraception. Antiwar protests came to a head in America in 1968; race riots erupted in the large cities. The solid identities and sense of purpose on which the society's corporate élan had been based started to collapse as the missionary effort expanded.

CIF and the aspirations surrounding it unravelled. In 1967 Illich published an article castigating North American missionaries not for their efficiency—the virtue that Peter Dunne thought they could contribute to Latin America—but for their insensitivity to Latin American culture.[90] The diatribe hit Jesuits at a time, immediately after Vatican II, of uncertainty about what might be salvaged from their Counter-Reformation mission, and when the United States was in the midst of a bout of self-criticism. The fury went deeper than the polarization between left and right, touching on questions of historical continuity and personal identity for which neither practical nor ideological fixes were at hand.[91]

The Jesuits had begun the expansion of their overseas activities in the late fifties, at a time of success but also incipient debility in the North American church. In Europe theological innovators were calling into question the Thomistic synthesis, and an urbane skepticism had started to filter into seminaries in the United States. The material foundations on which American Catholicism had rested—the communities of devout immigrants, knit together in solidarity against a Protestantism now becoming less hostile than indifferent to Catholic mores—were eroding with social mobility. The principles that seemed secure when Catholics were pitted against a hostile majority carried less conviction when transported outside this subculture, and in any case the environmental buttresses of the subculture itself were wearing away, and so was the certainty of the ideas themselves. These structural changes in the advanced industrial society of the United States were as devastating to the composure of the Society of Jesus as the poverty of the peasantry and urban proletariat in Latin America.

The enormity of the task that the Jesuits had undertaken made them uneasy from the outset. A belief in the kind of managerial and technical practicality espoused by Peter Dunne, and updated by Jesuits in Latin America with a view to gearing scarce resources toward maximum productivity, could be commended for its modesty and common sense in the face of mammoth odds.[92] Outsize ambition was checked by prudence. Even on a modest scale, the movement away from parish work and high school education, that were the traditional bailiwicks of the society in Latin America, raised questions about retooling, the tradeoffs of building on existing strengths as compared to exploring new territory, and similar issues. What did Jesuits know, for example, about community organization, in or outside the United States?

Yet even realism needed a self-confidence to drive and sustain it, and the intellectual and structural underpinnings of such assurance had started to come undone in the late fifties and early sixties, just as the enterprise got under way. Expectations ran high, then came crashing down. In 1971, at Casa Xavier, a Jesuit retreat house outside Mexico City, a postmortem was held.

> They were, many of them, the brightest hopes of the U.S. church of the sixties. Their special crusade began in the clear, hopeful days of John F. Kennedy, of armies for peace and alliances for progress, of a church that stood rock firm, of a pope whose heart seemed big enough to hold the world. It ended quietly in the gathering darkness of a fortress presidency and a troubled pope, a church that was offering options instead of answers, and a war in Vietnam that was tearing the United States apart.[93]

VI

The prolongation of the postwar economic boom in the United States stimulated enthusiasm for missionary work among the Jesuits and other religious orders. Fascination with the missions captured the idealism of younger cohorts of religious, whose immigrant roots trailed into the past. Adventure and sacrifice and the chance to make their own mark magnetized many of them.

Toward the end of the 1950s, in the final years of the pontificate of Pius XII, American Jesuits began searching for new directions. Their interests had always extended beyond parish boundaries, and some Jesuits now sensed that a parochialism of the imagination might be limiting even activities, such as college teaching, that had earned them prestige. An irony of the achievements of the brick-and-mortar era of American Catholicism was that it bred restlessness in its products. Younger Jesuits began to feel that they were outgrowing the old localism of the high schools and colleges. The attraction of the missions compensated only in part for uneasiness about the rationale of religious life.

The enclaves themselves were breaking up while the mentalities that surrounded and lingered after them ripened for criticism. The demographic supports of tradition withered just as they came in for attack by upcoming cohorts of Jesuits; the miasma of stale beliefs seemed to burn away like morning fog. A static legacy suddenly changed, and there were odd slippages between social realities and ideological captiousness. The sympathy expressed in the pages of *America* for the underprivileged of the Eisenhower era came a decade or two late for many working-class Catholics. The launching of the great missionary effort on the part of the Society of Jesus in the 1950s corresponded not with the apex of old-style evangelical fervor and triumphalism but with a tentative ecumenicism and with a skepticism regarding missionary imperialism. The successes of Tridentine Catholicism —in particular, sound schools supported by a loyal laity—had been consolidated in the United States. But expansion did not continue on the basis of the same worldview; the beginnings of self-criticism came instead. Targets that once seemed clear became elusive.

The American Jesuits who thrust themselves into a global arena did so partly because they believed that they could make more of a difference in Latin America than in the United States, where the institutional operations of the society appeared to be on autopilot. The globalization of Catholicism occurred at a time when the functions and identity of the priesthood became objects of doubt and of a scrutiny that generated few practical outlets. Between the global scope of the Society of Jesus and the personal reappraisal of many Jesuits, meaningful roles grew sparser and less secure; saturation with institutional routine conspired to augment individual anxieties. The next step in the evolution of the order was unclear.

CHAPTER

9

"A Strange Shift in the Affairs of Men"

I

In 1950 a young Jesuit social scientist published an article documenting the increase in the number of students majoring in business administration in Jesuit colleges and universities. The schools of commerce and finance, founded soon after the turn of the century, were now in full expansion. Through the end of World War II these faculties had accounted for a bit more than 10 percent of total enrollments. After the war, with the return of the veterans and the release of a desire to catch up with the good life, the proportion jumped to about 25 percent. By the 1950s slightly less than 40 percent of the students in Jesuit colleges and universities could be grouped under the traditional liberal arts curriculum.[1]

Choices were opening up. The interest in international work and the eagerness for business training were both indicative of the demographic changes that American Catholics were undergoing as economic assimilation proceeded. The multiplicity of options for doing things, for choosing among various lines of work and leisure, implied a new heterogeneity within the Catholic community. Catholics who once counted themselves lucky to find employment began shopping around for careers and meaning as well as for consumer items.[2]

The occupational differentiation and growing mobility of Catholics accentuated two disquieting trends as postwar prosperity took off into the 1950s. With economic mainstreaming American Catholics kept the ritual—attendance at Sunday Mass stayed high—but left some of the formal teaching of the church behind. Attention to the social *magisterium* had been selective at best. The papal social thought that had taken shape in the last decades of the nineteenth century and that had been refurbished during the

277

1930s had never lost its exoticism in the United States. During the forties and fifties it provided an even less satisfactory understanding of the American condition. A few ideas about the corporatist organization of business and labor, like those propounded by Bernard Dempsey, caught certain facets of a productive system that did not correspond to the liberal economic paradigm postulating individual actors in an open market, and in a general way the corporatist model gave reason for caution regarding wholehearted acceptance of the American way. But Catholic social theory did not deliver the alternative comprehensive view, either on normative or empirical grounds, to which it once laid claim. Its grand and static principles had little to say about social change, nor could the essentially European categories of the encyclicals encompass a society as large and diverse as that of the United States. The *magisterium* was encumbered by jargon that had some meaning and appeal if set in a national system of Catholic political parties, labor unions, and business associations. But American Catholicism was mapped into local clusters. In the absence of larger organizational referents, and in the midst of an economic boom that gave no reason to fix what wasn't broken, the doctrine floated in an intellectual and institutional limbo. It led neither to action nor to new ideas. Jesuits found themselves at a loss for concepts that might make sense of the structural flux of the postwar era and the sheer size of American success. There was no distinctively Catholic framework to bring to bear on the sweeping experience of assimilation. Most of the Jesuits' intellectual energies continued to be focused elsewhere.[3]

Another, concrete cause of bafflement emerged during this period. As the demographic ground shifted out from under Catholicism, and as the magisterial abstractions of Catholic social thought hovered in a Platonic empyrean, the psychological bases for practical action and person-to-person assistance began to slip away. A rationale for social action that claimed to apply fixed principles to good works was plainly a pious simplification. Some Jesuits felt that they had to work around if not against the institutional impedimenta and theoretical paraphernalia of Catholicism to get their job done. For a few radicals the establishment of the church was either irrelevant or an obstacle to social ministry.

For most Jesuits, however, the problem was much less tidy and confrontational. The scale and complexity of the demographic and intellectual changes affecting the environment of American Catholics had no precedent in the experience of the Society of Jesus. A depersonalization of social relations compounded the dissociation of social doctrine from the ministrations of the Jesuits, and in particular from their identity as priests. The growing size of the colleges and universities was the most common example of this; another was the sophistication and increasing mobility of the constituents of the Jesuits. Postimmigrant Catholicism did not bring cultural stability. Custom and common sense no longer seemed quite so certain guides to the everyday demands of the religious vocation, and zeal and eclectic amateurism could no longer be counted on to master or even cope with changes on a larger scale.[4]

Jesuits had reason to be content. Their schools were expanding, manpower was growing, benefactors kept up their contributions. However, the dynamism of American society and the ambitions of the Jesuits themselves ruled out the attraction of resting on their accomplishments, which appeared to some as routine and even mediocre. The way beyond these achievements was a bit intimidating. American Catholicism had become more variegated. Simultaneously, the urge to proceed beyond the subculture grew.

Fears of centrifugal stress were manifested only intermittently and even less frequently comprehended. There was a suspicion that—even if problems of such magnitude were understood—the Society of Jesus might not be able to do much to resolve them. These anxieties had a way of working themselves out not through theoretical analysis or organized conflict but through conciliation and piecemeal improvisation. Labor-management cooperation was prized; the labor schools became institutes of industrial relations.

The settlement was uneasy. Some Jesuits felt that the stress on pragmatic compromise led to a neglect of hard thinking and to an unwillingness to confront issues, such as racial discrimination and the poverty of unorganized workers, that did not fit the canons of social peace. The labor relations framework seemed earnestly apolitical, suitable as a guide to clerical participation in conflict management, perhaps, but flawed as an analytical prism for understanding conflict in American society as a whole.

At another level conciliatory pragmatism seemed bland and mechanical even when it worked. It failed to address the barely articulated needs for personal meaning and expression that were stirring among younger cohorts of Jesuits and Americans generally. Apprehension about future directions, the fear of complacency, the apparently perverse dissatisfaction with success accumulated during the fifties. At some point the balance tipped. Emotion arose from unsuspected depths, welling up against a heavy moral code, and challenging the organizational authority and intellectual standards associated with it. The ideal of the politic, affable, manly, unsanctimonious Jesuit—tough in his asceticism but indulgent with others, careful not to make ordinary human beings feel inadequate in the presence of holiness—gave way to hints of puzzlement among Jesuits themselves about why their own afflictions should be bottled up, and the model of unflinching personal distance began to crumble. Action, intellect, and affect were moving farther apart.

II

Within a year after the Institute of Social Order was refashioned at West Baden the Society of Jesus responded to worries about the lack of Jesuits prepared for social ministry. The American provincials inaugurated an Institute of Social Studies (ISS) alongside ISO in St. Louis. The ISS was to be the research and teaching arm of the operation. Fr. Leo Brown, a Harvard Ph.D. in labor economics, became the director of ISS, which opened in September 1944. His mandate was to assemble a faculty of Jesuits who would provide training in sociology, political science, and economics for fellow Jesuits from across the country.[5]

Meanwhile, through 1946, ISO under Daniel Lord continued to hold annual conventions. With the end of the war another organization—the Office of Social Activities (OSA)—was set up. As its name suggested, ISA leaned toward action and application. Most of its staff was drawn from the sodality operations that Lord supervised out of a rambling old residence converted to an office building. They put their efforts into pamphleteering and keeping up the Summer Schools of Catholic Action. OSA was a conglomeration of discussion and prayer groups.

ISS languished. Of the eight trained men Father Brown thought would be assigned to teach at St. Louis, two showed up in the fall of 1944, together with about half a dozen Jesuit students. The abrasive advocacy of racial integration by one of the original faculty, George Dunne, had made him unwelcome among the St. Louis Jesuits, and he returned to the West Coast; the other instructor returned to his home province in less than a year. Three more Jesuits assigned to teach at ISS did not last much longer. By mid-1946 the staff had been reduced to one, Leo Brown himself.[6]

The slow start of the Institute of Social Studies and the amateurism of the Office of Social Activities prompted the provincials to call for another of what would become a series of reviews of ISO and its offshoots. Joseph Fitzpatrick was one of the Jesuits asked to evaluate the experiments. As a scholastic he had helped set up the labor school at Xavier in Manhattan, and in 1947 he was at Harvard, finishing a doctorate in sociology. Fitzpatrick sent a long memorandum to Brown that touched on three interconnected themes: the interest of Jesuits in the social apostolate, the location of ISO in a Catholic as compared to a secular setting, and the intellectual stature of the operation as compared to its action orientation.

Fitzpatrick gave his fellow Jesuits a largely negative review for their lack of social awareness. ISO had defined itself as a national movement; on paper it included all Jesuits in the United States. But almost all of them were busy in the schools, and the others were in parishes and retreat work. Routines such as these did not encourage critical consciousness and did not leave much time for social activism:

> If the parish priest, the high school teacher, the master of retreats haven't the slightest idea of social realities, are not interested in a vigorous program of social activity, they are not going to be sending to the ISO for information, direction, schemes, techniques, etc. Here is our major obstacle. In general, the attitude of Jesuits throughout the country is not only not with us; in many cases it is against us. When we even have the Province Director of the ISO in a whole province whose ideas on Negroes are not at all Christian, this being the green wood, what can you expect from the dry? . . .
>
> Reports I have gathered indicate that at Boston College, practically nothing is being done to get our social doctrine across. The boys I have talked to who are really interested meet no challenging criticism of modern American life, often meet ridicule of rural life, etc. . . . [T]he college is pretty weak as the center of vigorous Catholic social thought or activity. . . . I could repeat the same about many of our high schools, many of our parishes. When it comes to business schools, and law schools and medical schools, I have only gossip to go on; but if the gossip is correct, the situation is very sad.[7]

The apathy detected by Fitzpatrick was not confined to the Jesuits. An economic boom had begun, and the clients of Jesuit schools were as eager as other Americans to get ahead. The prospects for a major thrust in social ministry were suspended between the American way and the parochialism of most American Catholics.

The inclusiveness of ISO, covering all potentially interested Jesuits, confirmed the part-time and peripheral nature of the movement. The sectarianism that might have been instigated by a focused program of social ministry was avoided. But the strategy also mirrored the fuzziness of the *magisterium*. The program was supposed to be utilitarian, yet ISO wavered at the motivational borders of the society. It was difficult to convert latent interest among individual Jesuits into effective collective action. Dependence on spare-time voluntarism presupposed an idealism that could not be sustained in corporate form. Amateurism and voluntarism condemned the venture to disappointment. To the failings of inoperable idealism was added the drawback that supporting ISO constituted a drain on the financial and, potentially, the manpower resources of the society. If good works could not become self-supporting, ISO could not expect to receive support from within the order. Elevated to a moral pedestal, ISO became a target for scolding that failed to motivate individuals or mobilize organizational resources. It suffered from intellectual haziness, inspirational immaturity, and institutional indifference.

All these problems notwithstanding, Fitzpatrick nourished a hope in the capacity of the society and the schools in which Jesuits worked to distance themselves from an uncritical Americanism. With considerable misgivings, he argued that the Institute of Social Order could be self-contained, nurtured within and serving the Catholic subculture. He recommended that ISS remain housed at a Catholic educational institution. ISO might gain focus by delimiting its organizational boundaries and narrowing its constituencies. Effective specialization might come through training and service within the Catholic enclave. This, Fitzpatrick hoped, would inhibit the elitism and will-o'-the-wispish formalism of secular science:

> Work in a non-Catholic university gives a man a fine, disciplined training in a field. But he is out of touch with Catholic thought; he is not getting the Catholic angle to things; he must put up with a great deal of graduate school formality in courses and requirements that are all right for a professional degree man but have no direct bearing on the social apostolate. The ISS should be free to weed out the formalities and develop a system of courses that would give the student the real meat of social studies (Cath. & non-Cath.) and at the same time put him in touch with the best in Catholic tradition in the social field.[8]

"But where," Fitzpatrick asked, "is the integrated, organized development of a body of knowledge? . . . This is the central difficulty of the ISS. I don't know whether they can get around it." The Catholic point of view, a holistic perspective on a society on the verge of abundance, and indeed on societies in the throes of historical change, did not exist. "The Catholic angle," was elusive. There was no intellectual vision to keep up a distinctively Catholic center of social research and teaching. Fitzpatrick tried to straddle what he hoped was the possibility of maintaining a countercultural posture vis-à-vis American society, from the vantage point of a St. Louis University or a similar Catholic institution, and the power of ideas from outside this orbit. He was torn between what he saw as the remnants of moral rectitude and the fear of intellectual embarrassment.

> It is pitiful how far removed we are from the general channels of social thought in non-Catholic universities. [We should] carry on social research in the best modern methods in an effort to get at the SOCIAL FACT, the thing so sadly missing from so much of Catholic thinking.

> It is only when one sees non-Catholics go after social facts that one realizes how far removed from them we are ourselves. . . .
>
> What puzzles the outsider as he talks to ISS men is the rather haphazard, directionless nature of their studies. They do not seem to be subjected to the vigorous discipline of study which is routine in a good graduate school, and is essential to the making of even a mediocre scholar. Secondly, their rather serious lack of awareness of the ideas that are common coin in social sciences in outside universities. This is partly corrected by their going out to outside universities for summer courses.[9]

Fitzpatrick could not come up with a coherent solution for the impasse. For many Jesuits the social apostolate meant social work as an extension of pastoral activity. From this perspective social science tended to be looked upon as so much fine print, and professional preparation as largely a waste of time:

> I do not think that anything more is needed to start with than a genuine enthusiasm and zeal for the social apostolate, at least for the men at the grass roots. Most of our men who are now doing valuable, practical work started from scratch. They had nothing. . . . I do not see why any special training is required.[10]

Yet the enthusiasm and flexibility that had served the Jesuits well under simpler conditions were of dubious utility in the advanced industrial society that the United States was fast becoming. Implementation was now less a matter of on-the-spot tinkering and fixing. More than a decade of practical improvisation in social ministry, under the auspices of a vaulting idealism, had not gained social ministry respect in the pecking order of the Society of Jesus. In addition, at the level of shaping public policy, it was doubtful that zeal and good works would enable the Society of Jesus to influence social programs. The Jesuits could not lead by example and exhortation alone; they needed ideas. Fitzpatrick called up to the imagination a mixture of charismatic leadership and rigorous training that would restore a sense of purpose and competence to ISO.

> Above all the institute would need INDIVIDUAL MEN WITH GUIDING IDEAS AND A METHOD. . . . [We need] a MAN, AN IDEA, A METHOD. The great developments in modern social science came from men who had an idea and who developed a method of carrying it out. If I could take two or three professors with whom I have been acquainted, give them twenty trained Jesuits, they would turn out scholarly and scientific knowledge in ten years that would knock the country's eyes out. . . .

I do not know whether an institute like this can be just formed! It takes a certain amount of creative genius in the man who will direct it. Perhaps the meeting of a group of Jesuit scholars and their cooperative effort over a period of time will gradually develop a method and begin to produce. If it is just organized without a director who really knows what he is going to do with it, it may be a perfect bust.[11]

This was a wish list, not a set of policy recommendations that could be implemented according to plan. It depended on a chemistry of ideas, organization, manpower, and more of a tradition of competitive scholarship than American Jesuits had built up. The more Fitzpatrick thought about ISO, the more difficulties came to the surface.

The vastness of the enterprise was the main reason for its unmanageability. When they first tried to think through their systematic project in Christian social order, Jesuits in the 1930s ran aground of its sheer complexity. The better-trained and more critically aware Fitzpatrick had a similar premise in the back of his mind in appraising the performance and the future of the refurbished ISO. The one self-imposed constraint was to reserve the job of educating Jesuits in the social sciences to Catholic schools—a limitation that did not affect Fitzpatrick himself, since he took his doctorate from Harvard. Apart from this restriction, however, the agenda was limitless. ISO would be an omnibus organization for carrying out research, teaching, and action. Unity of thought, word, and deed would be preserved. The organizational model that Fitzpatrick envisioned was an alternative institutionalized culture. With all his doubts and qualifications, the spirit of ISO as seen by Fitzpatrick was very much like the ethos of the super-*collège* sketched by Thurston Davis. Intellectual excellence and ethical concern were to be as one, and their combination was to convert the benighted and the wayward. The plan drawn up by Fitzpatrick presupposed the continued existence of a Catholic enclave that was beginning to disintegrate.

For these reasons, Fitzpatrick's suggestions were tentative and partially contradictory. A few paragraphs after arguing for keeping the social science education of Jesuits an in-house affair, he acknowledged the "haphazard, directionless nature" of such studies within Catholic schools. At one level the ideas set down by Fitzpatrick made up a policy think piece, an aide-mémoire for the busy institution builder. At another, the memorandum was symptomatic of the ambivalence that Jesuits felt in shifting between a changing subculture and the enveloping Americanism of the postwar years.

A quite different set of recommendations came from Joseph Fichter, a Jesuit who was also finishing graduate studies at Harvard, with summer sessions at Chapel Hill, North Carolina, and the University of Chicago.

There was a Germanic bluntness to Fichter and a personal traditionalism that made him difficult to categorize ideologically. Throughout his career he remained his own man, a gadfly. Like Fitzpatrick, he was involved only intermittently with ISO. [12]

Almost all of Fichter's observations had to do with ideas about research; questions of teaching and implementation were handled implicitly. This was daring. Jesuits had been in the business of teaching for a long time, and many of them were men of action or at least worthy administrators. But scholarship of the kind that took them out of the library and into the field was a novelty. Concentration on this new area narrowed the focus and responsibilities of ISO. Fichter brought the scope of ISO further in line with feasibility by recommending that research themes emphasize traditionally Catholic subjects.

In fact the research plan that Fichter laid out for ISS reflected his own intellectual agenda, which was broad but not sprawling. Rather than take up, with a relatively antiquated methodology, topics that reflected a secular set of interests, he proposed to conduct scientifically advanced research in classically Catholic areas:

> In back of the plan for the ISS are two basic facts: (a) the Church of-
> fers the only orderly and practical solution for the integration of *family
> life*, the fundamental unit of all society. Labor problems and interna-
> tional affairs, which consume the time of many Catholic social think-
> ers are, in the ultimate analysis, important only in the event that our
> family life hangs together; (b) the Church itself is the only organized
> social structure in the world today that offers a hope for unity and sta-
> bility, and its fundamental unit *the parish* is the place where people
> live and work and practice social skills. [13]

Although Fichter assumed that the results of research would feed into teaching and implementation, he did not concern himself with how one operation would interact with another. He did not offer an organizational package. His primary concern was with the quality of research. He thought more like a project director than an institution-builder.

Fichter emphasized the importance of doing empirical studies of "the fundamental Catholic social problems in a practical and usable fashion. This idea," he noted, "seems to have degenerated into something like library research in moral and ethical questions." He advocated instead investigation

> at the grassroots of Catholic life, e.g., family life and parish life, the
> relative positions of Catholics in city, small town, rural areas, what is
> the need for informal lay leadership, what are the actual functions of
> parish organizations, differences of fertility according to residence and

why, the approach of ethnic and race relations that can be known only through actual research among *people*.[14]

In substance though not in method, Fichter's concept of the role of ISO was traditional and inward looking. It involved not only an emphasis on the family as the basis of social order but also a supposition that the Catholic enclave—the parish enfolding the family—was the organizing feature of Catholicism in America. This view was commonplace in the Northeast, the heart of the Catholic enclave. It was also germane to the comparatively backward South—Fichter taught in New Orleans—where Catholics constituted islands in the midst of a Protestant majority. While Jesuits themselves did not generally act as parish priests, Fichter suggested that their intellectual skills could be of use to pastoral ministry through the divulgation of research findings.

It was the priority that Fichter gave to research that foreshadowed change in the direction that American Jesuits would try to take toward social problems. At the close of 1948, Leo Brown replaced Daniel Lord as head of ISO. There were no more annual conventions. The numerous topical and procedural committees that were once thought to coordinate a nationwide movement encompassing all Jesuits were disbanded. So was the Office of Social Activities. ISS was absorbed into ISO, with the goal of advancing and disseminating research in the social sciences. Graduate training in the social sciences was encouraged. But no distinctive program of research of the sort imagined by Fichter emerged.

Fichter's memo represented a potential turning point in the development of social ministry in the Society of Jesus. In the thirties the basic supposition was that the wisdom of the social encyclicals could be taken as given and that their message should in principle be broadcast to the secular world, even if in reality this message was directed mostly at Catholics. Fichter wanted to reverse this process. His idea was to import the methods and the concepts of the secular sciences to learn more about Catholicism. This project came close to violating accustomed boundaries between the sacred and the secular. His proposal to turn the tools of social science toward the inner workings of the church invited criticisms of clinical harshness and suspicions of nosiness that were raised less often when the direction of inquiry was the other way around.

Although ISO made efforts to move in a direction compatible with Fichter's program, the attempt fell short. Fichter himself paid a price for pursuing the kind of research he outlined in his memorandum. In a few years he found himself under censure from the curia of the Society of Jesus, forbidden to continue the publication of his studies of Catholic parishes in the South.[15] His later studies that documented rising dissatisfaction among younger Jesuits were filed away.

III

In 1949 John Baptist Janssens, the Belgian who was chosen superior general by the twenty-ninth General Congregation after the war, wrote a letter to all Jesuits, urging them to greater efforts in the social apostolate. Janssens was conversant with the labor and youth work of Catholic Action groups in northern Europe. His moral conservatism and anticommunism were equal to his predecessor's, and his expression was impeccably dour. He was, however, willing to encourage his men to gain firsthand knowledge of poverty. He stressed the importance of personal experience and example in bringing the social *magisterium* to reality.

> Superiors should not be afraid to propose to me certain changes by which some of the novices' experiments may be adapted, wherever needed, to improve their formation. I have willingly granted permission already for novices, under certain conditions, to beg from door to door for the poor and to distribute in the hovels of the needy whatever alms they collect. In some places, too, I have allowed certain picked men to be sent into factories for a short time, to work with the men and share their life. And in more than one place, novices working as helpers in our retreat houses have, with great profit, come to appreciate members of the working class making their retreat there. . . . I shall allow the Tertians more readily than novices to go into workshops or factories, either for spiritual ministry alone, or even to work with the men themselves, provided they never be forgetful of their priesthood. By all means they should visit the working classes and the poor in hospitals, in institutions, and, under proper circumstances, even in their homes. They will learn to know the wretched state of their homes, their poor food and clothing, by actually seeing it; they will learn to know their ignorance, their lack of refinement and education; by actual experience they would see the difficulty—I almost said the impossibility—of true Christian virtue, which we ourselves could not cultivate in the same circumstances.[16]

These changes of emphasis notwithstanding, Janssens saw no need to revise the theoretical bases of social ministry. He was not ready to introduce substantial reforms in the methods of Jesuit training, any more than he was eager to allow Joseph Fichter to study the inner workings of the church, and he seemed to have little feel for the complexity of developments in the newer disciplines. The curriculum was crowded enough as it was. Instruction in social questions could be added on here and there, without substantially modifying the course of training. New facts might be gathered, and young Jesuits could be exposed to social deprivation, but none of this would alter the content of doctrine. "There is no need," Janssens claimed,

> for the introduction of new courses; but care should be had that the courses in ethics, in social economics, in moral and pastoral theology be applied to modern times and needs. . . . [I]t will be the professor's duty to supply what is lacking and thoroughly to explain the social doctrine of the Roman pontiffs, while treating in short summary certain other points in his tract which are easier or somewhat out-of-date. [17]

Many of Janssens's ideas about social analysis and action had already been vented by Wlodimir Ledochowski, and most of the others were conventional. He repeated the warnings about a Catholicism encircled by enemies—by "communistic atheists" and "liberal materialists" (capitalists). He reiterated the implicit scale of evil between a communism that was intrinsically wrong and "the abuses of capitalism" that were susceptible to reform. [18] He stressed proper motivation. "Social-mindedness" must stem from "the interior law of charity and love." Because the social apostolate sometimes took Jesuits outside the "time-honored ministries of the Society," the selection of men for these endeavors was to be confined to "certain Fathers of suitable talents, industrious, and of reliable and strong character." The less institutionalized the field of activity, and the more it relied on improvisation, the more secure Jesuits had to be in their convictions and self-control. [19]

Janssens emphasized the personal, indeed existential, aspects of social ministry. Organizational proposals and detailed planning of the sort that characterized previous forays in the area took second place, perhaps because Janssens had come to appreciate the unbridgeability of the gap between central control and local circumstances. Yet one new theme emerged and persisted in Janssens's writings. "To prevent our Society from justly being classified with the rich and the capitalists," he stated flatly, "we must direct with utmost zeal many of our ministries towards the poorer classes." [20] Numbers could make up in demographic weight, in strategic mass, for what the poor lacked in political and economic power. In estimating the relative importance of reaching out to the managerial and working classes, numbers became crucial:

> I think that there are two types of institutes which will be especially fruitful in social action; both are in harmony with the spirit of our So-

ciety. We should have, either separately or together, schools and courses for the employers in which they would be taught their rights and duties and schools and lectures on social doctrines for the better educated and more capable members of the working class. Since, as can be seen, the future leaders of labor will be those only who come up from the ranks, and since there is a paramount need to save many, or even the mass of labor, and lead them along the right paths, this second type of school seems to be more important and of greater moment now. This is especially true, if anywhere, of our missions in Asia and Africa.[21]

Two different conflicts were in evidence. One was the divide between capital and labor that marked the industrial societies of Europe. In these regions Janssens recommended that the strategic balance be nudged in favor of the more numerous working classes. In fact, however, the Jesuit labor schools that survived into the 1950s tended to provide training for more and more lower- and middle-management cadres as unions themselves took over educational tasks for their members.

The second division reflected the growth of population in less developed countries, many of which were at least nominally Catholic. Latin America headed the list of demographically critical areas, in contrast to a Europe that seemed saturated with clerical Catholicism. This demographic shift from North to South, Janssens believed, was the crucial movement in world Catholicism, perhaps more fundamental than the clash between capitalism and communism: "Italy has about 60,000 priests for 45,000,000 inhabitants; Brazil with the same number of baptized inhabitants but scattered over a territory thirty times as large has hardly 6,000 priests. This is but one example out of many."[22]

Like Ledochowski before him, Janssens rarely missed an opportunity to remind Jesuits of the need for scrupulous observance of the rules of religious community; he wrote often on the need to strive for perfection in "the inferior life" as a prerequisite for apostolic service.[23] Although Janssens's tone was a shade lighter than the relentlessly chastizing bent of his predecessor, he is still remembered by some Jesuits as belonging to the line of generals "with faces like German nuns." Also like Ledochowski, he had a taste for strategic calculations cast in geopolitical terms. But the postwar world differed from the waning days of the *ancien régime* and the times of economic depression that framed Ledochowski's tenure as general. Janssens developed a heightened sense of the structural transformations, particularly the demographic changes, that were reshaping the relations between Europe and the rest of the world.

Janssens did not promote significant changes in the way Jesuits approached social ministry, although he managed to reaffirm the importance of social ministry and thus to keep it from vanishing under the society's educational institutions. In the tone of his moral exhortations he was thoroughly traditional. The times, however, were expansive. His intuition was that the Society of Jesus could ride this growth and could move forward in the social field without diminishing its ties to tradition. There was a studied vagueness to the practical, organizational zone between Janssens's global perspective and his regular reminders about individual perfection in the spiritual life. The generality of his prescriptions did not quite blur an important anomaly, however. This was the assumption that Jesuits could somehow lead in social ministry without learning—that is, without picking up ideas that might challenge the old paradigm. Internal change in particular was rejected. Social ministry was still consigned to the practical and intellectually derivative.[24]

IV

As the fifties wore on, glimmers of profoundly changing social and cultural conditions spread among American Jesuits. Sustained prosperity brought relief from the deprivation of the thirties; success fueled further change. In the eyes of some Jesuits, however, progress was deceptive. Abundance and the acceleration of growth were disorienting for a worldview erected on scarcity and stability. The task of understanding and influencing events seemed daunting. The latter goal—of shaping policy—was not a preoccupation of many Jesuits, even of those with an interest in social issues. They saw themselves as implementers rather than innovators. But there was a need for some understanding of social developments in the postwar era, now that the corporatist formulas of the thirties had fallen out of fashion. As the subculture opened to outside influences, Jesuits began to sense, though rarely acknowledge, the inadequacies of the categories through which they had been trained to interpret the world. There were also glancing perceptions that to follow established institutional and intellectual patterns might not be an optimal or personally satisfying course, now that technologies for change were coming everywhere into view.

Just before Christmas 1958, a decade after sending his memorandum to Leo Brown on the state of ISO, Joseph Fitzpatrick delivered an address to the Jesuit students at Woodstock College in which he surveyed the trends that were transforming the parameters of the social apostolate. His theme was the falloff in the certainty of simpler times and the rise of doubt in the face of complexity. His presentation was a threnody on an earlier stage of industrialization in which Jesuits felt relatively at home, when their constituents were moving from a rural to an urban ambience.

Fitzpatrick chided the upcoming generation of Jesuits for their religious subjectivity and asocial absorption in the things of the spirit. "I believe you are more inclined to set aside reports about the teamsters and longshoremen," he observed, "in order to follow the latest developments in theology."[25] He then launched into an overview of the historical divide between the times when he came of age, during the depression, and the new world of the postwar period, during which his listeners had reached adulthood.

> It is indeed a strange shift in the affairs of men. . . . [I]n the depths of the depression, when hunger was a common thing on our city streets; when resources were limited and experience slight, men had a confident optimism about the social apostolate; whereas today, at the height of a prosperous era, when resources are relatively abundant and experiences rich, men are hesitant, doubtful and reluctant. . . . [These are] days of doubt, 1948 to the present, days when the dimensions of our world have been twisted and stretched by extraordinary events, and we have not quite determined how the social apostolate should be related to a changing world of which we know so little.[26]

Formerly, optimism and certainty had been kept up by what appeared to be the more personal, manageable proportions of social problems. Although Fitzpatrick did not dwell on the correlation, innocence might also have been encouraged by the ignorance and parochialism of some of the Jesuits who pioneered in labor relations during the thirties. Anticommunism had cast antagonists into bold relief. This mentality had lasted through the Cold War and was only beginning to fade by the end of the fifties:

> We had the conviction that we knew what social evils were. We could see them, in the exploitation of workingmen; in the lack of social responsibility in business; in the menace of communism. The social apostolate, therefore, was a well-defined task. We were to teach people what communism was; teach workingmen how to organize and manage their unions; teach employers the Catholic principles of social justice. The solution of the problems was being worked out dramatically all around us. The CIO came into its own when Lewis lead his followers out of the AFL convention in 1935. The auto workers were organized in the sit-down strikes of 1936. The Wagner act was declared constitutional in 1937. Minimum wage legislation was passed; and social security. The Spanish civil war broke out in July of 1936. Lenin had said clearly that, "The torch of Europe would burn at both ends." Moscow and Madrid were to be the two poles of the relentless axis of communism. Every hour of the conflict became for us a symbol, first of the failure to correct the social abuses that had led to the

conflict; secondly of the struggle of embattled Christians against the communist menace. We felt, as we manifested our interests in the social apostolate, that we were part of a dynamic movement that was doing things and getting somewhere. We were convinced that social justice was in the making.[27]

Causes overlapped then, or so it seemed. The conflict was titanic and clarifying. In recollection the defenders of the good—Catholics—were aligned against the forces of evil—Communists—along all fronts, politically, socially, and morally. In reality the struggle was as much a competition for influence over sectors of the middle and working class, involving secular fascists and democrats in addition to Catholics and Communists, as it was a direct, either-or combat between two antagonists only. Fitzpatrick's tone in reconstructing this bygone era was elegiac; his purpose seems primarily to have been to transmit a fond memory ("We had the conviction . . ."), not the facts, of a fight whose time had passed. The memory was no less poignant for being half true. Like his gibe at the self-concern of younger Jesuits, Fitzpatrick's representation of the closed mentality of a dualistic world implied polite criticism of its tunnel vision.

World War II, Fitzpatrick then stated, "put a sudden end to optimism, not only in the social apostolate, but in most other areas of life as well." It was not so much the war itself, horrible as it had been, but the magnitude of social change and the potential for ceaseless transformation—the mass mobilization and technological developments accompanying the war—that threatened to sweep aside the small world that Jesuits thought they had mastered. A dense parochialism, full of familiar detail, had given way to a globalism of indecipherable complexity:

> We realized that the problem that we had defined in measurable terms and for which we thought we had solutions, was actually only one small aspect of a world-wide problem of unbelievable proportions. Men lost all confidence that they had an answer; in fact, they began to realize they did not even know how to define the problem.[28]

"The problem," as Fitzpatrick saw it, was a function of half a dozen major transformations in social structure and politics. The first involved the magnification of the potential for destruction in armed conflict between the Soviet Union and the United States. Fitzpatrick was a sociologist, not an analyst of world conflict, and he relegated his exposition of the dangers of the Cold War to a single paragraph. His real interest was in societal changes that escaped Cold War antinomies.

Fitzpatrick focused on developments that were making for realignments between North and South, as well as West and East, and for shifts in the configuration of power within Catholicism itself. Foremost among these was population growth. "Latin America is growing so rapidly and the number of priests is growing so slowly that, if the trend continues, by the year 2000, Latin America may be predominantly pagan, with a few islands of Catholicism."[29] Since he was acting as a middleman in the experiments that envisioned first Puerto Rico, then Mexico, as "bridges"—training and cultural exchange centers—between the Catholicisms of North and South America, Fitzpatrick knew that the differential growth in population between the continents would curtail the hegemony of Anglo–Irish American Catholicism. Dispassionate analysis vied with personal experience in Fitzpatrick's presentation, and his words took on the eloquence of an engaged but helpless witness to the unfolding of a historical drama.

Several other macrochanges contributed to a weakening sense of control. Urbanization bred a "cultural disorganization" that threatened the communities in which Catholicism thrived. While they helped fortify American leadership of the capitalist world, "technological achievements" also promoted an increasing depersonalization and "white-collar way of life." One corollary of this complexity was especially disheartening for Jesuits with memories of the thirties:

> The labor unions are no longer the struggling campaigners they once were. . . . Many of them are big, well-established, sometimes powerful, and, in an embarrassing number of instances, more guilty of injustice than the employers whose injustices they professed to correct.[30]

Fitzpatrick saw that the "area of dramatic development today," generating the enthusiasm once reserved for the labor movement, was "in the field of integration, interracial relations." This was unknown territory for many Catholics, Jesuits included.

Fitzpatrick turned finally to a traditional focus of Catholic concern, the family. His list of social problems, starting with the global and massively structural, had worked down to the local, "probably the area of most effective social action today." It was here, Fitzpatrick suggested, that the balance between complexity and manageability still favored Jesuits with a practical slant on social reform.

The mention of the face-to-face nature of family relations was a gesture at offsetting the emphasis on massive structural transformations that weighed on the talk. The contrast between the fragility of the family—the vessel of a dimming past—and the huge insensitivity of demographics in the aggregate deepened the melancholy and bittersweet review of times past. Fitzpatrick stressed the importance of large-scale social changes partly to remind his audience of the solipsistic perils of existential currents then fashionable in Catholic intellectual circles. But, while his observations about the forces underlying recent social changes were sweeping, he did not hint at a theory of comparable proportions that might give a clearer sense of their interconnectedness. No grand integration was forthcoming.

Despite the sense of crushing complexity, Fitzpatrick made a stab at being proactive. He insisted on the importance of humble "tasks of the social apostolate on the local level, the tasks that do not need extensive organization, the tasks that every Jesuit can find all around him if he has the time to give to them . . . the family apostolate, close contact with the poor in order to assist and guide them, interracial and inter-group relations, work with youth." There was a prima facie urgency to problems in these areas. Jesuits needed motivation, not specialized training, to work effectively or at least to make a start at this level. The other priority was scholarship, for "social action is a dangerous or a futile thing if it is not supported by competent scholarship." Fitzpatrick argued that "large or small, social action will be increasingly effective in so far as it is guided by competent and scholarly knowledge."[31]

These were recommendations, not conclusions. They were practical but anticlimactic. The balancing of study and action was a standby of Catholic social thought; it had been a central theme of Fitzpatrick's earlier reflections on ISO. But even study and action were not quite the same as doctrine and application. The big change now was in the perception that the walls of the Catholic world within which these two approaches, whatever their labels, interacted or competed were falling down, and with them the boundaries of identity and the social foundations of self-assurance. Between small tasks devoted to the family and changes of global proportions no *via media* or firm Catholic community appeared.

Fitzpatrick gave his talk at the onset of the papacy of John XXIII, after the burial of the leader of the old regime, before the calling of the Second Vatican Council. At that moment the plaintiveness of an uncertain transition came through louder than did the gestures at pragmatism:

> I have told you nothing definite that could give you a sense of security; nor have I told you anything inspiring that can fire your enthusiasm. It would be unfortunate if we were too distressed about our doubts, or if we attributed our doubts to our deficiencies. Doubt and uncertainty are the characteristics of the entire world, and our own doubt and uncertainty simply reflect the all-pervading uncertainty of the times in which we live. The doubt and hesitation should not be taken as signs that there is little that we can do, but as signs that the much more to be done will require greater patience, more painstaking scholarship, and a greater daring that has its security in an abiding confidence in God.
>
> Your generation will have a task much more difficult than my generation had.[32]

10

Social Order, Social Change

I

Catholicism traditionally propounded a synoptic vision. It was supposed to be a way of life expressed not only in the quotidian fullness of ethnic subcultures but also in the form of a cosmopolitan *Weltanschauung*. Jesuits were expected to defend and broadcast both dimensions of this world. For about twenty years, from the mid-forties until 1963, a periodical entitled *Social Order* was published under the auspices of ISO. These years cover a time of rapid change in the structure of American society and in the disposition of the Catholic community within it, and the pages of *Social Order* contain a detailed record of the efforts made by the Jesuits to come to terms with these changes.

Social Order appeared ten times a year. Obliged to offer professional commentary and sage reflections on a practically unlimited range of topics, the Jesuits had to do so frequently. They showed curiosity about a variety of secular and religious matters, but they rarely managed to pursue any one subject in depth. As early as the 1930s Daniel Lord and others had begun to suspect that the intellectual system on which successful popularization depended might itself be naive. By the end of the fifties some Jesuits had become aware of the irony of a supposedly universal vision that perpetuated amateurism amid a parochial Catholicism.

Another facet of the same problem originated in the need to reconcile modern ideas about social issues with the traditional teachings of the church. This double chore imposed an anticipatory censorship. Novel lines of thought were not often pushed very far. A shallowness induced by haste and spreading thin was exacerbated by circumspection. Occasionally, as with John Courtney Murray, the tension found creative release. The more typical outcome seems to have been a think piece that wandered from point to point. Overt censorship was less of a problem than the draining of psychic energy on the embellishment of preconceived truths. Intellectual effort was almost never devoted to ideas that might lead in fresh directions.

At the outset of the fifties Fr. John L. Thomas, who was soon to gain a reputation as an expert in family sociology, wrote a review of *Catholic Social Principles,* a standard text on the subject that argued, as Bernard Dempsey did, for the coming-of-age of corporatism with the rise of the new industrialism of the United States. The tone of the review was gentle. All the same, Thomas taxed the author for a reluctance to question and think through basic premises.

> To take such a stand [that management and labor have reached an agreement on ends and values and are merely disagreeing over segmentalized problems within a mutually accepted social framework] when dealing with the reform of the whole social structure, as advocated in the encyclicals, is to beg the question. . . . To state the problem briefly: Are the social evils of the capitalist system due merely to the accidental malfunctioning of the system, or is the malfunctioning of the system inherent in its very nature? . . . This is a key point. Although the author is second to none in castigating the evils of the present economic system, he lacks incisiveness in his stand on how this system should be reorganized.[1]

Thomas did not specify what the alternative to the reigning system might be. But he suggested that the failure might lie not with this or that author but with the social doctrine that resorted to hortatory generalities or dug up strange blueprints when faced with particular applications:

> The Popes speak of deproletizing [*sic*] the masses, of reintegrating them into the corporate life of the nation, of setting up an order which will make possible their acquisition of private property, of reorganizing the institutions of society in such a way that they will serve the common good and not the private interests of the propertied classes.
>
> As the author points out, the reorganization of economic society according to the papal plan is to be along the lines of the vocational group system, or the "Industry Council Plan," as they choose to speak of it here in America. Again the treatment of this difficult subject lacks penetration since there is a seeming refusal to face the full implications of such a reorganization in an American setting. . . . If our capitalistic system is essentially different from the European system, is it not prudent to ask whether the I.C.P. is what is needed at this time rather

than stress on social legislation, better labor unions and improved collective bargaining techniques?[2]

Thomas was broaching the vital question of the institutional exportability of a Eurocentric doctrine. It was insufficient to leave the *magisterium* on the plane of indicative moralism; it was hard to imagine how the promulgation of values could work without organizational embodiment. The transfer of social programs involved politics.

Thomas raised the issue of organizational creativity but did not pursue its implications. He distanced himself from fantasies of literal applications of corporatism to the United States at the same time that he maintained a critical perspective on American capitalism. He drew back from any flirtation with social revolution and suggested that some sort of benign hierarchy, in spirit like the corporatism of the encyclicals, might smooth the edges of the market. His point of departure was not an analytical framework but a pang at the disappearance of institutional mechanisms foregone by economic modernization and mass democracy:

> It is almost trite to add that the present system lends itself to a concentration of wealth, and consequently, of power, unheard of in previous ages. This is a social fact. It need not necessarily constitute a social problem, however, since it is possible to conceive of a paternalistic society in which this power serves the common good and is accepted by all. . . . Can a capitalist aristocracy survive in a framework of social and political democracy? It is the rebellion of the embittered, dechristianized masses which has created the unrest so evident in Europe today. Day by day they are fashioning the answer to our question and it is in the negative.[3]

The reference to the lost historical possibility of a benign paternalism served to rouse a dozing audience with a learned curiosity, but the probing stopped there. The imagery short-circuited thought, which was not sustained long enough to determine what its practical consequences might be.[4]

Tergiversation in the pages of *Social Order* resulted not only from the silent maneuvers required to address myriad questions without offending ecclesiastical interests. It also reflected uncertainty about the readership to be targeted. In the Jesuit tradition, ideas for their own sake did not enjoy priority. Knowledge had somehow to be useful. The question became: Whom to reach? The answer seemed clear: Catholics interested but not expert in social and economic problems. The response ignored non-Catholics except as persons to be converted to the Catholic point of view. But the American Catholic community itself had become more diverse. Although there were still customers for the pamphlets in the racks at the back of the churches, and there was a scattering of readers for professional scholarship, it was the audience in between, made up of busy religious professionals and educated laypeople, that proved difficult to visualize and to reach. Most Catholics took their moral beliefs from the pulpit and the parochial schools and looked elsewhere for their political and economic opinions.

The difficulty was not simply that Catholics were changing and becoming generically modern. The crucial obstacle was that the doctrine had no means of making sense of change, particularly the transformations that were beginning to stir inside the church. Ideally, reform still meant the restoration of a bygone social order. By the 1950s, although little of this was taken seriously as the basis of social analysis, a mood of nostalgia inhibited exploration. Provocative sallies like Thomas's were admissible; a systematic challenge of the sort raised by John Courtney Murray was not. The undertone of wistfulness that ran through John Thomas's essays could also be found in many other attempts to understand contemporary America.

Fr. Philip Land had written his doctoral dissertation at St. Louis University on the theoretical foundations of corporatism. In the first half of the fifties, before leaving to teach economics at the Gregorian University, he published a series of articles in *Social Order* in which he struggled to elucidate the philosophical underpinnings of vocational orders and corporate assemblies.[5]

Land began by dealing with the most obvious drawbacks of the corporatist perspective in the American context: its foreignness and its predilection for hierarchy. He began by chipping away at the myth of utter completeness and immutability that had encrusted the *magisterium*. He distinguished between the changeless core and the flexible periphery of doctrine, reiterating standard notions, drawn from natural law theory, about universal, unchanging principles and practical applications:

> Some institutions, it can be remarked parenthetically, which are expressions of natural exigencies will have a common and unchanging element. This unchanging element seems to be the basis of the *jus gentium*. Men will largely concur in the first and most essential understanding of their common nature. It is when they elaborate these first approximations into an institution that they begin to diverge on many details.[6]

This was a standard invocation of the position that a universal, stable ethic guiding personal behavior could be detected underneath the variety of collective social and political arrangements. This ethic was foundational but not necessarily constitutive of public order in a literal sense. In a passage that echoed the line of argument John Courtney Murray was developing, Land stressed what he considered the traditional Catholic respect for institutional solutions specific to particular countries. This went beyond mere toleration, he suggested, to a positive appreciation of the autonomy of the political sphere. Simultaneously he emphasized the need for "the people" to decide on the political forms that suited them:

> Our first principle here is St. Thomas' dictum that people rightly accommodate the application of the natural law to themselves, "each state determines what is good for it." Given a right objective, the people work out for themselves and within the framework of their culture, the way in which they will achieve that objective. Any institution, to have validity and permanence, must be by and of and for a people.[7]

Land based his appeal for the reasonable adaptation of ideas for social reform on historical experience rather than on "the people" of democratic theory or an axiomatic schemata. Viable social arrangements were not set down by deductive reasoning. Nor were they the product of an impartial empiricism. The experience that was to be respected was Burkean, made up of mostly local wisdom and biases—customs, ways of life—tested over centuries. Hierarchical order might be accepted and even, as John Thomas proposed, granted legitimacy. But it could not be a paternalism imposed from above or abroad. It had instead to be the organic product of the mulling of institutional evolution.[8]

A complementary element in Land's thinking, besides the insistence on the precedence of local realities in shaping plans for social betterment, was contingency. Historicity and potential mutability marked institutional arrangements. Here his argument, like Murray's, was not in favor of particular political solutions but rather against the idea that any single solution could be generalizable through time and space:

> There is the temptation to believe that a static wisdom covers all life's contingencies. One is impatient with realities which will not reduce to simple and unequivocal formulae. Not only is there the temptation to assume that valid generalizations drawn from observation may be fitted to any particular situation; there is the further danger that these generalizations themselves will not have been formulated with reference to the concrete, historical world.[9]

Land's was an essay in demystification. His main target was the cake of custom that had fossilized into schematic abstraction and imperial prescription. In an important sense, however, Land was quite traditional. A corollary of his argument was that truths that fell short of axiomatic perfection were more or less ad hoc, passing localisms. There was philosophy, and there was arbitrary custom; logic and history. A science of the social as a middle ground was barely conceivable.

Between dogma and randomness there was a moral ethos decanted from experience, a decent pragmatism. Land had an infatuation with common sense that informed his thinking about middle-range issues and current affairs. The terrible simplifications of the abstracting intellect were the great danger. This mind-set could just as easily encourage absolute belief in market competition or communism as credulity in the transcendent virtues of feudalism.

Land was skeptical about models of industrial relations that masked exploitation. But this realism had a religious bent. It led him to call for the cultivation of bonds of community in the modern firm, not an invigorated competition, much less social revolution. His heart was in cooperation. Though he denied that "this idea of friendship through work is . . . mere romanticizing," he could not resist invoking the corporatism of the Middle Ages as the precedent for an updated version of labor-management cooperation. The firm could be a big family:

> Such bonds existed in the medieval guilds where master and workman not only worked together, but played and worshipped together on their patronal feast days. This affective side of friendship is present in the bonds that hold together such professional associations as those of doctors, lawyers, and trade unions. Actually many factories want this and seek to build a spirit of team work. [10]

Land refrained from advocating a return to ennobling austerity. By 1955 the American economic boom was undeniable, and he welcomed prosperity as a support for political democracy:

> The performance of the American system has been so satisfying . . . that socialism has never been able to gain a footing. . . . [A] renewal of abundance dissipated the last vestige of hope for revolutionaries. The AF of L has been vindicated for clinging to its middle-class character; the CIO steadily moved in that direction. [11]

The new era abolished traditional understandings of hierarchy, of an "artificial, divine-right stratification of men" in the polity and the market. But "it is just as arguable," Land added, "that a wide sharing in manners, mores and social communication is the surest foundation upon which to erect a true elite." [12] By temperament Land prized a social system of compassion and community, and such an arrangement could entail functional hierarchies as practical devices of governance and production. The "wide sharing" he advocated was less feasible in the heterogeneous United States than in the racially and religiously homogeneous settings conjured up by corporatist theory. [13] In fact, national-level political and social models did not excite Land very much. His effective though not always explicit focus was at a smaller, regional and local-institutional scale. Within this range participation as well as paternalism could be personal.

John Courtney Murray had justified pluralism as tolerance commendable for its results. It worked, and there was no civilized alternative to it. By the second half of the twentieth century monarchical absolutism seemed a decorative irrelevance, an anachronism defended by the papacy for the church but surely not a model for the wider world. It was monarchy that was tolerated, not pluralism that was tolerated by monarchy. There could be no question of resuscitating an outmoded political form in modern times.

The economic and social issues addressed by the papal encyclicals were of a different stripe. It was unclear whether their message was intended for Catholics only or directed at non-Catholics as well. In the latter case, awkward questions arose about dialogue between opposing worldviews. Political forms were superstructural in both Catholic and Marxist thought; economic systems touched the lives of more people closely. Disputes over constitutional principles tended to be symbolic. The advocacy of and opposition to specific social measures affected policies and produced real outcomes. "Forms" were changeable, like the surfaces of Platonic essences. But "systems" smacked of solider and more comprehensive entities.

Land did not come up with a theory of social change and diversity comparable to Murray's of political change and pluralism. His central appeal was to pragmatism and common sense, and to pastoral kindness and interpersonal sanity. This left him, unlike Murray, within a Catholic framework, without direct conceptual bridges to the secular world. Land's ideas—for example, about cooperation—presupposed a relatively homogeneous social environment that served to buttress mutualistic values. They were not easily transportable across cultural environments and economic systems. His thinking could more safely be treated as a local curiosity than as normative theory.

In part, however, these limitations may have been spurious. Land was struggling toward a picture of an intermediate realm of social activity above the level of atomized individuals and the family but below formal political institutions. Like Bernard Dempsey, he was searching for organizations on a human scale—workplace groups, for example—that took up more of the daily lives of ordinary citizens than political institutions but that were not predominantly private, as was the family. These organizations were local and hence "lumpy," idiosyncratic and difficult to export; they tended to get lost in translation. Yet versions of them—that is, their functional equivalents—were very widespread. Athletic clubs in Brazil, for instance, were rather different from associations of baseball fans in the United States; and church groups presented similar quandaries of crossnational equivalence. Nevertheless such collectivities bore some affinity to one another.

Land was exploring territory that was less peripheral to Catholic doctrine than political institutions but more expansive and flexible than the family, in which the absolutes of personal morality were thought to be graven as in stone. This region was made up of the panoply of second-tier, more or less voluntary associations between the state and the individual—"intentional communities" that were the linchpins of "subsidiarity." Their apparent failure to travel well—the difficulty which Land experienced in conceptualizing such organizations as meaningful beyond distinctive localities, each with their ways of life—may be attributed to blind spots in contemporary social theory as much as to an inherent lack of portability in the institutions themselves.[14]

II

Viewed in print, the *magisterium* still current in the fifties seemed fixed in the past. In practice, under a codified patriarchy, forgiveness and a kind of spiritual clientelism became the human rule. The operative manner of Catholicism swung between the absolute and the chaotically circumstantial, as Murray complained. The corresponding realities of ethnic politics were flexibility and favoritism. An elaborate haziness of social doctrine kept a studied distance from practice. This encouraged cautious reform and calls for getting the facts straight rather than either revolutionary ardor or imaginative analysis. The importance given to the pastoral aspects of social ministry in the absence of intellectual rigor depleted the field of excitement and challenge. The air of tinkering and of confidence in moderation was strong. The articles published by Leo Brown in *Social Order* and elsewhere extolled conciliation and the social benefits to be derived from compromise. They were consoling homilies rather than goads to thought.[15]

With the appointment of Fr. Edward Duff as editor toward the end of the fifties, an effort was made to enliven the magazine. Duff, who had written his dissertation on the World Council of Churches, rid *Social Order* of some of its hothouse style.[16] In 1957 he introduced a symposium on the theme of American abundance by noting that "the Joads of *[The] Grapes of Wrath* . . . are buying television sets on wages earned in the California aircraft industry."[17] (ISO, he mentioned, was "unencumbered by abundance.") While he insisted on the need to avoid "a diet . . . calculated to produce a sleepy complacency," Duff avoided criticisms of the American miracle from a corporatist standpoint. His attacks on unemployment and racial discrimination did not set contemporary conditions against the afterglow of medievalism; he tried to be forward-looking.[18]

The centerpiece of Duff's writing appeared as a pair of articles proposing

a drastic revision of "Catholic social action in the American environment."
He began traditionally enough with the premise that "we have from moral
theology insights providing clear directives in intrapersonal relationships."
In addition, he continued:

> We have . . . from the gospels and from the Fathers of the Church an
> inescapable insistence on the equal dignity of all men in a common
> destiny for whose attainment the goods of the earth were created. Thus
> we know that class conflict is essentially without logic and that the pri-
> mary function of any economy is to provide for the basic wants of all,
> beginning with the most disadvantaged.[19]

But this core of verities did not suffice as social doctrine. It was limited to
questions of personal ethics and "intrapersonal relations"—that is, to questions of "faith and morals." Impersonal forces conditioned issues of economic and political policy. These controversies could not be resolved by
analogy with dilemmas of individual morality:

> The question arises . . . whether we have at hand a developed body of
> social doctrine shaped for the analysis and the reform of contemporary
> American institutions. . . . It is not suggested here that we Catholics
> have no premises from which to take positions in the effort of social
> reform. What is being asked is whether there is as much content, spe-
> cifically applicable to the American scene, in Catholic social doctrine
> as our language sometimes suggests. It is simultaneously hinted that we
> have lived off positions packaged elsewhere and have failed to make the
> contributions to intellectual life of the universal Church which our
> American experience warrants.[20]

Duff answered the question in the negative: "My simple argument is that we
do not have today [a] developed body of Catholic social teaching, concretely
applicable to the American scene."[21]

The secular environment of the United States had reached a stage at
which dedication and practical ingenuity no longer sufficed for achievement
and power, and reflective Catholics were far enough along the way to
assimilation that they had to compete by the rules of this environment. The
critical litany that others had applied to the deficiencies of Catholic academia was now brought to bear on the social apostolate:

> The American economic system is rather a new thing for Catholic so-
> cial thought to contemplate. . . . [I]n social action work enthusiasm
> cannot replace brains. . . . Accurate knowledge of anything, not least
> of our own neighborhood, demands hard, persistent and individual
> attention. Editorializing is no substitute for analysis.[22]

Duff emphasized the limitations of direct action uninformed by analysis. Piecemeal measures were routine and inadequate. Person-to-person help was satisfying but inefficient. Neighborliness could be smug. He singled out for criticism the attachment to "the immediate relief of personal distress." Personally rewarding as they might be, such efforts did little to determine public policy. Anticipating the emphasis on structural change that was to gain attention with Vatican II, Duff contended: "We are committed to the reform of institutions, to changing the patterns of behavior and the conditions of existence that lessen the full measure of justice available to our fellow men."[23]

Duff's comments did not constitute an attack on the traditions of social Catholicism but a warning against extending into the present a pastoral approach that seemed to have worked well up through the thirties and forties but that was now suffering from intellectual fatigue. In bygone days

> the Church in America . . . launched a huge salvage operation to alleviate misery, to integrate the immigrant and to protect the flock. . . . In such a situation the primary concern of the Church was the corporal and spiritual works of mercy. Speculation about economic structures was a luxury beyond the scope of the Catholic minority; nor indeed was there the intellectual tradition or the intellectual resources for such an inquiry. Direct action through social welfare agencies of its own creation was the Church's historic confrontation of American society.[24]

The American church had played a significant role in supporting the rights of an immigrant working class and in fostering social mobility. In doing so, it earned the gratitude not only of the working class but also of business interests who looked upon the church's paternal incorporation of the poor as a stabilizing force during the stressful years of industrialization.[25]

Duff realized that the church's stand on social issues did not please all interests. When they proclaimed themselves in favor of national health insurance in 1919, the bishops were well in front of conservative Catholic and American business opinion generally. The bishops' position had been "systematically opposed by Catholic spokesmen when proposed as legislation, seemingly because of fears it would interfere with the substantial property stake in Catholic hospitals."[26] On other occasions, however, the rejection of the official Catholic position was inspired not so much by reactionary interests entrenched against the deserving poor as by a judgment that the remedies being proposed were ineffectual and possibly crackpot schemes. Duff's attitude to the countercultural undercurrent in Catholicism was mixed and indulgent:

There has always been a wistful advocacy of the vocational group organization (advocated in *Quadragesimo Anno*) as *the* Catholic contribution to social reform without much clarity as to the scope and practical
function of these *ordines*. . . . When the Supreme Court invalidated
the [National Industrial Recovery Act] in the spring of 1935, Catholic
leaders urged an amendment to the Federal Constitution that would
empower Congress to create such true *ordines*. . . . Industry councils
were also the remedy proposed during the Depression by the Reverend
Charles E. Coughlin, a radio orator with a national audience and a
frenzied following. . . . A more astringent gospel of voluntary poverty
and back to the land was preached (and, with the addition of pacifi-
cism [*sic*], is preached today) by Dorothy Day. . . . The single practical influence of the Catholic Worker movement, and it was
considerable, was not its program but the challenge of Christian Poverty and Service it forthrightly presented to young Catholics who,
trained in the amorphous movement, left to enter the trade unions,
journalism and politics.[27]

The glory days of social Catholicism—though not, Duff implied, of Catholic intellectual life—were the immigrant decades. By the 1950s the frame
of mind and orientation toward action characteristic of that era were
squeezed between a dull concentration on labor-management relations and
a fervor for anarchic simplicity. One was lost in routine, the other seemed
unduly personalistic. "Neither professors nor students are preoccupied with
the need of a *réforme des structures*," Duff commented. "Indeed, the phrase
seems untranslatable into English."[28]

Duff castigated the "deplorable provincialism" of Catholic attitudes toward social reform as outdated. At the same time he upheld core Catholic
values by chastising Americans for their permissiveness with regard to family
norms and sexual behavior. The nonnegotiable point, as it was for John
Courtney Murray, John Thomas, and Philip Land, was the permanence
and universalism of natural law guiding personal behavior. This was to be
the unyielding anchor in the swirl of political and social changes that went
on around American Catholics. Murray's moralism echoed in Duff, who
decried the "diminishing moral consensus among Americans" as he posed
rhetorical questions:

Am I being alarmist in noting that the nation which outlawed polyg-
amy as socially pernicious has now announced . . . that adultery is a
debatable idea, that if you like that sort of thing that is the sort of thing
that you like? Have we been a little naive in protesting that we are all
for pluralism—meaning, for us, the coexistence of creeds and a respect
for different cultural traditions—when our partners in the dialogue

mean by pluralism a relativism that mocks the possibility of a Public Philosophy?[29]

Duff distinguished between the serviceable past of social Catholicism and the repetition of this achievement that blocked progress. He dreaded the neoparochialism of complacency. Similarly, he reminded his readers of the fallacy of reducing public policy issues to choices between virtue and vice, even as he insisted on the perpetuity of ethical claims in the personal realm. Catholics had yet to recognize that economic and political disputes could not be handled by assuming a straightforward or face-to-face connection between collective institutions, public policy, and moral principles directed at individual behavior. The disjuncture between private morality and public policy—which some critics argued Irish American politicians had raised to a high art—could not be overcome by exhortations to abandon selfishness. In taking care of their own, through their schools and hospitals and parish associations, Catholics had succeeded in entering the mainstream. They had become competent in an impersonal world. But in Duff's view Catholics had merely reached a way station; they had not arrived. If they did not press on, Catholics were in danger of being absorbed as nonentities:

> If concentration on labor-management issues has in the past marked American Catholic social thinking and if an uncritical acceptance of a middle-class ideology known as the American Way of Life threatens to blur the clarity and particularity of the Catholic vision, it will be apparent why American Catholicism—apart from its impressive range of charitable institutions—has small influence on the direction of American society or the policies of the national government. [30]

Acceptance was making Catholics flabby. In default of an intellectually informed idealism that could take the place of self-satisfaction and sentimentality, conservative inertia and petty moralism had diverted the concerns of American Catholics to an unsophisticated anticommunism suspicious of newer movements favoring civil liberties, racial justice, and Third World causes.

Up to a point the social agenda sketched by Duff closely resembled the program of the New Frontier. Racial integration, Peace Corps–type projects, ecumenicism, and intellectual flair led the way. But Duff also gave priority to two areas that were not at the top of the Kennedy platform but were traditional to Catholic social ministry: the family and rural life. These were the touchstones of solid morality, now jeopardized more than ever—here Duff cited Will Herberg—by the "idolatrous civil religion of Americanism."[31] The fact that these areas stood apart from the dominant, industrial relations emphasis of the recent past pointed up the importance that Duff attached to the maintenance of specifically moral, personal standards as the basis of Catholic social action. At the heart of organized action on behalf of the downtrodden there had to be character.

Duff covered a good deal of ground, and the ground itself was shifting. Unsurprisingly, therefore, his ideas were not impeccably coherent. Yet his comments on the relation of current developments to old-line Catholicism revealed an underlying pattern. Three motifs stand out.

The constant was the insistence on personal rectitude. The sanctity of the family and the perils of the sins of the flesh were to be unswerving points on the moral compass of modern American Catholics. Duff directed attention to these areas with a light touch. He never devoted a separate article—much less a series of them or an entire book—to the topics, as John Thomas did. Furthermore, his complaint that American Catholics were insensitive to the institutional and structural aspects of social problems indicated that he had reservations about a privatism whose concern for sexual propriety could be as self-indulgent in its way as promiscuity could. His concern with personal morality was not obsessive. Yet he was unable to discern positive signs in changes in popular culture and the experimentation of life-styles that were already part of American culture in the 1950s. Even in benign or harmless form these explorations served only to distract from the responsible work of shaping a progressive civic consciousness and a participatory public spirit. The foundations of the Catholic contribution to the American way had to lie in sexual control and affective reserve.[32]

Moral continuity was necessary in order to welcome institutional change, with its rejection of the triumphalism of the immigrant ghettos, at bearable psychic cost. The shrinking of the ethnic enclaves took away the communal supports of Catholic identity. Interior discipline signified by integrity in personal morals, particularly in sexual and family matters, was needed to keep up a sense of the Catholic self. The organizational shell might be overhauled and even abandoned, but individuals must persevere in virtue.

A second dilemma in Duff's diagnosis concerned politics. Repeatedly he castigated American Catholics for clinging to a soothing industrial-relations model of conflict management and to a public administration view of social problem-solving. Duff stressed the difference between the service model of social action, directed at the tribal communities of the Catholic subculture, which he characterized as obsolete, and a more sophisticated model of political influence, directed at the formulation of policy, which had yet to be attained. He wanted to inject excitement as well as expertise into civic affairs. But he neglected to clarify what might be the distinctly Catholic features of this revivification, and he said nothing about the role of religious professionals in it.[33] This omission hid a potential contradiction. If Catholicism had something cogent of its own to add to public debate in America, it was a focus on moral issues. Yet Duff did not locate these controversies, fundamental as they might be to Catholics, at the cutting edge of the new American politics. Likewise, he was not forthcoming about the institutional vehicles, in or outside the parties and the unions, for mobilizing Catholic opinion. Neither the programmatic priorities nor the organizational form of American Catholic activism was self-evident.

The general problem grew out of the difficulty of orchestrating the idealism and moral probity of individual Catholics, now increasingly dispersed outside the parishes of inner cities, and of mobilizing these scattered forces for collective impact. There was a danger that Catholics would lose the political clout they had built up during the days of the ward bosses and sink into the quietism of personal concern that Joseph Fitzpatrick feared was overtaking younger Jesuits. A more specific implication of Duff's reasoning, one that may have kept him from clarifying possible routes to political influence, was that the decline of the old broker Catholicism meant a decline in the role of the priest as political arbitrator. The "age of the laity" was at hand.

Duff had gone some way toward discrediting the reduction of politics to personal conflicts pitting the good against the bad. In rejecting this simple way of joining personal morality and public interests, however, he failed to explain how the private and political spheres might be connected at all except by way of a Catholic specialization with the triad of divorce, abortion, and pornography. Organizational behavior could not be reduced to the orchestration of personal morals, yet somehow collective outcomes had to represent the public good.

A third problem was also skirted. The task as Duff saw it was to revive the intellectual dynamism of American Catholicism by letting its organizational relics wither away without damaging the ethical core. But it was not just the paternalism and the grind of labor-management relations, which many Jesuits agreed could be updated without damaging Catholic teaching, or Cold War shibboleths that got in the way of ampler participation by the faithful in domestic and international affairs. Complacency with the settlement of the management-labor divisions of the thirties and forties and the movement toward global issues both obscured subjective transformations that were occurring in the values of younger cohorts. There was as yet no framework to make sense of this restlessness. In the abundance of postwar America, modes of personal conduct and interpersonal relations once thought to be steadfast came into question on a large scale.[34] The shift was not merely another symptom of the perennial battle between the young and the old but a rearrangement of the terms of the struggle itself, brought on by prosperity and by technological advances in the media. In their efforts to situate the Catholic tradition within a modernizing America, the Jesuits had come to a crossroads where generational change and historical transformation met.

Duff's insistence on stability of character as a psychological precondition for dealing with structural and institutional change put him in the company of other reformist Jesuits of his generation. It maintained a link with a past of collective meaning as the demographic environment went into sudden metamorphosis. Duff had premonitions of the rise of a temper strong on conscience—a radicalism attuned to social injustice and political oppression—but weak on character as persistence and traditional moral probity.

For Duff conscience without character was un-Christian but comprehensible. What his antennae missed or only dimly perceived was the rise in sensitivity toward another dimension of personhood. For some Jesuits the creation of identity meant rebellion against the past. Creativity required a rupture with moral consistency, and conscience as social obligation took second place to the discovery of personal direction. In this respect, Jesuits were undergoing many of the same changes as their peers in the larger society, with an edginess distinctive to their decades-long retreat from modernism.

III

The labor schools set up by Jesuits and other clerics reached their peak in the late forties. In 1947 Leo Brown was able to count

> no fewer than ninety-eight education programs for workmen conducted under Catholic auspices. Twenty-four labor schools are associated with Catholic colleges or universities; sixty-four schools are sponsored by parishes or diocesan institutions. In addition, there are five forums, which are conducted much in the manner of labor schools, and five labor institutes.[35]

Leftist and middle-of-the-road forces were still fighting for control of the union movement. The internecine battles of the thirties broke out again after the hiatus of the war. The Jesuits still had a service to offer to Catholic workingmen who wanted to defend themselves and perhaps make good in these power struggles.

Less than a year after the war, the pastor at Saint Helena, a church in the Parkchester section of the Bronx, approached Philip Carey with a request for assistance in getting classes started for workingmen in the parish hall. Carey's family lived in the neighborhood, and he responded by enlisting the help of contacts made through the Xavier Labor School. The lecturers were mostly

Irish American, one was Italian American; some were graduates of Fordham, and some were semiskilled members of the muscle trade unions. While all the participants were manual laborers—Carey insisted that no one from the ranks of management was to matriculate—the men were generally a step above the dockworkers and sandhogs of Chelsea and Hell's Kitchen.

Carey kept a record of the activities at "District 7 Holy Name School." The emphasis was on conciliation and competence in organizational procedure. The idea was to stand up for one's rights through discussion and persuasion:

> Mr. Paul McDonough, member of International Brotherhood of Electrical Workers, Local 3. Mr. McDonough teaches a practical course in how to handle a grievance. "Some of the fellows were saying that Jack wouldn't be happy even when he gets to heaven. They say he'll demand a grievance committee to take his little problems up with St. Peter. I don't know about that. This I do know, that even in the best managed plants there will always be misunderstandings, there will always be problems. It's smart to let these come to the surface, to discuss and settle them before spontaneous combustion sets in. To be a good shop steward takes knowledge of the conditions of the industry, the contract between the parties, fairmindedness and immense amounts of common sense and tact. It takes know-how and experience.[36]

The strong-arm tactics of the roughhouse days were frowned upon. The Jesuits preferred parliamentary tactics to the paramilitary methods favored by some of the union factions. The line of civil assertiveness was taken by Michael Papalardo, of the United Association of Plumbers Local 2, who taught public speaking and covered Robert's Rules of Order:

> Monday morning quarterbacks and militants at the corner bar don't help the cause. But a man has to know the proper times to speak. He has to know the simple rules that govern the conduct of a meeting. He has to know the age-old rules that ensure democratic process, i.e., to guarantee free speech for all without allowing the meeting to become chaos.[37]

The same atmosphere prevailed downtown at the Xavier Labor School. The offerings had not changed much since the thirties and forties. Five instructors, including Carey, held two six-week sessions a year, one in the fall and one in the winter. The classes met once a week on Wednesdays. Each lasted forty minutes. The evenings began at 6:45 and ended at 9:45. In that time the men were able to sit in on four courses, with five-minute breaks in between. A typical schedule included (1) "Health, welfare and pension plans," (2) "You and labor laws," (3) "Parliamentary practice and tactics," and (4) "The mission of labor leaders." The classes usually began with about twenty men in attendance for each. Carey rated a course successful if ten were left by the end.[38]

Carey kept in touch with a nucleus of colleagues in the New York area and its fringes. He corresponded regularly with Fr. Dennis Comey, the former president of St. Peter's College in Jersey City, who ran a school of industrial relations in Philadelphia. Fr. Philip Dobson, the former director of the Xavier Labor School, had set up a similar operation in Jersey City; another Jesuit, Fr. William J. Smith, headed a labor school in Brooklyn.

The network of labor schools on the East Coast and in the Midwest was extensive enough to attract the attention of Jesuits in other countries.[39] As was typical during the postwar period, the Americans exported their expertise to their European colleagues. Fr. Edmond Kent, an Irish Jesuit, spent his year of tertianship, from the fall of 1948 through the summer of 1949, touring labor schools in the United States. When he returned he helped found the Jesuits' college of industrial relations in Dublin.

Most of the schools existed slightly above the hand-to-mouth level. Kent traveled from city to city, taking notes during the evening classes and "going around at night and cleaning up." As he described it:

> Phil Carey looked after me. I never had an idle moment. He'd never tell me exactly who these people were beforehand. He sent me to see Dorothy Day. She lambasted me, for being a priest. He knew bloody well I wouldn't have gone to see her on my own. They [Catholic Workers] were all a little off. But very informative, I can tell you.[40]

Carey himself continued to teach labor ethics. Even at its peak, the Xavier school was a modest operation. Its capacity might have grown had Carey taken up the possibility of affiliating with Fordham University, with an eventual set of offices in Lincoln Center. But he declined to expand, in part out of resentment at what he considered the professional respectability of white-collar do-gooders and in part because larger size meant a loss of control without a concomitant gain in influence. The unions themselves were growing, too, and Carey pitted a call for local involvement against their gigantism:

> The big national unions did service their members, but because the problems facing them became too complex, it was felt that the ordinary rank and filer wouldn't understand. As a result, his advice and approval was [sic] frequently wanted. More and more the gulf between the ordinary union member and the leader widened until the locals were straw houses from want of activity and the top leadership became politicos.

The labor movement needs participation by the ordinary man. It needs grass roots democracy to resist the modern trend in all organizations toward bureaucracy.[41]

In the late forties and through the Cold War, the labor schools kept up a vigorous anticommunism that added a combativeness and ideological appeal to their pastoral routines. In Brooklyn, a few blocks from Ebbets Field, Fr. William Smith ran the "Crown Heights Associated Activities," whose centerpiece was variously called the Crown Heights Labor School or School for Working Men. Born in Buffalo, the son of a grocer, in 1899, Smith came after ordination to teach at Brooklyn Preparatory School on the corner of Carroll Street and Nostrand Avenue in 1935. Two years later, just before the Xavier Labor School opened in downtown Manhattan, "I suddenly found myself in labor relations work."[42] Smith took pride in passing on confidential tips about Communist infiltration of the unions to the *Brooklyn Eagle*, the borough newspaper.

Smith liked to present simplified ideas forcefully, with a moral fervor and a brisk fluency reminiscent of Daniel Lord. He produced a combined newsletter and broadside entitled *Crown Heights Comment*, "written, mimeographed, put together, mailed and distributed—1,000 copies each week, 6 to 8 pages."[43] The bulletin, "dedicated to Christ the Worker, by and for His fellow workers," set the teachings of the social encyclicals in the "waiting-for-Lefty" language of Clifford Odets's eponymous depression-era play:

> The ultimate aim of the Catholic Labor School is to contribute to the reorganization of industrial society through the plan of vocational groupings. . . . The core of the encyclicals lies in the admonition to change our industrial relations from a system that is based on a policy of class-conflict to one conducted on the principle of cooperation. . . .
>
> A code for labor? There isn't any and there won't be any until two missing ingredients are tossed into the industrial relations pudding. They are the meat of justice and the sweetening of charity. That suggestion will be sneered at as a Pollyanna offering, something foreign and alien to the American way of looking at things, no more practical than a fifth ace in a poker game. O.K., Sophocles! What's impractical about it? What's so foreign about it? Why is it so stupid? If some atheist gets up on a platform and raves and rants about a materialistic program or some slick word-twister rams down the throats of unsuspecting youth a diabolical principle that cuts asunder the nature of a human being, that's supposed to be smart and practical. If I propose a sound thought of a religious nature, that dates me. I'm out of step with progress. I'm a reactionary. Well, open your ears, brother, and listen.[44]

None of the labor schools were exactly alike. Some stressed anticommunism more than others. In contrast to ISO, they were decentralized, answering to the provincial superior of the area in which they were located, and their small scale gave them a low-profile resilience that the national organization never enjoyed. Smith's setup was identified more with the parish than with the Jesuit high school that lent him work space, and this put him on the margin of the society's chain of command.

Localism was the paradoxical common denominator of the labor schools. Although in expansive moments they liked to see themselves as pilot projects that might be duplicated in other locales, the schools did not travel well. Much of Smith's time was taken up with church politics. The diocesan clergy and priests from other congregations, he claimed, were jealous of Jesuit activities in the labor field.[45] A few fellow Jesuits—among them Benjamin Masse at *America*—considered Smith a red-baiter, and this led to further bickering. These rancors were the normal stuff of neighborhood rivalries, like schoolyard scuffles, and they duplicated the faction fights within the unions themselves.[46]

After a decade of serving as chaplain and impresario to various labor and business groups in the Flatbush neighborhood, Smith was weary of the intrigues that had been partly fueled by his own temperament. Also, the school's attraction to the clientele was beginning to slide. In 1947 he reported:

> Attendance for the past term does not warrant the effort that must be put into [the school] to continue. The Wednesday night group for business and professional men has held up—185 registrations with an average attendance around 180. The Labor School classes—110 registrations with perhaps an average of 50 or 55 attending regularly.
>
> The quality of the students to date is less promising than in other years.[47]

The fractious habits of the locals, like the incorrigible drinking of the immigrants in Hell's Kitchen described decades before by William Stanton, exasperated Smith, whose fuse was short to begin with. He delivered himself of a trenchant piece of urban anthropology:

> Contrary to popular belief, it has been our experience that Brooklynites are not easily induced to cooperate in a sustained program of adult education in industrial relations. They are "belligerent" in places but not "militant." Some groups will "fight at the drop of a hat" but will not train for the encounter. Father Dobson and Father Corridan, I believe, will confirm this opinion and it has been one of our major obstacles.[48]

Before the forties were over Smith moved across the Hudson to join Philip Dobson in Jersey City. There he passed his time writing tracts and pamphlets on social issues.[49]

Since the total number of Jesuits active in the labor schools was small, and the schools themselves were spread around and peripheral to the work of the society, generalizations about the factors contributing to their success and failure are precarious. Most of them died with their founders, confirming their image as one-man shows. Nevertheless, an evolution can be detected in the longest-surviving schools. The institute at Spring Hill College in Alabama fits the successful pattern.

Fr. Albert Foley had been involved in ISO from its foundation. A member of the Midwest Anti-Communist Committee, formed in 1935–36 at the urging of Wlodimir Ledochowski, in the late 1930s and early 1940s he wrote a pair of biographies of Jesuit saints.[50] While studying in St. Louis for his master's degree in philosophy, Foley met Daniel Lord, who was then at the height of his career in pamphleteering and the mounting of pageants and about to take over ISO. Foley returned to St. Louis University in 1947, about a year and a half after Claude Heithaus and George Dunne had been expelled from the Jesuit community there: "The walls were still vibrating."[51] He wrote another master's thesis in St. Louis, this time in sociology, then left for the University of North Carolina at Chapel Hill to complete his doctorate in 1950.[52]

Foley was assigned to Spring Hill College in Mobile, his base on the Alabama coast. In a few offices at the college he set up an Institute of Race Relations; the space did double duty as an industrial-relations center.[53] With this operation under way, he spent the 1952–53 academic year at the University of Michigan, at the group dynamics program of the Institute for Social Research. There he studied practical methods of adult leadership training and democratic education supported by the National Education Association (NEA). The assortment of techniques traced its intellectual heritage to John Dewey and to social scientists exiled from Germany before the war.

By 1954, the year of the Supreme Court decision outlawing segregation, Foley was back in Mobile. The timing was propitious. Foley got his establishment up and running more than a decade after the original labor schools started in the thirties and more than a decade before the turmoil of the sixties. A new crop of social issues was emerging that did not bind him to the thirties or to a predominantly Catholic constituency.

The bread and butter of Foley's industrial-relations institute became a series of management training seminars entitled the Executive Development Program. This was an annual course for lower- and middle-level administrators. Foley gave talks to Rotary and Lions clubs on the group dynamics, human relations approach to corporate capitalism. Course fees provided revenues to sustain the institute. Foley's growing reputation as a mediator thrust him into civic affairs. He was appointed head of the State Advisory Committee on Civil Rights in 1960. During the sixties the institute gained further support through Great Society funding.

In one respect the institute at Mobile was very much like the labor schools elsewhere: It was largely a one-man operation. Otherwise, however, the Spring Hill experiment was fairly distinctive. Foley housed the institute at a Jesuit institution of higher education (he was professor of sociology at the college), and he cast it as an industrial-relations program, not a labor school. The operation was multipurpose, with a varied clientele and different sponsors. The success of the management training program enabled Foley to turn his talents and attention to race relations. He was seen as an educator and a mediator.[54]

About 20 percent of the population of Mobile was Catholic, a spillover from its historical ties with New Orleans. While not sizable enough to form a dominant presence, the constituency provided Foley with a reasonable base. This demographic factor, together with Foley's faculty position at the Jesuit college, gave him a strong public identity without confining him to the Catholic world. His operation was small but not strictly denominational; it was more open-ended and multipurpose than the Northern labor schools. The students who enrolled in the training programs at the institute brought a cross-section of religious affiliations. The programs themselves were shaped by participatory, group-dynamics ideas that bore traces of the conciliatory spirit of corporatism. Techniques of intrafirm bargaining were taught without a trace of medieval and hierarchical trappings. Aside from parts of the Third World, Alabama was more backward than most places that Jesuits worked in, and this enhanced the potential power of Foley's expertise. More often than not, as a local notable, he was called on to lead and mediate. His skills were in demand.

Thus at Spring Hill a number of factors converged to bolster the chances of success and longevity. The institute was ecumenical and eclectic. The operation was also translocal. It prospered as a regional outpost in a network of reformist foundations and government agencies. The multipurpose setup at Spring Hill was useful to a variety of progressive interests—local, regional, and national. To some elites at the national level it turned out to be a vital link in the spread of social change against entrenched parochialisms.[55] By contrast, most of the labor schools had relatively limited functions, with restricted clienteles who eventually found that they could obtain comparable benefits from the unions themselves.

By the end of the fifties the majority of the labor schools were offering some classes in industrial relations and had admitted clerical and other nonmanual employees, or they had shut their doors. The schools folded because the market in which they offered their services had shrunk and been penetrated by able competitors. They were typically one- or two-man shops that had outlived their usefulness as the unions gained competence during the war years and afterward. Political conditions had also changed. "Preoccupation with the anti-Communist approach," one observer noted, "left the Catholic program without a driving force after Walter Reuther came to office and routed the Communist element of the UAW."[56] Economically and culturally, too, the schools had less to offer. Full employment cut into their appeal, and the spread of television provided alternative recreation to the outings with the boys that the night classes had furnished in previous days. Leo Brown issued a postmortem in 1960:

> One of the most successful efforts of ISO in its early years, the labor-schools programs, was of diminishing usefulness. Industrial relations institutes were springing up all over the United States, and state and other secular universities were offering programs which were at least as attractive as our own labor schools. At the same time the need for such schools was rapidly diminishing. The inexperienced labor leaders of the 1930s had acquired experience. The unions, better established, became persuaded that they could provide their own educational programs. The obvious need for Jesuit activity in fields of social action had greatly diminished.[57]

Some of the labor schools, then, died of natural causes. Others reoriented their programs toward a white-collar clientele and survived into the sixties and beyond. A very small number of second-wave labor schools, like the institute run by Albert Foley, came into being in the fifties in the South, focusing on the key domestic issue of racial integration while keeping some attention on tasks concerning labor relations.[58]

IV

When ISO attained its peak manpower in 1951, the staff totaled ten Jesuits including the editor and assistant editor of *Social Order*. By 1960 the number of Jesuits assigned to ISO had dwindled to five. The next year a subcommittee appointed by the provincials recommended discontinuing publication of *Social Order* and cutting the staff of ISO further. The downsizing was put off by Father Janssens, who would not countenance a drastic curtailment of the social apostolate on the part of the American Jesuits in the same year that John XXIII had issued *Mater et Magistra* to mark the thirtieth anniversary of the previous social encyclical.[59] Ten years later, in

1971, having moved from St. Louis to the East Coast and having changed its name to the Cambridge Center for Social Studies, the operation was disbanded.

When the institute was reorganized in 1947 it set its sights not on action but on ideas. Original scholarship was to be the chief product and influence on policy the eventual result. The institute was supposed to advance sociological knowledge and to extend the application of Catholic thought to social policy without controverting the received teaching of the church. These presumptions became increasingly difficult to credit. While the norm persisted that the crux of the social *magisterium* should be approximately universal with respect to time and place, this criterion served less as a positive guide than as a stricture on adventurous thinking.[60]

The hope was that hard work and the requisite talent, supplied by Jesuits, would produce something very close to an unassailable synthesis of social thought. The talent was considerable, as was the zeal, but the output was largely mediocre. The logics of doctrine, scholarship, and problem solving did not so much collide, either fruitfully or in combat, as go their separate ways. By the end, around Vatican II, the Jesuits were shrewd enough to recognize that the doctrine, far from being immutable, was undergoing substantial renovation. Yet few Jesuits associated with ISO tapped into the anomalies between ideas and perceptions of social realities that provoke intellectual breakthroughs, and their religious and their secular sensibilities remained apart at the wellsprings of creativity.[61]

The schools of social work set up by the American Jesuits in the first half of the century provided a service: training in community organization, therapeutic intervention, and the like. The service was educational rather than direct; very few Jesuits were social workers or community organizers themselves. At the same time, practical rather than theoretical knowledge was transmitted. Though the schools did not fit the humanistic template of the liberal arts colleges, they did not pioneer in original thought. The schools of social work delivered a service—training in skills useful for white-collar occupations—and they succeeded on their own terms. Their clientele was composed of lower-middle-class Catholics striving after upward mobility. Graduates could do well by doing good. The schools had modest intellectual ambitions, acting as certifying agencies, professional gatekeepers, rather than stimulants of original analysis or creativity. They found an institutional home in the preexisting Jesuit educational apparatus.

The labor schools laid even less claim to intellectual creativity than the professional schools, nor were they capable of becoming paying or break-even enterprises for the Jesuits. They were probably less crucial to workers than the schools of social work and the faculties of commerce and finance were useful to lower-middle-class students. The payoff on both sides of the exchange was uncertain. Nevertheless, for about two decades, from the end of the thirties to the mid-fifties, they served a function, and they ceased to exist soon after the demand for their function slackened.

The labor schools were the second important experiment of the American Jesuits in supplying services relevant to social questions. Like the professional schools, albeit at a more rudimentary level, the labor schools instructed their students in practical techniques. The Jesuits involved in them came closer to direct action, less in the sense of political agitation than in lending a sympathetic ear to workingmen burdened with financial and personal worries. Many of the schools had a strong pastoral orientation. The effective parish was occupationally rather than territorially defined.

In the beginning, the clienteles of the professional and the labor schools alike were drawn mostly from the Catholic subculture. Even then, however, there were signs of heterodoxy. The professional schools admitted women long before Jesuit high schools and liberal arts colleges did so. After all, social work faculties trained members of the helping professions, and these professions were largely female. The labor schools catered to a clientele below the lower-middle-class and the upper fringes of the working class that fed the society's mainstream schools. Their programs were inspired by local conditions, not by directives from Rome. In contrast to the presuppositions that burdened ISO, such innovations did not depend on the existence of Catholic surroundings.

The professional schools survived; the labor schools disappeared. Although the ethnic and denominational composition of the market differed from that of earlier times, there was still a market for training in middle-level service roles. The older Catholic working class, which had been the backbone of blue-collar unionism, shrunk, and the unions themselves took over training in organizational and administrative techniques. Some of the labor schools, like the one in Brooklyn's Crown Heights, failed prematurely, done in by the personal failings of their directors. Others faded away after reaching a certain eminence, running out of functions to perform.[62]

ISO was ambiguous on all dimensions of institutional viability. On the one hand, it was supposed to be out ahead of the instructional service model that was the prototype for both the social work and the labor schools. On the other hand, original ideas were neither easy to come by nor promoted within the top-down structures of Tridentine Catholicism. In addition, the "civilian" constituency for an exercise in distinctively Catholic social thought and policy was uncertain, given the shifting demographics of American Catholicism. Intellectually, organizationally, and demographically, ISO was orphaned.[63]

CHAPTER

11

Crosscurrents

I

The American Catholic subculture flourished through the forties, fifties, and early sixties. Vocations mounted. The schools expanded at all levels. Although Jesuits felt overextended and, in areas like higher education, uneasy about competition from secular colleges and universities, there was no widespread sense of crisis. Growth and mobility outpaced the modest economy of the Catholic enclaves, yet success and assimilation were not expected to subvert religious or ethnic identity.

Alarms about the decline of spiritual values were sounded throughout the pontificate of Pius XII. The American response was to point with pride to the growth of Catholicism amid material abundance. Devotions were amplified; Catholics prospered in business. Contributions poured in. As the ethnic ghettos shrank, the rise of the Kennedys appeared to confirm the compatibility of the ethos of city neighborhoods with broader horizons and larger accomplishments. Catholics might feel queasy about sin, especially the sexual kind, but they were blithe about social attainment. Criticism of the American way or the Catholic subculture was uncommon.[1]

Mentalities that soon would appear incongruous coexisted. Assimilation confirmed the belief that Americanism and Catholicism were in harmony. On the surface, collective identity was not threatened. Neither self-consciousness nor irony was conspicuous in the American Catholic community. The presumption was of progress along the two dimensions of identity. The faithful could be more American and more Catholic at the same time.[2]

Criticism of the church—when it did not reinforce internal solidarity—passed unnoticed. The possibility that an authoritarian institution might

319

clash with a democratic milieu was no more a live issue among Catholics than the autocratic leadership of their unions was unsettling for members of the working class. The danger was hypothetical, a misreading of the informal pluralism of the American settlement. From inside the tribe, the figure of the rugged-but-gentle shepherd tending contented flocks had the appeal of an oasis of calm in the middle of the frantic city. Behind the heavy doors of huge churches votive candles glowed warmly in red cups, and in niches on the walls colorful statues stood like heavenly guests come for a long visit, and rituals that to outsiders looked like so much mystification—with chalices of emerald-studded gold, and calla lilies that seemed like ceramic swans, set in plush foliage around marble altars—had the density and permanence of familiar things. There was a celestial realism to it all.[3] The live-and-let-live attitude of Americans, Catholics and non-Catholics, about matters of religion scandalized those in the Vatican who worried about "indifferentism." In compensation, pluralism meant that outsiders would not pry into the internal affairs of the church so long as Catholics did not attempt to foist their views on others. The loyalty of American Catholics held firm to the United States and to the church.[4]

Ecclesiastical oppression was not strongly felt and even when it was, the means for venting resentment were oblique. By the start of the sixties the silencing of John Courtney Murray was lifted as quietly as it had been imposed. There was no need to celebrate the abrogation of a punishment that had been an in-house matter from the beginning; only embarrassment could come of publicizing it. In the interim between the coronation of John XXIII and the unfolding of Vatican II, Murray's rehabilitation proceeded without fanfare. His ideas had no visible effect on the political practice of American Catholics. As a lesson in political strategy, their impact on the Roman mentality would be greater than on that of Americans themselves, who took such concepts for granted. In the United States, Murray was seen as catching up with, rather than changing, reality.

The reconsideration of historical change, viewing it as something approaching a creative principle instead of as an imperfection to be lamented, was to have a much greater effect inside the church. The result would be to modify the views of Catholics about the inalterability of their religion. Murray ratified rather than revolutionized the thinking of American Catholics on the politics of the secular arena. With regard to the church itself, however, he helped change how Catholics thought about change.[5]

But for the time being, the conjunction of political liberalism and ecclesiastical authoritarianism was considered part of the normalcy of pluralism. Confrontational mobilization that upset everyday structures of authority, in the family and the church, was in the future. The stable prosperity of the fifties prepared the way for the optimistic liberalization of the early sixties.

Aside from the involvement of a handful of Catholics in the beginnings of the civil rights and peace movements, there were few signs of political radicalization.[6]

Economically and politically, then, Catholics underwent assimilation with eagerness. The process was not supposed to alter Catholicism.[7] Nonetheless a pair of other developments belied the smoothness of the evolution. These changes had more to do with cultural shifts than with struggles for power or financial gain. One involved a move away from a preoccupation with communal survival and collective defense toward a search for a spirituality or an aesthetic that reflected a yearning for a subjective, individualistic understanding of religion. This change was not in the direction of an enhancement of social conscience and it certainly did not reveal a desire on the part of educated Catholics for a return to the pieties of the "simple faithful." It had anti-institutional connotations. It was a quest for a less superstitious religiosity.[8]

The origins of the interest in a customized spirituality were mixed, and the results of the exploration were varied. The movement represented a step beyond the religious practices of the old neighborhoods yet took for granted the continued existence of this subculture as a background for development. The approach presupposed the enrichment rather than the abandonment of devotion along denominational lines.[9] But despite the positive signs—the increase in vocations, the burgeoning enrollments in Catholic schools—prosperity and mobility were subverting the settled way of life. As the supports of the Catholic subculture receded, a cosmopolitan, personalized spirituality became increasingly attractive. This side of the movement had an ecumenical slant. For some the impulse to shop around for psychic satisfaction eventually became more compelling than the urge to retain a Catholic attachment. Theological disputes would come to be looked upon as churchy, the tedious quibbles of a legalistic institution.[10]

Another development reflected greater awareness of cultural change as a collective phenomenon than as a problem of the solitary psyche. The emergence of television after the war propelled a mass culture that attacked parochial solidarities and the hierarchies that underpinned religious tradition. The media purveyed secularization in the form of a profane, consumer populism in which communal loyalties and habits of obedience to authority seemed to dissolve. Choices proliferated, and this proliferation was itself as heady as the new items of desire.[11]

Some Jesuits felt that the spread of consumer values was more insidious than disputes over political and economic issues; the latter might divide Catholics, while the former threatened to demolish traditional values themselves. Their perspective was an extension of the conservative critique of industrial materialism popularized by Husslein and his colleagues earlier in the century. They approached the problem from a different angle, however. Now the popular culture that had been seen as a bulwark of common sense, sobriety, and ordinary hierarchy was being deformed by commercial interests that had at their disposal the technology of the mass media. Jesuits who thought about such matters had lost conviction in conceits such as corporatism and medievalism as remedies for the afflictions of mass society. The vernacular hierarchies that maintained preserves of authority within pluralism—families, the schools, the church itself—were vulnerable to the seductions of the media. Vulgar modernism reached into the hearth.[12]

The political observations of Jesuit commentators like Fr. William Lynch were parenthetical to their absorption with cultural criticism. Lynch himself had little to say about public policy. Yet he was concerned with the privatization of life in postwar America, and for this reason he paid attention to the media as a social technology midway between individuals and political institutions. Privatization seemed to guarantee some protection from the intrusions of the media, yet it also meant withdrawal from community. Lynch and others were gravely suspicious of the paradoxical individualism of a mass society which they saw sinking into a uniformity of the extravagant and tasteless. Their anguish arose from the problem of collective articulation of an authentic and possibly tragic consciousness in an age of conformity and escape into personal expression. The attention that Lynch gave to the media stemmed from his anxiety over the obstacles to communication and creativity in a culturally flattened, atomistic society. This anxiety had its origins in the disintegration of Catholic identity.

II

As Catholics became increasingly absorbed into the ways of postwar America, pride in traditional virtues was layered over economic achievement and social acceptance. Regret for the loss of simpler times was voiced from a position of new respectability. Values associated with a recent past that was harsher as well as simpler could be cherished in memory even if there was no will to revive them in actuality. The tonality of remembrance was sentimental, and nostalgia was often mixed with a denial that the subculture was fading at all. Defensiveness retained a triumphalistic edge. No one wanted to return to the deprivations of immigrant days, yet that past was still within reach of memory, and something was missing in the new riches that turned imagination backward and refused to let go.

Fr. Robert Ignatius Gannon, president of Fordham University from the 1930s into the 1950s, expressed the bittersweetness of social ascent and vanishing origins in a flood of bold detail. A paragon of the gregarious, fluent Irish American cleric, head of an educational enterprise with numerous alumni and an ornament of the ethnic politics of New York City, Gannon was much in demand as an after-dinner speaker. He gave talks to the Friendly Sons of St. Patrick, the National Republican Club, the Policeman's Benevolent Association, the Holy Name Society, and similar groups. In addition to his writings on the value of the liberal arts and a biography of his friend Cardinal Spellman, two volumes of these colloquies, covering the quarter century from the late thirties to the mid-sixties, were published. [13]

Gannon was outsize in the conservatism of his message and the melodrama of his anecdotes. A key theme was the supremacy of religious idealism and the preservation of tradition over purely intellectual endeavor. Character came before brilliance. Scholarship for its own sake was useless and indeed suspect. With a vehemence reminiscent of editorials from the *New York Daily News* and the *Brooklyn Tablet* Gannon excoriated the rise of secular humanism.

> Anyone in a cap and gown can blast the presuppositions of life, can rob our sons and daughters of all the principles on which civilization depends—but let him as much as whisper "academic freedom, I've got my fingers crossed," and no professional educator dares to say a word of criticism. Of course, the liberals in the street, who may spell academic with a "k," set up the chant whenever a liberal on the campus wants to attack a policeman or forge a check. [14]

Gannon preached a tabloid conservatism. The audience he had in mind was not composed of intellectuals or the leaders of higher education but of Runyonesque common men discomforted, as he might put it, by the effete philosophizing of the doyens of American culture. They were the gruff but dependable salt-of-the-earth, the Catholic version of the stuff of WPA murals, that Gannon led his audience to envision. Many of his listeners had forsaken their overalls for three-piece suits but had not overcome the insecurities of the change. The contrast between solid but defensive success and intellectual snobbery was obvious and reassuring; it left no middle ground. The caricatures evoked by Gannon on both sides were as instantly recognizable as the sketches of celebrities that hung framed in the uptown restaurants that the men were now able to frequent. [15]

Speculative intelligence was identified with puerile schemes for molding social conditions without regard for practical consequences. Under the new secularism, pastoral sense, common decency, the milk of human kindness—all were absent:

> What are [the] ingredients [of the prevailing philosophy of education in America today]? First, Exaggerated Experimentalism, second, Pragma-

tism, third, Socialism—and of the three the first is easily the most dangerous. For the whole tendency of this particular experimentalism is towards cutting off the past, ignoring the accumulated experience of the human race, starting anew, as if no one had lived before us.[16]

"The men who shape our national education," Gannon warned, "are engaged in a perpetual scramble for novelties. As if we need novelties! We are nauseated with novelties. What we need are things that are old, things that have stood the test of a hundred generations, things that are immutable."[17] As Gannon saw it, the remedy for the blight of Deweyism and the leftist juggernaut was not new ideas but "discipline" and "humility," the virtues of endurance that he associated with peasant—particularly Irish peasant—society. As it happened, these traits were also inculcated by the methods of formation and education espoused by the Society of Jesus. But they were "anathema to the high priests of American education." Character, even when limited by ignorance, was a shield against ideology:

> The discipline should show itself externally in obedience to legitimate authority; internally, not only in trained intellects which can use a set of carefully selected tools, but even more in trained wills. . . . [T]he worst education that teaches self-control is better than the best which teaches everything else and not that.[18]

Gannon's fulminations against secularism were tempered by his realization that as a New Yorker he should take politic delight in diversity; he knew dozens of priest-and-rabbi jokes. Pedagogical conservatism was not peculiarly Catholic. Gannon's phobias tapped into anxieties felt by many in the postwar metropolis. He saw the need for schools to foster and preserve the moral fiber of students, even at the expense of their intellectual attainment, as a goal within the practical American grain. The perils of "empty churches and vicious schools" were equated.[19]

The priority of moral fortitude over education as intellectual growth fit an understanding of schooling as preparation for success that would contribute to the prosperity of the community rather than subject its values to critical scrutiny. Jesuits were in the business of training solid citizens; their reputation for learning did not mean that they produced scholars or cultural critics themselves. Gannon assured his audiences that a keystone of the American value system, respect for private property, was integral to the Catholic tradition. This legacy was not only compatible with but also conducive—though not equivalent—to capitalism. Jesuit schools fostered an appreciation of both economic rationality and patriotism:

> Our lives are centered, yours and mine, on two of the main fundamentals of civilization—the right to worship God and the right to pos-

sess private property. . . . If you read some of the textbooks on the social sciences used in some of our schools, you will conclude that the Constitution was never meant to be anything but a target for European radicals. . . . [T]oday the strongest organized minority in our own country is attacking directly—not so much religion, not so much the American way of life, as the right to private property. . . . By constant repetition and innuendo, private property is identified in people's minds with Capitalism—though Capitalism was one of the results of the sixteenth-century upheaval, and the right to private property goes back to the dawn of man.[20]

The sacredness of property came second only to moral virtue itself, and both took precedence over knowledge for its own sake. The danger to be averted was cerebration that lacked regard for economic common sense and ethical restraint. Covetousness could be offset by the residues of morality; the heart could restrain the covetous hand. The common enemy of morality and boosterism was intellectualism. Learning for its own sake or in the service of a naive pragmatism was defeatist and dangerous. Progressive education, idle speculation, and the like led to "Ph.D.-itis" and "the sin of bibliolatry"—to research and the accumulation of knowledge at the expense of teaching and the shaping of character.[21]

What was needed to combat such decadence was "supernatural Faith— simple, direct and complete."[22] Abstraction was deadening. Gannon found faith embodied not in a set of ideas that might counter the corrosive skepticism of modernity but in the living community formed by Irish and Irish American Catholicism. American capitalism built on rather than destroyed the bonds of sentiment and the virtues of steadfastness. These qualities did not form a rationally comprehensible ideology. They were instead an inheritance of strengths and endearing weaknesses associated with peasant resilience and the tang of a personalism that was close to the soil and the dangers of the sea. In America they were channeled into the service of prosperity.

Economic progress, Gannon argued, was compatible with traditional religion. In fact, modernization was not truly viable without the toughening remnants of agrarian piety. Jesuit education molded and sharpened the virtues of communal loyalty and industriousness in the service of growth. Labor discipline and a clerical professionalism were added to muscle power and political conservatism. By showing they were not quitters, Catholics became winners.

Gannon stressed the versatility and adaptability of tradition for economic ends. The aptitude for hard work that he saw among newcomers to the American enterprise boosted productivity. Moreover, the upbringing of immigrants in a harsh environment enabled them to see through political cant. Gannon was especially taken by the talent for realism and popular democracy shown by his fellow Irish Americans, whose pleasantness veiled a wisdom of the streets. In contrast to the bluntness and dour Teutonism of the Germans, for example, Gannon praised "the meekness and sweet reasonableness of the Irish," their charm and sense of humor.[23] Added to this affability was the political advantage of the "Irishman's natural aversion to communism." There was a shrewdness and tenacity in the subculture that saw through the "national fog in which all kinds of reds and pinks and starry-eyed dreamers became an amorphous mass of Communist Fronts with the most alarming influence" during the war and the period immediately following, so that "almost no Irish names have graced the lists of those who were betraying their country through all these years."[24]

Among the immigrant Irish, Americanism and Catholicism were fused. They were hard workers, stalwart patriots, and deeply religious. What to the English eye might seem like indolence and incivility were in fact strategies for overcoming at one and the same time the impersonalism of modernity and the privileges of the past. In contrast to the Germans, the Irish disliked regimentation—although they were capable of collective action and organizational loyalty—and their distaste for ostentatious hierarchy amounted to a rough egalitarianism. They appeared very much like the yeoman democrats of Joseph Husslein's medievalism or like "the good English," the indomitably merry men of Sherwood Forest. They were inured, Gannon felt, against the temptations of absolutism and totalitarianism.

> The Irish will not do the goose step for anyone. They prefer to jig and go to church and the church they prefer is still the Church where every class of people can mingle without self-consciousness and, what is more important still, without class-consciousness, either.[25]

Again and again Gannon emphasized not only the intrinsic goodness of preindustrial values but also their utility for balanced modernization. His themes were the continuity of tradition and its compatibility with the American way. Even the failures of the Irish were ingratiating and full of lessons for an authentic way of life. They were neither ruthless capitalists nor feverish socialists. Since they had tasted little of it or were so new to it, the Irish were practically unspoiled by worldly success. In politics they declined to be seduced by arid logic. They were inoculated against "this wild idea of absolute equality played up by the Soviet press . . . that came down from the Stoics through the mad men of the French Revolution."[26] The organ pipes were opened full for extolling the virtues and endearing flaws of the Irish. The story of defiance even in defeat cascaded toward an emotional crescendo like the finale of a George M. Cohan production number. The ideal of sacrifice even unto martyrdom outlasted both materialism and mere ideas.

> The true son of Erin is aroused and repelled by the hard core of atheism, of dialectic materialism, that unifies the theory and practice of the Kremlin. The cruelty of the Soviet and its appeal to certain intellectuals are rooted in its Godlessness. . . . Whatever can be said of Ireland, good or bad, this must be said: for centuries she has borne in her sacred flesh the mark of the five holy wounds. They were bloody during her long agony of crucifixion, they were shining on the day of her resurrection, and whatever the future may bring of blessings and trials, they will remain to the end the real source of her glory among the nations of the earth.[27]

Gannon made it plain that there was bravado in his condemnation of communism and his apotheosis of Mother Ireland. The comic wink was as readily appreciated as the bombast. Part of the charm of his performances consisted in getting carried away. The Irish, after all, specialized in being belligerent and impetuous at the same time. It was the gratuitousness of their generosity and the obstinacy of their sins that enchanted. "Then take this pet idea of Marx and Engels that when the proletariat is freed the state will wither away. What Irishman wants to see the state wither away and with it all the grand shenanigans of local and national politics?"[28] Gannon delivered after-dinner speeches, not philosophical disquisitions, and the talks were as much the verbal equivalents of barroom rows and weepy reconciliations as they were popularizations of higher things. Communication was a byproduct of expression. ". . . [W]e suggest a little blarney to take the poison out of an Age of Fraud. Blarney, of course, is not the final solution of anything."[29] Bluster was still preferable to the schemes of secular salvation propagated by the left and by intellectuals generally. "At our worst," Gannon conceded,

> we were loud, pugnacious and insolent; extravagant, too, and, like the Scotch and the English, too fond of strong drink entirely. But with these faults went some of the finest qualities of the human heart, and eternal principles, gentlemen, qualities and principles which the United States needs most desperately today.[30]

Gannon instructed by entertaining. His talks were sermons for an audience weaving in and out of sobriety. His stories were parables that served as guides to the good life; they were also fond depictions of the heroics and follies of one's own. The mix was impervious to criticism. The corniness and bathos—"putting a little hair on it"—were ritual excesses. Gannon excelled in the genre as an athlete played dazzlingly under fixed rules.[31]

The talents and heartwarming defects of the Irish were epitomized in the anecdotal history of a family whose matriarch was Mrs. Kelly, a driving kindly woman who "took in washing to support her husband and the rest of her children."[32] Around the turn of the century, when areas of the outer boroughs of New York were still sparsely settled,

> the badly planned Kellys . . . lived in a homemade tar-paper shack that was built in a rambling sort of way under an oak tree, down by the waters of the Upper Bay [in Queens]. But inside it was as clean as the heart of the mother that kept it, and the children, down to baby Barney, were all gentle and well-behaved. Even on week days, when they didn't wear much, they still had some of their mother's innate refinement and dignity. And on Sundays when they passed our house in single file, the tallest going first, on the way to St. Peter's Church, there weren't many in the parish who wouldn't be proud to own them. It meant, of course, that Mrs. Kelly had worked far into Saturday night to iron out their shirts and ruffles and press their pants and brush their hats, but it also meant that she kept her head unbowed amid sorrows that would have broken common clay.[33]

It was piety and fortitude such as these, together with a ramshackle spontaneity, that had made Ireland, "all things considered, one of the few truly civilized nations left on the face of the earth." A similar lesson could be drawn from the travails of Irish Americans. The hardships of the diaspora were vindicated in the end by success. Mrs. Kelly had "gone to her glory these many long years," raging like a Mother Courage out of a play by Sean O'Casey:

> The last I saw of her was the day herself and all her children, including the old man, were dispossessed from their tar-paper shack by the railroad and passed our house in single file on their way to the promised land in Bergen Point. Her parting words were these: "Gossoon, beware the horn of a bull, the tooth of a dog, the stallion's hoof and the smile of an Englishman."[34]

Her offspring prospered. Mary, "the daughter who came between Barney and Jim," married a Democratic politician named Jimmie Lyons and bore him eight children. After he died she married a Republican "and moved into the Fifteenth Assembly District—but she still goes to church."[35] Almost all the others did well in their way too.

> Danny is a Monsignor, Birdie is a school principal, Kate entered the convent but couldn't stay on account of her health and keeps house for Barney, who never married, but owns a slice of Far Rockaway and is

grand to the Sisters. Jimmie is a missionary Father and has a colored parish in the South, which the rest of the family has to support. Tim is the poorest of the lot. He's a college professor—and from what I can gather, a great and distinguished scholar of most discriminating views. He is never done shooting holes in Progressive Education. There's one they never mention and I won't mention him either. I don't know what's the matter with him. He may be down in Washington.[36]

There were enough dark patches in Gannon's portrayal of this quintessential immigrant family to make the melodrama morally convincing. The sentimentality stroked a maudlin tragi-comic nerve between the vaudevillian and the epic. It was popular opera, and Gannon was the lead tenor. Tipsy though they might be, the men ingesting roast beef, string beans, turnips, and potatoes in the dining halls of armories with elk- and moose-heads and regimental escutcheons on the walls responded with tears and laughter to weaknesses they could identify as their own. The event that made them laugh so hard they cried was a ritualized release; it expressed the sentiment that was forbidden to them elsewhere. The Irish meant well; there was not a mean streak in them. Their faults were not culpable transgressions but instead maneuvers, sometimes successful, sometimes hapless, to defend themselves and their values against uncomprehending and hostile surroundings. Only those with hearts of stone could blame these angels with dirty faces. Gannon recognized that "the purloining politician" was a fixture of machine politics, regarded as "part of the general overhead. . . . But when he had stolen the people's money he was satisfied. He never tried to steal their souls."[37]

This sort of corruption could be indulged on the supposition that it aided a certain redistribution of benefits. Furthermore, it did not promote sexual dissolution and it did not threaten the authority of the church. The real menace lay elsewhere, in the connivings of heartless reformers:

Now there is a new swarm abroad in the land. They call themselves liberals, all in a spirit of good clean fun, of course, just as Hitler called himself a Socialist—being almost as social as he is democratic. So, too, for people who do not agree with them, these liberals are the greatest slave-drivers in the world. They are not as crude or as simple as the ward-heelers with the big cigars. What they want is not so much our money as our children. They want our schools and colleges. They want the key positions in the civil service. They want control of relief and all the social agencies, and they are getting what they want. Later they hope, when they have the youth of the nation in their power, to eliminate all religion and all morality that does not conform to their peculiar ideology.[38]

Traditional religious devotion was not an impediment and could be a boon to worldly success; this was Gannon's refrain. Yet he stopped short of asserting that worldly success was a sign of moral superiority, a stance that would smack too nearly of establishment Protestantism. Acceptance was more elusive than success. The injury that rankled was an awareness that material achievement was necessary but insufficient to gain entry into the recesses of the truly influential. The tone of defiance in Gannon's speeches came from perplexity and resentment that the social rise of American Catholics had yet to gain them prestige in academic quarters and the arts. If Catholicism and in particular its Irish strain were not at odds with Americanism either economically or politically, then the implication was that it could not stand up in the highest cultural circles. The fate of Irish American Catholics, so it seemed, was to be liked by practically everyone and taken seriously by no one. Not until the stylish Kennedys came to power did the sense of exclusion lift.[39]

For Gannon the response to this perceived rejection took the shape of a retreat into the subculture. Against the intellectual hegemony of the academicians Gannon set deeper and more abiding cultural values. The struggle might yet be won, or the odds at least changed to the advantage of an embattled minority, if the place of combat could be shifted from the mind to questions of morality.

Gannon put his strategy in characteristically concrete and histrionic form. Catholic men competed well as breadwinners, but too many of them were worn out from their toils. Family men performed less than adequately in the cultural realm. The hunters and gatherers of the tribe returned exhausted from their labors, anxious to relax over drinks and talk ball scores with the boys. It was women, not men, who stayed at home, nurturing and protecting authentic values. The defenders of the faith and the saviors of civilization would not be, according to Gannon, "mere trailing men." As he put it:

> We are so used to the deadening compromises that a man meets with in the ordinary struggle for existence that we have dulled our powers of indignation. Not so the women. . . . Give the women a clean-up job of any kind and they will see it through to the end. Especially, I may say, the Women of Ireland and their daughers to the third generation. Let them once fully realize that this new and insidious political force that calls itself liberalism is aiming at their school, their Church, their home, their children—and we shall not have to do a thing but applaud their success.[40]

The glorification of Mother Courage as the font of morality had as its corollary a rejection of the standards by which Catholic males were judged by secular intellectuals to be second-rate. Success outside the home was bitter and hollow if they allowed themselves to be evaluated by alien rules. They were not humiliated exactly, but the pang at failing to enter the club where ideas and style counted rankled. At this level the American dream seemed unattainable, and the reaction was to term that part of it a swindle, a deceptive abstraction, and to return to Mother Church.

There is no record of Gannon having burst into "Mother Machree," and he stopped short of intoning "Ireland Must Be Heaven, for My Mother Came from There." The essential message was plain enough and powerful. Men could be chivalrous even if weak and not fully successful. The family was sacred. If it could no longer serve as the lodestone of social order, it stood as a shelter in a ravenous world. Mothers and daughters were the carriers of the ideal of simultaneous sweetness and strength, the Christian practical-sublime. Benevolence meant compassion for the defeated and solidarity in grief, the sentimentality of tribal bravery and stoicism, not generic altruism. Failure was forgiven in the home as sins were forgiven by the church. Both institutions would survive. There was a cyclical tenacity to them. No matter how long and far-gone the voyage, they would be waiting. They gave a meaning to sacrifice, and a consolation, that transcended achievement and defeat. The all-embracing sempiternal hierarchy was the church itself that sanctified women as acolytes of endurance and that comforted and did not threaten men.[41]

Even when he played too broadly at being the stage Irishman, there was little thought of urging Gannon to silence. His knowledge of the ways of the Irish American ethos that still prevailed among the Jesuits ensured him of affectionate respect. He was himself "a piece of work," bluff and stylishly raffish and not a little despotic, like a political boss. His biases remained at least as prevalent among the administrators of the Society of Jesus, who toned them down with institutional prudence. Gannon had few ideas, but this was not known to be a fatal deficiency among university presidents. His mawkishness was both studied and sincere. His defense was showmanship. The braggadocio was so considerable that the artistry was there for all who cared to see. He understood education to be one of the performing arts. Gannon's appeal went beyond both the pragmatism and the intellectual traditions of the society. His views were intonations and tokens of poignancy beneath the gruff masculinity of "trailing men" whose regrets and memories of struggle were intermittently more riveting than their success.

III

Robert Gannon's speeches evoked a turn-of-the-century, sidewalks-of-New-York Irish Americanism as it was starting to die away but well before it became a museum piece. He spoke to a generation with direct memories of that time, who warmed, as if listening to bedtime stories, to the telling of the tales and the drawing of the traditional lessons. Recognizing the artifice did not take away its magic, and bad acting could not take away fondness for the show itself. On the contrary, awareness that a mythic reconstruction of courageous mothers and of long-suffering and lovable rascals was required to quicken memories of a vanishing way of life made the after-dinner oratory all the more gripping. His sermons ranged over themes that were as vibrant in an urban Catholic setting as the variations of country western music were in the factory cities of the North like Detroit. For Irish Americans the recollections were as mannered as vaudeville patter; they were part of the Hibernian tribal rite.[42] A dim perception that the enclaves were disappearing, a touch of silent disappointment in the success that had been attained, and a knowledge among the men that they were older now and had lost a step or two, heightened the sense of loss and attachment and sustained the taste for anecdotal moralizing. The message was reassuring, the tone was comic and elegiac. Grandiose hope and the cares of ambition were off the agenda of middle age. There was a psychological realism to the bluster and the historical romanticism. Humor buffered masculine informality against the passing of youth and the growing up out of a way of life that had suddenly become tradition. Gannon offered distraction and compassion without condescension, and his defiance made up for some of his silliness. Gannon knew. Fairness and ethical injunctions were secondary to the expression of ethnic belonging.[43] He achieved a homely incandescence.

The situation of the Irish American subculture could be taken in still another way. It could be looked on not as a triumph of pluck and luck that gave comfort in a present that did not live up to visions of Camelot, but as an experience that conditioned and raised questions about alternatives for the future. This was the line of inquiry adopted in a sociological comparison of Irish and Irish American Catholicism carried out by Bruce Biever, a Jesuit graduate student at the University of Pennsylvania during the mid-sixties.

In Biever's eyes the faintly relaxed Catholicism of the Irish in America during the late fifties and early sixties was a foretaste of a possible future for the rigorously conservative Catholicism still extant in Ireland. The Irish American subculture was a peculiar attenuation of a tradition that was being distorted by economic growth. Lessons could be drawn from the comparison in both directions, backward and forward. The forces working to unsettle Irish Catholicism and the elements of tradition in the Irish American offshoot were similar to their counterparts across the ocean. Both in their ways were islands whose cultures were increasingly vulnerable to penetration.

Thus, American Catholicism might serve as a preview of the evolution of Irish Catholicism. By the same token, Irish Catholicism could be viewed as a depository of retrograde elements that existed in diluted form in its American counterpart. By the early sixties it had become an exaggerated variant of a dying culture, paradoxically flamboyant in its material austerity and moral strictness:

> Granted that the Irish have a "habit of loyalty" to the Church in their native ground, and granted that this loyalty has small intellectual content . . . the time of Irish insular safety is about to pass. Loyalty and social pressures may have kept orthodoxy to the guiding norm in the past, but the pressures from the outside, from urban, industrialized and religiously alive Europe are such that orthodoxy without intellectual foundation will invariably crumble and pass into skepticism or fanaticism. [44]

Fortress Catholicism had been sustained in the United States by ethnic defensiveness. In Ireland it was buttressed by a geographical isolation that had been overlaid with hatred of Protestantism and fear of foreign secularism. [45] The Catholic church both supported and benefited from this self-definition. As the material reinforcements of American Catholicism decayed, however, its intellectual vacuity became increasingly evident, and with the spread of the media and greater ease of travel the visible and invisible barriers separating it from modernism became more permeable. As Edward Duff and others had argued, the sacrifices and dedication that protected the subculture in the past—principally by fortifying a separate system of primary and secondary education—began to seem less useful for the postindustrial stage Catholicism in the United States was entering. Idealism and generosity might be as abundant as ever, but now they were in danger of losing direction. Though still capable of edification, the claim of pragmatism—of training for life—was slipping away from the stern and soothing precepts of the old system. The bathos of a Robert Gannon, his blustering tenderness, was no substitute for knowledge and skills. Education was now a prerequisite for economic productivity and social achievement. However, sophistication in the service of success was the enemy of tradition. A heightened critical capacity might not yet be turned against the economic and political system that was reshaping the terms of mobility, but it could also corrode the arcane strictures of Catholicism.

It was not only schooling that bred doubts about traditional Catholicism. Regardless of their formal education, Catholics could no longer be shielded from the incursions of secularism. The mass media, especially television, spread everywhere, propagating a consumerism and sexuality that threatened to undo the norm of frugal familism. [46] The combination of intellectual subversion at the top and the merchandising of values among ordinary Catholics placed the institutional church, of which the Irish American branch was the supremely devout and prosperous representative, in jeopardy. The conceptual scaffolding and the emotional sustenance of traditional culture were threatened at the same time. Skepticism and consumerism were clearing the way for secularization on a massive scale.

Biever's diagnosis was remarkable not so much for his depiction, extensive as it was, of Irish and Irish American Catholicism as for his judgment that the old apparatus was not worth defending in its current guise. Here he and Gannon parted company. In the United States, discipline and politeness, the predictable competence and courtesy, bred by the nuns in the lower echelons of the Catholic school system, had lost the exclusive hold on social purpose that they had when the need was to make legions of immigrants and their children presentable to industrial capitalism. The devotional habits, neatness, and good behavior that once served as a backdrop at home and in the classroom to punctuality and respect for authority at work now seemed a bit outdated, second-rate skills. The brand-name recognition was high; the products of Catholic schools were known commodities, with an edge in dependability. But as the demographic layers of identity began to peel away, a fearful obscurantism came blinking into the light.

In Ireland the gap between traditional culture and the prerequisites of advanced modernity seemed even more severe. Intellectual oppression and sexual obsession continued to dominate the Irish experience in the middle years of the twentieth century, a generation after these mechanisms had lost their rationale as defenses against an alien power. In Ireland, where piety and nationalism reinforced one another, neither had contributed to economic growth. Biever saw that this situation could not last much longer. The old ways were being diluted; even so, modernization might not take hold. Habit outlasted belief and defied rationalization.[47]

> This lack of freedom, personally and institutionally enforced by the clergy and the church (e.g., by the censorship of books, the personal invasion of first class mail of suspect persons, the absolute control over almost all news media with the single exception of television, etc.) has made for a climate that precludes new ideas and enforces only conformity to the present *status quo* and those small hints of progress which the church does not regard as a threat to its power base. In so doing, the church has progressively estranged the intellectual class . . . and has deprived itself as well as Ireland of that vitality both so desperately need by almost forcing the talented intellectual to seek his fortunes in some other country.[48]

Rather than winning over new generations, authoritarian methods induced an observance of externals that lacked conviction. In addition to being obsolescent as a model of work discipline, the hierarchical style failed

to provide personal, spiritual satisfaction to younger, more educated cohorts. To work at all the system had to be labor-intensive; a high clergy-to-
population ratio was needed, and even in priest-ridden Ireland the church
faced competition from the media. Biever noted that while the slipping away
of the Irish in America from religious practice was not yet an avalanche, the
trend would gain momentum in an impersonal society. Once the structural
incentives and institutional props of outward conformity had begun to
weaken, the psychic landscape offered refuge from social and spiritual stul-
tification. The appeals of assimilation were great.[49]

Biever faulted Irish and Irish American Catholicism on two grounds. He
directed his criticism at an anti-intellectualism that upheld an infantile
dependence and discouraged original thought. He also attacked the panoply
of social structures and institutions—the schools, the youth organizations,
the devotional group—that perpetuated this mentality. Politeness took the
place of civility. There was a curious evasiveness behind the good manners,
a shyness about the self that betokened a kind of intellectual virginity and
emotional paralysis. There was something not quite grown up, as George
Orwell had claimed, about this roseate Catholicism:

> In an Ireland which in the modern world has kept the faith, whose
> churches are filled to capacity and where the Sacraments are fre-
> quented regularly, there are two judgments often heard about the qual-
> ity of Catholicism in Ireland: it is a simple faith and a happy one. . . .
> [W]hile these are good and should be kept, are not there other quali-
> ties which should be present as well? Simplicity and happiness have
> their dangers as well as their positive points. . . . The educational sys-
> tem is praised for not producing many heretics or infidels, but is this
> the only goal towards which Catholic education looks? . . . [I]s this
> directly the product of Irish education at all, or is it not the fact that
> social pressures militate for a religious orthodoxy, no matter whether it
> is a deeply held intellectual conviction or not? . . . [I]t is more to the
> closed system mentality and practice of Ireland that religious orthodoxy
> is preserved than to any educational efforts.[50]

The criticisms mounted by Biever focused on an area left unattended by
John Courtney Murray, who had aimed his fire at national political institutions at one extreme, and on the other at the need to maintain traditional
forms of interpersonal hierarchy. The patriarchal family was to stay in place
to certify masculinity and by extension to preserve the social order. This
meant leaving the family alone, free from the meddling of government
reformers. As a sociologist Biever paid only glancing attention to political
organizations, and he saw no real possibility of intervening in the intimate
redoubt of religiosity that was the family. Instead he concentrated on the

middle ground, the institutional church itself. He was concerned with clergy-run secondary associations that, like the traditional family but at a more public level, prolonged an authoritarian subculture. Whatever legitimacy the brick-and-mortar style of institution building had enjoyed in the past, the sultanic manner of decision making associated with the parish world was now outmoded. The social institutions identified with the parochial environment of traditional Catholicism were moribund.[51]

If the demographic supports of old-style Catholicism were collapsing, and with them its institutional apparatus, what was to prevent secularization? The logic of Biever's approach stressed intellectual understanding and the internalization of faith. But what beliefs were these and how were they to be transmitted? What the message of the new Catholicism might look like, and what media might be used for expressing it, were unclear. What was clear was that the old order was vanishing. "In areas of rapid change and urgent social exigencies," Biever noted,

> in areas where specialized techniques have been tested and adopted by many nations of the world, the Irish clergy still are preaching fidelity to the sacraments as the answer to all social evils, and have taken what at times are startlingly naive principles and dogmatized them as "Catholic social doctrine," urging their acceptance with the threat of supernatural sanctions when at best they are tentatively proposed Papal suggestions or untested hypotheses of so-called "schools of Catholic sociology."[52]

The teaching of the church in social and other areas was on the verge of major change. The means of communicating and reinforcing this revised message were also being transformed. The disappearance of the social and institutional parameters of Catholicism raised the question of what was to remain at the core.

Biever sketched in two alternatives. One entailed the transformation of an authoritarian communalism into a voluntaristic program of social concern. The streak of individualism that had existed alongside the mutuality of the parishes was gaining ascendancy amid postwar consumerism and mobility. A new idealism was needed to restore the balance, without returning to the customary hierarchies:

> The vocation of the majority is to live in the world, and if they are taught that to live in the world is bad, if the emphasis is on drink as bad, if the emphasis is on sex as bad, if the emphasis is on the religious vocation as the only fully acceptable call of God, then it must not be surprising if many relegate religion to a separate compartment in their lives just enough to calm their fears, or on the other hand,

develop a type of religion that borders on the superstitious, and is really only a form of escapism. Religion is to be a way of life, not a series of questions and answers given for the purpose of an examination and then as quickly forgotten. . . . There must be an effort made to eschew the emotional, the authoritative, the sentimental, and more attention made towards inculcating a spirit of love toward Christ as a Man as well as God, and especially needed is vigorous emphasis on the social implications of Catholicism which are now totally ignored.[53]

This was the normative alternative, the direction in which Biever felt Catholicism should be headed. It combined social conscience with an existential authenticity free from servility. Competence and autonomy, self-reliance and sophisticated compassion were the watchwords. A revitalized Catholicism would not only pay more attention to public affairs. With the decay of external reinforcements, it would also perfect a deepened interiority.

The unstated difficulty was that the solution headed in two directions at once. It set as its goals a more profound subjectivity and a keener social conscience that together constituted a reformed "way of life." The way of life, however, with its communal supports had started to come apart. Social concern might be a diversion from questions of identity and sexuality that the breakdown of the old communal controls had forced to the surface. In any case such dedication to others would be hard to sustain without a firm sense of self. "There must be," Biever observed,

an appreciation given of the real meaning and purpose of life, *this* life as well as the life hereafter, an appreciation, likewise, of the Providence of God for each individual human being, an appreciation of the real nature of man, of original sin, of redemption, of the Mass, of the Mystical Body. . . . There must be a rethinking of the question concerning the attitude of Catholics toward sex, and the introduction of adequate, clear and frank sex instruction in the schools. In sum, the teaching of religion must be brought up to the manifest needs of the times, lifted out of mere rote memory and blind obedience, and integrated into the lives of the people.[54]

Catholics were headed down divergent tracks. Social action was one course, the search for identity another. Though it was a step in the right direction, liberation from a crabbed moralism did not provide this identity. Thus the second alternative that Biever conjured up for the development of Irish American Catholicism was not an integrated way of life comparable to the majesty on a small scale that was passing. The trend was toward a further compartmentalization and privatization of religion. In theory, under the new dispensation, the age-old split between the spiritual and the temporal realms might shrink. But the division between personal salvation, spiritual or otherwise, and collective melioration was not quite the same as this, and in practice public-spirited action and personal satisfaction tended to go separate ways. Social concern remained at the margin of a therapeutic spirituality that prized self-realization.[55] This emphasis on personal fulfillment over commitment to the collectivity matched the individualism of the American milieu. However objectionable from the Catholic standpoint, the ethos appeared to correspond to the material conditions and the dominant incentives of postwar capitalism. By contrast, a Catholicism of social concern lacked contextual reinforcement; at least, its supports were not self-evident.[56]

Rampant individualism may have been a dominant orientation of the times, but it was no more predetermined by the economics and social mobility of the postwar years than the presumptive mutuality of earlier times was enforced by the Catholic subculture to the exclusion of self-seeking behavior. Increasing levels of material well-being might also encourage—perhaps not in equal proportion but nevertheless stimulate—concern for questions of political participation, social justice, and the like. This type of movement had a restricted appeal even under the most propitious conditions, for American Catholics had felt insecure as a minority and they were at least as prone to stretches of conformism as to bouts of eccentricity and cultural resistance. The uncertainty came from the difficulty of determining what, if anything, might be distinctively Catholic about a heightening of interest in matters of public consequence. Assimilation afforded opportunities for idealism as it did for rank materialism, but for some Catholics it did so at the price of their identity.

Biever rejected a return to parochial solidarity. Yet it was difficult to visualize what organizational form a new, more rational mutuality would take.[57] For all its faults, the old subculture seemed to be more or less of a piece. The conjunction of neighborliness with petty ambitions and disappointments was one in its diminutive scale. The implication of Biever's analysis was that in the absence of comparably supportive conditions, a social consciousness that might go beyond this microcosmic world would require an ideological supercharge. It would need to be bolstered by a dissident vanguard. This was to be the route followed by Catholic radicals in the aftermath of Vatican II.[58]

IV

Popular Catholicism during the twenty years following World War II did not lack interiority. Its spirituality, however, was largely formulaic. Ritual was experienced by mostly silent recipients as prayer in rhythmic Latin and half-chanted, half-periodic English, in childish rhyming hymns ("Bring flowers of the fairest, bring flowers of the rarest") and long devotions, the rosary and the novenas, feast days, vigils, visitations to the Blessed Sacrament, incense, the polyphony of magic utensils and blessed integuments— thuribles and scapulars, cruets and ciboria, polished aspergilla, the rustle of vestments, and the chiming of bells rung by altar boys in white surplices and black cassocks or, for high Mass and on holy days, red cassocks.[59] In addition to the ceremonial offerings there was an abundant literature, purveyed mostly in pamphlet form, to encourage meditation and furnish solace. The pamphlets transmitted a catechetical piety that was practically unchanged from childhood to adulthood. Exemplary tales first composed in the twenties and thirties were reprinted through the 1950s. In 1946, parishioners could purchase for a nickel the fourteenth printing of "He Kept It White: A Story of the Eucharist" by Fr. Francis J. Finn, a Cincinnati Jesuit who had written the piece in 1936 and who was well known as a writer of inspirational stories for boys. Also available from the Queen's Work in St. Louis were such titles as "Hard-Headed Holiness," by Francis P. LeBuffe, S.J., and "Tips on Temptation," by Benjamin R. Fulkerson, S.J. Herbert O'H. Walker, S.J., offered an anthem to the complementarity of Americanism and Christianity in "Our Way of Life Must Prevail."[60]

Occasionally a more ambitious piece of spiritual literature appeared, aiming beyond old-style devotion and consolation. In 1958 the Queen's Work published a more-than-550 page pocket manual entitled *Mental Prayer*. The compendium set forth guidelines for moral growth under modern conditions. It had been compiled by students at the Jesuit theologate in St. Mary's, Kansas. They tried to duplicate the narrative interest of the older pamphlets while reaching a somewhat more educated audience. The contents, however, were a still strictly traditional popularization of doctrinal prohibitions. The emphasis was on the dangers of sex and on manliness as bravery and mastery. The readership seems to have been envisioned as composed neither of old ladies nor children but of adolescent males.

"There's no easier way to hell," it was claimed, "than sexual misbehavior."[61] Under a section labeled "Moral Sin Deserves Hell" the theologians related the story of Larry and Sheila:

[They] leave a party. It has been a swell party, the best in their ten months of going steady. Before going home they "park" awhile. In the back of his mind, Larry suddenly thinks of the warnings he had heard against going steady . . . but they won't apply to him . . . deliberately . . . he has never fallen into mortal sin . . . and then . . . fully . . . deliberately! Finally Larry takes Sheila home. He is nervous . . . he has committed his first mortal sin . . . he speeds . . . he doesn't see the other car . . . there is a terrible crash, like an explosion! The jaws of hell open, and Larry's soul plunges into the pit of eternal fire— unending torture—for one mortal sin.[62]

This cautionary tale of the beautiful and the damned reflected the climate of fifties Catholicism and the ambient technology. The proximate occasion of sin for sericeous cherubim was not a porch swing but an automobile.[63]

Going steady symbolized the minor peccadilloes that accumulated and led to one big sin. Character gave in to permissiveness. Just as experimenting with recreational drugs could lead to serious addiction, venial sins put Catholics out of condition and could eventually bring on disastrous results. Such transgressions became bad habits that dulled spiritual vigilance. It was the pattern of lassitude that had to be avoided. Spiritual flabbiness had to be controlled. "Dear Lord," the penitent was instructed to pray, "give me what it takes to stay in training for eternity." Continuing the analogy:

All season Joe had known it would come—his big chance—the opportunity to be a star tackle. So far he'd had a so-so season. "Not enough zip," the coach said. But now he was in the championship game . . . 30 seconds to go . . . his school was ahead by one point! Tyler of the opponents was almost clear. Only Joe stood between him and the winning TD. This would be Joe's victory! He stretched his legs, filled his chest with air, gave it all he had. It wasn't enough! His lungs hurt, his legs were heavy. Tyler outran him. Because of Joe . . . the championship . . . lost. Back in the locker room, nobody looked at him. Only the coach didn't know that Joe hadn't caught Tyler because he was out of condition. He'd broken training all season. Just a small beer here, a little cigarette there—nothing serious. But when the big test came, Joe didn't have what it takes, because he'd broken training.[64]

Admonitions to scrupulosity were interlaced with pep talks on character-building. Heavy breathing was for athletic, not sexual, exertions. *Mental Prayer* attempted to arouse a "fighting, fiery spirit." A phobia of softness was channeled into rigorous spiritual exercises. A combative idealism and virile generosity were to be channeled into self-possession and good works. A combination of restraint and activism, of virtue and courageous pragmatism, was the prototype. A frank but contained masculinity was the ideal. The stress was on chastity, as a sign of strength of character and as a conditioning for works of charity.

The athletic imagery in *Mental Prayer* accentuated the tone of competitiveness and toughening. References to a loving God were almost totally absent. The spiritual life was neither warm nor fuzzy. Nervous energy had to be disciplined and directed toward the conquest of self and the accomplishment of good works. *Mental Prayer* was a manual for spiritual combatants in training for the battle of life and aiming for the ultimate victory of salvation. Prayer sessions, like rapid workouts, might lead to temporary exhaustion and renewed vigor but not to contemplation and relaxation. Unflinching self-denial led to heroic service.

The timbre of the manuals written by Fr. Anthony Paone was altogether calmer, with no inkling of suppressed hysteria. Paone spent most of his Jesuit life teaching and counseling high school students, but he wrote for a general audience of adult Catholics. He projected an aura of steady holiness. The book that brought him fame in Catholic circles was *My Daily Bread*, "a summary of the spiritual life simplified and arranged for daily reading, reflection and prayer."[65] The size of a miniature missal, it was thick but small enough to hold in the palm of the hand.

The message and even the format of the readings—fifteen-minute chunks of traditional reflections—were similar to those of the snappier *Mental Prayer*. But Paone wrote in a slow rhythm, combining short sentences and long pauses. His style, modeled after *The Imitation of Christ*, was as unadorned as plainchant.[66] The question-and-response format was catechetical. The vocabulary was limited, the caesuras were almost palpable, the short-syllabled words echoed with the placid solemnity of the interior of a darkened church. The vowels and spondees had the vibrations of human sound. The voice was slightly elevated and the breathing could be heard in the rise and fall of the clauses and their picking up again. The effect was hypnotic. A simple calm conveyed at once an impression of transparency and depth.

> Human desires and emotions are natural to man. That means that they cannot be destroyed. They are made more perfect insofar as one succeeds in controlling and directing them by the grace of God. Thus, "dying to self" means the right use of human emotions and desires. They are to be followed insofar as they help us to fulfill God's holy Will, and they are to be controlled insofar as they hinder us from doing so.[67]

Paone taught a reassuring lesson. Salvation was in reach of those who practiced mortification and obeyed authority. Earthly satisfaction was transitory; so was temporal suffering. Hope lay in the reasonableness of the connection between spiritual effort and reward. God was a sensible father. He spoke with paternal balance to his children:

> Man's happiness does not consist in having a great deal. A moderate amount of this world's good things is enough for you if you are daily

working for Heaven. The more you see life from My viewpoint, the more you will realize that this earthly life is a cross. It has its trials, burdens, disappointments, and sorrows, all of which must be borne patiently. It is not easy to be a spiritual man, because the good things of this world continually appeal to your feelings. Learn to govern your feelings with the reins of reasons and grace. Control them with your intelligence and My commandments. [68]

The "passing desires and brief enjoyments of this earthly life" receded next to "perfect self-surrender." The central question (as it was for Ignatius) was "How does this help me for eternal life?"[69] The salvific calculus employed a utilitarian wisdom shorn of distracting spectacle. Paone dispensed comfort and instruction, simplifying the quandaries of redemption with a directness that nonetheless retained an air of awe and mystery.

Transcendence of earthly concerns—which meant union with the divine—was the great objective. It was the singular relationship, the dwelling with God, that mattered above all. "I hope to become a man of silence," Paone wrote in the voice of the supplicant, "one who prefers to talk to God rather than to men."[70] Time was a medium in which habits of self-discipline were to be developed. Except as they involved hierarchies between leaders and followers, that is, patterns of obedience and obligation, social relationships were ignored almost completely:

My child, unless you learn to control your feelings, you will always find it hard to obey those who have authority over you. Your feelings do not reason. They simply turn away from what is unpleasant, be it right or wrong. . . . An obedient horse can help man in his daily tasks, but a stubborn mule can do more harm than good. So is it with man's own nature. His reason and will, strengthened by grace, must guide his unreasoning appetites and desires to right action. [71]

The person was to be alone before God. This interiority meant a dying to life, a turning away from the temptations and the cares of the world. The world was cold and impersonal. God was warm. The passages of reflection and prayers of supplication came close to an Oriental weariness in their admonitions about the snares of the evanescent. Pain was not illusory, but it subsided in light of the eternal.

The indispensable relationship, the one between God and the individual, both mirrored and overcame the division between the eternal and the temporal. Like a medieval contract between master and liege, it was hierarchical and personal, and there was a reciprocity to it. God would not turn away from a loyal servant. Punishment there might be, but not betrayal.

The meditations set down by Paone were psychologically incisive. They were traditional in their insistence on the fugitive nature of the things of the world and the everlastingness of spiritual peace and retribution. They were also emphatic in attending to the need for intimacy with the divine. In this way the abstract and the immediate were joined. A personal God stood above an impersonal world and yet he dwelt within, " 'the still small voice' that is all a discreet and self-effacing God permits himself in dealing with his creatures."[72] This property was ambiguous. Personal union with a paternal God was as traditional a religious ideal as was rejection of the mundane. But individualism created a paradox, for it could be viewed as a religious sentiment that had become shunted toward self-seeking.

In his first book Paone, like most of his peers, seems to have taken the communal context of religious sentiment for granted. The social dimension of the relation between the individual and God was assumed to be stable. Attention could thus dwell on the solitary person. There was a shadowy corner, however. The talks with God suggested loneliness even in the thickest of communities. God's words sounded like those of a best friend with all the answers. No such intimacy and security were to be had between Catholics themselves. From Paone's perspective this confirmed the incompleteness of the merely human and the validity of the yearning for transcendental communion. God was kind yet demanding. In order to find fulfillment the amateur seeker should behave as much as possible like a religious professional, distancing the self from purely material entanglements.

Paone's second book, *My Life with Christ*, appeared in 1962, and it signaled a shift away from an absorption with the ladder-of-being approach, in which individuals ascended one by one above their physical nature to a heavenly father. As the subtitle, *Spiritual Meditations for the Modern Reader*, indicated, it was addressed to a more sophisticated audience. The simulated talks with a God who addressed the worshiper as "My child" dissolved into a vocabulary with a clinical, therapeutic cast. While individuals may die alone and have to face God and eternity on their own, Paone implied, people live together.

The reminders about the ephemerality of worldly pleasures in *My Daily Bread* had reinforced classical teachings regarding the hierarchy between heaven and earth. These admonitions, together with a mode of address that placed the reader in the role of a fundamentally good but wayward child, served also as a preparation for the inevitable disenchantment of adulthood. The disillusion to be avoided lay in the transition from exuberant innocence to gloomy maturity. Paone wanted to preserve the original innocence in altered form, by insisting on the illusoriness of material failure and hence on the spuriousness of disenchantment itself. Detachment brought peace.

The problem dealt with in *My Life with Christ* was different. The effort to preserve an immaculate spirituality by sheltering a childlike innocence from reality, directing it upward toward another world, was very nearly replaced by prescriptions for coping more directly with the anxieties of this world. The starting point was the aftermath of the death of childhood. The ideal of an emotional immunity to the attractions and sufferings of the world that had functioned as a psychic analogue to physical virginity receded. Spiritual salvation remained supreme, but social maturity and psychic health gained in importance.

Although the divinity depicted by Paone had always been accessible, individuals had constantly been reminded of the transitoriness of the physical world and of their personal unworthiness and helplessness. Whatever the value of self-abasement in developing a feeling of nearness to a forgiving God, humility might not be effective for coping with the world. It might in fact turn into a crippling incapacity.

> If I have achieved a reasonable self-esteem and a fair measure of moral strength, I can tolerate the pressure of . . . interpersonal relations. On the other hand, beneath my external front and intellectual camouflage, I may still be resorting to childish forms of self-defense. If I am unable to maintain my self-respect when others oppose, resent, or reject me, I am immature.[73]

In place of the dependence of the father-child tradition, there was less accent on guilt and more on self-acceptance and confidence. Paone warned against "a morbid memory of past sins."[74] He advocated a positive thinking that would help the individual come close to God and at the same time get along better with neighbors and colleagues. With an approach that was still overwhelmingly psychological, *My Life with Christ* was less an old-fashioned prayer book and more a set of counsels for improving both sociability and the chances of salvation. "Interpersonal relations" had become problematic; for some, friendships had gone haywire. Personal identity was separable from communal belonging, and self-esteem had to be achieved. The individual had to be constructed; in part, identity had to be created. An exclusive focus on redemption risked ignoring a crucial issue for mobile Catholics in the postwar America of fluid attachments and erratic encounters. The hope of the union of the solitary soul with God might give ultimate meaning. But self-respect and an optimism about personal interaction made the encroaching loneliness and insecurity of modern times bearable:

> I must be intelligently content to be myself, without unreasonable shame, blame, or self-disgust. My fears, sensitivity, envy, irritability, contempt, and hostility toward others, often proceed from my own deficient self-respect. If I have a proper sense of my individual value and personal dignity, I shall find it much easier to accept others as they

are, and to deal with them with interior peace, emotional strength, and moral conviction. As long as I am not reasonably content to be myself, I shall be uneasy, distrustful, and antagonistic with others.[75]

The childhood spirituality of reward and punishment, one that combined a desire to please with the fear of an all-powerful God, did not suffice for adults whose world was less magical and more complex. Although it might be reduced to a long hymn to individualism, the approach originally espoused by Paone could better be understood as a compelling simplification: The individual, alone, knelt before a personal God. It articulated the bond of hope that many Catholics felt, or tried to feel, in collective silence at Sunday Mass. Respite from the daily grind and a return to the mystery of the personal and to a primitive simplicity was what readers got from the private quiet time spent with Paone's early writing. It afforded an interiority within the security furnished by the richness of the liturgy and the tribal myths. The sensation was the same as the relief felt on stepping from a loud and crowded sidewalk into a nearly empty church on a workday afternoon. The oasis was breezeless. Silence was magnified. Motes drifted in shafts of light aslant dark columns as if blown by the breath of tradition.

Yet there was also a release-for-shut-ins quality to this way of praying. It did not speak to the associational longings of Catholics and to their social insecurities. This audience had probably not ignored *My Daily Bread* altogether; next to raucous complexity, simplicity enchanted. Nevertheless, there was something airless and quiescent about these pious dialogues. The missing element in the title, though not in the text, of *My Life with Christ* was human companionship:

> I shall better insure myself against misapplying Christ's teachings if I improve my understanding of human nature. I may then more easily avoid the misconceptions or immature idealism that compels some to make impossible demands on themselves or others; and I may better avert the inner anxiety, strain, fatigue, depression, and discouragement that often lead to tepidity and laxity in religious practice.[76]

Increased attention to the interpersonal did not require the abandonment of the themes of eternity and emotional control as routes toward salvation. "At best," Paone repeated at the start of the book, "our earthly life is an imperfect performance."[77] Still, although the selfishness that some Catholics saw unleashed with the emptying out of local communities might be despicable, it was not unnatural, and it would not do to mistake religion for an unrelieved lament on the failings of humanity. The search after a purity of grown-up motivation could be as chimerical as the attempt to recover an unsullied innocence of simpler times. *My Daily Bread* was written for the weary and those whom circumstances had worn down. *My Life with Christ* was addressed to the ambitious and the insecure; those with careers, those who were neurotic but not quite traumatized. From another perspective, the books could be seen as addressing different moods and moments of the same uncertain person:

> There are many motives that induce men to fulfill their religious obligations and follow the moral law in their daily life. These motives may range from the sheerest desire to avoid God's punishment to the purest wish to show more generosity to the all-lovable Creator. . . . These lesser motives are not to be despised as long as they are regarded in their proper place. The self-concern that moves men toward these benefits was created by God. It inclines men to reach for things which are necessary or helpful to their daily lives. . . . [Many people] often wonder whether they are "doing enough" to please God. In their good work, they needlessly question the purity of their motives. They believe that they are "wasting time" unless they are doing something that has a formal "religious" value.[78]

All of Paone's writings were in the self-help genre. His bent was practical rather than mystical; his moralism was instrumental. Yet this almost hypnotic pragmatism, the rhythmic, strophic longings and reassurances, took different forms. The transition from the devotional exercises of the fifties to the advice on interpersonal psychology of the sixties reflected an appreciation of the need for social skills as tools for survival during a period of subcultural decline. Guilt and negativism, not merely sin, were to be overcome. The decay of community heightened the need to work at creating and sustaining companionship. Networks had to be forged to supplement the ties that families and a fading subculture could no longer furnish so well.

Paone barely touched on social awareness as a concern for injustice. The message set out in his later writing was directed neither at escaping from nor changing the world. He offered instead guidelines for accommodation. Sociability became a requisite of spiritual health; a direct line to God was emotionally insufficient, and social action of the sort that Biever advocated was something apart. God might be reached through other persons; at any rate others were not simply distractions. In neither case did the institutional church play a prominent role. It was an organizational convenience and a conservatory of tradition, in the background of American spirituality.[79]

V

Terrible was a signature word of William Lynch, a contemporary of Anthony Paone's and like him a New Yorker. Toward the end of his life Lynch spoke of "a terrible urgency to be human" that he felt was "located at the heart of so much mental illness."[80] A quarter of a century earlier, in the book that brought him a measure of celebrity, he had written that "the new burden of a terrible increativity and a lack of human style in life may very well become the consuming theological issues."[81] A few years later, in his major work of literary criticism, he noted that "the weapons of art . . . are terrible and not merely ornamental."[82]

Having begun his career as a classicist, Lynch used *terrible* in the Greek sense to denote both the awe-inspiring and traumatic. Various connotations of the word reverberated around this classical understanding. The tragedy that evoked sensations of terror entailed the prospect of terminal failure: loss of the hope of redemption. In an existential sense religious terror meant contemplating the disintegration of identity, the madness of the helpless self: This was the ultimate nightmare.[83]

Lynch also used *terrible* more colloquially to refer to the tortuous struggle to overcome the extinction of the self. As a paragon of this struggle he had in mind a postromantic notion of artistic creativity. Modernization changed the audience for artistic expression and raised the stakes of the perennial struggle for creativity. A new consciousness had arisen that was uncertain of its public, practically alone in its subjectivity, yet aware that mere interiority did not suffice. Creative individuals risked sinking into autism, each in a delusory paradise that constituted a prison of the self. Recovery for Lynch, as less turgidly for Paone, meant the attainment of sociability: mutual communication among coherent selves. Salvation had somehow to be collectively intelligible. But the social codes that permitted comprehension were being drowned out in mass society. The self was inaudible, and the old collectivity was dangerously close to being drained of meaning.[84]

Conflicting themes ran through Lynch's work—he spoke often of *contrariety*[85]—and *terrible* was his shorthand for the stresses generated by these antinomies. For Lynch the most enervating of these appear to have been between individual visions, rich in their particularity but difficult to express, and a public terrain that was a kind of dimensionless abstraction. The animating tension of the authentic life could not be simply the striving of the solitary soul for union with God, for this could degenerate into false transcendence—a satisfaction that was pure in its privacy and finally crazy, a literal "idiocy" of the unintelligible. The individual was driven not only toward self-expression but communication with others.

The tragedy that obsessed Lynch was the failure to meet one or both of these drives. The need for expression and the capacity for communication were often dissociated. He was attuned to the fragility of the link between private creation and public statement, and it was this dual sensitivity that informed his interest in the modern media as well as the preindustrial arts.

He dreaded the collapse of artistic expression into a black hole of self-absorption, a nonplace where identity was unrecognizable. He also feared the dominion of a technology of mass communication that was emptied of meaning and that entertained by gimmickry.[86] In one of the last essays published before his death, Lynch reiterated a warning that coursed through nearly all of his writing—the word *terrible* appears again—about the dangers of conformity imposed by a slick totalitarianism and perhaps by a dead tradition as well as by the shallowness of the new.

> [Human imagining] must not be grievously limited or shackled or it will take on an inhuman and monstrous form. At the other extreme, there are ways of *imitating* the ideal life of the imagination, ersatz ways which are rooted in intensity and ecstasy and single-mindedness; they follow brilliant paths but come to the same inhuman and terrible end. Both the shackling of the imagination and the dazzling counterfeits for imagining are in reality severe forms of the disease of non-imagining.[87]

Lynch was fascinated by the arts, particularly literature and theater, as expressions of the irreducibly concrete and idiosyncratic that managed both to create and to communicate a sense of self. He contrasted this paradox of a radical specificity with the capacity for self-transcendence against abstract "angelism."[88] This was a hideously insensitive, impersonal universalism—a positivism without ambiguity, made up of implacably binary, either-or assertions. Lynch leaned to another, religiously high-strung, extreme. He viewed aesthetic expression as a way of objectifying "the profound worthwhileness of the fundamental abyss of being that is the human self—below all normal identifications of the self with precise categories."[89] At bottom, Lynch felt, there could be no fixed individual identity; at best, it was precarious. Fluidity was very nearly all. Life itself had to be a kind of art. The forging of a coherent self was the psychic equivalent of the artistic enterprise.

So there was an irradicably personal yet analogical art that tapped into the universal and the transcendent. At least there was the possibility of attaining it; art was a metaphor for redemption. Art had the capacity to deliver persons, through a symbolic communality, from the shells of individualism that separated them. Besides this, however, there was a vacuum within the individual into which the person might vanish, disintegrating into insanity, unable to communicate, lost in subtleties as sterile as the generalities of pure abstraction. Art was a delicate redemptive therapy for healing the lesion between an empty, solitary individualism and a tolerably common humanity. It could not be wholly rational or "univocal."[90]

For Lynch the ground between psychology and aesthetics was murky. Creativity was a mode of shaping character and of affirming a distinctive voice, an identity that was recognizable to others. The object produced, the artifact, was human. In this sense the process differed from the formation of character as ethical conscience. Lynch wanted to avoid the moralizing that extracted messages from works of art. Not all great literature was invested with religious symbolism or elevating lessons; every poem was not somehow a prayer. But Lynch also criticized the loss of hope brought on by portraying human experience in the light of a secular perfectionism and the dream of universality. This spurious transcendence was the flaw of the abstract idealism that afflicted modern tragedy. The dramas of Eugene O'Neill, for example, tended to be awash in "vague, mystical moods" that amounted to chronic depression at the unattainability of a redeeming myth. This led inevitably to histrionics and despair:

> Any true theology of the self which would make the self the scene for the action of God is in our day somewhat suspect, regarded as a fragile tradition incapable of sincerity or of "facing the facts." Nevertheless, this view of traditional theology does not prevent those who hold it from theologizing in their own special way.[91]

In modern times, with the abandonment of the divine, the expression of the attempt to recover personal authenticity and courage in the face of suffering and death inclined the artist toward hysteria and false release, rather than a purgative creativity or healing therapy. This engendered not only a rejection of religious transcendence but a failure to connect up with fellow humans. What passed for modern drama was solipsism that alternated between ideological posturing and emotional spectacle:

> For O'Neill, as for so many of his contemporaries, God, in whatever form, is a reality completely external to man. Man must leap to God by unfounded faith, by sudden, uprooted ecstasy, or even by hysterics, in order to escape from the self. His plays in general turn from despair to hope and faith with brilliant, melodramatic ease. The search for man and the search for God remain totally disconnected.[92]

High art was doubly crippled. It was socially adrift, and it lacked a theological base. For its part, popular culture was sullied by the machinations of the market. It had almost no intellectual pretensions and no sense of community. Lynch criticized the commercialization of art into mass escapism and manipulation; his attitude toward popular culture was largely one of disdain. *The Image Industries,* the first of his books to reach a sizable audience, was a philippic against the mélange of sweetness and exhibitionism that characterized the entertainment of the fifties. The media had great power to persuade. But their potential was consumed in a self-intoxication with technological glitter and merchandising.

Many of Lynch's observations on the mass media were critical common-places about their superficiality. A few of his asides revealed a tendency to impose standards of good taste on political reality. His desire to infuse personal expression with social intelligibility sometimes led to the reverse fallacy of judging public issues and political performance by aesthetic criteria. The result was a confusion of realms that generated portentous lamentations. Lynch occasionally succumbed to belletristic weariness. The unevenness expressed his intrapsychic drama more accurately, though still indirectly, than it captured the state of the popular arts. A recurrent pattern with Lynch was stretches of dryness and finger-exercise commentary jolted by outpourings, manic in their suddenness, of some originality but border-line intelligibility.[93]

Once in a while, even if the manner was hyperbolic, Lynch touched a nerve close to the one Joseph Fitzpatrick had brushed in noting the decline of social awareness among American Jesuits. Like Fitzpatrick, Lynch sensed that victory over the economic hardships of the thirties posed novel challenges that were disorienting in their complexity and amorphousness. The problem in the first place was to name them and to show how they touched individuals. Unlike Fitzpatrick, Lynch did not list a series of social problems in need of attention. Instead, in the manner of a literary theologian, Lynch grappled with the task of identifying and expressing the new difficulty. For him a shock of personal recognition was indispensable to understanding, even though more was needed for communication. The issue was one of recovering and articulating an anguish that, under new social conditions, threatened to implode in its own subjectivity.

In *The Integrating Mind* Lynch addressed not Jesuits only but "the few," those he took to be the American intelligentsia. The outlines of the malaise were visible, but its full nature and the way of dealing with it were not:

> A generation ago, when the problem of the nation was social injustice and the mood was social progress, you found yourselves allied with a vast bulk of the Christian and religious forces of the country and were emboldened by your mutual success. Today the problem and the agony faced by the people are intensely greater than the social question; the problem is one of survival and existence itself, and the anxieties that come from the deepest planes of existence. The liberal intelligence has been accused very often of being without those inward resources of the mind and the spirit that would enable it to handle the true tragic question, the question of death and human finitude with which we are now confronted.[94]

Aside from differences in phrasing, Lynch's complaint about the passing of an epoch in which social criticism was structured by a noble purpose that was shared by intellectuals and their lower-class constituents bore a striking resemblance to the nostalgia voiced by Husslein and others for an "integral" medievalism. *Authenticity* was a new but equally continental word for *organicism*. Whatever the phraseology, coherence of this sort could no longer be approximated, and Lynch was already of a generation for whom medieval revivalism had lost its appeal.

He looked over his shoulder at rather more recent times: at the last decades of immigrant Catholicism when enclaves of tradition thrived in the spaces left untouched by the Enlightenment. His lament was for the passing not of the Thomistic synthesis but of a world in which vestiges of the premodern and the elemental were still recognizable and not yet thought of as exotic throwbacks. This was the true grit of local humanity, incomprehensible in light of rationalization and progress. The social order sustaining this ethos was disintegrating, not least because of the onslaught of the media, and its intellectual core—the interaction between aesthetic and religious impulses—had shriveled.

The decline of cultural context did not by itself instigate the separation of public and ultimately private conflicts. The problem for Lynch was that, with the breakdown of the old culture, antinomies of whatever kind were more difficult to articulate through a common language. "Since the end of the seventeenth century," he continued,

> when you began to overthrow the classical order of the static and the status quo, all your victories—and I do not underestimate the importance of many of them—have been on the level of the political and the social and the temporal. Now you are not being asked to give up any of these desires, but you *are* being asked to go deeper and higher as well, where you may again in unity meet the conscience and needs of a people who are stricken as they have never been stricken before. Thus, where you stood on common ground with many of the people a generation ago, you do not today possess with them a common language. [95]

"The political and the social and the temporal" were the outer rings of Lynch's aesthetic world. The inner world differed from collective reality and institutions that changed and passed, and there was no metaphor to span the breach. The public stood apart from the private, and the personal itself was riven with tensions. The most terrifying split was between a becalmed classicism that hinted of immortality and whose clarity smacked of paralysis on the one hand, and on the other the reckless effusion of "this brilliant, this beautiful and wild god Dionysus," the Mediterranean demiurge, calling to perishable but reproductive action and enjoyment. [96] The contrast between the brightness of the light and the darkness of the images it cast was close to unbearable. If Lynch discerned the contradictory connection between the irrational feminine of John Courtney Murray's imaginings and the impulsive male creator he conjured up himself, he did not mention it.[97]

Lynch was not a systematic or even a logical thinker. "Practically my whole argument," he acknowledged, "has been based on . . . instinctive ruminations as a protest against the over-extension of the clear idea and the either-or or moralistic mentalities, as well as a defense of a metaphysics and theology based on the idea of the interpenetration of contraries and the complicated nature of reality."[98] He criticized existentialism for a simultaneous self-absorption and universalizing hubris in which social context and human specificity were lost. But he was apt to fasten on a dramatic mode of exposition himself; the clash of opposites that registered on his temperament was the stuff of theater. Lynch's style of humanism—his revulsion at mechanistic reductionism—equaled his hatred of disembodied idealism. This was the axis along which the private-public struggle was fought. But it did not quite get at the conflicts that tore at him from the inside. These antinomies were unspecified, glimpsed intermittently as if they were too terrifying to gaze on for long. A sign of this panic was a change in the beat of Lynch's prose. It went choppy, the words snapped down on a table. Then the flow returned, with statelier qualifications and nuance. Lucidity gave way to density and equivocation.[99]

Lynch kept returning to the tenuous linkages between artistic release and psychic health—"balance," as he called it, another borrowing from the Greek masters—and it was here that his deepest feelings and doubts were engaged. By contrast, his scattered political and social commentary suffered from a portentous conventionalism that was the artsy equivalent of the conformity for which he castigated American public life. When he wandered off to comment on politics, his *aperçus* usually showed the vapidity of the generalizations he decried as a mark of the "univocal imagination." His insights into the operations of the media were more acute, even though many of them too were composed of stock fulminations against the demise of regional arts and craftsmanship, cheap shots at the Californiazation of American culture. He railed against the neon abstractions of modernism and the relativism of contemporary philosophy.[100] Nevertheless, he understood that the new visual media broadcast a variety of images to larger audiences, and he sensed that the diversity of these images, even their incoherence and hollowness, came close to a rhetoric of vocables, the primordial nonsense, that attracted him in the precarious art that skirted insanity.

Creativity, or rather the extreme difficulty of creativity, was Lynch's theme. The mass media and questions of social justice and politics took second place to problems of communicative, human generativity. Having pointed to the near impenetrability and singularity of aesthetic acts, his characteristic manner was to chip away at the subject almost haphazardly, from various angles, as if to confront or even unequivocally to state the problem would be to trivialize it, to reify the ineffable. He came at the theme slantwise, and much of his meaning was in the eddies and parentheses of his logic. The opposite danger was terrifying. Dealing directly with the difficulties of aesthetic expression and communication could mean dredging up shapeless, unbearable forces. Lynch was like the painter whose splattered palette and disheveled studio were more revealing than the self-portrait he could never bring himself to finish. His was the awkwardness of half-acknowledged repressions.[101]

Lynch seemed almost always to be on the brink of artistic expression. An alternative, to which he occasionally gave in, was to aestheticize politics. More often he circled around the corners, exploring the borderlands between theology and art and the possibility that for a priest the person was the supreme artifact. He was not a creative artist. He was an occasionally insightful critic of artistic creation. His true subject was creativity itself.

Lynch's sensibility veered from the exquisite to the inarticulate. Art and religion converged in an amalgam of the sublime and the unspeakable, accounting for some of the alternation between the laconic and the histrionic in his writing. After hospitalization for psychiatric treatment, Lynch appeared to come to grips with his thwarted creativity and with an identity that slipped between categories.[102] His search for expression, affective as well as artistic, prefigured the itinerary followed by many Jesuits in the decades to come.

Although Lynch did not leave a program of action or devise a school of thought, he tapped into two main currents of Jesuit tradition. His failure to attain artistic creativity was compensated for by his understanding of art not as a literal source of moral instruction but as a liberating therapy. This was the next best thing to redemption. Some of his retinue were not unlike Paone's. They were the wounded who could barely articulate the source of their pain, and they recognized their confusion in his halting words. He was the tormented sophisticate whose stammering prose expressed the imperfect and the ineffable. The appreciation of art, and the communication of enthusiasm for it, could be a peak educational experience, no less fulfilling than creation itself. From one perspective Lynch was a failed artist; from another he was a great teacher. Parts of his life as well as his expertise went into this work. Not all works of art were inlaid with ethical guides, and not everyone could create original works of art. Yet the fabrication of self was for Lynch a human imperative, especially amid the detritus of modernism.[103]

The other link with Jesuit tradition came by way of the fascination that rhetoric and the layers beneath it exerted on Lynch. He was concerned both with communication and creativity. The classical conventions that permitted artists to articulate shared meanings were either lost or had become problematic. The result was a clotted expressivity captured by Lynch's own alternately terse and Gongoresque prose. The irony of the new media, according to Lynch, was that their enhanced power to communicate did not create meaning. On the other hand, without communication there could be no identity. This was a circularity of the analogistic imagination. For Lynch, identity went deeper than the words he could summon up. The solitary, stranded self was made visible, like sunken treasure, by receding community and the cold clarity of the new media.

VI

With the exception of Robert Gannon, the Jesuits discussed in this chapter display an anti-institutional streak. To varying degrees Bruce Biever, Anthony Paone, and William Lynch can be understood as cultural commentators in search of collective meaning in a privatized world. All of them saw the passing of the world they came from, and none of them envisaged the restoration of a comparable solidity. The new institutions were social networks and the media—diaphanous things—not the brick-and-mortar organizations and close hierarchies they had grown up with.

Although continuities with the past were not cut off completely, they were extremely difficult to retain. As mobility increased, so did the sense not only of a split between the private and public spheres, which seemed in memory to have been closely linked within the confines of the subculture, but also of multiple divisions in the self. Lynch was the master and victim of the awareness that identity might be meaningless.

To some extent the predicament merely reflected the fact that Catholics could choose many more paths than they could before; the inherited categories were too rigid and too few. Jesuits traditionally had not been afraid to sally forth from home. There was some question now, however, whether there was a home to return to, or even a goal in sight.

The assumption that held constant in the evolution of the manuals of popular devotion written by Anthony Paone was not only that individual salvation was attainable but also that a supportive community could be preserved. Social mobility increased the need for but did not destroy human communication. The shift from the traditional piety of *My Daily Bread* to the social therapy of *My Life with Christ* reflected hope in a benign modernity. Progress and piety could be at peace.

William Lynch was less optimistic. The fracturing of community raised questions concerning organizational control and the institutional hierarchy of Catholicism. For Lynch, existential issues of character—of individual conscience, of creativity and identity—were also thrust into prominence. These fragments of the naked self were obscure and unassembled; they might not constitute a whole. The subtext of Lynch's tortured subjectivity was not art but the spiritual hardship of the search for self. His writings circled obsessively around a vacant identity. The echoes of the pioneers of modernism—of Nietzsche and Joyce, for example—suggest how suddenly a sense of randomness could overtake traditional Catholicism. The precariousness of the self that is the leitmotiv of Lynch's work suggested that Catholic antimodernism had postponed but not avoided the encounter with psychic chaos.[104]

12

From Aquinas to the Age of Aquarius

I

In January 1957, just as his predecessors in the Missouri province had done every year back to the century before, the master of novices at Saint Stanislaus seminary in Florissant on the outskirts of St. Louis sent a review of the past twelve months to the general superior of the Society of Jesus in Rome. By custom the memorandum could not exceed two single-spaced pages. There were seven rubics, labeled in Latin: *cura spiritus et disciplina religiosa* (spiritual care and religious discipline); *cura valetudinis* (health care); *cura vitae intellectualis* (intellectual life), and so on. Under *observatio votorum* (keeping of the vows), the master of novices noted as he had the year before, "The observance of the vows is good. Poverty and chastity are well guarded and obedience flourishes."

There were some concessions to modernity and a laconic recognition of change. Under the Latin subheadings the report was set down in English, and the prose was plain. In 1957, under *administratio temporalis* (the management of temporal things), it was noted that "the chicken yard, orchard, and now the herd have been discontinued." During the same year "the change from coal to oil for the heating of the house . . . provided a more steady heat for the novitiate and this has been much better than former years."[1]

The suburbanization of the environs of the seminary, a once bucolic outpost with the Missouri River close by below bluffs, to the east, and the city and outlying townships toward the south and west, proceeded. In 1959, two years after the chickens and the cattle had been sold, the vineyard and winery were "discontinued."[2] The seminary began to import more of its staples. But "brother barber" continued to cut hair, "brother cook" to prepare meals, and so on.

At the time it was uncertain whether any of these modifications represented significant departures from past practice. The traditional way of formation, like the weather, had its surprises. The ebb and flow of human frailties were as steady as the liturgy and the cycles of the days and the seasons. A few of the fathers drank too much and were "a source of real disedification." There were some difficult personalities and many quirks. A new rector arrived in the late fifties with a fresh array of eccentricities:

> [He] has been singing Requiem Masses as often as he has been offered stipends. The result has been that by far too many of these have been sung recently . . . three, for example, in the one week preceding Christmas, when the interesting and fruitful proper Masses were displaced.[3]

Such troubles were normal fluctuations, signs of growth and decay, in the rounds followed by dozens of men living together. They were familiar perturbations, the stuff of gossip that made for a cozy solidarity. The foibles and frailties of the men built up the lore of the place, the deposit of humanity, under the severe ideals of the written counsels of perfection that were nonetheless apart from the harsh and unforgiving competitiveness outside. The ambience was domestic. Incidental deviations could be absorbed into the schedule and the customs of the community without bringing into question the system of training or the way of life in which it was embedded. Idiosyncrasy had its anointed place, and personal deficiencies were counterbalanced by the aura of accomplishment that emanated from the society's upward spiral, the expansion of its corporate ministries, and the achievements of individual Jesuits. They were the human ingredients of the cycle of sin and forgiveness that helped make the strictness of recrimination and punishment endurable. At home, behind the mythology, Jesuits did not have to be superhuman.

Several changes took place after the war, however, that separated the coming years from earlier times, and they led to irreversible upheavals in the training and the work of Jesuits. During the academic year 1945–46, enrollment in Jesuit colleges and universities throughout the United States stood at less than 35,000. The next year, with the return of the veterans, it more than doubled, to just under 80,000, and before the end of the fifties enrollment had surpassed 100,000. It continued to climb in the sixties as the progeny of the baby boom matriculated.

The increase in applicants to the Society of Jesus was appreciable but less spectacular. The low year had been 1944, when only 191 novices entered. After that, recruitment picked up. A yearly average of 300 men joined the Society of Jesus between 1945 and 1949; for 1950–54 this average grew to 306, and for 1955–58 it reached 344.[4] While the number of Jesuits was increasing, the Catholic population, especially the segment seeking higher education, was growing faster still. This accelerating imbalance would eventually force some Jesuits to wonder whether the model of clerical control of Catholic institutions that underlay the anxiety about religious vocations was feasible or desirable.[5]

Other transformations were subtler, coming in the guise of mundane alterations in the material and technological environment of the seminaries. The manorial remoteness of seminary life—set apart in the countryside, self-contained, with temporal coadjutors, the dutiful brothers, in attendance—could no longer withstand the variety of incursions from the surroundings.[6] The shrinking of this isolation was partly physical. What were once farmlands and woods nestled in rolling hills and pleasant valleys came within reach of subdivisions and shopping centers. Billboards and parking lots came within walking distance of Saint Stanislaus. But the most irresistible penetration was through the airwaves. Even if the seminaries had been placed farther away from the cities they could not have been shielded from the news and norms transmitted by radio and still more seductively by television.[7]

Outside curiosities were not simply temptations that Jesuits could avoid by shrouding themselves in the claustral accoutrements of the seminary. The society's activist tradition closed off the option of withdrawal. Cultural changes with an attractiveness and value of their own could not be ignored by an organization whose mission required engagement with secular realities. The Jesuits responded in several ways, partially at cross-purposes, to expansion and encroachment.

One tactic stressed regimentation of the monastic ideal. Defenses were tightened up. This approach had become obsessive with Zacheus Maher during the war years and it continued, with less conviction and uneven implementation, over the following two decades. Under Pius XII's papacy, the striving after a standardized spirituality that had been codified in Maher's baleful admonitions retained legitimacy; his rules were not taken off the books. In practice, however, the tenor of religious discipline hinged on several unwritten conditions. Enforcement depended on the inclinations of individual rectors. At the same time, burgeoning numbers encouraged impersonalism and a regulatory fetishism in the training process. Independently of the iniquities of the times and of the whims of individuals, the need to process a multitude of recruits encouraged routine and rigidity.[8] But large numbers also enhanced the possibilities of subterfuge. Legalism and evasion thrived on numbers. Paternalistic indulgence and genuine kindness on the part of superiors, and resistance through odd habits on the part of ordinary Jesuits, were systematic adaptations to the regulatory pattern. Jesuits sometimes griped like foot soldiers but did not yet challenge the rationale behind the operation. The scheme of things seemed inviolate. Gradually in the beginning, and then with greater frequency, the constant maneuvering within a thicket of rules drained the system of credibility.[9]

Another response was directed at the outside world, and it was more forward-looking than the first. The energies released after the war spurred Jesuits to compete aggressively with secular institutions. The effort to surpass non-Catholic rivals concentrated on the schools. The objective, one that had been set by Wlodimir Ledochowski in the mid-thirties, was to bring Jesuit colleges and universities up to par with their academic peers. The depression and the war had necessitated a postponement of this campaign. With the end of the war, and with sustained prosperity, the Society of Jesus tried to catch up in the "intellectual apostolate." A related arena in which the Jesuits gave battle was the mass media.

In both settings the goal was to come to grips with changes that were less and less manageable not only because of sheer numbers but also because of the incipient shifts in values that came with mass education and mass society. The insufficiency of resources was not merely a quantitative problem. Jesuits did not retreat from the task of confronting a diffuse secularism. But the terrain was unfamiliar and their equipment—a strenuous disciplined activism—was better suited to the campaigns of the past. Although the challenges they addressed were novel, the policies of control and competition remained in line with the two-pronged strategy of hierarchical discipline and steady assertiveness that had come to be identified as the characteristic style of Counter-Reformation Jesuits.

The decades following the war were notable as well for the neglect of an alternative, one that Jesuits did not talk much about then. This concerned the *vita affectiva*, the life of the heart. Communal solidarity was not lacking. On the contrary, bonding of this sort seems to have been so strong that it was taken for granted. While there were unhappy Jesuits, and those who bridled at authority, these cases could still be handled as symptoms of individual weaknesses. They were not thought to reveal flaws in the organization.

From the fifties to the sixties, however, traditional understandings of what constituted emotional support and psychic satisfaction lost plausibility. The standards by which authority was judged became more demanding, and expectations regarding personal fulfillment shifted upward. American Jesuits were so caught up in the effort to maintain the structure of authority within their organization and to increase the influence of the order that the nurturance of individuals was neglected. At about the same time, the cultural experience that new members brought with them to the society began to diverge from the criteria of sanctity and accomplishment accepted by many of the older men. A proliferation of life-styles sapped a common way of life. By the end of the fifties, the heroism of stoic understatement and the norm of emotional distance began to seem less bearable and even less noble in principle than when images of unblinking courage dominated the ideals of aspiring Jesuits. With the arrival of the sixties, estrangement from traditional ascetic practice and impatience with the demeanor of grim endurance were widespread. Moral compunction came to be identified with both an anti-intellectual pietism and a rigidity of the emotions. This was not simply a rebellion of youthful Jesuits. Some of the older men lost confidence in the traditional ways, and indecisiveness on the part of their mentors further disoriented the younger cohorts.

The heightened importance of emotional expression was brought about by transformations in three areas: by the erosion of the immigrant church, by the organizational growth of the schools, and by tremors in the intellectual foundations of Catholicism. As long as these structural, institutional, and cultural supports had been in place, Jesuits had reasonable confidence in their mission and they derived satisfaction and prestige from their work. The absence of these supports brought activism to a boil and contributed to frustration and burnout as well.

II

In his report for 1958, the novice master at Saint Stanislaus mentioned that "no ill effects seemed to have followed the discontinuing of the chicken-yard, orchard and herd." The innovation permitted greater efficiency in the allocation of the personnel integral to the preservation of the manorial style. "Already a few brothers have been made available for other houses by the change."[10]

But outside influences kept filtering in. The situation was not out of hand and not altogether novel, and it was difficult to tell what fraction of the reports reflected a trend upward in petty violations, in balance with the captiousness and alarmism of superiors with time on their hands and an eye for detecting inevitable departures from the rules. Ripples of misbehavior, though disturbing, did not have the appearance of a tidal wave. Nevertheless, with growing insistence, there emerged a sense of something extraordinarily difficult to handle, whether by reason of the changing character of the young Jesuits or because of bewilderment on the part of their leadership.

Disobedience and boisterousness seemed to be on the rise. There was the matter of the ball scores, which the novices, forbidden to listen to the radio, obtained by joining in league with the brothers:

A certain number of the older men and most of the younger brothers with vows could give a better example of silence. The younger brothers especially keep alive an interest in sports by supplying novices with scores. Silence could be much better observed in the kitchen, infirmary and by those who work in the garden. . . .

There is fidelity to spiritual exercises. Visiting, trips and correspondence are moderate.[11]

The increase in recruits complicated administrative chores and impeded attention to individuals. By 1958 the novice master complained that "the biggest hazard of the year has [been] the large number of novices." He described the situation:

Some years ago that difficulty was taken care of by the division of the Province. . . . [But now] we are back to the difficulty of large numbers. Solidly trained Jesuits simply cannot be produced on a mass production basis. The difficulty is enhanced by the fact that I have been appointed with no previous theoretical or practical training. With little or no time to read, it becomes difficult to do justice to the instruction of the novices. With constant pressure of crowds one's energy is constantly being drained. One has simply to do the best possible under the circumstances. But with the best of will one's best under the circumstances can be quite distant from the ideal of the Society.[12]

Quantity outran quality; this was the most obvious problem. There was also a hint that, regardless of numbers, the times were changing; the novice master was beginning to sense the inadequacy of his professional preparation. He not only documented the burden of handling numerous young Jesuits but also suggested that new conditions, stemming from the sophistication of the period and the prior exposure of the recruits to less authoritarian habits, controverted the long-standing assumption that a mature Jesuit could cope with almost any situation. Apart from these intangible premonitions, the numbers problem was genuinely formidable. The novice master displayed traditional scruples about the dangers of people-processing in the training of spiritual leaders.[13]

Because of the need to staff an expanding network of schools and other programs with Jesuits, however, there was little pressure to cap recruitment. Misgivings about dilution through growth came and went. The tendency was to dismiss such forebodings as defeatist. Jesuits had habitually stretched their resources thin. Some applicants were accepted without close evaluation, only to be dismissed early in the formation process. At first glance, aside from perhaps a greater incidence of mistakes caused by the crush of numbers, the reasons for admission and subsequent departure given in the

report for 1959 appear not to be very different from the factors that might
have been at work twenty or thirty years earlier:

> There is just a slight danger that with the recent division of the prov-
> ince more attention will be paid rather to the quantity than to the
> quality of the candidates. . . . [W]e have released ten of the large
> number who were admitted last year. . . . From these ten men many
> could have been screened by more careful probing into three areas of
> the examiner's questionnaire: 1) the firmness of their determination to
> become Jesuits (some are admitted who have no firmer will than to
> "give it a try") 2) their psychological fitness (we have no testing pro-
> gram in our Province and some are let through with a history of obses-
> sive scruples, fears, anxieties, depression, that sort of thing) 3) a proved
> habit of chastity (some are let through with unbroken habits of solitary
> sin).[14]

The tentativeness of the new men, the frankness of some of them in admitting that they were giving the religious life a try, did not necessarily signal
a diminishing of ardor or piety. But this conditionality stood in contrast to
the sense of permanent commitment and sacredness of the vows that was felt
to be the norm among previous cohorts of recruits. There was zeal but a
touch less certainty. The spirit of organizational adventure was still high,
but there was also an unaccustomed flirtation with personal experiment.
Although the rigidity of the rules guaranteed a commonality of experience,
there was an uneasy sense that younger and older men were reading this
experience in different ways. Soon the annual reports began to show an
awareness of the changing composition of the entrants, together with perplexity about how to deal with the fact that younger Jesuits shared fewer
assumptions and habits with the older generation.

The novice master was able to note in 1959 that "the spirit of the novitiate
is good. One half of the first year men is [sic] of mature college age. They
have shown more self-control than many of the younger high school men
we have been getting." The trend toward an increase in the average age of
the novices was presumably to the good. But the new recruits brought
fashions and expectations from a milieu that seemed strange to the older
men, even to those who had spent years educating boys. The reflex was to
press for greater adherence to protocol:

> The matter of the use of proper titles in addressing Ours has long been
> a vexing problem. We decided to tidy the thinking of the novices on
> the matter with a view to better observance. . . . The distinction be-
> tween formal and informal situations has clarified the whole situation
> so that there is now excellent observance of propriety in the use of

proper titles on the one hand, and great improvement in charity when our novices are at ease among themselves.[15]

The older recruits seem to have been less malleable than the ones who entered in years past fresh out of high school, and this problem was compounded by a shift in mentality among the younger Jesuits themselves. Caustic observation crept into the record of the effluvia of incident and trivia. Thus, on Wednesday, October 9, 1957, the scholastic charged with keeping the diary for the theologians at West Baden wrote:

World Series game #3—the sixth game of the Series. All tied up after six games, but no permission to hear the seventh game tomorrow. A Mr. Oliver Field, of the FBI of the AMA, gave a talk in the auditorium on "How to Recognize Medical Fraud." [Mr.] Robert Viola [S.J.] from Uruguay returned to So. America because this place was "too dead." (Where do *we* go if we do not like it here?)[16]

Tidying up tradition had lost some of its devotional appeal. Dwelling on picayune improprieties had become a ritual in itself. The tipping point had still not been reached, however. While concern was beginning to crop up among superiors themselves about rule-bound distortions in the spirit of the formation process, elaborations on monastic etiquette had not yet rendered authority ridiculous. Among many of the novices the tacit law of being a man by toughing it out still prevailed over the perception that the rules, instead of shaping character, might be childish.

As the sixties opened, signs of change started to converge. Although it had already begun to level off in the late fifties, the influx of candidates continued to be large, and by that time a majority of them entered the society with at least a year or two of college education. Little instabilities appeared; small problems piled up. There was an air of coming and going; superiors arrived and left in the search for Jesuits capable of dealing with the new men. Television increased the sense of agitation. The report for 1960 combined an air of surveillance with helplessness and acerbity at changes that now seemed on the brink of getting out of control. Jesuit *formatores*, the formation directors, were inching toward a recognition that fundamental changes might be at work beneath myriad minor complaints and evasions.

Many of the problems could still be blamed on the usual suspects—the irresponsibility of youth and the customarily difficult personalities. Besides, excoriations of the vileness of the contemporary scene were commonplace in the antimodernist repertoire, and it was standard practice to raise these condemnations to a crescendo in the face of the publicity the media gave to affronts against Catholic tradition. But some unknown portion of the turmoil was undeniably new. Alarmingly, a casual atmosphere seemed to be spreading among the ranks of the senior Jesuits. It was the extent of informality among the younger Jesuits and their failure to grasp how this American style might be at odds with the precepts of Catholicism, together with the indifference and even the receptivity of the older men to the casual manner, that seemed ominous. Thus, in 1960, according to the novice master at Florissant, "Here religious spirit and discipline are not as good as they used to be." He wrote:

> A large number of the younger brothers with vows and most of the fathers give small heed to silence and regularity. . . . The haustus period was singled out as being particularly bad. What will be done remains to be seen. Among the Juniors there is considerable let-down in discipline and during many weeks of the summer and some days of the Christmas period they were without anyone to care for them. They enjoy too much liberty and it is thought that anything is all right provided permission is granted for it. At regular intervals they spend two to three hours at a time watching athletic contests on TV. Two hours a day for three successive days they viewed the Davis Cup tennis. There are baseball games in the summer that run to eleven at night. . . . It is rather a shame after the difficult work of trying to establish in the novitiate a right sense of balance with regard to these things to see young men of promise so soon launched upon a future that will require that they spend several hours a day often during the week following these sports. Coming from a pastoral life where more liberty is taken with regard to these things, our Rector has not a "sense of formation of Ours" and does not easily seek, or take, or follow counsel in these matters. He seems more intent to me on maintaining personal popularity.[17]

Disapproval hardly prevented the novice master from detailing the symptoms of unrest rippling through the religious community. He transmitted dismay—an awareness of difficulties without remedy in sight, cut off from action. Having to deal with large numbers combined with incomprehension between generations to aggravate frustration on both sides. The paradox of a ritual intimacy emanating from the regularity of the traditional system was delicate and difficult to keep up. It presupposed not only a shared iconography but a roughly common meaning to the store of symbols, a greater continuity of culture across generations than obtained during the late fifties and early sixties. Instead of affirming tradition, the recourse to new rules conveyed a sense of desperate improvisation. The reinforcement that came from companionship in group testing was offset to some extent by the escape afforded by the same numbers. Efforts to articulate rules that used to express mostly unspoken values turned out to be counterproductive, with the frustrating effect of discrediting the larger notion of authority. The logistics might be managed, but meaningful ritual could not be invented overnight. The suspicion arose that obsession with spit-and-polish spirituality belied an emptiness of religious strategy.

Priority was supposed to be given in the formation of Jesuits to *cura personalis*—attention to persons as individuals, each with his gifts and peculiarities. Intentions mattered; yet feelings, "emotionalism," were hidden. Collective worship, private confession, and personal quirks expressed these undercurrents obliquely. Even eccentricity had its rituals. The familiar patterns had a soothing predictability. There was a tangibility, almost a clarity to the interiority identified with the old formalism of spiritual development and commonality of purpose that was rarely expressive of individual emotions in direct fashion but that transmitted a sense of easy harmony, like choral voices. By the early sixties, however, this corporate unison began to turn cacophonous.

Ideally, purity of motive was supposed to furnish the basis for judging behavior, apart from the success or failure or the efficiency of actions. Balancing this proto-subjectivity was the emphasis on discipline and corporate solidarity, and on the prudential consideration of "the greater good" that could override the wishes of individuals. The sacrifice of personal ambition for the sake of corporate effectiveness—team playing to the point of self-abnegation—was an irrefutable demonstration of spirituality. Organizational loyalty was more easily observable than interior motivation.

Formal control and individuality were not always at odds. Hierarchical command was conceived of and often experienced in personal terms. Permissions had usually to be obtained on a one-to-one and preferably on a face-to-face basis. Telephones were little used. But institutionalized personalism grew less workable as numbers increased and the surrounding environment became more complex and intrusive. The habit of construing organizational malfunctions chiefly as a reflection of personal failings—insufficient zeal, for example, or lack of judgment—persisted. This had a corollary in redoubled yet oddly half-hearted efforts at surveillance, born as much out of bewilderment as punitiveness, that in turn created incentives for ingenious evasions of, and perplexity at, the halting guidance and the uncertainty it signified.[18]

The costs of a heavily supervised spirituality mounted for guardians and trainees alike. It was difficult for Jesuits, both those who felt threatened by and those who promoted or tolerated the gestating changes, to pin down their significance at the time. The timeworn channels for guiding individuals had silted up, as if tradition were burying itself. A method of training that had built up over so many years and that had managed to handle so many men could not change direction quickly, and in any case it was not clear what new direction it should take.[19]

III

Jesuits who, like the novice master at Florissant, were engaged in formation had second thoughts about the huge numbers of entrants. But almost to a man the truly influential members of the society—the provincials themselves and the presidents of the high schools, colleges, and universities—welcomed this growth. Jesuit institutions had to be staffed primarily by Jesuits. The momentum of the schools was forward; therefore, the more recruits the better. The policy was not to cut back for the sake of a nebulous improvement in quality but to try to make room for a needed increase in size. The response had to be bold to measure up to the influx of recruits and the responsibilities of the society.

In 1957 the New York province finished the construction of a seminary complex on a hill, denuded of trees, overlooking the woods around the town of Shrub Oak on the eastern side of the Hudson Valley, an hour's drive from Fordham University in the Bronx. Title to more than three hundred acres in northern Westchester had been acquired just after the war, and a planning committee had been busy since 1949. In 1952 Cardinal Spellman turned the first shovel of earth. When it began operation in the fall of 1955, with the library still to be completed, the seminary was considered "an enduring memorial to the generosity of our friends and benefactors, and to the wisdom and planning of our Fathers."[20]

The size and decorative appointments of Shrub Oak made it the ecclesiastical equivalent of an ocean liner in the heyday of trans-Atlantic travel. The portico, carved in creamy marble in the Art Deco style of curving modernity, depicted scenes from the life of Ignatius and the exploits of the early Jesuits. The lines of the chapel inside were smooth. The marble altar was inlaid discreetly with gold, and along the columns and the walls were inscribed passages in Latin from the Old and New Testaments. The refectory was immense, capable of holding more than three hundred men at a sitting, with a soaring ceiling that amplified the clatter of dishes and tableware. The buildings might have trespassed from the sleek magnificence of Rockefeller Center into the quiet of exurban New York. The overall effect was bright, soaring, and a little hollow.

Shrub Oak was the Titanic of seminaries. When shut down in 1971, it had become notorious among Jesuits as "the single most disastrous scholasticate that we had in modern times in the United States." In the words of one Jesuit historian, the faculty was composed of

> very intelligent, very capable philosophers who, having taught philosophy for a good number of years in a particular way, had lost touch with the ethos, for want of a better term, of the young scholastic. And then, of course, you get a group of young men in the Society, highly intelligent, told to hone their critical acumen, and you get a self-perpetuating, self-generating, extrapolating disappointment.[21]

Years later, one of the original faculty members who stayed with the seminary until the end took the Shrub Oak experience as a parable of the forces behind the demise of the system of formation and by extension of the Catholic subculture with which it was entwined. In his view, much the same transformation that galvanized the youth movement at the end of this period cut into Shrub Oak, with an anguish intensified by the brittleness of the tradition that collapsed. At the root of the "extrapolating disappointment" undergone by young Jesuits was the attenuation of communal bonds that the immigrant ghettos had forged before the war:

> If I were going to put this as a very personal reflection, and this is very personal, if you want to see what was really going on from the fifties forward, not just in the Society but across the board in Western Europe and the United States, what you had there quite independently of the intellectual movements, what you had was a change of affectivity, which never got satisfactorily thematized at the intellectual level.
> Postwar: I'm talking about 1950, when things really began to get rough. A change in where people lived and how people lived. The vast move to suburbia in the United States, the increase of radio, television, the car. What that produced was a group of younger people who were in a strong sense *deracinato*. Their affectivity to the group had changed.
> The older ones felt intensely at home with their group and felt a great satisfaction in being in the group. And there were these tribal leaders, whose agreements were never written out, but you damn well better keep them. I would trust Frank Hague [the former mayor of Jersey City] far more than I would trust a guy in D.C. I didn't say that I thought Frank Hague was honest. I said I [would] trust him. I knew his loyalties. There was never any bad booze in Jersey City.[22]

It seemed in memory that there had been a time before the fifties, when affection went hand in hand with respect for authority—when local sentiment ruled and with it came allegiance to the sachems of the wards and parishes. These figures, respected for their dealings downtown, were treated with a certain reverence, after the fashion of beneficent, wealthy kin, for their accessibility in the neighborhoods. Although there were some mystery and awe to the politician and the priest who worked the Catholic enclaves, there seemed to be nothing impersonal about their power. Clientelism was a compound of deference to the local bosses and fear of the unexpected beyond the church, school, and precinct. The notables carried maps in their heads of the alleyways and shortcuts through the territories of the secular. They were brokers and patrons. Insecurity about the unknowns of the regions beyond the barrooms and barbershops of the enclave mixed with the prestige of the priest on the inside to reinforce communal solidarity and to offset resentments at the tyrannies of ecclesiastical ways. The priest was "one of ours," a member of the tribe. The church gave comfort and stood as a buffer against the uncontrollable forces of the larger world.[23]

The particulars noted by the philosophy instructor are presented lovingly but with irony; the wit is elegiac. A kind of resignation came from awareness that the destruction could not have been prevented in any case: "You can't argue with an avalanche."[24] The details have become antique and their interrelations almost inexplicable, because the worldview that gave them firsthand meaning has vanished. The recollected configuration floats like the smithereens of a lost world. It was a compendium of gossip and minor mysteries, an endless small town.[25]

> With the old Society there was a very real sense, and there still is, that the Society is not legalistic, the way the army is. With the superior, that's a very interesting relation. The superior is very close to you and very human. But if you're a good Jesuit, you never forget he's the rector. Not in the sense that he's got power, but he has the old sense of *auctoritatis*. He's got the responsibility.
>
> We had the lines we had to follow and everything else. But there was an awful lot of kidding around in the old Society, there was humor. There were shows put on by the theologians, there were all sorts of things. The faculty never came. A whole series of things, they're not in the books anywhere.
>
> Now you've got that change of affectivity toward institutions. When you had that old, if you want to call it that, familial or tribal thing, you felt at ease with that. It didn't bother you that much. It was like the old station master in the Austro-Hungarian empire. He *liked* to go out and salute when the express went through.[26]

The expectations of that small world were modest; it had an aura of reverence around authority. Within this framework battles could be won, troubles could be fixed, and even when they could not be remedied, individual tragedies had meaning. That world also had a place for its absurdities; they were part of its capacity to enchant. In recollection the most poignant of these was the yearning for the perpetuity of a way of life, a psychic stability and material security. The home that immigrants thought they had found at last turned out to be an evanescent adaptation of tradition. The suddenness of its disappearance left many Jesuits lost in a desolate landscape:

> You might realize that this is a little bit ridiculous. But when you moved, as the whole world moved, from that older society to a very changed one . . . people have changed their home, they've changed their style of life, they've changed their physical location toward the older members of the family, you have a very individualistic world. And what you have also, it's become very prosperous, no sense of inbuilt limits on what you can expect. When mothers were bringing up their kids in the thirties, the kid had to learn that he couldn't have ice cream every day. Or that, dear, you're not going to be able to go to college, you've got to realize that you've got to get a job. And people were part of that. Okay, we're working. That whole affectivity and authority.[27]

The vanished hierarchies were close—not usually intimate or expressive but packed, often without privacy and except in church without silence—and it was this closeness in small spaces—the family, the neighborhood, the parish—that gave them a measure of authority. Surveillance was mutual and many satisfactions were collective. The Society of Jesus was in harmony with and a little ahead of the urban enclaves of American Catholicism, coexisting with the wider individualistic democracy. Within that confined place the Jesuits had considerable standing:

> I put a lot on that sense of belonging, which was the way that the older Society worked. Not that America was not upwardly mobile. It was, but it wasn't that upwardly mobile. The sense of the extended family, the sense of what the extended parish community was, the sense of belonging to the Society, with its *esprit de corps* that endured. . . .
>
> Going back, say, forty years ago, how lay people looked on the Society, the most notable group of educated "official Catholics" were the Jesuits. They had a sort of prestige in the Catholic community. Now you've got neurosurgeons, all of this around. You're not going to get the same mystique. I mean, they may like the guy, but they're not as impressed.[28]

The subcultural ponds that supplied recruits to the Society of Jesus began to dry up with the prosperity and technological advances of the postwar era. The effort to stay up-to-date that impelled the Jesuits to compete with secular institutions put contradictory pressures on the traditions of formation at the interior of the society. The grandeur of Shrub Oak froze these contradictions like an ice palace:

> It was a nice shiny new house. But it was not a livable house. Too new, too shiny. I think they had an excellent faculty. I had gotten good training in formation and philosophy at Woodstock. But I don't think the scholastics were ever happy there. It was an institution which, given the whole period and the temper of the times, it was not going to succeed, no matter what you did.[29]

The nearness of Shrub Oak to the metropolitan excitement of the sixties aggravated the sense of being left out. Many of the scholastics shuttled to take graduate courses at Fordham in the Bronx or Saint John's University in Queens and returned at the end of the day to the dormitories perched above a village sprinkled with frame houses erected in the twenties and thirties, vegetable gardens, a gas station, and a grocery store. The setting bred resentments. Quaintness became suddenly insufferable:

> This would have been around '68, when everything was popping out. We had trouble in Shrub Oak. They didn't want to take their examinations. Because the faculty were not close enough or talking to them or anything else. Maybe right, maybe wrong. It's neither here nor there.
>
> Then I had occasion to go through Europe, because I was checking on formation. The same year there had been a blowup in the juniorate and philosophate in Spain, because the faculty "weren't interested in the workers." Then there was a blow-up in the philosophate in France, which was perfectly happy, because the scholastics there thought the noviceship wasn't being run properly. Now the point is these three communities were in no way in contact with each other. There wasn't a cell, or somewhere a guy organizing all of these things. In each case it was the whole atmosphere, '68.[30]

Several ideas separate this retrospective consideration of the prelude to the breakup of the old system from the observations set down by the master of novices at Florissant at the time the process was going on. The Society of Jesus was plainly at a turning point. A confluence of historical changes gathered force after the war. Confirmation that these changes would alter the Society of Jesus, instead of constituting another in a series of challenges against which Jesuits had rallied in the past, came finally with the tumble in recruitment and the departure of full-fledged members and men in training.

The premise of steady if always insufficient expansion and the clarity of struggle between identifiable good and evil no longer held.

A related perception was that the forces at work on the Society of Jesus were structural and spread over advanced industrial settings, rather than predominantly personal and local. The problems of upholding authority and retaining members were not unique to Jesuits. Whatever consolation might come from the awareness of sharing troubles with other organizations, however, was muted by the admission of a lack of mastery over an impersonal fragmentation of the cultural landscape.

Most striking, however, is the importance given to the nexus between traditional morality and emotional allegiance, between "that whole affectivity and authority." The severing of this bond sapped hierarchy of its power. Commitments became more frankly contractual and calculating. Authority that was already under attack on intellectual grounds and at the hands of social activists could not withstand the withdrawal of affective fidelity. In becoming less personal, it was demystified. This provoked a profound upheaval in the traditional ethical code, according to which morality had been inextricable from authority and authority had stood above the ruminations of mere intellect. The moorings of everyday identity had been loosened, and the great arc from custom to conscience was playing itself out.

The retrospective diagnosis of the philosopher is not aimed at problem solving. The reminiscences are evocative. Ideological recriminations are absent, and no providential interpretation is forthcoming. The note is one of mourning, but few regrets appear and no practical lessons are drawn. Specifics and complexity dominate. The finality of historical passage does not generate grand theory but releases instead a tenderness for individuals swept up in a massive transformation, as if they had been made refugees again:

> What people forget is that a whole series of things happened simultaneously. The old Church could have handled the Puerto Rican immigration to New York beautifully. The pastor would have got everything done, the nuns would all have been there, the parents would have been delighted, the little girls would have all worn uniforms. But you couldn't have the nuns, this breakdown, you can't handle *all* these things simultaneously. [31]

The stability of the institutions of immigrant Catholicism was briefer than what memory imputed to them. Similarly, doctrinal changelessness was thinner and less fixed among the Catholic populace generally than it was in the pages of catechisms that parochial school children were obliged to store up by rote. Even so, the scale of social interaction and expectations among

Catholics seemed smaller before midcentury. It was not only the fugitive nature but the comparative delicacy of the vanished world, the drying up of a live membrane over an organism in miniature, that caused a pang. This accounts for the afterglow of affection surrounding the small structures of authority and the quotidian hierarchies, as well as for the alarm about the fate of the family in modern times:

> The older people came from much more stable families, rock-solid. Now from the fifties on you get lots of families which were good families, but they were not as stable. They had moved out and were upwardly mobile. The father was working hard, he's pushing very hard, maybe he's drinking a little bit too much. But there wasn't the whole sense of support. The individual family and their links to the neighbors are much less stable. They're much further from the grandparents or if the grandparents do come out they're sort of guests of the parish. Everything is new, see. [32]

The weakening of hereditary supports, crystallized in the family that flourished surrounded by the parishes and dioceses, called forth the need for alternative sources of emotional sustenance. Two decades after the turning point, the philosophy instructor stressed the search for affectivity in the lives of Jesuits. In earlier times affection was expressed through collective, hierarchical means, transmuted in ritual and in predictable obedience to a personal authority. The recollection was that authority and emotional commitment went together. The formalism was "organic," patterned and womb-like. The effect was hypnotic. Understanding was secondary to acceptance and the sense of belonging.

Behind these ties of sentiment lay a reasonable exchange of services and a consensual, though quite temporary, social ordering. The transaction seemed to be humane and in balance. For a few years, there was a match between the aspirations of large portions of the Catholic subculture and the talents and dedication of the Jesuits. The Jesuits furnished welcome services, and in exchange they were given respect and support. They could realistically nourish the feeling that their skills and their effort made a difference. They stood at the top of a hierarchical subculture that represented the way society as a whole was meant to be. The realism of the arrangement in the abstract was less important than the satisfactions that came from meaningful work in a world with boundaries and relatively clear tasks.

The strategy was responsive to the needs of the mobile elements among immigrant and second-generation Catholics. The education the Jesuits provided also helped to undermine the parochialism of this subculture. During the years after the war, the system took on some of the rigidity and complacency of a success story wrought out of sacrifice. The enclave eroded from within, in part through the restlessness of Jesuits themselves and by reason of a skepticism encouraged by their educational methods. The disintegration of the old certainties was speeded by forces from the outside as well, such as the media. The lavish ceremonials lost their hold, and the sheltering hierarchies turned burdensome.

IV

Shrub Oak was to be a magisterial outgrowth of the Jesuit legacy of toughened spirituality and organizational wisdom. But by the time the cornerstone was laid in the late fifties the seminary expressed an anachronistic triumphalism more than the solidarity of a homogeneous community.

The drama of Shrub Oak brought to a pitch the tension between generations of Jesuits and, within individual Jesuits, the stress of trying to integrate what came to seem barely compatible goals. Antagonism between younger and older Jesuits was accompanied by half-articulated personal conflicts and interior struggles. Private confusion and public polarization sometimes mitigated and sometimes aggravated one another. Confrontation did not always clarify the issues at stake; some of the men were shouting down their own doubts and anxieties.

Jesuits understood that a crucial task for them in the decades following the war was to expand and somehow to modernize their institutions. This meant investing further in their schools.[33] The challenge was one of updating the society's corporate works. The converse of this set of problems was less obvious. It entailed not modernization in the sense of magnifying corporate identity and clout but the appropriation of tradition on the part of incoming cohorts of Jesuits. How were the younger men to make this tradition their own?

The end of the fifties coincided with the last years of the papacy of Pius XII. It also corresponded to an American Catholic version of a closing of the frontier. The physical infrastructure of American Catholicism was reaching saturation. Furthermore, after half a century of antimodernist polishing and tightening, the intellectual framework seemed all but complete. It wheezed and creaked but it was burnished to a brilliant finish. This created a double bind, one side of which was historical and the other more purely generational. The Society of Jesus had first to negotiate its way through the hazards of updating the culture of the enclaves without calling down the wrath of strict traditionalists. This maneuvering toward a viable medium affected older as well as younger cohorts of Jesuits, and had been something of a constant during the adventurous periods of the order's history. The other facet of the problem was more specific to the younger men. It entailed the difficulty of establishing an identity within a tradition that purported to have reached self-containment and stability.

The terms of the conundrum made for confusion. There was some split in beliefs along generational lines, with regard to sexuality and the expression of affect, for example. But there was also considerable agreement on doctrinal matters among younger and older Jesuits. This partial agreement did not engender continuity, however. Older Jesuits were used to being kept busy building and patching the society's physical works and ministering to the flock; their accomplishments made chores like these less challenging for the younger men. In addition, the bringing to perfection of a comprehensive Thomism that occupied the minds of Jesuits in the nineteen-twenties, -thirties, and -forties had by the late fifties lost much of its curiosity value for younger Jesuits. They had come to an institutional and a logical impasse. What was left to them was transmission rather than creativity. Rebellion and the rhetoric of revolution became appealing alternatives. These options baffled older Jesuits almost completely.

The experience of one Jesuit professor of philosophy who taught at West Baden in the late fifties and early sixties is representative of the trials of the more acute of the older men. He had come of age intellectually in the late 1930s. The codification of canon law decreed in 1918 laid down the obligation that philosophy be taught "according to the principles and doctrine of St. Thomas," "the angelic doctor."[34] From the perspective of a later generation the result was to thicken the antimodernist climate, foreclosing intellectual development. But for some bright Jesuits at the time, the injunction provided a chance to flesh out important answers and, so they believed, to raise significant questions. The system was closed but seemingly capacious, so that restrictions did not seem intrusive. The excitement lay in viewing it more as a method to be followed than as a compendium of pre-established truths.[35] The politics of organizational centralization that shaped the intellectual agenda was scarcely noticeable to youthful idealists. The quarter-century from the thirties to the fifties was

> . . . the high tide of the Thomistic revival. There was a requirement that all teachers in the seminaries, the scholastic seminaries, would be taught in Rome. So the professors went to Rome, and the Gregorian [University] had switched over from a broad Suaresianism to a neo-Thomism dominated by the French.
>
> The starting point, I guess—this was around the late twenties, '28, '29, something like that, well, it might have been earlier than that, as a result of the new code—was a list of 24 theses. Somebody published

a book saying this is the authentic doctrine of St. Thomas. They pretty well followed a strict Aristotelian-Thomistic line.[36]

In practice, regardless of the initial enthusiasm for reinvigorating the corpus of received truths, scholarship was understood as the embellishment of eternal verities. Thomism became "a fixed, infrangible plenum."[37] The method had only an intermittent capacity for connecting up with reality or indeed with other intellectual systems. The air of counting angels on the head of a pin became strong:

> I don't know how familiar you are with things like [the debate over] the real distinction of essence and existence. Well, at St. Louis, for instance, Fr. Henri Renard was one of the people who came back from teaching in Rome and was strong for the new Thomistic purity, as against some of the others [Suaresians] who were teaching at the time.[38]
> There were movements within Thomism. The "real distinction" would certainly be one controversy. The "principle of individuation by matter signified by quantity" would be another, and the "complete application of act and potency" as dividing all reality, and things of this sort. It was a pretty abstract thing, Thomism. The variations with Suaresianism from one view of it were very minor; from another view they were profound. Okay?[39]

Efforts to refine Thomism irritated conservatives and frustrated the adventurous. Skirmishing within the scholastic framework alarmed reactionaries. Some fairly orthodox theologians, including a few "transcendental Thomists," were put under a cloud.[40] Among the student Jesuits, however, a common reaction to the diet of scholasticism was not only a growing impatience with the medieval style of philosophizing and incomprehension of its content but an incipient anti-intellectualism. The instructor, who had begun teaching at West Baden in 1951, noticed the critical atmosphere when he returned from a tour of Europe at the end of the decade:

> My class in the history of philosophy, I think it was, followed a course in either metaphysics or natural theology. The teacher had actually gotten his doctorate at Fordham but he had done his theological studies at the Gregorian. He was an enthusiastic Thomist. I remember one year, when I came into class following his class—probably would have been '57—the class was very agitated. Previously this man had been one of the leading teachers in the faculty, and everybody liked his class. I remember one student asking me, halfway through the class he stuck up his hand, without any reference to what I was doing at all in the class. He said, "Do you think the church will ever change on St.

Thomas?" And I said, "Well." I weaseled out of it. I think I remember saying, "Would you want it to change?" and let it go at that. And I think I did say I didn't see any future in it [changing from Thomism].

Well, there was a lot of restiveness among the scholastics, especially against philosophy. It hadn't been the case before that, to my knowledge. The change between when I went on sabbatical and when I came back was 100 per cent, 300 per cent, something like that. When I had been there before, there was a good deal of enthusiasm about the place, its studies, everything else. When I came back there was restiveness all over the place.[41]

The "perennial philosophy" had turned problematic. Yet the Jesuit instructor took note of a more puzzling phenomenon. Why did criticism of Thomism build up so quickly when it did, in the late fifties, rather than earlier? If the approved philosophy propagated time-transcendent verities, what was it, not about these truths, but about the times or the new generation of Jesuits that caused them radically to question what had not seriously been doubted before?

You know the Spanish philosopher, Ortega y Gasset, *Revolt of the Masses?* I think someplace in there he talks about the spirit of a generation. That's the only thing I've been able to figure. You don't know where it comes from. You ride it out, but you don't know when it's going to go. During those four years, '57 to '61, this restiveness was all across the country. And by the time of '61, they were having workshops at St. Mary's, at Weston, at Woodstock, at Alma on, well, there was Vatican II and the Church today and the Society and so on and so forth.[42]

The philosopher saw the change as a puzzle in the history of ideas. His best guess as to the origins of the resistance to the received wisdom was that they were to be found in the temper of the times. The source of the transformation was elusive. A new era was born, as it were, by cultural parthenogenesis. The problem lay not with the conceptual scaffolding of scholasticism, for to admit that would be to imply the not-so-timeless nature of its methods and its teachings, but with the intellectual distemper of the age and the minds that were befuddled by it.

This reconstruction of events is equitably Platonic. It was not a question of imputing bad will to individuals any more than it was of faulting doctrine. The shift toward an adversarial mood englobed an entire generation:[43]

Bernie Wernert, he was master of novices in Detroit. He was at Colombiere, and he had been there for a number of years. A dozen years or so, something like that. And I remember his identifying a year, or a time, when the incoming class was just different from the class before. Challenging what was being done. Not only philosophy. At that time they weren't doing philosophy in that part of the training, the novitiate. It was just restlessness all over. Nineteen fifty-seven or so, it would be about then.[44]

The shift was painful for Jesuits of an earlier generation, like the philosopher, in charge of training new cohorts. Boredom with the traditional curriculum spread. Some young Jesuits tired of questioning specific pieces of official doctrine and began searching for alternative total systems. What the faculty did or said, or failed to do or say, no longer seemed to matter much. Many were sympathetic or helpful, but very few of them could lead.

The memories of this period retained by Jesuits and ex-Jesuits are not uniformly hostile or bitter. Oppression was not monstrous. Some of those who left, as well as those who stayed, speak with affection of instructors and superiors who tried to understand the changes, with an air of sympathy for people trying to find a way out of "the troubles" that were beyond their grasp. Control was slipping, and so was the sense of creativity.

No correlation emerged between the policies adopted by superiors and the incidence of departures. At Weston, the theologate of the New England province in the foothills of the Berkshires, separate libraries were maintained: one for the student Jesuits and the other, holding some publications restricted because of their potential for precipitating controversy, for the use of the faculty. It was an ordeal for the scholastics to obtain access to the forbidden literature. "Scandal" was prevented. As a result most of the Jesuits there were innocent of the work of their innovative colleagues, like Teilhard de Chardin. Roughly the same prohibitions prevailed in the Missouri province. At West Baden, however, many books and periodicals were spread around in small rooms that were difficult to police, and the rector there during the swing years of the late fifties and early sixties was a progressive who sought to clear away restrictions that perpetuated the unreality of the encapsulated environment.[45]

It was symptomatic of the period that old ways, normal for a time, supposedly permanent, came suddenly to seem bizarre in juxtaposition with the new. Among younger Jesuits boredom, incomprehension, and resentment grew. The West Baden theologians' diarist recorded the events of the week from October 19 through October 26, 1957, with an impatience cutting through the usual staccato:

> Retreat of Fr. J. Courtney Murray, S.J., of Church-State fame. He gave the community a thoroughly speculative retreat with very little down-to-earth motivation. Got a list of retreat confessors from the phil[osophers'] beadle. Posted spiritual bouquet sign about the fifth day.

On the evening of the last day I gathered the mail and with the help of the sub had it sorted in half an hour . . . [On Sunday, October 27] a house movie, "Solid Gold Cadillac," was shown at 7 P.M. . . . At 9 A.M. Fr. Murray gave a lecture to the stalwarts gathered in the auditorium on Church and State.[46]

What had once seemed like a slow, barely rippled river was now swift-moving and less predictable. The record of the last days of August 1959, reflects the eddying:

Aug. 16. [Fr.] Dorta-Duque blew in from Cuba, went to high school with Fidel Castro himself but wears no beard. "Janet Blair" show (The Chevy Show) was good entertainment. Full house as usual.

Aug. 20. Last day of clergy retreat. THE GREAT FATHER [Bernard] LONERGAN FROM THE GREGORIAN UNIVERSITY (teaches *de verbo* and *de trinitate* there) delivered a two-hour lecture plus discussion on the subject "THEOLOGY AND HISTORY" in Canisius Hall. Well-attended. Some were enthralled, some mystified, others fell asleep. I liked it.

Aug. 21–22. Nothing special.

August 23. Sunday. Father Coppens, Dean of the Theological Faculty of the University of Louvain, and Professor of Scripture (Old Testament with a specialty in "Messianism") delivered an interesting lecture in the auditorium at 10:30 am on the subject "The Scripture and Dogma Conflict in Theology," in rather heavily accented English. Fr. Hardon raised a question about "ipisissima verba" in his usual elusive phrasing. It took Canon Coppens several minutes to figure out the drift of the question, then he neatly sidestepped into a prudent, ambiguous position.[47]

Nearly a quarter of a century later one Jesuit who rose in the administration of the order recalled the clash between established mores and changing ideas at West Baden:

It was the long black line, so to say, everybody going to the dining room and looking, well. . . . We'd sit typically at dinner, about 175 people. You had three years of philosophers, four years of theologians, a large faculty, a group of brothers, some older men that were retired there. It was a big, huge house. It was just unimaginably big, with one superior. It was the classic sort of old-style seminary in Jesuit experience. So that was the environment in those years.

But then all these currents were coming in. . . . [Back in the novitiate] I'd been slipped books by this Latin teacher that we had who had done a lot of work, his own doctorate, in structural linguistics. He would feed me stuff. Well, that was already relativizing. I was already in the late fifties or mid-fifties, '57, '58, reading this stuff and feeling that sort of vision of things was correct, that [the other] just wasn't so. If cultures and languages were really different, then we had to live with that kind of world.[48]

Thomism was still taught but it was taken less seriously. As the substance emptied out of the old curriculum, a talented instructor might stir excitement and catch the attention of the scholastics with a reversion to the give-and-take of the Socratic method:

Mike Montague, I think, became a sort of focal figure in some ways. The older men, you can talk to people at Loyola [University in Chicago] and you will discover some very powerful negative feelings about Montague as somebody who in many ways they distrusted. He was involved all his priestly career with the formation of Jesuits. Well, for him, the question was much more important than the answer, and that was a viewpoint that I thought was right on target. "So, tell me what the question is. What's the problem before we get. . . ?" That was one of the difficulties with the whole manual scholastic approach, you got all these answers and you didn't know why you were getting the answers. We were in a mood to get the questions out on the table and they were going to be very interesting.[49]

This pedogogy was a promising departure from the adversarial mode of neoscholasticism, but the method did not provide a new world view. The intellectual substance of official Catholicism had begun to evaporate. Soon the scholastics had little in the way of doctrine to make their own or against which they might prove themselves.

The struggle with dogma started out as a battle largely along generational lines. The testing involved some disputation over doctrinal issues, but it was also, perhaps predominantly, a reflection of younger Jesuits' need to take possession of tradition. The legacy could not simply be handed down. By the end of the fifties the deposit of faith, as expressed in neo-Thomism, suffered from a surfeit of stability. The outcome of debate was certain, and the game lost interest. It provoked an anger outside the rules. The claim of perfection engendered a perverse logic. It was uplifting but not liberating. The dynamics of cultural transmission pitted new Jesuits against "the venerable fathers," practically regardless of their views.[50]

With the approach of Vatican II, philosophical and theological pluralism moved closer to acceptability. A corollary of this shift was that scholasticism, whatever else it was, could no longer claim to be a complete, authoritative system. Now relativism affected both older and younger Jesuits. During the period from just before the council through sessions that ran over the course of three years, when a new worldview was being ratified, the problem changed from one of psychological resistance to a finished body of knowledge to one of an intellectual emptying out that affected senior and junior Jesuits alike. For a time there was almost no authority left that could be challenged.

The rupture in the inherited ethos of Catholicism was not a matter of ideas only. While some Jesuits sought new intellectual paradigms and argued among themselves about alternative ideologies, others rejected intellectualism entirely. They became rebels with a cause, but practically without ideas. These men resented not only the social irrelevance but also the emotional detachment they perceived in the Jesuit manner. Cerebral flair was still prized above other skills in the order, even though hierarchical procedures had lost favor. "We had a big split," noted the administrator,

> which had all sorts of ramifications that I was oblivious to, between
> the hardnose intellectuals and the warm puppies, folks that were more
> into personal relationships. I suspect a number of folks were discover-
> ing sexuality, though not I think in any kind of problematic way. It
> was just that they were aware that there was more than just studying
> languages. This split that developed had also, I think, a lot to do with
> the group that was very bright. I suspect that what was really happen-
> ing is what they'll talk about in contemporary formation about being in
> touch with your feelings and that sort of thing. That little door was
> just starting to open because it was certainly nothing we ever talked
> about in novitiate. You were not encouraged to be in touch with your
> emotions, feelings. That was part of the old Catholic culture, that that
> stuff could only be bad. And I think that some of our professors were
> aware that this sort of vision of life, the heavy intellectual thing, was
> just too narrow and too problematic, and of course it was.[51]

The other avenue away from scholastic aridity, besides emotional exploration, was social conscience and political action. With the virtual disintegration of the Thomistic synthesis, which fell in on itself before it could be
properly attacked, the task of conceptual renovation had lost its antipode,
and Jesuit intellectuals floundered on shapeless terrain. By comparison,
social activism targeted antagonists in and outside the society. The contrast
focused and lent passion and ideological fervor to the social crusades that
attracted younger Jesuits. Furthermore, social issues and psychosexual concerns gained priority because they were both experiential. The intellectual
scene was more rarefied, its satisfactions less tangible. Analytically inclined
Jesuits lost influence to the advocates of personalism and activist pragma-

tism. They tended to look on both movements as self-indulgent or, in the case of the older men, they suddenly felt left behind:

> The folks that were rather viciously labeled warm puppies, it isn't that any of these people were dumb but they were, insofar as they were able to get interested in philosophy, they saw philosophy as opening up personal realities for them, and they would have been more attracted to some of the soft existentialists. Kierkegaard would be one. Artistic, esthetic. The people who were most strongly in the hard-nose intellectualistic camp really disliked that sort of stuff, and I think that personally for a number of them at that stage of their development, they found it very threatening. They were not into the interior, they were not into feeling emotion, that was stuff that was scary. They . . . we didn't know what to do with it.[52]

On the whole the three currents—the intellectual, the expressive, and the activist—went their separate ways. But there was probably more interchange and swings between the latter two, by way of a shared anti-intellectualism, than between either of these and the *pensadores*. Expressive and social concerns seemed more immediate. The life of the mind was ethereal and remote, like the pale classical heaven of scholastic cosmology.[53]

The social and psychosexual rebels combined idealism with action-oriented pleadings. Although they were not devoid of ideas, it was impossible to treat the movement of activists and personalists in purely conceptual terms as the emergence of a new vision out of the husk of old thinking. It could also be traced to the unraveling of the institutions of the inherited social order. This was evident to some of the *formatores*. These men were selected primarily for their piety and interpersonal acumen rather than for intellectual brilliance, and they were not given to abstractions:

> I was in charge of all admissions, all the testing for the Society [in province X] and so on. That's when I had to make a study of psychological testing to find out what if any weight I should give to that. I went through the literature, and my conclusion was that they were testing in terms of what they would call job satisfaction and competence and perseverance. A great deal of this had been done for the Protestant ministry and the Jewish rabbinate. What came up almost accidentally, as it were, the one common factor for perseverance and even effectiveness, was family background, stable family, encouraging family—just at about the time we were getting candidates in some numbers from broken families.[54]

As with the philosophy instructor who pointed toward the temper of the times, the explanatory focus was on the new generation of Jesuits rather than on flaws in a body of doctrine with pretensions to immutability. But the formation director was more concrete, singling out historical changes in family patterns that he felt lay beneath the atmospherics of rebellion. As he saw it, there was a more or less direct link between changes in society's affective institutions, mainly the family, and the expectations that men brought to religious life:

> Even with the best of the novices, there was not a real belief any more in lifetime commitment. Just as people began to feel this way in the area of marriage, I think new men coming in at this time had been infected by that distrust of the whole idea of lifelong commitment. [55]

The hesitancy of the scholastics corresponded to the rising volatility in marriage and family life. The actual causal mechanisms, however, were obscure and circuitous. The *formator* remained silent about the possibly independent impact of the collapse of philosophical certainty on the demise of religious commitment. Nor did he dwell on the possibility that recruits to the religious life might carry as great a passion for the absolute as their predecessors had, even if their hopes of achieving fulfillment were lower and their prospects for unhappiness therefore greater.

Nevertheless, as he sifted through his experience with Jesuits in training, the *formator* recognized that more than a cultural miasma or a broad debilitation of the family might be behind the turnover in personnel. New norms and habits of personal interaction were generated by the technology of postwar mass society. The old ways of sociability and of acculturation into adulthood were coming undone:

> Something happened up at the juniorate before some people would say the troubles started, when we had young men coming in questioning authority, questioning obedience, having a hard time relating to adults. We [the *formator* and an assistant] let it be known that every night, far from bothering us, any one of our students could simply drop around, if he just wanted to talk, that's all, shut-ins the way we were, like in a submarine life, we had no defenses.
>
> Thursday was the day off and you'd have boat rides up the Hudson and all that kind of thing. I had decided that almost every Thursday I had to sit down and go do some work. The juniors would come in and say, "Father, please come tonight." "It's not because I don't want to," I said, "you know that." "Oh yeah, unless you come, the day won't be a success."
>
> It was almost as though they were not relating to one another. It was the way a host would have to be to bring strangers together. I couldn't conceive of myself, at their age, as giving a damn whether a faculty

member came out on holiday or not. We might have been happy to have him, but we didn't need him one iota.[56]

The lateral ties, in the form of gangs and territorial clubs and cliques, fostered by the old neighborhoods had withered. Vertical ties between generations had also weakened. The coordinates of interaction were mutable and confused. Communal bonds and personal hierarchies were fractured. The story unfolds into a tale of youthful atomization that spread through the novitiates, then into the later stages of training:

> Whenever somebody down at Shrub Oak in philosophy began to run into problems with his vocation, one of the first things I'd say to him [was] "Have you shared this with your best friend?" At least with your best friend. Maybe nobody else; you don't go spreading it around to everybody but maybe with a best friend or two best friends. Because I know in my own time, my friends when I was going through would often share a problem like that. I would get a blank look, and I would finally say, "Who *is* your best friend?" And in a dismaying number of cases they couldn't put their finger on it.[57]

The solidarity that the formation director expected of successive cohorts of Jesuit recruits dwindled, he perceived, after the war. It was from undercurrents of psychological deprivation and loneliness that much of the radicalism and generational defiance of the sixties eventually surfaced. The common identity of the young was insecure. They had constantly to work at sharing in order to overcome their solitariness; it did not come spontaneously or in the same way the *formator* remembered his growing up:

> I related it to the first TV generation—in the beginning, these passive kids sitting in front of sets instead of relating very early to kids. Like I remember our neighborhood when I was growing up. We had the big family, the big backyard. Every night you were out there with your friends, softball game or God knows what other games we played, stickball, dozens of them, dozens of them! You were relating a mile a minute, and I had best friends, you'd stay over at his house, he'd stay over at yours. Whereas [later] the common coin of conversation, and I couldn't join in at all, was TV programs. This was the common coin. Almost as though they couldn't communicate except through what they shared originally sitting all by oneself.[58]

For many younger Jesuits, then, beneath the agitation that was soon to be directed against those in positions of authority, there existed a prehistory of socialization in a mass culture that had begun to invade the zone once occupied by families and peers. The fury vented against older Jesuits represented in some measure a clamoring for paternal attention and an outcry against depersonalization.[59]

Although the ironies of the abandoned system did not usually come in for extended scrutiny, there is a countervailing tendency to stop short of full-blown romanticization from the vantage point of the present. When they consider the dark side of the past, older Jesuits favor a combination of self-mockery and ambivalence. Hardship had meaning then, and suffering had recompense:

> It's always been an anomaly to me that people who constantly complained about their formation years criticized and resented the next generation. I don't know whether it was, "We suffered, you ought to suffer, too." But I think there was a sort of a sense of the value of the discipline of the time. Even if people complained about the discipline of philosophy and of theology and classes and so on, there was a certain pride in the leadership the Jesuit faculty had. And also, in the end, a sense of the value of the program itself.[60]

A generation after the conditions forcing change came to a head, Jesuits gained a humanity that was recessive in the heroics of the triumphalist era, and some of those who were young at the time remember the experience as a passage out of innocence toward an ambiguous maturity. The memories of both the dark and the bright sides are often tinged with regret. "It was as if we were the last ones to study alchemy," one Jesuit noted.[61] Only rarely is the transformation depicted as a straight flight from oppression to freedom.

In recalling the first inklings of change, one former Jesuit, who finished the course of training only to leave just before ordination, began to reconstruct the complexity of growing up in terms that confound the imagery of right versus left. Instead, the movement was from the quasi-idyllic community of childhood to the search for a cause, and then to a questioning of the utility of being a Jesuit:

> Marty [the novice master] allowed us to play basketball, which they didn't have in the old days because that would be [physical] contact. And classical music was allowed [on] Sunday afternoons. And that would have been frowned upon, too. Although you can't say a Jesuit has an animus against the arts by any means, there was a sense that it smacked too much of the esthete rather than rigorous training.[62]

The reinforcement and manipulation of sexuality and sexual identity were not subtle but they were mostly unspoken. This unmistakable indirection was characteristic of the times. It was expression, not discipline, that was aberrant. The rigors of formation were not overwhelming, however, in part because so many others faced the same demands. There was consolation in numbers. Camaraderie balanced introspection:

> The only paper I read in my two year novitiate was excerpts from the time when Pope Pius XII died [1958]. And that was an allowance. There was no radio, certainly no television. There was nothing really. You read spiritual books or histories of the Society.
>
> I should add immediately that I found none of that difficult or stifling. The spiritual exercises of St. Ignatius, that's interesting in itself. And books on asceticism and histories of the Jesuits I found fascinating. So I liked the structure of it, and I never found it dull or boring. I think other people did.
>
> There was always a lot of criticism in the novitiate and the formation of cliques, inevitably. You had all of these sort of intense little rivalries and things that you'd find in any other place. And people sort of finding out who they were, that sort of thing. I imagine it'd be the same for people in a bad platoon of the Marines; even the badness of it created a solidarity. It was probably the unloosening of that more than the continuation of it that is related to upheaval. Finally, I think, a basic conservative insight into human relations fits. The problem is, of course, how you transcend that and move it along at the same time.[63]

Solidarity sprung from a mixture of common testing and a positive idealism about contributing to a better world, from youthful optimism and from pride in belonging to a select group.

> There was that feeling. You go in a line, and there's about 70 people, you did feel part of a unitary vision, of people you knew who were gifted, were not crazy, and were just good decent people. As opposed to the culture, where you are watching what would happen so that you don't lose your edge. Here for the first time in your life you're with people where what helped you helped them, what helped them helped you.[64]

The community tried to make up in ritual and in emotive signposts what it lacked in personal expression. The same symbolic encounters were present for everyone, and it was through these recurrent passages that individuals entered into a life with a large share of collective significance and silent communication. The regularity of the religious life in particular engendered a feeling of security, which in turn encouraged contemplation that kept a link to the group and at the same time strived to transcend intimacy. Privacy was respected, yet identity was not a function of ideas nor quite a reflection of individual accomplishment but of a place in the achievements of the collectivity. The architecture of community held firm. Identity was tied strongly to assigned roles and a sense of familial belonging:

> It's almost tactile. As you ask me and I reflect back, I remember one night going to litanies. You went to litanies at nine, so you left the asetory [a study hall in which each scholastic had a desk and a chair] at five to nine. This fall night I guess it was a particularly quiet mood for myself, just walking in this long line of people, feeling a sense of solidarity, security. That life *wasn't* a contest, that life *was* a cooperation. It couldn't be sentimentalized, because you couldn't get too close to anyone.[65]

The structures in the wider environment that supported this version of the Jesuit way of life crumbled in the late fifties. The sense of ritual community and confident leadership could not survive outside the parochialism that Jesuits found increasingly limiting and that was disappearing anyway. Jesuits were not immune to the attractions of a fast-moving society, and they felt under an obligation to understand it and somehow to become part of it. The pull of the secular city was powerful. Before the countercultural movements of the middle and late sixties that absorbed the Catholic left, the ambiguous mixture of a yearning for assimilation and an idealism on the lookout for a cause were already propelling the Catholic subculture beyond its safe haven:[66]

> The Jesuits were particularly vulnerable because around that time there was the feeling that American culture was superior to American Catholicism. After all, what made Kennedy admirable was not his Catholic traits but his American traits. He was pragmatic, he was young, he was vigorous, he had a beautiful wife, he had great-looking children, and America seemed to be a great saga. And Catholicism . . . I think the experience of American culture in that period did more to affect the sensibilities of the American Catholic than all of the Protestant propaganda for a century before. The Society and the church were being judged by American culture and failing sadly.
>
> You looked around . . . I remember at Shrub Oak people were saying . . . you had the freedom marches, you have the civil rights movement, and here we are studying transcendental philosophy. It was the *culture.* It was part of the innocence of American culture, a supposed vitality. I mean, you no longer felt a superior moral person to be a Jesuit.[67]

V

The first sign of trouble for the Jesuits during the years following the war came as an ironic by-product of success, and it was defined almost exclusively in quantitative terms. Greater numbers of Jesuits were needed to staff and run an expanding number of Jesuit operations. Some Jesuits began to express concern about the overload on the classic system of training. Their worries were traditional. At the heart of the system, after all, there was supposed to be a stress on the fundamental interiority and personalism of the religious life. Vocations could not be mass-produced. In their old-fashioned way the novice masters, spiritual fathers, and other personnel involved with formation expressed misgivings that would later seem symptomatic of an excessive subjectivity.

During the 1950s Jesuits also became increasingly alert to the qualitative defects of the formation process. About a decade after new methods of biblical criticism had been legitimized, and well into the time of liturgical revival, tentative efforts were made to replace a mechanical Thomism with a more existential, less schematic scholasticism.[68] The attempts at philosophical renewal gave cautious recognition to intellectual pluralism. This project took up the energies of some Jesuits in their late thirties, forties, and fifties, but it did not stir comparable interest among Jesuits in training. Still, as a result of concern over the potentially alienating consequences of assembly-line training and awareness of the intellectual stagnation of the Thomistic synthesis, a transitional strategy began to take shape among some Jesuits of the postwar generation. Because of this shift, battle lines did not form exclusively around a strict generational divide, between hidebound reaction and youthful liberalism.

Despite this adjustment, however, the changes of the sixties devastated the Society of Jesus. Interacting with the quantitative and qualitative difficulties were exogenous and internal forces that disrupted the traditional order. The suburbanization of the Catholic immigrant community not only deprived the society of much of its demographic backup; the collapse of this protective covering also laid bare the need for affective sustenance. Questions of sexuality and of the attainment of male leadership that had previously been codified in the formal garden of ritual and in the satisfactions of the enclave were thrust into the open and made objects of self-conscious scrutiny.

The world that vanished was not entirely a lost Atlantis. Its existence was real and also mythified. It depended on communal fabrication as well as on the servicing of genuine needs. It was, or felt like it was, all of a piece. It was a miasma of particularisms overlaid with a rationality that gave the appearance of a system that was at least compatible with modernity. "Neoscho-

lasticism," as one historian has put it, "constituted the technical philosophical system that could be called upon to explain, justify, and elaborate
the interlinked but technically informal set of beliefs Catholics held concerning the nature of reality, the meaning of human existence, and the
implications of these beliefs for personal morality, social thought, public
policy, and so on."[69]

Multiple transformations were underway, and their logic was tangled. On
the one hand, younger Jesuits had to define themselves relative to a tradition
that had been handed over to them as the culmination of the wisdom of
their predecessors. Their desire to appropriate an impeccable legacy helps
explain the seemingly perverse obstinacy of the younger men in the face of
the tinkering instigated by the generation of Jesuits ahead of them. "What
happens," one Jesuit asked in retrospect, mixing dismay with irony, "when
your parents become your friends?"[70]

The sudden collapse of the Thomistic worldview added to the anguish of
the new generation of Jesuits by depriving them of the target of their alienation, and it raised the suspicion that the rationale of Catholicism was
conjured up like smoke and mirrors around a power structure that no longer
met social needs and the demands of human sentiment. Hierarchy and
authority had been surrogates for a changelessness that, Jesuits now were
told, was the product of historical circumstance. There was a hint of defeat
in a dubious cause. Some Jesuits turned away from intellectual pursuits
altogether.

At the same time as intergenerational dynamics reduced the possibility of
gradualism and rational response, they revealed the bases of objective conflicts. Jesuits did not simply project their disillusion on causes that were easy
targets for deeper frustrations. The working through of affective and sexual
alternatives became a focus of exploration in the religious life of the sixties.
So did engagement with social and political radicalism.

The heart of the quandary was how to change—a process now seen as
inevitable—without losing identity. In the thirties, when they began to
consider problems of adaptation to the postimmigrant future, Jesuits were
still able to hope that Catholic social doctrine needed only to be dusted off
for its perennial verities to shine through. In the fifties some progressives
flirted with slightly bolder possibilities. The overlay of custom had become
so encrusted with dysfunctional curios that cosmetic surgery, not just a brisk
cleaning, might be needed. Both strategies assumed that such change as was
required could be controlled.

The switch from classical stasis to historicism sanctioned by Vatican II,
together with the events of the sixties, indicated to the contrary that Jesuits
had little control over their destiny. Even if the turmoil of the sixties could
be dismissed as transient, deeper reflection on the historical trajectory of the

Society of Jesus suggested that a similar argument could be applied to the supposed stability of tradition. This history turned out to look more like a series of fragile equilibria rather than a steady or edifyingly purposeful course.[71]

The immediate experience of Jesuits in the sixties indicated how quickly small changes exposed larger stakes. In part this reflected the degree to which the ethos of the traditional way of life was embedded in the particulars of ritual and minute confirmations of stability. Tampering with symbolic habits, in conjunction with the loosening of the environment of the immigrant ghettos, unleashed furies. Modernization differed from the dream, signified by Shrub Oak, of growth and of smoothing over the discontinuities and irrational crags of tradition. Nothing revealed that the transformation of a way of life was at stake so much as the extreme difficulty of fixing parts of the mechanism without sending reverberations throughout the system. As the layers of institutional and rhetorical artifice ruptured, what came into view was not a transcendent steadfastness but spasms of raw emotion. Some of this found an outlet in radicalism with a hysterical edge, and some in a newfound sexuality.

Many Jesuits persevered, performing good works and being of service, with a humbler sense of their own powers, acknowledging that while the society could not retreat into a vanished tradition, it was not sure how to move forward. Three dimensions of change had come to a head. Vatican II forced a recognition of a lack of emotion, a lack of mastery, and a lack of meaning in the Society of Jesus as it had come to be constituted in the latter part of the twentieth century. It was of the essence of the old faith that these elements formed an integrated whole. The affective, the activist, and the intellectual bases of corporate religion in the Jesuit fashion all came in for doubt, and the restoration of belief in their unity was uncertain.

CHAPTER

13

The Schools

What greater or better service can I render to the state than to instruct
and train the youth—especially in view of the fact that our young men
have gone so far astray because of the present moral laxity that the utmost effort will be needed to hold them in check and direct them in
the right way? Of course, I have no assurance—it could not even be
expected—that they will all turn to these studies. Would that a few
may![1]

I

The tensions welling up in the Society of Jesus with the passage from the
forties to the fifties were seen at the time as the reflection of organizational
and intellectual problems, not as symptoms of the affective crisis that would
burst forth in the sixties. Attention focused on the intellectual thrust of the
schools run by the Jesuits and more generally on the life of the Catholic
mind in America. This debate ran through the pages of the Catholic press
during the late fifties and early sixties.[2]

The intellectual dimensions of the issue were bound up with the material
and social conditions of Catholic education—the physical plant; the administrative structures; the regional, urban, and suburban, middle- and lower-
middle-class clientele. For as long as they could remember, most Jesuits in
the United States had lived out their working lives in the society's network
of high schools, colleges, and universities; upward of 60 percent of Jesuits
not in training themselves were assigned to the schools of the order.[3] The
growth in higher education after the war combined with the preexisting

commitment of Jesuits to operations scattered across every region of the country to raise difficult questions about financing and academic direction.

It was in the colleges and universities rather than at the secondary-education level that problems were acute. Jesuits were not used to running big schools. Furthermore, habits of intellectual creativity were slight; Jesuits tended to see themselves primarily as teachers and character builders. The chores of administration and instruction left them with little time for speculative thought in any case. They were overworked and, by secular standards of scholarship, underproductive.

The increase in the number of students, together with the financially precarious situation of private higher education generally, compelled presidents and deans to devote most of their energies to management without a corresponding payoff in the intellectual sparkle of the schools. The imperatives of survival and absorption of numbers usually took priority over questions of academic excellence. "There is something insidious," lamented Fr. Paul Reinert, president of St. Louis University, "about the effect of administration on a man's mentality." He went into detail:

> Concentration on administrative minutiae, the constant headaches and the eternal problem of trying to keep the machinery running smoothly and of keeping everybody happy—absorption in this type of work in a very short time dries up a man's interests and initiative for genuine intellectual activity, so much so that eventually, even when he may find the time for scholarly work, he almost certainly will not use it. Nor can we argue that this all depends on the individual—that a man who is determined can really combine these two types of activity. . . . Administrative duties ruin the promise of productive scholarship and intellectual initiative.[4]

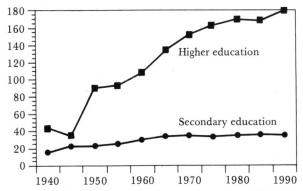

FIGURE 4. Enrollment (in Thousands) in Jesuit High Schools, Colleges, and Universities in the United States, 1940–90

By the 1950s the small, selective liberal arts college proposed as a paradigm by Thurston Davis, aloof from graduate training and from research, was no longer a realistic alternative to the expansion and onrushing complexity of Jesuit higher education. The *collège* model depended on the perpetuation of an enclave Catholicism that was entering into decline. It implied a return to a gentility, sheltered from the market and steeped in the classics, that could only be reproduced in the second half of the twentieth century by endowments beyond the Jesuits' reach. Davis also supposed that there existed a dedicated and intelligent minority who would prefer the seminarylike program he envisioned to the potentially more broadening offerings at non-Catholic campuses like Oberlin or Kenyon; it was assumed, with decreasing realism, that the best and brightest graduates of Jesuit high schools would go on to Jesuit colleges.[5] Although the model lingered as an ideal for a few of the order's small, bucolic campuses—the College of the Holy Cross in Massachusetts, for example, or Fairfield University in Connecticut—and in some of the undergraduate honors programs at larger universities, in fact the Jesuits plunged ahead with higher education on a large scale. They opted to keep up more than two dozen fair-size colleges and universities, spread throughout the country.

Sustaining these operations put inexorable pressure on manpower. The Jesuits renewed their efforts to develop the academic promise of their gifted men. The exigencies of wartime had reduced the annual number of Jesuits in "special"—that is, graduate—studies to fewer than one hundred. But by the academic year 1949–50 more than 250 were enrolled in graduate schools. The number slipped a bit over the following years, as provincial superiors called men back to their own territories, before they had completed their doctorates, to fill the teaching slots required to cope with the swarms of students. But by the end of the fifties, investment in graduate training was up again. The total surpassed 300 men in 1961, 400 in 1965, and exceeded 500 the next year.[6]

This deployment of manpower did not represent a wholehearted embrace of the secular sciences. On the average, Jesuits assigned to graduate work went to Catholic, and usually Jesuit, schools. Fordham, St. Louis, and the Gregorian University regularly headed the list. The norm was to concentrate in theology or in the traditional humanistic disciplines. Even so, both the proportion and the absolute numbers of Jesuits attending secular universities climbed.

The order had difficulty mounting a distinguished cadre of scholars in any one of the newer areas of academic specialization, but the spread across the humanistic disciplines was impressive, as befit a liberal arts tradition. The strategy produced teachers for perhaps half a dozen solid undergraduate schools. The trouble was that the extension of the Jesuit educational enterprise required several times this number, and manpower was inveterately spread thin. Jesuits customarily worked within their home provinces; there was no national market in educational positions. Each territorial unit of the American assistancy felt that it needed to have as many Jesuits in diverse fields as possible so that a critical number could be assigned to the various departments of their colleges and universities. Ideally, all department heads were to be Jesuits. When this was not possible, as was often the case, Jesuits were at least to chair key departments such as philosophy and theology. The effort to duplicate institutional facilities across regions was a major factor in the dilution of quality. The outcome was a chain of schools, many of which provided sound instruction largely to local students and none of which ranked among the top schools nationally.[7]

The ambition to excel academically was also held back by the desire to continue to furnish Catholic—that is, morally formative—schooling, at the secondary and college-and-university tiers of the educational pyramid. Traditionally, Jesuits had seen themselves as "pastors in the classroom."[8] With the onset of the postwar period it was impossible to maximize educational and formative objectives at all these geographical and functional levels simultaneously. Jesuit colleges and universities were diverse in size, location, and resources. In the abstract—that is, apart from the professional schools appended to them—they were seen as extensions of the high schools, providing a full spectrum of intellectual and ethical training. In reality the performance of the colleges and universities was squeezed between the offsetting goals of intellectual achievement and adherence to religious formation. The continued emphasis on moral instruction was the flip side of the affective and expressive undercurrent that was gathering force in the fifties.

Thus, while the paucity of financial and other material resources was clearly a dominant factor in preventing the colleges and universities of the Jesuits from entering the first rank, this shortfall was also the result of a collective decision to provide a panoply of educational services throughout the country. Service and teaching counted for more than intellectual originality, and these functions soon became partially captive to the revenue-producing professional faculties needed to provision them. And the other imperative that kept a lid on intellectual attainment was concern with the transmission of ethical values at the expense, if need be, of academic excellence.

This concern was evident at the highest echelons of the Society of Jesus. It also enjoyed a large constituency among rank-and-file Jesuits. There was an inclination to justify the less than satisfactory intellectual standing of the colleges and universities as a tolerable, if not altogether desirable, result of the priority assigned to the paramount goal of spiritual development. The moral perspective eschewed the movement toward academic growth in quantitative terms as vulgar, at the same time that it rejected learning for its own sake as secular elitism.[9]

After the war Fr. Vincent McCormick replaced Zacheus Maher as American assistant. Aside from laying out for John Courtney Murray the hazards of pressing forward on the topic of church-state relations—in effect, ordering him to silence—one of McCormick's obligations was to convey overall educational policy to Jesuits in the United States. In 1949 he delivered a dinner address to the annual meeting of the Jesuit Educational Association that crystallized this policy as a kind of masculine Grundyism.

McCormick placed the Jesuits at the cutting edge of tradition. He called up double-barreled images of "this militant, hierarchical Church, the Spouse of Christ our Lord, which God has strengthened, invigorated, by providing for it the aid of the Society of Jesus." He noted that no field was "of more vital importance to the Church than that of education." He reminded his listeners of the admonition of the previous pope, Pius XI, that education

> is a necessary function . . . of the family, the State and the Church, but it belongs preeminently to the Church; and the very nature of Christian education gives it a just claim to being preeminent in the divine mission of the Church.[10]

McCormick understood education as a vehicle of ethical training and only secondarily as a scholarly enterprise. The latter was an adjunct of the former. It was in light of this premise that he asked, "Is the Church militant today in these United States stronger, healthier, more robust for the help we are giving to its God-appointed leaders?" He was "tremendously impressed and consoled by the amount of spiritual direction being given to our students in high school, college and university." But there were problems. Secular values were penetrating Jesuit schools:

> The attainment of St. Ignatius' ideal can be seriously hampered if certain conditions are allowed to prevail. . . . I crossed the ocean with a graduate of one of our schools. . . . He was a man in his early thirties, a strong, virile type, alert, intelligent, at home with the priest. He had come from a solidly Catholic family. He recalled two outstanding professors of his time; one was a professed atheist, the other decidedly red in the color of his social theories. The head of one of our Schools of Business Administration was quoted to me as saying: "Don't talk to me about the *Quadragesimo Anno*. That letter has no place in this school while I am here." Some professors in a School of Education are admittedly of the philosophical tribe of John Dewey and the shelves of

the library offer a large assortment of books propagating his errors. In the Department of Philosophy a lay professor insists that a scientific study of psychology must be divorced from a Catholic viewpoint. An infiltration of Freudianism has been noted in the psychiatry section of a School of Social Service. And then one may ask if it is not very difficult to maintain a Catholic environment in a school, where more than fifty per cent of the students are non-Catholics and many of the professors are the same.[11]

McCormick pressed home his view that Jesuit education meant first and foremost moral formation. Scholarship had little autonomy; it was useful mainly insofar as it contributed to spiritual growth. Secular learning that contradicted Catholic doctrine, or more inclusively Christian values, or that had no distinctively ethical cast, was to be quarantined as the misguided, shallow opinion of a statistical majority without spiritual compass. Like that of Thurston Davis, McCormick's ideal academic setting was doctrinally and demographically Catholic. American culture was still hostile to Catholicism, and the Catholic subculture continued to operate according to a defensive logic.

The appropriate response, according to this logic, was not dialogue but the continued insertion of Jesuits into key administrative and academic positions. Concern about the loss of control over the educational process followed from the ongoing professionalization of the colleges and universities. With the success of their schools, as measured by growth, the Jesuits risked becoming swallowed up by larger and more complex institutions. After some point in the spurt of the student population toward the five-digit range—five to six thousand to a school was probably a manageable limit—moral and intellectual control became infeasible. McCormick concluded with a reminder that Father Janssens wished "no further expansion of present activities."

Few in the audience took this caution seriously. The ideal of maintaining the Catholic character of Jesuit education was unassailable. But the pressure to meet the demand for higher education was irresistible. In the absence of sizable endowments and wealthy alumni, the infusion of tuition payments, supported by the GI Bill, was a necessary condition for serious contemplation of qualitative improvement. Besides, the leaders of Jesuit educational enterprises were in tacit competition in the race for growth. Hometown pride was at stake. Social and financial incentives overrode calls to slow down.

There was also an intellectual argument in favor of growth, one that risked a shrinkage of organizational control even though it might expand the cultural influence of individual Jesuits in the longer term. The idea did not often find its way into print because it implied an attack on the finishing-school humanism and moral earnestness espoused by men like Thurston Davis. The idyllic enclave, remote from the marketplace of ideas, was an artifact of insularity and subject to its limitations. Traditional moral precepts might be preserved; what was also safeguarded was clerical control, and the correlation between this pair of priorities and intellectual excellence was moot. On the other hand, though far from disinterested, the advocates of expansion were not completely driven by the circular dynamic of numbers of students and the need for funding. They sought to overcome academic inbreeding. Their premise seems to have been that some Jesuit schools should welcome growth as a means of reaching a threshold of size that would foster diversity and internal pluralism. A corollary of this line of reasoning was that managing, rather than being overwhelmed by, the movement toward this goal would require a reassessment of the balance of power between Jesuits and lay colleagues.[12]

McCormick was aware of the distinction between organizational control and intellectual influence, even though he could not bring himself to countenance radical options such as encouraging Jesuit scholars to take positions at secular universities. In principle he saw the difference between education as an institutional enterprise, a series of services that threatened to become too much of a good thing, and the ideal of the intellectual competence of the Society of Jesus that enhanced the influence of the order. Accordingly, he was willing to give up some workaday routines "to release more of our men for more arduous fields and fields that promise results of more far-reaching good." Time off for research, even within a Jesuit school heavily committed to teaching, might result in intellectual credibility and influence over policy in the longer run:

> Such a field is that of scientific research, of scholarly productivity, from where our learning, profound and proven, can reach out to influence thought and conduct, to the greater strength of the Church, in the intellectual centers of the world. Such is the field not only opened but assigned to us by the Supreme Head of the universal Church in the institutes of Rome.[13]

The fallacy here was the same one the early planners of the Institute of Social Order had entertained in hoping for straightforward applications of Catholic principles. The attempt to create a two-track faculty, one for teaching and another for research, had fostered invidious comparisons when ISO was established at St. Louis University, and it did not produce compensating benefits. Besides this administrative difficulty, the store of Catholic expertise, "profound and proven," turned out to be a set of static truths in some areas, such as moral theology, and in other areas, such as the social sciences, virtually nonexistent, and in still other fields open to debate and revision and indistinguishable from the tentative hypotheses of secular knowledge. The trust McCormick placed in the readiness of the intellectual resources of the Society of Jesus rang true mainly within bastions of the American Catholic subculture like the small colleges purified to an ideal type by Thurston Davis and a few preserves such as the "institutes of Rome" (the Gregorian University) that corresponded to the West Point—but not the Oxford or Cambridge—of Catholicism.

McCormick fell victim to a triumphalism that was on the verge of obsolescence but that was not entirely myopic. Like many Catholics of his generation who grew up poor but who had experienced little sense of deprivation, he admitted no terms of comparison that might have allowed him to perceive that Jesuits and their students were inadequately educated by the standards of elite secular institutions. His image of the good school fitted the educational aspirations that immigrant parents, themselves without much schooling, had for children who would be the first in the family to go to college.[14] From the perspective of Jesuits who shared McCormick's philosophy, this image corresponded to a hierarchy of values topped by moral rectitude and guaranteed by clerical dominance; intellectual attainment, though important, had lower priority. For the immigrants and many of their children as well, critical thinking was less important than training in useful skills in preparation for "good, steady city jobs," and it was this clientele that stood behind the growth of the Jesuits' professional schools. Between these groups and many Jesuits of McCormick's generation there was a convergence of partially disparate—that is, idealistic and instrumental—interests. By contrast, it was quite uncertain whether truly large-scale research universities could either provide moral formation or deliver practical instruction.[15]

McCormick could cajole and he could make life pleasant or difficult for individual Jesuits, but he could not hold back the course of higher education in the Society of Jesus. His message was to build on the strengths of the past. Paul Reinert, the president of a university with a law school, a medical school, and the makings of an intellectual presence, gave the directives coming out of Rome a more dynamic twist. As a leading educational manager, he was eager to convince his colleagues that the Society of Jesus could play to its strengths—that is, continue its commitment to the colleges and universities in the face of demands for diverting resources elsewhere—not out of institutional inertia or to preserve a subculture of dubious intellectual stature but because modernized schools were the base from which the order could exercise its greatest impact on the larger society. Reinert was concerned that the general's injunction against "further expansion" might be taken as an excuse for assuming that the schools had accomplished their mission and for concluding that the problem of academic quality as defined by secular criteria was a side issue. Jesuits in search of new fields to conquer might abandon the classroom on the assumption that their job was done, missing the challenge of turning the schools from good colleges into competitive universities.

Reinert seized on a letter written by Janssens in 1947 on "the choice of ministries" to confirm the paramount role of education. The priority was not new, even if it was difficult to square exactly with Janssens's simultaneous interest in the social apostolate. The importance given within education to "scientific study and research" relative to teaching was novel, however.

> After placing scientific study and scholarship first in the list, and teaching in colleges and universities second, only then does Father General go on to enumerate and evaluate other types of work being carried on in the Society, putting missionary work third, then labors among the working class. . . . Here . . . we have the highest authority in the Society, the one who knows intimately all the Society's varied activities, one who speaks not only with the persuasion of logic and historical tradition but with an authority demanding our obedience of will and intellect—here the life of scholarship and teaching is officially put down as more important than every other type of work.[16]

Reinert and some other Jesuit educators of his generation—among them Fr. Robert Henle, who was to become president of Georgetown in the sixties; and Fr. Walter Ong, who would be elected president of the Modern Language Association (MLA)—wanted to make a few Jesuit universities into major research institutions. This would represent a significant departure from both the model of the small teaching college envisioned by Thurston Davis and from the assortment of sometimes mediocre undergraduate and professional schools that had sprung up helter-skelter under Jesuit auspices.[17]

The positive objective of raising the quality of Jesuit higher education as a whole proved almost as difficult as implementing Janssens's restriction against quantitative expansion. Concentrating resources would have required overcoming the regional interests of the various provinces, and yet the resources of each of the scattered colleges and universities were too small to establish a springboard for a leap toward excellence on their own. As it happened, improvements were eventually pushed through by dint of innovative management or came about by good fortune. A few large benefactors emerged, and professional fund-raising campaigns were launched. But the logic of academic specialization and professionalization worked against concerted efforts to turn Jesuit higher education around on a grand scale. The institutional and intellectual obstacles against forming a critical mass that might accumulate such resources were formidable. A coalition for radical change could not be assembled.[18]

Educational planning of national scope proved futile not only on account of organizational resistance but also because the dream presupposed a single model of excellence. The supposition that there should be a unitary mold for Jesuit higher education was in part a fiction serving to mask the uneven distribution of resources among the schools and their intractable diversity and in part a vestige of the conviction that, whatever the diversity of secular knowledge, a common ethical core pervaded the schools. As the schools began to lose the sleepy look of prewar days, they became less and less like one another. Disparities in size and resources increased; Georgetown University in Washington far outpaced Spring Hill College in Mobile. Frustration was built into a way of thinking that downplayed and had no way of exploiting the increasing scale and heterogeneity of the society's educational network. Conceptual uniformity had centralization as an institutional corollary. This did not work well for ISO, and in the case of more than two dozen existing colleges and universities it was wholly impractical.

Like the Thomistic idealization of monarchy as the best of all possible governments, the norm of the one best school was not pressed to a literal extreme. But the ideal of standardization continued to deprive pluralist thinking of respectability, and it put a cap on imagination and competition in the educational thought of the Jesuits. While practically everyone sensed that the norm was impracticable and indeed misguided in theory, an alternative dispensation had yet to come into view. By default, in the absence of consensus about intellectual directions, the inculcation of moral values remained the core priority about which it was impossible for Jesuits to disagree openly.[19]

The colleges and universities adopted a live-and-let-live policy, each going its own way regardless of guidelines set at the national level and, for that matter, increasingly beyond the influence of the provincial superiors who retained nominal control of the institutions in their territories. Despite misgivings in principle, decentralization was made possible by the fact that the schools did not depend on a single source for funding; Rome had no money to hand out to Americans. The schools catered mostly to local clienteles and, to a lesser but growing extent, were driven by national academic norms. The push toward higher quality entailed competition and a scrambling for funds not only between Jesuit and non-Jesuit institutions but also, insofar as they strove for national prominence, between Jesuit schools themselves. Small schools of high quality could not easily be cloned, and the successful promotion of a single model multiversity (or a few) would necessitate a severe cutback in existing commitments. Jesuit administrators were not alone in protecting their turf. There was no groundswell among students and alumni in favor of relegating a Fordham or a Creighton University to second-class status for the sake of building a Catholic Harvard or Yale. Although such factors did not prevent a modest coherence or the occasional emergence of charismatic educators with big ideas to try out in small arenas, they did rule out synoptic planning.[20]

II

The gap between the pedagogy of the Jesuits, enshrined in the *Ratio Studiorum*, and the knowledge explosion widened in the postwar years. As Fr. Gustave Weigel, a colleague of John Courtney Murray, saw it, the problem was not the core curriculum of the Jesuit schools. Training in the humanities remained an admirable and viable model. The rationale of humanistic education was not narrowly vocational but a broad preparation for life. Adaptability and versatility as well as integrity were the keynotes. In this, Weigel was of one mind with Thurston Davis. The trouble lay in a manner of instruction and an attitude toward learning that, at least beyond the high school level, had ossified. Mechanical formalities that passed for hallowed tradition had displaced authentic learning. "In any context we must speak the language of the situation," Weigel insisted. "Otherwise we cannot establish influential contact."[21]

Weigel, whose interests had turned to ecumenism, inveighed against the Protestant- and secularist-bashing, ritualized in the *disputationes*, that kept Jesuits from fruitful exchange with the larger world.[22] "The apologetic strain in Jesuit scholarship," he stated flatly, "is not a vital tradition." Rather, he said:

> It was the form the vital tradition took in a moment when it was meaningful. It is not meaningful today. The individual Jesuit teacher, mindful of the essence of the true tradition, must not be distracted by a pattern-relique which is not essential. Hume, Kant and Hegel are not so much "adversaries" as milestones in the development of philosophy and are to be treated that way.[23]

Weigel and his colleague Murray were kindred spirits; their rooms were on the same corridor at Woodstock College. Both recognized the importance of engaging their peers on the outside with an intelligible vocabulary. Their views might differ, but at least the parties would understand their differences. If a key objective of the Society of Jesus was to influence public affairs and the opinions of the powerful, Jesuits had to forsake gratuitous archaisms.

Questions of substance were also at issue. Weigel placed in the open his suspicion that the verbal pyrotechnics and logic chopping favored by some Jesuits might cover up their lack of anything to say. He reiterated the point, central to the methodology used by Murray in coming to terms with religious and political pluralism, that philosophical positions had to be situated in historical and cultural context. He was bothered by the tendency of Jesuits to get caught up with hackneyed maxims and to turn debate into an abstract "pattern-relique" without relevance to substantive contingencies. Not only was this language of discourse dead; the ideas themselves were husks of meaning:

> One danger inherent in the following of patterns instead of tradition is
> the elimination of time from questions to be studied. . . . The ques-
> tion raised in the 16th Century is not identical with the question as it
> faces us in the 20th. . . . To suppose that we can answer the current
> question by a simple return to the era when that question was first
> raised is an ignorance of the meaning of the question in its actual
> form.[24]

The artificiality of the polemical manner was not fatal; most academic discussion involved "artifices"—models, theoretical simplifications—of one sort or another. The problem lay in the tendency of Jesuits to forget that debates, to matter, had to be about something and had to engender a sense that they might actually have consequences for the testing and revision of ideas. Rhetorical abstraction perpetuated an intellectual virginity. Once in a while, Jesuits might lose or be mistaken. Not only this; the truths they clung to might not be as complete or as rock-solid as they supposed:

> One result of the elimination of time from the problematic is the ten-
> dency to reduce study to schematic verbalism and memorization. The
> real phenomenon as it stands vitally before our gaze is overlooked and
> in its place an older verbal formula for it is substituted. The teacher
> unconsciously begins to think that all questions were discovered and
> solved in the past. In consequence he conceives his true work to be
> the pulling together of the answers of our forefathers and arranging
> them in a logical synthesis. This synthesis is then the everlasting truth.
> All modern questions are resolved by referring them to this scheme
> and they are answered by deducing corollaries from yesterday's syn-
> thetic *depositum*. The present problem need not be examined in it-
> self.[25]

Weigel's peroration built up to a caustic judgment on the feats of memorization that had come to stand for intellectual achievement in Jesuit seminaries, where the reliance on instruction in Latin heightened the temptation to indulge in a play of words disconnected from testable ideas or tangible experience:

> In many a [Jesuit] student's mind the examination is nothing but a test of memory. . . . Good repetition is considered the goal of study. He thinks that a mark of excellence in study is given to a student not because he understands the reality he is talking about but because he has adequately memorized the scheme and in addition understands its logic. Acquaintance with the thing itself seems unimportant.[26]

"All this," Weigel concluded, "is verbalism, logicism, schematism and memorization."

Weigel focused on specific practices that all Jesuits were aware of, and this gave his critique an air of relevance and hopefulness that belied its negativism. It was impossible for Jesuits not to relate the generic condemnation of "logicism," for example, to encounters with certain bizarre instructors in the philosophates and theologates whose legendary quirks became fodder for irreverent mimicry. The lesson from experience was clear. In order to improve the quality of the schools under their direction, Jesuits would have to rethink the system used to educate their own men. By focusing on the embarrassing consequences of the methods that had grown up for training Jesuits, Weigel helped place the revamping of formation at the top of the agenda of the Society of Jesus. Instead of insisting, as McCormick had done, on subjugating learning to morality in the schools run for a lay clientele, Weigel recommended that the Jesuits modernize their conceptual and instructional methods. In this way, he implied, the credibility of moral exhortation would be strengthened. The message was that Jesuits should reform their own ways—in particular, they should update their intellectual skills—before trying to mold others.

Weigel's emphasis on a single, plainly important aspect of the system conveyed the hope that practical solutions might be found through critical assessment. He did not dilate on a supposed ethical breakdown, the ruinous secularization of Western civilization, and the like. He deplored instead the decline of intellectual standards within the Society of Jesus itself, attacking the educational practices of his peers, an area in which they were accustomed to take pride. The flaw, he argued, lay as much with the incompetence and mediocrity of poorly trained Jesuits as with the false gods of the secular world. The bad news was balanced by recognition of the possibility that, while the secular realm might be largely unmanageable, Jesuits could take steps to remedy their in-house failings.

Gus Weigel was a popular member of the Woodstock faculty and an eminent figure in ecumenical circles.[27] Although conservatives in the order took his criticism as so much liberal nagging—Weigel was very much in the

line of John LaFarge and John Courtney Murray, troublemakers with uncertain influence—there was reason to believe that he could contribute to
reforms that would be well received by younger Jesuits and by disgruntled
senior men.

III

Jesuit higher education was pulled in three directions during the postwar
period. The moralism of Vincent McCormick harkened back to a fortress
Catholicism that drew up the drawbridge against hostile surroundings. By
contrast, expansion in the size and scope of the Jesuit educational network
pushed Catholics toward assimilation. Some Jesuits felt that growth was not
only necessary to respond to the demands for mass education but was also
a prerequisite for academic excellence in the contemporary world. Finally,
in contradistinction to the tradition of moral formation and the trend toward
greater numbers of students, which were themselves in tension, there was
the new learning that defied integration or, as Weigel would have it, the
synthesizing impulses beloved by Jesuits. Whether they were purveyed in
small or large institutions, there was no guarantee that Jesuit pedagogy and
Catholic beliefs were compatible with the headlong advance and fragmentation of knowledge.

It was a set of essays written by Robert Harvanek, a philosophy instructor
and "prefect of studies" who was to become provincial superior of Chicago
in the mid-sixties, that sized up all three factors as they affected the rationale
and the operating structure of Jesuit education. The baseline for Harvanek
was a variation on the elite *collège* of the sort idealized by Thurston Davis.
It put a premium on "the traditional Jesuit humanistic goal of eloquence,
the art of excellent speaking and writing of worth-while thoughts."[28] The
setting conducive to the attainment of this goal was a small school in which
piety and learning, "the dual virtues of science and sanctity," could be
joined. The discipline required for growth in these two areas was also expected to develop habits of industriousness and mastery. "The whole man,"
mens sana in corporis sano, was to be perfected.[29]

Harvanek recognized that this ideal was a romanticization of Jesuit secondary education. Such a model may have been viable "when a high school
education was considered terminal and something of a privilege." To hold
it up as an exemplar at the present time, however, was to ignore "the
dynamism of the American ideal of universal education," which pushed
upward toward the spread of college and university education once the
completion of high school had become obligatory and no longer served as
an entrée into the middle class. Even at the high school level, according to

Harvanek, the growth in numbers attendant on mass education had the effect of encouraging objectives alien to the classical standards of Jesuit pedagogy.

At the same time that he expressed disapproval of these trends, Harvanek understood that they reflected not only ideological positions but also relentless social changes. The philosophy of progressive education was riding the tide of the growth of the work force. "The principal purpose of elementary and secondary education is [preparation] for life within the American democracy rather than intellectual and academic excellence."[30] Because he clung to the *collège* ideal, Harvanek ignored for the moment the portion of the market for training in practical know-how that Jesuit professional schools had captured with the rise of Catholics toward middle-class status. Acculturation in the standards and the skills of the American way differed from the inculcation of Catholic values and from the provision of an intense humanism for a select few, but it was increasingly on the basis of these services that Jesuits themselves had expanded their educational network in the United States.[31]

It was among the colleges and universities that the deleterious impact of growth was most keenly felt. Jesuits were more accustomed to teaching in and running "academies" than institutions of higher learning; most of their academic operations in Europe and elsewhere were confined to high schools. They felt comfortable with the smaller colleges typical of the years before the war that were closer to extensions of their high schools than full-blown universities. The familiarity of this cozy setting gave the utopian ruminations of Thurston Davis a sensible ring. That part of the tradition resonated not just in theory but in living memory as well.[32]

Educational expansion which Harvanek saw as inevitable ("size, in the American world, is a symbol of success . . . it is impossible to stand still when the whole culture is moving and growing") brought that arcadian world virtually to extinction and introduced problems of its own. As Paul Reinert and other advocates of growth admitted, the brick-and-mortar mindset, ceaseless fund-raising and the sheer headiness of change left little opportunity for the pursuit of higher interests. More than this, Harvanek argued, the pristine goals of Jesuit education were in danger of being displaced. The fading-away of the *collège*-style schools was not made up for by any discernible gain in control over the larger institutions:

> The growth in enrollment, though never fulfilling the individual institution's innate developing desire for a qualified student body needed to support its educational aims and total structure, nevertheless required larger plants and staffs. The cost of the operation went beyond the possibility of the Catholic community or the single wealthy benefactors to

support, and it became necessary to introduce community-wide modern fund collecting procedures.[33]

The days when Catholic schools were beholden to a very small number of individual, personally known sponsors and to a much larger number of small donations from members of what was still a community were giving way to faceless interests, mailing lists, data bases, and corporate power that threatened to blunt the Jesuits' mission:

> One result of this development was the tendency to place emphasis on the *private* character of our institutions. This had the double effect of softening Catholic social doctrine and stressing private enterprise, and of toning down the *Catholic* character of the institution in publicity while expanding its potential for *community* service.[34]

While Harvanek saw both as increasingly at odds with the surrounding culture, the colleges and universities could not be as self-sustaining as the high schools. They were more vulnerable to outside pressures. They required larger amounts of operating funds and capital investment, and the need for money placed them in danger of becoming hostage to shortsighted business interests. Jesuits, who had been trained to master their surroundings, and who had grown used to a good measure of autonomy vis-à-vis local bishops, found themselves in jeopardy of being crushed by the size and complexity of the institutions they had created. The colleges and universities assumed a life of their own, and they became increasingly impervious to attempts at coordination by the central offices of the Society of Jesus. They responded more assiduously to the policies and purse strings of the federal government, which took on a preeminent role in higher education after the war, and to regional economic forces. The bureaucratic and business environment deflected efforts that Jesuits might make to implement programs, such as "Catholic social doctrine." However much such ideas might be favored in principle, they were peripheral to the modus operandi of American higher education. Jesuits found themselves pincered between an ingrown parochialism and an indifferent gigantism.

Harvanek's exposition depended on a bit of roseate history that probably deepened his gloom about the future. While the argument could be made that the need to fund expansion made Jesuits hostage to moneyed interests with their own ideas about the ends of education, there was no evidence that Jesuit schools promoted the Catholic social *magisterium* any more strenuously in the thirties, when they were relatively small and impecunious, than in the fifties, when they were larger and on the make. Furthermore, it was not clear whether the problem was a genuine divergence in goals between Jesuit educators and corporate notables or instead a question of power sharing between manager-owners and the contributors of material resources.[35]

Harvanek was resigned to growth but he could not bring himself to view it as an opportunity. From his perspective, the confrontation was not only between quantity and the traditional Jesuit vision of education-as-formation, a kind of elitism of the spirit, but also between this ethical duty and the maximization of secular learning. He acknowledged the oxymoron that George Bernard Shaw had perceived in the very idea of a "Catholic university":

> As to the central function of the university, the pursuit of knowledge for its own sake and the extension of the limits of present knowledge and wisdom, this too must be the central function of the Catholic university. However, there is a problem here, the problem of Catholic humanism in general. The impulse of the Gospel is to draw men from earth to heaven, to put their heart, and their treasure, in the Kingdom of Heaven, to seek the things that are above. . . . [This] point[s] up the ambivalence in the Christian personality which does not permit him to be committed isolatedly to human knowledge and science.[36]

Placing secular knowledge below religious perfection in the hierarchy of educational values kept faith with the Jesuit view of knowledge as essentially instrumental. It was a means to salvation, not an end in itself. To be sure, Jesuits were not fundamentalists or crudely anti-intellectual, and the goal to which they sought to apply the means of formal education was not individual gain but ethical discernment. Furthermore, the humanistic disciplines—literature and history being the prime examples—were not only vehicles of moral instruction. They also provided playful escapes from stern readings of the salvific imperative. Unlike theology, these areas of learning did not have to be confined to a body of immutable truths, and in contrast to expectations for the social sciences, Jesuit humanists did not feel that they had to deliver practical advice. Not having to look over their shoulder to verify either the didactic correctness or the mundane applicability of their work, Jesuits in the humanities could give relatively ample rein to imagination without much fear of getting into trouble. They could shine.

Even here, however, behind the flights of fancy and the seductions of speculation, a moral agenda was customarily present. A wholehearted commitment to scholarship that made for the accumulation of new knowledge remained suspect. Applied research might be applauded but basic research—knowledge for its own sake—met with bewilderment. In one way or another, spiritually or materially, knowledge had to be applied. Utilitarianism of this sort might be an improvement on magical thinking, but it did not square well with an idle curiosity construction of the humanistic syllabus, and it perpetuated a forbidden fruit understanding of the limits and the dangers of intellectualism:

> There is a conflict with the way the secularist understands the pursuit of knowledge, and of new knowledge, for its own sake. Looked at metaphysically (not necessarily from the secularist's point of view), this pursuit must ultimately be rooted in man's desire for beatitude. It is basically a search for the ultimate. When the ultimate is found, when the relationship to beatitude is definitely established, then the dynamism of the pursuit of truth is fulfilled. The secularist will say that it is ended in the sense that it dies out. This is the reason for the secularist intellectual's hostility to absolute truth or to an irrevocable faith. To his way of thinking, attainment of absolute truth or an absolute faith is incompatible with the pursuit of truth.[37]

The unspoken ultimate here, behind the theological references to absolute truth, was stability. The supreme reward was a sense of closure and of coming home after a long search for the infinite. The regnant metaphor was that of spiritual odyssey rather than intellectual exploration. "The dynamism of the pursuit of truth" was supposed to terminate in timelessness and motionless calm. Change, like relativism, was defective, inferior. The life of the secular intellectual was guided by its own set of absolutes; the chief among these was knowledge itself. There was a fundamental incompatibility between this restlessness and fragmentation and the ideal of transcendent wholeness:

> The ultimate goal of anything a Catholic enters upon, and this is emphasized in Jesuit spirituality, is the glory of God and his service. Even the pursuit of truth is ordered to this further end. To the intellectual, again, this seems to be as much a prostitution of the profession of learning as is the pursuit of truth so as to be able to produce something which will result in financial or business profit. Even the philanthropic motive of the betterment of mankind is outwardly eschewed by the pure intellectual.[38]

Harvanek's portrayal of the contrast between secular and Catholic approaches to knowledge revealed a measure of stereotyping of outsiders as well as some insensitivity to members of the fold. The depiction of secular intellectuals as socially unconcerned might have been applied just as well to pious Catholics. The tendency for Catholics to indulge in aesthetic expression for the beauty of it, whether through quasi-liturgical or openly artistic means, without regard to practical or theological significance, went unnoticed. Pleasure of this sort was frivolous and possibly wrong. Neither of these currents quite fit within the ideal of instruction and edification, the high moral seriousness, that Harvanek took as the standard against which Jesuit pedagogy was to be judged:

> The secularist pursuit of truth in modern culture stresses almost exclusively the freedom of discovery of the scientist and intellectual. It is expected that this will go counter to inherited and traditional views and systems of value. It belligerently asserts its right to seek and discover and state the truth as it finds it. . . . But in addition to this, the basic disorientation of the secularist pursuit of truth from the religious context and goal of man gives an impulse to find truth in directions contrary to man's religious nature. This work of search and discovery must be redeemed. In other words, in addition to the direct pursuit of truth, it is one of the functions of the Catholic university to evaluate and purify as well as develop in a context of total truth the discoveries, views, and theories of the secular learning. This is particularly important and significant when the context of the total society in which the Catholic university is operating is not Catholic but pluralistic and secular. . . . [A] culture is incomplete and truncated unless it is informed by religion (and ultimately this must mean the true religion).[39]

Harvanek was back to the impeccable synthesis of simpler times, the earthly version of "beatitude." Resolution of the tensions between academic professionalism and the preservation of religious doctrine depended on a common recognition of a hierarchy of truth that could not, under pluralism and the segmentation of knowledge, be enforced. Harvanek acknowledged that such a consensus, while a logical possibility, was an unrealistic goal.

Something had to give. What separated Harvanek's analysis from the standard fare of defensive triumphalism was the honesty with which he pursued the consequences of his argument. The intellectual and ethical possibilities open to Jesuits, given their institutional commitments and traditional convictions, came down to three alternatives, in descending order of probability. The likeliest was "that which says that the decision and the commitment has [sic] already been made and that we are involved and cannot do otherwise than try to carry the venture forward as long and as well as possible." This meant capitulation or, more charitably, assimilation into the ways of secular academe. The process was beyond the control of the Society of Jesus. Catholic institutions might neither come up to secular standards nor retain their religious identity. They might evolve instead toward a mediocre middle ground.

The second option was a rationalization of the first, with improvements. It would foster the development of "a philosophy out of the exigencies of the situation and [would] maintain that the developing modern Jesuit lay university is achieving a great good, a greater good than was achieved by the small Jesuit liberal arts college with its theory of a select education of leaders, and a greater good than could be achieved by the small liberal arts college." The ideal of Thurston Davis and the drift toward assimilation were both rejected. Vigorous adaptation was the strategy. "The advocates of this new philosophy of Jesuit education," Harvanek wrote,

> have hope and confidence that with modern business and public rela-
> tion methods, plus increasing support from private and governmental
> sources, our Jesuit universities will be able to grow into institutions
> which will stand superior to many universities in the land, be equal,
> and perhaps be subordinate to only a very few.[40]

This was the optimistic, competitive path. It was modernizing, but with roots in the Jesuit habit of venturesomeness and acculturation to local conditions.

The third alternative was a reaffirmation of the ideal proposed by Thurston Davis. The role of the Jesuit university would be to

> [perform] the work of the more intensive Catholic higher education,
> recognizing that the less intensive, and the more laical education will
> be carried on in the secular universities, both state and private, as
> more and more Catholic students and professors enter into these insti-
> tutions and are accepted there. . . . It will mean that there will have to
> be a good proportion of religious and priests on the teaching faculty in
> disciplines other than philosophy and theology. . . . [T]he structure of
> the university will be guided by the necessity of having theology and
> spirituality present to all departments in an appropriate way. Theology
> will have to be the central department of the university. . . . [T]he
> university will revolve around the holy sacrifice of the Mass and . . . it
> will see its work as radiating out from this source and returning back to
> it.[41]

While this outcome was most improbable, Harvanek insisted that "it will make a difference what [the] ideal is." He shared with John Courtney Murray a respect for theory and a contempt for the merely expedient. Jesuits should at least understand what was happening to them even if they could do little to alter the situation; they should not try to finesse their losses.[42]

> It seems to be a matter of fact that thus far the decision has been taken
> in terms of the second response, at least on the part of the major com-
> plex universities. . . . Probably the judgment of reality will be that the
> third response is not possible and the first response is not satisfactory,
> and our institutions will go on without a good theoretical solution but

only a practical one. This is probably the way of existence of social phenomena in any event. The good that is possible is done. The good that is desirable is dreamed about.[43]

Discussions of the fate of Jesuit higher education were doomed to such forlorn conclusions as long as a "one best" institutional model, mirroring the criterion of hierarchy rather than a plurality of truths, stayed in place. It was not merely size or complexity but the fact of heterogeneity that tended to be looked on as unsatisfactory. Logic privileged one set of answers over others, as a device for preserving a nonnegotiable identity. Catholics had to defend and pass on their truth, not to test and revise it in exchange with outsiders. While they might bring ambivalence to a new pitch, Jesuits could not be single-minded and implacable in the pursuit of knowledge. Given this assumption, assessments of Catholic education in the United States were bound to be touched with melancholy, and some options were likely to be precluded. A fourth alternative, of clerical concentration in certain departments—in theology, for example, renamed religious studies— or in selected service functions such as campus ministry, in the midst of universities that were otherwise indistinguishable from most of their secular counterparts, remained in the future.[44]

IV

As the colleges and universities grew and as the sense of control over them diminished, evaluations of the course of Jesuit higher education flourished, and debate over the alternatives systematized by Harvanek expanded in print and in Jesuit rec rooms.[45] Jesuits worried less about their high schools. Rather than encouraging a debate over strategic issues—should the Society of Jesus commit its resources to research as against teaching?—the challenges facing the high schools prompted discussions in a how-to vein. How should a time-tested system of instruction for adolescent boys be adjusted to modern conditions? Altering the character of the schools was off the agenda; it was a matter instead of fine-tuning a proven system.

Through the 1950s and for several years into the sixties, Fr. Lorenzo K. Reed was "prefect of studies"—director of education—for the New York province of the Society of Jesus. With the decline in effective Jesuit influence over higher education, Reed turned most of his attention to the high schools. He produced a pair of guides for the Jesuit Education Association that encompassed the assessment of and the response to the changing situation of secondary education on the part of the Society of Jesus. The manuals are hands-on encyclopedias of pedagogical practice. They paint a vivid picture of how Jesuits actually dealt and how they felt they should deal with cultural flux in the postwar United States.[46]

Reed's was not a deductive or even a very rigorous mind. He was a shrewd and extremely resourceful tinkerer who shared with many Jesuits a perception of falling standards that he attributed to the spread of mass education and a laxity that went with the times. "A growing carelessness and vulgarity of speech, confusion of thinking, and the passivity of mind fostered by our present forms of entertainment are the intellectual ills of the age."[47] Views like these, reminiscent of the perceptions of disorderliness in the slums of New York that Jesuits had written down decades earlier, characterized Reed's philosophical leanings. But they formed only distant backdrop to the ingenuity he brought to the nuts and bolts of the high schools.

Reed devoted his energies mainly to the character-building goals of education. This was a function that he assumed could best be carried out by the clergy, who were specialists in moral formation, and it was a priority that had a greater chance of catching on among younger charges than older students, who were more or less beyond reach in large institutions. Reed subscribed to "the ends and means of Jesuit education" as were laid down by Father Ledochowski and Father Janssens in the thirties and forties.

> The goal established for our work in education is to lead our charges to the knowledge and love of God. Accordingly, our first concern must be that our students in the very process of acquiring learning also develop a truly Christian character. Hence in every one of our schools the moral and religious formation of our students according to the principles and directives of the Church must hold the place of first importance. By this means we shall prepare outstanding men for the family, for our country, and for the Church: men who in their individual spheres of action will be conspicuous for the right answer to the question, "Does this graduate possess a genuine and profound love of God, which motivates him above all else to shape his life to the service of God?"[48]

The emphasis on moral rigor was directed primarily toward personal improvement, but it also aimed at strengthening a sense of social obligation. The goal was "the unified and integral formation of the individual student under the twofold aspect of charity to oneself and to one's neighbor."[49] Reed was an institution builder, leery of schematic thinking. He was careful to phrase the "religious and social objectives" of Jesuit education in a language that drew on church teaching without offending the variety of its constituents. The stress was on the sharpening of individual conscience and on cultivating an ethic of social concern, rather than the formulation of specific programs for collective action or the promulgation of an explicit ideology:

In accordance with the directives of the Holy Father and of our Father General, as well as the needs of the times, great stress must be placed on the social consciousness of the individual student. This, however, must find its source and motivation in the religious formation of the student. Care should be taken not to confuse or identify social consciousness with the mere external features of social action. The objective of Jesuit education is always the integral, interior formation of the inviolable individual. [50]

The emphasis on the shaping of character was as unequivocal as the content of social education was vague. The approach presupposed a youthful audience that was open to idealistic appeals, and it depended for much of its content on shaping this impulse in opposition to social evils and political enemies that could broadly be defined as secular. The accent on the individual was a constant in the guidelines assembled by Reed. His was not, however, the unambiguous individualism of isolated competitors but rather a drive to attainment that presupposed the retention of a supportive subculture. Reed focused on the middle range—on the Catholic community with aspirations to betterment. His area was that crucial stage of the Catholic middle-class career whose context was secondary education. Forces beyond this range—the ethos of Americanism, for example—were touched on cursorily. The seductiveness of big-picture factors might be recognized, but dangers of such magnitude were not directly manageable. The hope was that Jesuit graduates, trained in modern skills and morally fortified, could achieve success without being absorbed by it. The objective was to encourage a sensible spirituality; character and competence were crucial.

This focus on the manageable middle ground helps account for Reed's persistent concern with the social and organizational psychology of teaching, learning, and school administration. His point of view was far less Olympian than Harvanek's. This perspective also underlay his fears, typical of the Catholicism of the period, of an encroaching collectivism and bigness, and it issued in reminders about the threat of government intrusion on a private sphere that englobed the economic, the educational, and the religious.

A rampant danger in the education trends of our times is the exaltation of "democracy" into a species of secular religion. One effect is to found social obligations upon a kind of statism, instead of upon man's threefold relationship to God, to himself, and to his fellow men. [51]

As a moral psychologist with administrative flair, then, Reed confined himself to conditions on a human scale that were subject to purposeful intervention and management. But he was also attuned to the distortions that entered into the Jesuit educational package and the self-serving ends to which it might be put. The individualistic premises of Jesuit pedagogy were ambiguous and could be put to a variety of uses. For many parents and alumni, the prestige of Jesuit schools reflected their role as an impetus to the social ascent of American Catholics from the working and lower middle classes into business and the professions. Social awareness was liable to remain dormant or lapse into sentimentality when it was not abandoned altogether. Although its ideological slant was quite indirect and its political effect impossible to document in any case, the concentration on self-discipline and assertive skills tended to be utilized selectively, leaning more to a competitive than to a service ethic. Reed was well aware that the clientele of the schools tended silently to screen out the socially inconvenient parts of the Jesuits' educational message:

> The attitude of most of our students toward the accumulation of wealth is truly disturbing: it is a major goal in life and a measure of ultimate success. In fact, their attitude differs very little from that of their secular counterparts.[52]

Theoretically, the remedy was to be found in a comprehensive philosophy of social order and justice thought to be contained in the encyclicals. At the everyday level, this might be combined with efforts at sensitizing students to the social *magisterium* in and outside the classroom. A practical difficulty with the plan was that few high school teachers, including Jesuits, were up on Catholic social doctrine; it was simply not very salient. The dangers and the lessons associated with sex and personal sin were easier to grasp than catechetical abstractions about social justice. There did not seem to be many incentives or even a distinct body of knowledge to catch the attention of the faculty and to commit large numbers of students to the cause of social justice.[53]

Reed nevertheless remained convinced that youthful idealism could be converted into social uplift. He put together a string of recommendations that gave the raising of social issues a legitimacy in Jesuit schools and that set the stage for a countercultural critique at odds with the civics-textbook patriotism that prevailed in the public schools. The overly generic and faintly weird tenor of papal social teaching might not be an insuperable problem and might even be turned to pedagogical advantage. The initial strategy was to elevate social concern on the Catholic agenda rather than get involved in potentially divisive theorizing. The approach sidestepped manifest ideology by stressing willpower and action over cerebration.

The time was ripe, Reed proposed, to reach beyond a concern with individual achievement and salvation toward matters involving collective welfare. He cast this change in the instructional agenda as the wave of the future, but it had evident ties to traditional communitarianism as well:

> Throughout the history of the Church contemporary conditions and problems have caused the emphasis in the Church's teaching to be thrown now on one aspect of religion, then on another. The Protestant revolt focused the emphasis on the nature of justification and the means of effecting it. Since the Council of Trent, our schools have been stressing man's duty to God. Today the papal encyclicals and the instructions of our Generals show the way to a change of emphasis— toward the duties of every man to his fellow-men. [54]

What the effort at consciousness-raising lacked in content might be made up for in zeal. The idea was to rally enthusiasm and to give legitimacy to the discussion of social issues. The energetic rhetoric was nearly the same as Jesuits had used among themselves in the 1930s. It repeated the need for a positive program but it was opaque about the specifics of alternatives to communism and American materialism.

> The urgency and universality of the problem call for a total effort, a saturation program. It is a radical program, in the sense that it is not a drive for charities nor a crusade against Communism, nor even a comprehensive labor program, but an all-out effort to establish a new social order according to the mind of the modern Popes. It is an attempt to understand the basic cause of the social evils and to build up an order in society so soundly based that these evils will crumble and dissolve. [55]

Compassion was to be united with the martial spirit of the Counter-Reformation, and both of these elements were to be joined to a respect for intellectual analysis. The strategy sounded like an extension of the Jesuit self-image to lay activists:

> Knowledge of facts and principles is essential to keep this social-mindedness from being a vague sentimentality. But when this knowledge has been infused with the enlightening and warming beam of light from religion, the right attitudes will grow, strong and sure. [56]

The program was not so much an alternative as an extension of the New Deal, close to the position of the progressive wing of the Democratic party. Reed resuscitated the tenor of the social policies that had captured the loyalties of American Catholics of his own generation. Equity, with an emphasis on class reconciliation, was the keynote. The platform was decked out with traditional values. Social-democratic goals were set alongside the traditional Jesuit focus on the training of leaders. Stability and hierarchy were to be consonant with social justice:

Father General Janssens has described the product: ". . . young men freed of that pagan mentality which adores riches . . . steeped in the charity which seeks above all the good of others and is ready to work with the Church in bettering the temporal and spiritual conditions of the greatest possible number of human beings." It is clear that the part our teachers are to play in the social apostolate is to exert a profound influence upon our students, supposedly the Catholic leaders of the future, to the end that they will be men well-formed in Catholic social teachings and men of action, inspired with the zeal and charity to make positive, effective contribution to the settlement of social problems and the building of the new social order. [57]

Continuity and reconciliation were given priority. The militancy of the program also required a certain aggressiveness that was cast as resistance against injustice. A toughness that might not be supplied by intellectual rigor would come from a zeal for justice that differed from mere charity. The imagery combined muscularity and compassion:

We should aim to develop . . . first . . . respect for and love of all men as brothers in Christ. Hence, the destruction of race and class prejudice. The second attitude is a zeal for justice, that all men receive the due reward of their labor, that there be a more equitable distribution of temporal goods, and a consequent and more universal sharing of spiritual goods.
. . . The third attitude we seek is a sense of responsibility to one's fellow-man, and a genuine concern for his welfare, a concern that is strong enough to take action. So many of our students, like their elders, feel that their only responsibility in life is for their own persons, to serve God adequately in their state of life and to save their own souls. [58]

The crunch came in fitting this message into a curriculum already crowded with "humanism, expression, and logical thinking." There were also conceptual difficulties. The preservation of hierarchy and the promotion of stability and social justice were not self-evidently consistent goals. But even if a compelling rationale could be developed for a reorientation of Jesuit education toward Catholic teaching on social justice, squeezing the program into the curriculum, given the formal and de facto priorities of the schools, was all but impossible.

The result was the cultivation of a free-floating idealism with an uncertain—and, in the event, adaptable—programmatic bent. The curriculum was not rearranged to accommodate separate courses in social doctrine. Instead, as happened in the seminaries, the recommendation was

somehow to infuse existing courses and extracurricular activities with social
awareness:

> Father General does not insist upon more hours of formal courses in
> social studies. Rather, he expects every teacher, already formed by so-
> cial consciousness, to be alert for every opportunity his subject presents
> for teaching principles, making applications, firing students with zeal
> for social justice. . . . The retreat master can channel his talks toward
> arousing social responsibility. . . . The various committees of the So-
> dality will brings its members into first-hand contact with the poor and
> the neglected and will give them a vivid realization of the social evils
> around them.[59]

The treatment of instruction in social justice took up only a few pages of
Reed's guidebooks. In the end, the manuals were about pedagogy and
school management. The arousal of social responsibility did not specify an
incisive vision of economic and political reality. Rather, the exhortations to
conscience supported a rough-and-ready sympathy for the underdog together with a pride in individualism and respect for authority. The democracy propounded by secular thinkers tended to be understood more as mass
rule than as representative government.

This combination of moral conservatism and social progressivism, alongside a skepticism regarding political liberalism and the Enlightenment generally, had characterized Catholic social thought since it took form at the
end of the nineteenth century.[60] In the American context, the mixture of a
left-of-center stance on labor-related questions and acceptance of authoritarian practices within organizations—a hallmark of the pluralist settlement
of the fifties—was beginning to show signs of wear. By the time Reed's
manuals appeared in the late fifties the social bases of support for blue-collar
Catholicism were already slipping.[61] Challenges to internal authority remained latent. The schools ignored these potential contradictions and continued to hone competitive skills and to reward the striving for mastery and
individual fulfillment.

For all this, Reed made sure that questions of social justice did not
disappear altogether from Jesuit high schools. A diffuse moralism, joining
the old virtues of self-control and discipline with criticism of public failings,
commanded respect. At least it had to be given a hearing. The ambience
was two-edged. A judicious tolerance of disagreement was a reasonable
mechanism for ensuring peace. The conciliatory mentality that was recommended as a guide to social conflict promoted diplomatic management. It
helped forestall controversy. On the other hand, ethical concern could not
be dismissed as an idiosyncrasy, particularly if the individuals advocating

social change had reputations for moral seriousness. In stressing the objective reality of social precepts, Reed drew on the natural-law legacy of Catholicism that separated opinion and personal power from principles. *Ad hominem* attacks on "difficult personalities" could be counterproductive. The abstractness that rendered these principles difficult to comprehend and to apply shielded them from the whims of individuals. It was improper to jettison this version of the rule of law on grounds of intellectual difficulty or material expediency. The content of social teaching might be ambiguous, but the legitimacy of ethical concern was secure. The irritant of conscience was not excised. [62]

V

It was through Reed's treatment of the psychology of teaching, not in the handling of social questions, that his educational manuals came alive. Most of the social material remained in an institutional limbo, without concrete expression. Practical applications were missing. This was not typical of Reed's approach. The pedagogical guides assembled by Reed harked back to the sixteenth-century *Ratio Studiorum,* a compendium of classroom lore that did not traffic in generalities. "The *Ratio* dealt little in expressed principles and much in methods and practices";[63] it was a system that took pride in flexibility. The angle of vision, intensely empirical, was the opposite of the deductive manner by which social principles were supposed to be derived.

When the scene was the classroom or the athletic field or when he turned his attention to staff meetings and extracurricular activities, Reed shone. He became a master of institutional psychology. He drew on the expertise accumulated by Jesuits in manageable settings. The schools prized experience as much as fixed tradition. In comparison to the almost completely enclosed seminaries, the students and some of the faculty were not Jesuits, and the tangible goal was human development rather than spiritual perfection. The ideal in both places was to develop an inner discipline instead of imposing control from the outside. But in the schools the Jesuits could not rely on the same panoply of supports that came with the total environment of the seminary; still, they had enough control to give them security to experiment. The give-and-take between directors, staff, and students could be fairly open. The Jesuits behaved like craftsmen customizing their tools and their techniques to an assortment of concrete tasks.

During the years following the war, the style of teaching and administration shifted further from surveillance to persuasion. The emphasis turned toward a human relations approach to getting things done. In Jesuit lore it was an extension of "personal care," with an admixture of prudence. The method mitigated the atmosphere of impersonal bureaucracy and the people processing that came with unbending rules:

> Not long ago it was common in some of our schools for principals and teachers to take solid satisfaction from the long list of students who failed and were eliminated from the school. They had the strange notion that a high mortality was evidence of a good school with high standards. This is a pernicious attitude, unworthy of schoolmen whose primary purpose is apostolic.[64]

Reed was mindful of the perils of resorting to a dictatorial manner that could not be enforced. Although he voiced the usual suspicions about an indulgent ("democratic") management style, Reed had enough experience with martinet administrators to understand the counterproductive consequences of such a style. His approach was eclectic. He was a fan of consultation and staff meetings. There were no sharp lines between professionalism, participation, and common sense. Intrafamilial collaboration and quarreling under paternal ministration was the basic model:

> "Democratic administration" has been carried to ridiculous lengths in some sectors of modern education. However, it would be unfortunate if the excesses drove the pendulum to the other extreme. . . . Surely a good staff or committee meeting directed by the principal can turn up more new ideas than the principal can single-minded. . . . [S]ubordinates will accept decisions more readily and will put their efforts into the execution more wholeheartedly when they feel that they have had a share in formulating the decisions.[65]

Reinforcement was designed to accentuate the positive. "We all thrive on praise and it warms our hearts to know that our superiors are aware of our efforts and our accomplishments." Inspiration by example was to be a motivating force. At close quarters, within the small community of the school, the behavior of Jesuits mattered more than either social abstractions or vast market forces. "The principal's idealism, his zeal for excellence, his pride of workmanship, and his wholehearted devotion to this work will set a level of achievement for teachers and students." Even decentralization was to be countenanced, in moderation:

> Effective delegation is a difficult and delicate matter and requires wisdom and skill. It is true that subordinates will do work of higher quality and will do it more effectively when the granting of authority and

responsibility quickens their initiative and arouses zest for accomplishment. . . .

If the principal keeps too close a hold on the work he has delegated, some will think he interferes, or that he lacks confidence in his delegates; if he keeps hands off, it will look to some as though he is unsympathetic or uninterested. As a matter of fact, some teachers cannot accept responsibility and so cannot be depended upon. Many young Jesuits lack a practical sense of management. . . . The principal has to guard against the consequences of inefficiency and irresponsibility. . . . [He] must keep in touch with the activities of his assistants and moderators. [66]

The prescription went beyond paternal kindliness to a commitment to human potential *avant la lettre*. Somewhat as the religious advice of Anthony Paone moved from an umbilical quietism to a spirituality of sociability, Reed kept refining his educational philosophy—less grandly, his rules of thumb—so that it could accommodate new classroom methods without patently menacing the prerogatives of the patrimonial manner. The choice of words was not merely cosmetic. He reinterpreted Jesuit pedagogy as a dialectic of control and empowerment.

The very first quality which the Society expects in its principals is leadership. This is an elusive quality, hard to analyze. It is closely interwoven with a man's personality. . . . Leadership implies a leader, a group, and a goal. . . . [The leader] has to teach and guide and help the individuals, developing the best that is in them, working at their side. . . . He has to inspire the group with enthusiasm for the goal. He has to carry them along with him toward the reaching of the goal.

Let this be guiding rule of every principal; let it be thoroughly realized and actuated; let it guide him through all the activities of administration like a radio beam to keep him on course: *The most important duty of the principal is to develop the people under him to their highest potential.* The gauge of success is the ability to enlist the top potentialities, energy and enthusiasm of the staff. It cannot be overemphasized that the principal's first concern is with *people*, not with things. [67]

The spirit that animated a curriculum inherited from the days when classical humanism reigned supreme was built up piecemeal out of bits of practical wisdom. The busy regularity of the high schools served to calm the anxiety, prevalent in the seminaries, about deducing practical applications from remote principles. The system was given; the curriculum provided a predictable structure. Continuity with the past was preserved; so was a feeling of community with Jesuit schools that shared virtually the same course of studies.[68] This freed energies for careful adjustment to particular cases. Moderate size permitted regular feedback. Within a stable framework the life of the high schools approximated as closely as might be expected an organically functioning system. Just as the linguistic drill, as much as the language itself and the training in discipline associated with it, constituted the real subject of Latin exercises, the ethic of service expressed by the Jesuits in their attention to students—the sheer time and energy devoted to teaching—probably made more of an impression than did expostulations on social responsibility. For all of the emphasis on *eloquentia perfecta*, on articulateness, much of the ethos of the high schools was unspoken. The moral tone was embodied in the imagery of daily action.[69]

The treatment of "scholastic deficiency" illustrates the Jesuits' case-by-case approach to instruction and formation. A working supposition was that once boys had been selected after passing admission tests, lack of ability was only rarely likely to be a fundamental problem. "God never expects us to do better than our best," Reed observed, "but parents often and teachers sometimes do." Motivation, and hence a sensitivity to the adolescent psyche, counted for more:

> We probably neglect interest and motivation more than any other phase of teaching. In the case of Latin, for instance,the boys have to "take it and like it." But if they do not like it, they will simply "take" it and no more. In educational matters, boys do not want the things they need and do not need the things they want. It is our business to reconcile the two. The root of failure for most of our boys is in the will, not in the intellect.[70]

Academic performance could be evaluated by combining letter grades and more discursive assessments, again with an emphasis on constructive criticism. The Jesuits' astuteness and attention to detail in helping students cope with the insecurities of learning paralleled in a down-to-earth way the diplomatic skills that, centuries earlier, had made some of their predecessors legendary papal emissaries. Of more immediate relevance was the implicit contrast between the persuasion and skill-through-repetition approach of the Jesuits and the emphasis on chastisement and athletics of other teaching orders, for example, the less delicate Christian Brothers. Although they regularly imposed staying-after-school penalties for behavioral infractions, the Jesuits generally refrained from physical punishment.[71] Understanding of the slowness and waywardness of hard cases was usual. Aside from its human decency, the sympathetic manner, together with the underlying seriousness of the Jesuits, had an element of snob appeal for the parents of students who had come out of a social background that had accustomed them to harsher treatment:

It seems better to phrase the traits in complete sentences. This will help to avoid misunderstanding and to lessen the possibility that traits will be checked on the basis of isolated incidents but will appear as habitual traits. Most existing checklists are too negative and too harsh. There should be items expressing commendations, as well as common failings.[72]

In instances when expulsion for academic failure was unavoidable, the procedure was to be handled with tact. Punitiveness to the student and his family was to be avoided, as was damage to the reputation of the school:

There will always be some failures, despite our best efforts, for each boy has a free will and the balance between his higher and lower appetites has been upset by original sin. We can't force him to study. When the boy cannot profit from our teaching any longer, or when he has resisted our best efforts to train him, we are obliged to dismiss him. . . . But let us keep our reasons in true focus. We do not dismiss him to enhance our reputation as a "good school."

. . . If we have nothing to be ashamed of on our part, and if we have kept in close touch with the boy's parents, the odium of dismissal can be reduced to a minimum. To protect the good name of the Society and the prestige of Catholic education, we must try hard to carry out the dismissal of students tactfully and amicably. . . . Students should never be dismissed curtly or abruptly without giving parents an opportunity to discuss the case. In such conferences, it is not prudent to emphasize the school's zeal for its standards. Parents should be brought to see that this action really looks to the student's own interest and welfare. . . . [T]he shock of dismissal and the opportunity to make a new start in another school often bring him to his senses, stiffen his character, and set him on the way of eventual success.[73]

The blend of strictness and sensitivity to individual differences was at the center of Jesuit high school education. The dominant style was a mixture of familial pushing and support; the manner was both stern and reassuring. The monitoring of performance was structured to build up self-confidence.[74]

Within the nurturant hierarchy, a key ingredient besides compassionate control was competition. The method of *emulatio*—training in and through competitiveness—went back to the earliest days of Jesuit education. Although most of the archaic variations had been abandoned by the 1950s, the overall stress on competition outlasted some of the specific components of the classical curriculum. Formal courses in rhetoric and logic, for example, had migrated to the underclassmen years of the colleges. In the high schools the approach had evolved into an assortment of group and individual games that were designed to elicit participation, as opposed to passive learning, and to accustom students to the tricks and rigors of competition itself. The playing field was as much in the classroom as it was outdoors. Reed praised the invigorating effects of competition in a passage that could have been lifted from Theodore Roosevelt:

> Much nonsense has been written about the harmful effects of emulation in the schools. The spirit of rivalry is in the fibre of the American boy. All his life he will be facing competition, which seems to grow fiercer as the years go on. To form the habit of flinching and shying away from competition will do the youth more harm than learning the attitude of welcoming it and facing it.[75]

The method relied on clear rules. Both the manner of battle and the outcome counted. The engagements were taken earnestly, and good sportsmanship was expected. They were exercises in assertive but courteous manliness. Losing toughened; winning was a lesson in style:

> Two precautions will eliminate the objectionable elements of rivalry and emulation. The *Ratio*, which uses emulation at every turn, always provides for competition *among equals*. It constantly pairs off individuals or groups of equal ability. Secondly, all meanness and ill-will must be avoided. A good competitor is magnanimous, striving to outdo his own best performance, not to glory in the defeat of a rival. It is significant that the rules for emulation were listed in the *Ratio* under heading "Incentives for Study."[76]

Although Jesuits could make it appear that they had devised as many words for *emulatio* as Eskimos had for snow, two shades of meaning—competition as practice to activate "diligent application" and competition in the more literal sense, as stylized combat—captured the principal nuances. One was a struggle with the self; the second was a struggle with others. Encompassing both functions—and keeping the activities from becoming either wholly solitary or wildly competitive—was the communal recognition that everyone shared the same predicament.

At least through the 1930s, the "chief forms of emulation" included a variety of games. *Decuriae* were made up of bands of ten students

> grouped according to ability and diligence. Each group has a captain, who hears recitations and memory lessons, keeps account of the performance, takes attendance, collects written assignments, and keeps order. Youths of the lower *decuriae* can displace those of the higher by superior performance.

In the ritual of *concertatio*

> the students of two classes on the same level are paired off for a series of single combats. The leading officers of one class may come to the aid of a classmate who is being hard pressed by his opponent of the other class. The winning class is determined on points and receives a trophy which it holds as long as it maintains its supremacy.[77]

After the war, these formalized contests fell out of favor among the scholastics who did the bulk of the teaching. The competitive spirit continued to be honed in debating clubs—interscholastic "oratorical contests" sponsored by the American Legion were popular—and other extracurricular activities, including sports.

The final element in the modus operandi of the high schools was drill, which might be more or less regimented, depending on the subject matter. The challenge came from the material itself instead of from direct competition with other students. The task involved mastery through memorization, repetition, analysis according to plan and categories, or some combination of these techniques. The systematic acquisition of learning skills was the goal, which in turn boosted the sense of mastery. The process might require

> memorizing declensions, learning a vocabulary list, understanding a rule of syntax or a scientific principle, comprehending a passage in a foreign language, or translating it or imitating it, mastering a technical process, tracing a trend in a period of history or summarizing the period, making judgment about the motives of a historical character, appreciating a piece of literature. Whatever the lesson may be, the content is clearly defined, the method is set forth, and the outcomes are expressed: "This is the subject matter; this is what you should be able to do as result of working with it; and these are the steps you should take in the process."[78]

Learning meant that students were to become familiar with ways of handling information presented in different forms. Discipline was to undergird adaptability. Some of the training was mechanical, as in language lessons. Other chores, like the interpretation of essays and poetry, were open to imagination and wordplay.[79] Drill in the narrow sense was a device suitable to the acquisition of skills and the building of confidence. In conjunction with the experience of competition, the feeling of completion and domination of the material was meant to build up a capacity to surmount obstacles and solve problems on one's own. This by-product of the more arduous tasks was analogous to the effect of muscle-building exercises designed to strengthen endurance. Successfully conjugating Greek verbs might open up unsuspected reserves of fortitude and prodigies of willpower.

Masculinity was defined both as the mastery of self and as competitiveness. Thus, dualism had a moral component. Sentimentality was oblique, a matter of bonding with one's own, and a base of compassion for others. The domination of self made for restraint; one did not go for the throat. It might also—although this went beyond the normal course toward what Jesuits thought of as the clerical path—lead to the discovery of self and new vistas of meaning.

VI

"We have an excellent product, Jesuit education," Lorenzo Reed wrote:

> We believe in it wholeheartedly, even as we realize that we can and should improve details here and there. We are not trying to sell it for profit, but to make it the instrument for saving souls and for promoting the greater glory of God.[80]

In the forties and fifties and until the cultural revolution of the sixties, the system of Jesuit secondary education worked satisfactorily. Labeling it a system risks inflating the formal underpinnings of an operation that had sifted and adapted the experience of Jesuits over the years. It was a collage of practical wisdom, a recipe more than a theory. Reed inventoried the parts of a living organism without fixing an abstract code to it.[81]

In the prestige ranking internal to the Society of Jesus, working in the high schools stood below teaching in the colleges and universities. However, it was in the high schools that experience, as contrasted with doctrine or principles, could be put to practical use with tangible results. Expertise was circumscribed and usable.

Concrete drill engendered habits of application, a palpable growth in reliability. Although this did not produce in a predictable way students with a markedly social conscience or a discernibly superior ethical sense, it was adapted—given the subtlety and sympathy of the Jesuits—to the age of the students and to the forging of self-esteem, as a step along the road toward character. Small gratifications might be immediate, but the larger lessons were that triumphs were partial and temporary and that one should win fairly. In balance with the reverse approach, manifested in efforts to flesh out preconceived social abstractions, practice in persistence generated a tangible orderliness.

Even during the most inward-looking and conservative days of ghetto

Catholicism, the system of secondary education was enlivened by the steady infusion of scholastics, whose periods of regency usually took the form of teaching in the high schools. This activity was part of their own education. More of the personnel in the high schools were Jesuits-in-training than was the case in settings such as parishes and universities, where religious staff members were almost exclusively priests. The enthusiasm of young Jesuits, combined with a store of know-how accumulated across centuries, imparted a chemistry to the schools that could not be derived from an academic blueprint and that could not be duplicated in the universities where Jesuit resources were dispersed.

The system loosened up in the fifties as the occasionally rigid discipline and rites of competition of earlier decades fell out of fashion. Jesuits in the high schools were as sensitive to parents as Jesuits in the colleges and universities were attuned to benefactors. The sometimes crushing punitiveness of schooling in the immigrant period receded in the prosperous era after the war. There was also a dawning awareness of the need for collegiality in dealing with lay colleagues. [82]

The scale of the high schools made innovation challenging but nonthreatening. There was a rough balance between the demands placed on the Jesuits, the goals they set for themselves, and their capacity for adaptation. Pedagogical methods were refined and customized without creating fears of runaway change. Even many of the particulars of the revered *Ratio* were ignored or forgotten. The system flourished not only because of the enthusiasm of young Jesuits, the wisdom of older ones, and a confluence of structural transformations—the burgeoning of a Catholic middle class that wanted its sons to be prepared for college, the ethnic communities that had not yet packed up for the suburbs—that for a while made private education in the cities a sought-after commodity. The arrangement also thrived because "the character"—the identity—of the schools was not in question. It was not intellectual certainty so much as a deep awareness of unalterable patterns beneath permissible changes that gave a sense of permanence. [83]

Jesuit high schools were controlled experiments as well as depositories of tradition. The security of being in charge of the fundamentals made innovation at the edges possible. Reed and the Jesuit Educational Association as a body were well aware of the difference:

Some principals and rectors take too literally the adage about the new broom, or listen too readily to every complaint about the existing order, and expect to please everybody by wholesale changes. In the interest of desirable unity and uniformity within a province or even within the Assistancy, there must be some limitations upon the autonomy of individual schools. Thus, certain changes in the character of the school, the curricula, the faculty, and other matters require the prior approval of either Father General or Father Provincial.[84]

There existed a clear hierarchy of the changeable and the immutable. The list of possible innovations "to be referred to Very Reverend Father Provincial"—the superior to whom the president of a high school answered—was extensive and in the context of the times, given the assumption that the Society of Jesus ran the schools in fact as well as in name, rather predictable. The items included "any changes in textbooks," "any change in tuition rates," "departure from province-established syllabi," "introduction of any new course," "reduction or increase of number of class periods regularly to be required of all students," "introducing, dropping, modifying obligatory attendance at daily Mass," and so on.[85] The length and detail of the list suggest that some principals were in the habit of bending the rules. Many prohibitions appear to be pointed reactions to previous transgressions, and it is hard to tell what effect yet another set of regulations might have had on hardheaded school administrators with a flair for solving problems expeditiously.[86]

More serious matters were sent correspondingly further up the chain of command. It was the short list of decisions that had "to be referred to Very Reverend Father General" himself that touched the core. This consisted of four items:

1. Establishment or suppression of a high school.
2. Introduction of coeducation.
3. Introduction of a curriculum that did not require any Latin.
4. Total elimination of Greek from the school.

Except for the question of the opening or closing of a school, these were symbolic more than functional matters. They set the parameters of institutional identity, bounded on the one side by the classics and on the other by sexual exclusiveness. The issue of dead languages was not completely ornamental. It resonated with academic habits from the society's founding days, and the belief was still widespread among the majority of Jesuits with scant training in science and mathematics that the study of Latin was an unrivaled device for disciplining mental processes. It was the question of coeducation, however, that was supremely delicate. This conjured up symbolic and institutional repercussions at once.

The mission of the schools was not in doubt; it was the saving of souls. In the shorter term this meant the improvement of life chances. Beneath this, where the operational and the symbolic were intertwined, was the identity of the schools. Jesuits were prone to see themselves as doers and to equate their work with their being.[87] Their identity was bound up with their institutions, and the most important of these were their schools. The schools were the incarnation of corporate identity. The palpable ethos surrounding this identity required the continuity of a classical tradition, or at least the ornaments of it, in the knowledge of Latin and Greek, and the preservation of sexual segregation.

Neither of these traditions was transparently practical. The contribution that single-sex schooling and training in classical languages were thought to make to the formation of leaders had been a staple of the prestige of elite private schools, and the customs were hardly unique to the Jesuits.[88] But by midcentury in America the connection between such requirements and career accomplishments no longer seemed so evident. Still, if the classics and sexual segregation were largely symbolic even for the Jesuits, their symbolism had institutional ramifications. For the Jesuits these customs served as a fixed point around which judicious and useful adaptations might be devised. They were supposed to furnish the stable foundation for a versatility that could cope with the modern world. Even if single-sex schooling did not have clearly discernible consequences for the educational attainment of students, it had organizational and psychological implications for the Society of Jesus. Unless Jesuit identity were maintained, assimilation meant absorption.[89]

As Vatican II approached, the social bases of clerical recruitment began to shift. Jesuits with their antennae tuned to younger men entering the order were picking up signals of changing aspirations. The society's intake was being transformed. Simultaneously, the colleges and universities were expanding faster than the Jesuits' capacity to keep their stamp on them. Few of the colleges and universities had much control over the influx of students. Their selection criteria were generally low. In addition, although they could assume that their higher education establishment promoted upward mobility, Jesuits had no way of tracing whatever ethical impact their colleges and universities might have.

The high schools were different. While there was more talk about the efficacy of moral formation at this level, attempts to confirm it systematically were disappointing. On the other hand, since their operating costs were modest, many of them could be pickier than the colleges and universities in their admission procedures. Numbers were kept fairly small. In addition the high schools kept substantial control over their curricula. Although they had difficulty expanding academic schedules to include new subjects, they could preserve traditional course offerings. The universities had begun to lose this struggle with the adding on of the professional schools and later with the growth of undergraduate enrollments.[90]

The high schools were preserves of institutional identity for Jesuits. Their results were hard to assess, and even their ability to dominate the inflow of resources would fall drastically with demographic changes in the cities. But inside, for a time yet, they were rather like collective works of art, reshaping patterns out of old forms. In the high schools Jesuits were tinkerers of genius.[91]

14

Harmonies and Antinomies

I

For much of the twentieth century the brightest thread running through the skein of writings by Jesuits on social issues consisted of meditations on the functions of the family and the role of women. The topics discussed in *America* magazine, *Social Order*, and other outlets of the Society of Jesus ranged over the political, economic, and literary landscape. Yet Jesuits as diverse as Joseph Husslein, John Rawe, John Courtney Murray, Joseph Fitzpatrick, and Robert Gannon returned to topics on sexuality, the position of women, and the functions of family life. These were the arenas where deep emotion and a hoped-for fidelity—prerational energies and the dream of stability—were supposed to meet. Family and gender themes were less central to the social and political thought of some Jesuits than others. They are conspicuous by their virtual absence, by the extreme indirection with which they are handled, in the writings of William Lynch, for example. Nevertheless, they made up the common ground that most Jesuits who commented on public affairs tried to cover. Politics and social issues had an ethical tincture, and social ethics was an extension, however circuitous, of a moral philosophy the center piece of which was sexuality and the family.

The treatment of moral and sexual issues was generally more consensual than the perspectives that Jesuits adopted on political and economic disputes. While the latter allowed for fairly open discussion, room for disagreement was restricted when it came to "matters of faith and morals."

A systematic contrast also prevailed in orientations toward the two sets of issues. In dealing with social controversies, Jesuits stressed the destructiveness and futility of class conflict, the importance of reconciliation between economic interests, and the desirability of harmonizing the functions of capital and labor. Class antagonisms were dangerous but ultimately super-ficial; hence, they were negotiable. There could be a diversity of views on specific policies, differing priorities might be attributed to issues affecting social justice, and measures that worked in one cultural setting might or might not be suitable in another. Universal principles were not at stake. At least so it was thought, if not broadcast, by centrist and progressive Catho-lics, including a few Jesuits, once the territorial claims of the papacy had come to be dead letters by the later part of the nineteenth century. Some forms of democratic consultation—preferably based on principles of corpo-rate rather than individual representation, although this could be waived—were not unpalatable. The slant was toward stability and pragmatism, and the overall imperative was social peace. These strands of realism, adaptabil-ity, and conciliation enabled John Courtney Murray to press for religious tolerance and political pluralism.

Issues concerning family life and sexual morality cut deeper and were charged with greater intensity. The basic intuition seems to have been that, while male and female were to form an indissoluble reproductive unit, their social roles were distinct. The separation of spheres implied an irreducible bifurcation of interests. Gender segregation also meant hierarchy. Notions of cooperation, reciprocity, and complementarity between the sexes were commonly invoked, and women were accorded some privileges, a measure of respect, and in the abstract even veneration—they were not chattel—but the word *equality* was rarely used, and then with a suspect connotation. Fundamental antagonisms, such as those between male and female, were to be overcome by an organic hierarchy with males at the head. This power differential lay at the center of social relations and it was the *cordon sanitaire* of natural hierarchy.[1]

Outside the realm of the family—in the area of Catholic economic the-orizing, for example—authoritarian learnings were offset to some extent by a streak of precapitalist populism. Its formulation was close but not quite equivalent to a refurbished paternalism.[2] The social *magisterium* was more remarkable for ambiguity than for consistency. It emerged over the course of a series of encounters between traditions of hierarchy and communalism, on one side, and on the other the liberal revolutions and working-class move-ments of the eighteenth and nineteenth centuries.[3] Shifts in the balance of power between religious and secular authorities, alongside the social mo-bilization precipitated by industrialism, altered the configuration of interests with stakes in doctrine. By the second half of the nineteenth century, the church could no longer pretend that it exercised much control over the institutional formulas of European politics. The Papal Territories were lost, and the pope declared himself "a prisoner" in the Vatican.[4] An offshoot of this decline in mundane influence was an accentuated rejection of materialism and a flight into idealism. The rhetoric of dogma sought higher ground. The declaration of papal infallibility was issued at Vatican I, a year before the confiscation of papal lands by Italian nationalists. The retreat from worldly power coincided with the elevation of a scholasticized Thomism to canonical status, and it encouraged the greatest outpouring of doctrinal pronouncements since Reformation times.[5]

The decay of the temporal power of the church drew clerical attention to regions within reach of ecclesiastical control. Sexual morality was the most prominent of these. This area comprised a concrete set of issues, not at all as stratospheric as some of those that engaged professional theologians, yet with vast symbolic resonance and with apparently practical, if indirect, implications for the solidity of the social order. Furthermore, such populist elements as existed in the family doctrine of the church reflected the habits of peasant and working-class males and the division of labor sanctified by middle-class domesticity. Catholic teaching on the family and allied subjects was probably closer to popular mores, and less class-biased, than was the social *magisterium*. Women were largely powerless, especially as their position shrank to an exclusive domesticity, and the potential for divisiveness along lines of gender remained latent.[6] The conservatism of the church on sexual and family matters had the advantage of cross-class appeal.[7]

The enhanced salience of sexual ethics and family morality did not, however, translate exactly into doctrinal uniformity or stability. Two rather different developments took place. One concentrated on matters of sexual propriety, taste, and the symbolism of everyday life. Canons of modesty in dress, for example, were handed down by requiring students to wear uniforms in Catholic schools. Regulations such as these stood as talismans of resistance against fashions in sexuality, and they also served as a mild rebuke against flaunting disparities of wealth.[8] Signs of interpersonal democracy were upheld, along with standards of a severe morality. The image to be cultivated was one of well-mannered reliability, respectful of authority and fringed with the refinement of one's betters, yet bound up with a populist air of neighborliness. The chief manifestation of the lace-curtain style was the affable yet sexually decorous demeanor of the Irish American and the German American subcultures.[9]

But even as this type of sumptuary semiosis held fast, a transformation was overcoming the context of family morality and allied domains. The change involved an alteration in the sociological framing of sexual issues. The linkages between these issues and ongoing societal shifts were attenuated. The moral substance and the symbolic reverberations of the controversies stayed about the same, but their social context came to be perceived differently. The change in vision corresponded to the decline in the political fortunes of the church and its recognition of the passing away of the agrarian ethos on which its sexual morality was based. In the United States the change was associated with a shift from an inward-looking perspective, limited to the Catholic subculture, toward one that contemplated more openly the hazards and attractions of absorption into the American way.[10]

At no time were moral issues thought to be completely cut off from questions of social order. But the connective tissue was increasingly stretched and the flow of influence from family to society came to be seen as reversed, as the political power of the church diminished. The traditional, predominantly Latin view held to a forceful, nearly unitary interpretation of the linkages between the micro- and the macrospheres. The family was a mini-government. The good state was an institution that protected the family and that itself abided by patriarchal norms. In the extreme, the main difference between the two in popular religious imagery seems to have been one of size. The Irish Republic, as envisioned in its 1937 constitution, and the austere corporatism of Portugal under Salazar, in which the state's revenues and expenditures were to be balanced like a family budget, approximated this ideal.[11]

The integralist paradigm of the family as government in nucleus, and of government as the family writ large, never enjoyed legitimacy in the pluralist, mobile climate of the United States.[12] A considerably more common rendering of the social role of the family was as an anchor of collective order. This view flourished in the ethnic enclaves. Marriage within the fold, and the propagation of large families with clear rankings of male and female roles, held the community together. The organizational soundness and normative continuity of the community, in turn, fostered a solidarity that paid off politically. Patriarchy that might be unacceptable outside the Catholic subculture could thrive within it. The hierarchical family and the community supported each other. If one changed, the other would, too. In addition, at the same time that it upheld communal bonds, the internally stratified family structure inculcated habits of discipline and application that were compatible with, and indeed supportive of, the work ethic of the economic system within which the enclaves functioned.[13]

The model of the family as social foundation depended for its plausibility, then, on the preservation of an encapsulating but paradoxical way of life. Besides a degree of mutualism and collective sentiment, it emphasized hierarchy and competitiveness. The success credited to effort and sacrifice would also come to be blamed for undermining the social bonds left behind by abundance.[14] Vaunted as tradition, the ethos was in fact short-lived. As the protective surroundings began to give away, and as the media penetrated the hearth, two divergent reactions surfaced. One was a subtle yet decisive shift toward a defensive privatization in which the family, bereft of most of its positive functions as a bulwark of order for a fragmented environment, came to be looked on as the last redoubt of virtue. The model reflected a feeling of encirclement, not influence outward. "Sex is here to say," a Jesuit political scientist wrote. "But the sexual moral standards of Christian civilization may not be."[15] This position was vigorously represented in the postwar era by the Jesuit sociologist John Thomas. Another stance was more equivocal about the trade-offs for the family and male-female relations in the process of assimilation. This ambivalence took form in the work of the Jesuit cultural theorist Walter Ong.

II

Questions of sexual morality, family life, and "values" were at the center of the social criticism conducted by Jesuits during the postwar years. In the periodical *Social Order*, the space given over to family issues and changes in moral standards was greater than that devoted to any other single topic.

Most of these writings were produced by John L. Thomas, a Jesuit sociologist trained at the University of Chicago. In addition to numerous scholarly and semipopular articles, he wrote a major book on *The American Catholic Family*.[16] Thomas's output is interesting not just for its extensiveness but for the persistence he brought to the task of reconciling the defense of traditional values with a social scientist's recognition of the economic and demographic transformations undermining the bastion of these values. The fact that his discussions of family life began to appear in the decades following World War II, as the underpinnings of the American Catholic environment were undergoing dramatic change, heightens their importance. His work is a meditation on the impending collapse of the way of life tied to first and second-generation immigrant families:

We came in as immigrants into a society which was Protestant, at least in the beginning. . . . The adjustment was pretty much defensive. We were ethnics of every variety. The point is that [for] these people, their first job was to survive. Survive in a Protestant country which is very, you know, they have their values and virtues, but they also have some extreme dislikes and fears. . . . So it led to a very defensive position in the church, and got worse, if anything. The church was quite open, I'd say, up until almost the end of the last century. Then they started tightening up. And Rome started tightening up, of course. I would say it wasn't until after World War II, up until then, they were living alongside American society, not in it. Their training was alongside of American society, not in it. Jesuit training was not in society, it was alongside of it. . . . That broke up in the fifties. It was going fast.[17]

The starting point of Thomas's analysis is the construct of sexuality not primarily as a personal phenomenon but as a relation enfolded in a hierarchical succession of larger collectivities. Although Thomas did not mention it explicitly, the metaphor of nested inner and outer rings in a Ptolemaic universe was integral to his sociological analysis. He concentrated first on the role of women within the family and, second, on the viability of the family within the economic and social environment made up of ethnic enclaves encircled by a largely secularized Protestantism. The continuity of religion was bound up not so much with doctrinal disputation or intellectual comprehension as with social reinforcements. Outside the wrappings of parish, neighborhood, and family, the individual was liable to become disoriented and to lose the faith. Demoralization, in its twin senses of anomie and of licentiousness, was likely to set in.[18]

The imagery of nested social units was in line with traditional thinking of the sort propagated decades earlier by Joseph Husslein. Thomas, however, directed his attention to the effects of larger structural transformations on the family and, by extension, on sexual mores rather than on the reverse connection that presupposed a causal impact of the family on the stability of the larger social order.[19] From both points of view the family was pivotal. Yet for Thomas, writing at a time when the denizens of the enclaves that had been built up under immigrant Catholicism were undergoing a second movement, toward full participation in the American way, realism lay in acknowledging that the dominant flow went from the social context to the smaller family unit rather than vice versa. The labor market, the driving of women out of the home to work, and an incessant consumerism were reshaping family life. The ethnic enclaves that once buffered the family from impersonal social forces were themselves shrinking and fading. Thomas retained a Catholic focus on the foundational nature of the family as a mechanism for transmitting religious values but he rejected the imagery of the family as a micromodel for larger institutions.

> The Catholic family, like other families, must work out a modus vivendi in an industrialized urban environment. . . . [S]ince Catholic families constitute a minority group, they are unable to control the institutional means necessary to implement their marriage and family values.[20]

Somehow, given the pervasiveness and relentlessness of modernization, Catholics had to come to terms with urban mores without abandoning the social patterns that made them distinctive. Thomas saw the Catholic family as a standard to be defended rather than as a model to be spread through society. Hence he did not have to concern himself, as Joseph Husslein or John Rawe should logically have done, with the question of how mini-utopias were to take hold in and reshape a hostile environment. The question of the aggregation of ideal social units, especially of primary groups like the family, into larger political institutions, always hypothetical in the American case, was by now theoretically as well as practically irrelevant. By the time Thomas undertook his studies of family relations, a Catholic monopoly of social customs was no longer tenable even as a normative yardstick. While most of his prescriptions for preserving the family and the place of woman in it were conservative, he did not seriously consider extending these standards across denominational lines, much less making them the law of the land. Thomas accepted the pluralist settlement. His conservatism was defensive, its objective not to attain political power but to preserve Catholic identity.

Thomas, then, like John Courtney Murray, was concerned with the fate of Catholicism in a pluralist setting. The economic plenty and political freedoms Catholics enjoyed were mixed blessings. The numerical growth of Catholics in the United States did not guarantee the survival of religious identity. Together with social mobility, such advances could lull Catholics into complacency. Catholics, their identity diluted by expansion and prosperity, were in danger of blending into the American cultural landscape. The enclaves they had arduously constructed might turn out to be little more than way stations along the road toward an inexorable assimilation:

> How does a religious minority which maintains distinctive concepts concerning the nature of man and his institutions secure the social realization of these concepts in a society which no longer accepts their validity as operative principles of organization and action? . . . [W]e desire to study how American Catholics can maintain their marriage and family ideals in a society which does not fully accept these ideals and which, consequently, establishes institutions and practices that either oppose or fail to support them.[21]

The complexity and rapidity of change in the United States threatened the maintenance of what Thomas called the "time-and-space-ignoring solidarity" of Catholicism.[22] A shared ideology was in danger of vanishing with the decay of support mechanisms for the family and the consequent breakup of familial routines and roles.[23]

As a Jesuit operating within a theological framework of unchanging precepts, Thomas posited the irrevocability of basic truths—the bans on contraception and divorce, for example. "The Catholic approach implies the existence of a set of absolute value premises which serve as unchanging points of departure in establishing practical programs for living."[24] Abandoning these beliefs was unacceptable. As a sociologist, however, Thomas recognized that beliefs and values were not Platonic absolutes, that they

required social and institutional reinforcement, and that the Catholic subculture was increasingly open to pressures from the outside. Moral principles were embedded in the intimate practices of household life. The values
associated with this subculture were at risk of being adulterated beyond
recognition in an unreflective process of assimilation.

Fear of seduction at the hands of the dominant culture lent Thomas's
thought a critical edge that went beyond the preservation of familial norms.
He warned of palliative approaches to industrial relations that gave workers
"a sense of participation" without inquiring whether "a sense of personal
importance and dignity is even compatible with the organizational requirements of the modern productive process" and he stressed the need for
resistance against "the pathology of normalcy."[25] Similarly, he denounced
the hucksterism and cynical sentimentality that merchandized sexuality and
consumerism in the name of family values, the rewards of honest down-
home toil, apple pie, and skies of Kodak blue.

But these suggestions of social radicalism were side issues. Thomas did
not pursue his insights in the direction of formulating an elaborate analysis
of labor relations.[26] Increasingly, his commentary became a lament for the
passing of the solidarity and uprightness of the Catholic way of life. The
principal target of his attacks was the decline of moral standards, which he
condemned through the years, recycling some of the phraseology that he
had used earlier against social injustice:

> Traditional views regarding the morality of pre-marital and extra-
> marital sexual relations are openly rejected in our all-pervasive mass
> communications industry, and receive only a vague, confused lip-
> service among a rapidly increasing proportion of people at all levels of
> society. . . . It is worth noting that although these various practices
> initially occasioned some shock, they soon came to be taken simply for
> granted. Most Americans evidently have learned to accept the nor-
> malcy of the morally pathological.[27]

Almost all of Thomas's scholarly energy was devoted to a search for social
mechanisms that might restore and bolster the moral fiber of the family
unit. He accepted the inevitability of a political pluralism in which Catholics existed as one among several communities, but he could not bring
himself to value moral pluralism as a positive development. This entailed a
relativism that became indistinguishable from permissiveness.[28] The defense of the family and of the roles and values embodied in the family
against the encroachment of an ethically oblivious pluralism was Thomas's
chief preoccupation. He viewed himself as an applied sociologist working
from unshakable postulates. The difficulty of reconciling these orientations
led to gloom about the prospects for the survival of a recognizably Catholic

culture in America. In turn, the deterioration of subcultural Catholicism deprived the American experiment of much of its moral ballast. Thomas shared with Murray a pessimism regarding the possibility of effective policy in the absence of ethical consensus:

> What has happened is the toleration of every form of "sex-tease" in a society which is incapable of developing uniform norms and behavioral patterns culturally channeling the legitimate expression of the reproductive drive. It is this combination of stimulation and confusion which has made the problem acute. In the final analysis, the loss of a common ideology paralyzes democratic action for there exists no common premises on the basis of which practical programs can be established.[29]

Thus Thomas looked on the family and the environment threatening it from two angles. One perspective was that of traditional moral theology and unchanging dogma. The other was by way of empirical sociology. The former was top-heavy with fixed principles; the latter was loaded down with facts and insights. Building a conceptual bridge between the ethical and factual domains was arduous, and for the most part Thomas gave up on the hope of a creative interchange that might transcend the limits of either one taken alone. Instead, a traditional Catholic moral framework provided an overarching perspective for his intellectual project, at the expense of systematic or exploratory ideas. The attention that might have been turned to the development of theory was diverted into the affirmation of doctrine.

The catechetical style followed from a supposition that the primary audience for his writings, even when they did not appear in textbook form, was composed of Catholic undergraduates. In principle, social facts could be sorted and hypotheses tested in light of middle-range theories that did not conflict with the ultimate truths of Catholicism. But the key theme of Thomas's work, the family, was so central to official teaching that some confusion between secular investigation and religiously inspired inference was difficult to avoid.[30]

On the other hand Thomas avoided simplistic condemnations of vice or exhortations to virtue. Fixation with doctrine did not prevent him from producing perceptive descriptions of the forces conditioning change in family structure. One such piece of analysis appeared in an analysis of "disintegrating factors" in marriage:

> In regard to Catholic marriages . . . this much is clear; the present trend toward greater equality and independence for women, implying as it does a weakening of the foundations upon which the prerogatives of male dominance in the marriage institution were based, has caused

many wives to be less tolerant and long-suffering than formerly. It is possible that the relatively high percentage of marriages which break up because of drink is as indicative of this trend as it is of any change in the drinking habits of the average husband.[31]

In passages such as these, the sociological mentality took over from the religious sensibility and from the habit of blaming a perceived social decline on personal failings. Moralism was suspended, at least as a first line of evaluation. An attempt was made to come to grips with an assortment of forces interacting to propel changes beyond the control and the consciousness-as-common-sense of single individuals.

However, when Thomas turned toward a more ambitiously speculative mode of interpretation, it was no longer a matter of estimating the relative weight of causal factors in marital breakdowns or of pinpointing the multiplicity of causes behind the decline of organized religion but of asserting the perpetuity of Catholic doctrine in the midst of variable theoretical shadings and in the face of probably irreversible social trends:

> Changes in the status and roles of women as well as modification of the family structure have operated to place the wife in a position of equality with the husband. Does this signify that the husband is no longer the head of the family, or if he is still considered to be the head, does the wife cease to have equality? Obviously, this problem would not rise in a society which considered males to be naturally superior nor is it likely to occur in a rural environment where the economic functions of the domestic unit clearly specify the different tasks of family members in a common enterprise. Modern changes, however, need not require the rejection of the husband's headship; they do demand a rethinking of what it means.[32]

In other words, changes in expectations and family practices could be accommodated insofar as they did not usurp habits of gender stratification. Despite its minority status, a hierarchical yet ample Catholicism was to selectively absorb rather than adapt fundamentally to secular change. The preservation of identity was at stake. Doctrine might be refurbished at the margins but the dogmatic core was irreconcilable with social trends gaining speed in the postwar period. Ideologies and sectarian causes would go out of fashion. Meanwhile, a comprehensive Catholicism might still be salvaged.

Thomas did not adhere to an obscurantist chauvinism. Male domination as personal aggression was primitive, lacking in nuance, and physically dangerous to women. His model acknowledged the beneficence of companionate relations for bettering the quality of life within marriage. And, although the fundamental aim of marriage remained that of reproduction,

Thomas was not insensitive to the possibly benign effects of more affectionate husband-wife relations on rearing and socialization:

> The pagan glorification of the male, which was in effect little more
> than the glorification of male passion, infiltrated even Christian prac-
> tice, limiting the restoration of the divine ideal of marriage effected by
> Christ. To be sure, modern women may continue one of the errors of
> the feminists by mistaking equality for identity with the male, but it is
> our contention that her present status offers her increasing opportuni-
> ties for personal development through companionship with the male in
> marriage.[33]

The deeper problem, however, was that marriage itself had become an
increasingly perishable commodity. For Thomas, discussions of various
types of family structure—more or less hierarchical, more or less egalitarian—took second place to the declining permanence of marital bonds
generally and, by implication, of personal commitment of any kind.[34] The
social ambience of American was increasingly hostile to the preservation of
Catholic values, and the stand that Thomas took was one of no surrender to
secularism in the essentials of Catholicism. In the conditions of the postwar
United States, this created a dilemma. The tangible barriers against secularization were being eroded by suburbanization; the homey ghettos were
disappearing. The material bases of Catholic spirituality—the neighborhoods and the social networks of the bars and union halls—were shrinking.
It followed, apparently, that Catholicism's line of defense had to be more
diligently intellectual and competitive than before. This was the strategy of
those who favored updating and expanding the colleges and universities.
The content of what was to be taught, however—the relation of this curriculum to Catholicism and to American modernism—remained unclear.

Catholic social thought itself seemed strange in the United States. Thomas sensed that the problem might not lie entirely with the exuberant
materialism of the American scene. The *magisterium* might be too Eurocentric to provide an overarching vision of the changing American social
structure. A tactical retreat was therefore in order. Instead of a panoptic
sociology, Catholicism could provide a theory of the family, the crucial unit
of social morality.[35] The church would specialize in bolstering the ethical
order, with the family acting as a microstructural lever for restoring cultural
norms compatible with Catholicism.

The recognition that demographic and structurally induced changes had
to be dealt with in organizational terms by individuals with limited resources
living in the here-and-now, rather than denied via psychic escape to an
idyllic medievalism, lent a reasonableness to Thomas's thought that raised
it above the mere defense of tradition. Unlike Husslein, Thomas had no use

for a lost paradise of social order. In a social program that called for the valuation of familial virtue, little needed to be exclusively Catholic. In addition, narrowing the analytical focus of his work to the family enabled Thomas to come up with a number of sociologically shrewd observations about the transformation of American social structures. His was an applied sociology in a dual sense. The immediate goal was the protection of the American family; the longer-range objective was to demonstrate the viability, if not the superiority, of Catholic moral teaching in a hostile environment.

The venture failed to catch on intellectually in part because of unlucky timing. The late fifties and early sixties, when Thomas produced the bulk of his ideas, witnessed a groundswell in favor of assimilation among American Catholics. These were years of optimism about the American way and of burgeoning curiosity about sexual expression. This was the gestation period for cultural upheaval. Thomas's sometimes Teutonic-sounding denunciations of Americanism fell mostly on deaf ears.

A related difficulty derived from the substance of Thomas's analysis. Even though he recoiled from easy condemnations of modernism, the picture that Thomas drew of the Catholic subculture was one of a benign authoritarianism. Once-compliant families were rejecting this milieu as opportunities improved to leave their parents' protected environs. The aspirations behind their mobility were not altogether misguided, as the studies of Andrew Greeley and others about educational attainment among Catholics demonstrated.[36] Thomas's was not a model to be received uncritically by educated Catholics skeptical of absolute claims that controverted the ordinary ambitions and common sense of their daily existence. Among growing numbers of Catholics, many of the appurtenances of parochialism had become tiresome, and accusations of "materialism" had come to sound almost as ritualistic as benedictions of medievalism.[37] Finally, because so much of his analysis dealt in descriptive terms with the situation of a minority which may have been troubled but which was not posing a threat of social disruption, the work of Thomas on the fate of the Catholic family aroused less interest in policy circles than it might have.[38]

Thomas let the gap between the social changes of the fifties and sixties and the adherence to unbending precepts of family and sexual morality stand. The ecology of homespun virtue was gravely threatened. He returned to his sociological conviction that the best defense against the incursions of secularism was organizational. This became the rationale for his insistence on the preservation of the institutional shields—the schools and the parishes—surrounding the Catholic way of life. The broader focus of Thomas's research beyond the family became the Catholic community itself, the subculture made up of mostly ethnic parishes strung together like fragile islands in a sea of Americanism. The parochial schools in particular constituted a built-in protection against the secular world. Their function was to reinforce the internalization of Catholic morality, specifically "the Catholic family ideal." Thomas insisted that the danger of familial disintegration had turned acute in the postwar period; he quoted a statement issued by the American bishops in 1949 to the effect that "the lethal danger to the family is neither chimerical nor remote. It is a present danger, more fearsome than the atom bomb."[39]

The ethnic subcultures, then, and their networks of schools and services formed environmental buffers against the blight of the cities, where most Catholics lived. The survival of these subcultures, Thomas admitted, was not automatic. The preservation required renewed efforts on the part of clerical authorities and religious practitioners:

> The parochial system is not self-sustaining. Besides the ever constant financial burden, there is the competition of the nonparochial school system and the steady inroads of indifference and secularism upon Catholic families. . . . [I]n order to establish, maintain, and enlarge the Catholic parochial school system, the clergy must not only plan and labor unceasingly, they must constantly encourage and exhort their parishioners to support the schools. In their sermons they must frequently stress the value of a Catholic education and the serious obligations of parents to provide this for their children. Catholic parents who support the schools must be praised. They must be made to feel that one of the finest heritages they can bestow on their children is the gift of a Catholic education.
>
> This constant emphasis on Catholic education is needed if the system is to endure.[40]

Thomas knew that suburbanization and social mobility were bound to damage the encircling stabilizers. Nevertheless, he felt that hard work and clerical prodding might prolong a recessive way of life. He envisioned a supraethnic, neoconservative countermobilization in defense of traditions that were increasingly despised by secular progressives:

> Although the Catholic family enjoys a maximum of religious freedom, many institutions such as civil divorce, and some accepted practices such as the use of contraceptive birth control, lend no support to the Catholic family ideal. Hence, Catholic families must formulate and put into practice particularly in the realm of chastity and family life certain moral ideals considerably at variance with the dominant culture. . . . [I]t was precisely because many ethnic leaders were distressed by the moral ideals and practices which they encountered in

the lower ranks of society that they reacted by building strong solidarity around the national parish and its organizations. With the gradual disintegration of these old solidarities, there is appearing increasing awareness among all ethnic families of a common bond of unity with other Catholic families.[41]

Thomas's program of bolstering traditional values appealed not only to Catholics who felt put upon or left behind by an America they found difficult to recognize and disdainful of the way of life they cherished. It also preserved a leadership role for the clergy. The task of preserving the *Volkstum*, the folkways and the familial morality of Catholicism, was tied to the dedication of religious professionals and the dominance of the ecclesiastical hierarchy. It promised to extend the life of Catholic Action.[42]

The program seemed to have the internal coherence of a utopian vision. Features that looked strained in isolation, such as the reliance on clerical control, made greater sense when their functions were understood as integral to the defense against a mounting external menace. Increasing secularization on the outside called forth redoubled devotion on the inside.

Even so, contradictions were detectable. One could be traced to the attempt to preserve absolute truth through the wisdom of the community. As a sociologist, Thomas understood that religious mores depended to a great degree on group support. He was somewhat less sensitive to the historical conditioning of religious beliefs that supposedly expressed unswerving truth. A Burkean guarding of tradition and great caution with respect to the pace of change qualified the notion of abstract verities. However respectful of custom, it belied a reading of Catholicism as a marble repository of the purely absolute. Abiding truths were historically contingent. A slowly evolving tradition was not equivalent to the universal, eternal, "time-and-space-ignoring" canon that Thomas understood to be the irrefragable essence of Catholicism. The distinction was slight if whatever change on either dimension—in historical custom or in deductive principle—might occur was imperceptible and practically indistinguishable from the other. Nevertheless, it left Thomas open to the criticism of indulging atavisms and shibboleths that had assumed the stature of givens by way of historical vegetation. They were neither axiomatic nor revealed truths. What was being defended was a quite untranscendental tradition, parts of which had grown to canonical stature, down arbitrary paths, out of random beginnings.

Another latent fissure came not from the long, organic evolution of communal memory but from formal education. Catholic schools were needed to uphold an equilibrium the subculture could not reach or maintain on its own. But the very quality of the educational system undermined the tradition that it was supposed to preserve. In the decades after the war,

teachers—including Jesuits who were supposed to be the best of them—
once used to training disciplined workers for economic competition, imbu-
ing them at the same time with fortitude and diligence, found themselves
caught between rebellion against outmoded strictures and a rising intellectual competence among their own creations. Habits of mind acquired in
Jesuit and other Catholic schools opened up occupational alternatives and
intellectual vistas that reduced the feasibility and the rationale for clerical
direction of a Catholic revival.

While much of his work anticipated the political counter-mobilization
that followed the legalization of abortion, Thomas's hopes for the preservation of a conservative Catholic ethics barely survived the sixties. An undercurrent of grieving that had not been far from the surface of his earlier
work became even more prominent.[43] For one of the final issues of *Social
Order* he wrote an article entitled "Early Teen-Age Dancing and Dating
Betrays Our Youth and Our Country." By this time, as the title indicates,
Thomas's dismay had clearly deepened. "The American people must realize
that the maintenance of our cherished way of life is radically incompatible
with the pseudopermissive, irresponsible cult of youth now in vogue."[44]
Although he had never pressed a positive connection between individual
morality and the health of the body politic, as Husslein and Rawe had done,
Thomas could not forsake the negative judgment that sexual license not
only wrecked the family but jeopardized the state of the nation. By the same
token, strong and hierarchical family structures and sexual continence were
necessary though not sufficient conditions for social stability. Sex, drugs,
and rock-and-roll were the ruin of the polity. It was the same position he had
expressed in the early fifties, warning that "our increasingly permissive attitudes toward sex can only lead to social anarchy and personal chaos."[45]

III

The plainness and concern with moral sobriety in John Thomas's writings
are reminiscent of the ambience of the northern Midwest that he shared
with Joseph Husslein. But Thomas touches only tangentially on the decline
of rural society; his principal theme is the fate of the family under industrialization. Just as other Jesuits—Leo Brown, for example—took the working class and labor relations as their main interests, Thomas fastened on the
Catholic family in the urban settings of the East Coast and in the region of
the Great Lakes. For these men, economic depression and the struggle for
security on the part of lower-class immigrants were shaping experiences.

A good deal of the plangency in Thomas's writings comes not just from
the decline of the religion of immigrant Catholicism but from the percep-

tion that the working class, the social conservator of that religion, had itself begun to recede during the postwar era. Two phenomena that in the eyes of European conservatives and radicals alike were supposed to follow opposite trajectories—the rise of the working class, the decline of religion—gave evidence of going downward in tandem in the United States. The pages of *Social Order* started to fill with commentaries on the problems of abundance in the 1950s as Jesuits began to puzzle over the unprecedented dilemmas of postindustrial society.[46] As John Thomas concentrated on the fate of the family in an industrial setting, Walter Ong examined the changes in traditional Catholicism in postindustrial society.

Unlike Joseph Husslein, John Courtney Murray, or John Thomas, Walter Jackson Ong has not been known primarily as a social analyst or political commentator. His prominence rested initially on his excavation of the work of Petrus Ramus, a Renaissance logician who influenced European instructional methods and the dissemination of ideas around the same time that the Society of Jesus was experimenting with the schools for which it would become famous. Ong singled out the innovations associated with Ramus as an instance of the larger transition from an oral to a print-oriented society.[47]

Even before the publication of his research on Ramism in the late fifties, however, Ong had begun to establish himself as a cultural critic of broad scope. He concentrated on the transition then stirring in American Catholicism from a subculture in which intellectual endeavor was still largely confined to the question-and-answer format of theological manuals toward a rapprochement with the fluid society of the years following the war, and he was instrumental in loosening the hold that the fanciful medievalism beloved by Husslein had on the Catholic mind.[48] He has continued to work the margins between the disciplinary demarcations of academia and the "deep reorganization of consciousness" implicit in the convergence of the Second Vatican Council, the transformation of the Jesuits, and the emergence of media technologies in advanced industrial society. Ong is the most recent in a line of Jesuit polymaths who, like Pierre Teilhard de Chardin, have attempted to reconcile the crosscurrents of tradition and modernity.[49] His creative period, again in contrast to the experience of Husslein or Murray, spans the pre- and postconciliar eras in roughly equal proportion. Many of the themes that are present in their work converge and are brought to a head in his writings.

While Ong's professional reputation was founded on a study of the work of a Renaissance scholar-teacher, his intellectual agenda has been shaped around a dialogue with modernity as culture and as the material equipment of culture. He has used the traditional Jesuit interest in the devices of instruction and communication, in "rhetoric," as an entrée into an analysis of the technology of learning and the management of discourse in the interests of social hierarchies. His work concerns the links between pedagogy and power, and he has tried to expose the subterranean politics of the humanist tradition.

Ong does not attend closely to the machinery of conventional politics, and his explicit references to questions of social justice are few; he has little to say about intermediate institutions.[50] In this respect his method differs sharply from the positivism-cum-moralism of John Thomas. The literary, artistic, and historical evidence that Ong draws on is often used as material for the interpretation of archetypal patterns in the collective representations of both high and low culture. Ong's interdisciplinary style has had as its substantive corollary an interest in the connections between apparently apolitical or merely interpersonal transactions, such as modes of teaching and learning, and their implications for the distribution of power at a societal level.[51]

In contrast to the Jesuits of Husslein's generation, and in line with the approach pioneered by John Courtney Murray and Gustave Weigel, Ong has purposefully engaged in dialogue with the secular world.[52] He has shown, in contrast to Murray, less disdain and indeed an ambivalent sympathy for cultural as well as political democratization. He is less literally sociological than Thomas and other conservative observers of the urban scene. But Ong is not, on the other hand, a philosopher or a historian of ideas. He has tried to distinguish between the consumer trinkets and the communicative technology of mass society, and between these physical objects and the norms conveyed by them. His analytical niche is that of a classicist and literary historian shocked into fascination with the implications of the new media for the breakdown of old hierarchies. From an expertise initially established in the pedagogical implications of the transition from oral to printed means of instruction and, more broadly, in the cultural strains of the shift from precapitalist to capitalist societies, Ong has concentrated on the ramifications of a subsequent, postmodern transition in material culture when modes of communication and expression are no longer so print-dependent.[53]

Ong has viewed the impulse toward and the limits on change in the institutional church from the vantage point of his expertise in early modern Europe. His historical sensibility is keyed toward the *longue durée*, a perspective that, together with his training in literature rather than the social sciences, may have contributed to the very minor role that political conjuncture has played in his thought. At the same time, the preoccupation with interpersonal technologies—with the evolving machinery of discourse—has enabled him to bring a social perspective to what might otherwise be considered a belletristic exercise in the history of ideas. Ong's style tends to the allusive, and his inferences sometimes take in entire civilizations. But his phenomenological analysis is pitched at the minutiae of interpersonal relations, specifically, at the functions of sexual conflict for self-definition.[54]

A persistent focus of Ong's work has been on the developing technological base of the diffusion of knowledge. In this respect and also in regard to the attention given to popular culture, his early writings anticipate the interest of modern literary criticism in the social context of artistic production. Ong has stressed how the medium—for example, vocalized speech as compared to written documents—in which rhetorical presentations are imbedded conditions not only the substance of communication, as his former teacher Marshall McLuhan insisted, but also how it constrains the characteristic ways of framing and storing ideas: how technology structures consciousness and identity. It is not only the content of information that is amplified, clarified, or restricted by the medium of expression; the conventions and paraphernalia of the media also influence the mental universes of communicators and receivers.[55]

Two claims are fundamental. One stems from the emphasis on the evolutionary nature of the material underpinnings of rhetoric. Technological changes revise sempiternal understandings of objective truth just as political developments undermined, for Murray, the vision of hierarchical government, changing it from a permanent standard to a temporary condition. The cyclical word of oral cultures, rooted in the turning of the seasons and agrarian ways of life, and the analytical world of print cultures, conveying a sense of permanence and categorical, virtually static truth, or of linear advance, have been layered on one another, and both are undergoing a secular process of further layering by new technologies.

The second idea is an extension of the first. A latter-day transition from printed to electronic forms of expression and transmission has contributed to a restructuring of the adversarial style built into classical rhetoric. The invention and spread of these channels of communication has meant not only general change in "cultural tool kits" but also a reorientation away from the presumed certainties and deceptive linearities—"the artificial securities of typography"—enshrined as canonical by combative, characteristically masculine modes of discourse. "The silent lifeworld into which man had moved with writing and print and, he thought, with Newtonian physics is no more."[56]

For Ong, print is allied with discipline, abstraction, and dominance. Oral cultures, on the other hand, tend to be associated with sensuality and concreteness. The contrast is analogous to the male-versus-female struggle that John Courtney Murray considered to be a foundation of identity and a precondition to civility. With this underlying correspondence as a preliminary, Ong takes the psychosexual implications of modes of communication and combat in new directions. In order to understand this, it is necessary to follow his account not only of the evolution of print from oral cultures but also of the growth of modern, post-print kinetic cultures from the detritus of both of these. Then Ong considers the consequences of this transformation in communicative technology for the forging of psychosexual identities at the basis of social relations.

The connection between modes of discourse, intimate hierarchies, and the forging of identity that stands at the center of Ong's thought was advanced first and perhaps most strikingly in his discussion of "Latin Language Study as a Renaissance Puberty Rite":

> When Latin passed out of vernacular usage, a sharp distinction was set up between those who knew it and those who did not. The conditions for a "marginal environment" were present. . . . [T]he marginal environment was one between the family (which as such used a language other than Latin) and an extra familial world of learning (which used Latin). . . . The cleavage between the vernacular world and the Latin world coincide[d] with the division between family life and a certain type of extrafamilial life and with a division between a world in which women had some say and an almost exclusively male world. . . .
>
> [I]n general, girls who were educated at home and not in schools could be quite literate without having any effective direct access at all to the learned world. . . . Closed to girls and to women, the schools . . . were male rendezvous strongly reminiscent of male clubhouses in primitive societies. [57]

The schools mirrored on a small scale a societywide system of stratification. The virtual exclusion of women from the classrooms of a modernizing Europe not only reinforced the larger hierarchy; the restriction was also designed to inculcate a psychology of emotional control during the passage from boyhood to manhood:

> It has not been sufficiently remarked how much Renaissance poetic and other language study finds itself wandering from the consideration of poetry or language to the consideration of courage, or of its opposite, softness or effeminacy. . . . The Jesuit savant Martin Antonio Delrio . . . explain[ed] how the lowly humane letters toughen the young boys who suffer from too great tenderness in age and mind, preparing them for the weightier disciplines of philosophy, medicine, law, and theology. [58]

Ong goes on to argue that the implicit link between Latin drill, the shaping of masculinity, and the fortification of gender hierarchy, far from being peculiar to Renaissance classroom practice, continued through the nineteenth and well into the twentieth century, especially in elite schools, as a discipline for "training the mind" or more accurately the will. The socializing methods of the better schools were forged around a combative rhetoric that was at once stylized and socially if not, toward the end, intellectually serious.[59] The social consequences of this pedagogy—in particular, the consecration of gender asymmetries—outlived the intellectual substance of what was taught. In this sense, for Ong, the method is the message.

The connection proposing "a better understanding of some curious and important momentums developed by past ideas and practices"—namely, the suggestion that social hierarchy, gender role, and sexual identity are linked and reproduced through stylized contests—is not carried over unimpeded into recent times. Traditional rites of masculine initiation and bonding in opposition to women have undergone decline. Ong ends his initial statement of the agonistic hypothesis not with a conclusion but with a series of questions

> [that] suggest matter for reflection—forward-looking, let us hope, rather than nostalgic—concerning the twentieth-century situation. Where are the rites de passage for youth today? Does a technological society have any? Should it have any? If so, what should they be?[60]

Toward the end of the seventies Ong pressed his examination of these issues. In *Fighting for Life*, subtitled significantly *Contest, Sexuality, and Consciousness*, he bound the postconciliar crisis in Catholicism directly to the demise of rituals of agonistic combat through which males had traditionally established their identities and selected leaders from among themselves:

> The development of the Roman Catholic ethos, as of consciousness generally over the last three millennia . . . has been that of a strongly masculinizing era, marked by . . . agonistic patterns. . . . Catholic theology in the West has been the last academic enterprise to abandon the agonistic proceedings and thought forms rooted in the ancient masculinized, residually oral academic world. The Roman Catholic Church clung longest of any group in the West to Learned Latin, the extrafamilial, sex-linked, distinctively male language that carried with it the old agonistic mind-set and thought forms. . . . As Latin ceased to be the medium of instruction, the agonistic economy of academia collapsed.[61]

The argument is illustrated by an assortment of examples drawn from a wide range of fields.[62] The most compelling turns out to be autobiographical, a retrospect of Ong's experience as a Jesuit-in-training, which is contrasted with the changes ensuant on Vatican II:

When I was studying theology at the Saint Louis University School of Divinity in the mid-1940s, the basic or main-line courses, such as moral theology and dogmatic theology, which formed the core of the curriculum, were all given in Latin. . . . In fact, the three-year philosophy course . . . followed by Jesuit scholastics, preparatory to theology, had remained as Latinate as theology into the mid-1960s, too. . . .

By the late 1960s, following the Second Vatican Council, Roman Catholic theology virtually everywhere in the West was loosening its connections with the Latin language. As it did so, certain spectacular correlative changes occurred, at times, it appears, rather automatically. Within two years, 1967 and 1968, the School of Divinity . . . (1) ceased using Latin as a language of instruction, (2) dropped the thesis method as a method of instruction, (3) dropped circles and disputations together with oral course examinations as integral parts of its program, and (4) admitted women students. So far as I know, no one involved in these changes adverted to what appears to be the fact from the evidence adduced here: they were hardly four changes, but in effect one. They moved theological instruction out of the age-old rhetorical, oral-agonistic world of male ceremonial combat.[63]

The collapse of the old ritualistic training involved erosion of the rules for establishing collective and particularly male identity. The outcome has been ambiguous. On the one hand, the legitimacy of a hierarchical order founded on gender discrimination has declined. Once-venerable means of securing male identity have lost conviction, as have the channels for conveying doctrinal certainties such as pyramidal models of ecclesiastical organization, and dogma itself seems less settled. "Basically, the Christian Church is not a body of doctrine or an 'institution' but a community with a shared memory."[64] On the other hand, the compression—the suddenness and intensity —of change appears to have called forth a yearning for fixity, at least in those areas such as the mores of sexual relations, if not the gendered differentiation of labor, in which identities have customarily been established. Some antinomies appear to be nonnegotiable. Both sides of the tension as well as some of the shades in between surface in *Fighting for Life*:

Given the reduced adversativeness in the Roman Catholic Church's stance since Vatican II, one might think that the Church could simply slough off various more or less agonistically toned masculine accoutrements. . . . [But] the Church's teaching is structured permanently in the deep feminine-masculine polarities that shift dialectically through time to produce, for example, today the needed and welcome ascendancy of the feminine in consciousness signaled most conspicuously by the women's liberation movements and also perhaps even more by

worldwide ecological concern, which regard the whole universe as a
house, a home. Since sex is a biological phenomenon, the masculine-
feminine dialectic is basically biological. . . . Catholic doctrine has a
biological base in the sense that the male-female relationship forms the
human ground in which redemption, freedom, and love take root.[65]

The central lesson here seems very close to Murray's. While doctrine that
was once thought to be revealed truth may "develop," there is at least one
underlying polarity, based on the biological difference between the sexes,
that is constant. The corporate hierarchies of Catholicism and, evidently,
the gender disparities on which these hierarchies largely rest are social
constructions. But there is also a biological component to sexual rivalry.
Whether this competition produces dominance or an inconclusive equality,
Ong does not say. Still, Ong is more explicit than Murray in hinting not
only at the possibility but also the desirability of change in the minisystems
of power and the social fabrications that are the cultural expressions of this
separateness and stratification:

> The Church is sexually defined. To the psyche, the Church is always
> feminine, Holy Mother Church. Psychoanalytically as well as theologi-
> cally there is no way to have a "Father Church."
>   The overwhelming femininity of the Roman Catholic Church from
> the human side suggests that a male clergy is basically not a character-
> izing feature of the Church so much as a countervailing feature. De-
> spite the masculine clergy, in macho cultures (of which there are
> many), where the male labors under more than the usual male insecu-
> rity, open association of males with Church services is relatively rare,
> so great is the threat of being swamped there in the feminine. In such
> cultures even an all-male clergy is likely to be regarded by other males
> as somewhat feminine because of the close alliance with the feminine
> Church.[66]

To the degree that the achievement of personal identity—particularly, of a
male identity for the priesthood—has depended crucially on shared protocols of sexual subjugation, the manner and the probability of attaining it are
increasingly problem-filled. The rules of struggle are not as clear-cut as they
once were. Though Ong argues that the struggle itself is timeless, a new
institutionalization has yet to come about:

> I suspect that what will happen is that there'll be some changes, but in
> the long run they'll be like many things in the Church, mostly ad-
> justed unconsciously and therefore very slowly, and there will be ac-
> commodations made to our new understanding. I think they already

are there, some of them. I don't see any way to make them, at this point, explicitly and articulately except to make them *a posteriori.*

If you shape up the issue, you may shape it up the way it's done in *Fighting for Life,* but that's complex and most people won't follow. But if you shape it up in a simplistic way, it strikes such terror in many people that you can't do anything with it. You'll spend all your time fighting people who really don't have anything to say. And that's, I guess, my reason for being in my own work rather irenic. I think the other styles are largely a waste of time. You fight these issues, hoping you can crush them. But by the time the news gets out, they're dead all on their own.[67]

IV

Institutions of the sort identified with industrial society—political parties, labor unions—receive short shrift in the work of Walter Ong. Even primary groups—notably, the family—are absent. Instead, his interests lie in the destabilization of the dyadic relations of everyday life, the dissolution of identity that hangs on these relations, and the myths about power and hierarchy embedded in technologies of communication. His concern has been with unspoken meanings and recurrent processes of domination and deference underneath the veneer of literacy and the codification of formal organizations.

Joseph Husslein, John Courtney Murray, and Walter Ong all show a sensitivity to linkages between political order, social change, and gender roles. It is also possible to discern a progressive unfolding of the connections they perceive. Writing in the decades after the turn of the century, Joseph Husslein proposed that family hierarchy was the bulwark of collective order. His fondness for a tapestrylike medievalism caused him to posit the Catholic ghetto as an ideal writ large, with the church monopolizing authority in public and private realms. Catholicism was, or should be, a way of life subsuming political, social, and sexual dimensions.

Writing a generation afterward, John Courtney Murray rejected the either-or standard of Catholic dominance in, or withdrawal from, politics as unworkable and undesirable. In the American case he greeted change in the public realm as a sign of political progress, and he saw pluralism and tolerance as the vehicles of this development. He was mostly silent on economic and social issues, but he stipulated an unchanging moral foundation—natural law—or, failing that, the preservation of a male elite whose masculinity was achieved by dominating women, as the anchor of Catholic identity under the tidal wave of assimilation.

For Walter Ong, the public sphere as conventional politics or public policy is scarcely present at all. Furthermore, he views the "battle of the sexes" as being essential not to Catholic identity but to the identity of males, especially clerics, in traditional Catholicism. The institutional church and Catholicism are differentiated. While the quest for identity through dominance by gender is ongoing and implies, according to Ong, a universal phenomenon that transcends cultural boundaries, it displays a special inflection in the Catholic world. Male leadership seems to be a prerequisite for the perpetuation of a patriarchal version of institutional Roman Catholicism, although not of some still to be specified emerging variant. The struggle is constant, but not the outcome. With Ong the existential, the communal, and the organizational dimensions of Catholicism have very nearly floated free of one another, and a new identity has yet to be achieved. The Renaissance humanism—the sense of mastery and creativity—that for Ong replaced the mysticism of medievalist nostalgia has itself lost much of its cultural thrust and meaning.[68] Whereas for Murray the danger to be met was an ethical relativism, the challenge for Ong has been to cope with nihilism, or perhaps less histrionically with a future struggling to define itself, in the midst of the collapse of inherited antinomies.

By the end of this progression, it would appear, the Society of Jesus has arrived at an impasse. The psychic pinions of its hierarchical style seem to have come undone. It may have reached the terminus in the evolution of a species of religious life.[69]

Intermission

How did the Society of Jesus really work? And how did it change? The order is a protean organization within an even more sprawling institution that is itself part of a variegated way of life. The action can be hard to follow. Where do the elemental patterns of the organization lie? In answering these questions I will proceed from the topical and the concrete, from commentary on the society itself, to more theoretical observations about its structural and symbolic environment.

For a time before Vatican II the Society of Jesus had two complementary elements in place: an apparently solid hierarchy and an almost palpable moral culture. One made up the society's command structure—the rules themselves. The other was composed of the legends behind the rules. These were the folklore and metanorms that portrayed the church as a family on which the larger community and perhaps the social order itself depended for stability and that took Jesuits to be versatile troubleshooters within that family. This institutional culture gave legitimacy to the nested, hierarchical structure, and the Society of Jesus in turn fortified the organizational context of the ethos.

Although the hierarchy seemed to behave, as far as anyone noticed, with aplomb, and although the ethos was dense and ubiquitous, Jesuits clung to a pair of practices so pervasive that they can best be described as normal irregularities. One involved ad hoc ventures—one- or two-man shows, sometimes larger—for getting tasks done: a department started, a classroom commandeered for labor school lectures, and so on. Jesuits could not simply follow rules; often they had to create roles for themselves. They improvised. Gradually, as their colleges and universities grew, as faculties and student bodies became more diverse, and as mobility pulled at the roots of the Catholic community, vertical models of education and scholarship became less tenable, as did the old patrimonial style of pastoral care. Networks— academic associations, invisible colleges, the marketplace of ideas—began to surround and cut into the domain of sempiternal truth.[1]

The formation of cliques based more on friendship than on work was another mild heterodoxy. These were affective rather than functional networks, and they avoided a strict construction of the prohibition against "particular friendships." Over and over again, groups of like-minded Jesuits formed in the nooks and crannies of the hierarchy, coming together on the basis of recreational interests, political views, literary tastes, or simply membership in the same seminary cohort.

Neither the networks nor the cliques were seriously anomalous. They formed the little tradition of the Society of Jesus, built up out of the desultory, creative delinquencies and irrepressible, semi-clandestine poking around of ordinary Jesuits. These adaptive accretions were as much a part of the operational code of the Society of Jesus as the formal hierarchy and the official heroic, side of its ethos.[2]

Informal understandings and ingenious shortcuts were in fact generated by the paternalism of the church militant and the expansion of the order. An imperialism of ideals encouraged a makeshift, autocratic decentralization. It was sometimes hard to distinguish the routine chaos of ecclesiastical administration and ambition from fortuitous triumphalism, epic improvisation, and a *historia calamitatum*.

The task networks probed where the hierarchy could not go and implemented what the hierarchy could not do. The cliques were bred by familiarity. They were the informal but immediately recognizable rituals of the society, expressed in athletic competition, irreverent humor, and mild carousing. The whiff of illegitimacy that hung about these ways of doing and being, like the opprobrium surrounding a black market, was dissipated by a recognition that they threatened neither the hierarchy nor the mythic structure of the society and in fact were part of the ecology of corporate survival and personal satisfaction. Such cliques and factions may have been marginal from a narrowly legalistic perspective but they were indispensable mechanisms by which the order adjusted to the environment and accommodated to the needs of its members. They reflected the common humanity more than the superhuman image of Jesuits. They were the white noise of the society, the steady hum of activity and comradeship, the small notations of Jesuit lives.[3]

However, while the networks and cliques that formed and reformed in the

Society of Jesus were for the most part pragmatic rather than symbolic or ideologically charged assemblages, and while they were tolerated and even encouraged by the managers of the order, at the end of the day there was no secure place for autonomous behavior, especially the sort that turned the networks and cliques into programmatic coalitions. Individual eccentricity might be acceptable; gatherings of free spirits were not. Developments in the postwar period strained the tacit understandings and fine-grained negotiations regarding organizational behavior to the breaking point. Flexibility geared toward adaptation was jeopardized by conflicts that challenged, with varying degrees of seriousness, the hierarchy itself.

In trying to figure out how the Society of Jesus actually operated during the years before Vatican II, it is tempting to conclude that the order alternated between militaristic rigidity and chaos, with nothing in between, or to throw up one's hands, in analytical exasperation if not in prayer, and admit that the whole venture appeared to muddle through miraculously. "Providence and the shifting sands of history," one Jesuit historian has written in this vein, "furthered the success of the enterprise."[4] A slightly more realistic fallacy is to treat deviations from the hierarchical ideal as so many haphazard cases set in a maze of circumstance.[5] However, it is possible to identify patterns of informal opposition and coalition building that thrived between absolute order and virtual anarchy and to isolate instances of conflict which escalated toward confrontation with authority.

The underlying parameters of conflict that surfaced in the Society of Jesus during these years cast hierarchical control against autonomous action, and intellect against moral precept. The quarrels described in the preceding chapters can be understood in light of selected combinations of these oppositions. The series of contretemps "rich in character and incident" that at first glance seems little more than random scuffles and brawls between strong and sometimes strange personalities takes on a certain regularity. The fixture in the pattern was hierarchical authority. The variation was provided by the increasingly explosive movements of the urge toward autonomous action, of intellectual dissent, and of moral compunction—that is, conscience—vis-à-vis authority.[6]

First, standoffs that were largely empty of moral or intellectual content occurred between authority and autonomous action. These were simply power struggles over resources other than the "immaterial" ones defined by intellect or ethics. Jockeying for advantage and battles over turf were unlikely, taken one by one, to upset the balance of dominion and deference; in the Jesuit parlance of the time, they were "neuralgic" nuisances. Eventually, however, in combination with growth in the size of Jesuit operations, their cumulative impact became unmanageable.

Second, subterranean, silent conflicts smoldered between intellect and ethics without involving or having immediate repercussions for either authority structures or avenues of action.[7] Individual Jesuits were not exceptionally guileful, but the web of authority encouraged an evasiveness in intellectual matters, a mental reservation, that kept some members of the order from opening up creative territory, even if such inhibitions did not prevent them from perfecting their gifts as transmitters of received knowledge. The tolerance of contradiction that went along with this tension encouraged a humanistic rhetoric rather than a scientific temper.

Third, the intellect-ethics division was more complex and less elevated than a Platonic dichotomy. In traditional Catholicism, particularly in its Irish American variant, ethics tended to mean sexual repression, covering not only moral injunctions but also emotional impulses, both of which might come into conflict with intellectual pursuits.[8] In the Society of Jesus of preconciliar times the opposition between moral control and emotional, particularly sexual, expression was treated as practically nonexistent. Control was supposed to be nearly absolute.[9]

In brief, seemingly innumerable embroilments can be reduced to a comprehensible few. The basic idea is that underlying many of the apparently haphazard scrimmages in the Society of Jesus were multiple, but finite, dimensions of difference: between intellect and ethics, between hierarchy and autonomous action, and, most seriously, between all these and emotional expression.

Consider the case of Daniel Lord or, better, the experience of the Institute of Social Order generally. A recurrent problem with this venture was the never-quite-acknowledged sense that it constituted an operation potentially outside the perimeters of the order. It was not an organization, like the schools, which those responsible for allocating manpower felt they could manage. The problem was not disagreement over ideas, much less moral dubiety. Instead the fear was that if ISO were to work, it would have to go off on its own, beyond the realm of Jesuit institutions already in place. The latent conflict was between authority and autonomy. In this respect, the tribulations of ISO represented a special case of the general challenge to top-down control posed by professionalization and organizational complexity. As long as the Catholic enclave delimited the administrative reach as well as the mind-set of the Society of Jesus, ISO could not escape the jurisdiction of the order. The tightness of this relationship became increasingly uneasy as the subculture eroded.[10]

John Courtney Murray posed a more spectacular threat to hierarchy. He represented an intellectually grounded challenge to institutional authority. An effort was made to handle his silencing deftly. The objective was to avoid impugning the conscientious stand of an individual Jesuit while signaling that his superiors were fulfilling their obligation of allegiance to the papacy by an act that could not be read as uncritical enthusiasm for censorship or as a sign of their own position on church-state relations; they were following orders. The rationalization was tortured. As it happened, the ignominy of the decision and the risk of diminished credibility in intellectual circles were curtailed by the fact that time was on Murray's side. Within a few years he was unsilenced.

The challenge to authority posed by George Dunne, Clyde Heithaus, and their scattering of allies at St. Louis University came from yet another direction. While the integration of the school involved, to a degree, questions of organizational autonomy, the core of the issue was framed as a struggle between an ethical principle and the Jesuit hierarchy. It was moral rather than organizational or intellectual. The superiors of the society could not accept being outflanked by having themselves cast on the morally indefensible side of such an issue, yet this was precisely where the attacks of Heithaus and Dunne were positioning them. The response was to hold to the moral course—to integrate St. Louis University—and to get rid of Dunne and Heithaus.

Both episodes and their consequences—complicity in the censorship of John Courtney Murray and the exiling of obstreperous Jesuits—represented grave challenges not only to the hierarchy but also to the traditional, often unspoken flexibility of the order. One crystallized around intellectual, the other around a moral challenge. In addition, alongside these dramatic confrontations, the ongoing differentiation of activities represented by ISO and by the professionalization of Jesuit colleges and universities presaged conflict between the hierarchical enforcement of rules and the logic of functional roles.[11] Issues that targeted authority from intellectual, moral, and pragmatic angles proliferated in the postwar years. The old-shoe style of authoritarianism and the expedient looking the other way that encouraged adaptability, black humor, and high spirits worked less well.[12]

Tensions crested in the sixties with a force that rearranged the terms of conflict itself. Confrontations came to be defined no longer only or even mainly as hierarchical authority versus freedom of action or intellect or moral fervor. Rather, authority was pitted against the expression of emotion, and in the extreme emotion was set against intellectual standards, the call of social activism, and traditional moral imperatives.[13]

For many Jesuits, including the majority whose commitment was less intellectual than Murray's, repudiation of the old ways was more a flight from the affective chill that surrounded rigorous obedience and an arid scholasticism and toward a modicum of emotional warmth, than an abstract contest between order and liberation or between loyalty and truth. The Society of Jesus as a "test of superhuman endurance and will power, a 'good show' performed by giants on the verge of tears," went into emotional meltdown.[14] There had been premonitions. In trying to comfort the disconsolate Pierre Teilhard de Chardin in the fifties, when his books were proscribed at the end of his career, a friend said, "Tell Father Teilhard someone loves him."[15]

II

> We used to have "the long black line," in cassock and biretta arrayed. And we went into classrooms and offices thus attired. We had a host of evident symbols and realities of a common life. They went from the Latin awakening—cry of "Benedicamus Domino"—to a whole pew nodding in weariness over night time litanies; they went from common syllabi to required textbooks. Those evident symbols are gone now; so, too, are many others. We shall have to use a lot of imagination to find new symbols and realities which can nourish the bonds of our companionship.[16]

The transformation of the Society of Jesus came in cascading waves. The traditional society had displayed a patchwork adaptability that allowed for functional improvisation and camaraderie as parallel realities alongside the prescribed hierarchy and the heroic mythology. After the war, however, the boundaries between creative and system-threatening tensions blurred.

First, the frustrating experiment with ISO crystallized a serious, possibly irremediable division between the maintenance of hierarchy and the requirements of reaching professional goals in an increasingly complex environment. Top-down control and the belief in authoritative precepts could not generate functional expertise. The issue was one of competence.

Second, stoic resignation on one side and the invocation of reasons of state on the other could not entirely avert the stigma associated with the silencing of the principal intellect in American Catholicism. The troubling implication of this faintly apologetic suppression of intellectual freedom lay not simply in the victimization of John Courtney Murray but in a dawning awareness that hierarchical authority had been invoked illegitimately. The affair called into question, once again, the intellectual probity of the order. It dramatized the corporate as well as the personal costs of bureaucratic control and the imperative of obedience.

Third, the challenge mounted in moral terms against the internal authorities of the society in St. Louis raised the possibility of a divorce between the hierarchical management of the order and ethical demands—in effect, between character as consistency and character as conscience. The issue was not one of incompetent or intellectually insecure leadership but of a structure of authority that might be temerarious or bankrupt on moral grounds. Even if the agitators for reform could be dismissed as hotheads, their cause was just. For a time, resolution of the conflict by a courageous decision on the part of the hierarchy, while Jesuits pressing for ethical zealotry were punished, succeeded in dispelling suspicions of a possible mismatch between the veneration of hierarchy and the maintenance of principle.

Finally, attacks on authority escalated toward an impasse pitting emotional release against hierarchy, and in some instances against intellect, involvement in social action, and inherited moral codes. This upheaval rearranged the adversarial terrain. The fundamental problem came to be seen not as the construction but as the liberation of the self.[17]

III

These crises, then, formed a spiral of seriousness, going from pragmatic to intellectual to moral to expressive attacks on the authority structure and ethos of the Society of Jesus. Sharp distinctions in such matters are bound to be somewhat artificial. But the pattern of escalation is reasonably clear.

Just as plainly, challenges to hierarchy emerged against a backdrop of structural, institutional, and cultural changes. The most conspicuous shift in the Society of Jesus, aside from the drop in numbers, was that from a rule-governed hierarchy to a role-driven network. The order maintained some leverage over its program of formation. But after that Jesuits had increasingly to enter a job market in which tenure was not guaranteed. Although superiors in the order were still able to pull men out of positions, they had greater difficulty assigning them to positions in the first place. This was a key sign of the metamorphosis from a predominantly hierarchical to a network mode of operation.[18]

For some Jesuits the expected slots were no longer out there, and alternative roles could not be quickly found. Neither security nor prestige was at hand. This stimulated a transition not from rules to roles but from both toward a search for community in which little groups were the building blocks of organization. The pursuit of intimacy became paramount. For a few, even this route failed. They left the order or turned into loners for whom the Society of Jesus retained only vestigial significance. Such wandering was not simply self-indulgence or the manifestation of delayed adolescence. It was brought on by the sharply reduced capacity of the Society of Jesus to provide meaningful roles to its members. The psychological explosion had structural causes.[19]

The symbolic environment of the order changed as well as its institutional infrastructure. The Society of Jesus is not only rule-governed and role-driven;

it is also dependent on meaning. One set of master metaphors has been that of the church as an enfolding family and the family as a shrine of personal virtue and social order. Another has portrayed Jesuits as pilgrims on a mission, both in and outside the church. The metaphors have expressed the symbiosis and the friction between the familial and the exploratory—the local and the cosmopolitan—sides of the order and, ultimately, between its feminine and masculine sides.[20]

By midcentury in America these symbols were flagging, largely because of changes in the social composition and gender roles of Catholics and also because of changes, such as the permeability of the Catholic enclave to the media, that were engulfing other subcultures in the United States as well. While this cultural shift had a distinctive edge among Catholics, it was not unique to their experience. The worldview into which the metaphors tapped declined along with the supersession of myths of domestic femininity and chivalric masculinity in American culture generally.[21] These customs had stood as a haven and a rebuke against the market and the demiurges of sexuality. One, the myth of domesticity, apotheosized a mechanism, the hierarchical family, by which Catholics reproduced materially. The other, taken to a pitch in the cult of male celibacy, glorified "virile men presented in a virile way"[22] and embodied the tradition by which the power structure of the church reproduced itself ideologically. By the sixties the contrasting visions of patient maternity and of heroic masculinity, implying a reciprocity between private and public spheres for the sake of a grand cause, had started to seem unworkable sacrifices and delusory ideals.[23]

IV

For many Jesuits the society orchestrated the frailties and goodwill of "weak men . . . from different places and cultures" in the service of evidently worthwhile goals.[24] The task was not emancipation from repression but the overcoming of the disordered self and, out of this, the constitution of corporate discipline and the achievement of good works.

Emphasis on character as consistency solved the intention-span problem. It channeled intermittent zeal into the performance of tasks by defining roles and setting orders to follow, giving a welcome clarity and sense of closure and hope to the striving after the infinite and the indeterminacies of service. For ordinary Jesuits the choice was usually not so stark as that between constancy and conscience. Beneath the baroque effusions, pragmatism, not manic exaltation, has marked the Society of Jesus. For many in religious life, crises of conscience tend to be infrequent in balance with the routine of self-management and ministering to others. Listlessness on the one hand—"acedia"—and impulse on the other were the failings that somehow had to be shaped into a method for action that might be of service.[25] In the end, the objective was not exceptional penetration into the souls of others or mere introspection into one's own but instead to find a useful slot and get on with benevolent work. Most Jesuits were foot soldiers, and they soldiered on. Prudence and reliability may not have made for "brilliancy," as Gerard Manley Hopkins put it, but the disposition provided a counterweight against improvident enthusiasms and the dithyrambic romanticization of religious life.[26] Dependable slogging was preferred to erratic inventiveness, and as long as the Jesuit enterprise kept an air of adventure that helped attract talented recruits from their schools this distinction did not seem like an either-or split.

For John Courtney Murray and a few colleagues—George Dunne and, later, Daniel Berrigan, for instance—crucial decisions may have been cast in terms of the tension between character as consistency and character as conscience. But for many other Jesuits the dilemma involved how to tailor adherence to the commands of superiors to the adaptations needed to get specific tasks done—in other words, how to mesh rules and roles.[27] Some Jesuits were not prepared to handle the increasingly complex and competitive nature of the tasks they faced in the postwar period. Obedience did not guarantee competence. A perception of the irrelevance of authority grew, and the confidence of Jesuits in their own problem-solving capacity fell.

What did these developments have to do with the crisis of affectivity and masculinity in the Society of Jesus? Regardless of whatever touchiness might be instrinsic to them, some issues become increasingly contentious in Catholicism for historical reasons.[28] The erosion of expertise meant a loss of prestige and confidence, and this institutional change coincided with a fading of the defining antinomies of the mythic culture of Catholicism. Concern for the fate of the family as an embattled bastion of virtue in a hostile world represented a comparatively conservative response to this confluence of changes; a projection of familial imagery onto the human community reflected a generally more latitudinarian posture.[29]

In either case, the transformation of the cultural and institutional order could not obscure, and indeed may have thrust attention on and called into question, the elementary particles of Catholic identity—sexuality and gender, the functions of women, the role of the celibate priesthood, and cognate issues. A realm of social relations that was once thought to be beyond or beneath politics turned out to be an arena in which questions of power and personal identity were worked through.[30]

V

The slide in manpower in the Society of Jesus and other religious congregations is the most clearcut change attendant on the Second Vatican Council. Religious vocations could not have continued to soar. The drop in vocations in the United States was coterminous with the evaporation of the vogue of male celibacy, particularly among Irish Americans. This demographic mainstay of clerical recruitment was more of a medium-term aberration than a solid tradition in Catholicism.

Even if increasing numbers of Jesuits had prolonged "the golden century," growth would likely have generated a reaction prompted by changes in the social and cultural profile of American Catholics.[31] Better educated and assimilated Catholics became less dependent on the Jesuits. The opening up of alternative idealisms and seductions, the sheer range of options, proved irresistible. The colleges and universities of the order became less attractive places to work for Jesuits put off by size and complexity. The Society of Jesus was caught between a peaking of recruits on the supply side and a softening of demand for its services, at least among its erstwhile clientele.[32]

Numerical decline may not signify catastrophe for the order. Some look on the drop not as a debacle but as an opportunity for rejuvenation and a chance to regroup. Imagine what American Catholicism might look like had the numbers of men and women in religious life continued to climb. It is not evident that such an increase would have been beneficial to the laity or healthy for groups like the Society of Jesus.[33] In any case, what is intriguing about the hypothetical experiment of ever-increasing growth is how it reveals the ambiguities embedded in presumably hard evidence about the Society of Jesus. A similar lesson would seem to hold even more strongly for the subjective processes that have been at work in the order.

Religious culture, however, is not just lofty fluff. The dynamics of culture emanate from the mundane intimacies of sexuality, patterns of familial authority, and pedagogical practice as well as from newer sources and technologies like the media.[34] Jesuits have operated in all these areas. On occasion they have waxed even more ambitious and have imagined that symbolic and normative schemata could shape the direction of change in economics and politics.

This book has been about the layered changes in the surroundings, the exterior, and the inside of the Society of Jesus. Two broad transformations have provided a context for understanding the fissures that developed among Jesuits during the years preceding the conciliar revolution. First, structural and institutional changes in advanced industrial society—increasing education, occupational mobility, the spread of the media, growth in the size of organizations—began to wear at the undergirding of the way of life on which Jesuits had come to depend. Second, these transformations in the demographic and organizational environment were accompanied by changes in the symbolic landscape of Catholicism and by realignments in Jesuit psychology.

In order to comprehend these changes, it is necessary to situate the Jesuits with respect to two related metamorphoses—the ambiguous nature of the modernization process in which they have been engaged and the shifting boundaries between public and private spheres. Both have been touched by cultural democratization.

VI

The new systems [of mapmaking] also involved substantial sacrifices. The new mapmakers and painters could no longer see around corners, or through the surface of the earth, or freely adjust the size and positions of their pictures to make them accord with their philosophical importance. Thus the medieval maps of the world (*mappamundi*) survived well into the Renaissance, sharing duty with the modern-minded Ptolemaic maps. The latter were better for finding one's way from one place to another, the former for understanding the purpose of the voyage.[35]

Organizations bear the marks of the time of their founding, and the Society of Jesus is no exception. Jesuits established themselves in early modern Europe as educators—as cultivators of human capital. Success in this broad niche complemented massive changes in two other domains—in the accumulation of physical capital and in the expansion and consolidation of nation-states—where Jesuits were hardly active at all. The Jesuits' focus on the development of human resources was no less important, for being an affair of *mentalités* and skills, than the bottom lines of the market and the state. Cultural influence was an overriding goal of the order.[36]

The Jesuits' flair for the systematic development of human talents set them apart from less adventurous and imaginative groups in Catholicism. Their educational mission preserved a thread of continuity from Renaissance humanism through the enlightened absolutisms of Europe, and it kept the church from sinking into obscurantism and superstition.[37]

Education remained the principal activity of Jesuits in the United States. Investment in human potential was as important to the Society of Jesus as was investment in capital resources to the expansion of a market economy and as the reinforcement of the government apparatus was to the political order.[38] A consensus grew up around the useful and wholesome connections between training in white-collar skills, mobility, and productivity. Apart from a few outspoken mavericks, Jesuit schools and their faculties stayed clear of politics in all but the most diffuse or local of senses. The schools served their students' social objectives by preparing them for the labor market; they also buttressed Catholic identity. The functions of the schools for the mobility and empowerment of immigrant and postimmigrant cohorts of American Catholics overshadowed the efforts of Jesuits in social action. The schools worked to deliver the prize of assimilation without the loss of faith.

Jesuits were proud of this educational achievement, but they worried about the forces their success unleashed. The knowledge that was supposed to be imparted in the *collège* of pristine imaginings combined utility and morality. Jesuit training not only transmitted know-how; it bolstered a sense of self. As their schools expanded after World War II, these two features of the educational system—roughly, competence and character—headed down separate and, for some, divergent paths.

The division between learning and moral formation was not seen as uniformly bad. Some Jesuits for whom the tension was creative were critical of tribal codes that seemed as gnarled and dark as the Victorian Gothic fretwork and gargoyles of their schools and churches, and it was not unusual for Jesuits to accept the expansion of knowledge in the sciences, which were on the whole peripheral to both their secondary and higher education curricula. But most Jesuits hoped that such developments would be offset by the steadfastness of moral truths and by a fair degree of fixity in the classical curriculum of the humanities. As it happened, differentiation between the instructional and doctrinal realms went on apace.[40]

The transformation was both social and moral. The Catholic identity that was instilled by the neighborhoods and by the schools fostered communal belonging. But there was an element of puerility to the faith of the enclaves. Badges of community were not equivalent to ethical probity. Custom was not character.[41] Inklings of mutability also began to emerge within the moral canon itself. In Jesuit colleges and universities, the humanities began to burst the template of scholasticism. A comparable uncertainty began to filter into the seminaries. The logistical and the mythical structures of Counter-Reformation Catholicism crumbled.[42]

VII

Jesuits devoted most of their energies to education in the United States not only because immigrants and their children furnished an abundant market in this field but also because the American political environment lacked the organizational outlets of Europe. The absence of confessional and militantly leftist parties was an unalterable constant of the United States that conditioned the incentives and options of Jesuits. Catholic social thought was exported to an American setting that departed from the organizational and ideological design of Europe. The absence of institutional receptacles added to the exoticism of a way of thinking whose hierarchical trappings irritated many Europeans as well as Americans. Foreignness itself was not crippling, for continental influences had helped to shape American creativity in the arts. It was some of the organizational contraptions of European politics, together with their ideological slant, that weighed social Catholicism down.[43]

Most Jesuits, then, neither felt the need for nor had the opportunity to copy a continental model that attempted to fuse political institutions, social policy, and moral principles. While this did not prevent a small band of American Jesuits from promoting programs of social analysis and action, it all but guaranteed that their activities would stay on the fringes of intellectual and institutional respectability.

Jesuits in the United States came to an accommodation with economic and political liberalism, mass participation, and later with the expansion of the role of government in social melioration. The progressive democratization of the political and socioeconomic realms that had pitted radicalism against reaction in much of Latin Europe was accepted by Jesuits in the United States with some theoretical but few practical misgivings. The upholders of a medieval pastoralism and the critics of industrialism, whose rhetoric accorded with scholastic discourse, were shown respect. They held the high, abstract ground. But in the workaday world of immigrant Catholicism and the corridors of practical accomplishment, their ideas were not taken seriously.[44]

John Courtney Murray anointed a settlement that had already been consummated. A key component of this accord was the understanding that the microstructures of authority of the Catholic subculture—the schools and especially the family—would remain untouched by the noxious side effects of industrialization and the democratic dispensation. These were the snug harbors of tradition in the storm of modernity. No incompatibility was thought to exist between popular hierarchy and impersonal democracy. In this Murray was of one mind with the advocates of pluralism, with the bosses of the urban machines and the labor unions as well as the theoreticians, who reconciled democratic competition between organizations with undemocratic stratification within organizations.[45]

With the passing of the immigrant era of Catholicism, politics entered the world of the American Jesuits in an unexpected and threatening way. Challenges to the ordinary hierarchies of social intercourse, particularly those ensconced in the family and gender roles, mounted during the postwar years and reached a crescendo with the sixties.[46] The schools, as they expanded, were caught up in professional and financial imperatives that shaped their direction largely beyond the control of the Society of Jesus. The cultural revolution that ensnared the family and neighborhoods, long thought to be preserves of private relations, was abetted by economic trends that penetrated the schools, which had formed a protective ring around the Catholic subculture.[47]

As for the family, Catholic tradition had viewed it as both a shrine of privacy and a sign of community. It was seen both as a support of political order and a refuge from and point of resistance against the depredations of political, economic, and cultural forces on the outside. The destabilization of family units, together with the increasing commitments of women outside the home, meant not only a breakdown of the underpinnings of social tranquillity but also the ruination of a vigorous legacy. All this smacked of an emancipation of the instincts that controverted Jesuit ideals of self-discipline and social continuity. It also implied a shattering of the time-honored separation of public and private spheres.[48]

The split in the imputed union between knowledge and morality as envisioned in Jesuit pedagogy coincided with the attenuation of the perceived links between family viability and collective stability. The pedagogy that Jesuits had developed over centuries and had adapted for an immigrant clientele—their formula for the development of human resources—came to be racked by internal countercurrents, by the growth in secular knowledge, and by economic forces reshaping American higher education generally. The intellectual primacy of Jesuits diminished. At about the same time, the mores of enclave Catholicism—particularly, the familial hierarchies, the protocols of sexuality, the domestic role of women—began to give way.[49] The moral conviction of Jesuits, their sense of emotional control as well as intellectual mastery, wavered. The transition between the small world of numerous households and familiar schools and the larger world of the market and public life became newly problematic.[50]

VIII

Somewhere in mid-voyage, the tragic and the comic clashed. The achievers, if they were lucky, laid aside their ego in favor of a lighter baggage. The machos, if they were lucky, gave ear to the feminine around and within. The frantic and the driven and appetitive, if they were lucky, discovered a still center, and dwelt there for a while. . . . We supposed it would be a good passage; but the supposition was very nearly our undoing. For again and again, the crossing ran close to disaster; and of all eventualities, we were least ready for this.[51]

The way of life that changed out from under the Jesuits was itself an unsteady alignment of transient forces. The impetus given to religious vocations by the cult of male celibacy was one of its major components. In the Catholic enclaves of the United States this amounted not so much to the ideology of gender aggression and domination typical of Latin versions of patriarchy as to an ethos of benign neglect with regard to women.

While the Irish American variant of Catholicism fitted the sexual prescriptions of Roman Catholicism it differed from the characteristically Latin mind-set that tied gender hierarchy to political and socioeconomic reaction.[52] Instead of the ideological polarization customary on the continent, a buoyant practicality drove American Catholicism. The restraint symbolized by chastened sexuality encouraged not only inner control but also the marketable virtues of diligence, thrift, and reliability. By combining self-discipline with training for adaptability, the educational approach of the Jesuits suited this pragmatism well. Catholic identity, founded mainly on ethical negatives and sexual taboos, was preserved without tying it to a narrow political or economic program. In any case, there were almost no partisan outlets for the ideological expression of sectarianism.[53]

Another circumstance fortifying the settlement of the years from the modernist crisis to the onset of Vatican II was the fact that upcoming cohorts of Jesuits still faced a challenging agenda. Most of the intellectual and certainly the theological weather of the antimodernist years was close to stifling.[54] But youthful energies could be channeled into an expanding educational network and numerous other tasks that the priest as patron could perform. Jesuits kept busy. Generational conflict was avoided; no serious challenge to the old order was mounted.

Toward the end of the postimmigrant period, however, as the fifties passed and as working- and middle-class Catholics were absorbed into the American way, the subculture presented fewer worthwhile opportunities to younger clerics, cultural tradition came to look like intellectual stagnation, and the diversion of energies into missionary activity did not suffice to sidetrack conflict across generational lines. The appeal of celibacy depended not only on its status as a sacrifice for the sake of personal salvation but also on a view of the priesthood as a heroic instrument for meaningful service that might not be performed otherwise. By the 1960s the credibility of both these views had declined.[55]

Finally, Jesuits brought a measure—for the brighter students, more than just a veneer—of cosmopolitanism, sophistication, and humanistic curiosity to an immigrant community of peasant and working-class stock. This was the essence of the classical curriculum, of the drill in Latin and Greek and the verbal and mental gymnastics in composition and philosophy.[56] Jesuits were gatekeepers to a wider world. In a few decades, however, not only did Jesuit pedagogy find itself outpaced by its rivals in secular education but many Jesuits were overtaken by the intellectual advances they had set in motion years earlier. As American Catholics came to intellectual maturity, the correlations between clergy and cosmopolitanism, and between the laity and parochialism, were reversed. Jesuits began to feel left behind.[57]

Thus a distinctive conjunction of dispositions toward sexuality and celibacy, of the capacity of institutions to absorb oncoming generations in meaningful tasks, and of the balance between clerical learning and the intellectual localism of an immigrant clientele, supported a way of life that transmitted an ample tradition. Given the adventitious configuration of these forces tradition evolved as Vatican II approached. The direction of this evolution was unpredictable, yet the fact that it was bound to change was no less organic than was the belief in slow or no change at all.[58]

IX

Part of the difficulty of understanding the Society of Jesus stems from the inadequacy of the categories that are brought to bear on cases whose political boundaries lack definition.[59] Here it is essential to recall the dual characteristics of the order. The Society of Jesus is both a socialization mechanism—an organization dedicated to perfecting the moral life of its members according to a set of norms—and a service agency, geared to furnishing help—for example, education—to others. The order is at once like a family and a formal organization. In the first instance Jesuits are concerned with "formation," and in the second with "apostolic action."[60]

Thus, one dimension of the Society of Jesus reflects norms and moral values and another taps organizational structure.[61] Crossing the two dimensions produces a hypothetical grid that situates the order relative to other types of institutions.

The quadrant to the upper right describes a hierarchical condition in which norms are not internalized. This is the ambience of surveillance and evasion, of the rule of "I-obey-but-don't carry out" (and of "disobey-but-don't-get caught") that characterized the Hapsburg empire in the days of the founding of the Jesuits.

The creation of the Society of Jesus represented an advance in organizational design. The order furnished a solution for inefficiencies of implementation and reduced the costs of supervision. Organizations under its control remained pyramidal; the externals of ceremony and control stayed in

Norms

		Internalized	Not Internalized
Structure	Hierarchical	Society of Jesus, cadre parties	Surveillance and evasion systems
	Nonhierarchical	modern, pluralist democratic, market systems	postmodern, self-interest maximization, hedonism

FIGURE 5. The "Classical" Society of Jesus Compared to Other Social Institutions

place; but norms were inculcated through a long process of socialization and training. Out of the internalized hierarchy came a sense of personal as well as corporate order that was supposed to be at once traditional and dynamic. A prompt and willing obedience was to be the Jesuits' supreme virtue. Their adherence to the model provided an outpost of reliability, an elite guard, for a rickety system.[62]

This was a model for the Society of Jesus itself, not a description of the institutional and cultural milieux in which Jesuits operated. The American environment was composed of the nonhierarchical but normatively constrained realm of Protestant individualism without intermediaries, of the market made feasible by an ethic of competition and honest work, of industrial democratic man. This was the pluralist world that John Courtney Murray came to terms with, in which a decentralized public order attained equilibrium and was presumably held together by respect for private traditions of hierarchy in miniature and deference to family values. These were the quotidian intimations of natural law.[63]

An alternative setting is formed by the detritus of a once-solid pluralism, the social and moral disarray of pluralism gone berserk that Murray feared. It is democratic in structure but no common norms are internalized except those of self-interest and the taste for pleasure seeking. This is the permissiveness and apparent nihilism, the ontological laissez-faire, that stand opposed to the classical Jesuit way of life.[64] Significantly, while the configuration fails as social design, it is also the abyss and anarchic font of creativity from which Jesuits like William Lynch attempted to retrieve a measure of psychic equilibrium.[65]

The typology locates the Society of Jesus vis-à-vis other organizational types and indicates its compatibility with alternative institutional arrangements. The combination of hierarchy and internalized norms—the "classical Jesuit way of life"—can be viewed as a depiction both of the ideal toward which the Society of Jesus itself strove during its heyday and of the self-image of Tridentine Catholicism as a "perfect society."[66] It represents a self-contained world approximated outside the order itself by the hierarchical family and the tight neighborhoods of the Catholic ghetto.[67]

The classical anatomy is considerably less adequate as a depiction of the postconciliar shape of the order. And as a political blueprint for entities broader than clerical institutions, the amalgam is confined to quasi-theocratic fantasies of government as a paternalistic family or, by way of analogy, to vanguard parties.[68] A democratic but normatively coherent pluralism, and a morally fragmented but structurally hierarchical authoritarianism, as well as a hierarchy in which norms of stratification are accepted, all appear to be consonant, or tolerably at odds, with the Jesuit ethos. Jesuit "militarism" is a special case within a spectrum of acceptable organizational formats.

The elasticity of the Society of Jesus suggests that as a culture or a network it may outlast the institutions in which Jesuits happen to be situated, even if its fate cannot be completely uncoupled from the fortunes of these host organizations. The quest for identity and the shaping of character are perennial; institutions are multiform. It is the contrast between the perpetuity of intrapsychic conflict and the mortality of institutions that makes for the odd combination of longevity and volatility in the Society of Jesus. In this sense the order is more of a culture that survives on contradiction than an organization that thrives on efficiency.[69]

X

Two related themes have been especially prominent in this study of the Jesuits. One has centered on the family as a metaphor of a larger collectivity. The other has emphasized the distinction between the shaping of character and the dilemmas of orchestrating individual virtues in corporate form.

In the United States few Jesuits supposed that political order might actually be fashioned by extending the patriarchal authority of the family toward American society. The task of coordinating individual talents and preferences was handled, not out of pious prescription, but pragmatically. Function, local demand, and a keen sense of the feasible compromised the rigidity of tradition and dictated the configuration of Jesuit schools. Adaptability was itself a tradition.

There was never any question of centralizing Jesuit colleges and universities into a smaller number of national schools, nor—although they shared some things such as a curricular emphasis on philosophy—did the schools develop according to a single model. Programs of social education, for example, took several forms: (1) labor schools, hived off from the mainstream of the educational system; (2) schools of social work, in effect, professional schools like the faculties of commerce and finance; (3) incidental courses devoted to social topics; and (4) the Institute of Social Order, the most ambitious attempt by the Society of Jesus to establish a think tank dedicated to research on social issues.

The idealized hierarchy that existed in the minds of Jesuits, with theology as the queen of the sciences, was operationally rather like a sloppy, animated pyramid, bulging this way and that at the sides. Institutionally, hierarchy was revered as a fiction that gave way to a plasticity of functions and the geographical diversity of "the works." The genuinely irreducible hierarchy was the interior one—the foundation of character and self-control on which both obedience and versatility were built, encased within the firm support of the Society of Jesus itself.

The supposition of a unique solution to the problem of organizational aggregation existed in the realm of honorable irrealism. While Jesuits were not indifferent to institutional design, such arrangements were looked on as relatively contingent and disposable. The philosopher king as the epitome of good government, supreme over less autocratic systems by virtue of a reasoned, natural superiority, was a Platonic vapor. By contrast, personal rectitude was compatible with a variety of organizational setups. In addition, a certain nearsightedness kept Jesuits from worrying about institutional optima. As long as character held steady, and as long as the familiar mechanisms of the neighboring social order stayed in place, politics would pretty much take care of itself.

The solution was not altogether harmonious. The training functions internal to the Society of Jesus were more hierarchical than the service activities geared to the outside. In neither case was there a hard-and-fast bottom line, and at least in the latter instance there emerged no single way of doing things. Nevertheless, the society's authority structure on the inside accorded less and less well with the variety of the order's work on the outside. There was sufficient indeterminacy in this incongruence to allow for flexibility and a humane, case-by-case pragmatism, at least before numbers overloaded the system. But the situation was also anomalous enough to spark principled resentment as well as exasperation with incidents of impracticality.

The system worked as long as it was self-contained. A signal feature of the Society of Jesus, one that supposedly complemented the propensity of Jesuits for restless peregrination, was that it was like a family. The order exercised great control over the training of its members and considerable influence over the Catholic subculture. Even when the interlocking between inner and outer rings loosened, as the ensemble of schools and other operations grew more complex and autonomous, hierarchy remained tolerable and even desirable to Jesuits who got more out of the socialization and caretaking functions of the society—spiritual comfort, companionship—than they could get elsewhere. However, when both the affective and the functional capabilities of the Society of Jesus began to falter, and as alternative satisfactions opened up, hierarchy lost much of its meaning. Suddenly Jesuits were left with a doubtful identity, shrinking roles, bureaucratic slots, and scant gratification.[70]

Despite the ultramontane pretensions of the Society of Jesus in Europe, the continental penchant for matching religious with expressly political organizations embarrassed Jesuits in the United States. The Irish model that dispensed with direct political control by suffusing social institutions with a Catholic ethos was more popular. The empire of the everyday pervaded the huge polyphony of the domestic and the sexual, where the faithful passed most of their lives, investing these mundane rites and trials with stupendous symbolism. Much of the power of this symbolic capital depended on the preservation of ghetto Catholicism and on a genial vagueness regarding interaction with the American way. When the boundaries of the enclave eroded, so did the influence of the Society of Jesus.

On the one hand, then, models designed for institutions with relatively unequivocal outputs can be misleading when applied to groups like the Jesuits. Conversely, the opacity of family metaphors as clues to the organizational mores of the Society of Jesus and to the links between Catholicism and the larger society should also be recognized. The emotional resonance of images of hierarchical families as supports of social and political order is one thing; the empirical plausibility of the perceived connection is another.[71] The containment of sexuality and the moral sobriety associated with strict upbringing, respect for paternal authority, and the like may enable individuals to take advantage of opportunities for advancement, thereby facilitating mobility, at the same time that mobility undercuts stability in the aggregate.[72]

The connection imputed between discipline and achievement has the appeal of an experiential maxim, and the nexus between sexual and social control has a plausible ring. As a nostrum for political order, however, the linkage is ill-defined and farfetched—unless one embraces latitudinarian standards of what constitutes the personal and the political.[73] Whatever practical lesson is embodied in the imagery surrounding the family may be the reverse of what Catholic traditionalists intended. Instead of viewing a small peg of society as a model for the whole, a case can be made for distinguishing between the family and putatively correlative matters in order to understand their components and interrelations in realistic detail. Otherwise, it is difficult to keep the pathology of splendid art and awful politics that has traditionally afflicted Catholicism from spilling over into policy debate. Joseph Husslein's "great woman problem" has turned out to be a welter of specific issues, covering divorce, abortion, contraception, reproductive ethics, and women's autonomy, among other controversies. Treating them as a seamless whole infuses moral issues with an ideological charge that borders on a spurious sacramentalism; recognition of their diversity would be equally catholic.

Two other loose ends are worthy of note. One concerns the psychology of change among Jesuits. The other has to do with the relation between the mythic structure of the Society of Jesus and the American way.

The transformation of the Society of Jesus has been stratified, swifter on the outside with regard to the political and social philosophy, slower on the inside in matters of sexuality and authority. Almost certainly this hierarchy of change is not peculiar to Jesuits. Although it would seem obvious that convictions bearing on intimate concerns should be slower to change than political opinions, evidence and theory about such a gradient is thin.[74] Besides, it is questionable whether sexuality stands in the same way at the core of folk wisdom about authority across Catholic cultures, and it is untrue that standards of sexual behavior are aligned with equal intensity vis-à-vis characteristic expectations on social and political issues even within Latin cultures.[75] Such information as is available suggests a fair degree of separation between the satisfactions and anxieties associated with perceptions of private and public realms.[76]

As for the interplay between the Jesuit variant on Catholicism and the American way, both mythic structures have altered, with some features becoming more salient than others.[77] Neither culture forms an undifferentiated bloc, and each has its imponderables and intractables. Disentangling the hodgepodge of sexuality and family life in Catholicism is rather like trying to get Americans to think straight about dreams of success and the distribution of wealth.[78]

The story can be read as the saga of metamorphoses in cultural syndromes whose internal pluralism is protean and whose interaction is at least as complex. While one is subject to fits of righteousness and the other to ideological schematics, they are, like expansive churches, polysemous rather than predictably sectarian. The permutations elude easy comprehension. "Catholicism" and "materialism" are labels not explanations. Nor do evocations of the stagey gloom of Roman Catholicism versus an American civil religion of porcelain humanitarianism improve understanding.[79] Both worldviews are compounds of transcendental aspirations and transnational activism. Both are collections of prolific localisms. While neither Americanism nor the Jesuit style emphasizes the contemplative-feminine, this sensibility is present, too.[80]

The Jesuit and American myths are as much driven pragmatisms as nebulous parables.[81] Jesuits developed ways of getting things done, "our method of proceeding," that adapted to different ways of life. As a monument to organizational hierarchy, the Society of Jesus became outmoded, and the educational expertise of Jesuits has diffused beyond its progenitors. Similarly, the American phantom of unfettered masculinity was lost in Vietnam, and the technological and economic prowess of the United States has receded, even as its political culture has spread. But these are murky hints for another day.

XI

"The trauma-inducing potential of serious historical study," one Jesuit historian has written, "must not be underestimated."[82] This story has been about a way of life that appeared hardly to change at all and then changed all of a sudden. The contradictions welling up in the Society of Jesus in the decades before Vatican II and the abrupt denouement of the years surrounding the council create a dual pathos.

On the one hand, a no-nonsense dissection of the glory years, when the Society of Jesus was the nonpareil of religious adventure and accomplishment, seems to reveal the limits to (and for some the futility in) the striving of Jesuits. In reviewing Francis Parkman's account of the exploits of the French Jesuits in seventeenth-century North America, a youthful Henry James drew attention, with a dash of antipapist hauteur but with the sting of insight, to the difference between strength of character and the flawed institutional context of Jesuit activities. "This touching story," James wrote,

> has peculiar and picturesque interest from the fact that the enterprise was, in a great measure, a delusion and a failure—a delusion consecrated by the most earnest conviction and the most heroic effort, a failure redeemed by the endurance of incalculable suffering. When the human mind wishes to contemplate itself as its greatest tension—its greatest desire for action, for influence and dominion—when it wishes to be reminded of how much it is capable in the direction of conscious hope and naked endurance, it cannot do better than read the story of the early Jesuit adventurers. . . .
>
> What is the moral? However well disinterestedness and self-immolation may work for individuals, they work but ill for communities, however small. The Puritans were frank self-seekers. They withdrew from persecution at home and they practised it here. They have left, accordingly, a vast, indelible trace of their passage through history. The Jesuits worked on a prepared field, in an artificial atmo-

sphere, and it was, therefore, easy for them to be sublime. However they, as a group—a very small group—might embrace suffering and martyrdom, the paternal Church courted only prosperity and dominion. The Church was well aware of the truth at which we just hinted—that collective bodies find but small account in self-sacrifice; and it carefully superintended and directed the fervent passions of the Jesuits. . . . In this circle they freely burnt themselves out. The Church could afford it on the part of the Catholic world at large, and as for individuals each had but his own case to manage.[83]

On the other hand, the precipitous downturn of the years right after the Second Vatican Council has the power of eliciting a sorrow, a Virgilian *pietas*, transcending judgments of right and wrong. The tremors of that transformation send forth the sense of haunted deliverance that Wallace Stevens expressed.

To see the gods dispelled in mid-air and dissolve like clouds is one of the great human experiences. . . . It was their annihilation, not ours, and yet it left us feeling that in a measure, we, too, had been annihilated. It left us feeling dispossessed and alone in solitude, like children without parents, in a home that seemed deserted, in which the amical rooms and halls had taken on a look of hardness and emptiness. . . . There was always in every man the increasingly human self, which . . . became constantly more and more all there was or so it seemed; and whether it was so or merely seemed so still left it for him to resolve life and the world in his own terms.[84]

Both passages touch on parts of what American Jesuits have gone through. One happens to be the product of a writer who in trying to overcome the magic realism of one of his predecessors indulged in a prosaic dirge, and the other flirts with verbal autointoxication. But both perspectives seem overwrought if taken as assessments of the encounter of the Society of Jesus with American culture.[85] Larry McMurtry, in evaluating the limits of recent research on the exploration and settlement of the American West, makes the point that such studies "often fail . . . because they so rarely do justice to the quality of imagination that constitutes part of the truth. They may be accurate about the experience, but they simplify or ignore the emotions and imaginings that impelled the Western settlers despite their experience."[86]

It may be that one can proceed only so far in the guise of the good pagan. This story has tried to follow Jesuits to the pit of their night, but it has not gone beyond that. In this respect it has been fully as conventional as studies of revolution that track the contradictions and the demise of the old regime but stop short of examining what follows. That is a different act of the drama, and the remainder of the script for the Jesuits in the American scene has yet to be written. Wendell Berry, in coming to terms with a flawed masterpiece of American literature, noted:

> The fulfillment and catharsis that Aristotle described as the communal result of tragic drama is an artificial enactment of the way a mature community survives tragedy in fact. The community wisdom of tragic drama is in the implicit understanding that no community can survive that cannot survive the worst. Tragic drama attests to the community's need to survive the worst that it knows or imagines can happen. . . .
>
> What is wanting, apparently, is the tragic imagination that, through communal form or ceremony, permits great loss to be recognized, suffered, and borne, and that makes possible some sort of consolation and renewal. . . . Without that return we may know innocence and horror and grief, but not tragedy and joy. Not consolation or forgiveness or redemption.[87]

Notes

PREFACE

1. Pál Kelemen, *Baroque and Rococo in Latin America*, 2nd ed. (New York: Dover, 1967), p. 43.

2. See James J. Hennesey, S.J., "Jesuit Provinces in North America, 1805–1955," *Woodstock Letters* 84 (April 1955): 155–69; and José Antonio Maravall, *Culture of the Baroque: Analysis of a Historical Structure* (Minneapolis: University of Minnesota Press, 1986).

3. Thomas Fleming, "She Made a Man of Him," *New York Times Book Review* (April 2, 1989): 13. Compare Mary Gordon, "'I Can't Stand Your Books': A Writer Goes Home," *New York Times Book Review* (December 11, 1988): 1, 36–38.

4. See Joseph J. Ellis, *After the Revolution: Profiles of Early American Culture* (New York: W. W. Norton, 1979); Mara Harington, *The Dream of Deliverance in American Politics* (New York: Alfred A. Knopf, 1986); Christopher F. Mooney, S.J., *Religion and the American Dream* (Baltimore, Md.: Westminster, 1977); and Ann C. Rose, *Transcendentalism as a Social Movement, 1830–1850* (New Haven, Conn.: Yale University Press, 1985).

5. Interview with Thomas H. Clancy, S.J., September 1, 1985. See also Simon Peter, S.J., "Alcoholism and Jesuit Life: An Individual and Community Illness," *Studies in the Spirituality of Jesuits* 13 (January 1981).

6. Clancy interview.

7. Quoted by Edward Kessler, *Flannery O'Connor and the Language of Apocalypse* (Princeton, N.J.: Princeton University Press, 1986), p. 60.

8. Richard J. Blackwell, *Galileo, Bellarmine, and the Bible* (Notre Dame, Ind.: University of Notre Dame Press, 1990); and Pietro Redondi, *Galileo Heretic* (Princeton, N.J.: Princeton University Press, 1987). Compare Robin Lane Fox, *Pagans and Christians* (New York: Alfred A. Knopf, 1987); and Judith Herrin, *The Formation of Christendom* (Princeton, N.J.: Princeton University Press, 1987).

9. Daniel Chirot, "The Rise of the West," *American Sociological Review* 50 (1985): 181–95.

10. Compare Amitai Etzioni, *The Comparative Analysis of Complex Organizations: On Power, Involvement, and Their Correlates* (New York: Free Press, 1961). There is a rough but suggestive correspondence between these changes

477

and the multiple connotations surrounding the title *Companía de Jesús*, the "company of Jesus," as the organization is called in the countries where it first gained prominence. Like a company geared for battle, the society has had its military aspects, most notably its tradition of obedience. It has also displayed features of a company in the sense of a business enterprise, showing an entrepreneurial zeal for creating and seizing opportunities and for institution building. Finally, the society reflects the root meaning of "company," a word derived from the Latin *cum* ("with") and *panis* ("bread"); Jesuits are a band of companions who eat together and form a community.

11. See for example Jerry H. Bentley, *Politics and Culture in Renaissance Naples* (Princeton, N.J.: Princeton University Press, 1987); Alan Charles Kors, "Theology and Atheism in Early Modern France," in *The Transmission of Culture in Early Modern Europe*, ed. Anthony Grafton and Ann Blair (Philadelphia: University of Pennsylvania Press, 1990); Robert G. North, S.J., *The General Who Rebuilt the Jesuits* (Milwaukee, Wis.: Bruce, 1944); and the essays in *The Enlightenment in National Context*, ed. Roy Porter and Mikulás Teich (Cambridge, England: Cambridge University Press, 1981).

12. Quoted by Maurizio Ferrara di Giampiero Mughini, "Mettiamoci in Corrente," *Panorama* [Rome] (April 13, 1989): 58.

13. Compare Jerome Bruner, *Acts of Meaning* (Cambridge, Mass.: Harvard University Press, 1990).

14. See Gilles Fauconnier, "Social Ritual and Relative Truth in Natural Language," in *Advances in Social Theory and Methodology*, ed. Karin D. Knorr-Centina and Alan V. Cicourel (Boston: Routledge & Kegan Paul, 1981); and Albert R. Jonsen and Stephen Toulmin, *The Abuse of Casuistry: A History of Moral Reasoning* (Berkeley: University of California Press, 1988). Compare John Bossy, "The Counter-Reformation and the People of Catholic Europe," *Past and Present* 47 (1970): 51–70.

15. Compare Norman Cohn, *The Pursuit of the Millennium: Revolutionary Millennarians and Mystical Anarchists of the Middle Ages*, revised and expanded edition (New York: Oxford University Press, 1970); Stephen Holmes, "The Secret History of Self-Interest," in *Beyond Self-Interest*, ed. Jane J. Mansbridge (Chicago: University of Chicago Press, 1990); and Herbert A. Simon, "Human Nature in Politics: The Dialogue of Psychology with Political Science," *American Political Science Review* 79 (1985): 293–304.

16. The holding in suspension of opposites also helps explain the penchant for eccentricity, anomaly, and absurdity—the air of peripeteia and a style of humor—that courses like a ritual through the adventures of the order. Just inside the entrance door of the Jesuit curia, the headquarters of the Society of Jesus on the Borgo Santo Spirito in Rome, is a large statue of Saint Ignatius, the founder of the order. Inscribed on the base of the statue in Latin is the command, "Go, set the world on fire!" Until a few years ago, a fire extinguisher was on the wall behind the statue.

17. See Mario Praz, *The Flaming Heart: Essays on Crashaw, Machiavelli, and Other Studies in the Relations Between Italian and English Literature from Chaucer to T. S. Eliot* (Garden City, N.Y.: Doubleday, 1958), pp. 131–32. Compare John Neville Figgis, *Political Thought From Gerson to Grotius, 1414–1625* (New York: Harper & Brothers, 1960), pp. 190–217.

18. Compare Mark Elkin, "A Working Definition of 'Modernity'?" *Past and Present* 113 (1986): 209–13.
19. See John Higley and Michael G. Burton, "The Elite Variable in Democratic Transitions and Breakdowns," *American Sociological Review* 54 (1989): 17–32.
20. See Reinhard Bendix, *Nation-Building and Citizenship: Studies of Our Changing Social Order* (New York: John Wiley & Sons, 1964); James D. Hardy,Jr., *Prologue to Modernity: Early Modern Europe* (New York: John Wiley & Sons, 1974); and Charles Tilly, *Coercion, Capital, and European States, A.D. 990–1990* (Oxford: Basil Blackwell, 1990).
21. See Aldo Scaglione, *The Liberal Arts and the Jesuit College System* (Amsterdam and Philadelphia: John Benjamin, 1986); H. O. Evenett, *The Spirit of the Counter-Reformation* (Cambridge, England: Cambridge University Press, 1968); and Michael Lee, ed., *Catholic Education in the Western World* (Notre Dame, Ind.: University of Notre Dame Press, 1967).
22. Quoted by Alvin Kernan, *The Death of Literature* (New Haven, Conn.: Yale University Press, 1990), p. 159.
23. Quoted by Robert Coles, *Times of Surrender: Selected Essays* (Iowa City: University of Iowa Press, 1988), p. 272.
24. See William B. Ashworth, "Catholicism and Early Modern Science," in *God and Nature: Historical Essays on the Encounter Between Christianity and Science*, ed. David C. Lindbert and Ronald L. Numbers (Berkeley: University of California Press, 1986); Michael J. Buckley, S.J., *At the Origins of Modern Atheism* (New Haven, Conn.: Yale University Press, 1987); and James Turner, *Without God, Without Creed: The Origins of Unbelief in America* (Baltimore, Md.: Johns Hopkins University Press, 1985). Compare Daniel Bell, "The Revolt Against Modernity," *Public Interest* 81 (1985): 42–63; Howard Brick, *Daniel Bell and the Decline of Intellectual Radicalism: Social Theory and Political Reconciliation in the 1940s* (Madison: University of Wisconsin Press, 1986); Robert N. Bellah, "The Triumph of Secularism," *Religion and Intellectual Life* 1 (1984): 13–26; John A. Coleman, S.J., "The Situation for Modern Faith," *Theological Studies* 39 (1978): 601–31; Denis Donoghue, "The Promiscuous Cool of Postmodernism," *New York Times Book Review* (June 22, 1986): 1, 36–37; and Nancy L. Rosenblum, ed., *Liberalism and the Moral Life* (Cambridge, Mass.: Harvard University Press, 1989). The Jesuits' insistence on joining morality and learning runs through all of their pedagogical writings. The following example is from Walter H. Hill, S.J., *Historical Sketch of the St. Louis University: The Celebration of Its Fiftieth Anniversary or Golden Jubilee on June 24, 1879* (St. Louis, Mo.: Patrick Fox, 1879), p. 152:

True education—complete education—consists of mental and moral training, and education is dangerous to the individual and to society unless it embraces these two parts. The history of the last two hundred years, with its bloody revolutions, its fearful crimes, its witness to the increase of disorders of the worst kinds in every grade of society, is enough to warrant the conclusion that mental development alone serves only to put deadly weapons in the hands of madmen for the destruction of their fellows.

The fixation of Jesuits with the union of knowledge and morality can be traced in large part to the priority given to action by the order. The emphasis has customarily been on somehow useful, and therefore moral, behavior. It should be noted that the dissociation between knowledge and conventional ethics takes several forms—for example, the Machiavellian, the Weberian (value-free science), the aesthetic (art for art's sake), and so on. It should also be noted that for some ("secular humanists") secularization does not in principle entail any such split.

25. See Peter Steinfels, "Catholic Colleges Chart Paths Still Catholic and Yet Diverse," *New York Times*, May 1, 1991, A1, 23.

26. "Professed fathers" take a fourth vow, of fealty to the papacy, in addition to the customary religious triad of poverty, chastity, and obedience, as a prerequisite to assuming positions of leadership in the order. See Donald A. Brown, S.J., *The Origins of the Grades in the Society of Jesus, 1540–1550* (Rome: Pontifical Gregorian University, 1971); and John W. O'Malley, S.J., "The Fourth Vow in Its Ignatian Context: A Historical Study," *Studies in the Spirituality of Jesuits* 15 (1983). Since the time of the Second Vatican Council, the status of the fourth vow appears to have changed. Previously, it seems to have been connected with "qualifying" Jesuits to become "superiors" within the hierarchy of the organization. In recent years this connection has loosened, and some "grade inflation" has probably set in, with an increase in the proportion of "professed fathers." At any rate, the commitment of fealty to the papacy remains. See John W. Padberg, S.J., "The Society True to Itself: A Brief History of the 32nd General Congregation of the Society of Jesus, December 2, 1974– March 7, 1975," *Studies in the Spirituality of Jesuits* 15 (May–September 1983).

27. Compare Jack Goody, *Development of the Family and Marriage in Europe* (Cambridge, England: Cambridge University Press, 1983); Tamara K. Hareven, "The Home and the Family in Historical Perspective," *Social Research* 58 (1991): 253–85; and Lawrence Stone, *Road to Divorce: England, 1530–1987* (New York: Oxford University Press, 1990).

28. See George Kateb, "The Moral Distinctiveness of Representative Democracy," *Ethics* 91 (1981): 357–74; and Joan G. Miller, "Culture and the Development of Everyday Social Cognitions," *Journal of Personality and Social Psychology* 46 (1984): 961–78.

29. See Joseph A. Tetlow, S.J., "The Jesuit University: A Community of Memory for Interpretation," Ignatian Anniversaries Year address, St. Louis University, April 4, 1991; compare Lynette Friedrich Cofer and Robin Smith Jacobvitz, "The Loss of Moral Turf: Mass Media and Family Values," in *Rebuilding the Nest: A New Commitment to the American Family*, ed. David Blankenhorn, Steven Bayme, and Jean Bethke Elshtain (Milwaukee, Wis.: Family Service America, 1991).

30. The scabrous literature is enormous in all European languages. Recent examples include John Gallahue, *The Jesuit* (New York: Stein & Day, 1973); and Eugene FitzMaurice, *The Hawkeland Cache* (New York: Wyndham Books, 1980). Three choice pieces, complete with dank, tenebrous cloisters and nocturnal clankings, are by Edmund Farrenc, *Carlotina and the Sanfedesti, or, A Night with the Jesuits at Rome* (New York: John S. Taylor, 1853); L. Giustiani, *Intrigues of Jesuitism in the United States of America* (Camden, N.J.: Franklin Ferguson, 1846); and Isaac Taylor, *Loyola and*

Jesuitism in its Rudiments (New York: Robert Carter & Bros., 1849). For a more extensive compilation, see Francis X. Curran, S.J., "Tentative Bibliography of American Anti-Jesuitania," *Woodstock Letters* 81 (July 1952): 293–304. For greater verisimilitude, see Robert Bireley, S.J., *Religion and Politics in the Age of the Counter-Reformation: Emperor Ferdinand II, William Lamormaini, S.J., and the Formation of Imperial Policy* (Chapel Hill: University of North Carolina Press, 1981); Robert Bireley, S.J., *The Counter-Reformation Prince: Anti-Machiavellianism or Catholic Statecraft in Early Modern Europe* (Chapel Hill: University of North Carolina Press, 1990); Elizabeth Jones, *Gentlemen and Jesuits: Quest for Glory and Adventure in the Early Days of New France* (Toronto: University of Toronto Press, 1986); and Paul P. Bernard, *Jesuits and Jacobins: Enlightenment and Enlightened Despotism in Austria* (Urbana: University of Illinois Press, 1971).

31. For a vivid analysis that sets the Jesuit style within the context of Renaissance pedagogy, with special reference to the Ciceronian manner that suspended contrapuntal patterns in a rhythmic movement to periodic resolution, see Paul F. Grendler, *Schooling in Renaissance Italy: Literacy and Learning, 1300–1600* (Baltimore, Md.: Johns Hopkins University Press, 1989).

32. Compare Michael A. Meyer, *Response to Modernity: A History of the Reform Movement in Judaism* (New York: Oxford University Press, 1988); and Gary Scott Smith, *The Seeds of Secularization: Calvinism, Culture, and Pluralism in America, 1870–1915* (Grand Rapids, Mich.: W. B. Eerdmans, 1986).

33. Compare Donald J. Wilcox, *In Search of God and Self: Renaissance and Reformation Thought* (Boston: Houghton Mifflin, 1975).

34. Turmoil has been so chronic throughout the history of the Jesuits that getting into trouble, both in and outside the church, might be interpreted as a latent function of the order. The society has been tolerated as a sensing mechanism, a probe that can be abandoned or retrieved, by an ecclesiastical establishment that itself is generally immobile and subject to a hardening of the organizational arteries. See Filippo Ceccarelli, "Ma che bella compagnia: Gesuiti/Radiografia di una roccaforte cattolica," *Panorama* [Rome] (March 22, 1987): 50–52; Francis X. Murphy, "Vatican Politics: Structure and Function," *World Politics* 26 (1974): 542–59; Richard N. Ostling, "Making Up With the Jesuits," *Time* (December 3, 1990): 89–90; John W. Padberg, S.J., "The Papacy and the Society—Often a Bumpy Relationship," *National Jesuit News* 11 (December 1981): 10–12, 20; and Lilian Parker Wallace, *Leo XIII and the Rise of Socialism* (Durham, N.C.: Duke University Press, 1966).

35. The agonistic style is hardly unique to the Jesuits. See for example William J. Bouwsma, *John Calvin: A Sixteenth-Century Portrait* (New York: Oxford University Press, 1988); S. N. Eisenstadt, *European Civilization in Comparative Perspective: A Study in the Relations Between Culture and Social Structure* (Oslo: Norwegian University Press, 1987); and Isaac Kramnick, *The Rage of Edmund Burke: Portrait of an Ambivalent Conservative* (New York: Basic Books, 1977); compare Peter Conn, *The Divided Mind: Ideology and Imagination in America, 1898–1917* (Cambridge, England: Cambridge University Press, 1983). See also Marjorie O'Rourke Boyle, "Angels Black and White: Loyola's Spiritual Discernment in Historical Perspective," *Theological*

Studies 44 (1983): 241–57; and George E. Ganss, S.J., ed., *Ignatius of Loyola: Spiritual Exercises and Selected Works* (New York: Paulist Press, 1991).

36. Compare Martha S. Feldman, *Order Without Design: Information Production and Policy Making* (Stanford, Calif.: Stanford University Press, 1989); and David Knoke, "Incentives in Collective Action Organizations," *American Sociological Review* 53 (1988): 311–29.

37. See Peter Berger and Thomas Luckmann, *The Social Construction of Reality* (Garden City, N.Y.: Doubleday, 1947); John B. Breslin, S.J., ed., *The Substance of Things Hoped For: Fiction and Faith* (New York: Doubleday, 1987); Alan Sica, *Weber, Irrationality, and Social Order* (Berkeley: University of California Press, 1988); David Tracy, *The Analogical Imagination: Christian Theology and the Culture of Pluralism* (New York: Crossroad, 1981); Robert Wuthnow and Marsha Witten, "New Directions in the Study of Culture," *Annual Review of Sociology* 14 (1988): 49–67; and Andrew M. Greeley in a speech given at the annual meeting of the Association of Catholic Colleges and Universities, quoted in *Chronicle of Higher Education* (April 10, 1991), B3:

> Most Catholics like being Catholic. They do not want to give up their Catholicism—the experiences, the images, the stories, the communities, and the rituals of their precognitive heritage. . . . In any conflict between propositional Catholicism, whether imposed by theologians, liturgists, and religious educators on one hand or the teaching authority on the other, and imaginative Catholicism, the latter win going away. . . . [T]he origins and raw power of religion are to be found in the poetic rather than the prosaic dimension of the self.

38. The fact that the Society of Jesus has diffuse goals makes it a different kind of organization from those with a clear bottom line, but no less of an organization. The system, such as it is, is more like a web or a coral reef, full of redundancies and diversions, than a machine whose parts are dedicated to optimizing a single function. See Charles Perrow, "A Society of Organizations," paper presented at the Center for Advanced Study in the Social Sciences, Juan March Institute, Madrid, May 22, 1989; compare Rosemary Haughton, *The Catholic Thing* (Springfield, Ill.: Templegate, 1979); Robert Nisbet, *Sociology as an Art Form* (New York: Oxford University Press, 1976); Erica Veevers, *Images of Love and Religion: Queen Henrietta Maria and Court Entertainments* (Cambridge, England: Cambridge University Press, 1989); and Lee Sproull, Stephen Weiner, and David Wolf, *Organizing an Anarchy: Belief, Bureaucracy, and Politics in the National Institute of Education* (Chicago: University of Chicago Press, 1978); see also Matila Ghyka, *The Geometry of Art and Life* (New York: Dover, 1977); and Robert Wuthnow, *Meaning and Moral Order: Explorations in Cultural Analysis* (Berkeley: University of California Press, 1987).

39. The logic of this situation is reminiscent of what political scientists call "nested games," The murkiness of the stakes in church politics—the absence of a common metric such as money or votes—makes it difficult to analyze in these terms, however; see George Tsebelis, *Nested Games: Rational Choice in Comparative Politics* (Berkeley: University of California Press, 1990). A fascinating

attempt to pin numbers on the payoffs in ecclesiastical legislative politics is by Salvador Gomez de Arteche y Catalina, "Grupos 'Extra Aulam' en el II Concilio Vaticano y su Influencia," Ph.D. dissertation, University of Valladolid, 1980. A handy introduction to the rules of the ecclesiastical game for the period covered in this study is by Elizabeth M. Lynskey, *The Government of the Catholic Church* (New York: P. J. Kenedy & Sons, 1952).

40. Compare William James Booth, "The New Household Economy," *American Political Science Review* 85 (1991): 59–75; Jan E. Dizard and Howard Gadlin, *The Minimal Family* (Amherst: University of Massachusetts Press, 1990); and Michael Mitterauer and Reinhard Sieder, *The European Family: Patriarchy to Partnership from the Middle Ages to the Present* (Chicago: University of Chicago Press, 1982).

41. Throughout his autobiography, Ignatius of Loyola, the founder of the Society of Jesus, refers to himself as "the pilgrim"; see Joseph N. Tylenda, trans., *A Pilgrim's Journey: The Autobiography of Ignatius of Loyola* (Wilmington, Del.: Michael Glazier, 1985). Compare Robert Darnton, "The Symbolic Element in History," *Journal of Modern History* 58 (1986): 218–34.

42. Compare Daughters of St. Paul, *Guide to the Revised Baltimore Catechism for Grade One* (Boston: St. Paul Editions, 1957); Bernard Hassan, *The American Catholic Catalogue* (San Francisco: Harper & Row, 1980); William J. Leonard, S.J., "Popular Devotions Remembered: 'The People Have a Certain Right to Be Vulgar,'" *America* (September 12, 1981): 119–21; John A. O'Brien, ed., *Understanding the Baltimore Catechism: An Official Edition of the Revised Baltimore Catechism No. 3* (Notre Dame, Ind.: Ave Maria Press, 1955); Peter Occhiogrosso, *Once a Catholic* (Boston: Houghton Mifflin, 1987); and John C. Stalker, *The Jesuit Collection of the John J. Burns Library of Boston College* (Boston: Boston College Library, 1986).

43. Compare Jay P. Dolan, "A Catholic Romance with Modernity," *Wilson Quarterly* 5 (1981): 120–33; Joseph C. Goulden, *The Best Years, 1945–1950* (New York: Atheneum, 1976); Richard T. Hughes and C. Leonard Allen, *Illusions of Innocence: Protestant Primitivism in America, 1630–1875* (Chicago: University of Chicago Press, 1989); Alan Harrington, *Life in the Crystal Palace* (New York: Alfred A. Knopf, 1959); Frank Levy, *Dollars and Dreams: The Changing American Income Distribution* (New York: Russell Sage Foundation, 1987); Henry R. Luce, "The First Great American Century," in *Culture and Commitment, 1929–1945*, ed. Warren Susman (New York: George Braziller, 1973); Irena Makarushka, "Subverting Eden: Ambiguity of Evil and the American Dream in *Blue Velvet*," *Religion and American Culture* 1 (1991): 31–46; and David S. Reynolds, *Beneath the American Renaissance: The Subversive Imagination in the Age of Emerson and Melville* (New York: Alfred A. Knopf, 1985).

44. See for example Robert H. Brinkmeyer, Jr., *Three Catholic Writers of the Modern South* (Jackson: University Press of Mississippi, 1985); Michael Kreyling, *Figures of the Hero in Southern Narrative* (Baton Rouge: Louisiana State University Press, 1987); Grady McWhiney, *Cracker Culture: Celtic Ways in the Old South* (Tuscaloosa: University of Alabama Press, 1988); and Michael O'Brien, " 'A Sort of Cosmopolitan Dog': Francis Lieber in the South," *Southern Review* 25 (1989): 308–22.

45. *Catholic Trivia: Pre-Vatican II Version* (Minneapolis, Minn.: J. Neill Tift, 1985).

46. Jonathan D. Spence, *The Question of Hu* (New York: Alfred A. Knopf, 1988), p. xviii.

INTRODUCTION

1. John D. Buenker, "Sovereign Individuals and Organic Networks: Political Cultures in Conflict During the Progressive Era," *American Quarterly* 40 (1988): 187–204; see also June Granatir Alexander, *The Immigrant Church and Community: Pittsburgh's Slovak Catholics and Lutherans, 1880–1915* (Pittsburgh, Pa: University of Pittsburgh Press, 1987); Kevin Christiano, *Religious Diversity and Social Change: American Cities, 1890–1906* (New York: Cambridge University Press, 1988); and Robert V. Hine, *Community on the American Frontier* (Norman: University of Oklahoma Press, 1980).

2. See Harriet Friedman, "World Market, State, and Family Farm: Social Bases of Production in the Era of Wage Labor," *Comparative Studies in Society and History* 20 (1978): 245–86; Steven Mintz and Susan Kellogg, *Domestic Revolutions: A Social History of American Family Life* (New York: Free Press, 1988); and Stephanie Coontz, *The Social Origins of Private Life: A History of American Families, 1600–1900* (London: Verso, 1988).

3. Daniel Berrigan, S.J., "Lew Cox Dies," *National Jesuit News* (February 1987): 16.

4. For an assessment of the Second Vatican Council as a revolution in cognitive maps, the *locus classicus* is John W. O'Malley, S.J., "Developments, Reforms, and Two Great Reformations: Towards a Historical Assessment of Vatican II," *Theological Studies* 44 (1983): 373–406. For the background of Tridentine Catholicism, see Trevor Aston, ed., *Crisis in Europe, 1560–1660* (London: Routledge & Kegan Paul, 1965); John Bossy, *Christianity in the West, 1400–1700* (New York: Oxford University Press, 1985); R. Trevor Davies, *The Golden Century of Spain, 1501–1621* (London: Macmillan, 1937); Kaspar von Greyerz, ed., *Religion and Society in Early Modern Europe, 1500–1800* (London: George Allen and Unwin, 1984); Hiram Haydn, *The Counter-Renaissance* (New York: Charles Scribner's Sons, 1950); and Paul Oskar Kristeller, *Renaissance Thought: The Classic, Scholastic, and Humanist Strains* (New York: Harper & Brothers, 1961).

5. See George Huntston Williams, "John Paul II's Concepts of Church, State, and Society," *Journal of Church and State* 24 (1982): 463–96.

6. See John Bossy, "The Counter-Reformation and the People of Western Europe," *Past and Present* 47 (1970): 51–70; Jean Delumeau, *Catholicism Between Luther and Voltaire: A New View of the Counter-Reformation* (London: Burns and Oates, 1977); R. J. W. Evans, *The Making of the Hapsburg Monarchy, 1550–1700* (Oxford: Clarendon Press, 1979); Peter Partner, *Renaissance Rome, 1500–1559: A Portrait of a Society* (Berkeley: University of California Press, 1976); Loren Partridge and Randolph Starn, *A Renaissance Likeness: Art and Culture in Raphael's Julius II* (Berkeley: University of California Press, 1980); and Gerhard Oestrich, *Neostoicism and the Early Modern State* (Cambridge, England: Cambridge University Press, 1982). Compare Wolfgang

Schluchter, *The Rise of Western Rationalism* (Berkeley: University of California Press, 1987); and Michael Walzer, *The Revolution of the Saints: A Study in the Origins of Radical Politics* (Cambridge, Mass.: Harvard University Press, 1965).

7. Thomas H. Clancy, S.J., *An Introduction to Jesuit Life: The Constitutions and History Through 435 Years* (St. Louis, Mo.: Institute of Jesuit Sources, 1976); and Leonard Krieger, *Kings and Philosophers, 1689–1789* (New York: W. W. Norton, 1970).

8. See Joseph M. Becker, S.J., "Changes in the U.S. Jesuit Membership," *Studies in the Spirituality of Jesuits* 9 (1977); and Francesco Farusi, S.J., "The Society in Numbers," *Documentation* (Rome) (April 1987–April 1990). The decennial breakdown was compiled by the Chicago province of the Society of Jesus.

9. Robert N. Bellah, "The Five Religions of Modern Italy," in *Varieties of Civil Religion*, ed. Robert N. Bellah and Philip E. Hammond (San Francisco: Harper & Row, 1980); Susan Berkowitz, "Familism, Kinship and Sex Roles in Southern Italy: Contradictory Ideals and Real Contradictions," *Anthropological Quarterly* 57 (1984): 83–92; Peter Brown, *The Body and Society: Men, Women and Sexual Renunciation in Early Christianity* (New York: Columbia University Press, 1988); Joseph F. Byrnes, "Explaining the Mary Cult: A Hypothesis and Its Problems," *Journal of Religion* 68 (1988): 277–85; David D. Gilmore, ed., *Honor and Shame and the Unity of the Mediterranean* (Washington, D.C.: American Anthropological Association, 1987); and Marina Warner, *Alone of All Her Sex: The Myth and the Cult of the Virgin Mary* (New York: Alfred A. Knopf, 1976).

10. See Colleen McDannell, *The Christian Home in Victorian America, 1840–1900* (Bloomington: Indiana University Press, 1986); compare Barbara Leslie Epstein, *The Politics of Domesticity: Women, Evangelism, and Temperance in Nineteenth-Century America* (Middletown, Conn.: Wesleyan University Press, 1981); Walter J. Fraser, R. Frank Saunders, Jr., and Jon L. Wakelyn, eds., *The Web of Southern Social Relations: Women, Family, and Education* (Athens: University of Georgia Press, 1985); and Carroll Smith-Rosenberg, *Disorderly Conduct: Visions of Gender in Victorian America* (New York: Alfred A. Knopf, 1985).

11. See Brendan Bradshaw, "The Wild and Woolly West: Early Irish Christianity and Latin Orthodoxy," in *The Churches, Ireland and the Irish*, ed. W. J. Sheils and Diana Wood (Oxford: Basil Blackwell, 1989); Patrick J. Corish, *The Irish Catholic Experience: A Historical Survey* (Dublin: Gill and Macmillan, 1985); Kevin O'Neill, *Family and Farm in Pre-Famine Ireland: The Parish of Killashandra* (Madison: University of Wisconsin Press, 1984); and Gail Bederman, " 'The Women Have Had Charge of the Church Work Long Enough': The Men and Religion Forward Movement of 1911–1912 and the Masculinization of Middle-Class Protestantism," *American Quarterly* 41 (1989): 432–65. Compare Peter Brown, *The Cult of the Saints in Latin Christianity: Its Rise and Function in Late Christianity* (Chicago: University of Chicago Press, 1981).

12. Colman J. Barry, O.S.B., *The Catholic Church and German Americans* (Milwaukee, Wis.: Bruce, 1953), pp. 6–7, passim; and Mack Walker, *Germany*

and the Emigration, 1816–1885 (Cambridge, Mass.: Harvard University Press, 1964).

13. K. H. Connell, *Irish Peasant Society: Four Historical Essays* (Oxford: Clarenden, 1968); Colleen McDannell, " 'True Men As We Need Them': Catholicism and the Irish-American Male," *American Studies* 27 (1986): 19–36; and Thomas J. Curran, *The Irish Family in Nineteenth-Century America* (Notre Dame, Ind.: University of Notre Dame Press, 1980); compare Lisa M. Bitel, *The Isle of the Saints: Monastic Settlement and Christian Community in Early Ireland* (Ithaca, N.Y.: Cornell University Press, 1990); and Margaret Marsh, "Suburban Men and Masculine Domesticity, 1870–1915," *American Quarterly* 40 (1988): 165–86. A concise exposition of the social origins and repercussions of Irish celibacy is by Michele Dillon, *Debating Divorce: Values in Contemporary Ireland* (Pittsburgh: University of Pittsburgh Press, forthcoming). Conspicuously missing from all of this literature is an examination of homosexuality in Irish culture. Ireland, unlike many other Western societies, appears not to provide any traditionally acknowledged "place" for homosexuals. The relationship between this "non-presence" and the role of the institutional church remains to be explored.

14. Robert E. Kennedy, Jr., *The Irish: Emigration, Marriage, and Fertility* (Berkeley: University of California Press, 1973); Lawrence McCaffrey, *The Irish Diaspora in America* (Bloomington: Indiana University Press, 1976); and James O'Shea, *Priest, Politics and Society in Post-Famine Ireland: A Study of County Tipperary, 1850–1891* (Dublin: Wolfhound, 1983). See also Herbert Kaufman, *Time, Chance, and Organizations: Natural Selection in a Perilous Environment* (Chatham, N.J.: Chatham House, 1985). For a particularly insightful analysis of the roots of Irish altruism, see Daniel J. O'Neil, "The Cult of Self-Sacrifice: The Irish Experience," paper presented at the annual meetings of the American Political Science Association, Chicago, September 3–6, 1987. It should be clear that this logic is directed at understanding changes in the number of religious vocations as an aggregate phenomenon, not at the reasons for commitment to religious life in individual cases.

15. See Mary T. Hanna, *Catholics and American Politics* (Cambridge, Mass.: Harvard University Press, 1979); and Seymour Martin Lipset, "Radicalism or Reformism: The Sources of Working Class Politics," *American Political Science Review* 77 (1983): 1–18.

16. See Owen Dudley Edward, "The Irish Priest in North America," in *The Churches, Ireland and the Irish*, ed. W. J. Sheils and Diana Wood (Oxford: Basil Blackwell, 1989); and Hartmut Keil, "German Immigrant Workers in Nineteenth-Century America: Working-Class Culture and Everyday Life in an Urban Industrial Setting," in *America and the Germans: An Assessment of a Three-Hundred-Year History*, vol. 1, *Immigration, Language, Ethnicity*, ed. Frank Trommler and Joseph McVeigh (Philadelphia. University of Pennsylvania Press, 1985).

17. Nathan Glazer and Daniel Patrick Moynihan, *Beyond the Melting Pot: The Negroes, Puerto Ricans, Jews, Italians, and Irish of New York City* (Cambridge, Mass.: MIT Press, 1964).

18. See Martin E. Marty, "The Catholic Ghetto and All the Other Ghettos," *Catholic Historical Review* 68 (1982): 185–205.

19. See James G. March and Johan P. Olsen, *Rediscovering Institutions: The Organizational Basis of Politics* (New York: Free Press, 1989).

20. Compare John H. Ehrenreich, *The Altruistic Imagination: A History of Social Work and Social Policy* (Ithaca, N.Y.: Cornell University Press, 1985); and Lori D. Ginzberg, *Women and the Work of Benevolence: Morality, Politics, and Class in the Nineteenth-Century United States* (New Haven, Conn.: Yale University Press, 1990).

21. See Lewis Coser, *Greedy Institutions* (New York: Free Press, 1974); compare Martha S. Feldman, *Order Without Design: Information Production and Policy Making* (Stanford, Calif.: Stanford University Press, 1989).

22. See George Lakeoff and Mark Johnson, *Metaphors We Live By* (Chicago: University of Chicago Press, 1980). An acute interpretation of this movement toward fusion, that captures both its tactile and its figurative elements, can be found in the essay on Gerard Manley Hopkins by Seamus Heaney, *Preoccupations: Selected Prose, 1968–1978* (New York: Farrar, Straus, Giroux, 1980), especially p. 91: "Hopkins's holy book was the New Testament, its commentary was the *Spiritual Exercises* of St. Ignatius Loyola, its reality was in his own experience of conversion and vocation to the Jesuit rule. His intellect was not forced to choose between perfection of the life or of the work but was compelled to bring them into congruence."

23. A different approach to the construct of way of life, based on the work of the anthropologist Mary Douglas, is found in Michael Thompson, Richard Ellis, and Aaron Wildavsky, *Cultural Theory* (Boulder, Co.: Westview, 1990). It is a nice question whether the properties of mastery, meaning, and emotional support can be rank-ordered, if we are to speak of organizational structure at all, with mastery being the indispensable element on which the others build. Meaning and emotional support appear to be more important to organizations like the Society of Jesus than to other "practical" organizations, even if Jesuits cannot dispense with efforts to control their environment. A condition in which the communal properties of meaning and emotional support displace corporate mastery cannot last for long; see Gerald A. Arbuckle, "Suffocating Religious Life: A New Type Emerges," *The Way* (supplement on "Religious Life in Transition") 65 (Summer 1989): 26–39.

24. The origins of the importance attached to obedience and character go back to the founding of the order. From its inception the Society of Jesus placed a premium on mobility. In early modern Europe, in the slipshod empire of the Hapsburgs and on its outer reaches, the organizational design of the Jesuits constituted a social invention. Mobility was counterbalanced by obedience. The more dispersed Jesuits were across regions, countries, and continents, the more loyal they were supposed to be to a central command structure.

A willing, prompt obedience—ostensibly instilled in Jesuits over their extraordinarily long course of training—was more efficient than a conformity that had repeatedly to be imposed from the outside. External means of control were fitful under the hierarchical centralization of Latin Catholic Europe, particularly as it underwent rapid geographical expansion. The match between a hierarchical social structure and bureaucratic centralism seemed close, but it was not functional. So endemic were departures from directives, despite the apparently organic match between civil and state hierarchies, so notorious was the corruption of the chain from command to implementation, that the Spanish captured the pathology—a pervasive culture of surveillance and evasion—in the paradox *Obedesco pero no cumplo*—"I go along but I don't follow through."

Displays of deference and protestations of piety did not get the work done; the cycle of capricious individualism and retribution was cumbersome and costly. What was institutionalized was not merely the hierarchical structure of society but the worldly-wise expectation of a gap between *el país legal* and *el país real*. A demimonde of cynicism and informal pragmatism flourished beneath the acquiescent protocols. The emergence of autonomous interests was stymied, but the system legitimized a sub-rosa flexibility. In one respect, the organizational design and moral ethos of the Society of Jesus fitted within the hierarchical tradition of Latin social structure. The novelty of the design consisted in overcoming a series of drawbacks that formal hierarchy exacerbated—namely, passive resistance, procrastination, corruption, and other types of noncompliance—as the decentralization caused by mobility made supervision all the more infeasible. See Louisa S. Hoberman, "Hispanic American Political Theory as a Distinct Tradition," *Journal of the History of Ideas* 41 (1980): 199–218; A. W. Lovett, *Early Hapsburg Spain, 1517–1598* (New York: Oxford University Press, 1986); Colin M. MacLachlan, *Spain's Empire in the New World: The Role of Ideas in Institutional and Social Change* (Berkeley: University of California Press, 1988); and Anthony Pagden, *Spanish Imperialism and the Political Imagination: Studies in European and Spanish-American Social and Political Theory, 1513–1830* (New Haven, Conn.: Yale University Press, 1990).

25. Compare Stephen L. Collins, *From Divine Cosmos to Sovereign State: An Intellectual History of Consciousness and the Idea of Order in Renaissance England* (New York: Oxford University Press, 1989); Harvey Goldman, *Max Weber and Thomas Mann: Calling and the Shaping of the Self* (Berkeley: University of California Press, 1988); Jacques Le Rider, *Modernité viennoise et crises de l'identité* (Paris: Presses Universitaires de France, 1990); and Jeff Weintraub, "The Theory and Politics of the Public/Private Distinction," paper presented at the annual meeting of the American Political Science Association, San Francisco, August 29–September 2, 1990.

26. Compare Nichole Woolsey Biggart and Gary G. Hamilton, "The Power of Obedience," *Administrative Science Quarterly* 29 (1984): 540–49; Avery Dulles, S.J., "Authority and Conscience: Two Needed Voices in the Church," *Church* 2 (Fall 1986): 8–15; Seymour Epstein, "The Stability of Behavior: On Predicting Most of the People Much of the Time," *Journal of Personality and Social Psychology* 37 (1979): 1097–1126; Robert H. Frank, *Passions Within Reason: The Strategic Role of the Emotions* (New York: W. W. Norton, 1988); Herbert C. Kelman and V. Lee Hamilton, *Crimes of Obedience: Toward a Social Psychology of Authority and Responsibility* (New Haven, Conn.: Yale University Press, 1989); William G. Ouchi and Alan J. Wilkins, "Organizational Culture," *Annual Review of Sociology* 11 (1985): 457–83; and Terrence W. Tilley, "Power, Authority and Life in Catholic Cultures," *Books and Religion* (Fall 1989): 5, 26–31. The dichotomy between character as constancy and character as conscience is a simplification. Later there will be occasion to introduce a third term, *competence*, to signify the flexibility that Jesuits have

customarily displayed in nonroutine situations, while preserving their "identity" and without entering "crises of conscience." Compare Arthur L. Stinchcombe, *Information and Organizations* (Berkeley: University of California Press, 1990), pp. 32–72.

27. See A. Lynn Martin, *The Jesuit Mind: The Mentality of an Elite in Early Modern France* (Ithaca, N.Y.: Cornell University Press, 1988); Brian O'Leary, S.J., "Living with Tension," *The Way* 61 (1988): 35–47; and Louis J. Puhl, S.J., ed., *The Spiritual Exercises of St. Ignatius* (Chicago, Ill.: Loyola University Press, 1951). Compare David Maybury-Lewis and Uri Almagor, eds., *The Attraction of Opposites: Thought and Society in the Dualistic Mode* (Ann Arbor: University of Michigan Press, 1989).

28. The simplification stems from ignoring, for the moment, the culturally variable ways in which male identity becomes an achieved rather than an ascribed trait. The point will become important in understanding the sensitivity of issues surrounding male ascendancy in Catholic religious life. See David D. Gilmore, *Manhood in the Making: Cultural Concepts of Masculinity* (New Haven, Conn.: Yale University Press, 1990); compare Pierre Bourdieu, *The Logic of Practice* (Oxford: Polity Press, 1990), p. 200, passim.

29. Compare Jon Elster, "Weakness of Will and the Free-Rider Problem," *Economics and Philosophy* 1 (1985): 213–65; Ernest R. Hull, S.J., *The Formation of Character* (St. Louis, Mo.: B. Herder, 1921); John O'Neill, "The Disciplinary Society: From Weber to Foucault," *British Journal of Sociology* 37 (1986): 42–60; Thomas C. Schelling, *Choice and Consequence* (Cambridge, Mass.: Harvard University Press, 1984), pp. 57–112; and James Q. Wilson, "The Rediscovery of Character: Private Virtue and Public Policy," *Public Interest* 81 (1986): 3–16.

30. See Philip Caraman, S.J., *The Lost Paradise: The Jesuit Republic in South America* (New York: Seabury, 1976); Nicholas P. Cushner, *Jesuit Ranches and the Agrarian Development of Colonial Argentina, 1650–1767* (Albany: State University of New York Press, 1983); R. B. Cunninghame Graham, *A Vanished Arcadia: Being Some Account of the Jesuits in Paraguay, 1607 to 1767* (London: William Heinemann, 1924); and Magnus Mörner, ed., *The Expulsion of the Jesuits from Latin America* (New York: Alfred A. Knopf, 1965); compare Antonello Gerbi, *La Disputa del Nuevo Mundo: Historia de una Polémica, 1750–1900* (Mexico City: Fundo de Cultura Económica, 1960); and Antonello Gerbi, *Nature in the New World: From Christopher Columbus to Gonzalo Fernández de Oviedo* (Pittsburgh, Pa.: University of Pittsburgh Press, 1985).

31. See Elizabeth Jones, *Gentlemen and Jesuits: Quests for Glory and Adventure in the Early Days of New France* (Toronto: University of Toronto Press, 1986); John Bernard McGloin, S.J., *Eloquent Indian: The Life of James Bouchard, California Jesuit* (Stanford, Calif.: Stanford University Press, 1949); James P. Ronda, "Black Robes and Boston Men: Indian-White Relations in New France and New England, 1524–1701," in *The American Indian Experience, a Profile: 1524 to the Present*, ed. Philip Weeks (Arlington Heights, Ill.: Arlington Heights, 1988); and François Roustang, S.J., ed., *An Autobiography of Martyrdom: Spiritual Writings of the Jesuits in New France* (St. Louis, Mo.: B. Herder, 1964).

32. See Robert J. Henle, S.J., ed., *Proceedings of the Conference on the Total Development of the Jesuit Priest*, 4 vol., University of Santa Clara, August 6–19, 1967, mimeo; compare Amartya Sen, "Goals, Commitment and Identity," *Journal of Law, Economics and Organization* 1 (1985): 341–55.

33. Berrigan, "Lew Cox Dies."

34. Paul Droulers, S.J., *Politique Sociale et Christianisme: Le Père Desbuquois et l'Action Populaire: Debuts—Syndicalisme et Integristes, 1903–1918* (Paris: Editions Ouvrières, 1969); and John LaFarge, S.J., "The Action Populaire as It Functions in France," *America* (January 7, 1939): 316–17. A few years later, in 1910, the Catholic Social Guild began operations in England under the direction of Fr. Charles Plater, S.J. See the somewhat patronizing retrospective by Paul Fitzpatrick, "Education and Social Engagement: The Lessons of the Catholic Social Guild," *The Month* 21 (1988): 649–56.

35. Austin G. Schmidt, S.J., ed., *Selected Writings of Father Ledochowski* (Chicago: Loyola University Press, 1945), p. 907.

36. See Wilfredo Fabros, S.J., *The Church and Its Social Involvement in the Philippines, 1930–1972* (Quezon City, Luzon: Ateneo de Manila University Press, 1988).

37. See Thurston N. Davis, S.J., "What is 'America'?" in *Between Two Cities*, ed. Thurston N. Davis, S.J., Donald R. Campion, S.J., and L. C. McHugh, S.J., (New York: America Press, 1962); Gerald P. Fogarty, S.J., *The Vatican and the Americanist Crisis: Denis J. O'Connell, American Agent in Rome, 1885–1903* (Rome: Gregorian University Press, 1974); Michael V. Gannon, "Before and After Modernism: The Intellectual Isolation of the American Priest," in *The Catholic Priest in the United States: Historical Investigations*, ed. John Tracy Ellis (Collegeville, Minn.: St. John's University Press, 1971); James Hennesey, S.J., "Leo XIII's Thomistic Revival: A Political and Philosophical Event," *Journal of Religion* 58 (1978): 185–97; Lester R. Kurtz, *The Politics of Heresy: The Modernist Crisis in Catholicism* (Berkeley: University of California Press, 1986); and Thomas T. McAvoy, *The Americanist Heresy in Roman Catholicism, 1895–1900* (Notre Dame, Ind.: University of Notre Dame Press, 1963). Compare Stephen Kern, *The Culture of Time and Space, 1880–1918* (Cambridge, Mass.: Harvard University Press, 1983).

38. See Thomas T. McAvoy and Thomas N. Brown, *The United States of America: The Irish Clergyman/The Irish Layman* (Dublin: Gill and Macmillan, 1970); and C. E. McGuire, ed., *Catholic Builders of the Nation: A Symposium on the Catholic Contribution to the Civilization of the United States* (Boston: Continental Press, 1923). Compare Marvin R. O'Connell, *John Ireland and the American Catholic Church* (St. Paul: Minnesota Historical Society Press, 1988); and Charles Joseph O'Fahey, *Gibbons, Ireland, Keane: The Evolution of a Liberal Catholic Rhetoric in America* (Minneapolis: University of Minnesota Press, 1980).

39. David O'Brien, *Public Catholicism* (New York: Macmillan, 1989).

40. See John J. Bukowczyk, "Mary the Messiah: Polish Immigrant Heresy and the Malleable Ideology of the Roman Catholic Church, 1880–1930," *Journal of American Ethnic History* 4 (1985): 5–32; Kieran Flanagan, "Liturgy, Ambiguity and Silence: The Ritual Management of Real Absence," *British Journal*

of Sociology 36 (1986): 193–223; Margaret Mary Reher, *Catholic Intellectual Life in America: A Historical Study of Persons and Movements* (New York: Macmillan, 1989); Dolores Liptak, R.S.M., *Immigrants and Their Church* (New York: Macmillan, 1989); Béla Menczer, ed., *Catholic Political Thought, 1789–1848* (London: Burn, Oates and Washbourne, 1952); Ann Taves, *The Household of Faith: Roman Catholic Devotions in Mid-Nineteenth-Century America* (Notre Dame, Ind.: University of Notre Dame Press, 1986); and Irene Woodward, S.N.J.M., ed., *The Catholic Church: The United States Experience* (New York: Paulist Press, 1979).

41. See Steven Seidman, *Liberalism and the Origins of European Social Theory* (Berkeley: University of California Press, 1983); compare Robert H. Wiebe, *The Search for Order, 1877–1920* (New York: Hill and Wang, 1967).

42. See Ronald C. Newton, "On 'Functional Groups,' 'Fragmentation,' and 'Pluralism' in Spanish American Political Society," *Hispanic American Historical Review* 50 (1970): 1–29.

43. See Charles Maier, "The Politics of Productivity: Foundations of American International Economic Policy After World War II," *International Organization* 31 (1977): 607–33; Michael J. Hogan, *The Marshall Plan: America, Britain and the Reconstruction of Western Europe, 1947–1952* (Cambridge, England: Cambridge University Press, 1987); and Frank Wilson, "Interest Groups and Politics in Western Europe: The Neo-Corporatist Approach," *Comparative Politics* 16 (1983): 105–23. See also Oswald von Nell-Breuning, S.J., *Reorganization of Social Economy* (Milwaukee, Wis.: Bruce, 1977); Oswald von Nell-Breuning, "West Germany's Economic Revival," *Social Order* 9 (May 1959): 201–14; Bernard W. Dempsey, S.J., *The Functional Economy: The Bases of Economic Organization* (Englewood Cliffs, N.J.: Prentice-Hall, 1958); Joseph B. Gremillion, *The Catholic Movement of Employers and Managers* (Rome: Gregorian University Press, 1961); and Gustav Gundlach, S.J., "Solidarist Economics," *Social Order* 1 (April 1951): 181–85.

44. "Instruction of Very Reverend Father General on the Social Apostolate, October 10, 1949," Woodstock Press pamphlet, 1950. Even during this period, the formation (training) of Jesuits was not as militaristic as it is sometimes made out to be; see F. E. Peters, *Ours: The Making and Unmaking of a Jesuit* (New York: Richard Marek, 1981). Although much of the process was standardized, implementation of the rules varied a bit, depending on the person who happened to be in charge at the local level, and the seminaries could not be shielded from hints of cultural change, particularly with the spread of the electronic media. For a contemporary indication of the changes to come, see Karl Rahner, S.J., "A Basic Ignatian Concept: Some Reflections on Obedience," *Woodstock Letters* 86 (November 1957): 291–310.

45. This is not to say that the generally cautious posture of the Jesuits was unpopular among Catholics in the United States, many of whom were working-class conservatives. The Catholic subculture tended to support the Jesuits' work in education, which promoted mobility, and treated their efforts to improve the plight of labor directly with respectful indifference. See Richard Oestreicher, "Urban Working-Class Political Behavior and Theories of American Electoral Politics, 1870–1940," *Journal of American History* 74 (1988): 1257–86; and Robert H. Zeiger, *American Workers, American Unions, 1920–1985* (Balti-

more, Md.: Johns Hopkins University Press, 1986). Compare David O'Brien, "Social Teaching, Social Action, Social Gospel," *U.S. Catholic Historian* 5 (1986): 195–224.

46. John Courtney Murray, S.J., *We Hold These Truths: Catholic Reflections on the American Proposition* (New York: Sheed and Ward, 1960). See also Jacques Maritain, *Scholasticism and Politics* (New York: Macmillan, 1940); Jacques Maritain, *Reflections on America* (New York: Charles Scribner's Sons, 1958); and Joseph W. Evans and Leo R. Ward, eds., *The Social and Political Philosophy of Jacques Maritain: Selected Readings* (New York: Charles Scribner's Sons, 1955).

47. Gerald P. Fogarty, S.J., "Public Patriotism and Private Politics: The Tradition of American Catholicism," *U.S. Catholic Historian* 4 (1984): 1–14.

48. See Donald E. Pellotte, *John Courtney Murray: Theologian in Conflict* (New York: Paulist Press, 1976); J. Leon Hooper, S.J., *The Ethics of Discourse: The Social Philosophy of John Courtney Murray* (Washington, D.C.: Georgetown University Press, 1987); and Richard J. Regan, S.J., *American Pluralism and the Catholic Conscience* (New York: Macmillan, 1963).

49. Charles A. Fracchia, *Second Spring: The Coming of Age of U.S. Catholicism* (San Francisco: Harper & Row, 1980); William VanEtten Casey, S.J., and Philip Nobile, eds., *The Berrigans* (New York: Avon Books, 1971); Francine du Plessix Gray, *Divine Disobedience: Profiles in Catholic Radicalism* (New York: Alfred A. Knopf, 1979); and Daniel Berrigan, S.J., *No Bars to Manhood* (New York: Doubleday, 1970).

50. See Joseph M. Becker, S.J., *The Reformed Jesuits*, vol. 1, *Upheaval and Response: Changes in Jesuit Formation, 1965–75* (Chicago: Loyola University Press, 1991).

51. See Thomas Philip Faase, *Making the Jesuits More Modern* (Washington, D.C.: University Press of America, 1981); James L. Franklin, "Leader of Jesuits Backs Order's Activism," *Boston Sunday Globe*, October 9, 1988, 42; and Joseph Parkes, S.J., and Arthur Bender, S.J., eds., *The Spiritual Legacy of Pedro Arrupe* (New York: Province Office of the Society of Jesus, 1985). For a statement by the present head of the society that is generally in line with the views of his predecessor, see Peter-Hans Kolvenbach, S.J., "The Spiritual Exercises and Preferential Love for the Poor," *Review for Religious* 43 (1094): 801–11; for a more conservative statement, see the interview reported by Lucio Brunelli, "Kolvenbach: The Pope Can Count on Us," *30 Days* (February 1989): 6–15.

52. Berrigan, "Lew Cox Dies."

53. See Paul Droulers, S.J., *Cattolicesimo Sociale nei Secoli XIX e XX: Saggi de Stòria e Sociologia* (Rome: Edizioni de Stòria e Letteratura, 1982); and "Sviluppi Metodologici e Doctrinale nel Magistero Sociale della Chiesa," *Civiltà Cattolica* 140 (April 1, 1989): 3–16.

54. See Giacomo Martina, S.J., *Pio IX, 1851–1866* (Rome: Gregorian University Press, 1986); and Arno J. Mayer, *Dynamics of Counterrevolution in Europe, 1870–1956* (New York: Harper & Row, 1971).

55. In the United States the turning away from political conservatism was probably also facilitated by the preexisting social democratic sympathies of most Jesuits.

Through the postwar period the majority of American Jesuits saw themselves as New Deal Democrats, as did American Catholics generally; see Bruce F. Biever, S.J., and Thomas M. Gannon, S.J., eds., *General Survey of the Society of Jesus: North American Assistancy*, 5 vols. (Chicago, Ill.: National Office of Pastoral Research/Argus Press, 1969).

56. See Joseph B. Gremillion, ed., *The Gospel of Peace and Justice: Catholic Social Teaching since Pope John* (Maryknoll, N.Y.: Orbis, 1976); and John E. Tropman, "The 'Catholic Ethic' vs. the 'Protestant Ethic': Catholic Social Services and the Welfare State," *Social Thought* 12 (1986): 13–22.

57. See Jean-Yves Calvez, S.J., "The Church and the Economy," *Chicago Studies* 15 (1986): 177–87; Thomas M. Gannon, S.J., "Religion and the Economy: Alliance or Conflict?" *This World* 7 (1984): 66–82; and Peter Hebblethwaite, "The Popes and Politics: Shifting Patterns in 'Catholic Social Doctrine,'" in *Religion in America: Spirituality in a Secular Age*, ed. Mary Douglas and Steven M. Tipton (Boston: Beacon, 1983).

By quantitative criteria the political and social involvement of Jesuits, while appreciable, has been less widespread than the publicity accorded these activities might suggest. In the United States, the actual number of Jesuits engaged in social ministry of one sort or another has increased slightly, from a very low base. In 1965, of a total of 8,300 American Jesuits, only one-tenth of 1 percent could be classified as working in social ministry. By 1979, the most recent year for which figures are readily available and, given the temper of the times, probably a top year for social activism, the relative figure had climbed to 1.4 per cent, while the total number of Jesuits had fallen to fewer than 5,800. See Dean C. Ludwig, "Avoiding Spiralling Decline: The Effects of Reallocative Retrenchment Strategies on Admissions and Departures in Voluntary Organizations" (Ph.D. dissertation, Wharton School, University of Pennsylvania, 1984). The corresponding figures for the distribution of Jesuit manpower across ministries in other countries are probably not much different. Even in South Asia, where the Society of Jesus is growing, most Jesuits are at work in schools. In general, the statistics on Jesuits who are officially classified as working in social ministry almost certainly underestimate the order's movement toward social concerns within its still dominant institutions, that is, through scholarship programs for minorities, maintaining schools in what have become inner-city neighborhoods, and the like.

Furthermore, even though the association was ignored at the time, there was some continuity between the political opinions espoused by Jesuits after Vatican II and the Catholic *magisterium* on the social question that had started to take shape in the second half of the nineteenth century. Apparently novel policy recommendations were reminiscent of traditional attacks on the corrupting influence of capitalist materialism. The increased salience given to issues of collective concern, relative to individualistic understandings of spirituality and salvation, was at least as important as reversals of opinion on policies from conservative to progressive. Social justice rose on the agenda of the Jesuits, as expressed in the documents of the society. Implementation was problematic, however, not only because of opposition and puzzlement among Jesuits themselves but also because of the sluggishness built into organizations through which Jesuits worked and because of doubts and suspicions on the part of collaborators and benefactors. See Jean-Yves Calvez, S.J., and Jacques Perrin, S.J., *The Church and Social Justice: The Social Teaching of the Popes from Leo XIII to Pius XII, 1878–1958* (Chicago: Henry Regnery, 1981); Richard L. Camp, *The Papal Ideology of Social Reform: A Study in Historical Development, 1878–1967* (Leiden, the Netherlands: E. J. Brill, 1969); Michael Campbell-Johnston, S.J., "The Social Teaching of the Church," *Thought* 39 (Autumn 1964): 380–410; Ann Fremantle, ed., *The Social Teachings of the Church* (New York: Mentor, 1963); John W. Padberg, S.J., ed., *Documents of the 31st and 32nd General Congregations of the Society of Jesus* (St. Louis, Mo.: Institute of Jesuit Sources, 1977); and Michael J. Schulteiss, S.J., Edward P. DeBerri, S.J., and Peter J. Henriot, S.J., *Our Best Kept Secret: The Rich Heritage of Catholic Social Teaching* (Washington, D.C.: Center of Concern, 1987).

In estimating changes regarding social policy and action in the Society of Jesus, the pre-existing commitments of the order and the clientele of these activities must be taken into account. Through the period of immigrant and postimmigrant Catholicism, most Jesuits worked in schools populated by middle-, lower-middle-, and working-class students. These institutions were not in the same elite category as the prep schools and small colleges attended by the sons and daughters of wealthier Protestants. Currently, the activities of Jesuits in Third World countries—for example, in Nicaragua or El Salvador—and the people with whom they work resemble the services and clientele that Jesuits provided at schools like Fordham decades earlier. See Charles J. Beirne, S.J., "Jesuit Education for Justice: The Colegio in El Salvador, 1968–1984," *Harvard Educational Review* 55 (1985): 1–19; and Ilja A. Luciak, "Popular Democracy in the New Nicaragua: The Case of Rural Mass Organizations," *Comparative Politics* 20 (1987): 35–55.

58. See William A. Barry, S.J., et al., "Affectivity and Sexuality: Their Relationship to the Spiritual and Apostolic Life of Jesuits," *Studies in the Spirituality of Jesuits* 10 (1978).

59. See Margaret O'Brien Steinfels, "The Church and Its Public Life," *America* (June 10, 1989): 550–58.

60. Compare Arthur O. Lovejoy, *The Great Chain of Being* (Cambridge, Mass.: Harvard University Press, 1936); Michael Mitterauer and Reinhard Sieder, *The European Family: Patriarchy to Partnership From the Middle Ages to the Present* (Chicago: University of Chicago Press, 1982); and Wilfrid Parsons, S.J., "Social Thought of American Hierarchy," *Social Order* 2 (June 1952): 259–78. Hierarchies of issue sensitivity are not unique to Catholicism. A close parallel can be found in the layering of racial relations in the South. Blumer's distinction among the "outer," the "intermediate," and the "inner" color lines is analogous to political, social, and gender divisions in Catholic thought. See Hubert Blumer, "The Future of the Color Line," in *The South in Continuity and Change*, ed. John C. McKinney and Edgar T. Thompson (Durham, N.C.: Duke University Press, 1965).

61. It might be argued, then, that the social protest and political activism that took place among Jesuits around the time of Vatican II were byproducts of the psychological upheaval in the interior of Catholicism. The collapse of a medieval cosmology created unexpected anguish among religious professionals.

Jesuits displaced their torment at the loss of previously well-defined roles and status onto a secular world that happened at the time to be in tumult. Jesuits, so the explanation goes, were acting out. This is essentially the position taken by James Davison Hunter, "Religious Elites in Advanced Industrial Society," *Comparative Studies in Society and History* 29 (1987): 360–80; and David Martin, "The Clergy, Secularization and Politics," *This World* 6 (1983): 131–42.

The argument runs the risk of substituting the large-scale structural forces disrupting Catholicism from the outside with psychological factors eroding Catholicism from the inside. One type of reductionism replaces another. The fact that psychic change and resistance to it have been crucial to the Jesuits does not mean that either the causes of these changes or their consequences have been entirely subjective.

The factor common to the radicalization of Jesuits worldwide was an internal change: the evaporation of an archaic world view. See Philip Gleason, *Keeping the Faith* (Notre Dame, Ind.: University of Notre Dame Press, 1987); Robert F. Harvanek, S.J., "Philosophical Pluralism and Catholic Orthodoxy," *Thought* 25 (1950): 21–52; and Gerald A. McCool, S.J., "Neo-Thomism and the Tradition of St. Thomas," *Thought* 62 (1987): 131–46. The disappearance of this ideology, or at least the timing of its disappearance, could not have been predicted mechanistically from structural transformations such as urbanization, education, and other exogenous factors. Jesuit seminaries in New York, El Salvador, and elsewhere modified the old methods of training more or less simultaneously, with very brief lags. The intellectual upheaval spread across different social and cultural contexts with remarkable uniformity.

The factors that differed in the radicalization of Jesuits from country to country were external to the Society of Jesus. Three of these have been paramount. During the postwar period more Asian, African, and Latin American Jesuits were exposed to the deepening impoverishment of Third World populations than were Europeans and North Americans. See Alejandro Portes, "Latin American Class Structures: Their Composition and Change During the Last Decades," *Latin American Research Review* 20 (1985): 7–39. Another ingredient was the complement of this: the increasingly educated and affluent pool from which Jesuits were drawn in advanced industrial societies following the war. Yet it produced similar results. In somewhat the same way as it seems to have done with student cohorts in the secular world, abundance contributed to the radicalization of younger Jesuits at precisely the time that ideology was supposed to have ended. Prosperity primed a generation of young people to be sensitive to issues of poverty, discrimination, and the quality of life. See Daniel Bell, "The End of Ideology Revisited (Part One)," *Government and Opposition* 23 (1988): 131–50; and Ronald Inglehart, *Culture Shift in Advanced Industrial Society* (Princeton, N.J.: Princeton University Press, 1989).

Third, demographic trends indicated that the future of Catholicism lay in the Southern hemisphere. Strategic as well as philosophical considerations prompted a rethinking of allegiances under North American hegemony. A decisive change became apparent in the late 1940s. Just as the United States was entering into a period of unprecedented economic growth, its population was overtaken in size by that of Latin America. From a geopolitical perspective, the high tide of English-speaking Catholicism was receding.

Thus, the convergence of a cultural turmoil inside Catholicism, the disappearance of the scholastic worldview, with mounting structural dislocation, and the acceleration of population growth in Third World countries and, simultaneously, increasing affluence in Europe and North America rendered Jesuits receptive to modes of criticism and action which they were inclined to treat as mistaken and dangerous a few years earlier. See Herman Bakvis, *Catholic Power in the Netherlands* (Kingston and Montreal: McGill–Queen's University Press, 1981).

The interpretation stresses the confluence of several conditions in altering the course of the Society of Jesus. Yet if a single factor could be said to underlie these transformations, age—or rather the generational and historical changes that age incorporates—would be a prime candidate.

Consideration of age throws light on the reasons behind the breakdown of the intellectual structure of Catholicism. By the end of the fifties, the brick-and-mortar chores of American Catholicism—the building-up of the schools and parishes—had been essentially completed. See Harold A. Buetow, *Of Singular Benefit: The Story of Catholic Education in the United States* (New York: Macmillan, 1970); and Edward J. Power, *Catholic Education in America: A History* (New York: Appleton-Century-Crofts, 1972). The recipients of these efforts were no longer so dependent on the ministrations of the clergy and were moving out of the confines of the neighborhood subcultures to the suburbs. In addition, the cultural equivalent of the achievement of the Jesuits in the institutional sphere was an intellectual system that claimed to be rounded but that was incongruous in its stress on stasis, hierarchy, and completeness in the midst of societal change. Perhaps even more disastrously, it was inadequate to the psychic need of young Jesuits to make the *magisterium* their own. Once the institutional challenges of American Catholicism had largely been met, Counter-Reformation triumphalism left Jesuits little room to stretch and prove themselves either organizationally or intellectually. Then, suddenly, with the evaporation of the Tridentine synthesis, they had little to test themselves against. A common reaction was to move between alienation and anomie directed both at the church and against the world outside.

A characteristic of successful authoritarian systems is their capacity to solve the problem of elite circulation and leadership turnover. By the 1950s Catholicism had an abundance of clerical recruits but was failing to keep open the channels through which the ecclesiastical hierarchy might replenish its energies. See John Seidler, "Priest Resignations in a Lazy Monopoly," *American Sociological Review* 33 (1979): 763–83; and Joan M. Waring, "Social Replenishment and Social Change: The Problem of Disordered Cohort Flow," *American Behavioral Scientist* 19 (1975): 237–56.

62. See Anthony Downs, "The Evolution of Democracy," *Daedalus* (1987): 119–48; and Charles S. Maier, ed., *Changing Boundaries of the Political* (Cambridge, England: Cambridge University Press, 1987); Steven E. Ozment, *When Fathers Ruled: Family Life in Reformation Europe* (Cambridge, Mass.: Harvard University Press, 1983); Carole Pateman, " 'God Hath Ordained to Man a Helper': Hobbes, Patriarchy and Conjugal Right," *British Journal of Political Science* 19 (1989): 445–64; and Steven A. Peterson, *Political Behavior: Patterns in Everyday Life* (Newbury Park, Calif.: Sage, 1990).

63. See William D'Antonio, "Religion and the Family: Exploring a Changing Relationship," working paper, Cushwa Center for the Study of American Catholicism, University of Notre Dame, 1980.

64. Compare Joan Wallach Scott, *Gender and the Politics of History* (New York: Columbia University Press, 1988); Edward Shorter, *The Making of the Modern Family* (New York: Basic Books, 1975); and Arland Thornton, "Reciprocal Influences of Family and Religion in a Changing World," *Journal of Marriage and the Family* 47 (1985): 381–94; see also Robert N. Bellah, "Religious Evolution," *American Sociological Review* 29 (1964): 358–74.

65. See Richard Nuccio, "The Family as Political Metaphor in Authoritarian-Conservative Regimes: The Case of Spain," working paper, Latin American Studies Center, Amherst, University of Massachusetts, 1979.

66. See Susan Moller Okin, *Justice, Gender, and the Family* (New York: Basic Books, 1989).

67. This adaptability and respect for the differentiation of spheres can be found in some sources of the canon of Catholic traditionalism such as Thomism; see F. C. Copleston, S.J., *Aquinas* (London: Penguin, 1955); and Paul Sigmund, ed., *St. Thomas Aquinas on Politics and Ethics* (New York: W. W. Norton, 1988).

68. An ambitious and suggestive attempt to trace institutional and ideological patterns from family structures, and one that lapses into reductionism, is by the French anthropologist Immanuel Todd, *The Explanation of Ideology: Family Structures and Social Systems* (Oxford: Basil Blackwell, 1985); and *The Causes of Progress: Culture, Authority and Change* (Oxford: Basil Blackwell, 1987).

69. See Christopher Lasch, *Haven in a Heartless World: The Family Besieged* (New York: Basic Books, 1977); David Martin, *A General Theory of Secularization* (New York: Harper & Row, 1979); and Alan Wolfe, *Whose Keeper? Social Science and Moral Obligation* (Berkeley: University of California Press, 1989). Compare James A. Sweet and Larry L. Bumpass, *American Families and Households* (New York: Russell Sage Foundation, 1987).

70. See Joan Huber, "Macro-Micro Links in Gender Stratification," *American Sociological Review* 55 (1990): 1–10; and Robert Wuthnow, *The Restructuring of American Religion* (Princeton, N.J.: Princeton University Press, 1989).

71. See Eric O. Hanson, *The Catholic Church in World Politics* (Princeton, N.J.: Princeton University Press, 1987); and Johannes Schashing, S.J., "From the Class War to the Culture of Solidarity: A Fundamental Theme of the Church's Social Teaching," in *Vatican Two: Assessment and Perspectives, Twenty-Five Years After, 1962–1987*, vol. 3, ed. René Latourelle (New York: Paulist Press, 1989).

72. See James R. Kelly, "Catholicism and Modern Memory: Some Sociological Reflections on the Symbolic Foundations of the Rhetorical Force of the Pastoral Letter, 'The Challenge of Peace,'" *Sociological Analysis* 45 (1984): 131–44. The universalizing model is also reminiscent of visions that abounded for the spread of Christianity during the expansion of Europe; see John Patrick Donnely, S.J., "Antonio Possevino's Plan for World Evangelization," *Catholic Historical Review* 74 (1988): 179–98.

73. Even though Jesuits are usually identified more with education than pastoral

work, the importance of matters involving the family and sexuality should not be underestimated in connection with the Society of Jesus. The key question of the "parvity"—the relative lightness or seriousness—of issues in this area was taken up soon after the founding of the society. It was determined to be nonnegotiable, an absolute. The following summary is taken from Patrick J. Boyle, S.J., *Parvitas Materiae in Sexto in Contemporary Catholic Thought* (Lanham, Md.: University of America, 1987), pp. 14–15, 85.

The turning point in reference to parvity of matter in the sixth and ninth commandments occurred in 1612 with the proclamation of Claude Acquaviva, the General of the Society of Jesus. Up to that time the Holy See had not as yet addressed the question of parvity of matter in sexual sins directly. After 1612, with few exceptions it was more or less a closed question. In 1612, Acquaviva issued a decree aimed at those who taught that some slight pleasure *in re venerea* deliberately sought could be excused from mortal sin. His decree forbade all the members of the Society of Jesus from teaching this doctrine in any form. It further forbade Jesuits from showing themselves in any way supportive toward it or from counseling according to it. Acquaviva issued the decree for two reasons. The first was that the opinion in favor of parvity of matter in his mind was harmful to the reputation of the Society. He also believed that the purity of life which the Society demanded of its members and its externs required such a teaching. His second reason for promulgating the decree was that the learned and authoritative fathers of the Society with whom he had consulted in this matter considered it in practice to be a teaching totally false and very much opposed to the virtue of chastity. These authoritative and learned fathers arrived at this conclusion because of the inherent danger in holding the contrary doctrine and because of the impossibility of distinguishing in practice between light and grave matter.

Acquaviva was so insistent on the prohibition that he attached severe censures to the violation of the decree. The decree bound all members of the Society under the vow of holy obedience and its violation was subject to a number of penalties including excommunication. It also imposed upon all Jesuits by virtue of holy obedience the obligation of revealing the names of those Jesuits who failed to observe the decree.

Even though the decree was quite general and ambiguous in meaning, still it played a very important part in the development of the traditional teaching. For all practical purposes it spelled the end for the teaching of parvity of matter. At that time in history, many educational institutions were staffed by Jesuits, who were forbidden under the strictest censure to teach anything other then the traditional teaching. Secondly, even though the Decree was not an official doctrine of the *magisterium*, still the silence of the Church at that time in face of this decree, which it knew would have such great influence on the minds and spirituality of the faithful, has to be taken as approval of the teaching as presented by Acquaviva.

74. Quoted by John W. O'Malley, S.J., "To Travel to Any Part of the World," *Studies in the Spirituality of Jesuits* 16 (March 1984): 6–8.

75. For an example of literary splendor amid the shelves of writings produced by this tradition, see Hélio Abranches Viotti, S.J., ed., *Padre José de Anchieta,*

S.J. [1534–97], *Cartas: Correspondência Ativa e Passiva,* 11 vol. (São Paulo: Edições Loyola, 1984–   ). Compare the discussion of "the portable self" by Richard Sennett, "Fragments Against the Ruin," *Times Literary Supplement* (February 8, 1991): 6.

76. The symbiosis of the metaphors can be detected in a "purely American," non-Catholic context, exemplified by the 1954 motion picture "Shane." See Richard Severo, "A. B. Guthrie Jr. Is Dead at 90," *New York Times,* April 27, 1991.

77. John Barrett, S.J., "Now and Then," *St. Ignatius Magazine* (Winter 1990): 6.

78. This criticism is advanced persuasively with reference to ideologies of the family by Katherine A. Lynch, *Family, Class, and Ideology in Early Industrial France: Social Policy and the Working-Class Family, 1825–1848* (Madison: University of Wisconsin Press, 1988).

79. Gerald A. McCool, S.J., *Catholic Theology in the Nineteenth Century: The Quest for a Unitary Method* (New York: Seabury, 1977). The contemporary flavor can be sampled in such publications as C. F. Donovan, ed., *Our Faith and the Facts* (Chicago: Patrick L. Baine, 1922); P. Hehel, S.J., *Short Sermons on Catholic Doctrine: A Plain and Practical Exposition of the Faith in a Series of Brief Discourses for the Ecclesiastical Year* (New York: Joseph F. Wagner, 1902); Francis Hunolt, S.J., *Sermons on the Four Last Things: Death, Judgment, Hell, and Heaven* (New York: Benziger Brothers, 1897); Eusebius Nieremberg, S.J., *A Treatise on the Difference Between Temporal and Eternal* (New York: P. O'Shea, about 1800–1900); Edward J. McGolrick, *The Unchangeable Church: Her Heroes, Her Martyrs, Her Trials, and Her Triumphs* (New York: John Duffy, 1909); and Conde B. Pallen and John J. Wynne, S.J., eds., *The New Catholic Dictionary: A Complete Work of Reference on Every Subject in the Life, Belief, Tradition, Rites, Symbolism, Devotions, History, Biography, Laws, Dioceses, Missions, Centers, Institutions, Organizations, Statistics of the Church and Her Part in Promoting Science, Art, Education, Social Welfare, Morals and Civilization* (New York: Universal Knowledge Foundation, 1929). Occasional pieces were directed at a more enlightened audience; they attempted to walk a fine line between conservatism and outright reaction. The following passage from W. Wilmers, S.J., James Conway, S.J., ed., *Handbook of the Christian Religion for the Use of Advanced Students and the Educated Laity,* 2nd ed. (New York: Benziger Brothers, 1891), typifies this approach:

> The third appendix particularly will be found appropriate at a time when liberalism, albeit unwittingly, crops out at times even in Catholic circles, and necessarily calls forth criticism in the more conservative portion of the Catholic press. In such circumstances it is well that the educated Catholic laity should have a standard by which to judge what is, and what is not, liberalism in the odious sense of the word. (p. vi)

80. See Isaiah Berlin, "The Counter-Enlightenment," in *Against the Current: Essays in the History of Ideas by Isaiah Berlin,* ed. Henry Hardy (London: Penguin, 1978); John B. Killoran, "Maritain's Critique of Liberalism," *Notes et Documents* 21/22 (1988): 110–22; Alasdair MacIntyre, *Against the Self-Images of the Age: Essays on Ideology and Philosophy* (London: Gerald Duck-

worth, 1971); and C. Vann Woodward, "The Lost Cause," *New York Review of Books* (January 30, 1986): 26–29.

81. Michael P. Fogarty, *Christian Democracy in Western Europe, 1820–1953* (Notre Dame, Ind.: University of Notre Dame Press, 1957); Michael Fleet, *The Rise and Fall of Chilean Christian Democracy* (Princeton, N.J.: Princeton University Press, 1985); and John H. Kennedy, *Catholicism, Nationalism, and Democracy in Argentina* (Notre Dame, Ind.: University of Notre Dame Press, 1958).

82. Francis J. Burke, S.J., "Why So Many Vocations to the Society in the United States," *Woodstock Letters* 57 (1928): 179–84.

83. See Gerald P. Fogarty, S.J., *The Vatican and the American Hierarchy from 1870 to 1965* (Stuttgart, Germany: Anton Hiersemann, 1982).

84. Gerald A. McCool, S.J., "Neo-Thomism and the Tradition of St. Thomas," *Thought* 62 (1987): 131–46. Compare H. Stuart Hughes, *The Sea-Change: The Migration of Social Thought, 1930–1965* (New York: McGraw-Hill, 1975); and Melvyn Stokes, "American Progressives and the European Left," *Journal of American Studies* 17 (1983): 5–28.

85. See Alfonso Alvarez Bolado, S.J., *El Experimento del Nacional-Catolicismo, 1939–1975* (Madrid: Edicusa, 1976); William J. Callahan, *Church, Politics, and Society in Spain, 1750–1874* (Cambridge, Mass.: Harvard University Press, 1984); Louis Hartz, *The Founding of New Societies: Studies in the History of the United States, Latin America, South Africa, Canada, and Australia* (New York: Harcourt, Brace & World, 1964); Ralph Gibson, *A Social History of French Catholicism, 1789–1914* (London: Routledge, 1989); Manuel Revuelta González, S.J., *La Compañia de Jesús en la España Contemporánea: Supresión y Reinstalación, 1868–1883* (Madrid: Universidad Pontifícia Comillas de Madrid, 1984); J. S. McClelland, ed., *The French Right: From DeMaistre to Maurras* (New York: Harper & Row, 1970); Joseph N. Moody, ed., *Church and Society: Catholic Social and Political Thought and Movements, 1789–1950* (New York: Arts, 1953); Stanley G. Payne, *Spanish Catholicism* (Madison: University of Wisconsin Press, 1984); Karl Otmar von Aretin, *The Papacy and the Modern World* (New York: McGraw-Hill, 1970); Michael Sutton, *Nationalism, Positivism and Catholicism: The Politics of Charles Maurras and French Catholics, 1890–1914* (Cambridge, England: Cambridge University Press, 1983); and John D. Stephens, "Democratic Transition and Breakdown in Western Europe, 1870–1939: A Test of Moore's Thesis," *American Journal of Sociology* 94 (1989): 1019–77.

86. See Carl Strikwerda, "The Divided Class: Catholics vs. Socialists in Belgium, 1880–1914," *Comparative Studies in Society and History* 30 (1988): 333–59.

87. Compare Robert H. Wiebe, *Businessmen and Reform: A Study of the Progressive Movement* (Cambridge, Mass.: Harvard University Press, 1962); Frank M. Snowden, "On the Social Origins of Agrarian Fascism in Italy," *Archives Européennes de Sociologie* 13 (1972): 268–95; and James Weinstein, *The Corporate Ideal in the Liberal State, 1900–1918* (Boston: Beacon, 1968).

88. See James M. Bergquist, "German Communities in American Cities: An Interpretation of the Nineteenth-Century Experience," *Journal of American Ethnic History* 4 (1984): 9–30; William Barnaby Faherty, S.J., *Dream by the*

River: Two Centuries of Saint Louis Catholicism, 1766–1980, rev. ed. (St. Louis, Mo.: River City Publishers, 1981); and Robert W. Frizell, "Migration Chains to Illinois: The Evidence From German-American Church Records," *Journal of American Ethnic Church History* 7 (1987): 59–73.

89. See David Blackbourn, "Progress and Piety: Liberalism, Catholicism and the State in Imperial Germany," *History Workshop Journal* 26 (1988): 57–78; Alfred Diamant, *Austrian Catholics and the First Republic: Democracy, Capitalism, and the Social Order, 1918–1934* (Princeton, N.J.: Princeton University Press, 1960); Ralph Gleason, *The Conservative Reformers: German-American Catholics and the Social Order* (Notre Dame, Ind.: University of Notre Dame Press, 1968); and Hartmut Keil and John B. Jentz, eds., *German Workers in Industrial Chicago, 1850–1910: A Comparative Perspective* (DeKalb: Northern Illinois University Press, 1983); compare Timothy R. Mahoney, *River Towns in the Great West: The Structure of Provincial Urbanization in the American Midwest, 1820–1870* (Cambridge, England: Cambridge University Press, 1990).

90. See Mary E. Brown, "Competing to Care: Aiding Italian Immigrants in New York Harbor, 1890s–1930s," *Mid-America* 71 (1989): 37–51; Gary R. Mormino, *Immigrants on the Hill: Italian-Americans in St. Louis, 1882–1982* (Urbana: University of Illinois Press, 1986); John F. Sullivan, *The Externals of the Catholic Church: Her Government, Ceremonies, Festivals, and Devotions* (New York: P. J. Kenedy & Sons, 1918); and Ann Taves, "Context and Meaning: Roman Catholic Devotion to the Blessed Sacrament in Mid-Nineteenth Century America," *Church History* 54 (1985): 482–95.

91. Compare Lawrence J. McCaffrey, "Irish America," *Wilson Quarterly* 9 (Spring 1985): 78–93; and Lawrence J. McCaffrey, "Building an American Power Base: The Irish, the Cities, and the Church," *Loyola* [Chicago] 13 (June 1984): 15–18.

92. See Donald McCartney, *The Dawning of Democracy: Ireland 1800–1870* (Dublin: McGill, 1987); and Stephen P. Erie, *Rainbow's End: Irish-Americans and the Dilemmas of Urban Machine Politics, 1840–1985* (Berkeley: University of California Press, 1988). Compare Nathan O. Hatch, *The Democratization of American Christianity* (New Haven, Conn.: Yale University Press, 1989).

93. George G. Windell, *The Catholics and German Unity, 1866–1871* (Minneapolis: University of Minnesota Press, 1954).

94. Compare Tom Garvin, *Nationalist Revolutionaries in Ireland, 1858–1910* (Oxford: Oxford University Press, 1987). See also the analysis of "militant respectability" by Hugh McLeod, "Catholicism and the New York Irish, 1880–1910," in *Disciplines of Faith: Studies in Religion, Politics and Patriarchy*, ed. Jim Obelkevich, Lyndal Roper, and Raphael Samuel (London: Routledge & Kegan Paul, 1987). This is not to say that Irish immigrants were deferential, or to interpret political outcomes by way of a retrospective determinism, and the like. Regional variations in militancy were considerable, and degrees of activism and solidarity depended substantially on the ideological agendas of political entrepreneurs; rowdiness alone could not be equated with class belligerence. For interpretations of the tangle of reformist, radical, nationalist, and religious strains in the Irish matrix, see John W. Boyle, *The Irish Labor Movement in the Nineteenth Century* (Washington, D.C.: Catholic University of America Press,

1988); Emmet O'Connor, *Syndicalism in Ireland, 1917–1923* (Cork: Cork University Press, 1988); Daniel J. O'Neil, "Revolution and Religion: The Irish Experience," paper presented at the annual meeting of the American Political Science Association, Atlanta, August 31–September 3, 1989; and T. Desmond Williams, ed., *Secret Societies in Ireland* (Dublin: Gill and Macmillan, 1973). Compare David Blackbourn, *Class, Religion and Local Politics in Wilhelmine Germany: The Centre Party in Württemberg before 1914* (New Haven, Conn.: Yale University Press, 1980).

95. See Emmet Larkin, "The Devotional Revolution in Ireland, 1850–75," *American Historical Review* 77 (1972): 625–52; and Jonathan Sperber, *Popular Catholicism in Nineteenth-Century Germany* (Princeton, N.J.: Princeton University Press, 1984).

96. Jay P. Dolan, *Catholic Revivalism: The American Experience, 1830–1900* (Notre Dame, Ind.: University of Notre Dame Press, 1978).

97. See Les and Barbara Keyser, *Hollywood and the Catholic Church: The Image of Roman Catholicism in American Movies* (Chicago: Loyola University Press, 1984); and George Victor Martin, *Leo McCarey's The Bells of St. Mary's* (New York: Grosset & Dunlap, 1946).

98. See for example Albert Muntsch, S.J., *Social Thought and Action: A Series of Social Sermons* (St. Louis, Mo.: B. Herder, 1934).

99. See John Francis Bannon, S.J., *The Missouri Province S.J: A Mini-History* (St. Louis, Mo.: St. Louis University Press, 1977).

100. John H. Whyte, *Church and State in Modern Ireland, 1923–1970* (Dublin: Gill and Macmillan, 1971). See also John Newsinger, "Historical Materialism and the Catholic Church: The Irish Example," *Monthly Review* 37 (1986): 12–22.

101. See Klaus Ensslen, "German-American Working-Class Saloons in Chicago: Their Social Functions in an Ethnic and Class-Specific Cultural Context," in *German Workers' Culture in the United States, 1850 to 1920*, ed. Hartmut Keil (Washington, D.C.: Smithsonian Institution Press, 1988); and Christopher J. Kauffman, *Faith and Fraternalism: The History of the Knights of Columbus, 1882–1982* (New York: Harper & Row, 1982).

102. See Glen Caudill Dealy, *The Public Man: An Interpretation of Latin American and Other Catholic Countries* (Amherst: University of Massachusetts Press, 1977); and Paul Julian Smith, *The Body Hispanic: Gender and Sexuality in Spanish and Spanish American Literature* (Oxford, England: Clarendon, 1989). Whatever the practice in Rome, the connection between Irish and official Latin Catholicism was tight in this area; see Dermot Keogh, *The Vatican, the Bishops and Irish Politics, 1919–1939* (Cambridge, England: Cambridge University Press, 1986); and Katherine Walsh, "The First Vatican Council, the Papal State, and the Irish Hierarchy," *Studies* 52 (1982): 55–71. One of the key talismans linking the Irish and Latin churches was Rev. J. Donovan, trans., *The Catechism of the Council of Trent, Published by Command of Pope Pius the Fifth* (Dublin: Richard Coyne, 1829).

103. Compare Robert Emmett Curran, S.J., "The McGlynn Affair and the Shaping of the New Conservatism in American Catholicism, 1886–1894," *Catholic Historical Review* 66 (1980): 184–204; Philip J. Greven, Jr., *The*

Protestant Temperament: Patterns of Child-Rearing, Religious Experience, and the Self in Early America (New York: Alfred A. Knopf, 1977); and Timothy I. Kelly, "American Catholics," *Journal of Social History* 23 (1989): 155–66.

104. For a nuanced study of the mix of militancy and moderation in Irish American politics, see David M. Emmons, *The Butte Irish: Class and Ethnicity in an American Mining Town, 1875–1925* (Carbondale: University of Illinois Press, 1989); compare Leon Fink, *Workingmen's Democracy: The Knights of Labor and American Politics* (Urbana: University of Illinois Press, 1983); and Daniel J. Walkowitz, *Worker City, Company Town: Iron and Cotton Workers in Troy and Cohoes, New York, 1885–1886* (Urbana: University of Illinois Press, 1978).

105. See Timothy J. Meagher, ed., *From Paddy to Studs: Irish-American Communities in the Turn of the Century Era, 1880 to 1920* (New York: Greenwood, 1986). Compare Thomas C. Reeves, *A Question of Character: John F. Kennedy in Image and Reality* (New York: Free Press, 1991).

106. See Henry Steele Commager, *The Empire of Reason: How Europe Imagined and America Realized the Enlightenment* (Garden City, N.Y.: Doubleday, 1977).

107. David Noel Doyle, "The Irish as Urban Pioneers in the United States, 1850–1870," *Journal of American Ethnic History* 10 (1990–91), summarizes the contribution of the Irish and German American enclaves succinctly:

In most cities . . . the Irish outnumbered the Germans. In the voices and the faces of the city crowds, of the girls spilling from factory gates, and men leaving mines and docks, the cities were locales and centers of the Irish. Moreover, their fairly rapid . . . political and religious organization, by contrast with other groups, heightened their impact and that of their offspring. The political story is well known. The overall impact of their religious pattern is less known. In 1890, 62 percent of all city dwellers were unchurched, and in 1906, 53 percent, which made the effect of the Irish more direct on the relative Christianization of the American city. In 1890, the Irish-born and their children constituted around 50 percent of all Catholics; more if further Irish-descended numbers are considered. . . . With German-American Catholics they ensured an urban Catholic subculture receptive to the spiritual needs of myriads of southern and eastern Europeans who were shortly to begin general arrival. (pp. 51–52)

108. Compare Joel Perlman, *Ethnic Differences: Schooling and Social Structure Among the Irish, Italians, Jews, and Blacks in an American City, 1880–1935* (Cambridge, England: Cambridge University Press, 1988).

109. See for example W. J. Lockington, S.J., *The Soul of Ireland* (London: Ambrosden Press, 1919), dedicated to "Mary Myden Dheelish, Mother of the Mothers of Ireland"; Alfred O'Rahilly, ed., *A Year's Thoughts: Collected From the Writings of Father William Doyle, S.J.* (London: Longmans, Green, 1936); Robert Reilly, *Irish Saints* (New York: Avenel Books, 1964); Leo Richard Ward, *God in an Irish Kitchen* (London: Catholic Book Club, about 1935); and Walter Romig, ed., *The Book of Catholic Authors* (Detroit, Mich.: Walter Romig & Co., 1945); compare Joan M. Allen, *Candles and Carnival*

Lights: The Catholic Sensibility of F. Scott Fitzgerald (New York: Columbia University Press, 1978); and Charles Fanning, ed., The Exiles of Erin: Nineteenth Century Irish-American Fiction (Notre Dame, Ind.: University of Notre Dame Press, 1988).

110. See Leonard I. Sweet, "The Modernization of Protestant Religion in America," in Altered Landscapes: Christianity in America, 1935–1985, ed. David W. Lotz (Grand Rapids, Mich.: William B. Eerdmans, 1989).

111. See Gunther Barth, City People: The Rise of Modern City Culture in Nineteenth-Century America (New York: Oxford University Press, 1980); Samuel P. Hays, The Response to Industrialism, 1885–1914 (Chicago: University of Chicago Press, 1957); and Alan Trachtenberg, The Incorporation of America: Culture and Society in the Gilded Age (New York: Hill and Wang, 1982); compare Alexander J. Humphreys, S.J., New Dubliners: Urbanization and the Irish Family (New York: Fordham University Press, 1966).

112. See Michael D. Clark, "Ralph Adams Cram and the Americanization of the Middle Ages," Journal of American Studies 23 (1989): 195–213; and Bernard Rosenthal and Paul E. Szarmach, eds., Medievalism in American Culture (Binghamton, N.Y.: Medieval and Renaissance Texts and Studies, 1989); compare Umberto Eco, The Middle Ages of James Joyce (London: Hutchinson Radius, 1989); and Jacques Maritain, Art and Scholasticism and the Frontiers of Poetry (New York: Charles Scribner's Sons, 1962).

113. Steven A. Riess, "The New Sports History," Reviews in American History 18 (1990): 311–35.

114. See Sam B. Girgus, The New Covenant: Jewish Writers and the American Idea (Chapel Hill: University of North Carolina Press, 1984); Neal Gabler, An Empire of Their Own: How the Jews Invented Hollywood (New York: Crown, 1988); Jack P. Greene, Pursuits of Happiness: The Social Development of Early Modern British Colonies and the Formation of American Culture (Chapel Hill: University of North Carolina Press, 1988); James N. Gregory, American Exodus: The Dust Bowl Migration and Okie Culture in California (New York: Oxford University Press, 1989); Andrew R. Heinze, Adapting to Abundance: Jewish Immigrants, Mass Consumption, and the Search for American Identity (New York: Columbia University Press, 1990); John F. Kasson, Civilizing the Machine: Technology and Republican Values in America, 1776–1900 (New York: Grossman, 1976); Seymour Martin Lipset, The First New Nation: The United States in Historical and Comparative Perspective (New York: Basic Books, 1963); Seymour Martin Lipset, "A Unique People in an Exceptional Country," Society 28 (November-December, 1990): 4–13; Martin E. Marty, Pilgrims in Their Own Land: 500 Years of Religion in America (Boston: Little, Brown, 1984); David Mogen, Mark Busby, and Paul Bryant, eds., The Frontier Experience and the American Dream (College Station: Texas A & M University Press, 1989); and Henry F. May, The End of American Innocence: A Study of the First Years of Our Own Time, 1912–1917 (New York: Alfred A. Knopf, 1959).

115. See Robert N. Bellah et al., eds., Individualism and Commitment in American Life (New York: Harper & Row, 1987); Anthony P. Cohen, The Symbolic Construction of Community (London: Ellis Horwood and Tavistock, 1985); Wilson Carey McWilliams, The Idea of Fraternity in America (Berke-

ley: University of California Press, 1973); and R. Jackson Wilson, *In Quest of Community: Social Philosophy in the United States, 1860–1920* (New York: John Wiley & Sons, 1968). Perhaps the closest that this sensibility came to taking organized form was the Catholic Worker Movement, led by Dorothy Day. The group did not have much impact on Jesuits except for such figures as Daniel Berrigan. James Terence Fisher, *The Catholic Counterculture in America, 1933–1962* (Chapel Hill: University of North Carolina Press, 1989) captures the exquisite interplay between aesthetics and politics, and between conservatism and radicalism, among the eccentrics of preconciliar Catholicism. Compare Robert Coles, *Times of Surrender: Selected Essays* (Iowa City: University of Iowa Press, 1988).

PART ONE

1. Gregory S. Gastos, *History of the West Baden Springs Hotel* (French Lick, Ind.: Springs Valley Herald, 1985), p. 1.

2. The structure and grounds had been sold for one dollar to the Jesuits in 1934 by Charles Edward Ballard who, as Will Rogers noted, "wasn't even Catholic." Ballard survived the sale by two years. He was shot dead in a Hot Springs, Arkansas, hotel room by "Silver Bob" Alexander, his partner in the operation of the Palm Island Club at Miami, Florida. Ibid., 70. In 1964, on the verge of a depression of their own in recruitment, and in an attempt to modernize their training program by bringing it closer to urban centers, the Jesuits moved the seminary operation from West Baden to North Aurora, outside Chicago. The property was eventually sold, and developers once again tried to lure the tourist trade. See Mary G. Johnson, "West Baden Hotel Restoration Delayed by 'Procrastination,'" *Sunday Herald-Times* (Bedford, Ind.), June 22, 1986, 1, 16; and David Margolick, "New Magic Revives Old Indiana Spa," *New York Times*, February 17, 1985, 12.

3. See Gerald McKevitt, S.J., *The University of Santa Clara: A History, 1851–1977* (Stanford, Calif.: Stanford University Press, 1979).

4. Lois Gordon and Alan Gordon, *American Chronicle: Seven Decades in American Life, 1920–89* (New York: Crown, 1990).

5. Compare Michael A. Bernstein, *The Great Depression: Delayed Recovery and Economic Change in America, 1929–1939* (Cambridge, England: Cambridge University Press, 1987); and Robert Heide and John Gilman, *Dime-Store Parade* (New York: E. P. Dutton, 1979).

6. See Gerald P. Fogarty, S.J., "American Catholic Biblical Scholarship," in *Altered Landscapes: Christianity in America, 1935–1985*, ed. David W. Lotz (Grand Rapids, Mich.: William B. Eerdmans, 1989).

7. Thomas Sheehan, "Revolution in the Church," *New York Review of Books* (June 14, 1984): 35. "The Inspiration of the Divine Spirit" was issued after the Labor Day meeting at West Baden, on September 30, 1943. Another of Pius XII's encyclicals, *Mystici Corporis*, had been issued on June 29 of that year. It stressed the idea of the church as "a mystical body." With hindsight, it too seems forward looking. With Vatican II the "mystical body" came to be understood widely as "the people of God" rather than narrowly as the ecclesias-

tical hierarchy. See Avery Dulles, S.J., *Models of the Church* (Garden City, N.Y.: Doubleday, 1974).

8. See Edward Reiser, S.J., "Parochial and Allied Ministries in the American Assistancy," *Woodstock Letters* 72 (December 1943): 306–35.

9. See Thomas Gaffney Taaffe, *A History of St. John's College, Fordham, N.Y.* (New York: Catholic Publication Society, 1891); and Ralph Foster Weld, *Brooklyn Is America* (New York: Columbia University Press, 1950).

10. See Sarah Burns, *Pastoral Inventions: Rural Life in Nineteenth-Century American Art and Culture* (Philadelphia: Temple University Press, 1989); Ann Novotny, *Alice's World: The Life and Photography of an American Original, Alice Austen, 1866–1952* (Old Greenwich, Conn.: Chatham Press, 1987); James L. Machor, *Pastoral Cities: Urban Ideals and the Symbolic Landscape of America* (Madison: University of Wisconsin Press, 1987); and Elliot Willensky, *When Brooklyn Was the World, 1920–1957* (New York: Harmony Books, 1957). Compare John L. Spalding, *The Religious Mission of the Irish People and Catholic Colonization* (New York: Catholic Publication Society, 1880); and Mary Gilbert Kelly, O.P., "Irish Catholic Colonies and Colonization Projects in the United States, 1795–1860," *Studies* 29 (1940): 95–110.

11. See Jay P. Corrin, *G. K. Chesterton and Hilaire Belloc: The Battle Against Modernity* (Athens: Ohio University Press, 1989).

12. See, however, Leslie Woodcock Tentler, *Wage-Earning Women: Industrial Work and Family Life in the United States, 1900–1930* (Cambridge, England: Cambridge University Press, 1979).

13. See Elaine Taylor May, *Homeward Bound: American Families in the Cold War Era* (New York: Basic Books, 1988).

CHAPTER 1. PARISHES, PRISONS, AND SCHOOLS OF SOCIAL WORK

1. See Robert M. Crunden, *Ministers of Reform: The Progressives' Achievement in American Civilization, 1889–1920* (New York: Basic Books, 1982); William Hutchinson, *The Modernist Impulse in American Protestantism* (New York: Oxford University Press, 1982); Rivka Shpak Lissak, *Pluralism and Progressives: Hull House and the New Immigrants, 1890–1919* (Chicago: University of Chicago Press, 1989); and David Ward, *Poverty, Ethnicity, and the American City, 1840–1925: Changing Conceptions of the Slum and Ghetto* (Cambridge, England: Cambridge University Press, 1989). A graphic report on the persistence of the underground culture through the present is T. J. English, *The Westies: Inside the Hell's Kitchen Irish Mob* (New York G. P. Putnam, 1990). A nostalgic but nonetheless useful account of Hell's Kitchen around the turn of the century is by Tom McConnon, *Angels in Hell's Kitchen: Heartwarming Reminiscences of a Boyhood in New York's Turbulent West Side* (Garden City, N Y.: Doubleday, 1959). Some of the same flavor is captured for Brooklyn in Mary Ellen Murphy, Mark Murphy, and Ralph Foster Weld, eds., *A Treasury of Brooklyn* (New York: William Sloane Associates, 1949); for a popular hagiography of Brooklyn, see John Richmond and Abril Lamarque, *Brooklyn, U.S.A.* (New York: Creative Age Press, 1946). The figure of the dangerous but lovable urchin, the "angel with a dirty face," was transnational and part of the

urban folklore of Dublin as well as New York; see Fergal McGrath, S.J., *Tenement Angels and Other Stories* (Dublin: M. H. Gill, 1934).

2. William J. Stanton, S.J., "Mission in 'Hell's Kitchen,' New York," *Woodstock Letters* 29 (1900): 30.

3. Ibid., p. 31.

4. Ibid.

5. See Edward Swanstrom, *The Waterfront Labor Problem: A Study in Decasualization and Unemployment Insurance* (New York: Fordham University Press, 1938).

6. See the discussion of the "old-law tenements" by Nathan Silver, *Lost New York* (Boston: Houghton Mifflin, 1967), pp. 140–41.

7. Stanton's account, "Mission in 'Hell's Kitchen,'" includes the observation that

> everything went on smoothly enough the first week—the women's week—despite the hurried call we got one evening at supper to come into the house next door to ours to save a woman from the blows of an angry husband. The man was to be pitied, and not the woman his wife. She was intoxicated, as was her custom, and we returned to our abode in disgust, over our failure to keep her sober for even one week (p. 31).

For an ampler view, see Hasia R. Diner, *Erin's Daughters in America: Irish Immigrant Women in the Nineteenth Century* (Baltimore, Md.: Johns Hopkins University Press, 1983).

8. Stanton, "Mission in 'Hell's Kitchen,'" pp. 32–33.

9. While the dominant perception of Jesuits regarding the Catholic ghettos seems to have been one of chaos rather than class militancy, they appear to have been much less impressed by the possible presence of underlying patterns of cohesiveness in the slums; compare Gerald D. Suttles, *The Social Order of the Slums: Ethnicity and Territoriality in the Inner City* (Chicago: University of Chicago Press, 1968).

10. See James S. Olson, *Catholic Immigrants in America* (Chicago, Ill.: Nelson-Hall, 1987).

11. Dominic Cirigliano, S.J., "Protestant Activities in Our Parish," *Woodstock Letters* 49 (1919): 222–31, 340–49. See also Mary Elizabeth Brown, "The Making of Italian-American Catholics: Jesuit Work on the Lower East Side, New York, 1890's–1950's," *Catholic Historical Review* 73 (1987): 195–210.

12. Cirigliano, "Protestant Activities," p. 345. Over the years Cirigliano's work was judged so exemplary that he was eventually sent to the parish of St. Roberto Bellarmino in Rome to instruct Italian clerics in the art of being parish priests.

13. Jay P. Dolan, *The American Catholic Experience: A History from Colonial Times to the Present* (Garden City, N.Y.: Doubleday, 1986), especially pp. 127–346; and Dolan, *The Immigrant Church: New York's Irish and German Catholics, 1815–1865* (Baltimore, Md.: Johns Hopkins University Press, 1975).

14. See Paul Boyer, *Urban Masses and Moral Order in America, 1820–1920* (Cambridge, Mass.: Harvard University Press, 1978); Lary May, *Screening Out the Past: The Birth of Mass Culture and the Motion Picture Industry* (New York: Oxford University Press, 1980); Randall M. Miller and Thomas D.

Marzik, eds., *Immigrants and Religion in Urban America* (Philadelphia: Temple University Press, 1977); Henry Nash Smith, ed., *Popular Culture and Industrialism, 1865–1890* (Garden City, N.Y.: Doubleday, 1967); and Robert W. Snyder, *The Voice of the City: Vaudeville and Popular Culture in New York* (New York: Oxford University Press, 1989). Chapter 11 takes up a latter-day manifestation of this aesthetic in a discussion of the after-dinner speeches of Fr. Robert Gannon, longtime president of Fordham University.

15. The notion that Jesuits somehow relegated parish work to the secular clergy would be an exaggeration, however. The society's internal regulations—"the Constitutions"—contained prohibitions against accepting "the care of souls" as a regular activity of the order. Sometimes, however, when Jesuits wanted to open a parish church, they would be blocked by the local bishop. They were more often allowed "to have the college church." In addition, semiretired Jesuits often took on parish work.

16. The deprivation-and-depravity genre—the tales of violence, drunkenness, near-savage destruction, and primitive piety—are not dissimilar to the chronicles of the French Jesuits who worked among the Indian tribes of Canada and upper New York in the sixteenth and seventeenth centuries. A popularized history, written in much the same style as Stanton's, is by Francis Talbot, S.J., *Saint Among Savages: The Life of Isaac Jogues* (New York: Harper & Brothers, 1935). Fascination with local color and a certain *nostalgie de la boue* need not be equated with conservatism. As mentioned earlier, like some others who viewed urban squalor at firsthand, Jesuits were less frightened by the potential for class conflict than they were appalled at the sheer disorder of the proletariat. Compare Nell Irwin Painter, *Standing at Armageddon: The United States, 1877– 1919* (New York: W. W. Norton, 1987).

17. Kevin B. McGinn, S.J., "Early Years of the Jesuit Mission to the Islands of the East River, New York City," unpublished paper, New York province of the Society of Jesus, April 1984. The asylum, later the site of Brooklyn Preparatory School, was visited by Charles Dickens during his American tour.

18. Henri du Ranquet, S.J. (trans. Albert Muntsch, S.J.), "Social Work by the Jesuit Fathers in New York from 1860 to 1868," *Woodstock Letters* 51 (1922): 217–22.

19. Ibid., p. 221.

20. McGinn, "Early Years of the Jesuit Mission," p. 14. Perhaps because of the nature of his work, a full record of Ryan's accomplishments is difficult to reconstruct.

21. Superiors did not as a rule assign Jesuits to the missions—now called the international apostolate—by ordering them overseas under "holy obedience." But those who volunteered for the missions were usually granted their request. There were exceptions and mixups. A few American Jesuits volunteered for the missions and never got sent. One of these was a man whose blood brother, also a Jesuit, did not volunteer and was sent. A tired provincial, one suspects, confused the names and did not bother to correct the error.

   The number of American Jesuits working as missionaries never exceeded 5 or 6 percent of the total.

22. Calculating the survival rate of the professional schools would be a substantial project in itself, since records would have to be located on a province-by-

province basis. Impressionistic evidence suggests that while mortality was low among the professional schools, there was a good deal of turnover in other operations of the American Jesuits, such as parishes and even high schools. See "Chronology of Some Apostolic Commitments of the Missouri Province," *Our Human Resources: A Workbook for Reflection* (St. Louis: Missouri Province of the Society of Jesus, 1986), pp. 26–31.

23. Weekend retreats for workingmen were a feature of Jesuit activity from the first decade of the century. They did not, however, spin off into lectures on social topics, nor did they produce a constituency for the development of schools of social work, as happened with the retreats geared for Catholic professional men. In Europe, the *semaines sociales*—discussion groups on the social question for middle- and upper-middle-class Catholics—developed out of the retreat movement. See "A Workingmen's Retreat: Turin, 1908," *Woodstock Letters* 38 (1909): 36–46; and H. Walmesley, S.J., "Spiritual Exercises for Men and Working-Men," *Woodstock Letters* 40 (1911): 323–28.

24. "Obituary: Father Terence J. Shealy," *Woodstock Letters* 52 (1923): 86–104.

25. See Joseph M. McShane, S.J., " 'To Create an Elite Body of Laymen': Terence J. Shealy, S.J., and the Laymen's League 1911–1922," *Catholic Historical Review* (forthcoming).

26. When Shealy died, the *Brooklyn Tablet* wrote that "his dramatic denunciation of the sins of capitalism, his vehement attacks on present-day hypocrites, his sarcastic descriptions of milk-and-water Catholics, his mimicry of society personages, his invectives against the orgy of salaciousness that corrupts society, made such impressions on his hearers that they never forgot him." "Obituary: Father Terence J. Shealy," p. 100.

27. Ibid., pp. 90–91.

28. "Laymen's League for Retreats, New York," *Woodstock Letters* 42 (1913): 67–69. Woodlock's reminiscences and philosophical musings are contained in *The Catholic Pattern* (New York: Simon & Schuster, 1947).

29. Gerald C. Treacy, S.J., "The Beginnings of the Retreat Movement in America," *First Annual Conference* (1928): 13–19 (photocopy supplied by *Company* magazine).

30. See Giacomo de Antonellis, *Storia dell'Azione Cattolica dal 1867 a Oggi* (Milan: Rizzoli, 1987); and Gianfranco Poggi, *Catholic Action in Italy: The Sociology of a Sponsored Organization* (Stanford, Calif.: Stanford University Press, 1967).

31. Compare Roy Lubove, *The Professional Altruist: The Emergence of Social Work as a Career, 1880–1930* (Cambridge, Mass.: Harvard University Press, 1965); and Olivier Zunz, *Making America Corporate, 1870–1920* (Chicago: University of Chicago Press, 1990).

32. An excellent coverage of Shealy's occasional writings is by Joseph P. Chinnici, O.F.M., *Living Stones: The History and Structure of Catholic Spiritual Life in the United States* (New York: Macmillan, 1989), pp. 159–66.

33. See Joseph M. McShane, S.J., *"Sufficiently Radical": Catholicism, Progressivism, and the Bishops' Program of 1919* (Washington, D.C.: Catholic University of America Press, 1986).

34. George G. Higgins, "Joseph Caspar Husslein, S.J.: Pioneer Social Scholar," *Social Order* (February 1953): 51–53.

35. Husslein's early essays were collected under the title *The Church and Social Problems* (New York: America Press, 1912). Most though not all of Husslein's writings were theoretical. His book *The Catholic's Work in the World* (New York: Benziger Brothers, 1917) was subtitled A *Practical Solution of Religious and Social Problems of To-day*, and was written in a catechetical style.

36. *The World Problem: Capital, Labor, and the Church* (New York: P. J. Kenedy and Sons, 1918), pp. 37–41.

37. Ibid., pp. 171–72.

38. Ibid., pp. 10–11.

39. Ibid., pp. 20–21.

40. Ibid., pp. 83–84, 259.

41. Husslein, *The Church and Social Problems*, p. 196.

42. Ibid., pp. 3, 81.

43. *The World Problem*, pp. 152–53.

44. John A. Ryan and Joseph Husslein, S.J., eds., *The Church and Labor* (New York: Macmillan, 1920), pp. 220–39.

45. See Edward K. Spann, *Brotherly Tomorrows: Movements for a Cooperative Society in America, 1820–1920* (New York: Columbia University Press, 1989); and, for updates, Walter L. Adamson, "Economic Democracy and the Expediency of Worker Participation," *Political Studies* 38 (1990): 56–71; Robert D. Hershey, Jr., "Including Labor in the Division of Capital," *New York Times*, April 24, 1988, E-5; Robert C. Grady, "Workplace Democracy and Possessive Individualism," *Journal of Politics* 52 (1990): 146–66; and Frank L. Wilson, "Democracy in the Workplace: The French Experience," paper presented at the annual meeting of the American Political Science Association, San Francisco, August 30–September 2, 1990.

46. See Clark A. Chambers, *Seedtime of Reform: American Social Service and Social Action, 1918–1933* (Minneapolis: University of Minnesota Press, 1963); and Charles Forcey, *The Crossroads of Liberalism: Croly, Weyl, Lippmann and the Progressive Era, 1900–1925* (New York: Oxford University Press, 1961).

47. *Democratic Industry: A Practical Study in Social History* (New York: P. J. Kenedy and Sons, 1919), pp. 345–62.

48. See Bruce Kuklick, *Churchmen and Philosophers: From Jonathan Edwards to John Dewey* (Chicago: University of Chicago Press, 1986); T. J. Jackson Lears, *No Place of Grace: Antimodernism and the Transformation of American Cultures, 1880–1920* (New York: Pantheon, 1981); Richard H. Pells, *Radical Visions and American Dreams* (New York: Harper & Row, 1973); Robert Sklar, ed., *The Plastic Age, 1917–1930* (New York: George Braziller, 1970); and Gary Scott Smith, *The Seeds of Secularization: Calvinism, Culture and Pluralism in America, 1870–1915* (Grand Rapids, Mich.: W. B. Eerdmans, 1986). Husslein does not stand in the forefront of social thinkers of the time; his cultural range and political experience were limited. See, for example, Edward Abrahams, *The Lyrical Left* (Charlottesville: University Press of Virginia, 1986); Donald Meyer, *The Protestant Search for Political Realism, 1919–1941* (Berke-

ley: University of California Press, 1960); Thomas P. Hughes and Agatha C. Hughes, eds., *Lewis Mumford: Public Intellectual* (New York: Oxford University Press, 1990); and Carl Resek, ed., *War and the Intellectuals: Essays by Randolph S. Bourne, 1915–1919* (New York: Harper & Row, 1964). Nevertheless, some of his views—for example, those on such issues as the economic role of women and the male-headed household—were widely shared by mainstream conservatives of his time. See Ron Rothbart, "'Homes Are What Any Strike Is About': Immigrant Labor and the Family Wage," *Journal of Social History* 23 (1989): 267–84; compare Maurine Weiner Greenwald, "Working-Class Feminism and the Family Wage Ideal: The Seattle Debate on Married Women's Right to Work, 1914–1920," *Journal of American History* 76 (1989): 118–49. Finally, the medievalism that Husslein espoused and that surrounded his calls for economic justice and political community was not confined to Catholics and conservatives. It had more than passing appeal to some progressives, most notably, Randolph Bourne. See the insightful analysis by Casey Nelson Blake, *Beloved Community: The Cultural Criticism of Randolph Bourne, Van Wyck Brooks, Waldo Frank, and Lewis Mumford* (Chapel Hill: University of North Carolina Press, 1990), which serves to balance Abrahams's perspective cited above.

49. Richard E. Mulcahy, S.J., *The Economics of Heinrich Pesch* (New York: Henry Holt, 1952).

50. See Alfred Diamant, *Austrian Catholics and the First Republic: Democracy, Capitalism, and the Social Order, 1918–1934* (Princeton, N.J.: Princeton University Press, 1960); and John W. Boyer, *Political Radicalism in Late Imperial Vienna: Origins of the Christian Social Movement, 1848–1897* (Chicago: University of Chicago Press, 1981).

51. See Irving Howe, *Socialism and America* (New York: Harcourt Brace Jovanovich, 1985).

52. A study that persuasively connects family and gender hierarchies with fraternal organizations, male solidarity, and occupational clubs while remaining sensitive to historical contexts is by Mary Ann Clawson, *Constructing Brotherhood: Class, Gender and Fraternalism* (Princeton, N.J.: Princeton University Press, 1989).

53. Husslein, *The Church and Social Problems*, 176–82. Husslein was thinking particularly of the free spirits who made Greenwich Village their headquarters starting around the time of World War I. See Candace Falk, *Love, Anarchy, and Emma Goldman: A Biography* (New Brunswick, N.J.: Rutgers University Press, 1990).

54. Compare Walter L. Adamson, "Fascism and Culture: Avant-Gardes and Secular Religion in the Italian Case," *Journal of Contemporary History* 24 (1989): 411–35.

55. Henry Spalding, S.J., *Social Problems and Agencies* (New York: Benziger Brothers, 1929).

56. Ibid., p. 141.

57. Ibid., p. 301.

58. The same universe of discourse prevailed across a variety of areas until Vatican II. Although the topic is different, the assumptions about her readership made

by Kay Toy Fenner, *American Catholic Etiquette* (Westminster, Md.: Newman Press, 1963) are remarkably similar to Spalding's.

59. *Social Problems and Agencies*, p. 217.

60. See Jon C. Teaford, *The Unheralded Triumph: City Government in America, 1870–1900* (Baltimore, Md.: Johns Hopkins University Press, 1984).

61. Compare Lawrence Goodwyn, *The Populist Moment* (New York: Oxford University Press, 1980); and Russel B. Nye, *Midwestern Progressive Politics: A Historical Study of Its Origins and Development, 1870–1958* (East Lansing: Michigan State University Press, 1959). Although there were common ideological elements, denominational as well as regional differences kept the Jesuits and the populists, and fundamentalists, far apart. See George V. Marsden, *Fundamentalism and American Culture* (New York: Oxford University Press, 1981). Catholic solidarity against Protestant and largely Republican progressivism was not uniform, however. As a German American, Husslein was bound to have reservations—even if unexpressed—about the urban machines controlled by Irish Americans. While he busied himself with academic institution building, Husslein does not seem to have been involved in municipal politics. His intellectual efforts may have stemmed in part from a detachment from practical politics that contrasted with the tribal pragmatism of Irish Americans of the time.

62. See for example Donald T. Critchlow, ed., *Socialism in the Heartland: The Midwestern Experience, 1900–1925* (Notre Dame, Ind.: University of Notre Dame Press, 1987).

63. See William M. Halsey, *The Survival of American Innocence: Catholicism in an Era of Disillusionment, 1920–1950* (Notre Dame, Ind.: University of Notre Dame Press, 1980).

64. A leading figure in this later development is Fr. John Thomas, whose work is discussed in chapter 14.

CHAPTER 2. Social Principles and Political Tactics

1. "The Last Illness and Death of Very Reverend Father General Ledochowski," reprint from the *Memorabilia Societatis Jesus* (El Paso, Tex.: Revista Catolica Press, 1943).

2. See Barbara Jelavich, *Modern Austria: Empire and Republic, 1800–1986* (Cambridge, England: Cambridge University Press, 1987); Arno J. Mayer, *The Persistence of the Old Regime: Europe to the Great War* (New York: Pantheon, 1981); and Joseph Rotschild, *East Central Europe Between the Two World Wars* (Seattle: University of Washington Press, 1974).

3. Joseph A. Slattery, S.J., "In Memoriam: Very Rev. Fr. Wlodimir Ledochowski," *Woodstock Letters* 72 (1943): 7.

4. Austin G. Schmidt, S.J., ed., *Selected Writings of Father Ledochowski* (Chicago, Ill.: Loyola University Press, 1945), pp. 380–81.

5. "The Principles Governing the Social Apostolate of the Society, a Letter Addressed to the Provincial of the Province of Castile," in ibid., pp. 592–601.

6. John Pollard, "'A Marriage of Convenience': The Vatican and the Fascist

Regime in Italy," in *Disciplines of Faith*, ed. Jim Obelkevich, Lyndal Roper, and Raphael Samuel (London: Routledge & Kegan Paul, 1987).

7. Oswald von Nell-Breuning, S.J., "The Drafting of Quadragesimo Anno," in *Readings in Moral Theology No. 5: Official Catholic Social Teaching*, ed. Charles E. Curran and Richard A. McCormick, S.J. (New York: Paulist Press, 1986), p. 67.

8. Nevertheless, there were some organizational and programmatic parallels between corporatism and New Deal activities. See, for example, Diane Ghirardo, *Building New Communities: New Deal America and Fascist Italy* (Princeton, N.J.: Princeton University Press, 1989).

9. A hint of amiable bewilderment and perhaps even deadpan resistance on the part of the Americans to the cares of Europe may be detected in the following anonymous report that appeared under the title "France: Catholic Action in Philately," *Woodstock Letters* 63 (1934): 123.

To a watchful Jesuit philatelist, Father Weber, of the Apostolic School in Florennes, France, is due the credit for having thwarted the plan of the Soviets to circulate a foreign issue of "godless" stamps. The Vatican was informed, the papal nuncios appealed to the various governments, and the Universal Postal Union has refused to authorize stamps that might offend any recognized nation. Father Weber was rewarded by His Holiness with a special blessing and some very valuable stamps.

10. Schmidt, *Selected Writings of Father Ledochowski*, p. 907.

11. After Walsh died in 1956, his life and work were detailed in an extraordinarily long (fifty-page) obituary in *Woodstock Letters*. See Louis J. Gallagher, S.J., "Father Edmund Walsh," *Woodstock Letters* 86 (1957): 21–70.

12. See Edmund A. Walsh, S.J., *Total Empire: The Roots and Progress of World Communism* (Milwaukee, Wis.: Bruce, 1951); and Anna Watkins, ed., *Footnotes to History: Selected Speeches and Writings of Edmund A. Walsh, S.J., Founder of the School of Foreign Service* (Washington, D.C.: Georgetown University Press, 1990).

13. Edmund A. Walsh, S.J., to provincial superiors of the American Assistancy, December 2, 1936, five pp., Missouri Province archives.

14. Ibid.

15. Ibid.

16. Ibid.

17. Ibid.

18. The notoriety that later came to Walsh as a fervent anti-Communist did not controvert his pragmatism, for that expression of ideological conviction coincided with the effulgent Americanism of the postwar years. See Donald F. Crosby, S.J., *God, Church, and Flag: Senator Joseph McCarthy and the Catholic Church, 1950–1957* (Chapel Hill: University of North Carolina Press, 1978).

19. For a concise treatment of the transnational aspects of Catholic agrarianism, with an emphasis on the English Distributists, see Bernard Aspinwall, "Broadfield Revisited," in *The Church and Wealth*, ed. W. J. Sheils and Diana Wood

(Oxford: Basil Blackwell, 1987). A perceptive history of the intellectual currents within the back-to-the-soil and nativist aesthetics is by Cornelius H. Sullivan, "Regionalism in American Thought: Provincial Ideals from the Gilded Age to the Great Depression (Ph.D. dissertation, University of Chicago, 1977).

20. "Plan of Action for the Establishment of a Christian Social Order, Through Jesuit Activity," Chicago, June 1, 1935, nine pp., Missouri Province archives.

21. Ibid.

22. "Suggestions for a Jesuit Plan," 1935, six pp. Missouri Province archives.

23. A twenty-one-page pamphlet summarizing the plan was, however, published as An Integrated Program of Social Order (St. Louis, Mo: Queen's Work, 1935).

24. "Suggestions for a Jesuit Plan."

25. John F. Pollard, The Vatican and Italian Fascism, 1929–1932: A Study in Conflict (Cambridge, England: Cambridge University Press, 1985).

26. Tom Gallagher, "The Catholic Church and the Estado Novo of Portugal," in Disciplines of Faith, pp. 518–36.

27. Frank Fadner, S.J., "The New State of Portugal and Communism," Informationes et Notitiae 2 (January 1937): 20–22; and Francis J. Tierney, "A Christian Commonwealth in Portugal," Informationes et Notitae 2 (May 1937): 17–18.

28. See Giorgio Campanini, ed., I Cattolici e la Guerra di Spagna (Brescia: Morelliana, 1987); and Colin M. Wilson, Workers and the Right in Spain, 1900–1936 (Princeton, N.J.: Princeton University Press, 1984).

29. "Spain: News of Dispersed Jesuits," Woodstock Letters 61 (1932): 484–85. Sacrilege was added to atrocity. In addition to the human slaughter, Jesuits were shocked by pictures showing statues of the Sacred Heart of Jesus—a popular devotion promoted by the society—riddled with bullets. In Madrid, inside the Church of St. Francisco Borja (an early general of the society), across the street from the American Embassy, one can still view memorials to Jesuit chaplains killed in the Civil War. See José M. Sanchez, The Spanish Civil War as a Religious Tragedy (Notre Dame, Ind.: University of Notre Dame Press, 1987).

30. "Brooklyn: Silver Jubilee of St. Ignatius Church and Brooklyn Preparatory School," Woodstock Letters 62 (1933): 437–41. According to the report, Monsignor Belford went on to write

touchingly of the sacrifices our Fathers, Scholastics and Brothers have made, and the great good they are doing in fields afar as well as at home; and he pays an especial compliment to the Jesuits in Brooklyn, who, he says, are rendering great service not only in their high school and parish, but also in Kings County Hospital and Insane Asylum, and in their zealous care of the deaf.

31. Rallying around the Catholic cause meant not only supporting the Nationalists but also an absence of tolerance for Republicans and their supporters in the United States. Thus, the cardinal of St. Louis forbade the Jesuit university there to permit a lecture that was to be given by a "renegade" secular priest who favored the Loyalists. See José M. Sanchez, "Cardinal Glennon and Academic

Freedom at Saint Louis University: The Fleisher Case Revisited," *Gateway Heritage* 8 (1987–88): 2–11.

32. Compare Gilbert Allardyce, "What Fascism Is Not: Thoughts on the Deflation of a Concept," *American Historical Review* 85 (1980): 367–88, and the criticism by Stanley Payne and the response by Allardyce following the article; see also Walter L. Adamson, "Modernism and Fascism: The Politics of Culture in Italy, 1903–1922," *American Historical Review* 95 (1990): 359–90.

33. Minutes of Chicago-Missouri province meeting on Communism and Atheism, West Baden College, Indiana, June 22–26, 1935, nineteen pp., Missouri Province archives.

34. Ibid., p. 4.

35. See Philip Gleason, *Keeping the Faith* (Notre Dame, Ind.: University of Notre Dame Press, 1987), p. 19ff.

36. See Jeffrey Hart, *Reactionary Modernism: Technology, Culture, and Politics in Weimar and the Third Reich* (Cambridge, England: Cambridge University Press, 1984).

37. See Hugh McLeod, "Popular Catholicism in Irish New York, c. 1900," in *The Churches, Ireland and the Irish*, ed. W. J. Sheils and Diana Wood (Oxford: Basil Blackwell, 1989).

38. See Keith Harding, "The 'Cooperative Commonwealth': Ireland, Larkin and the Daily Herald," in *New Views of Cooperation*, ed. Stephen Yeo (London: Routledge & Kegan Paul, 1988); compare Kerby A. Miller and Bruce D. Boling, "Golden Streets, Bitter Tears: The Irish Image of America During the Era of Mass Migration," *Journal of American Ethnic History* 10 (1990–91): 16–35.

39. Minutes of Chicago-Missouri province meeting, p. 14.

40. See J. J. Lee, *Ireland 1912–1985: Politics and Society* (Cambridge, England: Cambridge University Press, 1989), p. 271ff. The foundational text of Catholic corporatism in Ireland is by E. Cahill, S.J., *The Framework of a Christian State: An Introduction to Social Science* (Dublin: M. H. Gill and Son, 1932).

41. Minutes of Chicago-Missouri province meeting, p. 14. The cooperative movement had gained respect in Jesuit circles as a result of its propagation through the adult education programs at Saint Francis Xavier University in Nova Scotia, starting in the 1920s. A retrospective overview is given by Martín Brugarola, S.J., "El movimiento social de Antigonish," *Fomento Social* 14 (July–September 1959): 305–10.

42. Compare Robert S. Fogarty, *All Things New: American Communes and Utopian Movements, 1860–1914* (Chicago: University of Chicago Press, 1990); and Ian MacPherson, *Each for All: A History of the Co-operative Movement in English Canada, 1900–1945* (Toronto: Macmillan, 1976).

43. See Jerome Blum, *The End of the Old Order in Rural Europe* (Princeton, N.J.: Princeton University Press, 1978).

44. See Frances Lannon, *Privilege, Persecution, and Prophecy: The Catholic Church in Spain, 1875–1975* (New York: Oxford University Press, 1987).

45. The Spanish situation in particular continued to be important to Jesuits in the United States. In 1938 Franco rescinded the decree of the republic expelling

the society. The American provincial superiors delivered a letter of thanks, "done into Spanish by Father Peter Arrupe, of the Province of Castile." The generalissimo in turn acknowledged receipt of the note in a style characteristic of the time and place ("American Jesuits Salute Franco," *Woodstock Letters* 63 [1939]: 103–13):

His Excellency who in the name of all true Spaniards has had to oppose the enemies of the country, by restoring to Spain the Society of Jesus with all its legal rights, merely interpreted the sentiments of all worthy Spaniards who are presently fighting with him to eliminate for all times from our soil the hordes of Moscow . . . the Leader is confident that all who are members of the Society of Jesus, in all their acts and all their works, will proclaim the truth of our cause, and will strive in the manner which seems practical to each, to combat the calumnious propaganda which our enemies are spreading at the cost of the wealth and the art they have so iniquitously stolen from us.

46. See, for example, Richard J. Evans, "Politics and the Family: Social Democracy and the Working-Class Family in Theory and Practice Before 1914," in *The German Family: Essays on the Social History of the Family in Nineteenth and Twentieth-Century Germany*, ed. Richard J. Evans and W. R. Lee (London: Croom Helm, 1981).

47. See Tom Garvin, *Nationalist Revolutionaries in Ireland, 1858–1928* (Oxford: Clarendon Press, 1987); and Nancy Scheper-Hughes, *Saints, Scholars, and Schizophrenics: Mental Illness in Rural Ireland* (Berkeley: University of California Press, 1979); compare Garry Marvin, *Bullfight* (Oxford: Basil Blackwell, 1988).

48. Minutes of Chicago Province ECSO meeting, May 25, 1935, two pp., Missouri Province archives.

49. Frederic Siedenberg, S.J., "History of ESCO–Chicago Province," June 1, 1935, four pp., Missouri Province archives.

50. See Steve Fraser and Gary Gerstle, eds., *The Rise and Fall of the New Deal Order, 1930–1980* (Princeton, N.J.: Princeton University Press, 1989).

51. "Suggestions for a Jesuit Plan," pp. 4–5 (capitalization in original). An implication of this way of posing the problem was that Jesuits would have to exercise extreme prudence if they were beholden to a few large benefactors. Otherwise–if, for example, most contributions came from "cleaning ladies who send only singles"—they might do as they please. This calculus of risk and principle has not been distinctive to the Jesuits; it illustrates the vulnerability of many private voluntary organizations.

52. See the essays in Philip Gleason, ed., *Catholicism in America* (New York: Harper & Row, 1970).

53. Lord first gained prominence during the late twenties as an adviser to the Hays Commission, which formulated the Motion Picture Production Code; see David A. Cook, *A History of Narrative Film*, 2nd ed. (New York: W. W. Norton, 1990), pp. 296–300; and Stephen Vaughn, "Morality and Entertainment: The Origins of the Motion Picture Production Code," *Journal of American History* 77 (1990): 39–65.

54. Minutes of the Chicago-Missouri province meeting on Communism and Athe-

ism, West Baden College, June 22–26, 1935, 19 pp., Missouri Province archives.

55. William B. Faherty, S.J., "A Half-Century of the Queen's Work," *Woodstock Letters*, 92 (1963): 99–114; and John J. Ryan, S.J., "The First Summer School of Catholic Action," *Woodstock Letters* 61 (1931): 103–13.

56. Lord did not have a traveling troupe; instead, he rounded up local talent for the pageants.

57. "The Queen's Work Presents the Social Order Follies, Book and Songs by the Producer, Daniel A. Lord, S.J.," November 20–27, 1938(?), Missouri Province archives, eight pp. During the early decades of the century theme pageants were popular in many parts of the United States where other forms of entertainment were uncommon, and Lord's productions drew on this tradition. See David Glassberg, *American Historical Pageantry: The Uses of Tradition in the Early Twentieth Century* (Chapel Hill: University of North Carolina Press, 1990). The longest-lasting example of this tradition in an entertainment capital was the stage shows at Radio City Music Hall in New York City.

58. Edward Dowling, S.J., "Is Democracy Doomed?" Social Order Monday Series, St. Louis, November 4, 1935, five pp., Missouri Province archives. See also Robert C. Hartnett, S.J., "Father Moorhouse F. X. Millar," *Woodstock Letters* 87 (1958): 134–64.

59. Starting in the 1940s, Dowling (1898–1960) became prominent as a promoter of Alcoholics Anonymous; see Robert Fitzgerald, S.J., "Fr. Ed & AA's Bill W.," *Company* 8 (Winter 1990): 7–9.·

60. See Alan Brinkley, *Huey Long, Father Coughlin and the Great Depression* (New York: Alfred A. Knopf, 1982); and Philip A. Grant, Jr., "The Priest in Politics: Father Charles E. Coughlin and the Presidential Election of 1986," *Records of the American Catholic Historical Society of Philadelphia* 101 (1990): 35–47.

61. Compare James C. Cobb, "The South's South: The Enigma of Creativity in the Mississippi Delta," *Southern Review* 25 (1989): 72–85; Drew Gilpin Faust, *A Sacred Circle: The Dilemmas of the Intellectual in the Old South, 1840–1860* (Baltimore, Md.: Johns Hopkins University Press, 1977); Lucina Hardwick MacKethan, *The Dream of Arcady: Place and Time in Southern Literature* (Baton Rouge: Louisiana State University Press, 1980); Jack Temple Kirby, *Rural Worlds Lost: The American South, 1920–1960* (Baton Rouge: Louisiana State University Press, 1987); Richard H. King, *A Southern Renaissance: The Cultural Awakening of the American South, 1930–1955* (New York: Oxford University Press, 1980); and Daniel Joseph Singal, *The War Within: From Victorian to Modernist Thought in the South, 1919–1945* (Chapel Hill: University of North Carolina Press, 1982).

62. For a sympathetic biography, see Joseph T. McGloin, S.J., *Backstage Missionary: Father Dan Lord, S.J.* (New York: Pageant Press, 1958).

63. See Daniel Aaron and Robert Bendiner, eds., *The Strenuous Decade: A Social and Intellectual Record of the Nineteen-Thirties* (Garden City, N.Y.: Doubleday, 1970).

64. See Jan Cohn, *Creating America: George Horace Lorimer and the Saturday Evening Post* (Pittsburgh: University of Pittsburgh Press, 1989); Stuart Ewen,

Captains of Consciousness: Advertising and the Social Roots of the Consumer Culture (New York: McGraw-Hill, 1977); Richard Wrightman Fox and T. J. Jackson Lears, eds., *The Culture of Consumption: Critical Essays in American History* (New York: Pantheon, 1983); and Roland Marchand, *Advertising the American Dream: Making Way for Modernity, 1920–1940* (Berkeley: University of California Press, 1985); compare Lawrence Birken, *Consuming Desire: Sexual Science and the Emergence of a Culture of Abundance, 1871–1914* (Ithaca, N.Y.: Cornell University Press, 1988). One of the best (and now neglected) early interpretations of this trend is by David L. Cohn, *The Good Old Days: A History of American Morals and Manners as Seen Through the Sears, Roebuck Catalogs, 1905 to the Present* (New York: Simon & Schuster, 1940). The figure with the greatest impact on Jesuit thinking about popular culture began to exert an effect a decade or so later; see Herbert Marshall McLuhan, *The Mechanical Bride: Folklore of Industrial Man* (New York: Vanguard, 1951). His influence is examined in chapter 14.

65. Luigi G. Ligutti and John C. Rawe, S.J., *Rural Roads to Security: America's Third Struggle for Freedom* (Milwaukee, Wis.: Bruce, 1940). Rawe was principal author of the book. For three decades Monsignor Ligutti was chief executive officer of the National Catholic Life Conference. In the postwar period Ligutti expanded his operations to the international scene. After Vatican II, Paul VI appointed him permanent observer for the Holy See with the United Nations Food and Agriculture Organization. See Raymond W. Miller, *Monsignor Ligutti: The Pope's County Agent* (Washington, D.C.: University Press of America, 1981).

66. In a letter reporting on his attendance at a meeting of the National Catholic Rural Life Conference in the mid-thirties, John LaFarge wrote that "a plan was set on foot to meet in the near future, I believe at St. Louis University, with representatives of the group with which Father Rawe has been in touch, the Southern Agrarians, etc., and to plan out a Catholic agrarian manifesto in collaboration with them." John LaFarge, S.J., to Samuel B. Horne, S.J., provincial superior of Missouri, October 28, 1936, Missouri Province archives. Earlier that year Rawe had attended a meeting of the Agrarians in Nashville that promoted closer ties between the Americans and the English Distributists. The next conference, planned at this meeting, never took place. Two other Jesuits—Edward Day Stewart from Spring Hill College in Mobile and Charles Chapman from Loyola University in New Orleans—also attended; Donald Davidson, Cleanth Brooks, John Crowe Ransom, and Allen Tate were among the Southern luminaries. Minutes of convention of the Committee for the Alliance of Agrarian and Distributist Groups, Nashville, June 4–5, 1936, Vanderbilt University archives; I am grateful to Sara J. Harwell for locating this file. Rawe and several of the Distributists contributed essays in 1936 to *Who Owns America?*, edited by Tate and Herbert Agar. See also Paul K. Conkin, *The Southern Agrarians* (Knoxville: University of Tennessee Press, 1988); John L. Stewart, *The Burden of Time: The Fugitives and the Agrarians* (Princeton, N.J.: Princeton University Press, 1965); and Twelve Southerners [John Crowe Ransom et al.], *I'll Take My Stand: The South and the Agrarian Tradition* (Baton Rouge: Louisiana State University Press, 1983 [originally New York: Harper & Brothers, 1930]).

67. Liguitti and Rawe, *Rural Roads to Security*, pp. 3–4.

68. Ibid., p. 11.

69. Ibid., p. 50.

70. Ibid., p. 65.

71. Ibid., pp. 102–3.

72. Ibid., pp. 105–6

73. Ibid., p. 234.

74. Ibid., p. 235.

75. Ibid., pp. 108–9.

76. See Alice Goldfarb Marquis, *Hopes and Ashes: The Birth of Modern Times, 1929–1939* (New York: Free Press, 1986); David P. Peeler, *Hope Among Us: Social Criticism and Social Solace in Depression America* (Athens: University of Georgia Press, 1987); Richard H. Pells, *Radical Visions and American Dreams: Culture and Social Thought in the Depression Years* (New York: Harper & Row, 1973); and Howard P. Segal, *Technological Utopianism in American Culture* (Chicago: University of Chicago Press, 1984). The ultimate mainstreaming of strands of agrarian innocence seems to have occurred during this period with the sexless animals and other lovable and sometimes scary creatures popularized by Walt Disney.

77. Barbara Wood, *E. F. Schumacher: His Life and Thought* (New York: Harper & Row, 1984). See Robert Bellah et al., *Habits of the Heart* (Berkeley: University of California Press, 1986); and Marty Strange, *Family Farming: A New Economic Vision* (Lincoln: University of Nebraska Press, 1988).

78. Ligutti and Rawe, *Rural Roads to Security*, pp. 258–59. It is no coincidence that Rawe's ideas bear a strong resemblance to the heavily agrarian and moralistic model approached by the political economy of Catholic Ireland from the twenties through the fifties. This similarity probably made Rawe's proposals seem less strange to some American Catholics. See Edward J. Coyne, S.J., "The Future of Agricultural Productive Co-operation," *Studies* 44 (1955): 40–48; and Trevor West, *Horace Plunkett: Cooperation and Politics: An Irish Biography* (Washington, D.C.: Catholic University of America Press, 1986). Compare David A. Hounshell, *From the American System to Mass Production, 1800–1932* (Baltimore, Md.: Johns Hopkins University Press, 1984). At least one Jesuit, Fr. Leo Robinson, who had a hand in promoting the Institute of Social Order, was of Scandinavian origin; see Leo J. Robinson, S.J., and Van Francis Christoph, S.J., *Introductory Sociology* (Chicago: Loyola University Press, 1943).

79. As happened with Husslein and many other Jesuit social commentators, the valid points developed by Rawe tended to get lost under his colorful anecdotes, when they were not ignored completely because they came from an evidently conservative source. Many of the same lessons that Rawe tried to get across can be found in such nonsectarian manuals as Joseph K. Hart, *Educational Resources of Village and Rural Communities* (New York: Macmillan, 1914). They can also be found in the left-wing criticisms of his contemporary Carey McWilliams, *Factories in the Field* (Boston: Little, Brown, 1939). Rawe's lack of sophistication, together with the usual anti-Protestantism of Jesuits of the

period, may have blinded him to important points of convergence between classical economic theory and his own views. See for example David McNally, *Political Economy and the Rise of Capitalism: A Reinterpretation* (Berkeley: University of California Press, 1988).

80. When he confined himself to small-scale recommendations, Rawe could be quite down-to-earth; see for example John C. Rawe, S.J., *Reading to Save the Home: A Key to Practical Literature for Homemaking, Home Building, and Productivity in Homes—A Bibliography of Five-and-Ten-Cent Pamphlets* (St. Louis, Mo.: Queen's Work, 1941).

81. Interview with Edmond Kent, S.J., Dublin, April 25, 1989.

CHAPTER 3. The Labor Schools

1. For a lucid chronicle of the New York labor schools, see Joseph M. McShane, S.J., "The Jesuits and Organized Labor in the City of New York, 1936–1988," paper presented at the Conference on American Catholicism in the Twentieth Century, University of Notre Dame, November 1–3, 1990.

2. Robert H. Zieger, *American Workers, American Unions, 1920–1985* (Baltimore, Md.: Johns Hopkins University Press, 1986); and Robert H. Zeiger, "Toward the History of the CIO: A Bibliographical Report," *Labor History* 26 (1985): 485–516.

3. See Richard J. Altenbaugh, *Education for Struggle: The American Labor College of the 1920s and the 1930s* (Philadelphia: Temple University Press, 1990); and Ken Fones-Wolf, *Trade Union Gospel: Christianity and Labor in Industrial Philadelphia, 1865–1915* (Philadelphia: Temple University Press, 1989).

4. Interview with Philip A. Carey, S.J., New York City, May 9, 1986. Compare Iver Bernstein, "What Did the New York City Draft Rioters Think They Were Doing?" in *New York City and the Rise of American Capitalism: Economic Development and the Social and Political History of an American State, 1780–1870*, ed. William Pencak and Conrad Edick Wright (New York: New York Historical Society, 1989). A colorful introduction to the ambience in which Carey worked is by Jeff Kisseloff, *You Must Remember This: An Oral History of Manhattan from the 1890s to World War II* (New York: Schocken Books, 1989), especially 475–552; see also B. A. Botkin, *Sidewalks of America: Folklore, Legends, Sagas, Traditions, Customs, Songs, Stories and Sayings of City Folks* (Indianapolis, Ind.: Bobbs-Merrill, 1954). Edward Van Every, *Sins of New York, as "Exposed" by the Police Gazette* (New York: Frederick A. Stokes, 1930), provides a contemporary analysis of the connections between myth and reality associated with the Tenderloin and adjacent areas of Manhattan. The title and subtitle of one publication from the early postfamine days of Irish migration crystallize a major theme of the Irish American enclaves in which Carey worked: Hugh Quigley, *The Cross and the Shamrock, or, How to Defend the Faith; An Irish-American Tale of Real Life—A Book for the Entertainment and Special Instruction of the Catholic Male and Female Servants of the United States* (Boston: Patrick Donahue, 1853).

5. Dorothy Day's confessor at the time was a Jesuit, Fr. James McCoy, who lived at Xavier. When he died in 1977 at the age of seventy-two, his obituary described the qualities that endeared him to the members of the Catholic

Worker movement (John Catoir, "Death Comes to a Holy Man," *National Jesuit News* [April 1977]: 15; see also Edmond Kent, S.J., "Dorothy Day: An Interview," *Studies* 39 [1950]: 176–86).

His room was bare. He wore the same pair of patched pants for the last four years. He had absolutely no interest in material goods, and he prayed constantly for the grace of holiness. . . . He could relate easily to the dregs of society: drug addicts, derelicts, criminals. He had compassion for the mentally ill. There was no one in trouble whom he would not encourage and treat as an equal. He was a simple person, unshockable, and always for the underdog. He was especially effective with people who had suffered at the hands of churchmen. He suffered greatly in that way himself. Jim will never be canonized, but he was a holy man.

6. Philip E. Dobson, S.J., "The Xavier Labor School, 1938–1939," *Woodstock Letters* 68 (1939): 267.

7. Neil P. Hurley, S.J., "The Catholic Evidence Guild of New York City," *Woodstock Letters* 82 (1953): 301–16; Philip A. Carey, S.J., typed notes, Xavier Institute of Industrial Relations, n.d. (1959?)

8. Equal in difficulty to Carey's ministry among the transit workers was that of his colleague John Corridan among the dockworkers. Corridan was the model for the labor priest played by Karl Malden in the movie *On the Waterfront*. See Allen Raymond, *Waterfront Priest* (New York: Henry Holt, 1955).

9. Dennis J. Comey, S.J., *The Waterfront Peacemaker* (Philadelphia: Saint Joseph's University Press, 1983).

10. Carey had written his master's thesis on "The Guilds and Modern Vocational Groupings." See Joshua B. Freeman, *In Transit: The Transport Workers Union in New York City, 1933–1966* (New York: Oxford University Press, 1989), p. 277.

11. See Alan Brinkley, "The Best Years of Their Lives," *New York Review of Books* 37 (June 25, 1990): 16–21.

12. See Shirley Quill, *Mike Quill—Himself: A Memoir* (Greenwich, Conn.: Devin-Adair, 1985).

13. Dobson, "The Xavier Labor School," pp. 271–72.

14. Joshua B. Freeman, "Catholics, Communists, and Republicans: Irish Workers and the Organization of the Transport Workers Union," in *Working Class America: Essays on Labor, Community, and American Society*, ed. Michael H. Frisch and Daniel J. Walkowitz (Urbana: University of Illinois Press, 1983), p. 263.

15. Toward the end of his career Quill himself reined in his radicalism. "Quill had not even a touch of a martyr's complex," Freeman writes. "He had started out in the United States as a common laborer and the fear that he could end up that way haunted him. He preferred the sins of the soul to the damnation of obscurity, powerlessness, and the mean struggle for survival" (Freeman, *In Transit*, p. 301).

16. James J. McGinley, S.J., *Labor Relations in the New York Rapid Transit System, 1904–1944* (New York: King's Crown Press, Columbia University, 1949), p. 320.

17. The inattention to ideology among the immigrants did not simply reflect cultural bias or ignorance. Irish Americans had left behind the structural context that bred agrarian radicalism in Ireland, and by the end of the nineteenth century the economic and demographic conditions that gave rise to the Land Wars had faded in any case. See Paul Bew, *Conflict and Conciliation in Ireland, 1890–1910: Parnellites and Radical Agrarians* (Oxford: Clarendon, 1987); and T. W. Moody, *Davitt and Irish Revolution, 1846–82* (Oxford: Clarendon, 1981).

18. McGinley, *Labor Relations in the New York Rapid Transit*, pp. 324–25. Compare Craig Jackson Calhoun, "The Radicalism of Tradition," *American Journal of Sociology* 88 (1983): 886–914.

19. Compare Herbert G. Gutman, *Work, Culture and Society in Industrializing America: Essays in American Working-Class and Social History* (New York: Alfred A. Knopf, 1976); and Jeffrey Haydu, *Between Craft and Class: Skilled Workers and Factory Politics in the United States and Britain, 1890–1922* (Berkeley: University of California Press, 1988).

20. See Robert D. Waldinger, *Through the Eye of the Needle: Immigrants and Enterprise in New York's Garment Trades* (New York: New York University Press, 1986).

21. The identification of religion with feudalism, obscurantism, and the like on the part of the urban intelligentsia helped confirm the Jesuits in their hostility to academic secularism and little-magazine bohemianism; see Alexander Bloom, *Prodigal Sons: The New York Intellectuals and Their World* (New York: Oxford University Press, 1986); and Terry A. Cooney, *The Rise of the New York Intellectuals: Partisan Review and Its Circle* (Madison: University of Wisconsin Press, 1986).

22. Dobson, "The Xavier Labor School," p. 275.

23. See Walter Galenson, *The CIO Challenge to the AFL: A History of the American Labor Movement* (Cambridge, Mass.: Harvard University Press, 1960); and Ronald W. Schatz, *The Electrical Workers: A History of Labor at General Electric and Westinghouse, 1923–60* (Urbana: University of Illinois Press, 1983). See also Herman J. Muller, S.J., *The University of Detroit, 1877–1977: A Centennial History* (Detroit: University of Detroit, 1976). Some Catholic labor schools operated for a time in these cities under the auspices of diocesan clergy.

24. See Joseph T. Clark, S.J., "Some Lessons Learned from Anti-Communist Activity," *Woodstock Letters* 67 (1938): 245–60; and Joseph P. Fitzpatrick, S.J., "Contact with 'Little People' Formed Xavier's Labor Priest," *National Jesuit News* (April 1978): 18.

25. Despite their inadequacies from a European point of view, the anticommunism of labor school priests like Carey gave a fundamental legitimacy to their efforts. Their approach differed from that of the worker priests who were active in France and Belgium after the war and whose activities were eventually suppressed by Pius XII. See Égide Van Broeckhoven, *Journal Spirituel d'un Jésuite en Usine: Du Temps des Études au Temps du Travail* (Paris: Desclée de Brouwer, 1976).

26. As far as I can determine, the history of the flirtation of American labor leaders

with corporatist ideas of European provenance has yet to be written. A major source of the story is the labor archives housed at the University of Pittsburgh.

27. See Anne Fremantle, ed., *The Social Teachings of the Church* (New York: Mentor-Omega, 1963); Etienne Gilson, ed., *The Church Speaks to the Modern World: The Social Teachings of Leo XIII* (Garden City, N.Y.: Doubleday Image, 1954); Philip Hughes, *The Popes' New Order: A Systematic Summary of the Social Encyclicals and Addresses, from Leo XIII to Pius XII* (London: Burns Oates & Washbourne, 1943); and Terrence P. McLaughlin, ed., *The Church and the Reconstruction of the Modern World: The Social Encyclicals of Pius XI* (Garden City, N.Y.: Doubleday Image, 1957).

28. Interviews with Philip A. Carey, S.J., New York City, May 9 and October 25, 1986. See David P. Peeler, *Hope Among Us: Social Criticism and Social Solace in Depression America* (Athens: University of Georgia Press, 1987).

29. An excellent study of the pastoral work of Carey and his colleagues at Xavier is by Joseph M. McShane, S.J., "'The Church Is Not for the Cells and the Caves': The Working Class Spirituality of the Jesuit Labor Priests," *U.S. Catholic Historian* 9 (1990): 289–304.

30. "Retreat to High School Children," typescript, seven "meditations" of three to four pp. each, n.d., probably mid-1940's, Xavier Labor School archives.

31. Ibid., meditation one.

32. Ibid., meditation six.

33. Ibid.

34. Ibid., meditation seven.

35. Ibid.

36. See Kerby A. Miller, *Emigrants and Exiles: Ireland and the Irish Exodus to North America* (New York: Oxford University Press, 1985).

37. Technically, ISO, which Delaney headed, was separate from the Xavier Labor School, staffed by Philip Dobson, Philip Carey, and others. The operations shared the same quarters, however. For an analysis of the politics of Action Populaire, see John W. Padberg, S.J., "Above and Beyond Party: The Dilemma of *Dossiers de l'Action Populaire* in the 1930's," in *In the Presence of the Past*, ed. Richard T. Bienvenu and Mordechai Feingold (Boston: Kluwer Academic Publishers, 1991).

38. See Charles Hugo Doyle, *Cana Is Forever: Counsels for Before and After Marriage* (Tarrytown, N.Y.: Nugent Press, 1949).

39. John P. Delaney, S.J., *Bulletin of Institute of Social Order*, New York, mimeo, December 1940, eleven pp., Missouri Province archives.

40. The sodalities Jesuits had founded in Europe in the sixteenth century had by this time become devotional clubs whose membership was made up almost exclusively of high school students. The Holy Name fraternities for the men and parish circles for the women were not renowned for their social awareness. See Edward Garresché, S.J., "Progress of the Sodality Movement," *Woodstock Letters* 48 (1919): 54–71.

41. See Anthony L. Ostheimer and John P. Delaney, S.J., *Christian Principles and National Problems* (Chicago: Sadlier, 1945); and Anthony L. Ostheimer,

The Family: A Thomistic Study in Social Philosophy (Washington, D.C.: Catholic University of America Press, 1939).

42. John P. Delaney, S.J., "Clearing House for Social Thought," *Jesuit Bulletin* (1943).

43. John P. Delaney, S.J., "Retreats for Workingmen," Service Bulletin, Institute of Social Order, mimeo, December 1941, eighteen pp., Xavier Labor School archives.

44. Ibid., p. 4.

45. Ibid., p. 7.

46. Ibid., p. 9. Talbot was a recovered alcoholic.

47. Ibid., p. 13.

48. Ibid., p. 17.

49. The title "American assistant" did not make Maher "head of the American branch"; there was no such position. Nevertheless, because Jesuits in the United States were practically cut off from Rome during the war, Maher, who resided in the United States for the duration, could exercise extraordinary powers when he chose to do so. While he could not overrule the American provincials, he was more than just a *primus inter pares*. He could also put off making decisions when it suited him, pleading lack of authority.

50. See Abel Athouguia Alves, "The Christian Social Organism and Social Welfare: The Case of Vives, Calvin and Loyola," *Sixteenth Century Journal* 20 (1989): 3–21.

51. In his first book Husslein stated the nothing-new case concisely (*The Church and Social Problems*, p. 195):

The Church proposes no social system as such, but she clearly defines all the social principles which must be adopted by any system which Catholics may accept without disloyalty to their religion. These principles can be found clearly formulated in such documents as the encyclicals of Pope Leo upon "Christian Democracy" and upon "The Conditions of the Working Classes." Yet even these writings are nothing more than present-day applications of the same unaltered and unalterable principles which have ever been acknowledged by the Church since the days of the apostles.

52. Compare Harry Specht, "Social Work and Popular Psychotherapies," *Social Service Review* 64 (1990): 345–57. I am grateful to Josefina Figueira-McDonough for calling this article to my attention.

CHAPTER 4. "Une Longue Patience": Social Order, Social Reform, and John LaFarge

1. See Abraham A. Davidson, *The Eccentrics and Other American Visionary Painters* (New York: E. P. Dutton, 1978).

2. John LaFarge, S.J., *The Manner Is Ordinary* (New York: Harcourt, Brace & Company, 1957).

3. See Sidney E. Ahlstrom, *A Religious History of the American People* (New Haven, Conn.: Yale University Press, 1972), p. 336ff; Robert Emmett Curran,

S.J., ed., *American Jesuit Spirituality: The Maryland Tradition, 1634–1900* (New York: Paulist Press, 1988); Gilbert J. Garraghan, S.J., *The Jesuits of the Middle United States*, vol. 1 (New York: America Press, 1938), pp. 9–34; and H. Shelton Smith, Robert T. Handy, and Lefferts A. Loetscher, *American Christianity: An Historical Interpretation with Representative Documents*, vol. 1, *1607–1820* (New York: Charles Scribner's Sons, 1960).

4. See R. Emmett Curran, S.J., " 'Splendid Poverty': Jesuit Slaveholding in Maryland, 1805–1838," in *Catholics in the Old South*, ed. Randall Miller and Jon Wakelyn (Macon, Ga.: Mercer University Press, 1983).

5. See the encyclopedic work by Edwin Warfield Beitzell, *The Jesuit Missions of St. Mary's County, Maryland* (privately printed, 1960), a copy of which is housed in the University of Notre Dame library.

6. See Eileen Boris, *Art and Labor: Ruskin, Morris, and the Craftsman Ideal in America* (Philadelphia: Temple University Press, 1986); compare Graham Hough, *The Last Romantics* (London: Gerald Duckworth, 1947); and Fiona McCarthy, *Eric Gill: A Lover's Quest for Art and God* (New York: E. P. Dutton, 1989).

7. LaFarge, *The Manner Is Ordinary*, pp. 204–5.

8. Ibid., pp. 132–34.

9. John LaFarge, S.J., "Memorandum to the Very Reverend Fathers Provincial, at the Annual Meeting, May 7, 1940," five pp., Missouri Province archives.

10. Ibid., p. 2.

11. LaFarge, *The Manner Is Ordinary*, p. 236.

12. Ibid., p. 238.

13. LaFarge, "Scope and Method of the Proposed New York Social Action Institute," seven pp., n.d. (probably 1939), Missouri Province archives.

14. Ibid., p. 2.

15. Ibid., p. 2.

16. LaFarge, "Memorandum to the Very Reverend Fathers" pp. 3–4.

17. See John LaFarge, S.J., *Communism and the Catholic Answer* (New York: America Press, 1936).

18. LaFarge, "Memorandum to the Very Reverend Fathers," p. 5.

19. Ibid., p. 2.

20. A telling evaluation of LaFarge that emphasizes the toll taken by his timidity and penchant for diplomatic maneuvering around progressive rivals outside and conservative opponents inside the church is by David W. Southern, "John LaFarge: The Dilemmas of a Catholic Interracialist in the Age of Jim Crow," paper presented at the Conference on American Catholicism in the Twentieth Century, South Bend, Indiana, University of Notre Dame, November 1–3, 1990.

21. "The Founding of the National Catholic Welfare Conference and its Final Approval by the Holy See, May 1, 1919–July 14, 1922," in *Documents of American Catholic History*, vol. 2, *1866 to 1966*, ed. John Tracy Ellis (Wilington, Del.: Michael Glazier, 1987), pp. 607–13.

22. Toward the end of 1943, after the West Baden meeting, Francis Talbot,

LaFarge's colleague at *America*, wrote to Monsignor Michael Ready at the National Catholic Welfare Conference to reassure him that ISO was not a power play against the interests of the bishops (Talbot to Ready, November 18, 1943, Missouri Province archives):

The Institute of Social Order was set up in 1939, more or less as an extension of the apostolate carried on by *America*. Last May, the Fathers Provincial of the American Assistancy decided to appoint Father Daniel A. Lord, S.J., of the Queen's Work, as the Executive Director, with Father John LaFarge, Father Lord and myself as the governing committee. . . . It was decided that no newspaper or magazine publicity should be given to the Institute of Social Order. It was to be regarded merely as a loosely bound organization of Jesuit scholars, teachers and social workers striving to study, understand and help solve the problems of our dislocated society. It was thought that such conferences as that held at West Baden and such committees functioning through the year would be a stimulus to our Jesuits in the United States. The results of our work would, of course, be made available to the N.C.W.C., the Hierarchy, the individual bishops, if they found the reports and conclusions useful. The whole spirit of the Institute is that of collaboration with existing organizations, not that of setting up a new organization.

23. LaFarge, "Scope and Method" pp. 2–3.

24. Ibid., p. 3.

25. LaFarge to Samuel B. Horine, S.J., October 28, 1936, Missouri Province archives.

26. LaFarge to Joseph F. Small, S.J., February 14, 1947, Missouri Province archives.

27. See Joseph B. Gremillion, *Diary of a Southern Pastor* (Chicago: Fides, 1957).

28. LaFarge, "Memorandum to the Very Reverend Fathers," p. 2.

29. See John LaFarge, S.J., *The Jesuits in Modern Times* (New York: America Press, 1928).

30. LaFarge, *The Manner Is Ordinary*, p. 130.

31. Ibid., p. 212.

32. Ibid., pp. 259–60.

33. John LaFarge, S.J., *The Race Question and the Negro: A Study of the Catholic Doctrine on Interracial Justice* (New York: Longmans, Green, 1943), 35–36.

34. The descriptor used at the time for this approach was not "structural" but "environmental." See John Mahoney, S.J., *The Making of Moral Theology: A Study of the Roman Catholic Tradition* (Oxford: Clarendon Press, 1987), 32ff.

35. *The Race Question and the Negro: A Study of Catholic Doctrine on Interracial Justice* (New York: America Press, 1937).

36. The following account is pieced together from information gathered in Rome in April, 1989, from Jesuits with whom LaFarge spoke about the incident toward the end of his life. "Uncle John," as his intimates called him, said nothing about the episode during his working career. The main lines of the story were first written up by Conor Cruise O'Brien, "A Last Chance to Save the Jews?" *New York Review of Books* 36 (February 1989): 27–28, 35.

37. See Roberto Sani, *Da De Gasperi a Fanfani: "La Civiltà Cattolica" e il mondo cattolico italiano nel secondo dopoguerra, 1945–1962* (Brescia: Morecelliana, 1986).

38. Most of the text was the work of Gundlach, who was responsible for seeing that it conformed to the then-approved scholastic categories of thought and organization. LaFarge contributed some ideas, however, particularly on the role of Catholic schools in alleviating racial injustice. The draft encyclical has never been published. The reasons given for withholding it from the public are that it has no official status and that parts of it would appear dated.

39. Paul Droulers, S.J., *Le Père Desbuquois et l'Action Populaire: Dans la gestation d'un monde nouveau, 1919–1946* (Paris: Éditions Ouvrières, 1980), p. 348, passim.

CHAPTER 5. "Men Astutely Trained in Letters and Fortitude"

1. The phrase is by Edna Kenton, ed., *The Jesuit Relations and Allied Documents: Travels and Explorations of the Jesuit Missionaries in North America, 1610–1791* (New York: Albert & Charles Boni, 1925), p. iii.

2. See John W. Padberg, S.J., "How We Live Where We Live," *Studies in the Spirituality of Jesuits* 20 (March 1988): especially 4–14; compare Slaves of the Immaculate Heart of Mary, *Saints to Remember from January to December* (Still River, Mass.: Saint Benedict Center, 1961); and John J. Delaney, ed., *Saints for All Seasons* (Garden City, N.Y.: Doubleday, 1979).

3. While there was considerable standardization in formation across the provinces of the United States (and indeed worldwide) by the beginning of the twentieth century, small differences were common and cherished. For example, the biretta worn by Jesuits of the New York province was distinctive in having a small triangle in the middle, which according to the pious signified the Holy Ghost. It was also said to be an added help in picking up the biretta. A more noticeable sign of membership in the New York province was the large wooden rosary worn from the loose belt that cinched the cassock.

4. Contrary to what is sometimes supposed, the period of regency had not been introduced by Ignatius at the founding of the society as an interlude of practical experience in order to overcome the monastic isolation of religious training. It emerged toward the end of the sixteenth century, under Claudio Aquaviva, the fifth superior general of the society, during a time of rapid organizational expansion. Aside from serving the purpose of providing "apostolic experience" to young Jesuits, the regency provided much-needed manpower to the growing number of schools under the charge of the society. Over time, in some provinces, the years of regency were extended to five—an abuse that was finally corrected in the 1920s by a directive from Wlodimir Ledochowski. I am grateful to John W. Padberg, S.J., for this information. See inter alia, William V. Bangert, S.J., *A History of the Society of Jesus* (St. Louis, Mo.: Institute of Jesuit Sources, 1972).

5. Ordination after only three years' study of theology was a traditional privilege granted by the Holy See to the Jesuits, probably because their course of training was so long. In 1989 the privilege was revoked.

6. "Tertianship" refers to a third trial period. The first is the short time right before

the novitiate, when the qualifications of candidates are examined. The second is the novitiate itself.

7. Time for retiring at the end of the day was uniform until regency, when scholastics might stay up all hours, working.

8. Jesuits never chanted litanies like monks. The prayers, referred to by some in their fatigue as "the heavenly who's who," tended to be mumbled at a very fast pace. One Jesuit set the regimentation described here in context with his comments on an earlier draft:

What you say is correct but it seems to me that this is true of many units of people, e.g., a married couple that finds "we like to dine late" are likely to do so for most of the years of their marriage, and if "we always go to the cottage for July fourth," they do so for several years. The idea of doing things at regular times I don't see as creating "a system that enclosed their lives." Having a common eating time—how else would it be done? I agree that we were "locked in" but I don't think that things like having a common time for meals is what did it.

What did? It's something like this—it was that "being on time for dinner" became sacrosanct, so that if you were aiding the dying but arrived one minute after grace had been said, you could be told *not* to come in. It was not as though you were joining your *family* for a meal, it was more like military inspection.

9. *Brother "Courtesy": A Little Magazine about Jesuit Brothers*, vol. 1 (January–March 1955). The division continued symbolically after death. At West Baden, the graves of all deceased Jesuits were marked by simple headstones, but coadjutor brothers were buried separately from priests.

10. Some lesser positions were open to nonprofessed Jesuits, and Jesuits who were needed to assume leadership roles in "the works" were sometimes speeded on their way to the fourth vow. Invariably, however, key positions—for example, provincial superior, president of a university, and the like—were reserved for professed fathers.

11. Since a crucial criterion for candidacy to fully professed status was intellectual, there was probably a slightly higher proportion of spiritual coadjutors among social activists than among those who taught in the schools. Statistical proof would require collating information from Jesuit "catalogs"—that is, personnel directories. Resentment at the intellectual/activist distinction with regard to the fourth vow appears in Padre J. Guadalupe Carney, *To Be a Revolutionary: An Autobiography* (San Francisco: Harper & Row, 1987).

12. Daniel L. Flaherty, S.J., "Reflections on a Golden Jubilee: The Society Has Joined the 'Pilgrim People,'" *National Jesuit News* (February 1979): 12.

13. John F. Sullivan, *The Externals of the Catholic Church: Her Government, Ceremonies, Festivals, Sacramentals, and Devotions* (New York: P. J. Kenedy & Sons, 1918).

14. "Grand Haustus," mimeo, probably 1933, one p., Missouri Province archives.

15. Interview with FD, May 29, 1985.

16. Ibid.

18. Interview with MN, August 20, 1988.

19. Ibid.

20. Interview with JD, June 4, 1985. The "conferences" referred to here were not one-on-one meetings but rather sessions, such as a "rules class," which the novice master conducted for all the novices.

21. Ibid.

22. Ibid. Rodriguez spent most of his life in the Society of Jesus as a director of novices. His classic, which took up three volumes, fell from favor after Vatican II. (In some provinces Jesuit novices had been required to read passages from "the three volumes of Rodriguez" for half an hour a day, for two years. When they finished, they were told to start over.) His brand of spirituality struck many Jesuits as excessive:

Upon the twenty-first of February in the year 1616, in a good old age, full of merits, he happily rested in our Lord, in peace. His death was not less universally regretted than his sanctity was esteemed. He was a great lover of retirement, an exact observer of the rules, and had a very great zeal for the salvation of souls. His self-abnegation was such that in all things he had but God in view. The time in which he was not engaged in the discharge of other indispensable duties, he spent in prayer and spiritual reading, adding to these pious exercises very frequent austerities, which he continued to the end of his life; and when it was once represented to him that he could not practise such penances without shortening his days, he answered: "An unmortified religious man is already dead."

(Alphonsus Rodriguez, S.J., [trans. Joseph Rickaby, S.J.], *Practice of Perfection and Christian Virtue*, vol. 1 [Chicago: Loyola University Press, 1929], p. viii.)

23. "Snippets from the Archives," *Chicago Province Chronicle*, 44 (May 1985): 169–71. The Latin means "May the blessing of God descend upon us and guide us always."

24. Interview with FD.

25. "The Story of a Hundred Years: St. Stanislaus Seminary, Florissant, Mo," n.d. (probably 1925), twenty-three pp., Missouri Province archives.

26. Booklet entitled *The Formation of a Jesuit Priest* (Boston, Mass.: Provincial's Residence, 1944), p. 5. Missouri Province archives.

27. Ibid., pp. 5–6.

28. Exact figures on attrition during this period are difficult to come by. The dropout rate seems not to have been higher than 20 per cent and was probably lower on the average across provinces. The big change came in the ten to fifteen years immediately following Vatican II, when substantial numbers of ordained Jesuits left the priesthood and when the number of entrants fell off.

29. *The Formation of a Jesuit Priest*, p. 10.

30. Ibid., 15–16. This account, in the words of one Jesuit recalling his seminary years, is "a lovely idealized description":

What I recall of disputations is that they were commonly thought to be rehearsed, with the defender having seen the objections beforehand, and all parties doing their best to get through the period while the rest of us sat and took in what we could of the Latin.

30. Booklet entitled *The Years Between* (Chicago: Chicago Province Office, 1944), p. 18. Missouri Province archives.

31. The *Ratio Studiorum* has a somewhat mythical status in Jesuit tradition. Few scholastics actually read the *Ratio*. They had only philosophy courses, plus some courses in their major (for example, English literature), until the time of their regency. The pedagogy was transmitted more by submersion in the experience of teaching. The majority of scholastics at the time were products of Jesuit high schools and hence familiar with the manner of instruction. See Paul Oskar Kristeller, *Renaissance Thought and Its Sources* (New York: Columbia University Press, 1979).

32. *The Years Between*, p. 19.

33. Interview with FD. " 'Fathers' Rec,' " another Jesuit recalled, "had a dim reputation. The story was recounted of one old Jesuit who died during the hour of recreation 'and they didn't notice till the bell rang at the end of the hour and they got up to leave'—an apt story, whether true or not."

34. Theologians' diaries, West Baden College, Chicago Province archives. Routine was jarred the next year with a turn that might have come from an Agatha Christie novel. On Sunday, September 14, 1947, the scholastic in charge wrote that "Glen Moore, one of our gardeners, was shot this morning near this home. His death is still a mystery." His funeral was held the following Wednesday ("at 11 a.m."), but there was "no solution as yet."

35. *The Years Between*, p. 22.

36. *The Formation of a Jesuit Priest*, pp. 27–28.

37. Ibid., 39.

38. William C. Repetti, S.J., "How Electricity Came to Woodstock," *Woodstock Letters* 84 (July 1955): 261–70.

39. Edmund G. Ryan, S.J., "An Academic History of Woodstock College in Maryland, 1869–1944," Ph.D. dissertation, Catholic University of America, 1964, p. 197.

40. M. F. Fitzpatrick, S.J., "The Birds of Woodstock," *Woodstock Letters* 46 (1917): 203–14.

41. Ryan, "An Academic History of Woodstock College," p. 212.

42. Compare Paolo Dezza, S.J., *La Filosofia Scolastica de Frente al Pensiero Moderno* (Rome: Pontifical Gregorian University Press, 1942).

43. Michael A. Fahey, S.J., "A Last Look: Woodstock Closing After 109 Years," *National Jesuit News* (April 1975): 4–5.

44. Personal communication, MJP, December 21, 1990.

45. James Conway, "Hilaire Belloc," *Spare Time Essays* 1 (November 1930): 13–17; Francis G. Reed, "The Law of Entropy and Order in the Universe," *Spare Time Essays* 1 (Christmas 1930): 9–14; F. Marshall Smith, "Our Economic Difficulties," *Spare Time Essays* 1 (February 1931): 3–11, and A. G. Schirman, "Hymnus ad Martyres Americae Borealis," *Spare Time Essays* 1 (April 1931): 17, in the Woodstock Library, Georgetown University, Washington, D.C.

46. Thomas E. Henneberry, S.J., "The Ideal Poet," *Spare Time Essays* 1 (April 1931): 5. The immediate target of Henneberry's attack is evidently the classic

essay by George Santayana, "The Absence of Religion in Shakespeare," collected in Irving Singer, ed., *Essays in Literary Criticism of George Santayana* (New York: Charles Scribner's Sons, 1956), pp. 137–48; another possible target is John Donne, a convert from Catholicism and a Protestant divine, who became the greatest English metaphysical poet of his time and a fierce polemicist against the Jesuits. See Donne, *Ignatius His Conclave*, Timothy S. Healy, S.J., ed. (Oxford: Clarendon Press, 1969).

47. Interview with FD.

48. Interview with MN, August 23, 1988.

49. It is tempting to condemn these aspects of the formation process as oppressive by postconciliar standards and by the norms of progressive socialization. The danger in this judgment comes from pulling the system out of context. For some purposes the system was not inherently oppressive, though it came to be counterproductive as it persisted in the midst of broader changes within the Catholic community, especially after World War II. In an essay on "Ethics, Law and the Exercise of Self-Command," the economist Thomas Schelling considers a paradox that is identical to the combination of personal care and authoritarian command prevalent in the Society of Jesus before this time:

> A difficulty with enforcing my vows is that there needs to be somebody with an interest in enforcing the rule on me. If you finance my business and I promise to return your investment, there is no need for the state to take any initiative; you take the initiative if I don't come through. But when I vow to do twenty push-ups before breakfast, even if there are techniques by which to establish whether or not I comply, there is no one to bother unless we make it in somebody's interest to spy on me and denounce me to the authorities.

> (See Thomas C. Schelling, *Choice and Consequence* [Cambridge, Mass.: Harvard University Press, 1984], p. 103.) A similar point is made by James M. Glass in discussing the politics of dependence and therapy (*Private Terror/ Public Life: Psychosis and the Politics of Community* [Ithaca, N.Y.: Cornell University Press, 1989])

> In the modern mental hospital, what Foucault calls the scrutinizing or "panopticon" mentality . . . has been transferred to a variety of methods. . . . A Foucauldian analysis . . . does ignore the very real fact that for the patients the therapies diminish psychological pain, and medications alleviate some of the more frightening symptoms in severe mental illness. . . . While Foucault conceives professional intervention as an exercise of power . . . the patient may demand it in the frantic search for relief from pain and for acknowledgment that the pain is real and terrifying. (p. 206)

50. Interview with MN, August 20, 1988.

51. See George E. Ganss, S.J., ed. and trans., *The Constitutions of the Society of Jesus* (St. Louis, Mo.: Institute of Jesuit Sources, 1970).

52. "Permissions," two pp., n.d. (probably late 1930s), Missouri Province archives.

53. "Selection of Faults for Chapters," two pp., n.d. (probably late 1930s), Missouri Province archives.

54. Personal communication, PXJ, January 8, 1991.

55. The visitation of 1943 became part of the lore of the American branch of the society, as did the legend that Zacheus Maher was a ferocious martinet. The stories surrounding the episode include an improbable one to the effect that the scholastics at a certain philosophate "nailed the windows of his room open so that the mosquitoes would eat him alive."

56. Zacheus J. Maher, S.J., "Memorial of the Informal Visitation to the American Assistancy, 1940–1943," mimeo, Missouri Province archives, p. 3.

57. Ibid., pp. 4–5.

58. Ibid., p. 8b. Several pages later (8m), this prohibition was qualified. "Ours are not to listen to broadcasts of baseball games, prizefights, and of football games in which Our schools or at least a Catholic school is not participating."

59. Ibid., p. 8b.

60. Ibid., p. 8f.

61. Ibid., p. 8l (emphasis in original).

62. Ibid.

63. Ibid.

64. Ibid., p. 8c.

65. Personal communication, MTP, October 2, 1990.

66. One measure of growth was the quantification of the *fructus ministerii,* the outcome of spiritual ministries. Tabulations of "visits to sick and prisons," "catechism explanations," "sermons," and so on were published in *Woodstock Letters* for each of the provinces of the American assistancy.

CHAPTER 6. Praxis

1. Maher to Lord, August 9, 1943, Missouri Province archives.

2. A text in wide use at Jesuit colleges and universities through the thirties and mid-forties was E. J. Ross, A *Survey of Sociology* (Milwaukee, Wis.: Bruce, 1932). It was part of the "science and culture series" edited by Joseph Husslein. The preface, written by Husslein, began:

A basic and systematic treatment of the entire range of "Christian social science," as Pope Pius XI has significantly phrased it, is herewith presented in the present volume. . . . With the providential appearance of the great Vatican documents dealing with almost every aspect of the social question the time was ripe for the production of what may be justly termed a Christian Sociology. Such a book has now been prepared. (p. ix)

Two appendixes were provided to list "a bibliography of Catholic books on sociology [and] useful periodicals" and "non-Catholic periodicals of use to the student of social problems." See also E. J. Ross, *Fundamental Sociology* (Milwaukee, Wis.: Bruce, 1939).

3. Daniel A. Lord, S.J., "The Greatest Revolutionary," outline for talk at "Social Order Monday," January 13, 1935, three pages, mimeo, Missouri Province archives.

4. Maher to Lord, December 27, 1942, Missouri Province archives.

5. Lord to Maher, January 7, 1943, Missouri Province archives.

6. See William Barnaby Faherty, S.J., "Breaking the Color Barrier," *Universitatis* [St. Louis University alumni magazine] 13 (Autumn 1987): 18–21.

7. LaFarge to Lord, September 21, 1943, Missouri Province archives.

8. This was also the age before the emergence of national episcopal conferences, which came into being around the time of Vatican II.

9. Lord to Peter A. Brooks and other provincial superiors, November 22, 1943, Missouri Province archives.

10. Leo D. Sullivan to Lord, December 3, 1943, Missouri Province archives.

11. Thomas J. Shields to Lord, December 3, 1943, Missouri Province archives.

12. James R. Sweeney to Lord, November 26, 1943, Missouri Province archives.

13. See Edward D. Reynolds, S.J., *Jesuits for the Negro* (New York: America Press, 1949).

14. Two typed pages of tabulations by province and response category, May 27, 1943, Missouri Province archives.

15. Reported in an interview with Albert Foley, S.J., Mobile, Ala., April 26, 1990.

16. The reprimand was delivered as a *dicitur culpa*, read out as a "declaration of fault" in the Jesuit community. The severity of the reprimand required Heithaus's expulsion from the community.

17. Much of the story is told by Faherty, "Breaking the Color Barrier." See also Faherty, *Rebels or Reformers: Dissenting Priests in American Life* (Chicago: Loyola University Press, 1988); and Jeffrey H. Smith, *From Corps to Core: The Life of John P. Markoe, Soldier, Priest and Pioneer Activist* (Florissant, Mo.: St. Stanislaus Historical Museum, 1977). Other parts are related in the memoirs of George H. Dunne, S.J., *King's Pawn* (Chicago: Loyola University Press, 1990). A sanitized account is given by John J. McCarthy, "Facing the Race Problem at St. Louis University," *Jesuit Educational Quarterly* 14 (October 1951): 69–80.

18. Where Peter Brooks, the Missouri provincial, got the inspiration to press his colleagues on the question of integrating St. Louis University in the first place is unclear; he may have been influenced by John LaFarge. But there is no record of contact between the two.

19. See Glen Jeansome, *Leander Perez: Boss of the Delta* (Baton Rouge: Louisiana State University Press, 1977).

20. See Ernest Kirtschten, *Catfish and Crystal: The Bicentennial Edition of the St. Louis Story* (Garden City, N.Y.: Doubleday, 1965).

21. Some official sanction for anti-racism could be extracted from *Mit Brennender Sorge*, the encyclical addressed by Pius XI to the German people in March, 1937; see Zsolt Aradi, *Pius XI: The Pope and the Man* (Garden City, N.Y.: Hanover House, 1958).

22. Dunne's parting shot was an article that became a landmark in the Catholic press, "The Sin of Segregation," *Commonweal* 42 (September 21, 1945): 542–45.

23. LaFarge to Maher, August 16, 1944, LaFarge papers, Georgetown University Library Special Collections Division.

24. Ibid. "Our Lady of Fatima," referring to the apparition reported by Portuguese peasant children during World War I, was frequently invoked in "prayers for the conversion of Russia." See William Thomas Walsh, *Our Lady of Fatima* (New York: Macmillan, 1947).

25. LaFarge to Maher, August 24, 1944, LaFarge papers, Georgetown University Library Special Collections Division.

26. Compare Lowrie J. Daly, S.J., "St. Ignatius of Loyola and the Courtier Type," *Woodstock Letters* 89 (1960): 231–39.

27. LaFarge to Maher, August 24, 1944, emphasis in original. As far as I have been able to determine, the first African-American to join the Society of Jesus in the United States, Carl Shelton, began his noviceship in the Missouri province during the academic year 1945–46.

28. Ibid., emphasis in original.

29. Ibid. .

30. Maher to the provincials of the American assistancy, May 3, 1945, LaFarge papers, Georgetown University Library Special Collections Division. The author may have been Fr. John Courtney Murray.

31. LaFarge to Maher, June 3, 1945, LaFarge papers, Georgetown University Library Special Collections Division, emphasis in original.

32. Ibid.

33. Ibid., emphasis in original.

34. LaFarge to Maher, June 21, 1945, LaFarge papers, Georgetown University Library Special Collections Division.

35. The activities of American Jesuits in the field of race relations are touched on in research conducted by John T. McGreevy of Stanford University; the provisional title is "American Catholics and the African-American Migration, 1919–1970."

36. Paul A. Fitzgerald, S.J., *The Governance of Jesuit Colleges in the United States, 1920–1970* (Notre Dame, Ind.: University of Notre Dame Press, 1984), pp. 37–39, passim.

37. "Status of Graduate Studies in the Assistancy, 1944–45," *Jesuit Educational Quarterly* 7 (June 1945): 57–59.

38. Maher to Lord, January 10, 1943, Missouri Province archives.

39. Maher to Lord, January 26, 1944, Missouri Province archives.

40. Ibid.

41. Lord to Maher, February 1, 1944, Missouri Province archives.

42. Ibid.

43. LaFarge to Maher, June 7, 1945, LaFarge papers, Georgetown University Library Special Collections Division.

44. Ibid.

45. LaFarge to Maher, September 27, 1943, LaFarge papers, Georgetown University Library Special Collections Division.

46. Ibid.

47. Ibid.

48. LaFarge to Maher, August 24, 1943, LaFarge papers, Georgetown University Library Special Collections Division, emphasis in original.

49. Ibid., emphasis in original. LaFarge added that "Fr. J. C. Murray agrees with me in this synthesis."

50. Ibid.

51. *Played by Ear: The Autobiography of Daniel A. Lord, S.J.* (Chicago: Loyola University Press, 1956), 241. Lord was here quoting, approvingly, a talk by a Jesuit tertian director. See also Leo P. Wobido, S.J., "Father Daniel A. Lord, 1888–1955," *Woodstock Letters* 84 (July 1955): 261–70.

52. Jesuits continued to press for the integration of their schools and to monitor progress toward this goal; see for example Donald Campion, S.J., "Negro Students in Jesuit Schools, 1950–1951," *Jesuit Educational Quarterly* 13 (March 1951): 248–53.

PART TWO

1. See Christopher Thorne, "Fighting for the Status Quo," *Times Literary Supplement* (April 7–13, 1989): 371; and Geoffrey Perrett, *Days of Sadness, Years of Triumph: The American People, 1939–1945* (Madison: University of Wisconsin Press, 1973).

2. Thurston Davis, S.J., "Blueprint for a College," *Jesuit Educational Quarterly* 6 (October 1943): 74–82. Compare Charles M. O'Hara, S.J., "The Expanse of American Jesuit Education," *Jesuit Educational Quarterly* 2 (June 1939): 14–18; and John P. Rock, S.J., "The Classics and the Catholic Tradition," *Jesuit Educational Quarterly* 4 (March 1942): 168–75.

3. See also Francis Patrick Donnely, S.J., *Principles of Jesuit Education in Practice* (New York: P. J. Kenedy, 1934); John W. Donohue, S.J., *Jesuit Education: An Essay on the Foundations of Its Idea* (New York: Fordham University Press, 1963); and William McGucken, S.J., *The Jesuits and Education* (Milwaukee, Wis.: Bruce, 1931).

4. Davis, "Blueprint for a College," pp. 76–77. Compare William J. Bauer, S.J., "Jesuits Train Leaders . . . ," *Jesuit Educational Quarterly* 5 (March 1943): 250–54.

5. The ideal was probably most closely approximated by the College of the Holy Cross in Massachusetts. See James Leo Burke, S.J., *Jesuit Province of New England: The Formative Years* (Boston: Woodlawn Press, 1976); James Leo Burke, *The Expanding Years* (Boston: Provincial Office of the Society of Jesus, 1986); and Vincent A. Lapomarda, S.J., *The Jesuit Heritage in New England* (Worcester, Mass.: Holy Cross, 1977). Compare Brian Titley, *Church, State, and Control of Schooling in Ireland, 1900–1944* (Dublin: Gill and Macmillan, 1983).

6. Thurston N. Davis, S.J., "Major Trends in American Non-Jesuit Higher Education," *Jesuit Educational Quarterly* 18 (June 1955): 5–16.

7. See Guido Verucci, *La Chiesa nella Società Contemporanea: Dal Primo Dopoguerra al Concilio Vaticano II* (Bari: Laterza, 1988); and John H. Whyte, *Catholics in Western Democracies: A Study in Political Behavior* (Dublin: Gill and Macmillan, 1981).

8. At the time Davis wrote his article, and probably well into the sixties, graduates of Jesuit schools could be found in the political machines, civil bureaucracies, and small businesses of the cities of the Northeast, the Midwest, and in Los Angeles and San Francisco, and they could be counted on to lend a sympathetic ear about a variety of local hassles and issues that might bother the clergy, from parking tickets through medical care to zoning regulations. But this influence was more pedestrian than the kind Davis envisioned. It was the perceived stranglehold of ethnic Catholics and their clerical leaders on municipal government that was a primary target of Paul Blanshard, *The Irish and Catholic Power: An American Interpretation* (Boston: Beacon, 1953); and Paul Blanshard, *American Freedom and Catholic Power*, 2nd ed. (Boston: Beacon, 1958). As subsequent waves of graduates from Jesuit schools have been produced from the sixties onward (the recent period not covered in this study), alumni can be found in the higher reaches of American society—in Washington law firms, in the upper ranks of the federal government, in New York advertising agencies, publishing houses, and the like. This collectivity comes closer to what Davis had in mind as a cultural elite. But the "network"—too structured a word for a very loose conglomeration—hardly qualifies as a "Jesuit mafia," a tag more appropriately applied to a spectrum of the Filipino elite; see Robert L. Youngblood, *Marcos Against the Church: Economic Development and Political Repression in the Philippines* (Ithaca, N.Y.: Cornell University Press, 1990).

9. Personal communication, BT, November 12, 1990. Compare Peter Brooks, "Western Civ at Bay," *Times Literary Supplement* (January 25, 1991): 5–6.

10. See Andrew M. Greeley, *The American Catholic: A Social Portrait* (New York: Basic Books, 1977). Compare Robert Fishman, *Bourgeois Utopias: The Rise and Fall of Suburbia* (New York: Basic Books, 1987); and Daniel Horowitz, *The Morality of Spending: Attitudes Toward the Consumer Society in America, 1875–1940* (Baltimore, Md.: Johns Hopkins University Press, 1986).

11. See Ronald W. Schatz, "Connecticut's Working Class in the 1950s: A Catholic Perspective," *Labor History* 25 (1984): 83–101; and Neil Sullivan, *The Dodgers Move West* (New York: Oxford University Press, 1987).

12. Pictorial and capsule commentary on these times can be found in volumes six and seven of the This Fabulous Century series by Ezra Bowen et al., *1940–1950* and *1950–1960* (New York: Time-Life Books, 1970).

13. "Apostolic Letter of His Holiness, Pius XII, by Divine Providence, Pope, to His Beloved Son, Wlodimir Ledochowski, on the Fourth Centenary of the Foundation of the Society," *Woodstock Letters* 69 (October 1940): 294.

14. The phrase is from the report for 1956 of the master of novices at the Jesuit seminary in Florissant, Missouri. The source is the Missouri Province archives.

15. See W. T. Lhamon, Jr., *Deliberate Speed: The Origins of Cultural Style in the American 1950s* (Washington, D.C.: Smithsonian Institution Press, 1990); and Herbert Gold, ed., *Fiction of the Fifties: A Decade of American Writing* (Garden City, N.Y: Doubleday, 1961).

16. See Raymond Schroth, S.J., "Tough Choices on Campus: The Catholic Character of a University," *Commonweal* (March 28, 1986): 170–75.

CHAPTER 7. Political Change

1. See Vincent A. Lapomarda, S.J., *The Jesuits and the Third Reich* (Lewiston, N.Y.: Edwin Mellin Press, 1989); and Donald F. Crosby, S.J., *Men of God, Men at War: The Catholic Chaplains in World War II* (forthcoming). Compare Studs Terkel, *"The Last Good War": An Oral History of World War Two* (New York: Ballantine, 1984).

2. James B. Reuter, S.J., "He Kept Silence in Seven Languages," *Woodstock Letters* 75 (December 1946): 325. According to one Jesuit historian, Hurley was "a man of considerable status. Something of an unreconstructed colonialist, he had the sense to stay stateside after repatriation, where he helped get the war claims through Congress and received visiting Filipino dignitaries—many of whom had known him as prefect of discipline in his younger days." Personal communication, James Hennesey, S.J., January 3, 1991.

3. L. R. McHugh, S.J., "Hong Kong to Pearl Harbor," *Woodstock Letters* 75 (March 1946): 58–60. See also Edward Haggerty, S.J., *Guerrilla Padre in Mindanao* (New York: Longmans, Green, 1946).

4. See John Costello, *Virtue Under Fire: How World War II Changed Our Social and Sexual Attitudes* (Boston: Little, Brown, 1985); and Joseph C. Goulden, *The Best Years, 1945–1950* (New York: Atheneum, 1976). Compare Roy Emerson Stryker, *In This Proud Land: America 1935–1948 as Seen in the FSA Photographs* (Boston: New York Graphic Society, 1973). For a short biography of Carl Hausmann see James B. Reuter, S.J., "So Proudly We Hail: Father Carl Hausmann, S.J.," in John P. Leary, S.J., ed., *I Lift My Lamp: Jesuits in America* (Westminster, Md.: Newman, 1955).

5. The symbolic charge of Spain for Catholicism centered not only around the antagonisms of the Civil War but also on a polarization with deeper historical roots between Spanish intellectuals and the church; see Alfonso Botti, *La Spagna e la Crisi Modernista* (Brescia: Morcelliana, 1987); and Giorgio Campanini, ed., *I Cattolici Italiani e la Guerra di Spagna* (Brescia: Morcelliana, 1987).

6. LaFarge to Maher, April 9, 1945, LaFarge papers, Georgetown University Library Special Collections Division.

7. See Alfonso Botti, "Chiesa e Religione nella Guerra Civile Spagnola: Orientamenti della Storiografia," *Italia Contemporanea* 166 (1987): 73–83.

8. LaFarge to Maher, April 9, 1945.

9. LaFarge to Maher, November 27, 1945, LaFarge papers, Georgetown University Library Special Collections Division. *Fomento Social* [*Social Development*] was a periodical published by the Jesuits in Madrid.

10. At the time the economic situation in Spain, as in much of Europe, was desperate, and LaFarge feared that the intransigence of the regime in the face of deteriorating social conditions would force a replay of the anticlerical movements that had characterized Spanish politics earlier in the century. See Joan C. Ullman, *The Tragic Week: A Study of Anticlericalism in Spain* (Cambridge, Mass.: Harvard University Press, 1968). LaFarge's observations on Spain date from well before the economic boom engineered by Opus Dei technocrats in the early sixties.

11. See Alfonso Alvarez Bolado, S.J., *El Experimento del Nacional-Catolicismo,*

1939–1975 (Madrid: Edicusa, 1976); and Rafael Díaz Salazar, *Iglesia, Dictadura y Democracia: Catolicismo y Sociedad en España* (Madrid: Ediciones HOAC, 1981).

12. A hagiographical account is by Igino Giordani, trans. Thomas J. Tobin, *Pius X: A Country Priest* (Milwaukee, Wis.: Bruce, 1952). On the pontificate of Pius XII see Andrea Riccardi, ed., *Pio XII* (Bari: Laterza, 1984); and Andrea Riccardi, ed., *Le Chiese di Pio XII* (Bari: Laterza, 1986). The encyclical issued in 1950, *Humani generis*, had nothing to do with the never-released encyclical on racism, *Humanae generis unitas*, drafted by John LaFarge and Gustave Gundlach in 1938; see John Baptist Janssens, S.J., "Letter of Very Rev. Father General on the Encyclical 'Humani Generis,'" *Woodstock Letters* 80 (November 1981): 291–319. In a personal communication (February 12, 1991), Fr. Walter Burghardt pointed out that the promulgation of the doctrine of the bodily assumption of the Virgin, whatever its roots in the superstitions of earlier centuries, was supported during the 1950s by such figures as Graham Greene, who had been appalled at the blowing into smithereens of soldiers and civilians during World War II; see Philip Stratford, ed., *The Portable Graham Greene* (New York: Viking, 1973), pp 583ff.; and Graham Greene, *Ways of Escape* (London: Penguin, 1981), p. 109 *passim.*

13. See Michael Chinigo, ed., *The Pope Speaks: The Teachings of Pope Pius XII* (New York: Pantheon, 1957); and Robert C. Pollock, ed., *The Mind of Pius XII* (New York: Fireside Press, 1955). A recent compilation of papal discourses, arranged by the days of the liturgical year, is by Ulderico Gamba, ed., *Pensieri di Pio XII: per ogni giorno dell'anno* (Rome: Edizioni Carroccio, 1984).

14. John W. Padberg, S.J., "The General Congregations of the Society of Jesus: A Brief Survey of Their History," *Studies in the Spirituality of Jesuits* 6 (January–March 1974): 70–71.

15. John Courtney Murray, S.J., "The Problem of Pluralism in America," *Thought* 29 (June 1954): 165–208. Murray's life and thought are treated by Donald E. Pellotte, *John Courtney Murray: Theologian in Conflict* (New York: Paulist Press, 1976). For an overview of Murray's thought, see William J. Gould, Jr., "The Challenge of Liberal Political Culture in the Thought of John Courtney Murray," paper presented at the annual meeting of the American Political Science Association, San Francisco, August 29–September 2, 1990.

    Murray was not literally silenced. His superior in Rome, Vincent McCormick, the American assistant, did not directly order him to stop writing on church-state relations. McCormick "counseled prudence," aware that Murray had no genuine alternatives but silence or departure from the society. He notified Murray that any of his writings on church-state relations and religious freedom were to be submitted to Rome for "special censorship." This meant much greater scrutiny than was ordinarily the case with "provincial" censorship, by which Jesuit writings were reviewed at the province level. Murray decided that he could not operate under such rules, and so stopped writing on the indicated—that is, proscribed—subjects. I am grateful to Walter Burghardt, S.J., for this information; Burghardt was with Murray at Woodstock College when he opened the letter from McCormick. The following is excerpted from the text of a lecture Father Burghardt gave at the North American College in Rome in November, 1990:

It was a bleak spring day in 1955. I stood helpless in a room on the third corridor of the old Woodstock theological seminary in Maryland. Murray was sifting out the books on his shelves. *These* books would stay; they dealt with grace and the Trinity, with education or social issues, with the old humanities and the new atheism. But *these* books would go—back to the Woodstock Library: they dealt with religious freedom, with church and state. They would go because Murray saw no further use for them. His research was indeed incomplete, far from finished; but before he could publish further in these fields, before he could present his ideas to his peers for challenge and criticism, they would have to undergo a prior critique—in Rome. With his love for the Church of Christ and the Society of Jesus, he felt he could not disobey. But with his love for truth and for the human person, he did not see how he could operate in such claims. It was a bleak day, and my heart ached as I could only stand and look and listen—and wonder. His life's work seemed a shambles. And I thought of Francis Xavier writing from India in sheer frustration to King John of Portugal: "It is a sort of martyrdom to watch being destroyed what one has built up with so much labor."

16. Thomas T. McAvoy, *The Great Crisis in American Catholic History, 1895–1900* (Chicago: Regnery, 1957). An insightful discussion of the papal turn against "Americanism" is by Donna Merwick, *Boston Priests, 1848–1910: A Study of Social and Intellectual Change* (Cambridge, Mass.: Harvard University Press, 1973).

17. Murray to Vincent McCormick, S.J., November 23, 1953, Murray papers, Georgetown University Library Special Collections Division. See also James Hennesey, S.J., "American Jesuit in Wartime Rome: The Diary of Vincent A. McCormick, S.J. (1942–1945)," *Mid-America, An Historical Review* 56 (1974): 32–55.

18. Murray to McCormick, November 23, 1953.

19. Compare Baltasar Gracián y Morales, S.J., *The Oracle: A Manual of the Art of Discretion*, trans. L. B. Walton (London: J. M. Dent & Sons, 1953 [1647]).

20. Murray, "The Problem of Pluralism in America," pp. 204–5.

21. For a more nuanced view of the Spanish tradition of church-state relations, see Henry Kamen, "Tolerance and Dissent in Sixteenth-Century Spain: The Alternative Tradition," *Sixteenth Century Journal* 19 (1988): 3–23.

22. John A. Ryan and Moorhouse F. X. Millar, S.J., *The State and the Church* (New York: Macmillan, 1922); and R. C. Hartnett, S.J., "Father Moorhouse F. X. Millar," *Woodstock Letters* 87 (April 1958): 134–64. An earlier, practically unknown democratic theorist among American Jesuits was Charles Macksey. His doctoral dissertation, written in Latin, presented a series of arguments in favor of popular sovereignty; see Macksey, *De Ethica Naturali: Praelectiones Scholasticae* (Rome: Gregorian University, 1914). I am grateful to Robert Graham, S.J., for this reference.

23. Compare Brian M. Downing, "Medieval Origins of Constitutional Government in the West," *Theory and Society* 18 (1989): 213–47; and Hiram Haydn, *The Counter-Renaissance* (New York: Charles Scribner's Sons, 1950).

24. John Courtney Murray, S.J., *We Hold These Truths: Catholic Reflections on the American Proposition* (New York: Sheed and Ward, 1960). During the

early 1950s Murray taught for a year at Yale, an unusual step at the time for a Catholic scholar. Yale was then in the midst of the intellectual ferment surrounding the development of pluralist theory, most closely identified with the poltical scientist Robert Dahl, and this atmosphere may have encouraged Murray to press on with his ideas about religious toleration and political liberty. Professor Dahl has suggested that both he and Murray may have had a common influence in Francis W. Coker, who taught political theory at Yale during this period; Robert A. Dahl, personal communication, July 6, 1988.

25. Murray, "The Problem of Pluralism in America," p. 171. See also James H. Billington, *Fire in the Minds of Men: Origins of the Revolutionary Faith* (New York: Basic Books, 1980); Patricia U. Bonomi, *Under the Cope of Heaven: Religion, Society, and Politics in Colonial America* (New York: Oxford University Press, 1986); and Paul Wilstach, ed., *Correspondence of John Adams and Thomas Jefferson, 1812–1826* (New York: Bobbs-Merrill, 1925). Compare Garry Wills, *Inventing America: Jefferson's Declaration of Independence* (Garden City, N.Y.: Doubleday, 1978); and Gary Wills, *Explaining America: The Federalist* (Garden City, N.Y.: Doubleday, 1981).

26. Murray, *We Hold These Truths*, p. 51.

27. Ibid., pp. 51–52.

28. "America's Four Conspiracies," in *Religion in America*, ed. John Cogley (Cleveland, Ohio: Meridian, 1958), p. 24. Murray added, "To say this is not, of course, to endorse the concept of the fascist élite—a barbarous concept, if ever there was one. It is only to recall a lesson of history to which our own era of mass civilization may well attend."

29. Murray, "Reversing the Secular Drift," *Thought* 24 (March 1949): 36–46.

30. See David Hollenbach, S.J., et al, "Theology and Philosophy in Public: A Symposium on John Courtney Murray's Unfinished Agenda," *Theological Studies* 40 (December 1979): 700–15.

31. From a letter from Murray to Donald Wolf, S.J., July 20, 1958, quoted by Pellotte, *John Courtney Murray*, p. 57.

32. Murray, "The Problem of Pluralism in America," p. 167.

33. Interview with Joseph Becker, S.J., November 11, 1987.

34. Murray, *We Hold These Truths*, pp. 23–24.

35. "America's Four Conspiracies," p. 13.

36. In passages such as these that probe the psychology of political life, Murray shows the influence of extended conversations with his fellow Jesuit Fr. William Lynch, whose work is examined in chapter 11.

37. Martin Marty gives a somewhat different view of what Murray saw as the dangers threatening political discourse:

Murray was sure that his Catholicism was "the best and only true" church, yet he respectfully entered what he called the conversation with others. "Religious pluralism . . . is against the will of God, but it is the human condition; it is written into the script of history. It will not somehow marvelously cease to trouble the City." American pluralism seemed to him to be especially lamentable. "Many of the beliefs entertained within society ought not to be believed, because they are false; nonetheless men believe them." . . . Yet the priest readily agreed with the United States Supreme Court that it was not the function of government to resolve disputes between conflicting truths, "all of which claim the final validity of transcendence." Murray feared not the barbarian who came to the republican symposium in bearskins with a club in hand, but the person who wore a Brooks Brothers suit or academic robe and threatened others with scholarly footnotes that came from the ballpoint pen. The priest saw no choice but to keep the republican debate going, hoping that it might move some citizens past mutual confusion not to simple agreement but to better disagreement and from thence to a more civil argument.

While the interpretation is broadly valid, it is inaccurate to contend that Murray was untroubled by the demiurges of politics. See Martin E. Marty, *Religion and Republic: The American Circumstance* (Boston: Beacon, 1987), pp. 58–59.

38. *Woodstock Letters* 96 (Fall 1967): 421–27.

39. Ibid., p. 421.

40. Ibid., p. 425.

41. Ibid., p. 424.

42. Ibid.

43. The main lines of Murray's argument about the position of women are Aristotelian. Since most of Murray's writings have a rationalist bent, however, the origins of the impassioned nature of "The Danger of the Vows" form something of a puzzle. He was contemptuous of logical positivism and appreciated many of the Christian mystics. Although the evidence is not conclusive, traces of this influence can be discerned in the following recollection by Murray's longtime colleague Walter J. Burghardt, S.J., "Who Chilled the Beaujolais?" *America* (November 30, 1985): 360:

Two short sentences lay at the heart of his theology and his life. He took them from his beloved Aquinas, who had borrowed them from the elusive Pseudo-Dionysius. The first sentence: "Love makes for oneness"; the lover produces another self. In Murray's translation, "Love is the centripetal force." The correlative sentence: "Love makes for ecstasy" carries the lover outside him/herself. In the Murray version, "Love is a centrifugal force." The twin sentences summed up the heady synthesis of Aquinas: 1) God in His secret life; 2) man and woman as they come forth from God; 3) man and woman as they return to God in Christ. That insight—love as a force paradoxically unifying and "ec-static"—formed the core and motif of Murray's relationship with God and his activity for the human person.

44. Compare Garry Wills, *Roman Culture: Weapons and the Man* (New York: George Braziller, 1966).

45. See Murray to McCormick, July 22, 1958, Murray papers, Georgetown University Library Special Collections Division. In this letter Murray made a request, which was turned down, to have an article of his condemning religious monopoly translated and published in *Civiltà Cattolica*, the Vatican's Jesuit-run newspaper. Yet it was after this date, after approximately four years of enforced silence, that Murray began to publish his writings on church-state relations. The letter reads in part:

The occasion is the bid being made by Mr. Kennedy for the Democratic Presidental nomination. His office approached me indirectly some time ago on the question of a statement to be made on the perennially troublesome question: Can a Catholic support, in princple, the religion clauses of the Constitution? More recently Kennedy has decided not to make a statement unless he is forced by circumstances (it was Cardinal Spellman who told me this early in June). However, it may still be necessary; and the idea is to do better than Al Smith did. Again, the question of a Catholic for President has begun to be a journalistic issue. Harry Luce has asked my advice about an article that *Life* intends to run sometime in the fall. . . .

I do not adduce, as a reason for making this proposal, a desire to clear up my own ambiguous situation, though I would most heartily welcome such a clarification, one way or the other, since at the moment I do not know whether I am right or wrong. It seems fair to state that no effective guidance has come from Rome. Five propositions were sent, none of them unambiguous and none of them held by me. For the rest, a counsel of prudence, to keep silent. I have observed the counsel, under assent to its prudence. Only now I wonder whether the time has come for counsels of prudence to cede to the claims of truth.

46. Giuseppe Alberigo, ed., *Papa Giovanni* (Rome: Laterza, 1987); and Peter Hebblethwaite, *Pope John XXIII: Shepherd of the Modern World* (Garden City, N.Y.: Doubleday, 1987).

47. See Andrea Riccardi, *Il Potere del Papa da Pio XII a Paolo VI* (Rome: Laterza, 1988).

48. See Claudio Véliz, *The Centralist Tradition in Latin America* (Princeton, N.J.: Princeton University Press, 1980); Howard J. Wiarda, "Social Change, Political Development, and the Latin American Tradition," in *Promise of Development: Theories of Change in Latin America*, ed. Peter F. Klarén and Thomas J. Bossert (Boulder, Colo.: Westview, 1986); and Evelyn Huber Stephens, "Capitalist Development and Democracy in South America," *Politics and Society* 17 (1989): 281–352.

49. Compare R.W.B. Lewis, *The American Adam: Innocence, Tragedy and Tradition in the Nineteenth Century* (Chicago: University of Chicago Press, 1955).

50. Alfredo Acerbi, "Pio XII e l'Ideologia dell'Occidente," in *Pio XII*. See also Richard Wrightman Fox, "H. Richard Niebuhr's Divided Kingdom," *American Quarterly* 42 (1990): 93–101; Richard Wrightman Fox, *Reinhold Niebuhr: A Biography* (New York: Pantheon, 1985); and Robin W. Lovin, "Reinhold Niebuhr, Past and Future," *Religious Studies Review* 14 (1988): 97–102.

51. Pietro Scoppola, "Chiesa e Società negli Anni della Modernizzione," in Andrea Riccardi, *Le Chiese di Pio XII*.

52. Quoted by John L. Vessels, S.J., "The Movement for a Better World," *Social Order* 7 (February 1957): 50.

53. See Raymond Grew, "Catholicism in a Changing Italy," in *Modern Italy: A Topical History Since 1861*, ed. Edward R. Tannenbaum and Emiliana P. Noether (New York: New York University Press, 1974); and Massimo Olmi, *Pio XII* (Milan: Gruppo Editoriale Fabbri, 1983), pp. 30–32.

54. Vessels, "The Movement for a Better World," p. 50.

55. See Roberto Morozzo della Rocca, "Le Chiese Parallele: I Religiosi," in Riccardi, *Le Chiese di Pio XII*; and Ernest O. Hauser, "The Pope's Commandos," *Saturday Evening Post* (1958): 44–52. A strongly positive account of Lombardi is given by Armando Guidetto, S.J., *Le Missioni Popolari: I Grande Gesuiti Italiani* (Milan: Rusconi, 1988), pp. 364–66. An insightful critique of the ambience within which Lombardi worked can be found in Nicola Chiarmonte, "The Jesuit," in *The Worm of Consciousness and Other Essays*, ed. Miriam Chiaramonte (New York: Harcourt Brace Jovanovich, 1976). Compare Adrian Lyttleton, ed., *Italian Fascisms: From Pareto to Gentile* (London: Jonathan Cape, 1973).

56. See "The Strange Case of Fr. Lombardi," *The Tablet* (April 2–9, 1988): 395; and Giancarlo Zizola, "Roncalli e padre R. Lombardi," *Cristianismo nella Storia* (1987): 73–93.

57. Pellotte, *John Courtney Murray*, pp. 42–43.

58. Roberto Sani, *Da De Gasperi a Fanfani: "La Civiltà Cattolica" e il mondo cattolico italiano nel secondo dopoguerra, 1945–1962* (Brescia: Editrice Morcelliana, 1986).

59. See Jean-Yves Calvez, S.J., *The Social Thought of John XXIII* (London: Burnes & Oates, 1964).

60. In this respect Murray was vastly less ambitious than Pierre Teilhard de Chardin, his Jesuit contemporary who elaborated an evolutionary theory of cosmic scope. See Christopher Mooney, S.J., *Teilhard de Chardin and the Mystery of Christ* (Garden City, N.Y.: Doubleday, 1968). For a critical evaluation, see Stephen Toulmin, *The Return to Cosmology: Postmodern Science and the Theology of Nature* (Berkeley: University of California Press, 1982).

61. See Patrick W. Carey, ed., *American Catholic Religious Thought: The Shaping of a Theological and Social Tradition* (New York: Paulist Press, 1987).

62. Compare Wendy Lesser, *His Other Half: Men Looking at Women Through Art* (Cambridge, Mass.: Harvard Universary Press, 1991).

CHAPTER 8. Corporatism, Journalism, and Internationalism

1. See Herbert Gans, *The Urban Villagers: Group and Class in the Life of Italian-Americans* (New York: Free Press, 1962); and Thomas M. Mulkerins, *Holy Family Parish, Chicago: Priests and People* (Chicago: Universal Press, 1923). Compare James Q. Wilson and Edward C. Banfield, "Public-Regardingness as a Value Premise in Voting Behavior," *American Political Science Review* 53 (1964): 876–87.

2. See John H. Fenton, *Salt of the Earth: An Informal Portrait of Richard Cardinal Cushing* (New York: Coward-McCann, 1965); and James J. Walsh, *Our American Cardinals* (New York: D. Appleton, 1926). Compare Raphael M. Huber, O.F.M., ed., *Our Bishops Speak: National Pastorals and Annual Statements of the Hierarchy of the United States, 1919–1951* (Milwaukee: Wis.: Bruce, 1952).

3. Thomas P. Sweeney, S.J., *The Catholic Parish: Shifting Membership in a Changing Church* (Chicago: Center for the Scientific Study of Religion, 1974).

4. See Harold C. Gardiner, S.J., *Catholic Viewpoint on Censorship* (Garden

City, N.Y.: Doubleday, 1961); and Neil G. McCluskey, S.J., *Catholic Viewpoint on Education* (Garden City, N.Y.: Doubleday, 1959).

5. See for example James J. Berna, S.J., "Vocational Group Order: The Natural Structure of Society," *Social Order* 1 (November–December 1947): 157–61; James J. Berna, S.J., "Vocational Grouping," *Social Order* 1 (January–February 1948): 225–29; William N. Clarke, S.J., "Industrial Democracy in Belgium: A Milestone in the History of Labor-Management," *Social Order* 2 (February 1949): 49–68; Philip S. Land, S.J., "Guides for Social Reform: Vocational Order Must Spring from People," *Social Order* 4 (March 1951): 100–106; Quentin Lauer, S.J., "Co-Management in Germany: Toward Industrial Democracy," *Social Order* 4 (January 1951): 11–22; and Gerald C. Treacy, S.J., *Industry at the Crossroads: A Handbook on Industrial Relations Based on the Social Encyclicals of Pope Leo XIII and Pope Pius XI* (New York: Paulist Press, n.d.).

6. See C. J. McNaspy, S.J., "Catholic Workers' College: English Jesuits Train Workers for Union Leadership," *Social Order* 1 (March–April 1948): 266–68; "The Social Week in France: Study of Economic Science and Social Reform," *Social Order* 2 (October 1949): 368–69; and John LaFarge, S.J., "Maritain in the Americas," *Social Order* 7 (March 1957): 121–25.

7. Bernard W. Dempsey, S.J., *The Functional Economy: The Bases of Economic Organization* (Englewood Cliffs, N.J.: Prentice-Hall, 1958).

8. Ibid., pp. 105–6.

9. Ibid., pp. 86, 276.

10. Ibid., pp. 72–73.

11. Ibid., p. 284.

12. Ibid., p. 279.

13. Ibid., p. 306.

14. Compare Scott L. Bottles, *Los Angeles and the Automobile: The Making of a Modern City* (Berkeley: University of California Press, 1987); and Kenneth T. Jackson, *Crabgrass Frontier: The Suburbanization of America* (New York: Oxford University Press, 1987).

15. Dempsey, *The Functional Economy*, pp. 320–21.

16. Ibid., pp. 451–52.

17. Ibid., p. 452. Compare John Brooks, *The Great Leap: The Past Twenty-Five Years in America* (New York: Harper & Row, 1966); Thomas Hine, *Populuxe* (New York: Alfred A. Knopf, 1987); and Douglas T. Miller and Marion Nowak, *The Fifties: The Way We Really Were* (Garden City, N.Y.: Doubleday, 1977).

18. Dempsey, *The Functional Economy*, p. 450.

19. See Bernard W. Dempsey, S.J., "The Degree Program in Industrial Relations," *Jesuit Educational Quarterly* 10 (June 1947): 15–22.

20. Dempsey, *The Functional Economy*, pp. 450–51.

21. Compare Robert Wuthnow, "The Moral Crisis in American Capitalism," *Harvard Business Review* 60 (March–April 1982): 76–84.

22. Compare Daniel Bell, *The Winding Passage: Essays and Sociological Journeys, 1960–1980* (New York: Basic Books, 1980); and Ruth L. Smith and Deborah

M. Valenze, "Mutuality and Marginality: Liberal Moral Theory and Working-Class Women in Nineteenth-Century England," *Signs* 13 (1988): 277–98.

23. Dempsey, *The Functional Economy*, p. 293.

24. Ibid., p. 390.

25. Compare Charles R. McKenney, S.J., *Moral Problems in Social Work* (Milwaukee, Wis.: Bruce, 1951).

26. Dempsey, *The Functional Economy*, pp. 390–91.

27. See John Kenneth Galbraith, *American Capitalism: The Concept of Countervailing Power,* rev. ed. (Boston: Houghton Mifflin, 1956).

28. See for example John M. Culkin, "A Primer on Educational Television," *Jesuit Educational Quarterly* 22 (January 1960): 121–45; and Neil P. Hurley, S.J., *Theology Through Film* (New York: Harper & Row, 1970).

29. See Severyn T. Bruyn, *A Future for the American Economy: The Social Market* (Stanford, Calif.: Stanford University Press, 1991); and Charles F. Sabel, *Work and Politics: The Division of Labor in Industry* (Cambridge, England: Cambridge University Press, 1982).

30. See Lynn Dumenil, "The Tribal Twenties: The Catholic Reponse to Anti-Catholicism," working paper series 19, number 2 (Spring 1988), Charles and Margaret Hall Cushwa Center for the Study of American Catholicism, University of Notre Dame; and P. J. Mahon and J. M. Hayes, S.J., *Trials and Triumphs of the Catholic Church in America* (Chicago: J. S. Hyland, 1907).

31. Minutes of the annual meeting of provincial superiors, Gonzaga University, May 1–7, 1947, Missouri Province archives, p. 6.

32. These duties were divided with the growth of the schools after the war. The process is discussed more fully in chapter 13.

33. Minutes of the annual meeting of provincial superiors, New Orleans, April 30–May 6, 1946, Missouri Province archives, p. 1.

34. Ibid., p. 1.

35. Ibid., p. 5. "Fr. Vicar"—in effect, the interim superior general of the society—at this time was Norbert de Boynes, whose decisions were channeled through Zacheus Maher.

36. Minutes of the annual meeting of provincial superiors, Oak Park, Illinois, May 1–7, 1948, Missouri Province archives, p. 7.

37. Ibid., p. 16.

38. See Benjamin L. Masse, S.J., *Justice for All: An Introduction to the Social Teaching of the Catholic Church* (Milwaukee, Wis.: Bruce, 1964); and Benjamin L. Masse, S.J., *Religion and Economic Life* (Washington, D.C.: National Council of Catholic Men, n.d.).

39. Minutes of the annual meeting of provincial superiors, New Orleans, April 30–May 6, 1946. p. 4.

40. Minutes of the annual meeting of provincial superiors, New York, May 5–11, p. 8.

41. Minutes of the annual meeting of provincial superiors, New York, May 5–11, 1952, p. 10.

42. Compare Michael Goldfield, *The Decine of Organized Labor in the United*

States (Chicago: University of Chicago Press, 1987); and Martin Halpern, *UAW Politics in the Cold War Era* (Albany: SUNY Press, 1988).

43. See James P. Degnan, "J. F. Powers: Comic Satirist," in Daniel J. Casey and Robert E. Rhodes, eds., *Irish-American Fiction* (New York: AMS Press, 1979).

44. Minutes of the annual meeting of provincial superiors, New York, May 5–11, 1952, p. 8.

45. See Gerald P. Fogarty, S.J., "Francis J. Spellman: American and Roman," in *Patterns of Episcopal Leadership*, ed. Gerald P. Fogarty, S.J., (New York: Macmillan, 1989); and the more journalistic John Cooney, *The American Pope: The Life and Times of Francis Cardinal Spellman* (New York: Times Books, 1984); compare Michael Paul Rogin, *The Intellectuals and McCarthy: The Radical Specter* (Cambridge, Mass.: MIT Press, 1967); and Stephen J. Whitfield, *The Culture of the Cold War* (Baltimore, Md.: Johns Hopkins University Press, 1991), pp. 91–99.

46. For a description of the political atmosphere of Catholic journalism in New York at the time, see Alden V. Brown, *The Tablet: The First Seventy-Five Years* (Brooklyn, N.Y.: Tablet Publishing Company, 1983). Compare Raymond A. Schroth, S.J., *The Eagle and Brooklyn: A Community Newspaper, 1841–1955* (Westport, Conn.: Greenwood, 1976).

47. Minutes of the annual meeting of provincial superiors, New Orleans, May 4–10, 1953, Missouri Province archives, p. 11.

48. A detailed account is given by Donald F. Crosby, S.J., *God, Church, and Flag: Senator Joseph R. McCarthy and the Catholic Church, 1950–1957* (Chapel Hill: University of North Carolina Press, 1978).

49. Hartnett died at the Jesuit community at Loyola University, Chicago, where he had been living for some years, in 1987. Although difficult to verify, a common apprehension among his fellow Jesuits was that Hartnett had been removed from *America* at Cardinal Spellman's behest.

50. Minutes of the annual meeting of provincial superiors, Boston, May 3–19, 1953, Missouri Province archives, p. 7.

51. Ibid.

52. Minutes of the annual meeting of provincial superiors, Portland, May 3–9, 1955, Missouri Province archives, p. 8.

53. See Loren J. Okroi, *Galbraith, Harrington, Heilbroner: Economics and Dissent in an Age of Optimism* (Princeton, N.J.: Princeton University Press, 1988). The book, of course, was *The Other America*.

54. Compare the polished collection of articles from America edited by Thurston N. Davis, S.J., Donald R. Campion, S.J., and L. C. McHugh, S.J., *Between Two Cities: God and Man in America* (New York: America Press, 1962) with the blunter collection edited a decade earlier by Benjamin L. Masse, S.J., *The Catholic Mind Through Fifty Years, 1903–1953* (New York: America Press, 1953). See also Harold C. Gardner, S.J., *In All Conscience: Reflections of a Literary Editor on Books and Culture in America* (Garden City, N.Y.: Doubleday, 1959).

55. Some years later, Missouri province Jesuits ran into similar geopolitical obstacles when they were first assigned to the Patna mission in India, but "the

Midwest had enough non-Irish names to ease things." Personal communication, James Hennesey, S.J., January 3, 1991.

56. The sojourn inspired Dunne to write *Generation of Giants: The Story of the Jesuits in China in the Last Decades of the Ming Dynasty* (Notre Dame, Ind.: University of Notre Dame Press, 1962). Compare Jacques Gernet, *China and the Christian Impact: A Conflict of Cultures* (Cambridge, England: Cambridge University Press, 1985).

57. Prior to this administrative division, members of the English assistancy included (besides England) Belgium, Australia, Malta, Canada, and the United States.

58. Wilfrid Parsons, S.J., *Mexican Martyrdom* (New York: Macmillan, 1936). It was Parsons who suggested to Graham Greene the theme of the novel *The Power and the Glory*, about a reprobate priest fleeing government authorities in Mexico.

59. Minutes of the annual meeting of provincial superiors, New Orleans, April 11–12, 1928, Missouri Province archives, p. 6.

60. Minutes of the annual meeting of provincial superiors, Boston, April 3–4, 1929, Missouri Province archives, pp. 4–5.

61. Thus, in 1941, with the approval of the provincials, the Jesuit Educational Association's Committee on Latin American Cultural Relations recommended that more scholastics of the Latin American assistancy be brought to the United States to complete their studies, and in 1942, Fr. John Bannon, a historian who chaired the committee, was in touch with Nelson Rockefeller, then coordinator of Inter-American affairs for the Roosevelt administration. Minutes of the annual meetings of provincial superiors, Chicago, May 13–17, 1941, and Boston, May 5–8, 1942.

62. See Thomas J. M. Burke, S.J., *Beyond All Horizons: Jesuits and the Missions* (Garden City, N.Y.: Hanover House, 1957).

63. Peter Dunne and George Dunne were brothers. Peter was a considerable Latin Americanist, with a focus on the history of colonial Mexico. See Peter Masten Dunne, S.J., *Early Jesuit Missons in Tarahumara* (Berkeley, University of California Press, 1948).

64. Peter Masten Dunne, S.J., *A Padre Views South America* (Milwaukee, Wis.: Bruce, 1945), p. 138.

65. Ibid., p. 277.

66. Ibid., p. 266.

67. Ibid., p. 265.

68. Ibid., pp. 279–80.

69. See V. S. Pritchett, *The Spanish Temper* (New York: Alfred A. Knopf, 1954), especially pp. 74–81.

70. Compare C. Vann Woodward, *The Burden of Southern History* (Baton Rouge: Louisiana State University Press, 1960), especially the essays entitled "The Irony of Southern History" and "The Search for Southern Identity."

71. Dunne, *A Padre Views South America*, p. 283.

72. Ibid., p. 284.

73. James Hennesey, S.J., "Postwar Mission Work Developed and Shared," *National Jesuit News* (December 1974): 6.
74. Minutes of the annual meeting of provincial superiors, San Francisco, May 9–15, 1960, appendix, Missouri Province archives, p. 5.
75. Ibid., p. 16.
76. Ibid.
77. Ibid., p. 18.
78. See Manuel Foyaca, S.J., "El Pensamiento Político de Vladimir Ilich 'Lenin' en 1900," *Fomento Social* 25 (July–September 1970); 231–45.
79. Manuel Foyaca, S.J., "Crisis en Nuestra America," *Fomento Social* 19 (January–March 1964): 51–70.
80. See Joseph P. Fitzpatrick, S.J., "What Is He Getting At?" *America* (March 25, 1967): 444–49; and Joseph P. Fitzpatrick, S.J., *One Church, Many Cultures: Challenges of Diversity* (New York: Sheed & Ward, 1987).
81. Quoted by Gerald M. Costello, *Mission to Latin America: The Successes and Failures of a Twentieth Century Crusade* (Maryknoll, N.Y.: Orbis, 1979), p. 51.
82. In addition to Fitzpatrick, there were Emile Pin, then a Jesuit sociologist attached to the Gregorian University, and Renato Poblete, a Jesuit and chair of the sociology department at the Catholic University in Santiago, Chile.
83. Prendergast to Linus J. Thro, S.J., provincial of Missouri, April 18, 1963, Missouri Province archives. Prendergast himself was a missonary in Honduras.
84. Ibid.
85. Ibid.
86. Ibid.
87. Minutes of Conference on Latin America, Washington, D.C., February 12, 1962, Missouri Province archives. See also Francis P. Chamberlain, S.J., "Catholic Education in Latin America," *America* (May 20, 1967): 750–53.
88. Minutes of Conference on Latin America, p. 4.
89. Chapter 12 examines the crisis of clerical roles.
90. Ivan Illich, "The Seamy Side of Charity," *America* (January 21, 1967).
91. Illich left the priesthood in 1969, and the Cuernavaca center closed in 1976.
92. See Eugene K. Culhane, S.J., "Latin American Diary," *America* (February 18, 1967): 243: "The pessimism that was evident all over Latin America in the first years after Fidel Castro's revolution is giving away to hope and a determination to buckle down to slow, hard work."
93. Costello, *Mission to Latin America*, p. 168.

CHAPTER 9. "A Strange Shift in the Affairs of Men"

1. Raymond Baumhart, S.J., "Jesuit Topsy: The College of Commerce," *Social Order* 3 (May 1950): 215–18. Compare Raymond Baumhart, S.J., *An Honest Profit: What Businessmen Say about Business Ethics* (New York: Holt, Rinehart and Winston, 1968); and Baumhart, "It's Not Easy Being a Manager and a Christian," *America* (May 4, 1991): 486–89.
2. See William L. Doty, *Trends and Counter-Trends Among American Catholics* (St. Louis, Mo.: B. Herder, 1962); and Leo R. Ward, ed., *Catholic*

Life, U.S.A.: Contemporary Lay Movements (St. Louis, Mo.: B. Herder, 1959).

3. See Peter Kivisto, "The Brief Career of Catholic Sociology," *Sociological Analysis* 50 (1989): 351–61; and Loretta M. Morris, "Secular Transcendence: From ACSS to ASR," *Sociological Analysis* 50 (1989): 329–49.

4. See William H. Cleary, ed., *Hyphenated Priests: The Ministry of the Future* (Washington, D.C., and Cleveland: Corpus Books, 1969).

5. See Gladys W. Gruenberg, *Labor Peacemaker: The Life and Works of Father Leo C. Brown, S.J.* (St. Louis, Mo.: Institute of Jesuit Sources, 1981).

6. "A Summary Historical Sketch of the ISO," probably 1961, Missouri Province archives.

7. Fitzpatrick to Brown, May 30, 1947, Missouri Province archives. Compare John P. Delaney, S.J., "Social Leadership: The Challenge to Our Schools," *Jesuit Educational Quarterly* 3 (March 1941): 193–99.

8. Fitzpatrick to Brown.

9. Ibid.

10. Ibid.

11. Ibid., capitalization in original.

12. See Joseph H. Fichter, S.J., *One-Man Research: Reminiscences of a Catholic Sociologist* (New York: John Wiley & Sons, 1973).

13. Fichter to Joseph Zuercher, provincial superior of Missouri, June 26, 1947, Missouri Province archives, emphasis in original.

14. Ibid.

15. The only volume to appear was *Southern Parish: Dynamics of a City Church* (Chicago: University of Chicago Press, 1951). The censorship of Fichter's study, enforced by the Jesuit curia, was instigated by the complaints of diocesan clergy worried about offending their white parishioners. Fichter continued to publish numerous books and articles on religious topics, however. One of the most notable is *Parochial School: A Sociological Study* (Notre Dame, Ind.: University of Notre Dame Press, 1958).

16. "Instruction of Very Reverend Father General on the Social Apostolate," October 10, 1949, Woodstock Press pamphlet, 1950, pp. 7–9.

17. Ibid., p. 9. Compare Leo J. Robinson, S.J., "The Field of Social Studies in the Jesuit College," *Jesuit Educational Quarterly* 3 (June 1940): 27–29; and John P. Delaney, S.J., "Developing a Social Sense in Our Students," *Jesuit Educational Quarterly* 5 (June 1942): 44–52.

18. "Instruction of Very Reverend Father General," p. 21.

19. See John Baptist Janssens, S.J., "A Letter of Very Rev. Father General to the Whole Society on Continual Mortification," *Woodstock Letters* 82 (February 1953): 3–16.

20. "Instruction of Very Reverend Father General," p. 13.

21. Ibid., p. 11.

22. "Addresses of Very Reverend Father General John Baptist Janssens to the Congregation of Procurators, September 27–September 30, 1950," Woodstock College Press, 1951, p. 28.

23. Janssens, "On Fostering the Interior Life," December 27, 1946 (El Paso, Tex.: Revista Catolica Press, 1947). See also John Baptist Janssens, S.J., "Letter of

Very Reverend Father General to All Major Superiors and Rectors of Houses of Higher Study," *Woodstock Letters* 83 (1954): 321–30.

24. Follow-up efforts at rallying enthusiasm for social ministry were not lacking, however. See for example James J. McGinley, S.J., "Father Janssens' Letter De Apostolatu Sociali," *Jesuit Educational Quarterly* 14 (June 1951): 5–12; and Mortimer H. Gavin, S.J., "Application to Higher Institutions of De Apostolatu Sociali," *Jesuit Educational Quarterly* 14 (June 1951): 12–25.

25. Joseph P. Fitzpatrick, S.J., "New Directions in the Social Apostolate," *Woodstock Letters* 88 (April 1959): 115–116.

26. Ibid., p. 116.

27. Ibid., pp. 117–118.

28. Ibid., p. 124.

29. Ibid., p. 126.

30. Ibid., pp. 127–128. Compare Ronald W. Edsforth, *Class Conflict and Cultural Consensus: The Making of a Mass-Consumer Society in Flint, Michigan* (New Brunswick, N.J.: Rutgers University Press, 1986); and David Halle, *America's Working Man: Work, Home, and Politics among Blue-Collar Property Owners* (Chicago: University of Chicago Press, 1986).

31. Fitzpatrick, "New Directions . . . ," pp. 128–130.

32. Ibid., p. 130.

CHAPTER 10. Social Order, Social Change

1. John L. Thomas, S.J., "Catholic Social Principles: A Review," *Social Order* (February 1951): 82.

2. Ibid., p. 83.

3. Ibid., pp. 82–83.

4. In the context of the subculture of the time, Thomas's essay was still superior to many others that appears in *Social Order;* see for example John Doebele, S.J., "Pius' Basic Social Address: Man's Perfection the Object of Peace and Order," *Social Order* (November 1952): 397–403; Vincent A. Yzermans, S.J., "St. Pius X and the World of Labor," *Social Order* (September 1954): 297–99; and J. Edgar Hoover, "The Communist Party, USA," *Social Order* (September 1961): 296–301.

5. See Philip S. Land, S.J., "Prolegomena to Economic Communities," Ph.D. dissertation, St. Louis University, 1950.

6. Philip S. Land, S.J., "Guides for Social Reform," *Social Order* (March 1951): 103.

7. Ibid.

8. See Francis P. Canavan, S.J., *The Political Reason of Edmund Burke* (Durham, N.C.: Duke University Press, 1960).

9. Philip S. Land, S.J., "Practical Wisdom and Social Order," *Social Order* (November 1955): 393–94.

10. Philip S. Land, S.J., "Working Together: Toward a Fuller Idea of the Enterprise," *Social Order* (May 1952): 236–37.

11. Philip S. Land, S.J., "People of Plenty: A Review," *Social Order* (May 1955): 218.

12. Ibid., pp. 218–19.

13. Compare Timothy A. Tilton, "The Social Origins of Liberal Democracy: The Swedish Case," *American Political Science Review* 68 (1974): 561–71.

14. See, for example, Clifford Geertz, *Local Knowledge: Further Essays in Interpretive Anthropology* (New York: Basic Books, 1983); and Mark Granovetter, "Economic Action and Social Structure: The Problem of Embeddedness," *American Journal of Sociology* 91 (1985): 481–510.

15. See Leo C. Brown, S.J., "Towards Cooperation," *Social Order* (May 1952): 203–9; "Economic Theory and Social Policy," *Social Order* (January 1956): 21–31; and "Labor Arbitration," *Social Order* (February 1957): 62–69.

16. Edward Duff, S.J., *Social Thought of the World Council of Churches* (New York: Association Press, 1956).

17. Edward Duff, S.J., "Introducing a Symposium," *Social Order* (April 1957): 146.

18. Duff was far from an across-the-board progressive. His claim that "there is an absurd naïveté which points to peak production while failing to advert to the proportion of married women in the labor force with inevitable repercussions on normal family life" is indicative of the moral conservatism that underlay his views on social and political issues.

19. Edward Duff, S.J., "Social Action in the American Environment," *Social Order* (September 1959): 299.

20. Ibid., pp. 299–300.

21. Ibid., p. 302.

22. Ibid., p. 303.

23. Ibid., p. 304.

24. Duff, "Catholic Social Action in the American Environment," *Social Order* (September 1962): 302–3.

25. See David O'Brien, *American Catholics and Social Reform* (New York: Oxford University Press, 1968).

26. Duff, "Catholic Social Action," p. 305. See also Joseph M. McShane, S.J., *"Sufficiently Radical": Catholicism, Progressivism, and the Bishops' Program of 1919* (Washington, D.C.: Catholic University of America Press, 1986).

27. Duff, "Catholic Social Action," pp. 306–7.

28. Ibid., p. 301.

29. Duff, "Social Action," p. 304.

30. Duff, "Catholic Social Action," p. 310.

31. Will Herberg, *Protestant-Catholic-Jew* (Garden City, N.Y.: Doubleday, 1955).

32. Compare Alfred Kazin, "Sticking It Out" [review of Michael Harrington, *The Long-Distance Runner: An Autobiography*], *New York Review of Books* (March 16, 1989): 29–31.

33. See Robert C. Hartnett, S.J., "Comment on 'Catholic Social Action in the American Environment,'" *Social Order* (October 1962): 388–89.

34. See John Patrick Diggins, *The Proud Decades: America in War and Peace, 1941–1960* (New York: W. W. Norton, 1988); and Philip Rieff, *The Triumph of the Therapeutic: Uses of Faith After Freud* (New York: Harper & Row, 1966).

35. Leo Cyril Brown, S.J., "Catholic-Sponsored Labor-Management Education," *Journal of Educational Sociology* 20 (April 1947): 510.

36. Philip Carey, "Notes on District 7 Holy Name School," probably 1948–49, New York Province archives, p. 1.

37. Ibid.

38. During its days of greatest success, from the end of the war through the early fifties, the annual enrollment at the Xavier Labor School reached about 250 men. See Joseph M. McShane, S.J., "The Jesuits and Organized Labor in the City of New York, 1935–1986," paper presented at the Conference on American Catholicism in the Twentieth Century, Notre Dame University, November 1–3, 1990.

39. The account given above of the Xavier Labor School is extracted from a report made by a Spaniard, Martín Brugarola, S.J., "Organizaciones sociales catolicos en los Estados Unidos," *Fomento Social* 14 (January–March 1959): 61–71.

40. Interview with Edmond Kent, S.J., Dublin, April 20, 1989. See also Edmond Kent, "Dorothy Day: An Interview," *Studies* 39 (1950): 176–86.

41. Carey, "Notes on District 7," p. 2.

42. "Jesuit Labor School Head Brings Enthusiasm to Job," *Crown Heights Comment* (October 13, 1946), New York Province archives.

43. William J. Smith, "Crown Heights Associated Activities, First Semester, 1948, Report," New York Province archives, p. 1.

44. William J. Smith, "The Objectives of the Catholic Labor School Movement," *Crown Heights Comment* (January 22, 1946): 1, 4.

45. Smith to James P. Sweeney, S.J., May 18, 1940; and Sweeney, S.J., to Gerald Treacy, S.J., October 14, 1942, New York Province archives.

46. James Sweeney, his provincial superior, admonished Smith about his obstreperousness, particularly as it caused dissension within the ranks, in a good-natured way:

    Most people have admired your clear stand on the question of communists in the P.A.C. but too much publicity has been given to the differences of opinion expressed by yourself and Father Masse. When Jesuits cannot agree among themselves, the laity is bewildered and no good purpose is served. . . . I have been waiting for this battle between the Dodgers and the Giants to end because it is my judgment that Jesuits should not emphasize their disagreements in public. . . . Do not, however, let this injunction stop your good work. You can attack the P.A.C. all you like and you can criticize the New Leader and the Daily Worker, but you will have to spare your brethren on the mainland.

    Sweeney to Smith, March 1, 1945, New York Province archives.

47. William J. Smith, "Report on Crown Heights Associated Activities, Brooklyn, N.Y., November, 1947," New York Province archives, p. 6.

48. Ibid., p. 4. The latter reference is to John Corridan, the Jesuit who became known as "the waterfront priest" for his work on the docks of Manhattan; his base was the Xavier Labor School. Edmond Kent indicated (in the interview cited above) that Smith's ties with the world of labor, never secure because of his strident anticommunism, began seriously to deteriorate when word got out that he was writing a book that was part labor manual and part memoir. Kent quoted Smith as advising him:

"You have your choice. You can work with people, or you can write about them, but you can't do both. Because you'll make enemies. If there's any skullduggery, you'll learn about it from them. They give you that in confidence. The whole thing is bedraggled with disrepute."

49. See for example William J. Smith, S.J., *The Pope Talks About Labor Relations* (St. Paul, Minn.: Catechetical Guild Educational Society, 1955); and William J. Smith, S.J., *What Is Your "Social" I.Q.?* (New York: Paulist Press, 1951).

50. See Albert S. Foley, S.J., *St. Regis: A Social Crusader* (Milwaukee, Wis.: Bruce, 1941); also Albert S. Foley, S.J., *A Modern Galahad: St. John Berchmans* (Milwaukee, Wis.: Bruce, 1937).

51. Interview with Albert S. Foley, S.J., Mobile, Ala., April 20, 1990.

52. See Albert S. Foley, S.J., "Social Aspects of the Church in the Writings of Sorokin," master's thesis, St. Louis University, 1948. Foley's first master's thesis, written in 1936 was entitled "Anti-Epicureanism in Cicero's First Tusculan."

53. See Albert S. Foley, S.J., "Glimpses of the Interracial Apostolate," *Integrity* 5 (November 1950): 3–11.

54. See Albert S. Foley, S.J., "KKK in Mobile, Ala.," *America* (December 8, 1956): 298–99.

55. See Albert S. Foley, S.J, "Adventures in Black Catholic History: Research and Writing," *U.S. Catholic Historian* 5 (1986): 103–17.

56. Mark A. Fitzgerald, C.S.C., "Labor and Management Go Back to School," *Grail* (October 1954): 22.

57. Brown, "History of ISO," mimeo, Missouri Province archives, 1961, p. 8.

58. Besides the Spring Hill institute, the best-known variation on the original labor school format was the institute at Loyola University in New Orleans. See Thomas Becnel, *Labor, Church, and the Sugar Establishment: Louisiana, 1887–1976* (Baton Rouge: Louisiana State University Press, 1980); Clement McNaspy, S.J., *At Face Value: A Biography of Louis J. Twomey, S.J.,* (New Orleans: Institute of Human Relations, 1978); and John Robert Payne, "A Jesuit Search for Social Justice: The Public Career of Louis J. Twomey, S.J., 1947–1969," Ph.D. dissertation, University of Texas at Austin, 1976.

59. See Joseph N. Moody and Justus George Lawler, eds., *The Challenge of Mater et Magistra* (St. Louis, Mo.: Herder and Herder, 1963).

60. A significant effort to sort through this problem, aside from the essay by Philip Land already cited, was the joint article by Philip Land and George P. Klubertanz, S.J., "Practical Reason, Social Fact, and the Vocational Order," *Modern Schoolman* 28 (1951): 239–66.

61. See, however, Joseph M. Becker, S.J., *Shared Government in Unemployment Security: A Study of Advisory Councils* (New York: Columbia University Press, 1959); and Joseph M. Becker, S.J., *Guaranteed Income for the Unemployed* (Baltimore, Md.: Johns Hopkins University Press, 1968).

62. Compare Patrick J. Sullivan, *U.S. Catholic Institutions and Labor Unions, 1960–1980* (New York: University Press of America, 1986).

63. Compare J. M. Martin, *Catholic Social Action in Britain, 1909–1959: A History of the Catholic Social Guild* (Oxford: Catholic Social Guild, 1961).

CHAPTER 11. Crosscurrents

1. See however Andrew M. Greeley, *The Church and the Suburbs* (New York: Sheed & Ward, 1959); and Thomas F. O'Dea, *American Catholic Dilemma: An Inquiry into Intellectual life* (New York: Sheed & Ward, 1958). A parallel demographic shift was occurring among Protestant denominations; see Gibson Winter, *The Suburban Captivity of the Churches: An Analysis of Protestant Responsibility in the Expanding Metropolis* (New York: Macmillan, 1962). Compare Richard C. Braun, S.J., and Edward J. Fischer, S.J., "Jesuit Vocations in Our High Schools," *Jesuit Educational Quarterly* 17 (January 1955): 147–60.

2. Compare Geoffrey Perrett, *A Dream of Greatness: The American People, 1945–1963* (New York: Coward, McCann and Geoghegan, 1979); and Martin E. Marty, "The Idea of Progress in Twentieth-Century Theology," in *Progress and Its Discontents*, ed. Gabriel E. Almond et al. (Berkeley: University of California Press, 1982).

3. Compare Michael Young, *The Metronomic Society: Natural Rhythms and Human Timetables* (Cambridge, Mass.: Harvard University Press, 1988); and John P. Delaney, ed., *Saints for All Seasons* (Garden City, N.Y.: Doubleday, 1978).

4. See Emmet John Hughes, *The Church and the Liberal Society* (Princeton: Princeton University Press, 1944); Theodore Maynard, *The Catholic Church and the American Idea* (New York: Appleton-Century-Crofts, 1953); James M. O'Neill, *Catholicism and American Freedom* (New York: Harper & Brothers, 1952); and George Seldes, *The Catholic Crisis* (New York: Julian Messner, 1945).

5. For an earlier sally along these lines, see J. Rufus Fears, ed., *Selected Writings of Lord Acton*, vol. 3, *Essays in Religion, Politics, and Morality* (Indianapolis, Ind.: Liberty Press, 1985). Compare James Hennesey, S.J., *The First Council of the Vatican: The American Experience* (New York: Herder and Herder, 1963).

6. See Mel Piehl, *Breaking Bread: The Catholic Worker and the Origins of Catholic Radicalism* (Philadelphia: Temple University Press, 1982).

7. For early retrospective evaluations, see Philip Gleason, ed., *Contemporary Catholicism in the United States* (Notre Dame, Ind.: University of Notre Dame Press, 1969).

8. See Landon Y. Jones, *Great Expectations: America and the Baby Boom Generation* (New York: Ballantine Books, 1980); also Joseph Veroff, Elizabeth Douvan, and Richard A. Kulka, *The Inner American: A Self-Portrait from 1957 to 1976* (New York: Basic Books, 1981).

9. See Gerald Ellard, S.J., *The Mass of the Future* (Milwaukee, Wis.: Bruce, 1948). Compare Theodore Caplow et al., *Middletown Families: Fifty Years of Change and Continuity* (Minneapolis: Univeristy of Minnesota Press, 1982); and "Gonzaga Retreat House: The Miracle at Monroe," *Woodstock Letters* 82 (July 1953): 195–217.

10. See Andrew M. Greeley, *The Communal Catholic: A Personal Manifesto* (New York: Seabury, 1976); and Donald J. Thorman, *The Emerging Layman: The Role of the Catholic Layman in America* (Garden City, N.Y.: Doubleday, 1962). Compare Daniel Callahan, *The Mind of the Catholic Layman* (New York: Charles Scribner's Sons, 1963); and Daniel Callahan, ed., *Generation of the Third Eye: Young Catholic Leaders View Their Church* (New York: Sheed and Ward, 1965).

11. See William L. O'Neil, *American High: The Years of Confidence, 1945–1960* (New York: Free Press, 1986); compare James Q. Wilson, "A Guide to Reagan Country," in *Writers and Issues*, ed. Theodore Solotaroff (New York: New American Library, 1969).

12. Compare Patrick Brantlinger, *Bread and Circuses: Theories of Mass Culture as Social Decay* (Ithaca, N.Y.: Cornell University Press, 1983).

13. Robert I. Gannon, S.J., *The Cardinal Spellman Story* (Garden City, N.Y.: Doubleday, 1962). Although Gannon may have needed little prodding, it was commonly understood that Spellman leaned on him to produce this premature hagiography.

14. Robert I. Gannon, S.J., "An Educational Program for the United States," address at the 172nd annual banquet of the Chamber of Commerce of the State of New York, November 14, 1940, in *After Black Coffee* (New York: Declan X. McMullen, 1946), p. 18.

15. Recollections of Gannon surfaced, appropriately, in a biography of Vince Lombardi, the football coach who attended Fordham during the 1930s. See Michael O'Brien, *Vince: A Personal Biography* (New York: William Morrow, 1987), p. 39:

At Fordham intellectual virtues mattered less than character and moral development. "Men are not made better citizens by the mere accumulation of knowledge," said the *Fordham University Bulletin*. Knowledge was secondary because it had "no moral efficacy." Only religion could "purify the heart, and guide and strengthen the will." The principal faculties to be developed were the moral faculties. "Morality . . . must be the atmosphere the student breathes; it must suffuse with its light all that he reads, illuminate all that is noble, expose what it is base, and give to the true and the false their relative light and shade." The *Bulletin*'s philosophy was aggressively promoted by Reverend Robert I. Gannon, the Fordham president, who in 1936 condemned "the singleminded pursuit of the intellectual virtues." In contrast, said Gannon, Fordham devoted itself to the "character-building theory."

16. Gannon, "An Educational Program," p. 19, capitalization in original.

17. Ibid.

18. Ibid., pp. 19–20. Compare Joseph A. Murphy, S.J., "American Colleges and Character," *Woodstock Letters* 65 (June 1936): 224–41; and George D. Bull,

S.J., "Present Tendencies in Our Educational System," *Jesuit Educational Quarterly* 1 (June 1938): 5–13. Gannon's variations on the theme of character were embellishments of a constant in the Fordham tradition, rather like football at Notre Dame. In his closing address at the Fordham convocation in 1933, the Very Rev. Aloysius J. Hogan, S.J., then president of the university, spoke on "Really Educated Men—The Real Leaders," citing the late President Coolidge: "We do not need more material development; we need more spiritual development. We do not need more intellectual power; we need more character. We do not need more government; we need more culture. We do not need more laws; we need more religion." See "Fordham University," *Woodstock Letters* 62 (1933): 441–46.

19. Gannon, "Peace Through Business," address to the members of the International Business Conference, November 20, 1944, in *After Black Coffee*, p. 25. Compare Martin J. Smith, S.J., "Jesuit Education and Secular Universities," *Woodstock Letters* 58 (February 1929): 29–47. For a balanced critique of the practice of progressive education, see Lawrence A. Crimin, *American Education: The Metropolitan Experience, 1876–1980* (New York: Harper & Row, 1988).

20. Gannon, "Plato's Garden and the Reds," address at the dinner of the Real Estate Board of the State of New York, February 1, 1941, in *After Black Coffee*, pp. 5–6.

21. *After Black Coffee*, pp. 17, 67. Compare George E. Brantl, S.J., "Character Education in the Ratio Studiorum of 1599," *Jesuit Educational Quarterly* 9 (October 1946): 92–97; and Francis J. Donohue; S.J., "Return to Jesuit Progressivism," *Jesuit Education Quarterly* 3 (September 1940): 85–88.

22. Gannon, "Truth is a Fixed Star," address to the Friendly Sons of St. Patrick, 1944, in *After Black Coffee*, p. 105.

23. Gannon, "Plato's Garden," in *After Black Coffee*, p. 10. Compare Martin P. Harney, S.J., *The Legacy of Saint Patrick, As Found in His Own Writings* (Boston, Mass.: Daughters of St. Paul, 1972).

24. Gannon, "The Green Above the Red," address to the Friendly Sons of St. Patrick, Los Angeles, 1953, in *After More Black Coffee* (New York: Farrar, Straus, 1964), pp. 96–97. Compare Thubert M. Smith, S.J., "Education for Democracy," *Jesuit Educational Quarterly* 3 (March 1941): 200–6.

25. "Labor and the Priesthood," in *After Black Coffee*, p. 176. Compare Gerard F. Yates, S.J., "Jesuit Education and Democracy," *Jesuit Educational Quarterly* 3 (December 1940): 152–58. The idea that the Irish and Irish Americans might be averse to hierarchical rhetoric did not mean they were shy about public displays of national pride and religious devotion, as the tradition of the St. Patrick's Day parade indicates; see James M. O'Toole, "The Church Takes to the Streets: Public Demonstrations of Catholicism in Boston, 1930–1960," paper presented at the conference on American Catholicism in the Twentieth Century, University of Notre Dame, November 1–3, 1990.

26. "The Green Above the Red," in *After More Black Coffee*, p. 99.

27. Ibid., p. 100. Compare Richard Kearney, "Myth and Motherland," in Tom Paulin et al., *Ireland's Field Day* (London: Hutchinson, 1985).

28. Ibid.

29. Gannon, "More Blarney, Please," address to the Friendly Sons of St. Patrick, San Diego, 1961, in *After More Black Coffee*, p. 112.

30. "Truth Is a Fixed Star," in *After Black Coffee*, pp. 104–5.

31. Compare Calvin M. Logue and Howard Dorgan, eds., *A New Diversity in Contemporary Southern Rhetoric* (Baton Rouge: Louisiana State University Press, 1987); Steven A. Riess, *City Games: The Evolution of American Urban Society and the Rise of Sports* (Urbana: University of Illinois Press, 1989); and Robert W. Snyder, *The Voice of the City: Vaudeville and Popular Culture in New York* (New York: Oxford University Press, 1989).

32. Gannon, "The Women of Ireland," in *After Black Coffee*, p. 96. Gannon gave Mrs. Kelly no first name. According to the etiquette of the time among the Irish on the fringes of lace-curtain status, it was an appellation that her husband would rarely have used, any more than she would have used her husband's Christian name. "It took them a while," wags would say of Irish American married couples, "to get to know each other." Besides, the stark "Mrs. Kelly" allegorized the moral figure behind the family history.

33. Ibid., p. 97. Gannon's reference to the tar-paper shack was no exaggeration; see Richard Plunz, *A History of Housing in New York City: Dwelling Type and Social Change in the American Metropolis* (New York: Columbia University Press, 1990). Irishness, like character, was a virtually patented Fordham theme that Gannon played to the hilt. Just before the Depression hit, the university founded a short-lived "School of Irish Studies, the first serious attempt to establish an Irish Cultural Center in America. It was founded on the proceeds of a recital of Irish Poetry given at the Hotel Majestic. . . . Rev. Miles J. O'Mailia, S.J., is Dean of the School." "Fordham University Extension Centers," *Woodstock Letters* 58 (February 1929): 261–64.

34. Gannon, "Truth Is a Fixed Star," in *After Black Coffee*, p. 102.

35. Ibid., p. 103. The Fifteenth is the "Silk Stocking" district of Manhattan.

36. Ibid., pp. 103–4.

37. "The Women of Ireland," in *After Black Coffee*, pp. 98–99. Compare Herbert Asbury, *The Gangs of New York* (New York: Blue Ribbon Books/Alfred A. Knopf, 1928).

38. "The Women of Ireland," p. 99.

39. See Andrew M. Greeley, *The Irish Americans: The Rise to Money and Power* (New York: Harper & Row, 1981).

40. "The Women of Ireland," in *After Black Coffee*, pp. 99–100.

41. See Tom Inglis, *Moral Monopoly: The Catholic Church in Modern Irish Society* (New York: St. Martin's Press, 1987).

42. See Thomas G. Aylesworth and Virginia L. Aylesworth, *New York: The Glamour Years, 1919–1945* (New York: Gallery Books, 1987); Mayer Berger, *Mayer Berger's New York* (New York: Random House, 1960); M. Christine Boyer, *Manhattan Manners: Architecture and Style, 1850–1900* (New York: Rizzoli, 1985); Jimmy Breslin, *The World of Jimmy Breslin* (New York: Ballantine Books, 1969), especially pp. 213–32; Robert A. Caro, *The Power Broker: Robert Moses and the Fall of New York* (New York: Alfred A. Knopf, 1974); Clifford Edward Clark, Jr., *The American Family Home, 1800–1960* (Chapel

Hill: University of North Carolina Press, 1986); Earl Conrad, *Billy Rose: Manhattan Primitive* (New York: Paperback Library, 1969); Leland Cook, *St. Patrick's Cathedral: A Centennial History* (New York: Quick Fox, 1979); Harvey Frommer, *New York City Baseball, The Last Golden Years: 1947–1957* (New York: Atheneum, 1985); Hy Gardner, *Hy Gardner's Offbeat Guide to New York* (New York: Grosset & Dunlap, 1964); Pete Hamill, "The New York We've Lost," *New York* 20 (December 21–28, 1987): 61–65; John F. Kasson, *Amusing the Million: Coney Island at the Turn of the Century* (New York: Hill & Wang, 1978); Edo McCullough, *Good Old Coney Island: A Sentimental Journey into the Past* (New York: Charles Scribner's Sons, 1957); Edward McSorley, *Our Own Kind* (New York: Harper & Brothers, 1946); John Hull Mollenkopf, ed., *Power, Culture, and Place: Essays on New York City* (New York: Russell Sage Foundation, 1988); Pat O'Brien, *The Wind at My Back* (New York: Avon, 1967); Cleveland Rodgers and Rebecca B. Rankin, *New York: The World's Capital City—Its Development and Contributions to Progress* (New York: Harper Brothers, 1948); Robert A. M. Stern, Gregory F. Gilmartin, and Thomas Mellins, *New York 1930* (New York: Rizzoli, 1987); Leonard Wallock, *New York: Culture Capital of the World* (New York: Rizzoli, 1988); J. A. Ward, *American Silences: The Realism of James Agee, Walker Evans, and Edward Hopper* (Baton Rouge: Louisiana State University Press, 1985); Daniel J. Walkowitz, "New York: A Tale of Two Cities," in Richard M. Bernard, ed., *Snowbelt Cities: Metropolitan Politics in the Northeast and Midwest since World War II* (Bloomington: Indiana University Press, 1990); and Frank Weitenkampf, *Manhattan Kaleidoscope* (New York: Charles Scribner's Sons, 1947).

43. Gannon set forth his message in books that were less bombastic than his speeches; see Robert I. Gannon, S.J., *The Poor Old Liberal Arts* (New York: Farrar, Straus, and Cudahy, 1961); and *Up to the Present: The Story of Fordham* (Garden City, N.Y.: Doubleday, 1967).

44. Bruce Francis Biever, S.J., *Religion, Culture, and Values: A Cross-Cultural Analysis of Motivational Factors in Native Irish and American Irish Catholicism* (Chicago: Arno Press, 1976).

45. See Liam De Paor, "Ireland's Identities," in Mark Patrick Hederman and Richard Kearney, eds., *The Crane Bag Book of Irish Studies, 1977–1981* (Dublin: Blackwater, 1982); and F. S. L. Lyons, *Culture and Anarchy and Ireland, 1890–1939* (Oxford: Clarendon Press, 1979).

46. Biever, *Religion, Culture, and Values*, p. 516.

47. Compare David Bromwich, *A Choice of Inheritance: Self and Community from Edmund Burke to Robert Frost* (Cambridge, Mass.: Harvard University Press, 1989), p. 232, passim.

48. Biever, *Religion, Culture, and Values*, p. 497.

49. See David W. Lotz, ed., *Altered Landscapes: Christianity in America, 1935–1985* (Grand Rapids, Mich.: W. B. Eerdmans, 1989).

50. Biever, *Religion, Culture, and Values*, pp. 352–53.

51. See Clyde F. Crews, "American Catholic Authoritarianism: The Episcopacy of William George McCloskey, 1868–1909," *Catholic Historical Review* 70 (1984): 560–80; and Robert Emmett Curran, S.J., "Michael Corrigan: The

Conservative Ascendancy," in *Patterns of Episcopal Leadership*, ed. Gerald P. Fogarty, S.J., (New York: Macmillan, 1989).

52. Biever, *Religion, Culture, and Values*, pp. 262–63.

53. Ibid., p. 355.

54. Ibid., pp. 355–56.

55. Ibid., pp. 781–807.

56. Compare Robert Nisbet, *The Search for Community: A Study in the Ethics of Order and Freedom* (New York: Oxford University Press, 1953); and Robert Nisbet, *Twilight of Authority* (New York: Oxford University Press, 1975).

57. See Henry Winthrop, "Scientific, Intentional Communities Can Save Democracy and Religion," *Social Order* 13 (May 1963): 21–31; and Peggy Wireman, "Intimate Secondary Relationships," paper presented at the annual meeting of the American Sociological Association, San Francisco, September 4–8, 1978.

58. See James Colaranni, *The Catholic Left: The Crisis of Radicalism Within the Church* (Philadephia: Chilton, 1968).

59. See, for example, Francis P. Donnely, S.J., *Grains of Incense for the Thurible of Prayer* (New York: Hirten, 1934); and Donnely, *The Heart of the Mass: Prayerful Thoughts for the Sacrifice* (New York: Benziger, 1940). A striking depiction of this ambience is the aria in prose entitled "Memories of a Catholic Boyhood," pp. 15–37 by Garry Wills, *Bare Ruined Choirs: Doubt, Prophecy, and Radical Religion* (Garden City, N.Y.: Doubleday, 1972).

60. See Daniel A. Lord, S.J., ed., *Father Finn, S.J.: The Story of His Life Told by Himself For His Friends Young and Old* (New York: Benzinger Brothers, 1929); and "Father Francis J. Finn," *Woodstock Letters* 58 (February 1929): 119–25.

61. Theologians Sodality Academy, *Mental Prayer: Challenge to the Lay Apostle* (St. Louis: The Queen's Work, 1958). Compare William A. Carroll, ed., *Catholic Girl's Manual and Sunday Missal* (New York: Catholic Book Publishing Co., 1952).

62. Theologians Sodality Academy, *Mental Prayer*, pp. 80–81, hiatuses in the original.

63. See Beth L. Bailey, *From Front Porch to Back Seat: Courtship in Twentieth-Century America* (Baltimore, Md.: Johns Hopkins University Press, 1988); and Cynthia Golomb Dettelbach, ed., *In the Driver's Seat: The Automobile in American Literature and Popular Culture* (Westport, Conn.: Greenwood, 1976). Compare Fern K. Willits and Donald M. Crider, "Transition to Adulthood and Attitudes toward Traditional Morality," *Youth and Society* 20 (1988): 88–105.

64. Theologians Sodality Academy, *Mental Prayer*, p. 86. Compare Xenophon, *The Persian Expedition*, trans. Rex Warner (London: Penguin, 1949).

65. Anthony J. Paone, S.J., *My Daily Bread* (Brooklyn, N.Y.: Confraternity of the Precious Blood, 1954).

66. See Thomas à Kempis, *The Imitation of Christ*, trans. Leo Sherley-Price (London: Penguin, 1952).

67. Paone, *My Daily Bread*, p. 188. Compare Daughters of St. Pual, *Guide to the*

Revised Baltimore Catechism (Boston: St. Paul Editions, 1957); and Ralph L. Woods, ed., *The Consolations of Catholicism* (New York: Appleton-Century-Crofts, 1954).

68. Paone, *My Daily Bread,* pp. 76–77.

69. Ibid., p. 191.

70. Ibid., p. 220.

71. Ibid., pp. 58–59.

72. Timothy S. Healy, S.J., quoted in "Boston Graduates Cautioned on the Danger of 'Busyness,'" *New York Times,* May 21, 1991, C18.

73. Anthony J. Paone, S.J., *My Life with Christ* (Garden City, N.Y.: Doubleday, 1962), p. 147.

74. Ibid., p. 148.

75. Ibid., p. 205.

76. Ibid., pp. 316–17.

77. Ibid., p. 13.

78. Ibid., pp. 122, 236.

79. The change in terminology from Paone's first to second book suggests that he had become acquainted not only with the therapeutic literature but also with social commentary in the vein of David Riesman's *The Lonely Crowd,* with the distinction between tradition-, inner-, and other-directed personalities. Compare Editors of Reader's Digest, *The Art of Living* (New York: Berkley, 1980).

    Paone died on December 31, 1990, at the age of seventy-seven, having suffered from Alzheimer's disease for over a decade. By then, *My Daily Bread* had sold 1,350,000 copies; it continues to sell about 50,000 copies a year. See John M. McConnell, S.J., "Anthony J. Paone, S.J., (1913–90)," *America* (February 2, 1991): 109–10.

80. William F. Lynch, S.J., "On the Transformation of Our Images," *New York Images* 3 (Autumn 1986): 3.

81. William F. Lynch, S.J., *The Image Industries* (New York: Sheed & Ward, 1959), p. 7.

82. William F. Lynch, S.J., *Christ and Apollo: The Dimensions of the Literary Imagination* (New York: Sheed & Ward, 1960), p. 37. Compare Carl F. Schorske, *Fin-de-Siecle Vienna: Politics and Culture* (New York: Alfred A. Knopf, 1980).

83. Compare Gerald Roberts, ed., *Gerard Manley Hopkins: The Critical Heritage* (London: Routledge & Kegan Paul, 1987); and Charles Taylor, *Sources of the Self: The Making of Modern Identity* (Cambridge, Mass.: Harvard University Press, 1989).

84. Compare M. H. Abrams, *The Mirror and the Lamp: Romantic Theory and the Critical Tradition* (New York: Oxford University Press, 1953); and *Natural Supernaturalism: Tradition and Revolution in Romantic Literature* (New York: W. W. Norton, 1971).

85. For example, William F. Lynch, S.J., *The Integrating Mind: An Exploration into Western Thought* (New York: Sheed & Ward, 1962). See also the discussion of *reconciliatio oppositorum* in *The Image Industries,* p. 148, and of the

"interpenetrating reconciliation of . . . two contraries" in *Christ and Apollo*, p. 158.

86. See Vincent B. Leitch, *American Literary Criticism from the Thirties to the Forties* (New York: Columbia University Press, 1988), pp. 166–76. Compare Michael Löwy, "Revolution Against 'Progress': Walter Benjamin's Romantic Anarchism," *New Left Review* 152 (1985): 42–59.

87. William F. Lynch, S.J., "The Bacchae of Euripides: An American Parallel," *New York Images* 3 (Autumn 1986): 20.

88. Lynch, *Christ and Apollo*, p. 32. Lynch acknowledged his debt to Allen Tate, who originally formulated the distinction between the "symbolic" and the "angelic" imaginations in two essays written in 1951. See Allen Tate, *Collected Essays* (Denver, Colo.: Alan Swallow, 1959), pp. 408–54.

89. Lynch, *The Integrating Mind*, p. 90.

90. Lynch, *Christ and Apollo*, p. 118f. Though unacknowledged by Lynch, this line of reasoning is very close to the Joycean aesthetic; see Eugene Goodheart, *The Failure of Criticism* (Cambridge, Mass.: Harvard University Press, 1978), pp. 158–74. The understanding of aesthetic experience as a therapeutic appropriation of tradition was foreshadowed in Lynch's earliest publication, "Art and the Objective Mind," *Jesuit Educational Quarterly* 2 (September 1939): 78–82.

91. Lynch, *Christ and Apollo*, p. 93.

92. Ibid., p. 94. In a continuation of this passage Lynch summarized his view of the opposition between, in effect, a schizophrenic and an incarnational art:

This is a kind of theology, a kind of faith, a kind of leaping, which leaves the human situation untouched and in terms of which God is only being used as an escape. But all such escape is purely mythical. We cannot jump out of our skins, and if God cannot enter into the inmost part of us and our human reality, then all theology is a farce, a bit of magic which will never work or solve anything. All leaping is futile because leaping out of the human concrete is impossible.

93. Compare Judith N. Shklar, "Squaring the Hermeneutic Circle," *Social Research* 53 (1986): 450–73.

94. Lynch, *The Integrating Mind*, p. 49.

95. Ibid., pp. 49–50. Compare Vera L. Zolberg, *Constructing a Sociology of the Arts* (Cambridge, England: Cambridge University Press, 1990).

96. Lynch, "The Bacchae of Euripides," p. 20.

97. See also Leslie Paul Thiele, *Friedrich Nietzsche and the Politics of the Soul: A Study of Heroic Individualism* (Princeton, N.J.: Princeton University Press, 1990); and Alan Woolfolk, "The Artist as Cultural Guide: Camus' Post-Christian Asceticism," *Sociological Analysis* 47 (1986): 93–110.

98. Lynch, *The Integrating Mind*, p. 35.

99. A brief and reasonably accessible attempt by Lynch to resolve these tensions through sacramentalism—"a scandal to the rational mind"—appeared in an essay entitled "The Catholic Idea," in *The Idea of Catholicism: An Introduction to the Thought and Worship of the Church*, ed. Walter J. Burghardt, S.J., and Lynch (Cleveland, O.: Meridian Books, 1960).

100. Lynch, *The Image Industries*, pp. 47–48, and *Christ and Apollo*, p. 25f.

101. Compare Ilse Aichinger, *The Bound Man and Other Stories* (New York: Noonday, 1956). I am grateful to Nancy O'Neill for reminding me of this book. See also Cynthia Ozick, "A Master's Mind," *New York Times Magazine* (October 26, 1986): 52–113.

102. Lynch, *Images of Hope: Imagination as Healer of the Hopeless* (Baltimore & Dublin: Helicon, 1965).

103. Compare Howard M. Feinstein, *Becoming William James* (Ithaca, N.Y.: Cornell University Press, 1984). See also Gilbert Highet, "The Art of Teaching: Jesuits as Teachers," *Jesuit Educational Quarterly* 13 (March 1951): 207–10.

104. Compare David S. Luft, *Robert Musil and the Crisis of European Culture, 1880–1942* (Berkeley: University of California Press, 1980).

CHAPTER 12. From Aquinas to the Age of Aquarius

1. "Litterae Consultoris in Domo Probationis Sancti Stanislai in Provincia Missouriana," January 11, 1957, Missouri Province archives.

2. "Litterae Consultoris in Domo Probationis Sancti Stanislai in Provincia Missouriana," January 11, 1959, Missouri Province archives.

3. "Litterae Magistri Novitiorum in Domo Probationis Sancti Stanislai in Provincia Missouriana," January 8, 1960, Missouri Province archives.

4. Joseph M. Becker, S.J., "Changes in U.S. Jesuit Membership, 1958–1975," *Studies in the Spirituality of Jesuits* 9 (January–March 1977): 90–91.

5. The peak period of recruitment was the six years from 1959 to 1964, when the average number of entrants reached 372. In the aftermath of Vatican II, applications dropped precipitously. Thus, for the three-year period from 1965 to 1967, the average number of applicants was 224; for the two years 1968 and 1969, the average number was 134; and for the four years from 1970 through 1973, the average was 88.

6. Compare Gerald P. Fogarty, S.J., "The Geographical Location of the American Novitiate," *Woodstock Letters* 96 (Winter 1967): 133–39.

7. By the end of the fifties, television overcame the defenses of the Jesuit seminaries. Dated 1957, the following announcement at West Baden was entitled, in capital letters, "A MILESTONE." (The source is the Chicago Province archives):

Fr. Rector has graciously granted the theologians their own television set. . . . It is to be used under the following general condition—"two hours in the evening daily." Therefore, more precisely, DAILY 7:30–9:30 pm. Special requests for its use at other times should be made through the beadle, e.g., an afternoon ball game. Should any extra programming be granted, the schedule will be posted on the bulletin board in advance.
     Some remarks . . .

1. The set will be located in the speech room near the refectory.
2. The NBC channel is the only clear channel. Hence, to make things easier, the "choice" should be Channel 3.

3. Fr. Minister requests that once the buttons at the rear of the set have been adjusted no one fool with them.

8. The connection was recognizable in retrospect. A formation director of the postconciliar period observed, "Gone are the 'long black lines' and the battery of rules and policies which were in essence (if not always in consciousness) necessary 'traffic laws' for directing the movements of large numbers of people. Numbers . . . have a direct influence on life-style and spirituality." John O'Callaghan, S.J., "Jesuit Formation Today, Part One," *National Jesuit News* (January 1978): 5.

9. There is no evidence that the presence of ex-GIs among the first of the postwar novices affected formation procedures. These men were somewhat but probably not much better educated (the evidence is anecdotal) than their younger peers. It may be that their military experience prepared them for the course of training without giving them reason to question it. It was the entrance of greater numbers of more highly educated novices from the mid-fifties on that seems to have contributed more decisively to turbulence in the seminaries.

10. "Litterae Consultoris in Domo Probationis Sancti Stanislai in Provincia Missouriana," January 11, 1958, Missouri Province archives.

11. Ibid.

12. "Litterae Magistri Novitiorum in Domo Probationis Sancti Stanislai in Provincia Missouriana," January 5, 1958, Missouri Province archives.

13. Compare Charles Forest, S.J, "The First Trial of the Noviciate [*sic*]," *Woodstock Letters* 84 (April 1955): 131–44; and Peter Lippert, S.J., *The Jesuits: A Self-Portrait* (New York: Herder and Herder, 1958).

14. "Litterae Magistri Novitiorum in Domo Probationis Sancti Stanislai in Provincia Missouriana," January 11, 1959, Missouri Province archives.

15. Ibid.

16. Chicago Province archives.

17. "Litterae Consultoris in Domo Probationis Sancti Stanislai in Provincia Missouriana," January 6, 1960.

18. Compare Michael Hechter, *Principles of Group Solidarity* (Berkeley: University of California Press, 1987), p. 168f; and James Scott, "Resistance Without Protest and Without Organization: Peasant Opposition to the Islamic Zakat and the Christian Tithe," *Comparative Studies in Society and History* 29 (1987): 417–52.

19. The ambivalence and tentativeness of the time are expressed by Vincent T. O'Keefe, S.J., in his review of Gustave Weigel, S.J., A *Survey of Protestant Theology in Our Day* (Westminster, Md.: Newman, 1954). The review appeared in *Woodstock Letters* 84 (April 1955): 82. "It is indeed regrettable," O'Keefe wrote, "that whereas the early Protestants receive attention in Catholic dogmatic treatise, the contemporary *Novatores* [innovators] are scarcely mentioned. Barth, Brunner, Boltmann, Cullmann, Niebuhr, Nygren, Pittenger, Tillich, et al., who are definitely forming the Protestant mind of our day, mean little or nothing to our seminarians. . . . The Catholic theologian should be anxious to know what Protestant theology in our day has to say, and yet it is difficult to find a synthetic but authentic expression of the Protestant mind.

This is due to the fact that formulas used by different Protestants cannot be reduced to a unified system of categories because different Protestants use different categories and starting points which are irreducible. There is no perennial systematic skeleton proper to Protestant divinity." Compare Will Herberg, ed., *Four Existentialist Theologians: A Reader from the Works of Jacques Maritain, Nicolas Berdayev, Martin Buber, and Paul Tillich* (Garden City, N.Y.: Doubleday, 1958).

20. Francis X. Curran, S.J., "Loyola Seminary, Shrub Oak," *Woodstock Letters* 87 (February 1958): 42. Compare Albert Labuhn, S.J., "The Milford Novitiate," *Woodstock Letters* 88 (July 1959): 211–21.

21. Interview with PJ, December 7, 1984. The seminary was eventually converted into a drug-rehabilitation center funded by the state of New York.

22. Interview with MG, September 19, 1985. The resemblance of the evocation of times gone by with that of William Kennedy's Albany novels is striking; see George W. Hunt, S.J., "William Kennedy's Albany Trilogy," *America* (May 19, 1984): 373–75.

23. See Stephen P. Erie, "Bringing the Bosses Back In: The Irish Political Machines and Urban Policy Making," in *Studies in American Political Development*, vol. 4, ed. Karen Orren and Stephen Skowronek (New Haven, Conn.: Yale University Press, 1990).

24. Interview with MG.

25. Compare Paul M. Sacks, *The Donegal Mafia: An Irish Political Machine* (New Haven, Conn.: Yale University Press, 1976); and Amanda Dargan and Steven Zeitlin, *City Play* (New Brunswick, N.J.: Rutgers University Press, 1990).

26. Interview with MG.

27. Ibid.

28. Ibid.

29. Ibid.

30. Ibid.

31. Ibid.

32. Ibid.

33. See Darrell F. X. Finnegan, S.J., "Jesuit College Enrollment and Increasing Population," *Jesuit Educational Quarterly* 17 (June 1954): 41–49.

34. See "On Following the Doctrine of St. Thomas, Letter to the Universal Society, December 8, 1916," in Austin G. Schmidt, ed., *Selected Writings of Father Ledochowski* (Chicago: Loyola University Press, 1945), pp. 479–519.

35. See A. Robert Caponigri, ed., *Modern Catholic Thinkers: An Anthology* (London: Burns & Oates, 1960); James Hennesey, S.J., "Leo XIII: Intellectualizing the Combat with Modernity," *U.S. Catholic Historian* 7 (1988): 393–400; and Edward T. Gargan, ed., *Leo XIII and the Modern World* (New York: Sheed & Ward, 1961).

36. Interview with HR, May 29, 1985.

37. Walter J. Ong, S.J., "Realizing Catholicism: Faith, Learning, and the Future," Marianist Award Lecture, University of Dayton, January 26, 1989; see also Umberto Eco, "In Praise of Thomas Aquinas," *Wilson Quarterly* 10 (1986): 78–87.

38. See Vincent F. Dause, S.J., Maurice R. Holloway, S.J., and Leo Sweeney, S.J., eds., *Wisdom in Depth: Essays in Honor of Henri Renard, S.J.* (Milwaukee, Wis.: Bruce, 1966).

39. Interview with HR. See Frederick C. Copleston, S.J., *A History of Philosophy: Late Medieval and Renaissance Philosophy, The Revival of Platonism to Suarez* (Garden City, N.Y.: Doubleday, 1963).

40. See Dino Bigongiari, ed., *The Political Ideas of St. Thomas Aquinas* (New York: Hafner, 1953); Robert F. Harvanek, S.J., "Philosophical Pluralism and Catholic Orthodoxy," *Thought* 25 (1950): 21–52; and Gerald A. McCool, S.J., "Neo-Thomism and the Tradition of St. Thomas," *Thought* 62 (1987): 131–46.

41. Interview with HR.

42. Ibid.

43. While the perception of the simultaneity of change from one generation to the next pervades the recollections of Jesuits, examination of the historical evidence suggests a lag on the part of the American Jesuits of about a decade relative to some of their European counterparts. See Joseph A. Komonchak, "Theology and Culture at Mid-Century: The Example of Henri de Lubac," *Theological Studies* 51 (1990): 579–95; compare Martin C. D'Arcy, S.J., *The Sense of History: Sacred and Secular* (London: Faber & Faber, 1959); Avery R. Dulles, S.J., "Review, Johannes Hohlenberg, *Soren Kierkegaard* [New York: Pantheon, 1954]," *Woodstock Letters* 84 (April 1955): 186–87; Henri de Lubac, S.J., *Catholicism: A Study of Dogma in Relation to the Corporate Destiny of Mankind* (New York: Sheed & Ward, 1950); and Anton C. Pegis, ed., *A Gilson Reader: Selected Writings of Etienne Gilson* (Garden City, N.Y.: Doubleday, 1957). Compare H. Stuart Hughes, *The Obstructed Path: French Social Thought in the Years of Desperation, 1930–1960* (New York: Harper & Row, 1969).

44. Interview with HR. The chronology here is slightly incorrect, though the tenor of the story stands. Father Wernert was director of novices at Milford in Michigan from 1948 until 1959. He moved to Colombiere, outside Detroit, when the novitiate was opened there in 1959, and he held the job until 1963.

45. Even so, during this time of cautious liberalization, the West Baden seminary had its locked room, called "Gehenna," where a number of potentially injurious books were kept.

46. Chicago Province archives.

47. Ibid., capitalization in original. See W. Norris Clark, S.J., "Review of Bernard J. F. Lonergan, S.J., *Insight: A Study of Human Understanding*" (New York: Philosophical Library, 1957), pp. 374–75.

48. Interview with WB, June 6, 1986.

49. Ibid.

50. See George Riemer, *The New Jesuits* (Boston: Little, Brown, 1971).

51. Interview with WB.

52. Ibid.

53. The activist and expressive vertices were captured in the writings, respectively, of Harvey Cox, *The Secular City: Secularization and Urbanization in Theo-*

logical Perspective (New York: Macmillan, 1965) and Norman O. Brown, *Life Against Death: The Psychological Meaning of History*, 2nd ed. (Middletown, Conn.: Wesleyan University Press, 1988). See also Everett J. Morgan, S.J., ed., *Christian Witness in the Secular City* (Chicago: Loyola University Press, 1970).

54. Interview with BT, September 19, 1985.

55. Ibid. Compare William P. Bruton, "The Jesuit Scholastic in the Light of Social Psychology," *Woodstock Letters* 95 (Summer 1966): 288–304.

56. Interview with BT.

57. Ibid.

58. Ibid.

59. Compare Peter Clecak, *America's Quest for the Ideal Self: Dissent and Fulfillment in the 60s and 70s* (New York: Oxford University Press, 1983); and Christopher Lasch, *The New Radicalism in America, 1889–1963: The Intellectual as a Social Type* (New York: Alfred A. Knopf, 1965).

60. Interview with HR.

61. Interview with MN, September 18, 1990.

62. Interview with KRJ, June 5, 1985.

63. Ibid.

64. Ibid. Compare Wilson Carey McWilliams, *The Idea of Fraternity in America* (Berkeley: University of California Press, 1973).

65. Interview with KRJ.

66. See, for example, Edward J. Sponga, "An Ignatian Synthesis: A Phenomenological Evaluation of the Contemporary Jesuit in Search of His Own Identity," *Woodstock Letters* 92 (November 1963): 333–47; Daniel Degnan, "The Washington March: August 28, 1963," *Woodstock Letters* 92 (November 1963): 367–74; and George Devine, ed., *Theology in Revolution* (Staten Island, N.Y.: Society of St. Paul, 1970).

67. Interview with KRJ.

68. See for example Joseph W. Evans and Leo R. Ward, eds., *The Social and Political Philosophy of Jacques Maritain: Selected Readings* (New York: Charles Scribner's Sons, 1955).

69. Philip Gleason, "Neoscholasticism as Preconciliar Ideology," *U.S. Catholic Historian* 7 (1988): 405.

70. Interview with PM, October 5, 1985. Compare Samuel Osherson, *Finding Our Fathers: The Unfinished Business of Manhood* (New York: Free Press, 1986).

71. See John W. O'Malley, S.J., "How to Get Rid of History: Religious Revival and the Tyranny of the Past," *Woodstock Letters* 97 (Summer 1968): 394–412.

CHAPTER 13. The Schools

1. Cicero, preface to the second book of *On Divination*, quoted by R. M. Ogilvie, *Roman Literature and Society* (London: Penguin, 1980), p. 88.

2. See Editors of *The Commonweal, Catholicism in America* (New York: Har-

court, Brace, 1954); Thomas F. O'Dea, *American Catholic Dilemma: An Inquiry into the Intellectual Life* (New York: Sheed & Ward, 1958); and Rodger Van Allen, *The Commonweal and American Catholicism* (Philadelphia: Fortress Press, 1974).

3. The estimate is calculated from Dean C. Ludwig, "Avoiding Spiralling Decline: The Effects of Reallocative Retrenchment Strategies on Admissions and Departures in Voluntary Organizations," Ph.D. dissertation, Wharton School of Business, University of Pennsylvania, 1984.

4. Paul C. Reinert, S.J., "The Intellectual Apostolate," *Jesuit Educational Quarterly* 13 (June 1950): 75.

5. See Lorenzo K. Reed, S.J., "Colleges Attended by 1947 Jesuit High School Graduates," *Jesuit Educational Quarterly* 11 (March 1949): 242–49; and R. A. Bernert, S.J., et al., "Colleges Attended by 1954 Jesuit High School Graduates," *Jesuit Educational Quarterly* 18 (June 1955): 47–52.

6. "Status of Graduate Study in the Assistancy," *Jesuit Educational Quarterly*, various years.

7. See Christopher Jencks and David Riesman, *The Academic Revolution* (Garden City, N.Y.: Doubleday, 1969), p. 334f.

8. James Hennesey, S.J., in an address delivered at the National Assembly on Jesuit Higher Education, Georgetown University, Washington, D.C., June 1989.

9. See Allan P. Farrell, S.J., "Four Hundred Years of Jesuit Education," *Jesuit Educational Quarterly* 3 (December 1940): 117–27.

10. Vincent A. McCormick, S.J., "Ecclesiam Roborasti," *Jesuit Educational Quarterly* 12 (March 1950): 197–99.

11. Ibid., p. 201. It remained for Zacheus Maher to give an even more conservative reading of such matters. In an address to the National Catholic Laymen's Retreat Conference entitled "The Influence of the Retreat Movement on National Sanctities," published in *Woodstock Letters* 80 (February 1951): 1–11, Maher paraphrased and elaborated on the message of Pius XII:

Our own regions require compact companies of pious laymen who, united to the apostolic hierarchy by close bonds of charity, may help it with active industry, devoting themselves to the manifold works of Catholic Action. . . . Give me, cries Pius XII, in every parish a handful of laymen, alert, well-informed, devoted, and I will change the face of the earth. . . . All fields of human life, says the Supreme Pontiff, must be placed under the sweet empire of Christ, and the reason is clear: for all human relations, whether domestic, civil or social, whether industrial or professional, whether national or international, all, since they are pertinent to man, must necessarily have a religious and moral aspect, and as such, fall under the *magisterium* of the Church, the one and only divinely constituted guardian and expositor of faith and morals. . . . [A]ll these activities, if and when undertaken, must be carried out under the supervision of the hierarchy. . . . This point is clear beyond discussion. It is emphasized for the record.

12. See Lawrence C. Langguth, S.J., "Pro Limitation," *Jesuit Educational Quarterly* 17 (June 1954): 56–63; and Clement Regembal, "Pro Expansion," *Jesuit Educational Quarterly* 17 (June 1954): 50–55.

13. McCormick, "Ecclesiam Roborasti," p. 203. See also Walter J. Ong, "Scholarly Research and Publication in the Jesuit College and University," *Jesuit Educational Quarterly* 20 (October 1957): 69–84.

14. See the anonymous defense of Catholic higher education in "Boston College and Harvard University," *Woodstock Letters* 29 (1900): 337–39; compare Burton J. Bledstein, *The Culture of Professionalism: The Middle Class and the Development of Higher Education in America* (New York: W. W. Norton, 1976); Sherry Gorelick, *City College and the Jewish Poor: Education in New York, 1880–1924* (New Brunswick, N.J.: Rutgers University Press, 1981); James Michael Lee, "Catholic Education in the United States," in *Catholic Education in the Western World*, ed. James Michael Lee (Notre Dame, Ind.: University of Notre Dame Press, 1967); David O. Levine, *The American College and the Culture of Aspiration, 1915–1940* (Ithaca, N.Y.: Cornell University Press, 1986); and James W. Sanders, *The Education of an Urban Minority: Catholics in Chicago, 1833–1965* (New York: Oxford University Press, 1977).

15. Compare Christina Hoff Sommers, "Ethics Without Virtue," *American Scholar* (Summer 1984): 381–89; and Eugene J. Devlin, S.J., "Character Formation in the Ratio Studiorum," *Jesuit Educational Quarterly* 15 (March 1953): 213–22.

16. Reinert, "The Intellectual Apostolate," p. 70.

17. See Robert J. Henle, S.J., "What Is Graduate Education?" *Jesuit Educational Quarterly* 15 (January 1953): 133–38; and Walter J. Ong, S.J., *Frontiers in American Catholicism* (New York: Macmillan, 1957); compare Walter J. Ong, "Yeast: A Parable for Catholic Higher Education," *America* (April 7, 1990): 347–49, 362.

18. In the early 1970s the colleges and universities broke off from the Jesuit Educational Association (which continued to serve as an umbrella organization for the high schools under the name of the Jesuit Secondary Education Association) and formed a loose federation called the Association of Jesuit Colleges and Universities.

19. Thus, for example, the longtime director of the Jesuit Educational Association, Fr. Edward B. Rooney, S.J., wrote in the foreword (p. vi) to *Christian Wisdom and Christian Formation: Theology, Philosophy, and the Catholic College Student*, ed. J. Barry McGannon, S.J., Bernard J. Cooke, and George P. Klubertanz, S.J. (New York: Sheed & Ward, 1964):

An unrelieved accent upon intellectuality to the neglect of personal and social morality, an insistence on intellectual freedom without moral restraints, is a hazardous policy to impose upon college students. Traditionally, church-related colleges have felt a definite commitment to the moral and spiritual development of their students. It may well be that in so doing they have made and are making their most distinctive contribution to American higher education. For in addition to their role as patrons and staunch defenders of the liberal arts training, the church-related colleges in the U.S. have historically, with the churches themselves, been the guardians of morality and the theological sources of mature spirituality. The nation as a whole, by the admission of detached observers, has profited from this influence. The decline of it is already causing a weakening in the moral fiber of the country and one hopefully looks for a new emphasis to bring into focus and balance once again the traditional values in which intellect and moral responsibility become partners in the collegiate enterprise.

20. See the five-volume report on Jesuit secondary and higher education by James L. Connor, S.J., John W. Padberg, S.J., and Joseph A. Tetlow, S.J., *Project 1: The Jesuit Apostolate of Education in the United States* (Washington, D.C.: Jesuit Conference, 1974–75).

21. Gustave A. Weigel, S.J., "The Heart of Jesuit Education—The Teacher," *Jesuit Educational Quarterly* 10 (June 1957): 12. See also Benny Kraut, "A Wary Collaboration: Jews, Catholics, and the Protestant Goodwill Movement," in *Between the Times: The Travail of the Protestant Establishment, 1900–1960*, ed. William R. Hutchison (Cambridge, England: Cambridge University Press, 1989). Compare George E. Ganss, S.J., "Ignatian Research and the Dialogue with the Contemporary American Mind," *Woodstock Letters* 93 (1964): 141–64.

22. See Gustave Weigel, S.J., *Catholic Theology in Dialogue* (New York: Harper Torchbooks, 1965); and Robert McAfee Brown and Gustav Weigel, *An American Dialogue* (Garden City, N.Y.: Doubleday, 1960). Weigel had served as professor of dogmatic theology at the Catholic university in Santiago, Chile, from 1937 to 1948 and had been dean of the theology faculty there from 1942 to 1948. In that year, he became professor of ecclesiology at Woodstock.

23. Weigel, "The Heart of Jesuit Education," p. 13.

24. Ibid., pp. 13–14.

25. Ibid., pp. 14–15.

26. Ibid., p. 15. Compare Francois de Dainville, S.J. [trans. J. Robert Barth, S.J., and John M. Culkin], "Saint Ignatius and Humanism," *Jesuit Educational Quarterly* 21 (March 1959): 189–208.

27. See Walter J. Burghardt, S.J., "Man For Others: Reflections on Gustave Weigel," *Woodstock Letters* 97 (1968): 604–7; and John Courtney Murray, S.J., ed., *One of a Kind: Essays in Tribute to Gustave Weigel* (Wilkes-Barre, Penn.: Dimension Books, 1967).

28. The similarity to the Arnoldian ideal of "the best that has been thought" confirms the closeness of Jesuit pedagogy to the Victorian classic mainstream of humanistic education; see Richard Jenkyns, *The Victorians and Ancient Greece* (Cambridge, Mass.: Harvard University Press, 1980).

29. Robert F. Harvanek, S.J., "The Changing Structure of the American Jesuit High School," *Jesuit Educational Quarterly* 13 (1960): 69–83; and Robert F. Harvanek, S.J., "The Objectives of the American Jesuit University—A Dilemma," *Jesuit Educational Quarterly* 14 (1961): 69–87. Harvanek used "science" in the Latin sense of "general knowledge" or "learning."

30. Harvanek, "The Changing Structure," p. 76.

31. Compare Robert B. Westbrook, *John Dewey and American Democracy* (Ithaca, N.Y.: Cornell University Press, 1991); and Jan C. Dawson, "The Religion of Democracy in Early Twentieth-Century America," *Journal of Church and State* 22 (1985): 47–63.

32. It is important to recognize how close in time "the good old days" were. The

following reminiscences of a Jesuit administrator (interview with HJR, June 21, 1985) capture the flavor of the prewar era and the changes that came soon afterward:

Our colleges were run pretty much like seminaries. We didn't have any girls around, and we had pretty rigorous rules, and we had mostly Jesuits teaching. . . . At St. Louis University, in the early twenties, the main library was never open. Students couldn't use it. They had a little library for the students. But for the main library you had to get a key from father minister, and the faculty could use it, and then they let the scholastics use it, and then, around '28 or '29, they opened it up and made it a real university library. . . .

Jesuits were still operating under the European usage of what a college is. In the early part of the century, very few people ever finished the whole program. We would graduate, maybe, five people with a bachelor's degree. Others would go through four years, or five years, or six years, and then drop out. Then the first real tensions came when a lot of people began seeing that we had to do something besides teach classics and philosophy. Prior to that, Jesuits would say "I've got the equivalent of a Ph.D. After all, I've got three years of philosophy, four years of theology." They just didn't know what a Ph.D. was. We had a provincial in the late twenties who began to send Jesuits to top-ranking non-Catholic universities for doctorates. Gradually, as he sent men to England, to Spain, to Johns Hopkins, these guys came back and they knew what a modern American university had to be. So, they began changing, getting departments going.

Fr. Husslein, for example, was a great innovator. He started the science-and-culture series of books. We said that he wrote more prefaces than any man in the history of the world. He went out and *recruited* books. He went out and found Catholics and said, "Why don't you write something on sociology? Why don't you write something on history?"

A tension built up because we were building these units, which had their administrators and so on, and traditionally the president had always been the rector of the community. The more spread out, the more diversified, the more organized the university became, the more difficult it became. A layman could relate to him as the president. I'd have to relate to him as my rector *and* my president, which of course was incompatible.

It became an impossible job. We had a president in 1940. Every requisition in the whole university had to go to his office. He spent his whole morning okaying little chits. Traditionally we thought, well, with a little tuition and dedicated Jesuits we can run these unversities on a shoe-string, which we did. It was all one. Our money was all mixed up. You had only one pocketbook. One pot. Money. We really weren't clear on the proper handling of gifts because we were so used to throwing it in the same box. Whether it was given for the Jesuits, or whether it was given for the medical school, that often got mixed up. We had to untangle all of that and get it down to make sure that the will of the donor was being observed, and we had some hassling over what the community would own and what the university would own when they were separated.

One of the first things we did [in the 1950s] was separate the consultors from the board of directors. Everything got more and more complicated.

You'd have a consultors' meeting, and then you'd have a directors' meeting. You'd be meeting, meeting, meeting. One reason was efficiency, and the other was [to resolve] a conflict because as consultors we were obliged to talk with the rector, perhaps about a problem: very difficult, personal, spiritual matters. This would get mixed up with talking about a professor and his promotion. It just was not compatible, and we realized that, and we split things up.

Compare Paul Horgan, "The Father President," in Horgan, A *Certain Climate: Essays in History, Arts, and Letters* (Middletown, Conn.: Wesleyan University Press, 1988).

33. Harvanek, "Objectives of the American Jesuit University," p. 73.
34. Ibid., emphasis in the original.
35. The terms of the debate gradually shifted toward issues of power-sharing until, in the mid-sixties, St. Louis University became the first Jesuit institution of higher learning to install a cleric-lay board of governors; see Paul C. Reinert, S.J., "First Meeting of a Board," *Jesuit Educational Quarterly* 30 (October 1967): 112–17; and Paul C. Reinert, S.J., *To Turn the Tide* (New York: Random House, 1972).
36. Harvanek, "The Changing Structure," p. 81.
37. Ibid.
38. Ibid.
39. Ibid., pp. 82–84.
40. Ibid., pp. 85–66. Harvanek was thinking of Paul Reinert and others of similar bent.
41. Ibid., p. 86.
42. The college and university presidents were unsympathetic to Harvanek's position papers. He wrote the memoranda when he was director of studies for the Chicago province at the solicitation of the Jesuit Educational Association, of which the administrators were the most powerful members. Harvanek recalled that "I wasn't so much opposed as not wanting it to happen without a conscious choice. I wanted to avoid just attrition, and so I kind of forced the issues." Interview with Robert Harvanek, May 29, 1985. See also Paul A. Fitzgerald, S.J., *The Governance of Jesuit Colleges in the United States, 1920–1970* (Notre Dame, Ind.: University of Notre Dame, 1984), p. 160f.
43. Harvanek, "The Changing Structure," pp. 86–87.
44. See Robert Hassenger, *The Shape of Catholic Higher Education* (Chicago: University of Chicago Press, 1967); and Joseph A. Tetlow, S.J., "The Jesuits' Mission in Higher Education: Perspectives and Contexts," *Studies in the Spirituality of Jesuits* 15, 16 (November 1983–January 1984).
45. See C. Edward Gilpatrick, S.J., "The Role of the Jesuit University," *Jesuit Educational Quarterly* 25 (March 1963): 210–22; and Robert Harvanek, "Comment on 'The Role of the Jesuit University,'" *Jesuit Educational Quarterly* 25 (March 1963): 223–26.
46. *Manual for Jesuit High-School Administrators*, 2nd ed., (New York: Jesuit Educational Association, 1957); and *Teaching in Jesuit High Schools* (New York: Jesuit Educational Association, 1957).

47. *Teaching in Jesuit High Schools*, p. 153. Compare Diane Ravitch, *The Troubled Crusade: American Education, 1945–1980* (New York: Basic Books, 1983).

48. *Teaching in Jesuit High Schools*, p. 1.

49. Ibid., p. 149.

50. Ibid.

51. Ibid.

52. Ibid., p. 152.

53. Reed's manuals were not classroom textbooks. At the time, there was no written material on social questions that was readily available to students. The key book in the area of ethics at the level of secondary education was by Francis B. Cassily, S.J., *Religion: Doctrine and Practice* (Chicago: Loyola University Press, 1942). The text had been in use since 1926, and it defined social ethics largely in terms of sexual morality, as the following passage (p. 7) suggests:

> The field of social contacts is a fertile one for the Catholic who is filled with the spirit of Catholic Action. Our pagan world needs the lessons of modesty and self-restraint which Catholics who know their religion and are not afraid to practice it can give. Some Catholic young men and young women, as well as those outside the Church, need to be taught that it is perfectly possible to have a good time without violating a single law of God or the Church. In fact, many Catholics by their exemplary conduct at social affairs preach the beauty of the Catholic faith as effectively as the most eloquent orator in the pulpit. If all Catholics imitated their example, the conversion of our country to the faith would be immeasurably easier.

54. *Teaching in Jesuit High Schools*, p. 151.

55. Ibid.

56. Ibid.

57. Ibid.

58. Ibid., pp. 151–52.

59. Ibid., p. 152.

60. See, for example, the writings of Thomas P. Neill, professor of history at St. Louis University, on culture and politics: *Liberalism* (Milwaukee, Wis.: Bruce, 1952); and his textbook entitled *The Common Good: Christian Democracy and American National Problems* (Garden City, N.Y.: Doubleday, 1956). Compare Wilfrid Parsons, S.J., *Which Way, Democracy?* (New York: Macmillan, 1939); and Thurbert M. Smith, S.J., "Education for Democracy," *Jesuit Educational Quarterly* 3 (March 1941): 200–6.

61. See Seymour Martin Lipset, "Working Class Authoritarianism," in Lipset, *Political Man: The Social Bases of Politics* (Garden City, N.Y.: Doubleday, 1960); and Wilfrid Sheed, *Three Mobs: Labor, Church and Mafia* (New York: Sheed & Ward, 1974).

62. This ambiguity may help to account for the null results in documenting any improvement on the average in social awareness among Jesuit students attributable to their high school experience during the fifties and sixties. See Center for Applied Research in the Apostolate, *The Alumni of 1965 Report Back*

(Washington, D.C.: Jesuit Secondary Education Association, 1974); the study was directed by Joseph Fichter. There is anecdotal evidence to suggest that a few students distinguished between the ideological atmosphere of the schools—a kind of New Deal Democratic-going-on-suburban-conservative—and the ethical earnestness of the Jesuits themselves. Joseph Califano's recollections of the postwar atmosphere at Holy Cross, a small Jesuit college that in many ways resembled a high school, capture the combination of strictness and moral concern:

Holy Cross in the late 1940s and early 1950s was decidedly conservative. . . .
If General MacArthur had run for President, he would have captured more than 90 per cent of the vote. We were all too Irish- and Italian-American middle class to be Republican, but the class of 1952 was full of those Democrats the party has long since forfeited to the G.O.P. . . . What the Jesuits did give me, and what I shall be eternally grateful for, is a moral compass with which to confront so many of today's infernally complex issues; a conscience that pricks when I gloss over the difference between right and wrong; a mental and moral process to help get to the right questions.

Joseph A. Califano, Jr., "A Jesuit Educaton Revisited," *America* 160 (May 20, 1989): 470–71.

63. *Manual for Jesuit High-School Administrators*, p. 171.

64. Ibid., p. 100.

65. Ibid., p. 18.

66. Ibid., pp. 22–23.

67. Ibid., pp. 16–17. Emphasis in the original.

68. The same textbooks for core subjects were used throughout the schools. Final exams in selected subjects, such as Greek and Latin, were standardized for high schools within a province.

69. The impact of teaching by example seems to have been a part of the high school keenly remembered by students. The following passage from the memoirs of a former health minister in the Irish Republic typifies this phenomenon:

I was most impressed of all by the fundamental principle of Jesuit life, which they made no attempt whatsoever to inculcate in us, and which was the direct antithesis to the elitist beliefs which we were encouraged by them to hold. This was the pattern of personal self-imposed discipline observed by the Jesuit fathers, the novices, and the brothers of the Society. . . . Their lives exemplified the capacity for self-discipline, the qualities of humility and self-abnegation, the impressive ability to submerge themselves "ad majorem Dei gloriam" for the welfare of the Order and the success of their life's mission. . . . The Jesuits appeared to accept honors and demotion unemotionally, without question or complaint. They showed all the discipline of their soldier founder. . . . A solitary rootless life was implicit in unexpected moves and transfers from one institution to another. There was also real poverty—pittance tobacco money, threadbare clothes, frayed cuffs. . . . We saw the bare tables within the linoleum-covered and uncurtained rooms, the breviary with a few books, the simple crucifix above the prie-dieu. They owned no personal possession; comfort was a small fire and a ration of tobacco or cigarettes.

Noël Browne, *Against the Tide* (Dublin: Gill and Macmillan, 1986), pp. 53–55.

70. *Teaching in Jesuit High Schools*, p. 103.

71. "Jug" was a common punishment. Sometimes it involved walking on the school grounds in file in elongated circles for half an hour to an hour; more intellectually inclined Jesuits mandated the memorization of poetry.

72. *Teaching in Jesuit High Schools*, p. 99.

73. Ibid., pp. 100–101. Dismissal for poor academic performance differed from "expulsion" for delinquency—for example, for chronic cheating, behavior problems, and so on. In both cases, however, the final procedure was invoked only after a number of less drastic measures had failed. Prior to expulsion, a student would probably have been assigned demerits, would have undergone "detention" (been kept after school in "jug"), would have been suspended, and would have been placed on probation. The rule was to preserve flexibility (p. 260):

These are cases for cool judgment and earnest prayer. But in spite of the danger of criticism on the score of favoritism it seems better to judge each case on its merits rather than to have a fixed and automatic penalty of expulsion for certain offenses.

Whether delinquents should be expelled dishonorably or dismissed without prejudice is another difficult question. The main criterion would seem to be the resultant of two forces—the good of the individual and the good of the group. Christian charity would seem to demand that the youth be allowed to make a fresh start, so long as his association with a new set of companions will not seriously threaten harm to them.

74. Two organizational devices were also used to insulate students from undue stress. Some schools were reputed to be academically more demanding than others, so that preselection into brainier and less intellectual environments took place. Second, at a few schools tracking experiments were established on the basis of entrance test scores, with students sorted into three areas over four years: the normal course which required Latin and a modern language; the engineering route that emphasized the natural sciences and German; and the "Super-Greek" curriculum that added Greek to the Latin and modern language requirements.

75. *Teaching in Jesuit High Schools*, p. 175.

76. Ibid.

77. Ibid., pp. 175–6.

78. Ibid., p. 172.

79. A literature text in common use during the postwar period was edited by Julian L. Maline, S.J., and Wilfred M. Mallon, S.J., *Prose and Poetry of England* (Syracuse, N.Y.: L. W. Singer, 1949). The selections were accompanied by detailed discussion questions, lists of words to define, topics for essays, and suggestions for related readings. Students were also assigned passages to memorize and quotations to identify with particular characters. See also Francis P. Donnely, S.J., *Model English* (Boston: Allyn and Bacon, various editions from 1920s through 1950s); and Francis P. Donnely, S.J. *Literary Art and Modern Education* (New York: Kenedy and Sons, 1927).

80. *Teaching in Jesuit High Schools*, p. 132.

81. A useful compilation of atmospheric pieces on (mostly) elementary and secondary schooling, including excerpts from James Joyce's fictionalized memories of his Jesuit education, is by Abraham H. Lass and Norma L. Tasman, eds., *Going to School: An Anthology of Prose about Teachers and Students* (New York: New American Library, 1980).

82. See Peter N. Stearns and Timothy Haggerty, "The Role of Fear: Transitions in American Emotional Standards for Children, 1850–1950," *American Historical Review* 96 (1991): 63–94.

83. If there was a lesson that the Jesuits failed to draw from their repertoire, it was one that they had no incentive at the time to acknowledge. A good deal of the impetus behind the success of the schools came not from permanent commitment but from turnover in personnel. The scholastics brought energy and a spirit of experimentation during their three-year stints. The benefits that this system of renovation gave the schools had long been recognized. It was a clear instance in which the maturation of individual talents—in this case, of the scholastics—contributed to corporate effectiveness. But the possibility that periodic changeovers and prolonged sabbaticals might be beneficial in a broader sense, to religious vocations in general, seemed to run counter to the prevalent ideal of lifelong vows and virtue as demonstrable endurance. The norm was still that of a sacrifice of egoism for the collective good. This constituted visible progress toward sanctity, and it was beneficial to the organization. As in a pre-industrial family, work tended to be looked upon as domestic labor, and constancy was prized over creativity.

84. *Manual for Jesuit High-School Administrators*, pp. 13–14.

85. By the 1950s, religious observances such as daily Mass were no longer obligatory in some of the metropolitan commuter high schools of the Jesuits. Such devotions were probably more common in the *collège*-type institutions of higher education like Holy Cross.

86. Inspection though not enforcement was the role of the prefect of studies in each province.

87. See John LaFarge, *The Jesuits in Modern Times* (New York: America Press, 1928), especially the chapter entitled "Laborare Est Orare."

88. See William F. Kelly, S.J., *The Jesuit Order and Higher Education in the United States, 1780–1966* (Milwaukee, Wis.: Commission for the Study of American Jesuit Higher Education, 1966); Mary Jo Maynes, *Schooling in Western Europe: A Social History* (Albany: State University of New York Press, 1985); and David Tyock and Elisabeth Hansot, *Managers of Virtue: Public School Leadership in America, 1820–1980* (New York: Basic Books, 1983).

89. The pedagogical consequences of single-sex versus mixed-sex educaton at the secondary level do not appear to be entirely symbolic. Such evidence as is available suggests that both males and females in single-sex schools do better academically than their counterparts in mixed-sex schools; see Cornelius Riordan, "Public and Catholic Schooling: The Effects of Gender Context Policy," *American Journal of Education* 93 (1985): 518–40. Compare David Tyack and Elisabeth Hansot, *Learning Together: A History of Coeducation in American Public Schools* (New Haven, Conn.: Yale Unviersity Press, 1990). See also

Gary G. Wehlage, "Dropping Out: Can Schools Be Expected to Prevent It?" in *Dropouts from School: Issues, Dilemmas, and Solutions*, ed. Lois Weiss, Eleanor Farrar, and Hugh G. Petrie (Albany: State University of New York Press, 1989).

90. See Laurence V. Britt, S.J., "Multiplication of Curricula," *Jesuit Educational Quarterly* 21 (October 1958): 94–101.

91. This sense of adventure in a confined space is captured by William J. O'Malley, S.J., *The Fifth Week* (Chicago: Loyola University Press, 1976), p. 110f.

CHAPTER 14. Harmonies and Antinomies

1. See John T. Noonan, Jr., *Contraception: A History of Its Treatment by the Catholic Theologians and Canonists*, enlarged edition (Cambridge, Mass.: Harvard University Press, 1986); compare Christine Bose, "Dual Spheres," in *Analyzing Gender: A Handbook of Social Science Research*, ed. Beth B. Hess and Myra Marx Ferree (Newbury Park, Calif.: Sage, 1987); William B. Faherty, S.J., *Living Alone: A Guide for the Single Woman* (New York: Sheed & Ward, 1964); Richard A. McCormick, S.J., *Notes on Moral Theology, 1965 Through 1980* (Lanham, Md.: University Press of America, 1981); and Rt. Rev. Msgr. Bernard O'Reilly, *Illustrious Women of Bible and Catholic Church History: Narrative Biographies of Grand Female Characters of the Old and New Testaments, and of Saintly Women of the Holy Catholic Church, Both in Earlier and Later Ages* (New York: P. J. Kenedy, 1899).

2. The flavor is transmitted by John Keating, S.J., ed., *Selected Papal Encyclicals and Letters, 1928–1932*, rev. ed. (London: Catholic Truth Society, 1933); and Rt. Rev. Msgr. Parkinson, ed., *The Pope and the People: Select Letters and Addresses on Social Questions by Pope Leo XIII*, rev. ed. (London: Catholic Truth Society, 1913).

3. See Arnold J. Heidenheimer, "Secularization Patterns and the Westward Expansion of the Welfare State, 1881–1981," paper presented at the annual meeting of the American Political Science Association, New York, September 3–6, 1981.

4. See J. Derek Holmes, *The Triumph of the Holy See: A Short History of the Papacy in the Nineteenth Century* (London: Burns and Oates, 1978); compare Béla Menczer, ed., *Catholic Political Thought, 1789–1848* (London: Burns, Oates & Washbourne, 1952); Joseph N. Moody, ed., *Church and Society: Catholic Social and Political Thought and Movements, 1789–1950* (New York: Arts, 1953); and Jean Neuvecelle, *The Vatican: Its Organization, Customs, and Way of Life* (New York: Criterion, 1955).

5. John W. Padberg, S.J., "Memory, Visions and Structure: Historical Perspectives on the Experience of Religious Life in the Church," in *Religious Life in the U.S. Church: The New Dialogue*, ed. Robert J. Daly et al. (New York: Paulist Press, 1984).

6. See for example John Demos, ed., *Past, Present, and Personal: The Family and the Life Course in American History* (New York: Oxford University Press, 1986); and Tamara K. Haraven, "The History of the Family and the Complexity of Social Change," *American Historical Review* 96 (1991): 95–124.

7. See for example Roger Lyons, S.J., *Our Place in the Christian Family: A Study of Papal Attitudes Toward Home and Family* (St. Louis, Mo.: Queen's Work, 1943).

8. See the remarkable compilation by Raymond B. Fullam, S.J., ed., *The Popes on Youth: Principles for Forming and Guiding Youth from Popes Leo XIII to Pius XII* (New York: David McKay, 1956). In practice, dress codes were directed at the control of the sexuality of girls more than boys; I am grateful to Sue Llewellyn for bringing up the importance of this difference. Compare Stephen Lassonde, "Sexuality and Religion in Anglo-American Culture," *Journal of Interdisciplinary History* 18 (1988): 471–79; and A. Norman Jeffares and Anthony Kamm, eds., *An Irish Childhood* (London: Collins, 1988).

9. See Robert C. Broderick, *The Catholic Layman's Book of Etiquette* (St. Paul, Minn.: Catechetical Guild Educational Society, 1957); and William V. Shannon, *The American Irish: A Political and Social Portrait*, 2nd ed. (Amherst: University of Massachusetts Press, 1989); compare Steven Mintz, *A Prison of Expectations: The Family in Victorian Culture* (New York: New York University Press, 1985); and F. M. L. Thompson, *The Rise of Respectable Society: A Social History of Victorian Britain, 1830–1900* (Cambridge, Mass.: Harvard University Press, 1988).

10. Compare Richard Sennett, *Families Against the City: Middle Class Homes of Industrial Chicago, 1872–1890*, 2nd ed. (Chicago: University of Chicago Press, 1984); and Alan Gowans, *The Comfortable House: North American Suburban Architecture* (Cambridge, Mass.: M.I.T. press, 1986).

11. See Terence Brown, *Ireland: A Social and Cultural History, 1922 to the Present* (Ithaca, N.Y.: Cornell University Press, 1985).

12. See, however, Sacvan Berkovitch, *The Puritan Origins of the American Self* (New Haven, Conn.: Yale University Press, 1975); Barbara Leslie Epstein, *The Politics of Domesticity: Women, Evangelism and Temperance in Nineteenth-Century America* (Middletown, Conn.: Wesleyan University Press, 1981); Jan Lewis, *The Pursuit of Happiness: Family and Values in Jefferson's Virginia* (Cambridge, England: Cambridge University Press, 1983); and Michael Zuckerman, *Peaceable Kingdoms: New England Towns in the Eighteenth Century* (New York: Random House, 1970). Compare Nicholas Canny and Anthony Pagden, eds., *Colonial Identity in the Atlantic World, 1500–1800* (Princeton, N.J.: Princeton University Press, 1987).

13. See Tamara K. Haraven, *Family Time and Industrial Time* (Cambridge: Cambridge University Press, 1982). Compare Mary P. Ryan, *Cradle of the Middle Class: The Family in Oneida County, New York, 1780–1865* (Cambridge, England: Cambridge University Press, 1981); and Desmond Bowen, *Paul Cardinal Cullen and the Shaping of Modern Irish Catholicism* (Dublin: Gill and Macmillan, 1983).

14. See Eli Zaretsky, *Capitalism, the Family, and Personal Life*, rev. ed. (New York: Harper & Row, 1986).

15. Francis Canavan, S.J., "Reflections on the Revolution in Sex," in *Amerian Catholic Horizons*, ed. Eugene K. Culhane, S.J. (Garden City, N.Y.: Doubleday, 1966), p. 12.

16. John L. Thomas, S.J., *The American Catholic Family* (Englewood Cliffs, N.J.: Prentice-Hall, 1956).

17. Interview with John Thomas, October 18, 1985.

18. Besides *The American Catholic Family*, see the textbook authored by Clement Simon Mihanovich, Gerald J. Schnepp, S.M., and John L. Thomas, S.J., *Marriage and the Family* (Milwaukee, Wis.: Bruce, 1952); and the collection edited by Ralph L. Woods, *The Catholic Concept of Love and Marriage* (Philadephia, Pa.: J. B. Lippincott, 1958).

19. See Steven F. Messner and Robert J. Sampson, "The Sex Ratio, Family Disruption, and Rates of Violent Crime: The Paradox of Demographic Structure," *Social Forces* 69 (1991): 693–713.

20. Thomas, *The American Catholic Family*, p. 28.

21. Ibid., p. 6.

22. Ibid., p. 8.

23. Compare Philip E. Converse, "The Nature of Belief Systems in Mass Publics," in *Ideology and Discontent*, ed. David E. Apter (New York: Free Press, 1964).

24. Thomas, *The American Catholic Family*, p. 297.

25. Ibid., pp. 18–19, 28.

26. Thomas had completed his Ph.D. at the University of Chicago in the 1940s; there much of the field work for his doctoral program involved interviews with union men who were mostly Catholic.

27. John L. Thomas, S.J., "A Sociologist Looks at the Future of the American Catholic Community," *Social Justice Review* 140 (September–October 1982): 142.

28. Compare Peter L. Berger, "Religion in Post-Protestant America," *Commentary* 81 (May 1986): 41–46.

29. Thomas, *The American Catholic Family*, p. 315.

30. A major effort toward systematizing the Catholic social viewpoint after the war was a textbook co-authored by Thomas, Leo Brown, and other Jesuits associated with ISO entitled *Social Orientations* (Chicago: Loyola University Press, 1954).

31. Thomas, *The American Catholic Family*, p. 239.

32. Ibid., p. 303.

33. Ibid., pp. 349–50.

34. See Philip Slater, *The Pursuit of Loneliness: American Culture at the Breaking Point* (Boston: Beacon, 1970).

35. This was very similar to the research strategy proposed by Joseph Fichter, outlined in chapter 9.

36. See, for example, Andrew M. Greeley, *Religion and Career: A Study of College Graduates* (New York: Sheed & Ward, 1963); and Joe L. Spaeth and Andrew M. Greeley, *Recent Alumni and Higher Education: A Survey of College Graduates* (New York: McGraw-Hill, 1970).

37. The crisis came in 1968, with the promulgation of the encyclical *Humanae Vitae*, condemning contraception.

38. Thomas was a pioneer in family studies, or at least a second-generation innovator, and the neglect of his work may be partially attributed to the comparative flashiness of class and later racial studies at around the time he did much of his important work. Some of Thomas's early findings—for example, regarding the

negative correlation between religiously mixed marriages and marital satisfaction—have been replicated; see Suzanne T. Ortega, Hugh P. Whitt, and J. Allen William, Jr., "Religious Homogamy and Marital Happiness," *Journal of Family Issues* 9 (1988): 224–329. The scope of this line of research is microstructural, stressing the quality of life of individuals within the family unit. It does not consider the question of the possible effects of degrees of endogamy and exogamy on societal and political stability.

39. Thomas, *The American Catholic Family*, p. 174. See also William A. Lynch, *A Marriage Manual for Catholics* (New York: Trident Press, 1964).

40. Thomas, *The American Catholic Family*, p. 387.

41. Ibid., p. 126.

42. See Daniel A. Lord, S.J., *The Sacrament of Catholic Action* (St. Louis, Mo.: Queen's Work, 1936); and the address by Robert Dwyer, bishop of Reno, *History of Catholic Action in the United States* (Washington, D.C.: National Council of Catholic Men, 1954).

43. Not all of Thomas's work during this period was ideological or polemical; he produced an empirical report on the state of organized religion, including ecumenical relations. See John L. Thomas, S.J., *Religion and the American People* (Westminster, Md: Newman Press, 1963).

44. *Social Order* 13 (January 1963): 24.

45. John L. Thomas, "Sex and Society," *Social Order* 4 (June 1954): 242.

46. See Michael Goldfield, *The Decline of Organized Labor in the United States* (Chicago: University of Chicago Press, 1987); compare Lawrence Birken, *Consuming Desire: Sexual Science and the Emergence of a Culture of Abundance* (Ithaca, N.Y.: Cornell University Press, 1988).

47. Walter J. Ong, S.J., *Ramus, Method, and the Decay of Dialogue* (Cambridge, Mass.: Harvard University Press, 1958). See also Jeanette Batz, "The Many Words of Walter Ong," *Universitas* (Fall 1988): 22–27; Randolph F. Lumpp, "Walter Jackson Ong, S.J.: A Biographical Portrait," *Oral Tradition* 2 (January 1987): 13–18; Elizabeth L. Eisenstein, *The Printing Press as Agent of Change* (Cambridge, England: Cambridge University Press, 1979); and Oswyn Murray, "The Word Is Mightier Than the Pen," *Times Literary Supplement* (June 16–22, 1989): 655–56.

48. See Walter J. Ong, *Frontiers in American Catholicism: Essays on Ideology and Culture* (New York: Macmillan, 1957); and his *American Catholic Crossroads: Religious-Secular Encounters in the Modern World* (New York: Macmillan, 1959); Robert D. Cross, *The Emergence of Liberal Catholicism in America* (Cambridge, Mass.: Harvard University Press, 1958); and "Transition in Catholic Culture: The Fifties," special issue, *U.S. Catholic Historian* 7 (Winter 1988).

49. See Walter J. Ong, "I Remember Père Teilhard," *Jesuit Bulletin* (Missouri Province) 46 (February 1967): 6–7, 17–18; Christopher F. Mooney, S.J., *Teilhard de Chardin and the Mystery of Christ* (New York: Harper & Row, 1965); and Donald P. Gray, "The Phenomenon of Teilhard," *Theological Studies* 36 (March 1975): 19–51. Compare Joscelyn Godwin, *Athanasius Kircher: A Renaissance Man and the Quest for Lost Knowledge* (London: Thames & Hudson, 1979).

50. For gestures in this direction, see Walter J. Ong, "An Apostolate of the Business World," in *Frontiers in American Catholicism*, and "The Religious-Secular Dialogue," in *Religion in America*, ed. John Cogley (Cleveland: Meridian Books, 1958).

51. Compare Richard Merelman, "On Culture and Politics in America: A Perspective from Structural Anthropology," *British Journal of Political Science* 19 (1989): 465–93. Although there is no evidence that the two were ever in contact, the attention that Ong pays to quotidian politics is paralleled by the excursions in cultural anthropology of the former Jesuit Michel de Certeau, *The Practice of Everyday Life* (Berkeley: University of California Press, 1984).

52. See Walter J. Ong, "The Renaissance Myth and the American Catholic Mind," in *Frontiers in American Catholicism*.

53. This path resembles the one followed by Marshall McLuhan, with some major differences. McLuhan began his career as a literary critic with a strong sympathy for Catholic medievalism and a deep allegiance to the Southern Agrarians. See Christopher Brookeman, *American Culture and Society Since the 1930s* (New York: Schocken, 1984); and Eugene McNamara, ed., *The Interior Landscape: The Literary Criticism of Marshall McLuhan* (New York: McGraw-Hill, 1969). By contrast, Ong from the outset made clear his dissatisfaction with the romanticization of preindustrial times. For a critique of McLuhan that stresses the agrarian connection, see chapter 6 in Daniel J. Czitrom, *Media and the American Mind: From Morse to McLuhan* (Chapel Hill: University of North Carolina Press, 1982); see also Karen Wright, "The Road to the Global Village," *Scientific American* 262 (March 1990): 83–94.

54. Ong summarizes his approach in *Interfaces of the World: Studies in the Evolution of Consciousness and Culture* (Ithaca, N.Y.: Cornell University Press, 1977), pp. 9–11:

The works do not maintain that the evolution from primary orality through writing and print to an electronic culture, which produces secondary orality, causes or explains everything in human culture and consciousness. Rather, the thesis is relationist: major developments, and very likely even all major developments, in culture and consciousness are related, often in unexpected intimacy, to the evolution of the word from primary orality to its present state. But the relationships are varied and complex, with cause and effect often difficult to distinguish. . . . From the time of my studies of Peter Ramus and Ramism, my work has grown into its own kind of phenomenological history of culture and consciousness, so I have been assured by others, elaborated in terms of noetic operations as these interrelate with primary oral verbalization and later with chirographic and typographic and electronic technologies that reorganize verbalization and thought.

55. See the correspondence with Ong in Matie Molinaro, Corinne McLuhan, and William Toye, eds., *Letters of Marshall McLuhan* (Toronto: Oxford University Press, 1987); Walter J. Ong, "The Mechanical Bride," *Social Order* 5 (February 1952): 79–85; and Walter J. Ong, *Orality and Literacy: The Technologizing of the Word* (London: Methuen, 1982). Ong gives an appreciation of McLuhan's significance in "McLuhan as Teacher: The Future Is a Thing of the Past," *Journal of Communication* 31 (Summer 1981): 129–35.

56. Compare Ann Swidler, "Culture in Action: Symbols and Strategies," *American Sociological Review* 51 (1986): 273–86. The last sentence is quoted from "Literate Orality of Popular Culture," in Walter J. Ong, *Rhetoric, Romance, and Technology: Studies in the Interaction of Expression and Culture* (Ithaca, N.Y.: Cornell University Press, 1971), pp. 284–303.

57. Ong, "Latin Language Study as a Renaissance Puberty Rite," in Ong, *Rhetoric, Romance, and Technology*, pp. 113–41. See also Elene Kolb, "When Women Finally Got the Word," *New York Times Book Review* (July 9, 1989): 1, 28–29.

58. Ong, "Latin Language Study," p. 129.

59. Compare Philippe Ariès and André Béjin, eds., *Western Sexuality: Practice and Precept in Past and Present* (Oxford: Basil Blackwell, 1988); Dennis Baron, *Grammar and Gender* (New Haven, Conn.: Yale University Press, 1986); Mark C. Carnes, *Secret Ritual and Manhood in Victorian America* (New Haven: Conn.: Yale University Press, 1989); Jack Goody, *The Interface Between the Written and the Oral* (Cambridge, England: Cambridge University Press, 1987); Harvey J. Graff, ed., *Literacy and Social Development in the West* (Cambridge, England: Cambridge University Press, 1981); Johan Huizinga, *Homo Ludens: A Study of the Play Element in Culture* (Boston: Beacon, 1955); and George A. Kennedy, *Classical Rhetoric and its Christian and Secular Tradition from Ancient to Modern Times* (Chapel Hill: University of North Carolina Press, 1980).

60. Ong, "Latin Language," pp. 104–41. Compare Ray Raphael, *The Men From the Boys: Rites of Passage in Male America* (Lincoln: University of Nebraska Press, 1988).

61. Walter J. Ong, *Fighting for Life* (Ithaca, N.Y.: Cornell University Press, 1981), pp. 169–70.

62. Compare George L. Mosse, *Nationalism and Sexuality: Middle Class Morality and Sexual Norms in Modern Europe* (Madison: University of Wisconsin Press, 1985).

63. Ong, *Fighting for Life*, pp. 137–39.

64. Ibid., p. 167. See also Avery Dulles, S.J., *Models of the Church* (Garden City, N.Y.: Doubleday, 1974).

65. Ong, *Fighting for Life*, p. 171.

66. Ibid., p. 178. Compare Robyn L. Muncy, *Creating a Female Dominion in American Reform, 1890–1930* (New York: Oxford University Press, 1991).

67. It is significant that in speculating on the indeterminacy of postconciliar Catholicism, Ong has recourse to both agonistic and conciliatory imagery:

> Of course, you can make and make statements that are true, but they are never in every way complete. Someone can always ask another question. But, in real life, asking another question may *not* be the thing to do because it may, here and now, only confuse the real issues—which are never purely intellectual.

Ong, personal communication, September 8, 1988.

68. Compare Lauro Martines, *Power and Imagination: City States in Renaissance Italy* (New York: Alfred A. Knopf, 1979), p. 306, passim.

69. See E. K. Francis, "Toward a Typology of Religious Orders," *American Journal of Sociology* 60 (1950): 437–49; and Raymond Hostie, S.J., *The Life and Death of Religious Orders* (Washington, D.C.: Center for Applied Research in the Apostolate, 1983).

INTERMISSION

1. See John A. Coleman, S.J., "A Company of Critics: Jesuits and the Intellectual Life," *Studies in the Spirituality of Jesuits* 22 (November 1990).

2. Compare the use of "ethos" as a guide and motive to action by Samuel L. Popkin, "Political Entrepreneurs and Peasant Movements in Vietnam," in *Rationality and Revolution*, ed. Michael Taylor (Cambridge, England: Cambridge University Press, 1988).

3. Compare Gilbert Sorrentino, "Hubert Selby," in Sorrentino, *Something Said* (San Francisco, Calif.: North Point, 1984), p. 114, passim.

4. Edmund G. Ryan, S.J., "An Academic History of Woodstock College in Maryland, 1869–1944: The First Jesuit Seminary in North America," Ph.D. dissertation, Catholic University of America, 1964, p. 235.

5. See the curious study by J. Solterer, "A Sequence of Historical Random Events: Do Jesuits Die in Threes?" *Journal of the American Statistical Association* 36 (1941): 477–81. Compare Hanna Fenichel Pitkin, *Fortune Is a Woman: Gender and Politics in the Thought of Niccolò Machiavelli* (Berkeley: University of California Press, 1984); and Philip Herring, *Joyce's Uncertainty Principle* (Princeton, N.J.: Princeton University Press, 1989).

6. See Robert F. Harvanek, S.J., "The Status of Obedience in the Society of Jesus," *Studies in the Spirituality of Jesuits* 10 (September 1978).

7. Compare John L. Stanley, *The Sociology of Virtue: The Political and Social Theories of Georges Sorel* (Berkeley: University of California Press, 1981).

8. In a limerick written in the 1930s to commemorate a birthday of James Joyce, Samuel Beckett refered to Ireland as "the hemorrhoidal isle"—a phrase that does poetic justice to the point. Compare Desmond Keenan, ed., *The Catholic Church in Nineteenth-Century Ireland* (Dublin: Gill and Macmillan, 1983); and Alfred O'Rahilly, ed., *A Year's Thoughts Collected from the Writings of Fr. William Doyle* (London: Longmans, Green, 1936).

9. See William Birmingham and Joseph E. Cuneen, eds., *Cross Currents of Psychiatry and Catholic Morality* (Cleveland, O.: Meridian, 1966); and Karl Stern, *The Third Revolution: A Study of Psychiatry and Religion* (New York: Harcourt, Brace, 1954).

10. ISO was in effect replaced by the Center of Concern in the 1970s. The Center, headquartered in Washington, was not officially a "work" of the Society of Jesus and did not draw its funding from it, although many of its leading figures were Jesuits. Interview with William F. Ryan, S.J., Ottawa, Canada, December 2, 1987. Father Ryan was the first director of the Center of Concern.

11. See Charles A. Gallagher, S.J., "State of Life or Career," *Jesuit Educational Quarterly* 21 (June 1958): 54–58.

12. Compare Eliot Friedson, *Professional Powers: A Study of the Institutionalization of Formal Knowledge* (Chicago: University of Chicago Press, 1987); and

Marshall W. Meyer, "The Growth of Public and Private Organizations," *Theory and Society* 16 (1987): 217–35.

13. Compare Morris Dickstein, *Gates of Eden: American Culture in the Sixties* (London: Penguin, 1989); Richard Gilman, *Faith, Sex, Mystery: A Memoire* (New York: Simon & Schuster, 1986); Michael Harrington, *The Politics at God's Funeral: The Spiritual Crisis of Western Civilization* (New York: Holt, Rinehart and Winston, 1983); and John L'Heureux, *Picnic in Babylon: A Jesuit Priest's Journal, 1963–66* (New York: Macmillan, 1967).

14. The phrase is from the interpretation of heroes in the novels and short stories of Hemingway by John W. Aldridge, *After the Lost Generation: A Critical Study of the Writers of Two Wars* (New York: Noonday, 1958), p. 41.

15. Quoted by Mary Lukas and Ellen Lukas, *Teilhard: The Man, the Priest, the Scientist* (Garden City, N.Y.: Doubleday, 1977), p. 323. Compare Charles Lloyd Cohen, *God's Caress: The Psychology of Puritan Religious Experience* (New York: Oxford University Press, 1986); and Martin D'Arcy, S.J., *The Mind and the Heart of Love: Lion and Unicorn, A Study in Eros and Agape* (New York: Henry Holt, 1956).

16. John W. Padberg, S.J., "Jesuit Higher Education: Too Abstract?" *National Jesuit News* (December 1983): 7. See also James M. Hayes, S.J., John W. Padberg, S.J., and John M. Staudenmaier, S.J., "Symbols, Devotions and Jesuits," *Studies in the Spirituality of Jesuits* 20 (May 1988).

17. See Carl R. Rogers, *On Becoming a Person: A Therapist's View of Psychotherapy* (Boston: Houghton Mifflin, 1961); and Abraham H. Maslow, *The Farther Reaches of Human Nature* (New York: Viking, 1971).

18. See William A. Barry, S.J., "Jesuit Formation Today: An Invitation to Dialogue and Involvement," *Studies in the Spirituality of Jesuits* 20 (November 1988); George B. Wilson, S.J., "Where Do We Belong? United States Jesuits and Their Memberships," *Studies in the Spirituality of Jesuits* 21 (January 1989); and Joseph A. Tetlow, S.J., "Homosexuality and Chaste Celibacy," *The Way*, supplement on "Religious Life in Transition," 65 (1989): 104–8.

19. Compare J. Craig Jenkins, "Radical Transformation of Organizational Goals," *Administrative Science Quarterly* 22 (1977): 568–86.

20. Compare Frances L. Restuccia, *Joyce and the Law of the Father* (New Haven, Conn.: Yale University Press, 1989); Kevin Sullivan, *Joyce among the Jesuits* (New York: Columbia University Press, 1958); and Bruce Bradley, S.J., "James Joyce: Embarrassment?" *Interfuse* [house organ of Irish province] (June 1982): 59–67.

21. See Ann Douglas, *The Feminization of American Culture* (New York: Alfred A. Knopf, 1977); and Elliott J. Gorn, *The Manly Art: Bare-Knuckle Prize Fighting in America* (Ithaca, N.Y.: Cornell University Press, 1986); compare Joseph Allen Boone, *Tradition Counter Tradition: Love and the Form of Fiction* (Chicago: University of Chicago Press, 1987); Karen Lystra, *Searching the Heart: Women, Men, and Romantic Love in Nineteenth-Century America* (New York: Oxford University Press, 1989); Margaret Marsh, "Suburban Men and Masculine Domesticity, 1870–1915," *American Quarterly* 40 (1988): 165–86; Janice Radway, *Reading the Romance: Women, Patriarchy, and Popular Literature* (Chapel Hill: University of North Carolina Press, 1984); H. Mark

Roelofs, "Huckleberry Finn: Paradigm of the American Male," paper presented at the annual meeting of the American Political Science Association, San Francisco, August 29–September 2, 1990; Steven M. Stowe, *Intimacy and Power in the Old South: Ritual in the Lives of the Planters* (Baltimore, Md.: Johns Hopkins University Press); and William R. Taylor, *Cavalier and Yankee: The Old South and American National Character* (Cambridge, Mass.: Harvard University Press, 1979).

22. The phrase is by Joseph Husslein, S.J., in his preface to *Wings of Eagles: The Jesuit Saints and Blessed*, ed. Francis J. Corley, S.J., and Robert J. Willmes, S.J. (Milwaukee, Wis.: Bruce, 1941), p. ix. Compare J. A. Mangan and James Walvin, *Manliness and Morality: Middle-Class Masculinity in Britain and America, 1880–1940* (New York: St. Martin's Press, 1987); and Ted Ownby, *Subduing Satan: Religion, Recreation, and Manhood in the Rural South: 1865–1920* (Chapel Hill: University of North Carolina Press, 1990).

23. Compare the chapter entitled "The Lonely Politics of Michel Foucault" by Michael Walzer, *The Company of Critics: Social Criticism and Political Commitment in the Twentieth Century* (New York: Basic Books, 1988).

24. The phrase, from the document known as "Deliberation of the First Fathers" who met in Rome in 1539, is quoted by Joseph Veale, S.J., "How the Constitutions Work," *The Way* 61 (1988): 3–20. See also John W. O'Malley, S.J., "The Jesuits, St. Ignatius, and the Counter Reformation: Some Recent Studies and Their Implications for Today," *Studies in the Spirituality of Jesuits* 14 (January 1982).

25. Compare Jean Delumeau (trans. Eric Nicholson), *Sin and Fear: The Emergence of a Western Guilt Culture, 13th–18th Centuries* (New York: St. Martin's, 1990); and Reinhard Kuhn, *The Demon of Noontide: Ennui in Western Literature* (Princeton, N.J.: Princeton University Press, 1976). See also J. C. W. Blanning, "The Role of Religion in European Counter-Revolution, 1789–1815," in *History, Society and the Churches: Essays in Honor of Owen Chadwick*, ed. Daniel Beales and George Best (Cambridge, England: Cambridge University Press, 1985); and Bernard M. G. Reardon, ed., *Religion in the Age of Romanticism: Studies in Early Nineteenth Century Thought* (Cambridge, England: Cambridge University Press, 1985).

26. "Brilliancy does not suit us." G. M. Hopkins, S.J., to R. W. Dixon, December 1, 1881, in John Pick, ed., *A Hopkins Reader*, revised and enlarged edition (Garden City, N.Y.: Doubleday, 1966), p. 387. For a judicious discussion of the tradeoffs between individual discretion and the rationality of forms of organizational control, see Alfred Stinchcombe, *Information and Organizations* (Berkeley: University of California Press, 1990), especially p. 345: "The standard operating procedure of the various parts of the organization . . . is not only a system for taking discretion away from smart individuals who might have guessed better in a particular situation; it is also a system for collecting information so that the ordinary people who are likely to be at the point of decision at the crucial time are moderately likely to take the right decision."

27. See the discussion of male caring in Francesca M. Cancian, *Love in America: Gender and Self-Development* (Cambridge, England: Cambridge University Press, 1987).

28. See, inter alia, Joan H. Timmerman, "Sexuality and Social Justice: The State of the Question," *The Way* 28 (1988): 206–21.

29. Compare R. Bruce Douglass, ed., *The Deeper Meaning of Economic Life: Critical Essays on the U.S. Catholic Bishops' Pastoral Letter on the Economy* (Washington, D.C.: Georgetown University Press, 1987); Judith A. Dwyer, S.S.J., ed., *"Questions of Special Urgency": The Church in the Modern World Two Decades After Vatican II* (Washington, D.C.: Georgetown University Press, 1986); Thomas M. Gannon, S.J., ed., *The Catholic Challenge to the American Economy* (New York: Macmillan, 1987); and Eugene C. Kennedy, *Tomorrow's Catholics, Yesterday's Church* (San Francisco: Harper & Row, 1988).

30. Compare Patricia Gurin, "Women's Gender Consciousness," *Public Opinion Quarterly* 49 (1985): 143–63; Andrew Kimbrell, "A Time for Men to Pull Together," *Utne Reader* 45 (May–June 1991): 66–74; and Hugo Rahner, S.J., ed., *Saint Ignatius Loyola: Letters to Women* (New York: Herder and Herder, 1960).

31. See, inter alia, George N. Schuster et al., *Catholicism in America: A Series of Articles from The Commonweal* (New York: Harcourt, Brace, 1954). Compare Patrick W. Carey, *People, Priests, and Prelates: Ecclesiastical Democracy and the Tensions of Trusteeism* (Notre Dame, Ind.: University of Notre Dame Press, 1987).

32. See John Seidler and Katherine Meyer, *Conflict and Change in the Catholic Church* (New Brunswick, N.J.: Rutgers University Press, 1989); for the English experience, see Michael Hornsby-Smith, *Roman Catholic Beliefs: Customary Catholicism and Transformation of Religious Authority* (Cambridge, England: Cambridge University Press, 1991). Here, as throughout the book, the Second Vatican Council is treated as one among several causes of the transformation of the Jesuits. The objective is not to "explain" the origins of the council itself.

33. For varying perspectives see Gerald A. Arbuckle, S.M., "Refounding Congregations From Within: Anthropological Reflections," *Review for Religious* 46 (1986): 538–53; Helen Rose Fuchs Ebaugh, *Out of the Cloister: A Study of Organizational Dilemmas* (Austin: University of Texas Press, 1977); Paul Hendrickson, *Seminary: A Search* (New York: Summit, 1983); Dean R. Hoge, Joseph J. Shields, and Mary Jeanne Verdieck," "Changing Age Distribution and Theological Attitudes of Catholic Priests, 1970–1985," *Sociological Analysis* 49 (1988): 264–80; Courtney Leatherman, "With Fewer Priests and Nuns, Colleges Agonize Over Hiring Lay Presidents," *Chronicle of Higher Education* (January 16, 1991), A15–17; John W. Padberg, S.J., "The Jesuit Question," *The Tablet* [London] (September 22, 1990): 1189–91; John W. Padberg, S.J., "The Society of Jesus Is Not Quiet," *America* 163 (September 29, 1990); Sandra M. Schneiders, *New Wineskins: Re-imagining Religious Life Today* (New York: Paulist Press, 1986); David Toolan, S.J., *Facing West From California's Shores: A Jesuit's Journey into New Age Consciousness* (New York: Crossroad, 1987); Paul Wilkes, "The Hands That Would Shape Our Souls," *The Atlantic* 266 (December 1990): 59–88, and *Why We Are Jesuits: The Upcoming Generation* (Rome: Centrum Ignatianum Spiritualitatis, 1980). Cutting the period of research off in the 1960s—with the exception of a few spillovers toward recent times (as in the consideration of some of the later

writings of William Lynch and Walter Ong)—places examination of these aftermath issues outside the scope of the present study. This may have the effect of accentuating departures from the Society of Jesus and of downplaying the numbers that remained. It is as if a dependent variable—in this case, numerical increase/decrease—were truncated so that only part of its range was visible. The impression is hard to avoid, since the variable moves over time.

34. See Jeffrey C. Alexander and Steven Seidman, eds., *Culture and Society: Contemporary Debates* (Cambridge, England: Cambridge University Press, 1990); Niklas Luhmann, *Love as Passion: The Codification of Intimacy* (Cambridge, Mass.: Harvard University Press, 1986); Thomas Scheff, *Microsociology: Discourse, Emotions, and Social Structure* (Chicago: University of Chicago Press, 1990); Michael Schudson, "How Culture Works," *Theory and Society* 18 (1989): 153–80; Gwendolyn Wright, *Moralism and the Model Home: Domestic Architecture and Cultural Conflict in Chicago, 1873–1913* (Chicago: University of Chicago Press, 1980); and Kenneth Gergen, *The Saturated Self: Dilemmas of Identity in Contemporary Life* (New York: Basic Books, 1991).

35. John Szarkowski, *Photography Until Now* (New York: Museum of Modern Art, 1989): 17–18.

36. See Miquel Battlori, S.J., *Cultura e Finanze: Studi sulla Storia dei Gesuiti da S. Ignazio al Vatican II* (Rome: Edizione di Storia e Letteratura, 1983); D. G. Thompson, "French Jesuit Wealth on the Eve on the Eighteenth-Century Suppression," and Thomas M. McCoog, S.J., " 'Laid Up Treasure'; The Finances of English Jesuits in the Seventeenth Century," both in *The Church and Wealth: Studies in Church History*, ed. W. J. Sheils and Diana Wood (Oxford: Basil Blackwell, 1987). Compare Roland Barthes, *Sade Fourier Loyola* (New York: Farrar, Straus & Giroux, 1976); and John A. Hall, *Powers and Liberties: The Causes and Consequences of The Rise of the West* (Berkeley: University of California Press, 1986).

37. Compare Jacob Viner, *Religious Thought and Economic Society* (Durham, N.C.: Duke University Press, 1978); Raymond Grew and Patrick J. Harrigan, "The Catholic Contribution to Universal Schooling in France, 1850–1906," *Journal of Modern History* 57 (1985): 211–47; and Keith Thomas, *Religion and the Decline of Magic* (New York: Charles Scribner's Sons, 1971).

38. Compare Stuart M. Blumin, *The Emergence of the Middle Class: Social Experience in the American City, 1760–1900* (Cambridge, England: Cambridge University Press, 1989); Stephen Skowronek, *Building an American State: The Expansion of National Administrative Capacities* (Cambridge, England: Cambridge University Press, 1982); Martin J. Sklar, *The Corporate Reconstruction of American Capitalism, 1890–1916* (Cambridge, England: Cambridge University Press, 1988); and John W. Donohue, S.J., *Work and Education: The Role of Technical Culture in Some Distinctive Theories of Humanism* (Chicago: Loyola University Press, 1959).

39. Compare R. Emmett Curran, S.J., "Confronting 'The Social Question': American Catholic Thought and the Socio-Economic Order in the Nineteenth Century," *U.S. Catholic Historian* 5 (1986): 165–93; Robert Bruce Mullin, *Episcopal Vision/American Reality: High Church Theology and Social Thought in Evangelical America* (New Haven, Conn.: Yale University Press, 1986);

Melvyn Stokes, "American Liberalism and the Neo-Consensus School," *Journal of American Studies* 20 (1986): 449–60; and George M. Thomas, *Revivalism and Cultural Change: Christianity, Nation Building and the Market in the Nineteenth-Century United States* (Chicago: University of Chicago Press, 1989). See also Francis X. Curran, S.J., *Major Trends in American Church History* (New York: America Press, 1946); and Albert J. Nevins, M.M., *Our American Catholic Heritage* (Huntington, Ind.: Our Sunday Visitor, 1972).

40. See Norval D. Glenn, "The Trend in 'No Religion' Respondents to U.S. National Surveys, Late 1950s to Early 1980s," *Public Opinion Quarterly* 51 (1987): 293–314; Philip K. Hastings and Dean R. Hoge, "Religious and Moral Attitude Trends Among College Students, 1948–84," *Social Forces* 65 (1986): 370–77; Francis J. Sweeney, S.J., ed., *The Knowledge Explosion: Liberation and Limitation* (New York: Farrar, Straus and Giroux, 1966); and Edward Wakin, *The Catholic Campus* (New York: Macmillan, 1963).

41. Compare Christopher Lasch, *The True and Only Heaven: Progress and Its Critics* (New York: W. W. Norton, 1991); Ray Oldenburg, *The Great Good Place* (New York: Paragon House, 1990); Allan Silver, "The Curious Importance of Small Groups in American Sociology," in *Sociology in America*, ed. Herbert S. Gans (Newbury Park, Calif.: Sage, 1990); and Michael Walzer, "The Communitarian Critique of Liberalism," *Political Theory* 18 (February 1990): 6–23.

42. See Edward A. Goerner, "The Future of American Catholicism and the End of the Natural Order," unpublished ms., University of Notre Dame, 1984; R. B. Kershner, *Joyce, Bakhtin, and Popular Culture: Chronicles of Disorder* (Chapel Hill: University of North Carolina Press, 1989); and Raymond A. Schroth, S.J., et al., eds., *Jesuit Spirit in a Time of Change* (Westminster, Md.: Newman Press, 1968).

43. Compare Olaf Hansen, *Aesthetic Individualism and Practical Intellect: American Allegory in Emerson, Thoreau, Adams, and James* (Princeton, N.J.: Princeton University Press, 1990); John Higham and Paul K. Conkin, eds., *New Directions in American Intellectual History* (Baltimore, Md.: Johns Hopkins University Press, 1979); Hugh Kenner, *A Homemade World: The American Modernist Writers* (New York: William Morrow, 1975); Henry F. May, *The Enlightenment in America* (New York: Oxford University Press, 1976); and Edward S. Morgan, *Inventing the People: The Rise of Popular Sovereignty in England and America* (Boston: W. W. Norton, 1988).

44. Compare James Gilbert, *Designing the Industrial State: The Intellectual Pursuit of Collectivism in America, 1880–1940* (Chicago: Quadrangle, 1972); and Cecelia Tichi, *Shifting Gears: Technology, Literature, Culture in Modernist America* (Chapel Hill: University of North Carolina Press, 1987). For a rare contemporary eclogue that captures the feel of "the immigrant bucolic," see the cameo of Brooklyn set in contrast to Manhattan, entitled "Southeast of the Island: Travel Notes," in *The Collected Short Prose of James Agee*, ed. Robert Fitzgerald (New York: Ballantine, 1970). See also Barry Jacobs, "Sentimental Journey: Brooklyn After the Dodgers," *New York Affairs* 7 (1983): 139–48; Kate Simon, *Bronx Primitive: Portraits in a Childhood* (New York: Viking, 1982); Thomas Kessner, *Fiorello La Guardia and the Making of Modern New York* (New York: McGraw-Hill, 1989); Norval White, *New York: A Physical History*

(New York: Atheneum, 1987); Bernard J. Coughlin, S.J., *Church and State in Social Welfare* (New York: Columbia University Press, 1965); Richard Guy Wilson et al., *The Machine Age in America, 1918–1941* (New York: Abrams, 1986); and William F. Drummond, S.J., *Social Justice* (Milwaukee, Wis.: Bruce, 1955).

45. See Robert A. Dahl, *Democracy and its Critics* (New Haven, Conn.: Yale University Press); and Hugh McLeod, "Building the 'Catholic Ghetto': Catholic Organizations, 1870–1914," in *Voluntary Religion: Studies in Church History*, ed. W. J. Sheils and Diana Wood (Oxford: Basil Blackwell, 1986). Compare Richard L. Bushman, *From Puritan to Yankee: Character and the Social Order in Connecticut, 1690–1765* (Cambridge, Mass.: Harvard University Press, 1967); Thomas L. Dumm, *Democracy and Punishment: Disciplinary Origins of the United States* (Milwaukee: University of Wisconsin Press, 1987); Paul A. Carver, *Another Part of the Fifties* (New York: Columbia University Press, 1983); Marty Jezy, *The Dark Ages: Life in the United States, 1945–1960* (Boston: South End Press, 1982); and William J. Grace, S.J., *The Catholic Church and You: What the Church Teaches and Why* (Milwaukee, Wis.: Bruce, 1955).

46. See Richard King, *The Party of Eros: Radical Social Thought and the Realm of Freedom* (Chapel Hill: Univeristy of North Carolina Press, 1972); and David O. Moberg and Dean R. Hoge, "Catholic College Students' Religious and Moral Attitudes, 1961 to 1982: Effects of the Sixties and Seventies," *Review of Religious Research* 28 (1986): 104–16; compare Stanley Coben, *Rebellion Against Victorianism: The Impetus for Cultural Change in 1920s America* (New York: Oxford University Press, 1991).

47. Compare Jacquelyn Dowd Hall et al., *Like a Family: The Making of a Southern Mill Town* (Chapel Hill: University of North Carolina Press, 1987); Joshua Meyrowitz, *No Sense of Place: The Impact of Electronic Media on Social Behavior* (New York: Oxford University Press, 1985); Rita Seiden Miller, ed., *Brooklyn USA: The Fourth Largest City in America* (New York: Columbia University Press, 1979); and Stanley Wenocur and Michael Reisch, *From Charity to Enterprise: The Development of American Social Work in a Market Economy* (Urbana: University of Illinois Press, 1989).

48. See Duane F. Alwin, "Religion and Parental Child-Rearing Orientations: Evidence of a Catholic-Protestant Convergence," *American Journal of Sociology* 92 (1986): 412–40; compare Anthony Copley, *Sexual Moralities in France, 1780–1980: New Ideas on the Family, Divorce, and Homosexuality* (London: Routledge, 1989); and Walter J. Fraser, Jr., R. Frank Saunders, Jr., and Jon L. Wakelyn, eds., *The Web of Southern Social Relations: Women, Family, and Education* (Athens: University of Georgia Press, 1985).

49. See William V. D'Antonio, "The American Catholic Family: Signs of Cohesion and Polarization," *Journal of Marriage and the Family* 48 (1985): 395–405; compare Sherry B. Ortner and Harriet Whitehead, eds., *Sexual Meanings: The Cultural Construction of Gender and Sexuality* (Cambridge, England: Cambridge University Press, 1981).

50. See Richard D. Alba, "The Twilight of Ethnicity among American Catholics of European Ancestry," *Annals of the American Academy of Political and Social Sciences* 453 (1981): 86–97; and Robert E. Sullivan and James M.

O'Toole, eds., *Catholic Boston: Studies in Religion and Community, 1870–1970* (Boston: Archdiocese of Boston, 1985). Compare Ronald Tobey, Charles Wetherell, and Jay Brigham, "Moving Out and Settling In: Residential Mobility, Home Ownership, and the Public Enframing of Citizenship, 1921–1950," *American Historical Review* 95 (1990): 1395–1422; and Virginia Scharff, "The Ghosts of Suburbia," *New York Times*, May 24, 1991, C19.

51. Daniel Berrigan, "Lew Cox Dies," *National Jesuit News* (February 1987): 16.

52. See J. G. Peristiany, ed., *Honor and Shame: The Values of Mediterranean Society* (London: Weidenfeld & Nicolson, 1965); and Jill Dubisch, ed., *Gender and Power in Rural Greece* (Princeton, N.J.: Princeton University Press, 1986); compare Jan Wojcik, "About Men: A Going-Away Present," *New York Times Magazine* (June 23, 1985): 52.

53. See, however, Thomas Albert Kselman and Steven Avella, "Marian Piety and the Cold War in the U.S.," *Catholic Historical Review* 72 (1986): 403–24. Compare Andrew Walder, *Communist Neo-Traditionalism: Work and Authority in Industry* (Berkeley: University of California Press, 1986); and Desmond Bowen, *Paul Cardinal Cullen and the Shaping of Modern Irish Catholicism* (Dublin: Gill and Macmillan, 1983).

54. See Gerald A. McCoot, S.J., "Twentieth-Century Scholasticism," *Journal of Religion* 58 (1978): 198–221.

55. See Richard A. Schoenherr and Andrew M. Greeley, "Role Commitment Processes and the American Catholic Priesthood," *American Sociological Review* 29 (1974): 407–26; and Raymond A. Schroth, S.J., "The Trouble With the Younger Men: A View From the Bridge," *Woodstock Letters* 94 (Winter 1965): 45–54. Compare David Wyatt, *Prodigal Sons: A Study in Authorship and Authority* (Baltimore, Md.: Johns Hopkins University Press, 1980).

56. See Christa R. Klein, "Jesuits and Boyhood in Victorian New York," *U.S. Catholic Historian* 7 (1988): 375–88; compare David I. MacLeod, *Building Character in the American Boy: The Boy Scouts, YMCA, and Their Forerunners, 1870–1920* (Madison: University of Wisconsin Press, 1983). See also Walter J. Burghardt, S.J., "Homer on Park Avenue," *Woodstock Letters* 68 (June 1939): 114–37; and Michael Rosenthal, *The Character Factory: Baden Powell's Boy Scouts and the Imperatives of Empire* (New York: Pantheon, 1986).

57. See Frank L. Christ and Gerald E. Sherry, eds., *American Catholicism and the Intellectual Ideal* (New York: Appleton-Century-Crofts, 1961). Compare H. Stuart Hughes, *The Sea Change: The Migration of Social Thought, 1930–1965* (New York: McGraw-Hill, 1975).

58. It is important not to reduce the turmoil of the sixties, in which the Jesuits were caught up, to a singular effect of the postwar baby boom or to conclude that the "youth revolution" is a permanent fixture of American life. If the 1940 census is taken as a baseline, it becomes evident that the trend is for the elderly (sixty-five years of age and older) segment of the population to grow more rapidly than younger cohorts. For example, in 1940, the number of persons sixty-five years of age and older came to slightly more than one-quarter (27 percent) of the number of persons fourteen years of age and younger. By 1980 the corresponding percentage had climbed to 50 percent. See *U.S. Census of*

Population, U.S. Summary, Characteristics of the Population, Vol. II, Part I, 1940–1980 (Washington, D.C.: U.S. Government Printing Office, 1981); Felicity Barringer, "What Americans Did After the War: A Tale Told by the Census," *New York Times,* September 2, 1990, E1, 5; and Gary Schwartz, *Beyond Conformity and Rebellion: Youth and Authority in America* (Chicago: University of Chicago Press, 1987).

59. See Clarke E. Cochran, *Religion in Public and Private Life* (New York: Routledge, 1990); George Lakoff, *Women, Fire, and Dangerous Things: What Categories Reveal About the Mind* (Chicago: University of Chicago Press, 1987); and Charles S. Maier, ed., *Changing Boundaries of the Political* (Cambridge, England: Cambridge University Press, 1987).

60. George I. Carlson, S.J., "'A Faith Lived Out of Doors': Ongoing Formation of Jesuits Today," *Studies in the Spirituality of Jesuits* 16 (September 1984); and Bernard J. F. Lonergan, S.J., "The Response of the Jesuit, as Priest and Apostle, in the Modern World," *Studies in the Spirituality of Jesuits* 2 (September 1970).

61. The difference is comparable to the division between the core documents of the Society of Jesus: respectively, the Spiritual Exercises and the Constitutions. See Antonio M. de Aldama, S.J. (trans. Aloysius J. Owen, S.J.), *The Constitutions of the Society of Jesus: An Introductory Commentary on the Constitutions* (St. Louis, Mo.: Institute of Jesuit Sources, 1989). See also Joseph A. Tetlow, S.J., "The Fundamentum: Creation in the Principle and Foundation," *Studies in the Spirituality of Jesuits* 21 (September 1989).

62. See Joseph N. Tylenda, S.J., ed., *Counsels for Jesuits: Selected Letters and Instructions of Saint Ignatius Loyola* (Chicago: Loyola University Press, 1985). Compare John Howe, "The Nobility's Reform of the Medieval Church," *American Historical Review* 93 (1988): 317–39; Steven Hughes, "Fear and Loathing in Bologna and Rome: The Papal Police in Perspective," *Journal of Social History* 21 (1987): 97–116; and Anthony Pagden, *Spanish Imperialism and the Political Imagination: Studies in European and Spanish-American Social and Political Theory* (New Haven, Conn.: Yale University Press, 1990).

63. See J. S. Whale, *The Protestant Tradition: An Essay in Interpretation* (Cambridge, England: Cambridge University Press, 1959). Compare Raymond Baumhart, S.J., *Ethics in Business* (New York: Holt, Rinehart and Winston, 1968).

64. See Harry Eckstein, "Civic Inclusion and Its Discontents," *Daedalus* 113 (1984): 107–46; Greil Marcus, *Lipstick Traces: A Secret History of the Twentieth Century* (Cambridge, Mass.: Harvard University Press, 1989); Richard Sennett, "Destructive Gemeinschaft," *Partisan Review* 43 (1976): 341–61; and Edward A. Tiryakian, "Sexual Anomie, Social Structure, Societal Change," *Social Forces* 59 (1981): 1025–53, compare Brigitte Berger and Peter L. Berger, *The War Over the Family: Capturing the Middle Ground* (Garden City, N.Y.: Doubleday, 1983); James Finn, ed., *Private Virtue and Public Policy* (New Brunswick, N.J.: Transaction, 1990); James B. Gilbert, *A Cycle of Outrage: Juvenile Delinquency and the Mass Media in the 1950s* (New York: Oxford University Press, 1986); and Elaine Showalter, *Sexual Anarchy: Gender and Culture at the Fin de Siècle* (New York: Viking, 1990). See also the statement by Sar A. Levitan, quoted by Martin Tolchin, "A Defender of 'the Welfare

System,'" *New York Times*, July 31, 1985, 8: "Permissiveness is the key word. We gave up on old-fashioned standards like punishment for crime, and family values. A society needs law and order. We opened up college to everybody, not just those who could benefit." Compare this with the statement of Tom Hayden, who attended a Jesuit high school in Detroit: "The word, always the word. The Jesuits taught me that first you write words of grandeur, then perform the deed. That changed, of course, as SDS became more radical, uninterested in ideas. But the belief in ideas nourished us at Port Huron, and with me it hasn't changed." Quoted by William L. Chase, "Still Idealists After All These Years," *U.S. News and World Report* (June 15, 1987): 60. For an empirical perspective, see Duane F. Alwin, "From Obedience to Autonomy: Changes in Traits Desired in Children, 1924–1978," *Public Opinion Quarterly* 52 (1988): 33–52.

65. Compare Suzette Henke, *James Joyce and the Politics of Desire* (New York: Routledge, 1990); and Robert Ornstein, *The Moral Vision of Jacobean Tragedy* (Madison: University of Wisconsin Press, 1960).

66. See James Brodrick, S.J., *Robert Bellarmine: Saint and Scholar* (Westminster, Md.: Newman Press, 1961). For a rounded update see John Patrick Donnelly, S.J., and Roland J. Teske, S.J., eds., *Robert Bellarmine: Spiritual Writings* (New York: Paulist Press, 1989).

67. Compare Louis J. Kern, *An Ordered Love: Sex Roles and Sexuality in Victorian Utopias—The Shakers, the Mormons, and the Oneida Community* (Chapel Hill: University of North Carolina Press, 1981).

68. See Lewis A. Coser, "The Militant Collective: Jesuits and Leninists," *Social Research* 40 (1973): 110–28. I am grateful to José A. Moreno of the University of Pittsburgh for calling this article to my attention. Compare Kenneth Jowitt, "An Organizational Approach to the Study of Political Culture in Marxist-Leninist Systems," *American Political Science Review* 68 (1974): 1171–81. The Society of Jesus of the very earliest days was less autocratic than the tightly structured organization it became, especially with its restoration in the nineteenth century. The "classical amalgam" I refer to is the autocratic one. For a study of the somewhat looser tradition, see Louis Châtellier, *The Europe of the Devout: The Catholic Reformation and the Formation of a New Society* (Cambridge, England: Cambridge University Press, 1989).

69. "Networks" and "cultures," like "movements," have a free-floating connotation in comparison to solid-sounding "organizations." The suggestiveness of the network imagery deserves to be clarified in response to some obvious questions, such as "Network of what?" It is significant that the area where the Society of Jesus is growing most rapidly, South Asia, is one that harbors a Catholic minority with a tangible institutional framework of schools and hospitals much like the organizational set-up found in the American Catholic enclaves of decades past. In addition, elements of Indian culture provide traditional roles for male celibates. See Walter Fernandes, S.J., *The Indian Catholic Community* (Brussels: Pro Mundi Vita, 1980); and Owen M. Lynch, ed., *Divine Passions: The Social Construction of Emotion in India* (Berkeley: University of California Press, 1990).

70. The following excerpt, entitled "Going Home," from Joseph Conrad, was printed without comment in *Woodstock Letters* 79 (May 1950): 155, evidently as a pointed observation on stoicism and solitude:

We wander in our thousands over the face of the earth, the illustrious and the obscure, earning beyond the seas our fame, our money, or only a crust of bread: but it seems to me that for each of us going home must be like going to render an account. We return to face our superiors, our kindred, our friends—those whom we obey and those whom we love; between those who have neither, the most free, lonely, irresponsible and bereft—even those for whom life holds no dear face, no familiar voice—even they have to meet the spirit that dwells within the land, under its sky, in its air, in its valleys, and on its rises, in its fields, in its waters and its trees—a mute friend, judge, and inspirer.

71. See Charles H. Reynolds and Ralph V. Norman, eds., *Community in America* (Berkeley: University of California Press, 1988).

72. Compare Michael Hout, *Following in Father's Footsteps: Social Mobility in Ireland* (Cambridge, Mass.: Harvard University Press, 1989); and Alan Macfarlane, *The Culture of Capitalism* (Oxford: Basil Blackwell, 1987).

73. Compare Susan Dwyer Amussen, *An Ordered Society: Gender and Class in Early Modern England* (Oxford: Basil Blackwell, 1988); and Rosalind Mitchison and Leah Leneman, *Sexuality and Social Control: Scotland, 1660–1780* (Oxford: Basil Blackwell, 1989).

74. See Philip E. Converse and Gregory B. Markus, "Plus Ça Change . . . The New CPS Election Study," *American Political Science Review* 73 (1979): 32–49.

75. Compare for example Roberto DaMatta, *Carnivals, Rogues, and Heroes: An Interpretation of the Brazilian Dilemma* (Notre Dame, Ind.: University of Notre Dame Press, 1991); Peter McDonough, *Power and Ideology in Brazil* (Princeton, N.J.: Princeton University Press, 1981); Richard G. Parker, *Bodies, Pleasures, and Passions: Sexual Culture in Contemporary Brazil* (Boston: Beacon, 1990); and Brendan Walsh, "Marriage in Ireland in the Twentieth Century," in Art Cosgrove, ed., *Marriage in Ireland* (Dublin: College Press, 1985).

76. See for example James Hurley, Barbara Carroll, and Brian R. Little, "A Typology of Lifestyles," *Social Indicators Research* 20 (1988): 383–98.

77. Compare Herbert J. Gans, *Middle American Individualism: The Future of Liberal Democracy* (New York: Free Press, 1988); and Henry F. May, *The End of American Innocence: A Study of the First Years of Our Own Time, 1912–1917* (New York: Alfred A. Knopf, 1959).

78. See William Form, *Divided We Stand: Working-Class Stratification in America* (Champagne: University of Illinois Press, 1986); and Nan L. Maxwell, *Income Inequality in the United States, 1947–1985* (Westport, Conn.: Greenwood, 1990). Compare Loren Baritz, *The Good Life: The Meaning of Success for the American Middle Class* (New York: Alfred A. Knopf, 1989); and George Gilder, *Wealth and Poverty* (New York: Basic Books, 1981).

79. Compare Thomas L. Haskell, "Capitalism and the Origins of the Humanitarian Sensibility, Parts I and II," *American Historical Review* 90 (1985): 339–61, 546–66; Henry F. May, *Ideas, Faiths, and Feelings: Essays in American Intellectual History, 1952–1982* (New York: Oxford University Press, 1983); and William L. Vance, *America's Rome*, vol. 2, *Catholic and Contemporary Rome* (New Haven, Conn.: Yale University Press, 1989).

80. See James T. Kloppenberg, "The Virtues of Liberalism: Christianity, Republicanism, and Ethics in Early American Political Discourse," *Journal of American History* 74 (1987): 9–33.

81. Compare Thomas P. Hughes, *American Genesis: A Century of Invention and Technological Enthusiasm, 1870–1970* (New York: Viking, 1989); and Francis Sweeney, S.J., *Bernadine Realino, Renaissance Man* (New York: Macmillan, 1951).

82. James Hennesey, S.J., "Grasping the Tradition: Reflections of a Church Historian," *Theological Studies* 45 (1984): 161.

83. Henry James, "Francis Parkman: The Jesuits in North America," *The Nation* (June 6, 1867), reprinted in *Literary Reviews and Essays on American, English and French Literature*, ed. Albert Mordell (New York: Grove, 1957).

84. Wallace Stevens, *Opus Posthumous* (New York: Alfred A. Knopf, 1957), pp. 206–7.

85. The predecessor was Nathaniel Hawthorne. For a more balanced assessment, see Francis Jennings, *The Ambiguous Iroquois Empire: The Covenant Chain Confederation of Indian Tribes with English Colonies from its Beginnings to the Lancaster Treaty of 1744* (New York: W. W. Norton, 1984). See also Xavier Rubert de Ventós, *El Laberinto de la Hispanidad* (Barcelona: Planeta, 1987); and Francis Jennings, *Empire of Fortune: Crowns, Colonies and Tribes in the Seven Years War in America* (New York: W. W. Norton, 1988). Toward the end of their lives both James and Stevens were drawn to Catholicism.

86. Larry McMurtry, "How the West Was Won or Lost: The Revisionists' Failure of Imagination," *New Republic* (October 22, 1990): 32–38; and Larry McMurtry, *In a Narrow Grave: Essays on Texas* (Albuquerque: University of New Mexico Press, 1968).

87. Wendell Berry, "Writer and Region," in *What Are People For? Collected Essays of Wendell Berry* (San Francisco: North Point, 1990), pp. 24–25. The touchstone of Berry's meditation is *Huckleberry Finn*. See also Geoffrey Hawthorn, *Enlightenment and Despair: A History of Sociology* (Cambridge, England: Cambridge University Press, 1976); Dolores Hayden, *Redesigning the American Dream: The Future of Housing, Work, and Family Life* (New York: W. W. Norton, 1983); Alejandro Portes and Rubén G. Rumbaut, *Immigrant America: A Portrait* (Berkeley: University of California Press, 1990); Richard B. Sewall, *The Vision of Tragedy* (New Haven, Conn.: Yale University Press, 1959); Ann Swidler, "Love and Adulthood," in *Themes of Work and Love*, ed. Neil Smelser and Eric Erickson (Cambridge, Mass.: Harvard University Press, 1980); and Mary Gordon, *Good Boys and Dead Girls and Other Essays* (New York: Viking, 1991), pp. 3–23.

Index